# SchNEWS

## AND

# SQUALL

"HA HA HEE HEE AHA HA HA"

**DISCLAIMER: SchQUALL; the SchNEWS/SQUALL book is for entertainment purposes only. Honest.**

**SchQUALL** the SQUALL and SchNEWS book is published by Justice? June 2000.

**ISBN: 0 9529748 3 5**

Printed by Calverts, following last-minute censorship by Information Press, Oxford - who pulled out because of our too-hot-to-handle content...

British Library Cataloguing in Publication Data; a catalogue record for this book is available from the British Library.

Typeset, in myriad, by **The Font Is Ours**

**Cover Pics:**
Front
*Anti-GM action, Watlington* and *June 18th, City of London* by Nick Cobbing
*Solstice at Stonehenge* by Ivan Coleman
Back
*Intercontinental Caravan* and *Kissing - June 18th, City of London* by Nick Cobbing

**SchNEWS** is a free, weekly information sheet printed and published by volunteers in Brighton. It is obtainable by sending first class stamps (one for each issue) or donations (in UK pounds, payable to "Justice?") to SchNEWS, c/o On The Fiddle, P.O. Box 2600, Brighton, East Sussex, BN2 2DX, UK. Alternatively you can get it via email - register by visiting the web site at http://www.schnews.co.uk/ or email us your request.

**SQUALL Magazine Online** is a regularly updated alternative news and culture service freely accessible and intra-searchable at http://www.squall.co.uk/

**SQUALL Download** is an A5 hardcopy magazine published roughly every month and securable by subscription only. The subs rate is £7 for six issues or £12 for twelve issues (These prices include p +p). Cheques payable to "SQUALL" and addressed to SQUALL subs, P.O. Box 8959, London, N19 5HW, UK. The project is run by volunteers and is entirely non profit making so please include extra stamps or finance if possible.

**Your turn now:** please send in yer photos, cartoons and so on, from actions and events as they happen. They might go down in history, or at least in next year's annual! (Put yer name and address on 'em, and a brief blurb describing the event and anything else we should know.)

# SchQUALL

## contents

# An Introductory Rant by Rob Newman on SchNEWS and SQUALL

**From the free and blissfully anti-copyright SchNEWS and SQUALL I steal all the material I need to make big money at corporate-sponsored comedy shows and rake fat fees from prime-time television slots (once I've removed all the controversial anti-capitalist bits and that). They're grrrr-eat!!!!**

The soaraway readership enjoyed today by SchNEWS totally vindicates its change of direction back in the mid-nineties. It's hard to recall now, but back then SchNEWS was a pretty ordinary magazine covering mainly interior design, fashion catwalks and celebrity chefs. Market research, however, had identified new and exciting possibilities in a growing sector called "radical, anti-capitalist, eco-consciousness."

SQUALL, meanwhile, fluked it by an incredible stroke of luck which has now, of course, passed into journalistic legend. One day their horoscope writer had her train home cancelled and wrote a scathing attack on privatised railways. That evening, as luck would have it, their travel-editor was held in a Turkish jail for inadvertently photographing the Kurdish village of Hasankeyf (as backdrop to soft-porn shots of Joanne Guest). He wired back an angry piece. Such was the positive post-bag to these two articles that SQUALL's editorial board widened its next issue's attack to the whole system of profit, whereby the earth and all its people are condemned to serve the interests of a tiny corporate elite, and what capitalism calls democracy is merely the safety valve of privilege and property, whereas grassroots, participatory anarchism is closer to the true democratic ideal. Heady stuff!

Even though some media analysts and shareholders had doubts at first, the timing of SchNEWS & SQUALL's shifts of direction could not have been better. Here's why...

In Britain, people have been absolutely deserted by the news-media who have given up on any and all notions of journalistic responsibilty. The most servile intellectual class in the Western world has sold us down the mercury-polluted, phosphate run-off river. They have in their knowing, worldly-wise, sophisticated way just rolled over and swalllowed.

Every single ideological orthodoxy of the "new" capitalism is presented as fact, any questioning of this perfect system is opinion. We live in a land where the Financial Editor of The Guardian can say that Wall Street saved the world from recession by taking the financial burden on itself, and not be laughed out of his job. In any functioning democracy he would have to walk barefoot through the slums of Manila, the slave-plantations of South Carolina and the Lincolnshire barley-belt wearing a sandwich board on which his words were written. We live in a land where twice in one programme, a Radio 4 presenter calls for increased military aid for Columbia - the country Amnesty International cites as the world's number one human rights abuser (and co-incidentally the recipient of one half of the total US foreign military aid budget). Where Westminster gossip passes for political coverage. Where Burson Marsteller, Satan's Little Helper and the world's biggest PR firm, can become joint partners with ITN and rely on obedient commissars not to mention it.

And why would they? Why bother, when much of what passes for news is corporate propaganda or just straight advertising anyway? The top PR firms send out Video News Releases or VNR's (packaged to look like news items) which go straight to air (and best of all we pay for it.) Hence BBC News 24 stories about the wonderful service offered by amazon.com, and the incredible Tesco price-slash lead-story. Hence the new "more thoughtful" approach to GM. (Turns out it's not giving pollution a life of its own after all.) You can play propagando bingo by matching whole

sentences from TV and broadsheet newspapers with whole sentences from corporate press releases out of Pfeizer, IMF, Hyundai, WTO, or BAe.

And why would they? After all, the selection-mechanisms of the institutions they work for naturally choose only those who can really spread their butt cheeks wide for the NASDAQ money-shot. Reporting of May Day, for example, showed the speactacular class bias of our media elite. "Inevitably, some innocent passers-by were caught up in the chaos" said one TV news reporter over a shot of a protestor split up from her child by the TSG riot-cops, who wouldn't let her cross their lines to get her kid. I had seen this woman earlier when everyone was gardening, but guerilla gardeners can't be ordinary people with children, can they?

As Mark Thomas put it, the news-media have sacrificed analysis for access. And as Ken Loach said, "Humphries and Paxman set an extremely Conservative and reactionary agenda within which they can pose as radicals."

On the rare occasions the advertising / corporate press "cover" environmental, poverty and human rights stories, they do so as if they were all unrelated. SchNEWS and SQUALL's brilliant internationalism reports all struggle and injustice like it's part of one struggle against one injustice, one tyranny. Almost as if all our many different social, ecological, spiritual and personal problems have their roots in the same system. Phew!

Where the broadsheets make what's simple confusing by usingshow-off technical jargon, upside-down corporate bias and bluster, SQUALL and SchNEWS intelligently put needlessly obscure stuff into the clear, everyday language of someone down the pub. In fact it's uncanny how much of SchNEWS reads just like someone down the pub. Almost as if most of it was indeed written by people who've just come out the pub. One of those pubs that gets closed down and replaced with a franchise theme-pub.

Short on theory, long on facts and research, SchNEWS and SQUALL have, along with Undercurrents, Corporate Watch, Earth First! Action Update, and many more, contributed to the best-informed, sharpest resistance movement ever. WTO and IMF delegates sneered that protestors on the streets simply didn't understand what was going on. The fact is that those outside actually knew much more about what's going on than those in-side - despite the best efforts of the corporate media - and that because of the worldwide, exponential growth in grassroots publications.

The single best thing about SchNEWS and SQUALL, though, is how they are absolutely indivisible from the whole grassroots protest movements they both inform and are shaped by, inspire and are inspired by. Every writer and researcher, gluepot paster and glue-sniffer at SchNEWS and SQUALL are also activists. For example, it was [NAME DELETED] who, as we know, single-handedly organised the [DATE DELETED] carnival in the city of [DELETED]. And although her face is hidden by a balaclava, that famous Seattle Police Department photo of someone [DESCRIPTION OF ACTIVITY DELETED] is of none other than [NAME DELETED], yes, that's right, the one who with the [DESCRIPTION DELETED] who lives at [ADDRESS DELETED] with [NAME DELETED] and [NAME DELETED] and has been building contacts with the [NAME OF ROGUE ARAB STATE AND ITS MAD DICTATOR COLONEL DELETED].

The next ten years are the most crucial in human history. The tyranny of corporate world-take-over will stop at nothing. More and more people are realising with horror that even in the face of imminent ecological collapse they are still meant to believe there is no alternative to the killing machine of global capitalism. The challenge facing grassroots organisers now is, I reckon, to build a broad, diverse, mass movement (but not a mass party). The alliance in Seattle was so broad that it became impossible for the state to ghetto-ize protestors as being 'NOT LIKE YOU'. They were everyone. From Raging Grannies to disaffected black youth, from construction workers to family farmers. These words of Egyptian activist and writer Nawal El Saadawi describe where we might want to go from here, with a little help from our friends at SQUALL and SchNEWS:

*"My cousin Zeinab looks old and sick, when I hold her hand I can feel horny knots and cracks caused by long years of labour with a hoe. She whispers: When I was a child I dreamed of escaping from this awful life but now I've lost hope. Now there are no jobs, and our debts keep growing. Now we eat fava beans canned in California instead of growing enough ourselves. I see her eyes questioning... Can I tell her that 443 people (men) own as much wealth as half the people of the earth? ....Can I tell her that the peoples of the world are learning how to work together and that many Seattles everywhere, in the North and South are my wish, and my hope?"*

Or to put the same thing another way, here's Frank Manckiewicz, ex Vice Prez at Hill & Knowlton PR:

*"The big corporations, our clients, are scared shitless by the environmentalists. I think they are wrong about that. I think the big companies will have to give in only at an insignificant level. Right now, the big corporations are too powerful, they're the establishment. The environmentalists will have to behave to be like the mob in the square in Rumania before they prevail."*

We have our instructions.
**Robert Newman**

# SchNEWS

*Printed and Published in Brighton by* **Justice?**

http://www.schnews.org.uk/

# FIFTH BIRTHDAY SHOCKER!

Who would have thought in those halcyon days of the Courthouse community centre, squatted to highlight the nasty Criminal Justice Act looming on the horizon, that it would come to this? A few people decide to mimic the news, reading out bits of information while getting their hair cut. Then some bright sparks decide to put the spoken word on paper "cos Brighton needs a news-sheet." Hey presto! SchNEWS is born (no we can't remember why it's called that either, or maybe never knew...) But five years on and we're still here.

Despite the Criminal Justice Act (CJA) being well established on the statute books people protesting and putting on free parties just haven't taken the hint, and have carried on regardless. As for SchNEWS, it has grown from a scrappy bit of A4 with a no advertising - no compromise policy – to well, eh, a scrappy bit of A4 with a no advertising and no compromise policy! Along the way we've branched out from just writing about the CJA with it's arrestometer, to taking on the whole damn world.

Making links with all sorts of groups in struggles ranging from striking dockworkers, to the granarchists on the live export direct action frontline, to indigenous peoples fight against multinational nasties, to anarchist pie throwers.

Going on mass to Geneva to the Peoples Global Action first conference and meeting all those inspiring people from around the world and realising that all our struggles are the same - that no issue is single. The multinationals based in the west, are the very same companies that are doing the damage to the peoples of the so- called third world.

## AND THE NEXT FIVE YEARS?

SchNEWS is run on a voluntary basis. No one gets paid tho' we do manage to blag into gigs and festivals for free (to spread the word of course) and when our treasurer's not looking, raid the petty cash tin for biscuits.

Our stories originate from dodgy anarchist filth mags to the Financial Times (no, really), from conversations in the pub to the internet. We try and be as accurate as possible and chase people up to verify the stories. And since the idea of SchNEWS is not to believe the written word, but get up off your arse and go and see things for yourself, articles are often first hand accounts from our very good selves as we storm all over the country causing trouble/saving the world/having a laugh.

As for who keeps us going. Well even with free office space kindly donated by the Levellers, we still reckon to be spending around £20,000 a year on printing, stamps, telephone, computers, envelopes, stationary, e-mail accounts … and rely on subscriptions and our readers generosity to keep us afloat.

*...and finally...* SchNEWS is an open collective, we are always looking for new people to get involved, so if you like reading the news the mainstream tends to ignore (or at best talks about the lifestyle rather than why an action is going on) take a look in the next column and see if anything grabs your fancy.

## WAKE UP! WAKE UP! IT'S YER TYPICAL SCHNEWS WEEK

**Monday afternoon:** We get up to 350 emails a week, and someone has the fun job of going though all these, answering queries and deciding which ones might become stories.

**Wednesday:** Start writing and researching SchNEWS, go through all the mail, decide roughly what we are going to cover this week.

**Thursday:** More writing, except it's usually a bit more frantic cos we've got to get it all finished and checked by early evening before the pubs shut.

**Thursday evening:** Desk Top Publishing crew come in and do their stuff, someone managing to crush a tonne of information into two bits of A4.

**Friday 10 am:** Hot off the press. A bleary-eyed person prints up the SchNEWS at The Resource Centre.

**Friday mornings:** The web-masters do their thing and put it on our site (currently getting 1,200 hits a day) and send it out to all our e-mail subscribers (currently 2,600 and growing at 15 a day.)

**Friday afternoons:** The mail out crew, stuff envelopes and send it out to all our paper subscribers. (We've currently got 500 subscribers, 80 of these copy and distribute, whilst various organisations, bookshops and people get bundles to hand out. Prisoners get SchNEWS free.) While this is going on SchNEWS is being distributed to various places around Brighton (about 2,000 copies.)

**Saturday:** If people are about then SchNEWS is handed out to passers by in the North Laines.

**And there's more:** During the week the subscription database is constantly being updated, letters answered, book orders posted, journalist queries answered (unless it's any of Murdoch's papers where we tell the caller to fuck off.)

**Still interested?** Then give the office a call. We have regular training days, but if you can't wait for them, give the office a ring now. Don't let the fact that SchNEWS comes out every week lull you into a false sense of security. We constantly need more people to get involved.

We guestimate SchNEWS reaches around 30,000 people a week. Not bad for a scrappy no-adverts no-compromise bit of A4.

## Subscribe!

# SQUALL

*SQUALL Magazine began life in 1992 when a particularly virulent Criminal Justice Bill was first touted by a regime which stood diametrically opposed to diversity, new culture and civil liberties. The Bill threatened to stomp all over vital grass roots UK culture, and even the more liberal elements of our Oxbridge-dominated media proved too busy arranging the vol-au-vents to take any notice. Indeed many of these vessels of hot air thought the dinner party would go smoother if the lowlifes were quietly and swiftly removed.*

So SQUALL decided to make a stand in the place where we lived. To go one step further than simply diagnosing the dearth of integrity or genuine impartiality in British media and establish a new media forum. SQUALL........ a storm to stir the sediment......from the Scandinavian word 'skvala' meaning to shout. In the words of The Clash.....Excuse me if we have to shout but while we were talking we saw you nodding out......

The magazine rapidly grew into a major hardcopy broadsheet presenting investigative analysis of the issues behind direct actions and other subjects of social concern ignored by the mainstream. Factual accuracy and a non-ranting accessible style helped SQUALL reach a diverse audience.

*"If SchNEWS is yer tabloid, SQUALL is yer broadsheet".*

The SQUALL website began way back in the mists of cyber time (1995) but in 1998 it became the primary medium through which SQUALL presented material to an even wider audience. Never ye mind though all you hardcopy lovers, 'cos SQUALL produces a monthlyish A5 magazine packed with concise material just right for the bus and the bog. SQUALL Download presents some of the pick of the latest web material plus some exclusive bits'n'pieces.

SQUALL Magazine online is now a regularly updated forum for radical quality journalism and photography at www.squall.co.uk. An ever deepening, intra-searchable encyclopaedia presenting investigative, factually reliable news and analysis accessible even to a wandering eye.

The pool of writers, photographers, designers and editors who sweat themselves dry to produce SQUALL do so voluntarily. The motivation for involvement is thus kept separate from money, ensuring the emphasis remains unfettered by the commercial millstones which drown other media sources. We still need money to collate, present and distribute the material of course by we can say with confidence that SQUALL is a mammon free zone. If you don't know what mammon is then we recommend you become familiar with the word....cos it sums up a lot of what's happening around us.

Whilst some of SQUALL's photo and article contributors earn a living in mainstream media they see their contribution as a way of exercising their art and principled concern on SQUALL's web pages. Other people who work for SQUALL wouldn't touch the mainstream with a sterilised barge pole, sure in the knowledge that many of those who populate this arena are irredeemably scurrilous and contagious to boot.

SQUALL encourages anyone interested in principled journalism to contribute photographs and articles.
If British media is unacceptably unrepresentative then SQUALL seeks to proffer a medicine for the malaise. A set of guidelines for photographers, feature writers, news short journo's and subbers are available from SQUALL. Write, specifying your area of particular contributory interest, to SQUALL, Garage Style, PO Box 8959, London N19 5HW.

SQUALL Download (A5 monthly hardcopy) is available on subscription for £12 for 12 issues (includes P&P). Write to SQUALL Download, PO Box 8959, London N19 5HW. Cheques payable to SQUALL. This magazine is non-profit making so please include any additional finance or stamps you can afford to help ensure its survival and thrival. You can contact SQUALL by writing to the above address or by e-mailing us at info@squall.co.uk

Respect is more than a word. But like muscle, it wastes away when unexercised.

MAMMON ~ FREE ZONE

# A GENETICALLY MODIFIED CROP CIRCLE

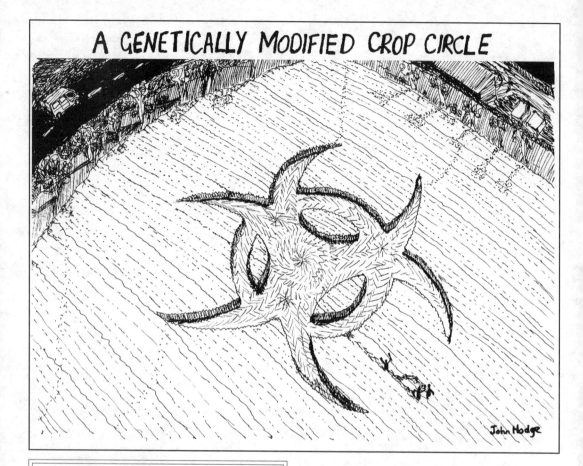

John Hodge

## SQUOTES

"You have been telling the people that this is the Eleventh Hour, now you must tell them this is the Hour. And there are things to be considered... This could be a good time! There is a river flowing now very fast. It is so great and swift that there are those who will be afraid. They will try to hold on to the shore. They will feel they are torn apart and will suffer greatly. Know the river has its destination. The elders say we must let go of the shore, push off into the middle of the river, keep our eyes open, and our heads above water.

And I say, see who is in there with you and celebrate. At this time in history, we are to take nothing personally. Least of all ourselves. For the moment that we do, our spiritual growth and journey comes to a halt. The time for the lone wolf is over. Gather yourselves! Banish the word struggle from your attitude and your vocabulary. All that we do now must be done in a sacred manner and in celebration. We are the ones we've been waiting for."

***Oraibi Arizone Elder - Hopi Nation***

WAKE UP! WAKE UP! IT'S YER SOMETHIN FOR NOTHIN

# Weekly SchNEWS

*Printed and Published in Brighton by Justice?*

**Friday 19th Feb 1999**   http://www.schnews.org.uk/   **Issue 201**   **Free/Donation**

# MODS AND SHOCKERS

*"Parliament is being besieged by them. We have our own crop of genetically modified lobbyists."* Alan Simpson, Labour MP

As SchNEWS went to press New Labour were stubbornly refusing to call a five year ban on genetically modified organisms (GMO)despite the outcry against 'frankensteins food' growing louder every day. Meanwhile the bio-technology companies must be holding their collective (three)heads in their hands. Last year the biggest and baddest of them all, Monsanto, spent one million pounds on an advertising campaign, yet support for gmo's plummeted; leaked memo's from the company confirmed that just when they thought it couldn't get any worse it did, again and again and now support for gmo's has hit rock bottom.

So what do you do when you've lost the argument with the public? You take the advice of PR company Burson Marsteller, the greenwash specialists, and fast spinning cog in the propaganda machine of the new world order. Yer good ol' neighbourhood perception managers advised EuropaBio- the main lobby organization for the European BioIndustry back at its first cake-divvying session in 1997- to leave any public debate to "those charged with public trust - politicians and regulators - to assure the public that biotech products are safe". Now SchNEWS would never accuse the party of the people from being hand in glove with big business; the following list is just an uncanny co-incidence.

**David Hill**, one of the top media men for the **Labour Party** until a year ago, now works for Monsanto's PR company Bell Pottinger. **Cathy McGlynn** is also employed by Bell Pottinger after six years of working as an adviser to **Jack Cunningham Labour MP** (who chairs the Cabinet committee on biotechnology and says a ban on gmo's would "not be sensible")

**Lord Sainsbury**, the billionaire whose supermarket empire sells unlabelled genetically modified food with abandon is **New Labour Science Minister**

The genetic food company Zeneca has an executive on the Dept of Healths Committee on the **Toxicity of Chemicals in Food**. Their Chief Executive **Peter Doyle** is also on the **Department of Trade and Industry's** Biotechnology Research Council.

Novartis, a rival of Monsanto and Zeneca, sponsored last years **Labour conference**, paid for a training session to tell new MPs how to behave and has one of its ex-employees, **Nick Palmer**, sitting in the Com-
p

mons as the **New Labour MP for Broxtowe** (Novartis gives him £5,000 a year to be its Parlimanetary adviser) And surely it can't be true that **New Labour** offered genetic engineering companies including Monsanto, millions of pounds in inducements to expand their UK operations?

Or that companies involved in GM food have met government officials and ministers **81 times** since Labour came to power. An analysis by Friends of the Earth showed **Monsanto's executives** secured 17 audiences with ministers in Blair's first year in office - **one meeting every three weeks.**

Still, even if Labour do slap on a ban, Monsanto and Zeneca have threatened to appeal to the European Union, reckoning the British authorities have no power to halt genetic research if it has been given the go-ahead by the EU.

So it's back to Tory Blair who reckons the food is healthy, tasty, heaven sent dietary bliss and will settle for nothing else, for himself or his family. He must have been drooling when on Thursday activists delivered four tons of mutant soya beans to his doorstep.

*"I wouldn't eat it willingly...It is commercially driven and we are like a guinea pig generation."* Dr.Mae Wan Ho, reader in biology at the Open University.

So *forget* the arguments that we have been genetically modifying crops for thousands of years (look mate, sticking the anti-freeze gene from an arctic fish into strawberries is a whole different ball-game from natural breeding processes which take years); that GMO's are gonna feed the world (the World Health Organisation say we already produce one and a half times what the world needs to feed itself, it's just a shame that market forces mean the poor can't afford to buy it); that genetic crops are more environmentally friendly because they use less pesticides! (get a grip - they actually need more pesticides and disturb the balance of the soil. We haven't a clue what would happen if these crops cross-breed with wild-plants, produce superweeds, create novel toxins, eradicate the wildplants that our native insects and birds depend on to survive in our countryside. In fact all over the world when non-indigenous species have been introduced into new environments they have caused long term damage.)

The fact is that this massive bio-tech experi-

ment is the only avenue left if intensive farming systems are to have any chance of survival. The SchNEWS alternative is small-scale organic farms which would wrestle food production away from the multinationals, would create jobs, would safeguard and improve the environment, would improve health, would put a greater percentage of the population back in touch with the land. Just take a look at the million wetland rice farmers in the far east who have shifted to sustainable agriculture, where group-based farmer-field schools have enabled farmers to learn alternatives to pesticides whilst still increasing yields. While in the USA farmers are applying sustainable technologies so well they have higher yields than conventional farmers, without relying on toxic chemicals or the lame assurances of the gene age peddlers.

How many times do we have to say it, big business is only interested in profit, government is only interested in sucking up to big business.

**The Monsanto Monitor**
P.O. Box 92066, 1090 AB Amsterdam, Holland. Tel: +31-20-468 2616; Email: biotech@aseed.antenna.nl

**Genetix Update,**
PO Box 9656, London, N4 4JY Tel 0181 374 9516 - www.envirolink.org/orgs/shag/action. GEN can also supply a list of genetic crop sites around the world

**Nationwide Food Survey**
Beacon House, Willow Walk, Skelmersdale, Lancashire, WN8 6UP
Produce 'How to Avoid Genetic Foods' www.wkweb4.cableinet.co.uk/pbrown/index

**"The Unbottled Gene"**
A week of evening talks in London from Monday 8th to Friday 12th March 1999
For details of venues ring 0171 254 6863
www.//members.tripod.com/UL_Forum_on_GE.

**Grow yer own!**
Organic food is the only food that under EC legislation cannot contain gmo's. Unfortunately it's still pretty expensive, so why not start growing your own fruit and veg. Find out how by sending a SAE to the Henry Doubleday Research Association, Ryton Organic Gardens, Coventry, CV8 3LG Tel 01203 303517
* On Wednesday Monsanto and Perryfields Holdings Ltd, were given a pathetic £17,000 fine plus costs after breaking safety regulations in Lincolnshire. A six-metre border designed to stop the escape of GM pollen was found to be inadequate. As pollen can travel for miles and bees don't know the difference the borders are a joke.

---
**REBEL ALLIANCE**
Tuesday 23rd Feburary 7 pm upstairs at the Hobgoblin Pub, London Rd
(please note date change!)
---

@ANTI-COPYRIGHT - INFORMATION FOR ACTION

## KURDISTAN

What's behind the recent wave of embassy occupations and demonstrations across the globe by Kurds, protesting at the arrest of the leader of the PKK, Abdullah Occalan ? Much has been made of their 'illegal' tactics (invading foreign embassies etc) and the PKK's status as 'terrorists', but what hardships have motivated such resistance?

The Kurds are the biggest stateless people in the world, numbering 20 to 25 million spread over 200,000 square miles including parts of Iran, Iraq, Syria, but mainly Turkey, where they are a sizeable minority. The current war- going on since 1984- in south east Turkey has seen over 22,000 Kurds killed, and forced 3 million to flee the country. Amnesty have reported numerous human rights abuses, and Turkey had the second highest expenditure in the world on conventional arms during 1992-96; over $6 billion in 1996 alone. So why does the West turn a blind eye to these atrocities, whilst getting self-righteous about the problems in Kosova?

Could it be that Turkey has huge arms deals with the US and Germany, or that in 1997 the British company Vickers sent 800 tanks to the Turkish regime? The Campaign against the Arms Trade is calling for an arms embargo on Turkey and implementation of Robin Cooks' so-called 'ethical' foreign policy. But the West doesn't want to rock the boat in Turkey- they are an important NATO ally. Air bases in SE Turkey are used by British and US planes to police the no-fly zone over Iraq. Only last week Iraq's foreign minister Tariq Aziz met the Turkish authorities to ask them to stop the flights. They refused, but made it clear that they wanted a favour in return from the West. Could Occalan have been handed over as a thank you present? His capture is clouded in confusion. He was staying in the Greek embassy in Nairobi, and soon after leaving, mysteriously ended up in Turkish custody. It is unclear whether the Greek authorities deliberately handed him over. Greek and Turkey are old rivals, and the affair caused such an outcry in Greece that 3 cabinet ministers have had to resign. Nairobi, where Occalan was captured is also the main base for US intelligence in Africa (what a coincidence!).

As Schnews went to Press, the embassy siege in London had finished, and all the occupants had been arrested under the Prevention of Terrorism Act.

Kurdish Information Centre: 10 Glasshouse Yd., London EC1A 4JN (0171 250 1315)
**Given that all schools and universities in **Kosova** have been closed since 1989 by the Serbian authorities, a group of students are doing a tour of the UK from the 15th to 27th March. They will be talking at universities in London, Derby, Leicester, Manchester, Bradford, Edinborough and Aberdeen. Can they talk at your University? Ring 0161 2260404 if interested.

**The Diggers Working Week**
Between Saturday 20th - Sunday 28th March at a venue near Brighton All hands are needed to help out making, preparing and repairing - canvas structures (they've got an industrial sewing machine), portable compost toilets, kitchen resources, banners, defenses, etc.for a large scale land occupation. If you wanna get involved ring 0961 373 385.

## SchNEWS in brief

There's a national demonstration to **defend asylum seekers** rights and protest at new legislation on asylum and immigration going through parliament. Saturday 27th February @12 noon, Embankment, London, (Embankment tube). Contact 101 Villa Rd., Birmingham, B21 1NH, 0121 5546947 email: cair@ncadc.demon.co.uk ***Citizen Smith** - a new squatted Sunday afternoon veggie café has opened in North West London at 161 College Road, Kensal Green, London NW 10. Contact 07931 980534 www.members.tripod.com/citizensmith/hello/ ***The latest set of **Corner House** briefings are available on subjects such as racism, conflict and globalisation. Contact Corner House, PO Box 3137, Station Rd., Sturminster Newton, Dorset, DT10 1YJ Tel 01258 473795 http://www.icaap.org/Cornerhouse ***WANTED-films**! Whether it's a 90 minute feature, pop video or 30 second experimental animation. Deadline is 26th February . Send to RIL Independent Film and Video Festival, 53 Carnew St., N.C.R., Dublin 7, Tel +353 1 8681466 email:FESTIVAL@EMC23.TP *** **WinVisible** (women with visible and invisible disabilities) have a number of pamphlets and leaflets available. Send SAE for a list to Crossroads Women' Centre, 230a Kentish Town Rd., London, NW5 2AB Tel 0171 482 2496 *** Natural Selection is a web search engine specifically designed to find and twist far right and racist sites on the net, using **ridicule as a weapon.** More details check out http://www.mongrel.org.uk/ email: info@mongrel.org.uk *** **The Equality Housing collective,** based in Oxford, squats empty buildings and brings attention to housing problems . They are currently occupying a disused nursing home in north Oxford owned by the council, and with the help of local kids have made many improvements to the building. Despite recent favourable talks leading to potentially permanent occupation, the council have decided to try and repossess the building anyway. Contact 07775 700732 *** Saturday 27 is a Day of Action for sanctions to be removed against **Iraq**. Meet 1-3pm, Piccadilly Gardens. More info 0161 834 8301 *** If your in Brighton, there will be a talk about **sanctions** on 22nd Feb. 2pm at the University of Sussex, A1 lecture theatre. Speakers will be George Galloway MP, Sabah Al-Mukhtar (leading Arab voice on international law) and Mailan Rai (Voices of the Wilderness campaign)

**Oi - Global Capitalism - No!**
On Saturday 27th February from 10am there will be a gathering for people participating in actions on **June 18th** actions against globalisation. It's at the(squatted) United Reform Church, Church Street, Stoke Newington, London N16 - with a social in the evening.

**Oops!** In SchNEWS 200 we missed out how to get on the June 18th list; send an email to listproc@gn.apc.org with your email address and the following line: subscribe J18DISCUSSIONS ** There's also a June 18th discussion in Glasgow 3-4 April.Contact-counterInformation (Autonomy) c/o 28 King Street, Glasgow G1.

**Stop-press:** Greenpeace have occupied towers at Livepool docks to stop gmo's coming into the port.

## INSIDE SCHNEWS

In November last year two members of a Czech anarchist group were brutally attacked by a group of at least five neo-nazis in a Prague club. One of the two was knocked out after a short fight, while the other, Michal Patera, was injured. Fearing for his life, Michal drew his legally owned gun and fired at his attackers. One of the fascists was shot three times, and the others withdrew for a moment. Michal managed to escape, but was arrested shortly after by the police. For defending his life, Michal is now charged with "attempted murder motivated by ideological conviction" and faces 25 years in prison, with at least one year in "protective custody" before his case goes to trial. None of the attacking neo-nazis faces even minor charges.

This is the fourth time in a few years that the Czech authorities have thrown a victim of fascist terror in jail on charges of murder or attempted murder for defending his life. The Czech anti-fascist movement has also had to raise large amounts of money to cover lawyer fees, and is now skint. If you can help send donations to SF International Secretariat, PO Box 1681, London, N8 7LE (cheques payable to NELSF)

**Letters of solidarity to:** Michal Patera (1976), PO Box 5, 14057 Praha 4, Czech Republic, or send them by email to the Defense Campaign: sam20uj@axpsu.fpf.slu.cz

## ...and finally...

Lambeth Council are not having an easy job with their plans to gentrify Brixton, as squatters have realised that a barricade a day keeps the bailiff at bay. The 121 centre is an 18-year old autonomous squat in the heart of Brixton, open as a bookshop, advice centre, meeting space for radical groups etc. A notice of eviction was served for last Monday, and according to the Inspector of Operations for Brixton police, the bailiffs were expecting to stroll in, remove the door and brick up the space. Oh dear! What they weren't expecting was for 70 anarchists to be dancing in the street at 6.30am to a sound system, behind barricades in the roads, with the warning cry of a WW2 air raid siren blaring from the rooftop. (In fact the fort proved so effective that a number of activists woke up on Valentines morning to find themselves barricaded inside the building , asking passers by if they could borrow a ladder!) Offices in the town hall were later occupied until police came and broke up the party. While local residents were supporting 121, three other squats in the area were evicted that morning. The Lambeth evictor is ruthless, and help is needed in defending the buildings. It doesn't take much…at another squat, open for 10 years as a workshop, bailiffs were greeted by lots of locals sitting in armchairs in the street who told them the house was crammed with people (ahem!). The bailiffs left crying, *"but you promised this property would be empty this morning, you people are supposed to be peaceful types!"*

Get a copy of the South London Stress! Contact 121 Railton Road, Brixton London, SE24, tel 0171 978 8214email mark261@hotmail.com

**disclaimer**
SchNEWS warns all tomatos not to think they are arctic fish. You can't swim and you will drown.

# THAT MAKES ME CROSS

LOTS OF PUBS AND SHOPS IN BRIGHTON WHERE I'D HANG OUT ALONG WITH OTHER SOCIALLY UNDESIRABLES HAVE RECENTLY BEEN SHUT DOWN AND RE-OPENED AS SHITE POSH WANK PLACES I CAN'T AFFORD ANYTHING IN! JUST SOME EXAMPLES (OF MANY!):

before: **JUBILEE ARCADE**

THIS CONSISTED OF LOTS OF STALLS WITH CHEAP USEFUL STUFF.

after: NOW IT'S A THEATRE AND POSH "CAFÉ-BAR"! **KOMEDIA**

TONITE: ANOTHER PRETENTIOUS PLAY 7.30pm

before: LOTS OF SCUMMY AND MEAN LOOKING BODS WOULD HANG OUT AT THE GREEN DRAGON PUB...

after: NOW, THEY FOUND SOME SOURCES OF LIGHT AND IT'S: **the office** café bar

I'M NOT SAYING SMALL BUSINESS IS BETTER THAN BIG BUSINESS - IT'S ALL CAPITALISM. BUT I'M SICK OF BECOMING MORE & MORE EXCLUDED FROM AN INCREASINGLY LIFELESS AND ARTIFICIAL TOWN CENTRE!

— Bomb the Yuppie Bars!

ISY 99

# BLANKING THE ORGANIC

**SQUALL**

Where Do You Want To Grow Today?
--
I Wanna Go Home
Underground Update
Features
Squall Pics
Frontline Communique
✓ The State Its In
Squotes
Resources
Links
From Our Correspondence

We kid you not....One of SQUALL's reporters was recently offered an entire flock of sheep for nothing by a Herefordshire farmer keen to off-load her worthless burden. It is now possible to buy an adult Welsh sheep for as little as ten pence. With farm incomes plummeting by 50 per cent in the year up to June 1999, conventional non-organic agriculture in the UK is in its death throes and the cries of anguish voice loud from the countryside. In an effort to assuage the swelling discontent (used as a political weapon by pro-hunting lobby groups like the Countryside Alliance), Tony Blair recently found £150 million to compensate Britain's suffering farmers. But whilst the Government publicly laments the tragedy by throwing elastoplast money at a seemingly hopeless situation, it continues, inexplicably, to ignore an agricultural salvation prospering in the wings.

For whilst chemically-injected sheep munch unprofitably on chemically-soaked pastures, sales of organic produce have doubled over the last two years. Annual consumer spending on organic food in the UK rose 40% last year to £390 million and is expected to top £1 billion within the next two years.

So it was an announcement worthy of some incredulity when the Government said in August that finance to help farmers convert to organic had run out and that no further money will be available for at least 18 months. An exasperated National Farmer's Union slated the move as "ludicrous". In early November, the affects of the French beef ban in France forced the Government into finding a further £10 million for the organic conversion scheme as a short term palliative but such small amounts of cash are singularly failing to connect British agriculture with the organic boom.

And so it is that 70% of organic food bought in the UK is imported from abroad, with both British farmers and consumers paying the price. A recent opinion poll conducted by the Soil Association revealed that consumer willingness to purchase organic food - booming though it is - is still hampered by high prices. How much lower would it be if we grew it ourselves? How much more could we afford to eat organic?

According to the EU's farming commissioner, Franz Fischler, British farmers are "failing to capitalise" on the booming consumer demand for organic produce: "In some member states the success of organic farming is overwhelming. In others, like the UK, it unfortunately still lags behind." An estimated one per cent of British farmland is run organically compared with ten per cent in Germany and Austria.

The problem for British farmers is that it takes five years of non-chemical application to achieve organic status for land; a period of time which requires financial support. The conversion grants given to farmers by the UK government to facilitate such changes have always been among the lowest in Europe. Now the money has run out all together.

The major UK supermarket chains on the other hand are now hailing organic produce as the new saviour; making hasty readjustments to both retail strategy and marketing. Sainsbury's may have been trailing in the UK's supermarket profit league lately but their rapidly increasing organic sales now lead the current supermarket 'go organic' boom. It is a trend not lost on a British retailing industry bracing itself for the takeover of Asda by the world's largest retail business, Wal Mart. The American retail colossus is about to arrive on British shores with massive bulk purchase potential, aggressive marketing and wide-scale dramatic price cuts on popular supermarket products. Whilst the UK's most profit-successful supermarket chain, Tesco, are putting themselves in the ring for a price match, the other UK supermarket companies realise Wal Mart's immanent foist on British retailing is a serious and potentially terminal threat.

Iceland, Marks and Spencers and Sainsbury's are amongst those already redirecting their advertising focus to show off organic credential, undoubtedly aware that specialising in such produce may be the only sanctuary from Wal Mart's market invasion.

### So where does this leave the Government?

According to Helen Browning, chair of the Soil Association: "By inadequately funding the [conversion] scheme the Government has lost a crucial opportunity to revitalise the beleaguered farming industry in this country in a sector where the potential is obvious to everyone." Everyone that is except the government itself. So why the blind eye?

Lamentable differences in the Government's allocation of agricultural cash provides the clues. This year's exhausted government grants for organic conversion amounted to a paltry £6 million with just £2.2 million spent on organic farming research. In contrast, the Government shelled out £52 million agricultural biotechnology research in 1998.

Blair's US driven globalisation myopia has squandered both political attention and direct financial support on facilitating the US biotech industry's drive towards genetically-modified agriculture and away from the irrefutable potential of organic farming. Both the Soil Association and organic farming in general, stand expressively in diametric opposition to everything genetically-modified farming is about.

*Pic: Tom Pilston*

**"Here - bite my finger - it's more nutritious"**

Public concerns about genetically modified foodstuffs are now so great that both the national media and the the British supermarket industry have stepped off their usual safety fence and avowedly embraced the 'No to GM food' campaign; an issue which was only propelled into public consciousness after over a year of crop-ripping direct action back in 1997/8.

Preoccupied with facilitating big business, Tony Blair is the last to acknowledge the point. Meanwhile, the whole country is losing out on a sustainable agricultural future because of a government which fights more for the rights free-trade globalised big business than it does for its own nation's long term health.

**WAKE UP! WAKE UP! IT'S YER MODIFIED BEANSTALK...**

# Weekly SchNEWS

*"it's one goddam thing after another"*

Printed and Published in Brighton by **Justice?**

**Friday 25th February 1999**  http://www.schnews.org.uk/  **Issue 202 - Free / Donation**

# OOH, AMERICA - WHAT BIG LIES YOU HAVE!

*"Over the past two years the US has flooded the world market with unregulated and unlabelled genetically-engineered grain. It is clear it wants to continue this practice and will sabotage any efforts to set international rules for GE crops."* **Louise Gale, Greenpeace**

More than once upon a time, an evil mutant wolf (neither beautiful nor noble, so no complaints, wilderness types) called the USA wooed, deceived then shat upon the Little Red Riding Hood of a free world. Well guess what, boys and girls - the furry bastard is back. Blink and you might have missed it, but on Wednesday a world wide agreement that would have put safeguards on the trade of genetically modified organisms (GMO's) was sabotaged and no, there's no prizes for guessing the villain of the piece.

Over 135 nations of the world were at Cartagena, Colombia to agree upon an International Biosafety Protocol, a binding set of international safety standards concerning the trade of GMO's. The Agreement would have forced exporting nations to tell countries whenever any GMO's were going to turn up at their docks. It would mean that biodiversity and environmental safety would be- shock, horror- put above the interests of industry, and provide protection for developing nations.

But surprise, surprise. America - alongside other members of the "Miami Group" (US, Canada, Australia, Argentina, Chile, and Uruguay, now dubbed the "Miami Vice" of grain exporters) - did the dirty and scuppered the plans, clearing the way for the biotech companies to take even greater control of the food chain. As Ricarda Steinbrecher, representative for Women's Environmental Network (W.E.N.) at the negotiations argues, *"Biodiversity and safety are the big losers at these negotiations. Trade has got the upper hand and is dictating a Bio-Trade Protocol."*

The US kindly decided to piss in the world's pint-pot on two counts. Firstly, worried that little niceties like clear labelling on international shipments might help citizens boycott products, they refused to allow things like soya beans and corn, which account for 90% of the world trade in GMO's to be included in the negotiations. The "health-conscious" Yanks insist that any safety tests

felt necessary by ungrateful little third-world nations would have to be carried out domestically - beyond the resources of many nations, who were hoping the Protocol might give them the time and knowledge to develop their own laws. Secondly, the US was insistent on the inclusion of Article 31, part of the Protocol relating to other international agreements, which all the countries wanted deleted. This would mean that, in the event of a conflict of interests between the World Trade Organisation and the Protocol, the interests of business would win out. Did the US play fair? We think not, as Dr. Steinbrecher points out: *"The Ethiopian delegate, representing some countries of the so-called 'Third World' was locked in a room with two delegates from the developed world for over seven hours without any break or contact*

*with other 'third world' countries. He is under immense pressure."*

Even more unbelievable is that the US didn't even have a formal delegation in Colombia. It is not even part of the Convention on Biological Diversity, so what was it doing there? Turns out the posse of bullyboy gatecrashers - sorry, *powerful lobby group* - was a bunch of Arthur Daley sales reps from biotech companies including Monsanto, Novartis, Agro-Evo, Pioneer, Rhone Poulenc and Global Biotech Forum who came, in the words of Greenpeace spokesperson Louise Gale, *"with one task - to torpedo the negotiations."*

The delegate from Mauritius joined 63 countries in condemning the negotiations, *"We came here to negotiate, but found ourselves most of the time in corridors or in front of*

*locked doors, not knowing the state of play. We cannot accept this draft that was thrust down our throats without discussion."*

The scuppering of the Protocol leaves countries that want to block the import of GMO's out on a limb - if they make an individual stance they could face the wrath of the World Trade Organisation.

And what, you may wonder, is Britain's stance on this? Well, after initial lip service to outrage, Bill C. got on the blower and now "we" are pressing for compromise along with the US.

As W.E.N. say, *"Consumers... don't want to be bullied by big industry and the USA. Without a strong protocol, we are all the losers."*

The same old *Un*-fairy tale, eh readers? For more bed-time reading, contact Womens Environmental Network, 87 Worship Street, London, EC2A 2BE. Tel: 0171 247 3327 or visit http://www.greenpeace.org/

## KVAERNER KREW

**Protester:** *"Do you consider the Economy to be more important than the environment?"*
**Kvaerner Construction:** *"..Yes!"*

That's strange, as their delightful brochure boasts that "...we see the protection of the environment... as our prime concern... we act as a single globally-functioning business with a single identity world-wide."

The Kvaerner owned company, Midland Expressway Limited (MEL), are the consortium wanting to build Britains first toll motorway, the Birmingham Northern Relief Road (BNRR). While the Alliance Against The BNRR were in the High Courts appealing the decision for the go-ahead for the 27 mile motorway, 30 activists payed a visit to their offices, complete with banners, fire juggling and general chaos. Kvaerner may have difficulty getting an estimated £600-700 million from the city following the financial failures of their other toll roads in America and abroad. A camp is still on route, contact Mike on ..01922 416110, or Birmingham FoE..0121 6326909 for more info.

**Learn to Desk Top Publish for SchNEWS!** We're running a training day on Monday 22 March. Absolute beginners 10.30 am - 12.30 pm, others 1.30 - 3.30 pm.(We can handle 4 people per session; book now!) SchNEWS is desperate for more people to DTP on Thurs evenings. Competent? Patient? Get in touch.

## Fortress UK

While Tory Blair this week talked of a "more tolerant, more inclusive Britain" after the publishing of the Stephen Lawrence report, the second reading of New Labour's Immigration and Asylum Bill eased its way through parliament. Words such as 'tolerance' do not spring to mind in the new way asylum seekers, often fleeing torture and persecution, are going to be dealt with when they arrive here. The Bill includes:

❖ Withdrawing all benefits from asylum seekers and their families and introducing a system of cashless vouchers worth about £30 to exchange for food (forget clothes, toiletries, medicines, household goods etc.)

❖ Remove local authorities' obligations towards them under the National Assistance, Homelessness and Childrens Acts.

❖ Scatter asylum seekers in designated accommodation around the country; no matter that it might mean they are seperated from family and/or friends or housed in areas without proper support facilities such as services for torture survivors.

❖ Giving immigration officers new powers to enter and search premises and arrest asylum seekers, in some cases without a warrant 'using reasonable force if necessary'

❖ Extend the use of detention and finger-printing on arrival to the UK

❖ Some bail hearings to be tried via a live TV link!

❖ Reduced appeal times.

❖ Introduce a whole new range of criminal offences for people who help asylum seekers.

Still, as the Refugee Council points out, *"Most asylum seekers come here for purely selfish reasons: to escape death."* Refugee Council 0171 582 6922.

***DEMONSTRATE t** his Saturday against the Asylum Bill: 12 noon, 27 February, Embankmank (a minibus is going from outside St.Peters Church, Brighton at 10am.)*

* 335 pages of the Stephen Lawrence case and no mention of police corruption. Funny that. But what of Duwayne Brooks, who was with Stephen at the time of his murder? After officers said he was anti-police they then reckoned he was in danger and needed their protection. So they assigned him the same copper who had been seen drinking on 3 occasions with the father of David Norris - one of the racist scumbags accused of killing Stephen. Norris is a big time gangster, currently serving 8 yrs for drugs and arms, suspected of at least one murder with a reputation of jury nobbling and intimidation of witnesses. Duwayne had a breakdown and couldn't give evidence at the private prosecution or even turn up at the public inquiry.

* If readers want to see our double-page interview with someone from the Lawrence Family campaign send an SAE for issue 177 or check out our web-pages.

## Freedom For Tibet Week

March 10 1999 is the 40th Anniversary of the Tibetan National Uprising, when the Tibetan people rose up against the Chinese occupation of their country. Thousands of Tibetans were killed by the brutal surpression of the uprising with the Dalai Lama also being forced into exile.

For a full programme list of the week, which runs from 4-13 March, contact the Free Tibet Campaign, 1 Rosoman Place, London EC1Y OJY. Tel.0171 833 9958.

## SchNEWS in brief

Nobody likes paying for public services, do they, Gordon Brown? Apart from the people of **Milton Keynes** that is, who have voted in a referendum to increase their council tax bills by almost 10%. Faced with the prospect of deep cuts in schools, libraries and home help budgets a turn-out of almost 45% said yes to more public services. Bloody revolutionaries. ** The **U'wa people** live high in the cloud forests of Colombia and believe that their purpose in life is to protect the earth Bloody radicals. Of course, as you would expect their lands are now threatened by evil oil giants. One of them Berito KuwarU'wa is coming to the UK on 28th March @ Earth Centre, Denaby Main, Doncaster, DN12 4DY 01709 512000. ** **Permaculture** Introductory Weekend 13-14 March. Contact NatureWise 0171 281 3765. ** **International Women's Day**-Rally for Mothers Against Disappearances! Saturday 6th March, 4pm Trafalgar Square. ** Discuss **Ghetto Politics** with **London Anarchist Forum,** 8pm, Conway Hall, 25 Red Lion Square, London, WC1R 4Rl (nearest tube Holborn).The Forum meet at same place, same time every week Tel 0181 847 0203. ** Benefit evening for Workers Aid for **Kosova** Friday 5th March, 8pm-12pm, The Yard Theatre, Hulme with Attila the Stockbroker,. Tickets £6/4. ** **The Centre for Alternative Technology** has recently won the British Environment and Media Awards. for best website. Check it out *www.cat.org.uk*** Genetic Engineering Network** Office needs help urgently. If you've any have time to spare call 0181 374 9516.

## Bosses that bug us

Sick of your boss sticking their nosey beak into your business? Well have a read of "Surveillance and Privacy at Work" by Michael Ford. Today a quarter of a million people are drug tested every year by companies. Businesses are investing in Big Brother interviews, demanding potential employees to release their most intimate secrets like psychological makeup, sexuality, religion, bra size etc. It's not just prisoners that are being fitted with electronic tags, but also your average Joe Public call centre worker. This infra red equipment designed by AT&T follows a worker the minute he gets into work, knows when he's off his PC, and can even track him into the bog. Ford's book goes into the whole world of pervy boss spying antics and calls for extra legislation to make this practice illegal. Contact: Institute of Employment Rights, 177 Abbeville Road, London, SW4 9RL (it's a steep £20 order it from the library.)

## Resistrance is useless

Those free party people activists RESISTRANCE are holding another one day spectacular on Sat 13th March at the New Trinity Centre, Bristol. Entitled "An alternative thinkers gathering", day-time has stalls, Kebele Kulture veggie café and a wide-range of speakers (hey even SchNEWS will take to the stage). Social in the evening includes bands Baby Head and Dubmerge followed by an all-nighter techno party. Last years event was excellent. Details 07970 337638

Avon calling! Construction is underway on the Avon Ring Road (Bristol's answer to the M25). The campaign has squatted a field near the route and need more people. Anyone who can handle a spanner is urged to get on down there! The campaign has good local support and a secure camp.For details and directions contact 0836 653723.

Ashton Court Quarry Campaign, Bristol are celebrating one year anniversary of protest with a week of action on February 27-March 5 starting with a "BIG" free party on the 27th. Contact Campaign Mobile:07970 423834.

## Portsmouth Three

Hampshire police love hunt saboteurs, and welcome them to their Police Benevolent Fund all-night fund-raising parties. No, actually they don't; but they did set up a full-time CID incident room for them, for over 4 months. A week on Monday these efforts come to a head when begins the Portsmouth trial of 3 sabs charged with *conspiracy to commit violent disorder.* Funny, this one....

Violence had been mounting from supporters of the Hursley Hambleden foxhunt. When things kicked off again at a meet of the hunt, no-one was charged (on either side) for actual assault or damage, despite plenty of police having been in the area. But the cops were as keen to use the opportunity to gather intelligence on sabs as the hunting lobby were to make PR capital from it. The police took first pickings, arresting 42 sabs, raiding homes and workplaces and seizing clothes, phones, video cameras and vehicles. Then the media to moved in; the Evening Standard reportage furthering its propaganda effort against the anti-hunt Foster Bill.

Thus the web of conspiracy unfolds. We can infer the old bill had tipped off the hunt about the planned large-scale sab, as (unusually) present were pro-hunt surveillance teams and the regional press officer of the Countryside Movement (doubtless keen to canvas support for that organisation's concern for rural Post Offices). Another tip-off:

*Demo outside Portsmouth Crown Court, 1:00pm, Monday March 1 (1st day of trial, and National Day Of Acton Against All BloodSports). Prosecutions in Britain are never politically motivated. Be there to admire the Hampshire officers' dedication to the quest for justice.*

* **Defence Campaign**, Box H, 67 Fawcett Rd., Southsea, Hants, PO4 ODH

## ...and finally...

A company trying to continue its 5 year perfect safety record showed its workers a film aimed at encouraging the use of safety goggles on the job. According to *Industrial Machinery News*, the film's depiction of gory industrial accidents was so graphic that 25 workers suffered minor injuries in their rush to leave the screening room. 13 others fainted, and one man required 7 stitches after he cut his head falling off a chair while watching.

**disclaimer**

## Subscribe!

Keep SchNEWS FREE! Just send 1st Class stamps (e.g. 20 for next 20 issues) or donations (payable to Justice?) **Ask for "Originals"** if **you can make copies.** Post *free* to all prisoners. **SchNEWS, c/o on-the-fiddle, P.O. Box 2600, Brighton, East Sussex, BN2 2DX.**

*Tel/Autofax:* +44 (0)1273 685913    *Get e-SchNEWS every week by email:* schnews@brighton.co.uk

# ASSEMBLIES OF CELEBRATION, ASSEMBLIES OF DISSENT

Jim Carey reviews the recent political history of Travellers, city kids, raves and festivals and reveals the multi-tactic approach used in attempts to annihilate an emerging culture of celebration and dissent.

SQUALL

Where Do You Want To Grow Today?
---
I Wanna Go Home
Underground Update
**Features** ▶
Squall Pics ▶
Frontline Communique
The State Its In
Squotes
Resources
Links
From Our Correspondence

When the Criminal Justice and Public Order Act began its passage through parliament in 1993, there were many who were genuinely flabbergasted. Why were travellers, squatters, ravers, political protesters and public assemblies considered so much of a threat to the nation that new criminal law was required? As Home Secretary in 1992, Kenneth Baker broadcast the government's opinion thus: "We will get tough on rapists, tough on armed robbers and tough on squatters". Such farcical juxtapositions became a feature of the passage of the new law and an indication of the extent to which the government were prepared to go in persuading the British public that such activities were harbouring nests of parasitic criminals. Such selective demonisation was nothing new of course, though few thought that it would manifest itself in such overtly draconian fashion. That a "series of repetitive beats" should become the defined target of criminal sanctions, reinforced the impression that the Nazi penchant for targeting cultural undesirables was now finding new expression in the UK. Far from an isolated incident however, the Criminal Justice and Public Order Act was merely one of the more overt measures in a long term strategy of annihilation.

The networking hub of the UK's so called 'underground' culture were the unlicensed public festivals which had been proliferating across the British Isles since the early seventies. Primarily designed to provide financially accessible community celebrations, these gatherings also harboured active expressions of rising public dissension; populated as they were by an outflux of disaffected youth from inner cities determined to create a new life for themselves outside the market-myopic. The largest example of these gatherings took place annually at Stonehenge around the date of the summer solstice; the longest day.

Having begun as a small gathering in 1974, the Stonehenge Solstice Free Festival attracted 30,000 people to its last uninterrupted incarnation in 1984. The political significance of this 'Mother' of all festivals was exacerbated by its location. Not only were 30,000 people gathering without the presence of the police, they were doing so in the highly Conservative county of Wiltshire on one of the largest military training grounds in the UK. To the British establishment this was a flagrant challenge, and one which, much to their annoyance, was getting larger every year. Furthermore, with environmentalism as a prominent feature of festival culture, those attending the gatherings - including the swelling ranks of British travellers - began involving themselves in direct action, the main focus of which concentrated on nuclear energy and weaponry. Between 1980-1984, convoys of travellers took part in public operations known as Cruisewatch. This involved the overt tailing of mobile Cruise missiles, transported from silos in Wiltshire to secret locations in neighbouring counties. This was a particularly sensitive area for the government. Secretly located nuclear missiles formed a major part of the UK's nuclear deterrent tactics, with mobility designed to confuse the Soviets in the event of an attack. Anti-nuclear campaigners argued such manoeuvres brought the possibility of nuclear war even closer and effectively blew the government's cover by following the missiles everywhere they went.

The term 'Peace Convoy' was a generic term coined largely by the media and, with the continual involvement of travellers in anti-nuclear demonstrations, it was a term that stuck. In June 1982, a 'peace convoy' left Stonehenge to support the nuclear weapons protest outside Greenham Common in Berkshire; holding an impromptu festival on the perimeter and cutting the fence. In September the same year, another convoy incorporated the Sizewell B nuclear reactor in Suffolk into its itinerary of East Anglian festivals. Once again they established themselves in the car-park and stayed for a week. In 1984, the significance of these stand-offs was brought to a head when another peace convoy took part in a

THESE ROMANS ARE CRAZY!!!

STONEHENGE
SOLSTICE RITUAL
*FREE FESTIVAL*
JUNE

"BRING A FRIEND OR TEN !!"

large demonstration outside the US Cruise Missile base at Molesworth in Cambridgeshire. Along with other contingents of anti-nuclear protesters, travellers occupied a perimeter site for five months; planting and reaping crops whilst a group of Quakers built a Stone Chapel of Peace. Following a High Court possession order granted in February 1985, the entire protest camp was finally evicted using soldiers from the Royal Engineers regiment. Significant to the political escalation resulting from these protests, the eviction was attended by the then Minister of Defence, Michael Heseltine, famously arriving on site dressed in a camouflage flak jacket. Meanwhile the festival circuit harboured an increasing multitude of campaign groups - particularly those connected with the environment - assembling en masse, distributing information and discussing action. Up until 1985, these burgeoning assemblies of alternative living and dissent stood successfully defiant in the face of Margaret Thatcher's designs on an ultra-efficient market mono-culture. In 1985, however, the 'Peace Convoy' and its associated culture became the target of a multi-strategic campaign of annihilation, inaugurated with blood at Stonehenge.

## The Battle of the Beanfield

It is difficult to convey the extent and affect of the berserk circumstances which occurred on June 1st 1985, but their socio-political ramifications were immense. A convoy of travellers' vehicles left an impromptu park-up site in Savernake Forest to head towards Stonehenge. Seven miles from the Stones, and still some way out of the newly imposed four and half mile High Court exclusion order, police blocked the convoy with three lorry loads of gravel. After a short standoff, the acting Deputy Chief Constable of Wiltshire, Lionel Grundy, gave orders for his men to begin attacking the vehicles and arresting drivers. When word swept through the convoy that police were smashing windscreens at the front and back of the line of vehicles, travellers pulled off the A303 and into an adjacent grass field. At this stage, many travellers were keen to return to the Savernake Forest site, but were told by Wiltshire Police that those wishing to leave the scene could only do so without their vehicles (homes). After a tense wait, the pressure cooker finally exploded when over 1000 police, drawn from five constabularies, charged into the field wielding truncheons. In an effort to escape, the convoy drove from the grass field into the adjacent Beanfield looking for a way out. A huge number of riot police charged in behind them to commit their now infamously one-sided carnage, inappropriately referred to as the Battle of the Beanfield.

break new bounds in the scale and intensity of its violence. We saw police throw hammers, stones and other missiles through the windscreens of advancing vehicles; a woman dragged away by her hair; young men beaten over the head with truncheons as they tried to surrender....the police operation became a chaotic whirl of violence...basic rules of police behaviour were abandoned. The identification numbers of most officers were concealed by flame- proof overalls....I saw a young man's glasses swiped from his face and front teeth break under the raining blows." The only national television camera crew in the Beanfield was from ITN. Reporter Kim Sabido spoke to camera: "What we the ITN camera crew and myself as a reporter have seen in the last 30 minutes here in this field has been some of the most brutal police treatment of people that I've witnessed in my entire career as a journalist. The number of people who have been hit by policemen, who have been clubbed

**The Battle Of The Beanfield 1985**

Public knowledge of the events of that day are still limited by the fact that only a small number of journalists were present in the Beanfield at the time. Most, including the BBC Television crew, had obeyed the police directive to stay behind police lines at the bottom of the hill "for their own safety". One of the few journalists to ignore police advice and attend the scene was Nick Davies, Home Affairs correspondent for The Observer at the time. He wrote: "All of us were shocked by what we saw: police tactics which seemed to

Pics: Ben Gibson

whilst holding babies in their arms in coaches around this field, is yet to be counted...There must surely be an enquiry." However, when the item was nationally broadcast on ITN news later that day, Sabido's voice-over had been removed and replaced with a dispassionate narrator. The worst film footage was also edited out. When approached for the footage not shown on the news, ITN claimed it was missing.

"When I got back to ITN during the following week and I went to the library to look at all the rushes, most of what I'd thought we'd shot was no longer there," recalls Sabido. "From what I've seen of what ITN has provided since, it just disappeared, particularly some of the nastier shots." Some but not all of the missing footage has since re-surfaced on bootleg tapes and was incorporated into the 'Operation Solstice' documentary shown on Channel Four in 1991. A similar story of missing visual evidence transpires when trying to track down the images taken by photojournalists. Ben Gibson, a freelance photographer working for the Observer that day, was arrested in the Beanfield after photographing riot police smashing their way into a traveller's coach. He was later acquitted of charges of obstruction although the intention behind his arrest had been served by removing him from the scene. Most of the negatives from the film he managed to shoot disappeared from the Observer's archives during an office move. Fellow photographer Tim Malyon narrowly avoided the same fate:

"Whilst attempting to take pictures of one group of officers beating people with their truncheons, a policeman shouted out to 'get him' and I was chased. I ran and was not arrested." Malyon thought his film was safe after storing it with London solicitors' firm Birnbergs. However, despite the fact that his photographic negatives were never supposed to have left Birnbergs' possession, they too disappeared. Fortunately, some of Ben Gibson's and Tim Malyon's prints have recently resurfaced and are printed here.

One unusual eye-witness to the Beanfield nightmare was the Earl of Cardigan, secretary of the Marlborough Conservative Association and manager of Savernake Forest (on behalf of his father the Marquis of Ailesbury). He had travelled along with the convoy on his motorbike accompanied by fellow Conservative Association member, John Moore. As the travellers had left from land managed by Cardigan, the pair thought "it would be interesting to follow the events personally". Wearing crash helmets to disguise their identity, they witnessed what Cardigan described as "unspeakable" police violence. Cardigan provided eye-witness testimonies of police behaviour during subsequent prosecutions brought against Wiltshire Police, including descriptions of a heavily pregnant woman with "a silhouette like a zeppelin" being "clubbed with a truncheon" and riot police showering a woman and child with glass.

"I had just recently had a baby daughter myself," Lord Cardigan told SQUALL. "So when I saw babies showered with

Stonehenge Festival 1983

glass by riot police smashing windows, I suppose I thought of my own baby lying in her cradle 25 miles away in Marlborough." After the Beanfield, Wiltshire Police approached Lord Cardigan to gain his consent for an immediate eviction of the travellers remaining on his Savernake Forest site. "They said they wanted to go into the campsite 'suitably equipped' and 'finish unfinished business'. Make of that phrase what you will," says Cardigan. "I said to them that if it was my permission they were after, they did not have it. I did not want a repeat of the grotesque events that I'd seen the day before." Instead, the site was evicted using court possession proceedings, allowing the travellers a few days recuperative grace.

As a prominent local aristocrat and Tory, Cardigan's testimony held unusual sway, presenting unforeseen difficulties for those seeking to cover up and re-interpret the events at the Beanfield. Wiltshire Police responded to the event with the now familiar tactic of prosecuting for assault the very people they had assaulted. In an effort to counter the contrary impact of Lord Cardigan's testimony, several national newspapers began painting him as a 'loony lord', questioning his suitability as an eye-witness and drawing farcical conclusions from the fact that his great-great grandfather had led the charge of the light brigade. The Times editorial on June 3rd claimed that being "barking mad was probably hereditary".

As a consequence, Lord Cardigan successfully sued the Times, the Telegraph, the Daily Mail, the Daily Express and the Daily Mirror for claiming that his allegations against the police were false and for suggesting that he was making a home for hippies. He received what he describes as "a pleasing cheque and a written apology" from all of them. His treatment by the press was ample indication of the united front held between the prevailing political regime and complicit national media sources, with Lord Cardigan's testimony as an unplanned-for spanner in the plotted works: "On the face of it they had the ultimate establishment creature - landowning, peer of the realm, card carrying member of the Conservative Party - slagging off police and therefore by implication befriending those who they call the powers of darkness," says Cardigan. "I hadn't realised that anybody that appeared to be supporting elements that stood against the establishment would be savaged by establishment newspapers. Now one thinks about it nothing could be more natural. "I hadn't realised that I would be considered a class traitor; if I see a policeman truncheoning a woman I feel I'm entitled to say that it is not a good thing you should be doing. I went along, saw an episode in British history and reported what I saw."

Largely as a result of his testimony, police charges against members of the convoy were dismissed in the local magistrates courts. However, there was no public enquiry. Of the 440 travellers taken into custody that day, 24 went through the gruelling five year process of taking Wiltshire Police to court for wrongful arrest, assault and criminal damage. They finally won a four month court case at Winchester Crown Court in 1991, but received compensation almost identical to the legal costs incurred in the process. As Lord Gifford QC, the travellers' legal representative, put it: "It left a very sour taste in the mouth". To some of those at the brunt end of the truncheon charge, the violence left a devastating legacy. Alan Lodge, a veteran of many free festivals, was one of the 24 travellers who 'successfully' took Wiltshire Police to court following the Beanfield incident: "There was one guy who I trusted my children with in the early 80's - he was a potter. After the Beanfield I wouldn't let him anywhere near them. I saw him, a man of substance at the end of all that nonsense wobbled to the point of illness and evil. It turned all of us and I'm sure that applies to the whole travelling community. There was plenty of people who had got something very positive together who came out of the Beanfield with a world view of fuck everyone."

The violent nature of the police action drew obvious comparisons with the coercive police tactics employed on the miners strike the year before. Many observers claimed the two events provided strong evidence that government directives were para- militarising police responses to crowd control, a view confirmed by Sir Peter Imbert, ex-commissioner of the Metropolitan Police: "A subject of concern is the move towards paramilitarism in the police. I accept that such a move has occurred." Indeed in the confidential Wiltshire Police Operation Solstice Report, released to plaintiffs during the resulting Crown Court case, it states: "Counsel's opinion regarding the police tactics used in the miners' strike to prevent a breach of the peace was considered relevant." An edition of the Police Review, published seven days after the Beanfield, also revealed: "The Police operation had been planned for several months and lessons in rapid deployment learned from the miners' strike were implemented." Such heavy handed tactics were 'justified' at the time by a farcical passage from the confidential police report:"There is known to be a hierarchy within the convoy; a small nucleus of leaders making the final decisions on all matters of importance relating to the convoy's activities. A second group who are known as the 'lieutenants' or 'warriors' carry out the wishes of the convoy leader, intimidating other groups on site." If the paramilitary policing used on the Miners Strike was a violent introduction to Thatcher's mal-intention towards union dissent, the Battle of the Beanfield was a similarly severe introduction to a new era of intolerance of travellers, festivals and public protest.

# Manufacturing a case for public order law.

At the 1995 Big Green Gathering Festival, Inspector Hunt, a member of Wiltshire Police force for 20 years, told a reporter from SQUALL: "Stonehenge Festival grew too large and out of control, the Beanfield was just the beginning of the process of dealing with it. The laws that came after were even more effective." The following year saw the imposition of the Public Order Act 1986, giving police powers to break up any gathering of twelve vehicles or more. This new legislation not only provided the authorities with powers to stop convoys, it also had seriously detrimental implications for both festivals and traveller sites all over the country. On June 3rd that year, Douglas Hurd - then Home Secretary - described travellers as "nothing more than a band of medieval brigands who have no respect for the law or the rights of others."

On June 5th, Margaret Thatcher told the nation that the British government was "only too delighted to do anything we can to make life difficult for such things as hippy convoys" . On the same day, a cabinet committee was formed to discuss new legislation to deal with travellers and festivals. Chaired by Home Secretary, Douglas Hurd, the committee was comprised of the Secretaries of State for Transport, Environment, Health and Social Security, and Agriculture.

Meanwhile, convoys assembling to celebrate that year's Solstice were chased around several counties by police, before finally finding some temporary respite on a site at Stoney Cross in the New Forest. Four days later, Hampshire Police mounted the 4am 'Operation Daybreak' to clear Stoney Cross. Sixty Four convoy members were arrested and 129 vehicles impounded after police came on site armed with DoT files on every vehicle. The police also came armed with care orders for the travellers' children, though a tip off reached the camp beforehand and the children were removed. The Battle of the Beanfield and the increasingly hostile political climate which followed, had a dramatic affect on the travelling community, frightening away many of the families integral to the community balance of the festival circuit.

In 1987, a few hundred people stood on the tarmac beside Stonehenge, having walked the eight miles from an impromptu site at Cholderton. As clouds smothered the Solstice sunrise, those who had walked the distance were kept on the road, separated from the Stones by rows of riot police and razor wire. As the anger mounted, scuffles brokeout.

A year later the anger had tangibly increased and once again at Solstice dawn there were some who found the situation too unacceptable. This time the scuffles were more prevalent with concerted efforts made to break through the police cordon. Secreted around the area, however, were thousands of waiting riot police and as the frustration of the penned in crowd grew, numberless uniforms came flooding down the hill to disperse the crowd with a liberal usage of truncheons and riot shields. Andy Smith - now editor of the magazine Festival Eye - finally received a £10,000 out of court settlement from Wiltshire Police in 1996 for a truncheon wound to the head received after he tripped and fell at Stonehenge in 1988. The numbers of people prepared to travel to Stonehenge and face this treatment naturally dwindled, resulting in a concentration of those who were prepared for confrontation in defence of what was considered as a right to celebrate solstice at Stonehenge. Successive large-scale police operations backed by the Public Order Act 1986, became stricter in attempts to stop anyone from reaching the stone circle at Solstice. Each subsequent year, however, there were those who hugged hedgerows and darted between the beams of police helicopters in order to be in view of the Solstice sunrise at Stonehenge.

# Destroying the alternative economy

Up until 1985, the free festival circuit had provided the economic backbone of traveller's year long itinerary. Traditionally the three cardinal points in the festival circuit were the May bank holiday, the August bank holiday and Solstice. Without the need for advertising, festival-goers knew to look out for these dates in expectation that a festival would be taking place somewhere. The employment of two bank holidays as specific festival times allowed workers the opportunity of attending a festival without the inevitable bleary Monday back at work. By selling crafts, services, performance busking, tat and assorted gear, travellers provided themselves with an alternative economy which lent a financial viability to their itinerant culture. Evidence suggests that the political campaign to eradicate festivals was in good part aimed at breaking this economy. A working party set up by the Department of Health and Social Security published a report on Itinerant Claimants in March 1986 stating: "Local offices of the DHSS have experienced increasing problems in dealing with claims from large groups of nomadic claimants over the past 2 or 3 years. Matters came to a head during the summer of 1985 when several large groups converged on Stonehenge for a festival that had been banned by the authorities. The resulting well publicised confrontation with the police was said to have disrupted the normal festival economy and large numbers of claims to Supplementary Benefit were made."

"As soon as they scared away the punters it destroyed the means of exchange," recalls traveller Alan Lodge. "Norman Tebbit went on about getting on your bike and finding employment whilst at the same time being part of the political force that kicked the bike from under us." In the years that followed, the right wing press made much of dole scrounging travellers, with no acknowledgement that the engineered break up of the festival economy was a major contributory factor.

Another ramification of this tactic was even more insidious and ugly. At the entrance gate to the 1984 Stonehenge Free Festival, a burnt out car bore testament to the levels of self-policing emerging from the social-experiment. The sign protruding from the wreckage proclaimed: "This was a smack dealer's car". However, dispossessed of their once thriving economy and facing incessant and increasing harassment and eviction, the break down of community left travellers prone to a destructive force potentially more devastating than anything directly forced by the authorities.

"At one time smack wasn't tolerated on the road at all," recalls mother of six, Decker Lynn. "Certainly on festival sites, if anybody was selling or even using it they were just put off site full stop."

Pic: Nick Cobbing

Heroin, the great escape to oblivion, found the younger elements of a fractured community prone to the drug's clutch and its use spread amongst travellers like myxamatosis. Once again traveller families were forced to vacate sites which were falling prey to the heroin, further imbalancing the battered communities and creating a split between 'clean' and 'dirty' sites.

"I don't park on big sites anymore," says Lynn, who still lives in her double decker bus. "Heroin is something that breaks up a community because people become so self-centred they don't give a damn about their neighbours." Many travellers report incidences of blatant heroin dealing going untouched by police, whilst other travellers on the same site were prosecuted for small amounts of hashish. The implication of these claims were that the authorities recognised that if heroin took hold of the travelling community, political designs on the destruction of the travelling community would take care of itself.

"So many times people got away with it and there were very few busts for smack," recalls Lynn. "They must know smack is the quickest way to divide a community; united we stand and divided we don't."

The other manifestation of community disruption was the emergence of the so called 'brew crew'. These were mainly angry young travellers feeding themselves on a diet of special brew and developing a penchant for nihilism, blagging and communal disrespect. In the previous years of a more healthy festival culture, the outflux of youth from the inner cities was well met, absorbed and often healed.

"To start with it was contained," says Decker Lynn. "Every family had its problems but the brew crew was a very small element around 1986, and very much contained by the families that were around. But there was large number of angry young people pouring out of the cities with brew and smack and the travelling community couldn't cope with the numbers." The so called 'brew crew' caused constant disruption for those festivals still surviving on the decimated circuit and provided an obvious target for slander hungry politicians and right wing media.

## Raves and the new blood

Towards the end of the eighties a new cultural phenomenon emerged in the UK resulting in an injection of new blood and economy to the festival scene. Rave parties were similar to free festivals in that they were unlicensed events in locations kept secret until the last possible moment. Such events offered similar opportunities for adventure and began attracting huge numbers of young people from the cities. Some of these parties differed from the free festivals in that they were organised by groups such as Sunrise, who would charge an entry fee and consequently make large amounts of money in the process. Not all such rave parties were of this nature however, and the free festival scene began to merge with the rave party scene producing an accessible hybrid with new dynamism.

Once again political attention was now targeted against these new impromptu rave events, resulting in the Entertainment (Increased Penalties) Act 1990. Introduced by John Major's Personal Private Secretary, Graham Bright MP, this private members bill brought in massive penalties of up to £20,000 and/or six months imprisonment for the organisers of unlicensed events. Once again this legislation had a dramatic affect on the free festival/rave scene, pushing event organisation into the hands of large commercial promoters with the necessary sums required to pay for licences and policing.
Indeed, a report called 'Leisure Futures', produced by market analysts the Henley Centre in 1993, gave some indication of how worried commercial entertainment businesses had become over the explosion of rave culture. Estimating that British ravers were worth a potential £1.8 billion a year to the entertainment industry, the report confirmed that rave culture was posing a "significant threat" to the market share of drinks retailers, breweries and pubs. Richard Carr, then chairman of Allied Leisure, the entertainments section of the alcohol conglomerate Allied-Tetley-Lyons, had already voiced his concern about rave culture in 1992, describing it "a major threat to alcohol-led business."

A web of mutual interests involving parliamentary lobbyists Ian Greer Associates, Sir Graham Bright MP and one of the UK's largest alcohol-led businesses Whitbread (whose headquarters are situated in Bright's Luton constituency) opened up powerful conduits to political influence. In 1993, Ian Greer's firm helped Whitbread set up a beer club in the Houses of Parliament. With over 125 member MPs it is the largest industrial club in the palace. As a consequence of legislation directed against raves, the nature of festival and rave promotion swung away from its community-based orientation, as big business attempted to commercially harness the public's desire for adventurous festival/parties in the countryside. According to Tony Hollingsworth, ex-events promoter for the GLC and now part of a £multi-million commercial festival outfit Tribute: "The motivation behind these festivals is no longer passion, it is commerce." Relative to the people-led festivals, critics argue that the commercial festival scene now offers little more than another shopping experience, where an attendant wallet is valued and encouraged far more than participation.

## Castlemorton Common

By 1992, leaked documents from Avon and Somerset Constabulary demonstrated the existence of Operation Nomad. A Force Operational Order, marked 'In Confidence', revealed: "With effect from Monday 27th April 1992, dedicated resources will be used to gather intelligence in respect of the movement of itinerants and travellers and deal with minor acts of trespass." An intelligence unit set up by Avon and Somerset Police produced regular Operation Nomad bulletins, listing personal details on travellers and regular festival goers unrelated to any criminal conviction. The Force Operational Order issued by the Chief Constable also stated: "Resources will be greatly enhanced for the period Thursday 21st May to Sunday 24th May inclusive in relation to the anticipated gathering of travellers in the Chipping Sodbury area."

This item referred to the annual Avon Free Festival which had been occurring in the area around the May bank holiday for several years, albeit in different locations. However, 1992 was the year Avon and Somerset Police intended to put a stop to it. As a result, the thousands of people travelling to the area for the expected festival were shunted into neighbouring counties by Avon and Somerset's Operation Nomad police manoeuvres. The end result was the impromptu Castlemorton Common Festival in West Mercia, another pivotal event in the recent history of festival culture.
West Mercia Police claim they had no idea that an event might happen in their district and were therefore powerless to stop it. However, observers questioned whether it was possible that Avon and Somerset Police had not informed their neighbouring constabulary that they were pushing travellers their way in Operation Nomad.
In the event, a staggering 30,000 travellers, ravers, festival-goers and inner city youth gathered almost overnight on Castlemorton Common to hold a free festival that flew in the face of the Public Order Act 1986 and the Entertainment (Increased Penalties) Act 1990. It was a massive celebration and the biggest of its kind since the bountiful days of the Stonehenge Free Festival.

The authorities used Castlemorton in a way which led people to suggest it had been at least partly engineered by the authorities themselves. The right wing press published acres of crazed and damning coverage of the event, including the classic front page Daily Telegraph headline: "Hippies fire flares at Police" . In the following morning's Telegraph, the editorial headline promised "New Age, New Laws" and within two months, Sir George Young, then Minister for Housing, confirmed that new laws against travellers were imminent "in reaction to the increasing level of public dismay and alarm about the behaviour of some of these groups." One revealing feature appeared in the Daily Telegraph following the festival at Castlemorton. Headlined "From ravers to travellers: a guide to the invaders", it profiled four individuals under the headings 'The Squatter', 'The Raver', 'The Traveller' and 'The career Traveller' - a significant early indication of what was to come. Indeed, the outcry following Castlemorton provided the basis for the most draconian law yet levelled against alternative British culture. Just as the Public Order Act 1986 followed the events at Stonehenge in 1985, so the Criminal Justice and Public Order Act 1994 began its journey in 1992, pumped with the manufactured outrage which followed Castlemorton. By the time it reached statute two years later, the CJA, as it came to be known, included criminal sanctions against assembly, outdoor unlicensed music events, unauthorised camping, repetitive beats, squatting and 'aggravated trespass' (public demonstrations). The law also reduced the number of vehicles which could gather together from 12 (as stipulated in the Public Order Act 1986) to six.

The news-manufacture used to prepare the public palate for the coming law was incessant, with media descriptions of travellers including "a swarming of human locusts" in the Daily Telegraph and "These foul pests must be controlled" in the Daily Mail .

# Police Surveillance and Benefit Clampdowns

The year after Castlemorton Common, the police set up Operation Snapshot, an intelligence gathering exercise on raves and travellers designed to establish a database of personal details, registration numbers, park up sites and movements. This information was used as a backbone for an ongoing intelligence operation begun by the Southern Central Intelligence Unit (SCIU), operated from Devizes in Wiltshire and initially co-ordinated by PC Malcolm Keene. The SCIU held regular meetings with representatives of all the constabularies of Britain.

Leaked documents revealed that Operation Snapshot had estimated there to be around 2,000 traveller vehicles and 8,000 Travellers in the UK. In the minutes of a meeting held at Devizes on March 30th 1993, the objectives of the operation included the development of "a system whereby intelligence could be taken into the control room, and the most up-to-date intelligence was to hand"..... "capable of high speed input and retrieval and dissemination of information". The meeting was attended by constabulary representatives from Bedfordshire, Avon and Somerset, Devon and Cornwall, Dorset, Gloucestershire, Dyfed-Powys, Cambridgeshire, Hertfordshire, Kent, Norfolk, Northamptonshire, South Wales, Gwent, Staffordshire, Thames Valley, Warwickshire, Surrey, Suffolk, West Mercia, West Midlands and the Ministry of Defence (Hampshire and Essex sent apologies). The National Criminal Intelligence Service (NCIS) also had representatives at the meetings, and requested that the NCIS should be allowed "to move in with the Southern Central Intelligence Unit for one or two weeks during the Solstice".

They were all asked and all agreed to provide the Southern Central Intelligence Unit with "any information, no matter how small on New Age Travellers or the Rave scene". The leaked minutes revealed the Operation Snapshot database was initially constructed to hold one million items of information . After a short period, the Northern New Age Traveller Co-ordination Unit, designed to cover the north of Britain, was established and operated from Penrith in Cumbria.

p

Further intelligence information was gathered via social security offices. The working party report on Itinerant Claimants, prepared for the DHSS in 1986, advised that "in the interests of advance warning and the safety of staff, we recommend better liaison with the police." A 1993 internal Benefits Agency bulletin headed 'New Age Travellers' and marked "not to be released into the public domain", stated: "Offices will be aware of the adverse reaction from the media following the treatment of claims from this client group last summer [Castlemorton]. Ministers are concerned that the Benefits Agency and Employment Services take all necessary steps to ensure that claims from this group are scrutinised carefully." The bulletin reports that a National Task Force had been set up to "monitor the movements of such groups of Travellers" and to "inform relevant District managers of their approach and numbers". In the back of the bulletin is a list of telephone numbers for all the regional police contacts in both the Northern New Age Traveller Co-ordination Unit and the Southern Central Intelligence Unit. Every constabulary in the country, including the Ministry of Defence police had at least one but usually several such designated co-ordinators. In 1995, the Benefits Agency conducted a census of New Age Traveller benefit claimants including their personal details. A leaked copy of the results suggested there to be 2000 such claimants. In July 1996, more leaked documents revealed that the Agency was once again asking regional offices to carry out a census, the results of which are as yet unrevealed . Following the introduction of the Job Seekers Allowance Scheme in October 1996, benefits could be halted if "appearance" or "attitude" "actively militates getting a job". The implications for the further selective targeting of the traveller community were obvious.

# Increased surveillance and DiY mutation

The extraordinary lengths taken by the authorities to annihilate travellers, raves and festivals are a testament to the treatment meted out to cultural minorities outside the acceptable hegemony. The use of legislation, intelligence targeted harassment, benefit clampdowns and news-manufacture were consistantly deployed as a multi-tactic approach stretched out across many years. Such strategies are often executed hidden from even the glance of public scrutiny; with the length of time over which they are deployed, serving to diffuse recognition of their mechanism and ultimate intention. What is clear, however, is that rather than seek to democratically accommodate an expanding community culture, Margaret Thatcher's government and those who replaced her sort instead to annihilate it. Although the battered survival of both travellers and free festivals demonstrates that they did not fully succeed, their jackboot approach left a lot of pain in its wake.

*Sources quoted in body text:*
(1) 'Operation Solstice' Channel Four 7/11/91 made by Neil Goodwin and Gareth Morris *(2) Written statement by Tim Malyon 4/6/85* (3) The Observer 9/6/85 *(4) Interview with Lord Cardigan SQUALL No.14 Autumn 1996* (5) 'The case against para-military policing' by Tony Jefferson (pub Open University Press 1990) *(6) Police Review 7/6/85* (7) Daily Telegraph 6/6/86 *(8) Hansard 5/6/86* (9) Times 6/5/86 *(10) 'Nomadic Claimants - Report of Working Party' Department of Health and Social Security HQ9RD9)* March 1986 (11) Independent 17/8/92 *(12) The Observer 20/10/96* (13) Force Operational Order 36/92 - 'Operation Nomad' issued by Chief Constable of Avon and Somerset Constab. "in confidence".*(14) Daily Telegraph 26/5/92* (15) Daily Telegraph 27/5/92 *(16) Daily Telegraph 7/6/93* (17) Daily Mail 27/5/92 *(18) leaked minutes quoted SQUALL No. 14 Autumn 1996* (19) Income Support Bulletin 24/93 Benefits Agency ("not for public domain") *(20) The Guardian 19/7/96* (21) SQUALL No. 9 Winter 1995 *(22) 'The Security Services' HMSO 1995* (23) Hansard 17/3/97 Col:417

# URBAN DESERT

WAKE UP! WAKE UP! WE COULDN'T MAKE THIS STUFF UP

# Weekly SchNEWS

### Printed and Published in Brighton by Justice?

Friday 6th March 1998    http://www.schnews.org.uk/    Issue 203    Free/Donation

# PARKING MAD

*"There is a time for words and a time for action. Now is the time for action."*

Harry, a local campaigner currently up a tower during the eviction

As SchNEWS went to press the eviction of the protest camp at Crystal Palace entered its third day. The site is surrounded by hundreds of security and police, main roads have been closed off, but protestors reckon the eviction could last for at least another ten days.

The Grade II listed park, on the highest point in London, is about to be carved up to make way for a £56 million, 20 screen multiplex cinema with 9 bars/restaurants, various retail outlets with concrete ramps leading cars up to the largest rooftop car–park in Britain! 12 acres of the park and 150 trees will disappear under the building which has been likened to an 'airport terminal.' This blot on the landscape will be visible for miles.

*Despite the fact that there was no environmental impact assessment; the Wildlife and Countryside Act was broken and the EU Habitat Directive ignored John Prescott gave the venture the green light saying there was no need for a public enquiry. Since taking over the park from the G.L.C. in 1986 Bromley Council have deliberately run the park down hoping any development would be welcomed by locals. However, the Councils claim that the development will "capture the essence of Paxtons work" hasn't washed with the locals who complain that the consultation process left a lot to be desired. The trashing of Crystal Palace, however, is being repeated around the country. The London Wildlife Trust estimate that sixty wildlife sites in the capital have been threatened by development this year alone.*

Not that architect Ian Ritchie cares. He told disgruntled residents "I'm glad people don't like it – it confirms my belief that it is a good design."

The complex aims to attract people from across South London and as Croydon councillor Adrian Dennis points out, "It is a car led development".

One of the boroughs bordering the site, Southwark, despite having the lowest car ownership rates in the country, suffers some of the worst air pollution rates in northern Europe, and will be hit further by the development with thousands of visitors expected.

In fact Bromley Council's own traffic advisor when asked by a local person how they could cope with the extra traffic replied 'It will be best to avoid the area'. Bit difficult when you live there.

Southwark is also the most densely populated district in northern Europe – here more than anywhere people need open spaces. Still, councillor John Lewis, a supporter of the development reckons "People don't want change and will find any excuse to hinder progress. There is a hard core group of people who want a museum and more trees in the park."

More trees in a park – good god, whatever next. As one protestor Storm Porrum told SchNEWS "Parks are the lungs of any city and we don't want our breathing space encroached upon by a development that will only add to pollution by increased car use."

### A little history

The Park lies on what was once Penge Common, a patchwork of common land dominated by the Great North Wood. The area was still wooded and rural when the Great Exhibition housed in the 'Crystal Palace' building was moved from Hyde Park to Sydenham Hill in 1852. Over the years the Palace, built by Joseph Paxton became run-down until it burnt down in 1936 after a cigarette was dropped during an orchestra rehearsal. The resulting fire was seen across south east England. The grounds of the Palace became parkland and various Acts were passed by parliament to ensure that the land was held as recreation space for the people.

### Directions to the camp:

It's at the corner of Crystal Palace Park Road and Westwood Hill. By train: Crystal Palace or Gypsy Hill station direct from Victoria then walk up the hill. No.3 bus from Brixton or No. 63 to Kings Cross to Palace.

Contact the Crystal Palace Campaign 0181 693 8200

## CRAP ARREST OF THE WEEK

For talking to a shop-keeper! After having the cheek to ask a Nottingham ASDA store manager about genetically modified food labelling, a man was told he could either "starve to death, or shop somewhere else". None to pleased with the reply, the disgruntled customer went back the next day and handed out leaflets about the mutant foodstuffs, when he was arrested on suspicion of "tampering and poisoning Asda food products"! (hey, does that mean we can charge Monsanto and their ilk?) The man was released without charge a few hours later.

## CASUAL KILLERS PT2

The Simon Jones Memorial Campaign swung into action again on Wednesday invading the Department of Trade and Industry and occupying the lobby for an hour to demand the prosecution of employment agency, Personnel Selection.

Simon Jones was sent by Personnel Selection to work for Euromin on the docks. He received no health and safety training despite being asked to do one of the most dangerous jobs in the country. Within two hours he was dead. Nearly a year on and despite every legal channel being exhausted as well as a series of high-profile actions no-one has been prosecuted over his death.

Meanwhile on the same day in Parliament George Galloway MP thundered "James Martell's (Euromin manager) contempt for the laws of health and safety in this country, his greed and hunger for profit, his negligence and carelessness, slaughtered this young man just as clearly as if he had pushed him off the dock with his own hands."

Simon's death highlights the spread of low-pay and casualisation across Britain; as a spokesperson from the Memorial Campaign told SchNEWS "If you want to kill someone, the easist way to get away with it is to do it at work."

Simon Jones Memorial Campaign, PO Box 2600, Brighton, E.Sussex, BN2 2DX www.simonjones.org.uk

\* Tony Blair has declared in the Register of Members Interest that the Freedom Group of Companies has seconded an employee to work in his constituency office for 15 hours a week.The company advises business on how to convert staff contracts into freelance jobs.

\* A gorilla from the Welsh Socialist Alliance recently tried to get a job at Staff Sign recruitment agency in Wrexham, after hearing the firm paid peanuts. Apparently the recruitment agency boss went bananas.

## CRAP APPOINTMENT OF THE WEEK

*"Appointing the former boss of the Countryside Landowners Association to head the Countryside Agency is like putting an alcoholic in charge of a pub."*   Kate Atkinson, Rambler's Association

**What is the CLA? Sounds like a people's democracy movement doesn't it?**

**DON'T BE A NANA!** The Countryside Landowners Association is the exclusive club which, as their own promo blurb enthuses, is *"a force to be reckoned with, constantly lobbying ministers and government departments"* to safeguard the interests of private landowners. In fact, its headquarters are in exclusive Belgravia Square, London, in property owned by the Duke of Westminster, Britain's largest landowner. Last year the Right to Roam movement, headed by the Rambler's Association and the Land Is Ours seemed on the verge of victory with the Blair's pledge to introduce laws forcing landowners to open up their land. So abhorrent were the squirearchy at the prospect of picnicking families and courting couples interrupting a Saturday afternoon's bloodfest, that the Countrside Alliance was formed in the blaze of publicity which guaranteed that the Stoogestry for State got the message. A year on, and a bill backed by the Rambler's Association would, if passed, remove all farming subsidies and government grants from landowners who obstruct footpaths or refuse to provide public access. No-one could be more aware of the duty of landowners to share the wealth of nature's bounty with the people than Ewen Cameron, the former president of the CLA and handpicked by Blair himself to chair the new Countryside Agency, which will oversee the whole Right To Roam programme. Indeed it's almost poetic that Cameron is the same Somerset potato farmer who planted spuds over a public right of way through his farm in 1996. *"Trust me, I'm a landowner"*. I think not. * Pack yer sarnies for the next South Downs Mass Trespass Meet 10am Brighton Train Station March 21.

## CRAP JOB OF THE WEEK

Heard the one about the 'Sustainable Aviation' research post at Manchester University held by Professor Callum Thomas and funded by, eh, Manchester Airport!

Air transport is believed to be responsible for 5% of 'greenhouse gases', so Schnews decided to investigate this apparent conflict of interest. Upon questioning, Prof. Callum declared *"yes I'm a fat cat ...(but )it is very important for decisions made by society to be based on sound science."* Obviously, the fact that his funding body has an interest in getting a positive light for aviation will not affect his research in any way, and he will of course produce the soundest, unbiased science.

## LOONY LAMBETH

On Wednesday night, over 100 local people were stopped from entering a Lambeth Council meeting held to discuss cuts in local services, including special needs schools, playcentres, youth and community centres. The cops were called, the street barricaded but the council did not change their tune. When SchNEWS tried to discover what's happening in Lambeth, the council gave us the runaround, complaining that the different committees have little contact with each other. *"It's difficult to find anything out,"* one confused official told us. These cuts continue the process of gentrification of Brixton, but people aren't taking this lying down. Local disabled activists are occupying the Lambeth Centre for Independent Living, and the 121 Centre, Railton Road, still faces eviction  For more info contact the 121 Centre on 0171 274 6655, email mark261@hotmail.com.

## SchNEWS in brief

The trial of the three **Portsmouth hunt sabs** up on charges of conspiracy (see SchNEWS 202) has been postponed for the time being. Contact Defence Campaign, c/o Box H 167 Fawcett Rd, Southsea, Hants. Tel  0411 166 533 ** **Goldsmith College** students are occupying their lecture building after 8  students were expelled for not paying their tuition fees. They are in court today to fight a possession summons. Meetings are in the Whiteland Building, Goldsmith College, Dixon Road New Cross SE1  5pm every day. Contact 0181 692 1406/0797 9896545 **Having problems explaining the problems of Free Trade? Why is the World Bank so destructive? What is the IMF? What resistance is there world wide ? **Undercurrents** have produced a radical 12 minute video exposing the truth. Entitled "WASHES WHITER!" it's £10 plus £1.50 p+p from undercurrents, 16b Cherwell St, Oxford OX4 1BG Tel 01865 203662 www.undercurrents.org ** **MAI-DAY** ACTION on Sat May 1st in Birmingham, needs imagination, music, ideas, street entertainment, banners, donations etc to set the city alight with fun and frolics. Contact 0961 810356 to get involved *** ****The Network of Socialist Alliances** Conference will be held on Saturday 27 March at the Union Club, 723 Pershore Rd, Birmingham. Contact 32, The Green, Long Lawford, Rugby CV23 9BL. Tel 01788 569766. **There's a **whistle-blower** march outside vivisection lab Huntingdon Life Sciences on Sat 20th March 11 am outside Huntingdon Tescos, Ring Road (A141) Tel 0589 026435 www.fortunecity.com/greenfield/shell/279/ ** **National Anti-Fur Day**: Sat March 6th. Brighton Animal Rights Coalition demo outside Karen Millen boutique, Nile Pavillions, Nile St, 12pm- Brighton's last fur stockists!!**What a shame – but apparently the new road surface on the **Newbury Bypass** is cracking up with pot-holes appearing; oil and mud is filling the balancing ponds and the police complaining the slip-roads are too short *** It's **International Women's Day** this Monday (8th) and the Crossroads Women's Centre have organised some events over the coming month. Sunday 14th March there's a Mothers Day Celebration and Protest 1pm; 26th March video and talks celebrating the sans-papiers (without papers)third anniversary – both events at the Women' Centre. Meanwhile this Sunday there's various events at Hove Town Hall 11 am – 4pm. Join the global women's strike 8th March 2000"for a new millennium that values women's work and women's lives". Contact Crossroads, 230a Kentish Town Rd (entrance on Caversham Rd.) London NW5  0171 482 2496

## SNORT FAIR!

Our crazy Californian chums in the city of Huntington Beach (a.k.a Surf City) have signed a deal with Coca-Crapa giving the dodgy scum exclusive rights for ten years to display their corporate logo in parks, on benches, even on police and fire stations. Coca-Wankas competitors Pepsi has been banned from sale in all but a few outlets. However, Pepsi are close to signing a similar deal with California's state capital, Sacramento, that "will send a tidal wave of Pepsi over Coke's Huntingdon Beach deal," says an executive, who no doubt enjoys surfing in his toilet.

*  What have McDonalds, Coca-Cola and Wrigleys all got in common? They all gave £25,000 last year to the Tidy Britain Group who every April organise the National Spring Clean. Y'know where people go round woods, ponds etc. clearing up all the excessive package generated by organisations like - well, eh McDogshit, Coke and Wrigleys. Hey and guess what? The chairman of the Tidy Britain Group is Peter Stokes formerly of 'The Real Thing'.

## INSIDE SCHNEWS

"The pie is cast. We shall not rest until justice, as well as dessert, is served" - Agent Apple of the Biotic Baking Brigade.(BBB)

Three members of the BBB have been imprisoned for the anarchic and blatantly anti-social, not to say extremely violent, act of pieing San Francisco mayor Willie Brown. Having already pied the Chief Executive Officers of Monsanto and Maxxam, last November the BBB launched their act of humiliation at Mayor Brown, for his continued collusion with developers at the cost of local poor and homeless people. "Poverty is violence" said Justin Gross, one of the three sentenced. Rahula Janowski suffered a broken collar bone in the fracas that ensued when Mayor Brown ordered the Cherry Pie 3 arrested by his mayor's police guard. The judge complied with Mayor Brown's demand for the maximum sentence of six months for simple battery. This from a Mayor known for his (unpunished) violent outbursts.

Write to the Cherry Pie 3:
**Rahula Janowski #1818075**
,c/o SF County Jail 8, E Pod,    425 7th St.SF, CA 94103
**Justin Gross #1818071**c/o SF County Jail 8, B Pod    425 7th St.SF, CA 94103
**Gerry Livernois** has not been sent down yet due to medical reasons.

The BBB could really use some financial support. Cheques and money orders can be made out to Jeff Larson and sent to: Friends of the BBB: 3288 21st #92, San Francisco, CA, 94110, or contact <bbb_apple@hotmail.com>.

* "…They Will Never Get Us All!" a new booklet of writings and poetry by US Anarchist prisoner and jailhouse lawyer Harold H Thompson is available for £1.80 from Huddersfield ABC, PO Box 12766, HD13XX.

**Stop-press :** The first two protestors to be charged under the Criminal Justice Act 'trespassory assembly' laws yesterday had their convictions over-turned in a landmark ruling. More next week.

## ...and finally...

It isn't usual for SchNEWS to be lost for words, so we thought we'd throw it out to our readers. An ordinary Wednesday at SchNews Towers, when who should phone but Chief Inspector Mike Flynn from Sussex Police HQ. "Can you help me," quoth the voice of Law 'n' Order, explaining he'd been put in charge of compiling the 'National Guide To Public Order Policing'. Keen to stress his (yawn) 'sense of fair play', CI Flynn doesn't just want the views of the goons with batons. Oh no. He wants to know how YOU feel. "I'm interested in 'alienated groups' expectations of the police," he enthused. Can you help the friendly copper, readers? Don't get too carried away, though: "I know some people might wish we just disappeared altogether. Hey, can we talk real world here?"

CI Flynn is of the opinion some of us may have had 'good experiences' of public order policing. He wants to know about them. "Perhaps some people have even had negative experiences of police in such situations",he added, more plausibly. "Perhaps they have low expectations of us." Surely not? "Tell me about them too."

Well, he asked for it. If you'd like to assist CI Flynn with his enquiries (we know you're itching to) his direct number is 01273 404345; fax 01273 404229. "Please don't hesitate to call".

### disclaimer

## Subscribe!

Keep SchNEWS FREE! Just send 1st Class stamps (e.g. 20 for next 20 issues) or donations (payable to Justice?) **Ask for "Originals"** if you can make copies. Post *free* to all prisoners. **SchNEWS, c/o on-the-fiddle, P.O. Box 2600, Brighton, East Sussex, BN2 2DX.**
Tel/Autofax :  +44  (0)1273  685913   *GET IT EVERY WEEK BY E-MAIL:*  schnews@brighton.co.uk
whatever next - the Evening Argus supporting the Simon Jones Memorial Campaign! Really.

WAKE UP! WAKE UP! IT'S YER COOL BANANA !

# Weekly SchNEWS

*Printed and Published in Brighton by Justice?*

Friday 12th March 1999  http://www.schnews.org.uk/  Issue 204 Free/Donation

# KILLER CORPS GO BANANAS

*"Has the world gone mad or is it me?"*

Dave Brock- *Master of the Universe*

Late last year, the guardians of freedom and democracy felt compelled to mount a tactical trade offensive against small Caribbean farmers, as a golden thankyou to Carl H. Lindner, the Chief Execution Officer of Chiquita Brands International, who donated $500,000 dollars to Democrat funds.

Only hours after receiving this philanthropic gesture the Clinton administration lodged a complaint with the World Trample Organisation (WTO) charging the EU with having a 'discriminatory' approach to importing bananas. That is, the EU support the Caribbean economies which rely on banana exports for survival, in preference to the economies of the expansionist corporations which have controlled Central America's "banana republics" with an iron fist for decades.

The US is now threatening action against a range of European business from Italian light fittings to Scottish cashmere sweaters, in response to the $520 million US banana giants Chiquita, Dole and Del Monte claim they 'lose due to unfair trade' each year. Chiquita alone is worth $14 billion.

Like one of those baby fishies that just gets bigger and bigger by eating all the smaller baby fishies in the same creek who think it's harmless cos it looks the same as them, the US Killer Corps have gone to war on their allies.

The ACP banana trade is rooted in colonialism which has left Caribbean economies dependent on exports to Europe for survival

Now small Caribbean farmers are facing ruin because the Chiquita-Dole cartel, which own massive plantations in Latin America, effectively act as price setters.

*"Take a drive around the island and the decline is evident. Everybody you speak to will tell you that the banana industry is heading for the rocks. Just a few years ago there were 6500 banana growers, these days there are only between 3000 and 4000 in an atmosphere of total uncertainty"*

Windward Islands Farmer's Association.

The real costs of banana production are not included in the current retail price. Banana production in the Windwards is characterised by smallholders, who grow their fruit on family owned farms. The system is labour intensive, and use of agrochemicals is low. Despite the pressures, banana quality from the Islands is on the up. Bananas are Britain's most popular fruit and consumption is increasing. In a fair world you would think there would be room for the smallholders. But Chiquita has 70%

of the EU banana market and wants the lot.

*"The market is now governed solely by the classic supply and demand mechanism. Within the new system, only the most competitive producers will be able to supply the European market."* Banana Link

So let's look at the world of banana dollars and see if we like it.

● Transnational business methods in the 'banana republics' have followed a familiar pattern of eviction, exploitation and negligence.

● In Guatemala, a union officer organising Chiquita plantation workers was shot dead in 1994 while other trade unionists received death threats.

● In Honduras, in 1996, an entire village of 600 people in a banana plantations was bulldozed by troops. Chiquita said the land was no longer suitable, and people must be evicted so it could be sold - then they leased it to a former employee who continued with slashed labour costs. Chiquita was later revealed to have bought food and fuel for the army unit carrying out the clearances.

● And last week Chiquita laid off 6000 workers in Honduras and Guatemala only 120 days in the wake of a hurricane. They have received no financial assistance for the last two months. The company is trying to get unions to agree to lower wages and reduced social benefits. 'Banana dollar' production requires massive capital investments in the form

of roads, irrigation and drainage. Plantations have an unhappy history of low-wages, limited worker's rights, poor working conditions and high levels of agrochemical use.

Frequent applications of the pesticide DBCP (banned in the countries which produced it) together with inadequate protection, has led to more than 20,000 cases of male sterility amongst workers. Both Chiquita and Dole are involved in legal cases brought by those affected. For every ton of bananas shipped, two tons of waste are left behind while an average Costa Rican consumes an incredible 4kg of pesticides a year, eight times the world average. Chiquita's track record is one of aggression, intimidation and brutality in pursuit of massive profits

SchNews ain't 'avin it and maybe you ain't either, so this weeks alternative is to discriminate like fuck against Chiquita and support fair trade bananas by buying those labelled Windward Islands (5 Isles bananas) We do not recommend readers find out where Chiquita CEO Lindner lives, buy a Chiquita banana, tie up the slimeball, and shove said banana, now coated in a powerful fixative up the tosser's rectum.

**World Development Movement,**
25 Beehive Place, London SW9 7QR
0171 737 6215 - www.oneworld.org/wdm
**Banana Link**
38-40 Exchange St, Norwich NR2 1XA

## PARK PRANKS

The protest camp at Ashton Court Park in Bristol is calling it a day. For nearly a year protestors have tried to stop the expansion of Durnford Quarry into the park. With the meadow 'translocated' and blasting imminent, it was time to say goodbye, but not without the last few laughs.

Ashton Court was given to the people of Bristol in 1959 with the condition that nothing be done that '*would detract from its value as a recreation ground or prejudice the enjoyment of the people'*. Realising that turning the park into an open quarry and destroying the habitats of rare orchids and other wildlife might just 'prejudice their enjoyment' of it, two protestors abseiled into the quarry and occupied a ledge above a load of explosives that were due to be detonated five minutes later. They were evicted by police after 32 hours and are in court at the end of the month. Meanwhile the quarry manager had his lawn translocated onto his driveway – and a daffodil planted on the roof of his car. Translocation means digging up everything and placing the land elsewhere. Surprise, surprise, it never works but it makes for good greenwash!

## RIGHT TO STAND
### on roadside victory

All at SchNEWS towers can sleep soundly tonight, safe in the knowledge that we are free to stand on the verge next to the road-side and not fear arrest. The Lord Chancellor decided last Thursday to uphold the quashing of the conviction of two people who were hanging out round Stonehenge one summer solstice, and nicked under the trespassory assembly section of the Criminal Justice Act (CJA). The clause was originally intended to make assemblies of 20 or more people a criminal offence, but the ruling could make this unworkable.

However, before you get carried away with all these new rights, and run out there to stand on your nearest road-side, beware! You can only do so if you have a "reasonable purpose", or the " activity in question does not amount to a public or private nuisance and does not obstruct the highway by unreasonably impeding the primary right of the public to pass and repass"(got that) Rest assured, we can continue to protest peacefully, while our lungs fill up with carbon monoxide.

## RIGHT TO WALK
### in the countryside shocker

While you're recovering from the shock of discovering that you can stand on the verge of the A303, there's more! Jump for joy, Michael "Swampy" Meacher ,this week announced a right to roam across 4 million acres of open land in the UK. It is surely only a matter of time before all land in the UK is collectivised, and we live in anarchist communes, eating root vegetables, sharing stories of the revolution.

However, don't get too excited, as there's no timetable for legislation, and it could get amended beyond all recognition by House of Commons committees, or by those well known guardians of the freedom to access, the House of Lords. Richard Moyse from Land Is Ours told SchNEWS *"It's a start, but not entirely satisfactory"*.

Meanwhile the Local Access Forums could end up a bureaucratic nightmare over-seen by the Countryside Agency, which as we pointed out in last weeks SchNEWS is headed by landed gentry bod and former president of the Country Landowners Association, Ewan, ('just like putting an alchoholic in charge of a pub') Cameron.

**\*Mass Trespass** Sunday March 21st Meet Brighton Station 10 am <u>sharp</u>. Six miles walk. No dogs. £5 travel costs. Tel 01273 620815

\*Sat April 3rd **land occupation** somewhere in the south of England, to celebrate 350th anniversary of Diggers occupation of St.George's Hill.

The Land Is Ours, Box E, 111 Magdalen Rd., Oxford,OX41RQ    Tel    01865    722016 www.oneworld.org/tlio

#### SECURITY GUARDS ROB LOCAL SHOPS

As SchNEWS went to press, the eviction at Crystal Palace entered its tenth day with people still down the tunnels trying to stop a massive leisure complex being built in the park (see SchNEWS 203). While Bromley Council moan about "professional protestors…preventing those in the surrounding area who are unemployed and unskilled from the opportunities that will…" blah, yawn) they stay stony silent about the fact that some private security guards from Pilgrim Security have been nicked during the eviciton after robbing the local off-licence and petrol station.

There's a massive party planned this Saturday (13th) Meet 12 noon at the Palace Paarde. Contact the Campaign 0181 693 8200

## SchNEWS in brief

We kid you not – after lasts weeks SchNEWS revelation that **McDonalds** gives cash to the Tidy Britain Group comes this little gem. Operation Eyesore is a new campaign "designed to encourage improvement in London's most tired and neglected areas." People can nominate their favourite blots on the landscape by picking up leaflets from ….any central London McDeadly. ** McDogshit is planning to build a giant 1,000 diner restaurant which will dominate the approach to the **Millenium Dome**. When Tony Blair was asked why the so-called showcase of British culture should be sponsorcd by " a great big American fast food corporation, which would probably try to reduce it to a large McDome and fries" he replied that the project needed all the sponsors it could get. *** The **Erotic Oscars** male and female striptease artistes semi-finals are on 31st March at Improv, 161 Tottenham Court Rd., London, W1P . £10/6 conc. Money raised will go to the Leydig Trust – helping disabled people find partners *** SchNEWS has unconfirmed reports from Topshop that they are withdrawing their **kipper tie** range after they were found to contain genetically modified organisms *** There's a **'Kitsch Bitch'** exhibition at The Last Chance Saloon all this month featuring freaks, monsters and a host of fanatics and revolutionaires 88 Lower Marsh, Waterloo, London, SE1 7AB (Waterloo tube) Ring 0171 7717466 for opening times *** **Lyminge Forest** in Kent, has now been occupied for two years to stop the RANK corporation destroying 500 acres of green belt land for a leisure complex. There will be a gathering on Sunday 21st March from 12 noon looking to create a **NO SINGLE ISSUE SITE**, uniting different campaigns and creative stuff. Contact Jani on 0171 231 0181 or 9797025 3931 *** Yesterday saw the first ever conviction of a mink fur-farmer for animal cruelty. The farmer who had all his mink released by the ALF recently was fined a pathetic £5,000. If you want to really rub it in there's a demo outside his Windmill Mink Farm, Shaftesbury Rd, Child Okeford, Dorset on Sunday 21st March 11.30 am e-mail: caft@caft.demon.co.uk***On Saturday 20th March theres another day of action **Hillgrove Farm**, against cat-breeders for vivisection, meeting at the main gates 12 noon. There are also skills days for animal rights campaigners in Brighton and Birmingham on Sunday 28th March – advice on running an effective campaign, using hidden cameras, and how to deal with all those friendly coppers. For more info call 0121 632 6460. *** On the same theme, two activists charged with **'conspiracy to commit criminal damage'** after a genetic crop site was trashed will be in Plymouth Crown Court on Monday 29th March and request 'loud and colourful support'.*** **The End is Nigh** West London Anarchists and Radicals are organising a ' not yer normal' benefit night on Friday 19th March at the Venture Centre, 103A Wornington Rd, (Westbourne Park tube) 8 – 11pm. **The prison service may have to pay up to £1 million in compensation to higher waged inmates who were charged for board and lodging under a policy introduced by the last Tory government. **

Following on from last year's Mayday event in Bradford, there will be a three day **Easter Rising** in Glasgow on April 2nd-4th for discussing global capitalism, multinationals, consumerism, and (more excitingly) how to oppose it all. Contact CI [autonomy] on 0141 810 3001 or e-mail radfest@yahho.com ** Free Range Activism Network is running a day workshop on **landfills**, how they work, how they get built, and the risks to the environment and human health they present. 11am to 4.00pm, Sat. 20th March at The Stewponey' pub, Stourton, nr. Stourbridge. Contact Chris Smart on 01384 877020 email mobbsey@gn.apc.org

## RUSSIAN REVOLUTION DEJA VU

A Workers' Collective Committee has taken over a machine-building plant in Yasnogorsk, a town of 20,000 people near Moscow. The 4,200 workers are battling the Communist Party local authority and the (Yeltsinite) privatization program for the plant. In 1990, the factory was turned into a joint stock company in which the workers held a majority of shares. Last September the workers and shareholders of the plant dismissed the Administration at a general meeting. When the "owners" of the plant refused to recognize the results, the workers seized control. A Soviet-stylee Workers Collective was set up and now oversees admin, production, selling, all finances, distribution of wages and the town as a whole. Last December 10,000 people from Yasnogorsk marched to block the railway line into Moscow to support demands for the release from prison of the worker-elected directors of the factory and to stop the privatization move. It was only the mobilization of special police forces which prevented the workers from paralyzing one of the main railways in Russia. The Yasnogorsk workers say, "This is our revolution" and are appealing for international solidarity in the fight against the trend towards private property and global capitalism.

### RIP

Once again the message from Colombia is 'Don't fuck with the oil barons.' Two years ago the U'wa people won a law suit to stop US firm Occidental Petroleum (working with Shell of course)from drilling in their lands. They had threatened mass sucicide believing that if oil('the blood of the earth') was extracted it would mean the end of the tribe. Helping them with their legal battle and deeply committed to the Uwa people, was Terence Freitas who along with Ingrid Washinawatok and Lahe'ena'e Gay were kidnapped last week on their way to the reserve. Their bodies were found bound,blindfolded and bullet ridden. No one has yet claimed responsibility for their deaths.

SchNEWS dedicates this weeks issue to them.

* Berito KuwarU'wa from the tribe will open the Earth Centre near Doncaster on March 28th. Contact 01709 512000

## ...and finally...

Heard the one about Hunt Liason Police officer from Wiltshire who got together with his mates from the Countryside Alliance and Master of Fox Hounds Association and produced, after 'lenghty consultation' a code of conduct for hunt protestors "which everyone agreed was the way forward". Apart of course Hunt Sabs and the League Against Cruel Sports (LACS), who seem to have been overlooked in the 'lenghty consultation' process. The code includes gems like

*"Do not attempt to intefere with the hunt, engage in any form of sabotage be it direct action or subtle tactics (ie use of whips, horns, sprays, shouting/yelling or the use of your vehicle in any manner to obstruct/cause nuisance to the hunt".*

*"In the interests of safety should an injured fox be required to be dug out and humanely destroyed a 50 metre exclusion zone will be in force."*

Which would just about make hunt sabbing totally ineffective… Talking of coppers,the first hard evidence (if any was needed) that foxes suffer stress and exhaustion from being hunted came early in February, when a fox being chased by a hunt, sought refuge down a rabbit hole. 'Copper' the fox was eventually rescued by sabs and taken to a vet and is now recovering. SchNEWS wishes 'copper' well - tho' we think the idea of sending 'Get well soon cards' a little odd. Wouldn't it prefer a nice juicy….

**disclaimer** "Cone on punk, make my day!"

## Subscribe!

# WHO'S POLICING THE POLICE?

SQUALL

Where Do You Want To Grow Today?
--
I Wanna Go Home
Underground Update
Features
Squall Pics
Frontline Communique
The State Its In
Squotes
Resources
Links
From Our Correspondence

For the first time in its history, a prominent European Committee for the Prevention of Torture (CPT) has been censored by a nation under investigation. And that nation is us. Si Mitchell reviews the implications of the CPT's damning indictment of police malpractice in the UK and reveals why Jack Straw is so keen for the cover up.

On December 16 1994, two police officers arrested Shiji Lapite, a Nigerian asylum seeker on suspicion of possession of drugs. One officer applied a neck hold and the other admitted kicking the suspect in the head. Lapite died from asphyxiation. An inquest jury returned a verdict of unlawful killing, but the CPS refused to prosecute the officers responsible, claiming insufficient evidence for a realistic prospect of conviction. The Police Complaints Authority decided not to push for disciplinary action. The decision not to prosecute Lapite's killers, along with those of another man who died in custody, Richard O'Brien, and the exposed torture of Derek Treadaway at the hands of the West Midlands Serious Crime Squad, triggered a visit to Britain from the Council of Europe's Committee for the Prevention of Torture (CPT) in September 1997. In March 1998, the CPT submitted its subsequent report to the British Government. The convention under which the committee operates allows the nation state concerned power to veto their reports. The Government (who has given conflicting answers to parliamentary questions about the report's whereabouts) sat on the document until Jan 13, when a censored version - complete with blanked out text - was finally released. No one, not even notorious human rights abusers like Turkey, has censored a CPT report before. We had the choice of not publishing at all or publishing this abridged form, said Mark Kelly of the CPT. Raju Bhatt, the solicitor who represented both Lapite's widow and Treadaway, described the document as a damning indictment of modern democracy. He says the process for investigating police officers is no more than an exercise in mitigation, designed solely to clear their names.

THE POLICE COMPLAINTS AUTHORITY (PCA), IS DESCRIBED AS ILL EQUIPPED TO CARRY OUT THE WATCHDOG ROLE IN WHICH IT HAS BEEN CAST.

The report (even minus the deleted memos sent by Metropolitan Police lawyers to high-ranking officers) is brutally critical, raising serious questions about the independence and impartiality of the procedures presently used to process complaints about police misconduct. Out of the 10,243 complaints lodged against the police in England and Wales during 1996/97 only 141 (0.4 per cent) resulted in criminal and/or disciplinary proceedings. In the same period only a single Metropolitan police officer was convicted of an offence against a yearly background of around six thousand complaints. The Police Complaints Authority (PCA), is described as ill-equipped to carry out the watchdog role in which it has been cast. The PCA disputes these figures, saying over half of the complaints are granted 'dispensation', or withdrawn by the complainant. This happens if a complaint is considered repetitious, malicious, is filed more than twelve months after the incident, or if it is not 'reasonably practical' to carry out an investigation. We neither see or want to see the majority of complaints, said an agitated Authority spokesman who disputed the CPT's claims that there is little public confidence in the PCA's independence. He said the committee had failed to understand the British criminal justice system. The CPT's visiting team comprised two UK lawyers and a British trained High Court judge. On January 13, the outgoing Met Commissioner, Sir Paul Condon, called for a truly independent complaints authority. The CPT criticises the substantial degree of influence the police retain over the entire complaints process. Both the PCA and the Crown Prosecution Service (CPS) are entirely reliant on evidence gathered by the police, in most cases by officers employed by the same force as that under investigation. As the report says: In the vast majority of cases the investigating officer will be a police officer from the force about which the complaint is being made, although the chief officer may exceptionally decide to appoint a police officer from another force..The majority of cases are unsupervised by the PCA. The role of 'chief officers', it says, needs to be reviewed. At present they are expected to oversee the disciplinary process from beginning to end, including appointing an investigating officer and determining what disciplinary action, if any, to take. It is doubtful whether any single officer is able to perform all of these functions in an entirely independent way, says the report.

I'VE ASKED MY SOLICITOR TO SUE SOUTH WALES POLICE, O'BRIEN TOLD SQUALL. BUT I DON'T THINK ANY ACTION WILL BE TAKEN. I'VE NEVER SEEN A POLICE OFFICER DONE YET FOLLOWING A MISCARRIAGE OF JUSTICE CASE.

....A staunchly left New Labour Party ... but yet an amicably right wing New Labour Party...

p

Despite being bound by the Crown Prosecutors Code, which states a charge must be brought whenever there is a realistic prospect of conviction or it serves the public interest, the CPT found that the unwillingness of the courts to convict police officers has created a reluctance [within] the CPS to bring charges against them. This in turn has led to a higher standard of proof being required to charge police men and women, than is required for the rest of the population. The CPS said that the Glidewell. Macpherson and Butler inquires (all published since 1997) have covered much of this ground. Judge Gerald Butler QC described the system used by the CPS for selecting who to prosecute as confused, inefficient and fundamentally unsound. Despite numerous recommendations, Raju Bhatt points out: We are yet to see much action from Jack Straw's action plan. Michael O'Brien of the Cardiff Newsagent Three, had his conviction for murder quashed in December 1999. He spent 11 years in prison during which time his daughter and father died. I've asked my solicitor to sue South Wales police, O'Brien told SQUALL. But I don't think any action will be taken. I've never seen a police officer done yet following a miscarriage of justice case. Paddy Hill, who spent 18 years for the 1975 Birmingham pub bombings in jail before his conviction was overturned, points out that there have been over 300 exposed miscarriages of justice since the Guildford Four were released in 1985, yet the system has not been improved. They're just getting better at covering their tracks, says Hill.

## THERE'S NO STATUTORY TIME LIMIT ON CRIME. BUT IF ANY CHARGES ARE BROUGHT AGAINST POLICE OFFICERS, THEY GO SICK AND THEN THEY RETIRE. THEY GET EIGHTY PER CENT OF THEIR WAGE, AND THEY ARE OUT OF TROUBLE. PADDY HILL
- One of the Birmingham Six

Hill and O'Brien are in the process of setting up a Miscarriage of Justice Organisation (MOJO) which will offer legal, forensic and support services to victims of bad justice. They plan to launch it in June. Unlike the rest of the population, police officers have retained the 'right to silence' in their disciplinary procedures. A Home Affairs Select Committee inquiry in December 1997 recommended that this be brought into line with standard criminal proceedings. It concluded: There is a great deal of justified dissatisfaction with elements of the disciplinary and complaints system. Other proposals by the Select Committee, endorsed by the CPT report, include greater independence in police adjudication panels (at present often consisting of a single senior officer sitting in private) and greater commitment in establishing if an officer is genuinely sick, when seeking retirement. Paul Barrat of the Association of Chief Police Officers (ACPO) said: When an officer has served 30 years, they have the right to retire. According to Paddy Hill this is a ruse to escape disciplinary action: There's no statutory time limit on crime. But if any charges are brought against police officers, they go sick and then they retire. They get eighty per cent of their wage, and they are out of trouble.

## THE COMMITTEE ALSO CALLED FOR THE CROWN PROSECUTION SERVICE TO BE REQUIRED TO GIVE DETAILED REASONS WHEN IT DECIDES NOT TO PROSECUTE OFFICER AND THE POLICE COMPLAINTS AUTHORITY SHOULD BE REPLACED BY A FULLY-FLEDGED INDEPENDENT AGENCY.

The Police Federation says its officers are not above the law. But as Jimmy Robinson, cleared for the murder of newspaper boy Carl Bridgewater in 1997, says: The CPS took no action against the eleven officers in my case, despite Ap-

peal Court judges urging them to do so. Unable to gain satisfaction in the criminal justice system many have chosen to pursue their grievances through the civil courts. In 1996/97 the Met paid £2,658,000 in damages (either awarded by, or settled out-of, court), in over 1,100 civil actions. The PCA's spokesman pointed out that the standard of proof is lower in a civil court, with the decision reached on the balance of probabilities compared to the stricter criminal standard of beyond reasonable doubt. However the CPT maintain that the gravity of these cases make the courts seek a very high degree of probability and distinguishing between the two standards, does not explain the failure to bring charges against officers whose conduct has been called into question in civil proceedings. The CPT studied four cases in detail where substantial payouts had been made following allegations of assault by officers. The one consistent thread was that no action was subsequently taken against any of the officers concerned. Despite the police being under legal obligation to initiate an investigation and send the results to the CPS, no senior Complaints Investigation Branch (CIB) officer questioned could recall this ever happening. In one example, the civil court even turned up eyewitness evidence - of a man being mauled by a police dog while handcuffed - that the CPS had overlooked

## THE POLICE COMPLAINTS AUTHORITY IS DISCREDITED AND IS A DISCREDIT. RAJU BHATT
- defence barrister

In conclusion the CPT recommended a review of all cases in the last two years that resulted in a payout in excess of £10,000. In each case, it says, the decision not to bring disciplinary/criminal charges should be reconsidered. The committee also called for the CPS to be required to give detailed reasons when it decides not to prosecute officers and the PCA should be replaced by a fully-fledged independent agency. The PCA is discredited and is a discredit, says Raju Bhatt, adding that it is widely accepted the authority will be replaced. However it is less a question of who will police the police, but how they will be policed and how they are seen to be policed. Bhatt says he understands officers have a difficult job to do. But to do it they need public confidence. To get that they must be seen to be answerable to the rule of law and subject to fair and impartial investigations. Transparency is the key. That's what we need. He believes the situation is not helped by the Government dragging its feet on implementing promised changes, or by the continued resistance towards prosecuting those who even Sir Paul Condon has described as bad officers. ACPO says it has introduced measures to significantly reduce pensions for officers discharged for misconduct. However, ACPO's Paul Barrat was unable to give an example of this actually happening. A Judicial Review last year compelled the CPS to explain their decisions not to prosecute in the Lapite, O'Brien and Treadaway cases. However legal manoeuvering and the passage of time scuppered any potential convictions. Treadaway's was granted £50,000, only to die within a month of the hearing. The police have issued guidelines discouraging the type of neck hold which killed Lapite, though they stress it is not unlawful. As with any use of force, the question to be considered is: 'Was it reasonable in the circumstances?' Lapite's widow, ground down by years of fighting, has chosen not to fight on, but to try and rebuild a life for herself and her children. Justice? asks Paddy Hill. They haven't got the integrity or intelligence to spell it let alone dispense it. The Home Office say they will respond to the CPT's report in February.

*To view the entire, though censored, CPT report check: http://www.cpt.coe.fr/en/press/20000113en.htm For more background information on miscarriages of justice check Getting away with it in the SQUALL features section.*

WAKE UP! WAKE UP! IT'S YER SICK AS A CARROT

# SchNEWS

weekly

*Printed and Published in Brighton by Justice?*

**Friday 18th March 1999** http://www.schnews.org.uk/ **Issue 205 Free/Donation**

# HERBAL HIGHS

Unless a much bigger international coalition can be formed … to save health freedom – we will see it stripped from us as the drug companies play a game called 'boiling the frog slowly'" - John Hammell (The Life Extension Foundation).

Imagine walking into your local health food shop to get some herbal remedies or vitamin supplements. Well, if certain people get their way you won't be able to.

The Government has been secretly working on a proposal that would give the Medicines Control Agency (MCA) sweeping new powers to classify health products as medicines. Don't be surprised if you don't know anything about this. The government's consultation period wasn't exactly extensive with only a few weeks for objectors to put their side. When SchNEWS decided to have a ring around to find out what people involved with health and medicine reckoned to the proposal, most didn't know what the hell we were talking about (nothing new there then).

Thanks to Britain's membership of the European Union (EU), the only criteria the MCA needs to apply are:

*Can the product alter physiological function?

*Is it being used for medicinal purposes?

Seeing as anything you eat or drink has an effect on your body, this covers everything.

Previously a product had to be either unsafe for human consumption, or else its manufacturer had to make false medicinal claims before it could be banned. In theory, under the new EU regulations, even glucose, coffee and brandy could be classified as medicinal. This back-door plan will mean that if small businesses want to license a product they will have to fork out between £80 000, for a single-ingredient product, and £2 million, for a multi-ingredient product in order for them to go through testing procedures. Everything from cancer chemotherapy drugs to simple vitamin preparations would be treated the same.

*"Clearly this is but yet the latest stage of a concerted effort by the powerful pharmaceutical industry to halt the growing interest in 'alternative' medicine"*

**Ann Wills (British Anti-Vivisection Association)**

By restricting what nutritional supplements people can take, the government is telling us that we don't know our own bodies and aren't sussed enough to make decisions about our own health. As Penny Viner of the Health Food Manufacturers Association points out

*"This proposal will achieve the situation whereby the MCA will be acting as policeman, judge and jury without any checks and balances"*

So who the hell are the MCA? They are a QUANGO, funded by taxpayers and run by people appointed by ministers. By 1996 a third of public expenditure (£50billion) and three quarters of civil servants had been quangoed. It's hard to find the status of quangos: they can be Non-Departmental Public Bodies, Next Steps Executive Agencies, private companies, government departments, trusts, public companies, or a mixture of any of these. They can refuse to answer any questions over the phone by hiding behind their protected status and are only in the phone book under their supervising department's name. So here you are: the MCA's phone number is 0171 273 0392.

• • • • • • • • • • • • • • • • • • • • •
Internationally, the drug companies are trying to stitch us all up by saying a level playing field is needed for global commerce. To achieve this, countries must agree on common rules. A German proposal calls for (1) no dietary supplements to be sold for preventive or therapeutic use, (2) dosage limits set by the commission, and (3) preventing nations from setting their own standards. This proposal is being pushed by three German companies - Hoechst, Bayer, and BASF - who were formed when IG Farben was disbanded after the Nuremberg War Trials due to their role in manufacturing the poison gas used in the Nazi concentration camps.
• • • • • • • • • • • • • • • • • • • • •

So is SchNEWS getting its herbal knickers in a twist? To see what will soon happen here we only have to look across the pond to Canada and America where supplements have been withdrawn following similar pressures from the multinational drug companies.

According to Christopher Whitehouse of Consumers for Health Choice *"The implications are much more serious... It is not the law that has changed, but that the MCA is saying that it is going to be the most ruthless regulator in Europe"*

Oh dear - someone pass us a cup of Camomile tea.

**Society for Promotion of Nutritional Therapy**, P.O.Box 47, Heathfield, East Sussex TN21 8ZX Web: http://visitweb.com/spnt

**Consumers for Health Choice**, 9 Old Queen St, London SW1H 9JA

**What Doctors Don't Tell You**, 4 Wallace Rd, London N1 2BR Web: www.wddty.co.uk

## Revolting Students

Three Colleges and Universities in London have been occupied over the past couple of weeks, as students grew militant in the face of chronic underfunding . Funnily enough Tony Blair's promise to make education a top priority hasn't materialised for students. Not content with continuing phasing out grants, New Labour introduced tuition fees. However, when students started getting expelled for not doling out over £1000 a year in fees, they reacted. At Goldsmith's College in South London, 8 were expelled for non-payment, so they staged a week long occupation, ending only when the College gave in and re-instated the students from Easter.

At University College London (UCL), things were a bit more full on. Over 300 students occupied buildings in protest at the planned expulsion of non-payers. The occupation started at 1 pm on Thursday, UCL issued a Court summons by 9pm and the case was in Court the next morning. By 6pm that evening the bailiffs (who were paid triple time) turned up with sledge hammers. This eviction may be related to the fact that Mikhail Gorbachev was due to speak in one of the buildings occupied!

The students' union at UCL covered the college with posters disowning the occupation and wanted to liaise with the management. A student from UCL said " the Union's procedures are official, but not democratic. What have they done to secure the future of those who cannot pay?" The student welfare officer at UCL was *even* seen having a pint in the bar while students were being dragged out!

Meanwhile, over 100 students at Camberwell School of Art have been in occupation for over a week to protest against the lack of resources and increasing risk to students' welfare from dodgy Health and Safety practices. Management are refusing to reply to their demands until they concede. They are due in Court at 10am , Friday,.

Contact the occupation: 07930 662 416.

* Campaign for Free Education, PO Box 22615, London N4 1WT. Tel: 0958 556 756 http://members.xoom.com/nus_cfe/

**STOP-PRESS**
As SchNEWS went to press, students at UCL had sacked their executive officers after a vote of no confidence.

# THE EXXON FILES

## SchNEWS in brief

It was just past midnight on March 24th, 1989, when the oil tanker *Exxon Valdez* ran aground on Bligh Reef in the icy waters of Prince William Sound. Nearly 11 million gallons of crude leaked into the water, blackening 1,500 miles of the magnificent Gulf of Alaska coastline. 250,000 seabirds, 2,800 sea otters, 300 harbour seals, 250 bald eagles and as many as 22 killer whales were killed.

Ten years on from the most damaging oil spill in history, and the effects of the *Valdez* continue. According to a recent report by the state-run Oil Spill Trustee Council, which monitors the effects of the tanker accident, of the 28 species listed in the report, only two - the bald eagle and the river otter -are considered "fully recovered" a decade later.

However, another disaster soon followed that had nothing to do with the choking black mass that coated the pristine arctic wilderness. The Valdez disaster has become in the text-books of the public relations companies, a prime example of how *not* to handle the press and public. Forget the oil-spill, what Exxon needed was some green-wash.

*"It is easier and less costly to change the way people think about reality than it is to change reality"*

Morris Wolfe , PR consultant

Green-wash is the term used for corporations who make a big song and dance about chatting to mainstream environmental groups, spend millions on adverts telling the world how green they are, while behind the scenes doing everything they can to oppose any laws which might harm their profits. This is commonly known as having your cake and eating it, or what John Stauber, of PR Watch magazine calls the "good cop/bad cop" approach.

The father of greenwash, E. Bruce Harrison, is a strong advocate for corporate-environmental 'partnerships'. *"It's smart on two levels: it avoids legal problems, and it widens your options,"* he wrote in the 1993 book 'Going Green: How to Communicate Your Company's Environmental Commitment.' In chapters with titles like "Mental Greening: The Habit of Thinking Like a Good Guy' and 'What to Do When You're Attacked by an Activist Group,' he suggests that companies meet with citizens who criticise them, listen but reveal little information, and research their opponents, even if it means hiring private detectives to spy on them.

So while the Valdez oil spill continues to pollute the gulf of Alaska, Exxon continue to drag their feet in paying $5 billion damages to the 30,000 Alaskans affected by their recklessness. Meanwhile, the company's vice president for environment and safety reckons that while the oil spill was unfortunate, exhaustive studies by the company and so-called independent scientists had found no long-term harm. Strange then that the Oil Spill Trustee Council have discovered that oil spills cause a hundred times more damage than previously thought and oil pollution of less than one part per billion is sufficient to kill marine life. Salmon and herring with half-formed tails, twisted spines and grossly distended stomachs are

---

still being caught in Alaska's Prince William Sound. 'There are still patches of heavy oil pollution out there, and traces of these are still killing fish,' said Dr Bruce Wright of the US National Maritime Fisheries Service in Alaska. 'It is not the local impact that is the real problem,' says Wright. 'Our work indicates that even microscopic amounts of oil that get into any stream or bay are going to kill fish. This is a problem for the whole world.' Swilling out a tank of diesel fuel or an out-board engine will have deadly consequences, he added. 'Even rain falling on car parks will flush oil that has leaked from engines and carry it into drains and then into streams and bays. Marine life will be killed off even if only tiny traces of oil are present.'

'The Valdez disaster provided us with a perfect laboratory. We are able to compare fish that were born in polluted parts of the Sound with those born in areas unaffected by oil,' said Wright.

The scientists' study suggests that no coastal region can ever be protected from oil pollution. In plain English this means that 'green' and 'oil company' are two words that can never be compatible.

---

Companies like Exxon (called Esso in Europe) now pay public relation firm front groups (nicknamed 'Astroturf ' groups) that support their interests. Astroturf groups often hide their real agendas behind warm and fuzzy names to try to, as one PR man admitted in a New York Times interview, come over all "good-guyness."

One of Exxon's favourites is the Global Climate Coalition, who lobby governments to oppose any international climate change treaties, that could wreck oil companies profits. A couple of years back the Exxon chairman addressed a large international gathering in China and urged developing countries to sort out their environmental problems by "increasing…the use of fossil fuels". The logic being that economic growth will pay for the mess caused by…economic growth.

---

*Joseph J. Hazelwood, skipper of the Valdez when it crashed is finally returning to Alaska to begin a community service program, picking up litter on the streets of Anchorage.

**International Day of Action** against Exxon-Mobil Wednesday 24th March. Contact Friends of the Earth 0171 490 1555

*Read '**Global Spin**' - the corporate assualt on environmentalism by Sharon Beder (Green Books)

* **Corporate Watch** Issue 8 out now, digging the dirt on your favourite multinationals. Essential. £3 + 50p+p PO Box E, 111 Magdalen Rd., OX4 1RQ www.oneworld.org/cw

## Court in a maize

The two women charged with 'conspiracy to cause criminal damage'are appearing in Plymouth Crown Court on 29th March 9.30am. They are defending themselves over the trashing of a genetically modified site which they admit to, but say it was in the public interest. The mutant maize was growing next to an organic farm and near bee hives so cross-pollination could easily occur. A large demo is expected. Get down there! Contact 07970 873643

---

The Crossroads Women's Centre, are hosting **Sans -Papiers**, immigrants without papers third anniversary celebration, on Friday 26 March at 7pm, with big screen footage of recent protests around Europe. The centre is at 230a Kentish Town Road NW5 Tel: 0171 482 2496 ** Get on down to the Guilford **Technival** on 4th April at Maltings Bridge Sq Farnham. Six room festival featuring acts from Megadog and Pendragon. Tickets £6.80 adv. Box office 01252 726234. **If you're interested in permaculture design then get in touch with **Naturewise** who do working weekend courses.Call 0171-281 3765 ***Free **permaculture courses** if you're on benefits in mid Wales. Contact 01970 832044 ** Brighton and Hove **Wood Recycling Project** is open at Regent Street, Brighton, selling timber saved from landfill - 01273 570500 **Culture Vulture** is a wicked little 'zine that rips out the still beating heart of consumerism and feeds it to the dogs. Get it from CattleProd, Box 39, 82 Colston St BS1 5BB or www.gn.apc.org/cattleprod ** Last week the **Wild Greens**, the direct action youth wing of the Green Party jumped the fence at the Crop and Food Research Centre near Christchurch, New Zealand destroying an experimental G.M.potato crop & ruining the $200,000 research project. The experiment involved mixing the genes of potatoes with genetic material from toads and silkworms to make the potatoes rot resistant. www.econation.org.nz/ ** Protest at a genetic crop site near Edinburgh on Sunday 28th March Contact **Fife Earth First!** 01334 477411 ** Next meeting of the **Inter-Continental Caravan** is on 24th March at Strike, Top floor, 11-29 Fashion St, London E3 at 7 pm **

---

Ever wished you could get SchNEWS off the web and print it out so it looks like the real thing? Well now you can. All you need is an internet connection, Web browser, the Acrobat Reader and any old printer. See our web-site for more info.

---

## ...and finally...

The Queen Mum could be in for a bit of an eye-opener this summer, if plans for a mass disrobing outside Buckingham Palace take place. Organiser Vincent Bethel reckons that *"Society is mentally ill"* and forcing people to hide their body's isn't helping.

*"It is a fact that humans have genitals"* (can't argue with that one)

*"Would you like to live in a healthy world, a healthy environment, among healthy happy human beings?"* (well, yeah that sounds good)

*"Theoretical humanism is a misnomer, theoretical humanitarianism is a paradox, theoretical love is utterly preposterous."* (eh, you've lost us)

Now SchNEWS isn't against people getting their kit off if they want, but maybe well stick with the beach. Still if you want to 'protest naked for the right to be naked in public'on June 8th contact 208 Foleshill Rd., Coventry, CV1 4JH

**disclaimer**

SchNEWS warns all readers to remember to keep on swallowing the corporate truth pills while chanting "profits are good, profits are god", then you will feel content. Honest

---

## Subscribe!

Keep SchNEWS FREE! Just send 1st Class stamps (e.g. 20 for next 20 issues) or donations (payable to Justice?) Ask for "Originals" if you can make copies. Post *free* to all prisoners. SchNEWS, c/o on-the-fiddle, P.O. Box 2600, Brighton, East Sussex, BN2 2DX.

Tel/Autofax: +44 (0)1273 685913 *GET IT EVERY WEEK BY E-MAIL:* schnews@brighton.co.uk

WAKE UP! WAKE UP! IT'S YER AXE WEILDING

# Weekly SchNEWS

Printed and Published in Brighton by *Justice?*

A SYSTEM 65 MILLION YEARS IN THE MAKING

GOVERNMENT

DINOSAURS STILL RULE THE EARTH

| Friday 26th March 1999 | http://www.schnews.org.uk/ | Issue 206 | Free/Donation |

# FORESTS FOR THE CHOP

*"The agreement reflects an economic agenda which prioritises unsustainable corporate profit-making over the maintenance of healthy ecosystems."*

Friends Of The Earth

What would your solution be if SchNEWS told you that an area larger than Mexico had been deforested between 1980 and 1995? More forest protection? Don't be daft. Last week negotiations took place in Geneva at the World Trade Organisation (WTO) to kick off a wood trade free-for-all which would effectively trash what's left of the world's forests.

So who is behind all this? Surprise, surprise, it's the good 'ole apple pie United States, strongly supported by their paper and wood product industries! They're pushing for a WTO agreement, which could strip the world's remaining natural forests of any existing protection, while boosting consumption of forest products and increasing logging. SchNEWS wasn't surprised to hear the US Trade Representative at the W.T.O talks in Geneva, Charlene Barshefsky, used to be a lobbyist for the Canadian Timber Industry.

This little story (and SchNEWs readers might be going all deja vu about these trade agreements) started in 1995 when negotiations between GATT (General Agreement on Tariffs and Trade) and APEC (Asian Pacific Economic Co-operation Forum) failed, and the WTO was asked to join a forest products free trade agreement. A quick look at deforestation rates in APEC countries is enough to raise a few concerned eyebrows... between 1990 and 1995 the annual deforestation rate of APEC countries was more than twice the world average. Doesn't really inspire confidence eh?

Peru, Russia and Vietnam joined APEC in 1998...worrying as Russia has the most remaining frontier forests of all the world's countries; Peru the fourth most; meanwhile, Vietnam's frontier forests are the third most threatened in the world.

The Forest Industry reckons that protection laws reduce their profits, this is reason enough for them to push the WTO to pass new laws removing such petty obstacles to their progress. WTO have been described as having 'uniquely powerful tools' and are obviously not afraid to use them! The Director General said "We are writing the constitution of a single global economy".

Minor inconveniences that may arise from this attitude include the probable importa-

tion of destructive pests on wood products.

One such pest is the Asia long-horned beetle which has killed thousands of trees across the United States since it was imported on untreated logs and packaging material.

Another probable bummer is that the removal of tariffs will mean no distinction between wood products that are harvested by sustainable methods and the logging of old-growth and endangered trees. Basically, Joe public will have no way of knowing whether they are buying the last remaining rainforest or not.

As per usual the worlds press are falling over themselves to tell us about this charming little agreement- and it could be law by November when the WTO meet in Seattle. So what can we do about it?As the WTO obviously consider our world's forests a resource to be plundered, we can only suggest a spot of direct action-go and plant some trees!

* Trees For Life, The Park, Findhorn Bay, Forres IV36 OTZ, Scotland. Tel:01309 691292

* For info. on sustainable living, contact the Permaculture Assoc. BCM Permaculture Association, London, WC1N 3XX. Tel: 01654 712188 Web http://www.btinternet.com/~permaculture.uk

If you are interested in fighting against the WTO agreement, contact karen@aseed.antenna.nl. This woman has all the information ammunition you will need!

Recommended reading: "Profit Over People" by Noam Chomsky.

## SCARY STATISTICS

* Every hour, at least 4,500 acres of tropical forests fall to chain saws, machetes, flames or bulldozers, and another four plant or animal species become extinct.

* Half the world's original forest is gone.

* Only 22% remains as undisturbed 'primary' forest.

* Less than 10% of temperate forests remain.

* Half the world's tropical forests have been cleared.

* Chile's native forests-one third of the world's remaining temperate rain forests-will be completely deforested in just 20 years if current practices continue.

* At least 200 million hectares of forest were lost between 1980 and 1995 - an area larger than Mexico says the 1997 United Nations Food and Agriculture's State of the World's Forests report.

## CRAP ARRESTS OF THE WEEK

**For walking around with your hands in your pockets.** Conrad Samuels was walking along a street in East London when he was told by a police officer to take his hands out his pockets. He refused. On being asked where he was going, he replied " This is a free country and I can walk where I like." Oh no you can't - your nicked.

**For walking on a flower bed!** A supporter of the Movement Against the Monarchy (MA'M) was in Basildon, Essex trying to disrupt a visit by the Queen, when they were nicked. However, after the cops couldn't match the footprint, they were later released without charge.

MA'M, PO Box 14672, London E9 5UQ www.geocities.com/CapitolHill/Lobby/1793/Index.

---

## Why do we need forests?
* To prevent global warming
* To stabilise climate change
* To ensure a steady source of clean water
* To prevent floods and serve as windbreaks (stops soil erosion and desertification)
* As a source of fuel, food, medicine, beauty and recreation

---

## MR. LIBERAL JOINS THE BANKERS

"The feminist agenda is not about equal rights for women. It is about a socialist, anti-family political movement that encourages women to leave their husbands, kill their children, practice witchcraft, destroy capitalism and become lesbians." . . . according to the world view of Dr Pat Robinson, a right wing extremist with whom the Royal Bank of Scotland has just announced a business link. Over 100 people recently demonstrated outside the Edinburgh branch. You can tell them what you think about Mr.Reasonable by ringing 0131 442 7777.

# ERT GO HOME

Ever heard of the the European Round Table of Industrialists(ERT)? Thought not. Well, these are the people (made up of various multinational bosses) that pushed the European Commission to adopt the Trans European Networks(TENs) project.

The aim of TENs is to expand and build new roads, high-speed railroads and airports. As you would suspect TENs gets the thumbs up from the road and industry lobby, but has been described by others interested in a rather more sustainable future, as an 'environmental nightmare'.

A SEED Europe have organised a Transport Action Day on the 27th March. This will co-incide with the offical meting of EU Transport Minsisters.Actions are promised all over Europe. For a Transport action pack contact Frank van Schaik, c/o A SEED Europe, Postbus 92066, 1090 AB Amsterdam, Netherlands. Tel + 31-20-668-2236 email: frank@aseed.antenna.nl

## BUNKER MENTALITY

The eviction of the protest camp at Crystal Palace (see SchNEWS 203) ended on Monday, with two people Animal and Ken, spending 19 days in an underground bunker! The Grade II listed park could soon be home to a £56 million, 20 screen multiplex cinema with nine bars/restaurants, various retail outlets with concrete ramps leading cars up to the largest roof-top carpark in Britain. According to local papers, an extra million pounds has been spent by Bromley Council on the eviction.

One of the bunker residents, Animal, is currently in remand awaiting sentencing relating to the Manchester 2nd runway campaign. Send love letters, magazines, cards etc. to Eleanor Hutson, SX2145, HMP Newhall, Dialwood, Flockton, Wakefield, WF4 4AX

Crystal Palace campaign 0181 693 8200

## ON THE BUSES

Britain's first toll motorway came another step nearer completion this week, when the High Court refused to allow the protestors' legal challenge to go ahead. The Birmingham Northern Relief Road would be a 27 mile, 3 lane motorway bypassing Birmingham to the North, would devastate local wildlife and communities, and would do little to reduce congestion. This is all bit ironic, considering it happened around the same time that Prescott announced more incentives to increase bus use, and boasted that 15% of his weekly journeys were by bus. Well done John , you must be really roughing it, only using your chauffeur driven cars 85% of the time!

## SchNEWS in brief

Guess wot? The National Year of Reading is part-sponsored by **The Sun** newspaper ** Demonstrate against **Hillgrove Farm's** continued breeding of cats for vivisection on Saturday April 17th from 12 noon. Transport is available from all over the UK – for details call 0121 632 6460 ** **EuroDusnie, Lieden,** The Netherlands . What started off as a three day counter-EU summit in April 97 has grown into an anarchist collective with four buildings squatted around the town. On the week of 27th March – 4th April a celebration of the two years is planned. For more info call 00 31 (0)71 5173019 or **www.dsl.nl/eurodusnie** ** **Med TV** the only independent Kurdish Channel in the world, has had it's licence revoked by the Independent TV Commission. Complain to the commision by ringing 0171 255 3000 or faxing 0171 306 7800 ** **Stop the Asylum Bill** public meeting 16th April 7.30 pm Friends Centre, Ship St., Brighton ** Will **alternative economic institutions** ever challenge capitalism, or are they only useful in covering up its failures? The answer to this question and more at the Secular Hall, Humberstone Gate, Leicester on April 24th . More details from T.Hooley, English dept., Univ.of Leicester, LE1 7RH email caw4@le.ac.uk **

**Red South West** is a decent mag covering lots of left-wing subjects an interesting way! Wow. Send a quid + SAE to Exeter Left group c/o The Flying Post, PO Box 185, Exeter, EX4 4 EW ** Transport is going from Brighton to the opening of the trial of the **Totness Two**, charged with trashing a genetically modified crop site. Page 0336 760424 if you want a lift! **

Don't forget the Global Days of Action against **Monsanto and genetically** modified foods on April 15-30.Info- www.jps.net/dcasner Tel 0181-374-9516, Genetix update, c/o PO Box 9659,London, N4 4JY ** **McBurger Off!** Anti McDonalds benefit gig featuring special guests Chanter (Folk-Rock)at the Royal Standard Music Venue, Blackhorse Lane - directly opposite Blackhorse Lane (Victoria Line) tube station - Walthamstow E.17. 29th April 8pm ** Shout out for more people to get down to the the squatted **121 Centre** in Brixton which has now been in occupation, behind barricades, for eight weeks. They are expecting eviction any time soon, so why not pledge a three hour shift? Events are still happening daily. 121 Railton Road, Brixton, London SE24 Tel 0171-274-6655 ** Last week more than a million people demonstrated in **Mexico City** including electricity workers fighting privitisation and students protesting against the introduction of fees ** Last week one of the **Southdowns Hunt Sabs** received a broken arm in five places at the very last meet of the West Kent Fox Hunt (they are folding and will now be taken over the Old Surrey and Burstow hunt). Sabs arrived to find the place swarming with red coats and about 150 riders - some of whom decided to ride at sabs and broke a woman's arm. Despite a four wheel drive full of cops less than 10 yards away they saw nothing. As for the press always portraying hunt sabs as violent, in the last season about 15 hunt supporters were found guilty and convicted in the courts - only one hunt sab. Contact Hunt Sab Association 01273 622827 ** On the 27th March the Tameside care-workers will have been out on strike for a year. 250 of them were sacked by a Labour Council after they refused to accept worsening pay and conditions. There will be a demo and rally from Astley Rd., Stalybridge. Contact 0161- 308-2452

**Looking ahead to June 18th an internet broadcast is being set to coincide with the Global day of action. Contributions are needed Tel: 07788-491899/e-mail,Capitalism sux@hotmail.com. or write to Box 6, Greenleaf Bookshop, 82 Colston St, Bristol, B51 5BB.

## Inside SchNEWS

"What I realised after the end of this case is that I never, or almost never, have been involved in a trial which has ended in a conviction where I am certain, or almost certain, that the defendents are wholly innocent, and are wholly wrongly convicted." – defence solicitor Gareth Peirce.

Samar Ali and Jawad Botmeh, two Palestinians accused of bombing the Israeli Embassy and Balfour House in London in 1994, are still protesting their innocence. Both are being held as Class A (highest security) prisoners on twenty year sentences, after which they will face deportation.

The two were convicted in 1996 on circumstantial evidence only. Since their conviction, more evidence showing the unfairness of the trial has come to light. In November 1997 it was revealed in the Mail on Sunday that MI5 had received a warning prior to the bombing which was ignored. The source of the warning pointed in a different direction to Samar and Jawad but this evidence has never been made public. In 1998 Paul Foot revealed in Private Eye that another MI5 official had cast more doubt on their convictions. There is also evidence that the jury were exposed to biased journalism and TV documentaries.

An appeal date has now been set but the defence is being refused access to even more important evidence which could be important to the outcome of the case. A campaign for justice for the two was launched in 1997 and are calling people to picket the appeal on 29th March at the Royal Court of Justice, Strand, London WC2 .

Contact BM FOSA, London WC1N 3XX or www.freesaj.org.uk

## SQUATS GOING ON

**Hackney Squat Evictions** are continuing without court orders. Using the elctricty board and the police, the council has been evicting people on suspicion of having illegally supplied electricity and smashing meters and toilets to make buildings uninhabitable. Protesters who occupied the Estates Management offices last Friday were told they couldn't speak to the man responsible for the evictions, as no-one knew which of his TWO houses he was at! When they did get to speak to someone they were told that the council would do 'everything legal' to keep squatters out of Hackney's thousands of empty properties, as part of their 'zero tolerance' policy. No-one could tell the protesters whether the council also had a 'zero tolerance' policy on homelessness.

## ...and finally...

Thanks to increasing work hours and the 24 hour society Britain is becoming a nation of 'border line retards' - according to the British Sleep Foundation.

So SchNEWS reckons this is as good a call as any, for people to get involved in the World Phone in Sick Day on April 6th. For this action, all you have to do is get on the blower, give some excuse for not turning up for work.

The brains behind the day, Decadent Action - the consumer terrorist organisation - are out to bring down capitalism by feeding it until it bursts. This involves a campaign of luxury living funded by shoplifting, credit and the DSS, all intended to push the country into hyper-inflation. According to the Decadent ones, phoning in sick is fast becoming "a genuine alternative to the organised strike."

Check 'em out at BM Decadence, London WC1N 3XX. England.
www.underbelly.demon.co.uk/decadent/

### disclaimer

SchNEWS apolgises to all our readers for going on about those nasty people at World Trade Organisation and their dirty little free trade agreements. Hey, we know sarcasm is more our style. We won't let it happen again. Honest

The Land Is Ours commemorate 350 years since the Diggers originally occupied St. George's Hill by laying a stone at the same site **(SchNEWS 207)**

Pic: Rob Todd

## 17th century Digger

## 20th century digger

Pic: Simon Chapman

"Beats sitting around in an armchair!" Stopping the Avon Ring Road - Bristol's answer to the M25

p

**Scenes in Kosovo after the fighting**

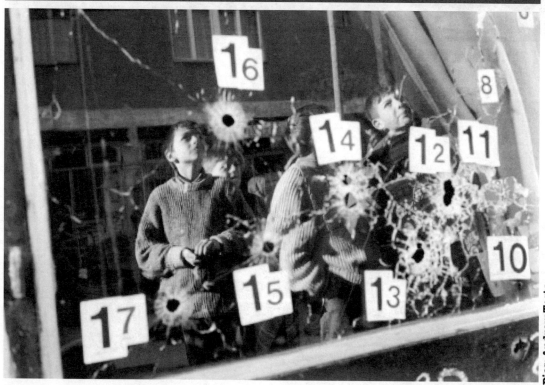

WAKE UP! WAKE UP! IT'S YER NEWS-SPEAK

# Weekly SchNEWS

*Printed and Published in Brighton by Justice?*

**Friday 9th April 1999**  http://www.schnews.org.uk/  **Issue 207**  **Free/Donation**

# WAR IS PEACE

"We are taking this action for one simple reason: to damage Serbian forces sufficiently to prevent Milosevic from continuing to perpetrate his vile oppression against innocent Albanian civilians"

**Tony Blair**

"The first casualty of war is always the truth" traditional

**On 24th March, two weeks after Poland, Hungary and the Czech Republic joined NATO, NATO launched massive air strikes against Serbia. As ever, superpower aggression was dressed up as a humanitarian exercise, this time to defend Kosovan Albanians from Serb terror. As ever, this was a lie. Since 1992 the desire of Germany, Britain and the United States to expand their influence into eastern Europe at the expense of an enfeebled Russia has brought war, genocide and 100,000 dead to the peoples of the former Yugoslavia. Those dying now in Kosovo and Serbia are the latest victims of these western powers' bid for control of the region.**

There is no doubt that Milosevic is engaged in mass murder of the majority ethnic Albanian population in Kosovo. Ethnic Albanians account for over 80% of Kosovo's two million population - well over one million of these Albanian Kosovans are now refugees, either inside Kosovo or in neighbouring countries. It is still unclear how many have been killed by the Serbian army, police and fascist paramilitaries.

Until 1989 Kosovo had been an autonomous province within Yugoslavia, but with the rise of nationalist hatred fuelled by the super powers, Milosevic was able to use his assertion of Serbian nationalism in Kosovo to grab power for himself in Serbia - and lay the basis for war, ethnic cleansing and genocide in Bosnia and, now, Kosovo. There is no doubt that Milosevic's warmongering, encouraged and payrolled by western powers when it suited them, needs to be opposed.

But NATO's attacks on Serbia are nothing to do with protecting Kosovan civilians - their plight is now worse than ever. For less than a tenth of the cost of one bomber, NATO could have supplied significant amount of arms to the Kosovan Liberation Army or supported what is left of the democratic opposition in Serbia. Of course, they did neither - because they are concerned with global power struggles, not the plight of those they cynically exploit to justify their warmongering.

If the United States, Britain and the other massive military powers currently bombing the former Yugoslavia were concerned with defending "innocent civilians" they have had numerous opportunities to do so recently - and not done it. In Turkey, the Kurds have had their villages burnt, their culture outlawed, their people killed and turned into refugees by the thousand without any action from NATO - maybe because Turkey is a key strategic member of NATO. When one million Rwandans were systematically slaughtered in a hundred days Clinton did nothing to prevent it because it did not suit US global interests to do so.

The air strikes NATO are carrying out are aimed at ensuring that Serbia, with its strong economic and political links to Russia, does not get in the way of growing western influence in the region. A staggering amount of air power is being used. 80 fighter bombers and 100 cruise missiles - costing £800,000 each - were launched on the first night alone. You can only wonder at the technology contained in the B2 stealth bombers, which cost $2.1bn each.

NATO tells us that these weapons are so expensive because of their ability to minimise civilian casualties - in fact, they are designed to increase their destructive power while minimising any risk to those using them. Each cluster bomb being dropped from an RAF Harrier jets, for instance, spreads 147 small bombs over an area of up to 100 acres - many do not explode, creating unregulated minefields wherever they are dropped. The RAF is currently dropping cluster bombs on Kosovo.

For four decades following the second world war, socialist Yugoslavia was able to maintain peace amongst the various nationalities making up the country. The Balkans had always been a region where major world powers fought out their battles at the expense of the local population. The anti-fascist militias that became the Yugoslav state after the second world war were determined to prevent the rise of national tensions and fascism in the area again.

The death of Yugoslavia's President Tito and the collapse of the Soviet Union in the late 80s allowed western powers to expand their influence in the region by encouraging the national tensions that would lead to the present horrors. They consistently backed local politicians stirring up national hatred - like Serbia's Milosevic and Croatia's Tudjeman - against those trying to keep Yugoslavia united.

...life, liberty and the pursuit of happiness.

DON'T INSULT OUR INTELLIGENCE

The powerful multinationals that NATO and control of natural resources - not Kosovan refugees. The peoples of the former Yugoslavia, like so many other millions of people from South America to East Timor, can expect no help from these warmongers except for PR purposes. Organising practical support for the victims of the war in Kosovo and building serious opposition to the multinationals' war machine in Britain is the only way we can show solidarity with the millions so cynically used to justify this latest European war.

Further reading: The Death of Yugoslavia by Laura Silber and Alan Little; Kosovo - a short history by Noel Malcolm.

Workers' Aid for Kosovo are involved in organising a convoy of food, medical supplies, toys, etc leaving for Kosovo on 20th April. You can help by organising collections, blagging/lending vehicles and going on the convoy. 0161 227 8184 for details.

"for action is the life of all and if thou dost not act thou dost nothing" Gerrard Winstanley.

## DIRTY DIGGERS

*"All the Commons and waste Ground in England, and in the whole world, shall be taken in righteousness, not owning any property; but taking the Earth to be a Common Treasury, as it was first made for all."* Gerrard Winstanley.

Landlessness, homelessness and poverty are nothing new. The Diggers were fighting for the right of the common person to make rent-free use of the common land way back in 1649.

350 years ago, British activists were already trying to reclaim their rights. The King, who officially owned all the land in England, had been defeated in the civil war leaving England's pastures potentially up for grabs so activist Gerrard Winstanley, with twenty of his poor and landless friends took posession of St Georges Hill at Walton on Thames. The Diggers used 'liberated' presses to produce pamphlets encouraging the poor to make use of common and waste land for cultivation and common grazing, attempting to raise consciousness of why so many go hungry while so few grow rich. SchNEWS can't argue with that – but unfortunately the government and landowners weren't impressed and got rid of them through a combination of legal actions, military intervention and mob violence.

350 years later and the Diggers are back! They have set up site on St George's Hill, ironically now a huge private estate for millionaires, and are demanding a permanent home for the Diggers' memorial stone and guaranteed public access to the hill. The squatters have now been served with an eviction notice, so try and get along this weekend.

SchNEWS spoke to local resident Cliff Richard, who expressed concern over possible 'Devil Women' on site, but was keen to offer his 'congratulations and jubilations' on the memorial site. Location details 0961 373385 The Land is Ours Office: 01865 722016 www.oneworld.org/tlio/

## GENETICS VICTORY!

*"This was a political, and in my experience, unprecedented decision. By withdrawing the case from the jury the Crown have accepted that there was compelling evidence that the defendents had a lawful excuse to remove the GM maize. The last thing the Crown wanted was to see a jury- a microcosm of society- acquit people who admitted taking direct action against GM crops."* Mike Schwarz, defence solicitor.

The two women who faced charges of conspiracy to cause criminal damage for removing GM maize from a test site have had their charges dropped, with the Crown Prosecution Service admitting that they were unable to prove that the two women did not have 'lawful excuse' to pull up the GM maize.

After nine months of preparation for the case, the Crown Prosecution Service decided to drop the charges four days before the trial was set to begin, announcing that " *for complex reasons the Crown intend to offer no evidence.* " They admitted in court that they actually overestimated the cost of the damage, that the figure of £605,000 was a bit exaggerated, its more like £5,000!!

Despite the pouring rain, 300 people turned up outside the court with banners and street theatre, with a bio-hazzard flag hoisted onto the Crown Courts mast.The defence solicitor stated that this was a green light for direct action…so lets get busy this summer!!Totnes Genetics Group Tel: 01803 840009www.togg.freeserve.co.uk

\* A genetic test site on the Scottish Agricultural College's Boghall Farm was trashed last week, despite a large police presence with horses and dogs.6 people were nicked but were released without charge

\* Don't forget April 15-20: Global days of action against Monsanto & genetic engineering.

## SchNEWS in brief

**Designer Babies** - From the elimination of genetic diseases to creating the perfect child - should we be tampering with our genetic-make up? Meeting on April 15th at the Royal Institution 21 Albermarle Street, London W1 7.30 p.m. \*\* Thought you'd all like to know that April 29th is **'Take Our Daughters to Work Day'**. Wanna know more, then check out www.gn.apc.org/daughtersday/ \*\* The **McLibel Two** stuck another two fingers up to the BigMac corporation last week, when three appeal court judges added to the list of accusations found in the Whats Wrong With McDonalds leaflet. Already charged with being responsible for cruelty to animals, exploiting children in advertising campaigns and paying workers a pittance, they now stand accused of promoting a diet which may lead to heart diseases! Contact McLibel Support Campaign, 5 Caledonian Rd., London, N1 9DX 0171 713 1269 www.mcspotlight.org/ \*\* **"The End is Nigh"**- an evening of Millenium Paranoia compered by Tony Allen & guests will be performed upstairs at the Hobgoblin on Sat. April 17 \*\* Fighting Shell in Nigeria: **Ogoni and Ijaw** Resistance talk and video session at Brighton Unemployed Centre, Tilbury Place (Behind the Edward Street AMEX Building) on April 14th, 7.30pm. \*\* **Whoops!** The phone number on the fliers for Brighton June 18th action group is wrong and should read: 01273 298192 \*\* Saturday 17th - Benefit party for June 18 International Day of Action with Dead Dog Mountain, Max Pashm, Praying for the Rain. 9pm till 3am at On the Rocks, 25 Kingsland Road, Shoreditch, London E2. Just £3 \*\* **Save The Shamrock Monkeys** have set up a National Demo For Laboratory Animals March in Brighton and wreath laying at Shamrock on Sat 24th April. \*\* **No More Bombings!** Lift the Sanctions!(Libya & Iraq) April 17th, London: March and Rally for Peace and Justice: 1pm assemble Hyde Park Corner; 3pm Rally in Trafalgar Square. Tel: 0171 436 4636.\*\* **Movement Against the Monarchy** have had a few scenes cut from their upcoming programme "Get Rid of the Royals". Apparently the BBC's lawyers were worried that some scenes were a little treasonous (heaven forbid!). Watch it on BBC 2 on April 13th at 7.30 pm \*\* The **SQUALL** Crew presents 'Commotion'- djs from Squall, Exodus and Under One Sun play underground sounds of house, drum&bass and eclectic beats at the Pembury Tavern - junction of Amhurst Road and Dalston Lane london E9 Friday April 23rd. Just £1 \*\***Project Censored** Yearbook: Censored 1999' highlights the hot stories that the mainstream press ignored. And the top of the censored list? It's the Multilateral Agreement on Investment - that nasty little 'free trade' agreement that would have nullified human, environmental and labour protection laws in all countries that signed it.\* Don't forget **Street Party** outside 121 Centre,Railton Rd, Brixton 2pm Saturday 10th Info 0171-274-655

## Inside SchNEWS

Lindis Percy is currently serving a nine month sentence for putting 'invalid' stickers up on illegal bylaw signs that run around the US Menwith Hill in Harrogate Yorkshire. While the MoD sponsored NSA (National Security Agency) Spy Base has been busy feeding military intelligence and data through to the Western War Machine killing thousands in the Balkans, Lindis has just come out of a week in solitary confinement for refusing to be strip searched on entering the prison. Lindis needs all the support she can get as she is being restricted visitors, given harsh routine psychological tests and is getting ill through all the strain. To cap it all she can even hear fighter jets taking off from the nearby bases at USAF Lakenheath and Mildon Hall. Write to:- LindisPercy (CF9734), HMP Highjpoint, Stradishall, Newmarket, Suffolk, CB8 9YG

## PENSIONER POWER!

When the Church of England wanted to pull down the Community Centre on Gloucester Rd in Bristol 15 years ago, local pensioners stepped in and occupied the premises. After 5 years they arranged a lease, and ever since volunteers have been running the centre on a non profit basis, available free to skint organisations, finding places for the homeless and organising a bread run. The centre is also used by Hare Krishnas, Buddhists, and a music school that caters for 100 Sikh children.

Despite the fact that the 6 other local churches are never exactly packed with punters the C of E. wants to take back the centre and rent out the rooms to raise cash. Charitable souls that they are they promise zero tolerance of other religious groups so presumably the sikhs, buddhists and krishnas will be out on their collective arse. The pensioners even offered to buy the premises but the C of E is still determined to evict them so the sagacious squatters took their tale to the top, petitioning the Archbishop of Canterbury by chaining themselves to his railings outside Lambeth Palace! Their case goes to court on April 19th. Tel. 0117 944 4401.

## ...and finally...

*"I've always wanted to actually hit an arms dealer, and then turn 'round and say 'well if I didn't do it, someone else would."* - Mark Thomas

Tired of hearing about massacres of people in far-away countries while you sit helplessly at home? Sick of seeing TV footage of people being shot at by the shock troops of dodgy regimes? Ever wished you could hit back at those arming such tyrants? Then read on… this year, some of the world's biggest arms dealers are handing us ample opportunities to deal them some determined blows. They don't only hang out in remote countries, these firms have events and premises in this country too. So it's open season on the industry that equips mass murderers and torturers the world over….

**April 28** - Two firms, British Aerospace (BAe) and Alvis/GKN are having their Annual General Meetings in London on this Wednesday. Two for the price of one - come and play! All you need is a single share; with an offer like this, you just can't lose.

**BAe** is Europe's biggest arms manufacturer, and with the planned £7 billion merger with GEC-Marconi there's no better time to give them hassle. Come and meet the guys in suits who are about to sell 16 Hawk attack fighter planes to Indonesia, and who are flogging 200,000 assault rifles for the Turkish military. Or perhaps you'd like to speak to the top people at **Alvis**, whose Scorpion tanks have been used on the streets of Jakarta against unarmed protesting students.

**No-one goes away empty handed…** If you can't make it to the AGMs on that day, BAe and Alvis are giving you the chance to visit them in one of their many centres of manufacturing excellence around the country. To ensure maximum impact try to organise actions hitting them at these places at around the time of April 28. Targets at the following locations:Hampshire, Stockport, Nottingham, Bristol, Plymouth, Lancashire, Humberside, London & Coventry.

**September 14-17** - the even bigger one. Defence Systems Equipment International (DSEi) is the title of the UK's one-stop bombs ' n' guns emporium, to which you can be sure many of your top torturers will be coming along. And the best gag is - we ourselves bankroll it with a cool quarter of a million of taxpayers' money. Put those dates in your diaries, May 15 (Manchester, Friends Meeting House) and May 29 (London, Conway Hall, WC1).

Take a well-aimed pot-shot or two at your favourite arms dealers this year. These not-to-be missed opportunities are brought to you by Campaign Against the Arms Trade. Call them on 0171 281 0297www.gn.apc.org/caat

## Subscribe!

Keep SchNEWS FREE! Just send 1st Class stamps (e.g. 20 for next 20 issues) or donations (payable to Justice?) **Ask for "Originals"** if you can make copies. Post *free* to all prisoners. SchNEWS, c/o on-the-fiddle, P.O. Box 2600, Brighton, East Sussex, BN2 2DX.
*Tel/Autofax :* +44 (0)1273 685913 *GET IT EVERY WEEK BY E-MAIL:* schnews@brighton.co.uk
Don't forget Street Party outside 121 Centre,Railton Rd, Brixton 2pm Saturday 10th Info 0171-274-655

# SO WHAT IS THIS GENTRIFICATION?

Despite being far too long a word to roll off the tongue, gentrification explains a lot of the changes happening right here in Brixton. Lambeth Council (*in all their infinite wisdom – Not!*) are selling off properties to raise capital (what we call money) but the "development" of Brixton does little to help local people or shops (surprise, surprise). The council are, just like the rest of the country, in a mad race to sell-off and privatise as much of our neighbourhoods and services as possible – cutting funding to vital resources like Libraries and Centres while raking in a profit from mad shopping and tourist schemes that dispossess and disempower local communities. None of this money goes to help US, in fact they are trying to price us out of our own area, like in some parts of Islington, Hackney and Tower Hamlets and now Brixton, to make our areas yuppie playgrounds!

DON'T BE FOOLED! The development of Brixton and the criminalisation of groups like the homeless and squatters are just the tip of the iceberg. If the police and the council have their way, once Brixton has been "cleansed", rents will soar and people will be forced out of their own neighbourhoods. Local shops will either "make" or "break" with hefty new RATES to accompany the new poncy clientele, and many will be bought out or bust. So we have a situation where first they kick out the undesirables and homeless on the streets with new police powers, then they evict all the squatters, AND THEN GUESS WHO IS NEXT?? **Watch your back, your Council is on the loose.**

South London Stress, 27th March 1999

# 121 RAILTON RD, BRIXTON

**Reclaim the Streak, street party on 10th April, 1999**

# TEKNIVALS IN FRANCE

**1. The Transport**

France is currently enjoying a big free party scene – or Teknivals as they're called in Europe. The scale of these events is huge, with as many as 5-10,000 people, and up to forty sound systems – and most parties are tolerated by the authorities... unlike some here in Britain. Party people of all ages and backgrounds come together in a unified feeling of resistance. Unlike here, there had been no free festival/party scene until the turn of the 90's when Spiral Tribe left England and inspired people across Europe to set up their own parties. Squatting is popular in France, but - like in a lot of places - many young people are still seen as unpoliticised.
In France the May Day teknival has become the biggest of the year. Check out: www.freetekno.org United Systems party line: 020 8959 7525

**2. The Power**

**3. The People**

**4. The Party**

Pics: Aubin Thomas

WAKE UP! WAKE UP! IT'S YER

# Weekly SchNEWS

*Printed and Published in Brighton by Justice?*

JUSTICE
FOR ALL

**Friday 16th April 1999**  http://www.schnews.org.uk/  **Issue 208  Free/Donation**

# HILLSBOROUGH

## 10 YEARS ON

*"I've followed Liverpool for over 50 years and what I saw that day at Hillsborough will stay with me till the day I die. We could see something was wrong even as the match started, the pens behind the goal looked packed, although there was plenty of space either side. We couldn't believe the scenes we witnessed, we were in deep shock as it became obvious that things were wrong. Why weren't the police helping? I watched them come on with police dogs, whilst younger supporters ferried the dying and injured on advertising boards. They were heroes, yet the media portrayed them as thugs and animals. It's not right that 10 years later most of those responsible have never been charged with a criminal offence; what kind of country are we living in?"*

Pensioner who was at Hillsborough.

Ten years ago on April 15th 1989, Liverpool were playing Notts Forest in a FA Cup semi-final at the Hillsborough Stadium in Sheffield. As kick-off approached, the ancient turnstiles at the football ground became a bottleneck as five thousand Liverpool fans tried to get in. When the police eventually opened the main gates, instead of directing the fans to the open terraces they sent them into a crowded pen.

*"I was at the front of the pens, and you could see people were dying. I asked, pleaded, with a copper to open the gates. He just looked at me as if I wasn't there. Some who tried to climb out were pushed back in, maybe to die"*Hillsborough Survivor.

96 Liverpool fans lost their lives and 400 were injured that day in the Leppings Lane terraces- crushed to death against the jail-like railings, which became twisted from the pressure. As people tried to get on the pitch, the police pushed them back, thinking there was a pitch invasion. At 3.06 pm the game was finally abandoned.

What followed was a monumental and arrogant cover-up of inadequacies and incompetence, which one supporter described as an 'active propagation of mistruths' as the police sought to hide their mistakes.

The subsequent inquiry by Lord Justice Taylor left no doubt where the blame lay: *"The main reason for the disaster was the failure of police control."*

Not however according to the SUN newspaper, which, in the aftermath of the tragedy, dragged its gutter self to new depths. In a front page spread editor Kelvin MacKenzie blamed the tragedy squarely on Liverpool supporters:

*'Some fans picked pockets of victims.'…'Some fans urinated on the brave cops' 'fans beat up PC giving kiss of life.'*

During the thirty-one days of the Taylor inquiry no one mentioned hooliganism.

Nearly two years later, an 80 day inquest, verdicts of accidental death were reached. But as the Hillsborough Justice Campaign pointed out *"Senior South Yorkshire police officers were responsible They committed a criminal act when they threw open exit gates for the fans to enter the stadium,. they should have delayed the kick-off that day."*

Then in December 1996, Carlton TV's "Hillsborough" ripped apart the inquest decision that the victims suffered only accidental death. They unearthed evidence that a camera, which the police claimed was not working, held vital evidence that people were being crushed. This footage mysteriously vanished. It highlighted the fact that more fans might have survived if  medical treatment had been available sooner. It exposed police lies, such as blaming fans for forcing a gate open to get in the ground . There were allegations of cops putting pressure on people giving evidence at the enquiry. And Still no police officers have yet to face any disciplinary hearing.

*"Unfortunately, the facts concerning Hillsborough haven't been told – all we've had is the usual manipulation of facts to be served up by the media circus – football supporters become SCUM and ANIMALS, easy scapegoats. South Yorkshire police were rubbing shoulders with journalistic filth before the bodies of the dead grew cold. I'll never forget what the S\*\* printed. I remember burning a copy with my father. I'll never forgive those journalists, they could have refused to print the police's lies."*

Liverpool supporter

As Trevor Hicks -who lost his daughters at Hillsborough- said *"We got two disasters at Hillsborough : the one on the day and one that's happened since. There was evasion and an orchestrated cover up against us from the beginning. Nothing has been done willingly."*

\# The Hillsborough campaign are calling for a boycott of the Liverpool v Sheffield Wednesday football match on 8th May

\# The High Court gave the go ahead in March for two police officers to go face charges of manslaughter and wilful neglect of duty in court

\# A campaign against The Sun got under way with sales slumping by almost 40% costing £10 million a year. The boycott is still going on

Hillsborough Justice Campaign, 134 Oakfield Rd., Anfield, Liverpool, L4 OUG Tel 0151 260 5262  Recommended reading 'Hillsborough, the Truth' by Phil Scraton (Mainstream)

## WHO KILLED BLAIR PEACH?

*"As the police rushed past him, one of them hit him on the head with a stick..He tried to get up, but he was shivering. He couldn't stand. The police came back and told him'Move!Come on, Move!'They were very rough with him and I was shocked because it was clear he was seriously hurt. He was in a very bad state and he couldn't speak. Then he just dropped down."* Mr.Parwinder Atwal

On 22 April 1979 5,000 people marched from Southall to Ealing Town Hall to hand in a petition of 10,000 signatures demanding that the National Front (NF) should not be allowed to come into their  town and insult their community. The next day 4,000 cops arrived to deal with the 20,000 people who had turned out to oppose the fascists. The police brutally attacked the protesters. Blair Peach and his friends were trapped…at least six witnesses saw a riot cop  club Blair Peach in the head, he later died. No inquiry took place and no one has ever been charged with his murder.

Blair Peach was a white school teacher in East London, active within the South Hackney and Shoreditch branch of the Anti Nazi League. His murder became a symbol of establishment incompetence and police brutality. *"his death….exposed how black people were treated by the police, and how both black and white people were affected by racism….It united people who saw that the National Front was a threat to our democracy."*

The Scarman Report in 1981 sugggested the 'bad apple' theory- that a few police 'let down the force' but the police force themselves are not intrinsically racist. The report suggested 'race awareness training'….Stephen Lawrence's case is just one of many incidents which confirm a blatant lack of such awareness to date. Muhammad Anwar, of the Centre for Ethnic Relations at Warwick university explained  *"You cannot isolate one incident, just as you cannot isolate one institution, but these all contribute to an accumulated perception of how the police treat black people. Many of today's young people weren't even born when these incidents took place, but they learn from parents and community leaders. You cannot separate attitude from experience. They are just as important as each other."*

On Sat 24 April there's a  Demo Against Racism in Southall Park. Meet 1pm @ Dominion Centre, The Green, Southall. Coaches from Brighton outside the Royal Pavilion at the Old Steine at 10.30am Tickets £7/5 for sale at the Peace Centre. For Information Tel: 0181 980 3601.

## TUBEWAY BARMY

Reclaim the Streets! On Sat 1st May its time to transform the tube! Meet at Tower of London, 2pm,Saturday 1st May with your party-pants on. Bring food and drink and fun and games-The Party Line terminates at Clapham Common May Day Festival.

For too long has the tube been the stomping ground of the wealthy, an unattainable luxury for those on low incomes. The government's privatisation plans put profit before passengers as always through the intended full-scale sell off of the tube.

London's tube system is already the most expensive in Europe and fares will spiral out of reach of poorer pockets as private profit is increased at our expense. Anti- strike legislation has put paid to any arguments from the underdog, consequently workers suffering attacks against their pay and conditions are only likely to make an impact through 'unofficial' action.'

So on 1st May let's turn the tube into a Place to Party! Show your solidarity and revel against the fat cats. Bring food, drink, musical instruments, decorations, toys, games, masks, banners and flags. Further information: Reclaim The Streets: 0171 281 4621.

* Transport from Brighton, tickets from Peace Centre, Gardner Street

### MAY DAY EVENTS

**\*INTERNATIONAL WORKERS MAY DAY MARCH.** Meet 12 noon Clerkenwell Green to Trafalgar Square. 100 years of celebrating trade union rights, human rights and international solidarity. + May 2nd, May Day International Evening-music from around the world at Subterania, 36 Acklam Rd, London W10(Ladbroke Grove)4-11pm

**Reclaim May Day** The Oyster House 6-11pm, Locksway Road, Milton, Portsmouth. £3/2. Featuring bands and DJs. Food 6-8pm.

**Cannabis Coalition** Beltane Ganja day. Celebration of Cannabis March and free-festival on Clapham Common. Meet noon Brixton Ritzy. Tel: 0171 737 6289 mayday@schmoo.co.uk

**Nottingham May Day events** 26th April to 1st May. Program available from **Mushroom Bookshop**, 12 Heathcote St, Nottingham

**Bradford May Day**. Tel: 01274 734160 1in12@legend.co.uk

**\*DIY Resist Global Action.** B'ham. Fight back against global economic power.. Meet 11am outside NatWest HQ. Colmore Row, City Centre.

**Manchester mini reclaim the streets.** Meet Midday, 30th April at University Students' Union, Oxford Road. 0161 2245153 mfox4rhm@fsl.art.man.ac.uk

**Hull reclaim the streets** Saturday 8th May, meet at Pearsons Park (off Beverly Rd) 12noon

**\*Finally**, for those of you who are sick to death of all the politics, fuck it all off and get with the **Vegan Organic Network.** Permaculture, forest gardening, community gardening, etc. May 1-2 at 'Fresh Horizons', 50 Ditton Court Rd, Westcliff On Sea, Essex. Tel: 01702 303259

### INSIDE SCHNEWS

Mumia Abu-Jamal, black rights activist and award winning radio journalist on death row for the past 16 years, has been subject to state oppression since he joined the Black Panthers. He was wrongly arrested in 1981 for killing a Philadelphia cop. In '95 files were finally exposed proving that minority citizens were being routinely framed. Abu-Jamal's years' work exposing state terror led to over 300 victims' convictions being reversed, but even when it became national news his own was not. Mumia again faces imminent execution. Mass demos on 24th April, his birthday. Contact Mumia Must Live! BM Haven, London, WC1N 3XX. www.Mumia.org

## SchNEWS in brief

The **National Front** are planning a march in Worcester on the 24th. The Anti-Nazi League are planning a counter-demonstration, assemble at the Guildhall at 1pm.For confirmation:Tel.: 0171-2844040,e-mail:editors@s-light.demon.co.uk **\*\***This months 'special issue' of **The Ecologist** is full of information on the growing climate crisis, the political and corporate response, and what the hell we should be doing about it. Our planet is being sabotaged, inform yourself and take action! For copies ring 01403 786726 **\*\*Kosova Aid Convoy** benefit @Sussex Arts Club, Ship St, Brighton this Sunday ( 18th) 7.30pm with Tartan Amoebas + DJ's Ghecko and Hair Bear.£5/3 **\*\***There is another benefit gig for People's lifeline for **Kosova** on 29th April at New Madeira Hotel, Marine Parade, Brighton. 8-2 with talks and videos £3 **\*\*No Pasaran.** Get cultural with the Stroud Football Poets compelling accounts of the Spanish Civil War. Sat 24th April, 8pm. Hexagon Theatre, Kingsfield School, Brook Rd, Kingswood, Bristol. Tickets£4/3 - Tel: 0117 9711540 **\*\***Alternatively, you could motivate yourselves to march from Westminster Cathedral to the BNFL office in Buckingham Gate to remind them about the **Children of Chernobyl** who are still suffering as a result of the world's worst nuclear disaster. Tel 0171 6072302 **\*\*No Smoke Without Fire** is a guide for people who believe they are the victims of a miscarriage of justice, containing advice starting from the moment of arrest through to post-release care. SAE to: Liberty, 21 Tabard St, London SE1 4LA. Tel 0171 403 3888**\*\***Thespionage presents **'TICK-A-TEENTH? because dealing can be murder-'** Another tale from the front-line, for those that know the score. At The Komedia, Gardener St, Brighton. Tues 27 and Wed 28 April 8pm 01273 647 100. The Akademia, Manchester St, Brighton. Fri 14th & Sat 15th May 7.30pm 01273 607 171. Tickets £5/4 **\*\*Conference on Iboga** A talk by Dan Lieberman on the therapeutic uses of Iboga (a psychoactive plant from the Congo Basin). Used by the Bwiti in their 3-5 day initiation ceremonies it has been especially effective in treating opium addiction. At the Akademia, 14-17 Manchester St. Tel: 0181 3878824 ethnobotany@iafrica.com**\*\***The contract for the **Avon Ring Road** has been awarded to Christiani Nielsen, the Leamington-based outfit responsible for the Wells relief road and the nasty evictions at Dead Woman's Bottom. Work is expected to start on Apr 19; the protest camp is gearing up for action. Contact the camp on 0836 653 723 or 0797 999 0389 or STARR at 84 Colston St, Bristol BS1 5BB **\*\*World Day for Laboratory Animals** is Sat April 24 with a national march in Brighton. Meet Preston Park at noon followed by wreath laying at Shamrock Farm ** First-ever National Animal Rights demo at **Medical Research Council**, the Ridgeway, Mill Hill, London. The labs here were infiltrated several years ago and such cruelty exposed that top profs had to resign: the experiments still continue- let's stop them. 11am, Fri April 23. Nearest tube Mill Hill East, then 240 bus. More info: Soraya 0181 888 4971; Chrissie 0181 203 2325/ 0467 471111**\*\***Party at **Lyminge Forest** West Wood protest camp, 24/5 Apr. The battle is nearly won!!**\*\* Third Battle of Newbury** are suspending their monthly meetings until 2nd Sep, due to lack of cash** The camp at the **B'ham Relief Road** need tarpaulin & wood, sorry no tel no as one of the dogs buried the mobile**Don't forget: this Saturday (17) Benefit gig with comedian **Tony Allen** @ Hobgoblin London Rd upstairs 9pm. £1.50 **

---

**SIMON JONES MEMORIAL CAMPAIGN**
Meeting next Thursday 22nd April 7.30pm upstairs at The Hobgoblin. 01273 685913

---

## Watching me, watching you.

Each person in this country watches an average 4 hours of TV a day; that's a quarter of the waking life of everyone spent staring at a piece of furniture. Scary, but we ain't seen nothing yet.

How about a TV that watches you? Every time you click the remote control of a new Digital TV, the set notes what you are watching and for how long, and then relays this information to the service provider. As you explore the interactive new world of entertainment a file is being compiled of your interests and viewing habits, name, address, bank details... This will then be sold to the multi-national corporations, so they can target you with specific products, or to any other organisation who wants it.

The happy advertisers of TV's 'digital revolution' promise more "viewer power", but in fact the opposite is true. Pilot interactive TV projects have created programmes that are designed to extract even more information from people, through on-screen quiz shows and questionnaires. Matthew Timms, head of programming at Two Way TV says viewers are happy to answer personal questions:

*'They tend to be fairly honest... because somehow they feel they're sitting there, it's just them and the television, even though the reality is it's got a wire leading straight back to somebody's computer..."*

And there's more in store. The service providers can send new software to your telly at any point, without telling you, and they're working on the idea of artificial intelligence programming so the box can respond to the information it gleans about you. It could sell you products you might like, suggest programmes to watch, work to increase your viewing, or your children's...turn off, tune out and drop off drop the thing out of a twelve storey window.

22-28th April is International TV-Turnoff Week, coordinated in this country by White Dot. They encourage you to *"Take a healthy break from TV and you'll find out what you really enjoy doing."* More information on this and the leaflet "Spy TV" about digital telly from White Dot, PO Box 2116, Hove, East Sussex, BN3 3LR; www.whitedot.org

## SHIT HAPPENS

April 19th-25th is Real Nappy Week - did you know that British parents throw out 8 million disposable nappies a day, that's over 800 000 tonnes a year of nappy waste - all have to be disposed of. For every £1 spent on nappies, the taxpayer pays 10p to get rid of them.The Real Nappy Association and Women's Environmental Network are trying to expose the environmental damage caused by nappy waste and promote alternatives. Councils are joining in, giving away free real nappies and encouraging use in maternity wards. Apart from the volume of waste, the campaign is concerned with the ingredients of disposable nappies, which are not subject to govt controls and include at least one chemical removed from tampons in 1985 because of its link to toxic shock syndrome. Real Nappy Association, PO Box 3704, London SE26 4RX, 0181 299 4519

## ...and finally...

Tomatoes around the country are going all gooey over drum and bass. Growers have found that blasting the fruits with loud bass-heavy music which helps to dislodge the pollen, which falls on the sigmas and a baby tomato is born. Ahhh. "Music with a stong beat is best" reckons Alan Parker, chair of the Tomato Growers' Association "Even growers whose taste inclines more towards Radio 3 recognise the merits of drum and bass. We have not compiled a tomato top 10 yet, but it is safe to say Simply Red will be in there".

SchNEWS has unconfirmed reports that Monsanto is trying to splice a DNA gene from Goldie into tomatos.

**disclaimer** SchNEWS warns all readers that their TV is full of disposable shit. Honest!

WAKE UP! WAKE UP! IT'S YER 'ON THE PISTE' (YET AGAIN)

# Weekly SchNEWS

### Printed and Published in Brighton by *Justice?*

**Friday 23rd April 1999**     http://www.schnews.org.uk/    **Issue 209**    **Free/Donation**

# BALACLAVA BOVVER

Just when you thought that there weren't enough nasty laws to keep us in our places, along comes The New Crime and Disorder Act , which came into effect this month. Democracy is now surely safe with this new law which amongst other things, makes wearing masks on demonstations illegal, and creates new Anti-Social Behaviour orders to deal with bad people. Here is your survival guide to the new powers the forces of darkness now posess

### Masking up illegal

Sections 25-7 of the new act dictate that a Police Officer of inspector rank or above can order you to de-mask on a demo if s/he fears "serious violence or disorder in his/her area". They also have the power to confiscate and destroy materials used to mask up with- so don't take your brand new tops. Failure to de-mask can land you in the nick for up to a month.

On a hunt sab in Dorset last month, the cops declared the whole county an area of potential serious disorder in order to force sabs to de-mask. Amongst items confiscated were hooded tops and a copy of the local paper that one shy sab was using to preserve his modesty! But fear not, when quizzed by SchNEWS our friendly Dorset cops informed us that they would only use the legislation where appropriate, and if it was a cold December morning on a peaceful demo then you could wear your scarves in safety. Well that's alright then.

Thames Valley Police used the act at last weekends anti-vivisection demonstration at Hillgrove Farm. The police went back on a previous agreement not to perform searches on the day, forcing 41 people to unmask and nicking one man who refused to do so. Some might say it's a wee bit unfair, since cops often have their faces covered on demos, and seem to mysteriously lose their ID numbers. But of course, police don't need to conceal their identity, as they would never do anything wrong, would they?

### Anti Social Behaviour Orders

Sections 1-4 of the Act cover the Anti-Social Behaviour Orders (ASBO). When someone is suspected of anti-social behaviour, a senior police officer or local authority can apply to the courts for an ASBO which is done in a civil rather than criminal court, so they need less proof to get one. The hearing can also be held without the person affected by the ASBO being there to defend themselves. Once they get it, they can not only force the person to stop the "anti-social" behaviour, but can also get more wide-ranging restrictions on their actions, even if it's not directly relevant to the ASBO, such as curfews or exclusion orders. The order runs for at least 2 years, but can be extended for indefinite periods. Violation of an ASBO can land you with up to 5 years in the nick.

These orders are being hailed as the way to deal with "neighbours from hell", but animal rights groups fear the new law will be used against them in the same way that the anti-stalking laws have . The definition of anti-social behaviour is so wide-ranging that you can have an ASBO slapped on you if your behaviour causes "alarm or distress, or harassment to one or more people". Wouldn't it be spooky if protestors at Hillgrove or Shamrock started getting ASBOs issued against them?

### Wider definition of terrorism

Just when you thought it couldn't get any worse, those nice guardians of our freedom in the Labour government have published their 'Legislation against Terrorism' Consultation Paper which will protect us all from international terrorism, with the use of even more draconian laws. The Paper suggests, amongst other things, that there is a "continuing need for counter-terrorist legislation for the foreseeable future." This is regardless of the threat of terrorism in Northern Ireland How odd then, that it was a Labour government that introduced the first Prevention of Terrorism Act in 1974, promising that it was only a temporary measure, brought in after the Birmingham pub bombings. Well apparently the "time has come to put that legislation onto a permanent footing" Whoops!

This Consultation paper also proposes to widen the definition of terrorism as "the use of serious violence against persons or property, or the threat to use such violence to intimidate or coerce a government, the public, or any section of the public for political, religious or ideological ends." If it wasn't obvious enough, they intend to use this definition to include animal rights activities, and "indigenous groups prepared to engage in serious violence to further their cause (e.g. independence for a certain region, or environmental concerns)". So watch out all you Cornish nationalists and anti-open cast campaigners. Finally the paper proposes that the powers of stop and search and detention that exist in Northern Ireland should be extended to the rest of the UK. So a copper can arrest you to "prevent acts of terrorism" and hold you for up to 28 days without trial.

But before you all get too paranoid and give up direct action, and start to write dodgy anarcho news-sheets, they're only bringing in such laws, because they realise how effective direct action is. So bear in mind the London Animal Rights News editorial "Whilst we should monitor the situation, it in some way reflects the success our movement has had. It shows that animal abusers see us as a force to be reckoned with."

## ROBERT HAMILL RIP

" In Northern Ireland this case has the sort of impact for many that the Stephen Lawrence case has in London" *Jeremy Hardy*

On 27th April 1997 Robert Hamill left a Catholic social club in Portadown after a family nightout.. A Royal Ulster Constabulary (RUC) landrover parked nearby had been warned that a group of loyalists were hanging around. Seeing the RUC presence and knowing that they had been alerted to possible trouble, Robert and his family made the fatal mistake of assuming that the police would keep the peace, and they could safely walk past the lurking Loyalists. The mob, of about thirty, knocked Robert down then gave the men a serious kicking. The women ran to a nearby RUC vehicle, begging for help. They received NO response, though the attack took place in full-view of the officers . The police said they feared for their safety even though they carry guns. No arrests were made, no crime scene declared. After twelve days in a coma, Robert finally died.

Roberts family have been taunted ever since the attack by RUC vehicles beeping their horns, one time swerving close enough to hit a brother's ankle; also by Loyalists chanting " Where's Robbie Hamill", while miming holding someone by the hair and kicking and stamping on their head.

Of the six men who were eventually arrested, five were released without charge due to insufficient evidence. Although there were CCTV cameras overlooking the scene, the RUC claim nothing of any relevance was recorded. It took 10 days and 5 press statements for the police to come close to admitting the truth. Initially the RUC said *"Police moved in to separate (two) groups…bottles were thrown… and the police themselves came under attack "*, this bears little resemblance to the truth.

One man, Paul Hobson, 22, was recently acquitted of Roberts' murder but convicted of causing an affray, he could be back on the streets in less than six weeks! Roberts family, realising that no-one else is going to do anything about this, are collecting funds to pay for a private prosecution.

* Donations and messages of support to: Robert Hamill Justice Appeal Fund c/o 8 William Street, Lurgan, Co. Armagh, BT66 1JA.

* In a recent TV documentary 'Loyalists' reporters were told that thousands of documents containing detailed information on 'suspects' were passed onto Loyalist death squads by the RUC and British Army.

Read 'The Committee: political assassinations in Northern Ireland by Sean McPhilemy

* Since July 1998 Catholics living in Portadown, Northern Ireland have been living under a state of continuous siege, since the Orange Order were banned from marching through the Garvaghy Road. Residents are harassed daily by Orange Order demos and other violent acts. A support group in Britain has now been set up Friends of the Garvaghy Road, BM Box 5519, London, WC1N 3XX Tel 0181 442 8778 email fgr@brosna.demon.co.uk

* Demonstrations by the South Armagh Farmers and Residents Committee continue. Despite the Good Friday agreement they live in the most militarised area in Western Europe. Within an area under ten miles in radius there are 30 spy posts and five military bases with 3,000 troops assigned to the area. That's one for every eight people in South Armagh.

* A helicopter flying for just one hour costs the equivalent of a nurse's wages for 4 months. Official figures show that 30,000 flying hours were recorded last year in N. Ireland - enough to pay around 6,000 nurses.

* Good Friday Agreement discussion meeting 1pm Sat 8th May St.Margaret's House, 21 Old Ford Rd., Bethnal Green, E2 Tel 0171 833 3022

## SchNEWS in brief

The Big Issue is launching a campaign to end the Home Office's inhumane practice of issuing **food vouchers** to asylum seekers They're printing coupons over the next four weeks for you to send to Jack Straw. Support line-0171526 3305**American news group Cable News Network (CNN) have agreed to show an Adbusters advert as part of **"TV Turn-Off Week."** ABC, CBS and NBC however, told Adbusters to get lost.International TV Turn Off Week runs from 22-28th April and is co-ordinated in the UK by White Dot, PO Box 2116, Hove, E.Sussex, BN3 3LR www.adbusters.org **Stop the War!** Brighton and Hove campaign, meeting every Monday, 7.30 pm , Friends Meeting House, Ship St. Protest every Sat. 12 noon, Clocktower, Brighton. National Demo, London, 8th May, coaches will be organised**Come to the opening of the new **Unemployed Workers Centre.** 1st May 1pm, 4 Crestway Parade, Hollingdean. Food, stalls, music etc.** **Whitehawk Hill Allotment Gardeners Association** (WHAGA) are a co-op working a 1/2 acre of disused allotments at Whitehawk Hill. They want to expand to open up more derelict land for organic growing in a cooperative way and need to show they have support in the wider community. Ring Karl Heyman 292215 to put your name on the waiting list for Whitehawk Hill*** **Newcastle Community Green Festival,** FREE environmental event. May 1+ 2 Tel: 0191 232 1750 ** A woman is due in court next month charged with writing '**don't bomb Iraq'** on the dockyard walls at the Royal Naval Base in Portsmouth. As they point out "People in Iraq need our solidarity, not bombs and sanctions" so turn up outside the court hearing wearing black. Portsmouth Magistrates' Court, Thursday 6th & Friday 7th May 9.30am Contact Portsmouth Anarchist Network, Box A, 167 Fawcett Rd., Southsea, Hampshire, PO 4 ODH **If you saw the TV programme **Movement Against The Monarchy** (MA'M) and you want to know more about those trouble making anti-royalist scum go to a MA'M meeting on May 2nd 2-5pm Conway Hall, Red Lion Square,Tube, Central London ** Protesters camped along the route of the proposed **Birmingham Northern Relief Road** have sent us their new contact no. after their dog buried their mobile last week: 07931 161761**Demonstrate against **student fees** in Huddersfield on Wednesday April 28 Meet 11am outside Students Union**The National Front** plans to march through Worcester this Saturday have been cancelled. Shame.

## BLOODY TREES

A protest camp has now been set up at Cedars Wood after Manchester Airport PLC started felling trees. The airport authorities wanted to chop down the wood because those blasted trees will get in the way of the radar for the new runway. Permission was given by the owners, National Trust, who are, once again, breaking their own rules.

The protesters are expecting eviction soon,despite the fact that the House of Lords have still to decide on the woods future. Contact 01226 764279 Site mobile: 07931 931850

## Inside SchNEWS

In March, prisoner activist **Kenny Carter** was placed in solitary at Full Sutton gaol in the interests of 'Good Order and Discipline'. Although he had committed no offence, the guv decided that his presence on 'normal location' was *"objectionable"*. He was segregated because of his campaigning for prisoner rights. Kenny spent years on the 'ghost-train', being constantly moved around until his arrival at Full Sutton in 1998 where he was segregated immediately . After 3 months he was allowed into an ordinary wing but remained a target for prison staff . Four months later, Kenny was back in segregation where he remains. It's important that he is supported by all who share his vision of a society free from brutal prison systems and dehumanised prisoners. Write letters of support to Kenny Carter ,AD3434, HMP Full Sutton, Moor Lane, York Y04 1PS. Letters of protest to the governor at the same address.

*Benefit gig for **Michal Patera**, a member of the Czech anarcho-syndicalists, Sat 1st May @Arsenal Tavern, Blackstock Rd, 10 mins from Finsbury Park, with Steve Cope, the Doleclaimers and North London anarcho-syndicalist choir. 8pm 'till late £5/2.50 unwaged. Michal is currently facing 25 years hard labour after defending himself from attack by 5 neo-nazis. None of the attackers have been charged. Funny that! Over a third of Czech police are members of racist organisations.

## WORKERS MEMORIAL

April 28th is Workers Memorial Day, a day to remember workers around the world who have been killed, disabled or injured at work. The day not only highlights the preventable nature of the vast majority of workplace accidents and ill health, but promotes campaigns for safety at work. In the UK alone about 500 people are killed every year in work and road traffic accidents. An estimated 20,000 more die each year from work related illness.

One of these deaths was Simon Jones, who one year ago went to work at Shoreham docks for Euromin Ltd. for the first and last time. Sent by a temping agency to do one of the most dangerous jobs in the country with no health and safety training. He was helping to unload a ship when the grab of a crane crushed his skull. He died instantly.

A year on and despite every legal channel being exhausted as well as a series of high-profile direct actions no-one has been prosecuted over his death. In Parliament George Galloway MP said Euromin manager James Martell's *" contempt for the laws of health and safety in this country, his greed and hunger for profit, his negligence and carelessness, slaughtered this young man just as clearly as if he had pushed him off the dock with his own hands."*

*Wed 28th April protest outside the Health and Safety Executive HQ, London (South side of Southwark Bridge) Transport leaves Brighton from St.Peters Church at 11 am £1/50p concession

Simon Jones Memorial Campaign, PO Box 2600, Brighton, BN2 2DX www.simonjones.org.uk

## ...and finally...

Get yer laughing-gear round this one!Vegan Condoms are available to delight the discerning in their search for kosher kontraception. Comdomi's exciting new range of cruelty-free jonnies (best avoided by S&M freaks) have something to tickle everyone's fancy; 'Nature' for down-to-earth types, Flavoured for the discerning palate,-Schnews imagines a tasty tofu flavoured option, simply marinade in soy sauce for optimum results-, Noppy. for the adventurous, and Hand-Painted Fun for arty types. Schnews just hopes they taste better than your average vegan meal!! Contact Condomi 0171 277 6630

**Disclaimer:** SchNEWS warns all readers not to be shy. Always be prepared to give up your clothing to friendly police officers, who only want to get to know your particulars better. You will then be cool. Honest.

# Seeing The Back Of Hillgrove and Shamrock

**The grass-roots animal rights movement has truly revealed its power over the past year with the closure of two major suppliers of animals to the vivisection industry. A combination of high-profile campaigning, public support, direct action and a hell of a load of determination has seen the end of Hillgrove Farm and Shamrock Farm.**

Hillgrove Farm was a family-run business breeding and supplying cats to vivisection labs worldwide for over 30 years. Based near the small village of Witney in Oxfordshire it had been the target of a small low- profile campaign for many years. The closure of beagle-breeders Consort Beagles in July 1997 gave the animal rights movement the boost and confidence to take on establishments such as Hillgrove, and the Consort campaign had been an opportunity to try out various methods, old and new. Long-term activists had said that the feeling of power generated at Consort demos was something they hadn't seen since the mid-80s. Thousands of activists had gone to Consort on a regular basis not just to express their disgust at the vivisection industry that mutilates and murders millions of animals (and people through the drugs it produces) but to go further, and try and rescue animals and cause as much damage as possible to property in order to close the place down.

Many of those involved in the Consort campaign turned their attention to Hillgrove, notorious for supplying kittens as young as 13 days to a whole list of torture labs. In time, daily demos and night vigils were held at the entrance to the farm, regional and national demos were organised on a regular basis, and firms supplying all sorts of materials to the 'Farm' were persuaded to stop their dealings. Concerned members of the public flooded Hillgrove with phone calls and faxes during office hours so that genuine customers couldn't get through. Mr Brown and his wife found themselves receiving all sorts of things they had never ordered, from books to porcelain statues of Elvis (sent to them after people had 'mistakingly' put Brown's address on the 'send no money now' forms found in magazines). When Brown received a letter bomb courtesy of the Justice Department it was clear he had become a major target.

Amazingly, even after a huge ten-foot fence was erected around the premises, which was patrolled by CCTV cameras and security guards, Mr Brown's wife was still trying to run her bed and breakfast business! The ads continued to claim a "friendly atmosphere" without mentioning the thousand cats at the back of the farm waiting to be shipped to labs, and the thousands of masked and angry protesters! Eventually, the bed and breakfast business had to fail after holiday bureaus, the Caravan Club and guide-books all removed Hillgrove from their listings, adding to the financial pressure. The Advertising Standards Authority even banned the Browns from using the word "friendly" to describe their B&B and self- catering holidays due to the constant presence of demonstrators!

National demos at Hillgrove were events that anyone who attended will never forget. It was a time when grass-roots activists were largely in control and the police could have very little impact. Who could forget the demos surrounding World Day for Laboratory Animals where thousands of people tried to storm the farm, ripping down fences and pelting Brown's house with rocks that smashed probably every window as well as extensively damaging his roof. Protests such as this were attended by up to 400 cops and cost £100,000 each time to police. By the end of the campaign over £1.5million had been spent policing the protests. Although the large police presence prevented activists getting to the cats during most demos, earlier on in the campaign some activists did manage to rescue cats during a daytime action. Later, one intrepid activist who happened to be walking around Hillgrove one daytime found a carrying box in a vehicle and decided to take it away for closer examination - inside were four six-week old kittens about to be sent to a lab.

The campaign attracted people from all walks of life, young and old, who felt equal outrage at Brown's activities. Local support came in with 95% of people voting to close down Hillgrove in one local newspaper poll. During one trial at Witney Magistrates court, the chair of the Magistrates commented that many of them supported the protesters!

With both the Shamrock and Hillgrove campaigns, activists were determined to stay ahead of the police. When exclusion orders were issued, preventing protests at the farms, campaigners instead went to the city centres of Brighton and Oxford. There was no way they were going to simply go home, they had a message to take to the public and they certainly made it heard. If the police think that by stopping campaigners from going to the hell-holes that they will simply give in, then they have been proved wrong. This not only gave the public a chance to hear the message, but they also saw first hand how the police treat protesters, and it was often people out shopping who were attacked by police. It was during the Hillgrove campaign in particular that journalists and photographers were harassed and attacked by police. Despite carrying official press cards a number of photographers were arrested and had films confiscated. Home Secretary Jack Straw got dragged into the fight when it emerged that his having a country cottage as a "weekend retreat" just half a mile from Hillgrove may have been the reason for such restrictive exclusion orders banning protests and the massive police presence. Friends in high places ...

Shamrock (GB) Ltd was another company that had long been a target for animal rights activists, but it wasn't until campaigners took a leaf out of the book from the Consort and Hillgrove campaigns that things really started to move. Shamrock was set up in 1954 to supply wild caught primates for vivisection, later starting its own breeding colonies at the site in Small Dole, West Sussex. Like Hillgrove, Shamrock also supplied labs all over the world. The new improved campaign kicked off in November 98, and despite 45 years in business it only took 15 months for some extremely dedicated activists to finish the company off.

In the early 90s an undercover investigator from the BUAV worked at Shamrock, keeping detailed diaries of goings on and filming conditions. He exposed the day to day brutality, where monkeys were punched, pulled out of the cages by their tails, and being repeatedly stabbed with a needle to try and take a blood sample. The BUAV estimated that in the 10 years up to 1992 Shamrock had sold 40-50,000 monkeys to labs. With the vast majority being wild caught this represents some 250,000 monkeys when deaths during capture and shipping are taken into account.

Once the campaigns really got going there was no stopping them. The companies were hit from every angle. If someone supplied a product to Hillgrove or Shamrock they were persuaded to stop. A constant presence at the premises made day to day business uncomfortable. Those staff who weren't wise enough to leave immediately found themselves receiving mass demos outside their homes. One Hillgrove worker finally gave in after her house was taken over for the day by a bunch of cops awaiting a home demo - apparently the mess they made with their muddy size elevens was

sure of Hillgrove but the snowballing of an anti-vivisection campaign that no-one seems able to stop.

These two establishments existed because of money. There were big bucks to be made in supplying cats and monkeys to labs. When you start to have an impact on that profit the incentive for carrying on is weakened. When you have to pay for constant security guards and spend thousands on new security measures that means less profit at the end of the day. And when you find it difficult to find anyone to work for your company, and you keep getting your property trashed, it doesn't seem like a good line of business to be in after all.

The main lesson learnt from these campaigns is 'keep at it'. Right from the start those involved most knew it could take many years of a long hard battle until they won, but they were determined to not give in until they had reached their goal. Animal Liberation is not an unachievable goal, we have to put all we have into it because we know we can - and will - get there.

So where does this leave us now? Hillgrove and Shamrock are closed but animals are still being poisoned, burned and mutilated in their millions in the name of 'science'. These campaigns make vivisection unprofitable. Closing down animal breeders will make it more difficult - and more costly - for labs to get hold of animals. Vivisectors will look elsewhere for employment and those thinking about working in animal torture may think otherwise. Millions of people have been informed about the realities of animal experiments. When vivisection becomes less profitable those companies currently testing on animals will look at non-animal methods of testing as a cheaper way of getting their products onto the market. The whole animal abuse industry has been shaken to the core by these campaigns. We've still got a long hard battle ahead, but no-one ever said this would be easy.

There are now two major anti-vivisection campaigns operating on the same lines that need your help:
- Save the Newchurch Guinea Pigs: PO Box Evesham, Worcs, Tel: 01902
- Stop Huntingdon Animal Cruelty: PO Box 381, Cheltenham, Glos, GL50 1YN. Tel: 0121 632 6460

For information on grass-roots animal rights campaigns contact ARCNEWS on 01902 711 935 or james@arcnews.demon.co.uk, or see www.arcnews.co.uk

just too much! Lynda King, vet and Managing Director of Shamrock, knows more than most people what it's like to take on the animal liberation movement. It has been reported that at the stroke of the new millennium as she and her friends were singing auld lang syne some uninvited guests improved her ventilation by smashing all her windows. Not long afterwards an arson attack on her garage destroyed two cars.

Rumours had abounded for some time about the closure of Hillgrove, but it wasn't until 13th August 99 that it was finally confirmed. The RSPCA went in that night to take away all 800 cats to RSPCA centres for rehoming. The RSPCA had criticised the campaign against Hillgrove all along, and even after its closure they continued to defend not only Chris Brown but also his

> "Thank god there are people willing to sacrifice their liberty for the sake of defenceless animals, and prove that common humanity does still exist in this so-called civilised country."
>
> Marilyn Tyrrell, 94-year old Hillgrove supporter - Oxford Mail 27.1.98

business of supplying cats to labs. In April 2000 the RSPCA even appointed ex-Shamrock vet Paul West as their assistant chief veterinary officer! This is a man who was criticised for his treatment of animals at Shamrock by even the Home Office.

The closure of Shamrock came more suddenly and surprisingly. On 9th March campaigners met to plan the next stage of the campaign. They had no need - Shamrock released a press statement on 10th March announcing they would close as soon as the remaining monkeys could be "humanely relocated". Although this turned out to be a lie as all the monkeys have been sent to labs, no more animals will suffer there anymore.

The strength of these two campaigns came from the diversity of people involved and the diversity of actions. From the pensioners writing letters to the younger activists risking their liberty to cause financial pressure, everyone played their part. We are all in it together and we can all do something to achieve animal liberation. A lot of people were arrested during protests against Hillgrove, and several served prison sentences for various "public order offences". But their sacrifices helped achieve not just the clo-

WAKE UP! WAKE UP! IT'S YER SUMMER PARTY AND PROTEST

# Weekly SchNEWS Capital

Printed and Published in Brighton by *Justice?*

Friday 30th April 1999     http://www.schnews.org.uk/     Issue 210   Free/Donation

# FAT CAT SLIM

*"The Private Finance Iniative means paying more for less."* Dr.Jean Shaoul, accountancy expert Manchester University.

Public services sold off to big business. Private firms in our schools. Worse pay and conditions for workers. Adverts on fire-engines. Who could possibly be behind such dastardly schemes? New Labour silly.

Welcome to the world of the Private Finance Initiative (PFI), which in plain English means privatisation by the back door.

### FIRST THEY CAME FOR THE TUBE...

The London Underground is already the most expensive in Europe, and with plans for it to be sold to private companies, fares will spiral even higher. As with the fragmentation of British Rail, health & safety will be put at risk, services will be cut, and large scale redundancies and casualisation are on the cards.

### THEN THEY CAME FOR OUR SCHOOLCHILDREN......

In Haringey four private companies have been short-listed under the PFI to take over schools, including Rentokil Initial (who in the past have been removed from one in three of its school cleaning contracts).

School buidlings will effectively be privatised, as private companies will take control for up to 30 years, and they will decide how schools will be used outside of school hours, to make profits.

In Haringey this will mean the privatisation of cleaning, caretaking and repair and maintenance work, threatening jobs, pay and conditions. Despite widespread opposition, the Council is pushing ahead spending £250,000 just to prepare its bid.

If that's not enough New Labour have also come up with Education Action Zones, allowing big business to get involved in running education. In Sheffield the main sponsors are Midland bank and Yorkshire Water. Meanwhile in Surrey, the council have announced plans to privatise the teachers of one of its schools.

### THEN THEY ATTACKED OUR BRAVE FIREFIGHTERS....

*"It's privitisation through the back door. All companies work for profit and this is just not appropriate within a public service."* Fire Brigade Union spokesperson

Fire-fighters are on the brink of their first national strike since the seventies over plans to break up the national framework, which sets a minimum standard of working conditions around the country and replaces it with "local bargaining." Fire-fighters rightly see this as a first step towards privatisation. One union spokesperson commented *"We've seen what damage local bargaining has done to our public services,our railways and our ambulance service. First they carve up the workforce then they sell bits off and the public end up paying for a worse service."*

Just to show how keen they, the London Fire Brigade this month made a multi-million pound Private Finance Inititave deal to fund their fire-fighting fleet and equipment.

And there's more...London are also looking into the raising cash through private sponsorship, which could include advertising on the side of fire engines!

### NEXT IT WAS THE HOSPITALS

*"It's (the PFI) like taking out a mortgage from a loan shark to buy a house which you already own - and then discovering, 25 years down the line, that the property has been repossessed by the lender anyway".* Francis Wheen, journalist .

Dryburn hospital in Durham due to open in 2001 will be built, financed and owned by a private sector consortium, Consort Healthcare. In return for use of the hospital, the local health service trust will pay the consortium £7 million every year for the next 30 years. Consort will also provide most of the hospital's ancillary staff, at a cost of an extra £5 million a year.

Offically, PFI schemes are given the go-ahead only if they offer better value for money than other options. But a study by the union UNISON shows that the cost of the PFI scheme over 30 years will be over £22 million more than if the public sector had built and owned the hospital.

There will also be a reduction in services with only half the hospital beds originally planned and a 22 per cent cut in clinical staffing budget over the next two years

\* Workers at the University College Hospital in London recently went on a two week all out strike over privitisation plans.

### THEN THEY WENT FOR THE HOUSING BENEFIT DEPARTMENTS

Housing Benefit and Council Tax staff in Brighton and Hove are preparing to take strike action after the Council revealed it's plans to sell off their department to a private company called Capita. The announcement , made only three weeks ago, was followed by an immediate meeting where 180 people voted unanimously for a strike ballot to defend their jobs, and two mass pickets of the Town hall while the issue was debated left Councillors in no doubt as to what the mood was.

The proposals, which will remove the entire Housing Benefit operation to Falmer, will mean an inevitable drop in the quality of the service: long delays in processing claims, no local service points, no flexibility when it comes to overpayment demands. Capita have a past history of incompetence(in one mistake 4,600 pensioners were accidentally sent a letter informing them that their housing benefit was being cut, along with an increased council tax demand!), lying about their efficiency rates -and redundancies.

The most interesting thing about the company is that Labour Council leader Lord Bassam lists a consultancy with Capita in the House of Lords Register of Interests! When news of the privatisation broke, Capita's shares rose 39p-more money for Bassam's chums.

The Council, worried that this is becoming a local election own-goal have decided to 'review' the decision-a stalling tactic if ever there was one. But with Unison deciding to introduce a voluntary levy on all it's Brighton and Hove members to support a prospective strike, the Council may have bitten off more than it can chew.

---

A recent report which studied 41 local authorities involved in Private FinanceIinitiative schemes, has concluded that 150,000 jobs will be transferred to the the private sector in the next 10 years. Job losses are estimated at 30,000.

---

### LIFE AFTER PRIVITISATION

*"Strikes in the future are not just going to be won by the withdrawl of labour - they are going to be won by employing other methods. Having people like Reclaim The Streets(RTS) involved could go a long way to winning other disputes in the future. RTS get publicity and cause the bosses serious financial distress - and they can't be sacked."* Steve.

Steve Hedley was on strike with other railway maintainance workers and engineers over pay and conditions. Since privitisation the companies that bought British Rail have been making around £1million a day profit and Railtrack a similar amount. Meanwhile maintenance workers are taking home around £135 a week after tax for a 37-39 hour week.

During the dispute Steve was at Euston Station on a picket line when a scab van drove straight at the picket line. On its way past it was alledged that a wing mirror was cracked on the van and Steve was blamed. However two independent photographers and even Railtracks own CCTV showed that Steve wasn't the person. Still, the Railtract sub-contractors sacked him and even though the case was thrown out of court, the company have refused to give him his job back.

### SKY CHEFS DISPUTE

Last November 273 airline catering workers at Heathrow airport were sacked just three hours after going on an official one-day strike over worsening pay and conditions. People on holiday pay or sick that day were sacked.

The company LSG Lufthansa SkyChefs are the biggest airline catering company in the world serving 260 air-lines with pre-tax profits of £2.2 million in 1997. Meanwhile sacked workers doing a 60 hour shift could expect a take-home pay of just £220 a week.

The strike, which has received virtually no press, is seen by many as a pointer to the future. If Skychefs get away with it, then all their workers will eventually be forced to work under worse conditions for longer hours and less pay

There's a mass picket on Monday 3rd May 9 am - 1 pm at Fagg's Rd off the A30, south end of Heathrow airport. Assemble opposite the 'Green Man' pub (5 mins walk from Hatton Cross tube station.)

### THE STRIKE SUPPORT GROUP

aims to give financial aid to workers in struggle, give striking workers resources to print and publish their own leaflets etc., and to physically support pickets and other demonstrations of workers in dispute.

For a copy of their newsletter send SAE to 145 Imperial Ave., Victoria Rd., London, N16 8HL Tel 0171 249 0041 They meet every Monday at the CockTavern, Phoenix Rd., London NW1 at 7.30 pm

Reclaim the Streets 0171 281 4621; rts@gn.apc.org

Haringey Against Privatisation, c/o PO Box 8446, London, N17 6NZ

Campaign Against Tube Privatisation 47c Wadeson St., Bethnal Green, London, E2 9DP- Tel 0181 981 8065

Anarchist Trade Union Network PO Box EMAB, 88 Abbey St., Derby DE22 3SO

MAY 1ST IS INTERNATIONAL WORKERS DAY

## MAY DAY/BELTANE

The celebration of Beltane heralds the start of the summer in the pagan calender - signifying the death of winter and the return of the warm weather. *BEL-TENE:*'A goodly fire'. Traditionally people jumped the fire together and alone to purify, to cleanse and to bring fertility. The *TEIN-EIGIN,* the sacred fire, was kindled after all the fires in the community had been put out. Beltane is the celebration of the sacred marriage. A festival for friends and lovers, for joining energies together and for honouring that union. It is a time to honour sex in it's raw state as part of the cycle, nature and the expansive energy of this time. So get out into the fields, light a fire and indulge in some loved-up beltane celebrations.

## THE HAYMARKET MARTYRS

May 1886 and 80,000 workers and their families walk down Chicago's Michigan Avenue in the world's first ever May Day Parade. At the same time 340,000 workers in 12,000 factories across the US down tools to demand an eight hour day in order to spread work among the thousands made unemployed by new 'labour saving' machinery. The next day Chicago police attack peaceful strikers with guns and clubs, killing and wounding several. On May 3rd 6,000 striking lumberworkers march to the aid of strikers at the Mcormick Harvester factory who have been locked out over a wage dispute. When pickets try to stop scabs from entering the plant, the cops attack again, opening fire killing four and wounding many others. Outraged at this a protest is called for the next day at the Haymarket Square.

The meeting was peaceful and a shower of rain soon sent away most of the crowd. However, with only a few hundred people remaing the police once again attacked - a bomb was thrown and exploded among the police who immediately opened fire. Several cops and many workers were killed.

It has never been discovered who threw the Haymarket bomb, but it was certainly none of the eight anarchists who were put on trial for it. Six of them were not ever there! Yet the trial with biased judge and hysterical press ensured a guilty verdict and condemned 5 of the 8 to death. Despite worldwide protests Parsons, Spies, Fischer and Engels were hanged on November 11th (Ling had committed suicide the previous day). Six years later the state governor released the survivors from jail, admitting that there had no evidence to link any of the 8 with the Haymarket bomb.

On 14th July 1889, on the 100th anniversary of the Bastille Day, an American delegate at the International Labour Congress in Paris proposed that May 1st be officially adopted as a workers holiday. This was unanimously approved and since then May Day has served as a date for international solidarity.

## PROTEST CAMPS

**AVON RING ROAD** Trying to stop Bristol's answer to the M25 being built. People with experience of tunnelling would be most welcome, as would anyone else. Directions: from Bristol train station catch the 48 or 49 bus to the end of the route (Sainsburys), go down the hill and turn right. The camp is another minute's walk, and is opposite the security compound. Tel: 0797 999 0389.

**BIRMINGHAM NORTHERN RELIEF ROAD** Camps set up to try and stop England's first toll motorway. Directions: From the centre of Birmingham take the 105 or 105A bus to Roughley Terminus. Carry on walking in the direction the bus was going, past a beech wood on the left and past Turf Pits Lane. They could use materials for treehouses plus some tarpaulin. Tel: 07931 161761.

**LYMINGE FOREST** After battling against the Rank organisation for a couple of years (who want to build a massive leisure complex), the camp has almost won against the entertainment giants. Rank have lost interest, but there's a rumour that planning permission may be sold to Center Parcs.

The local council in Kent wants to sell the land, but will have to do so by August. Tel: 01303 257046.

**FASLANE PEACE CAMP** Still hassling the Trident base next door, after 16 years the camp is still going strong. Contact: 01436 820901.

**MANCHESTER** A camp has been set up to stop Manchester Airport PLC cutting down trees at Cedars Wood. A few days ago nearly 30 cops raided the camp without a warrant and arrested 5 people and nicked off with boltcroppers and tools (replacements most welcome!). More people are needed to keep the two camps going, local support is still strong. There is a stay of execution till October when the House of Lords will make their decision. A party is planned for June 21st. Tel: 07931 931850

## WOMENS PEACE CAMPS

**SELLAFIELD Womens Peace Camp**. 16 Sholebroke Ave, Leeds. LS7 3HB. Tel: 01132621534. Email ( marked clearly for the peace camp) cornerstone@gn.apc.org

**ALDERMASTON** Womens Peace Camp. Contact Helen, 33 Heron Rd, Bristol. 0117 9393746

**MENWITH HILL** Womens Peace Camp. Outside Menwith Hill US NSA Spy Base, Kettlesing Head Layby, A59, Harrogate. HG3 2RA. Tel: 01943 468593

**GREENHAM COMMON WOMENS PEACE CAMP.** Yellow Gate, Greenham Common, Newbury, Berks. Tel: 01374 136728. Between7-9.30pm only.Permanent camp outside main gate of Greenham Common. Organises information about and actions against, the production of trident at Aldermaster and Burghfield.

## FREE PARTY GUIDELINES

Despite the best efforts of the authorities, people are still putting on free parties up and down the country. Here's a few do's and dont's just in case you stumble wide-eyed across one.
*Be prepared to be self sufficient. Facilities will be minimal.
*Park sensibly, keep site roads clear.
*Be friendly to local residents, ramblers etc.Smile you're at a free party!
*Bury your shit!!
*Don't trash the site - take a bin bag
*Fires - use dead not live wood (it don't burn in any case).
*Make a donation - if someone passes a bucket round, don't be a mean git. It costs money to put on a free event.
*Know your rights - Get yourself a BUST CARD, 10p from Release. Advice line 0171 729 9904 *Emergency Help Line 0171 6038654* *Enjoy yourself - and don't let the party poopers get yer down!*

# ITS YER SCHNEWS PARTY
# AND PROTEST SUMMER GUIDE

## MAY........

Mon 3 LLANTRISANT FREE FESTIVAL Mid Glamorgan, S.Wales; 0973 399220 ...Sat 8th and Sun 9th STREETS OF BRIGHTON FESTIVAL on-the-beach including The Firestarter Stage with Zion Train, Head-Mix collective, Max Pashm, the supergroove Jazz Skiffle Sensation, Kyras Tortoise and the phenomenal, unmissable, legendary Lucy Wild Blues(viva villcabamba sista!) Tel: 0181 986 9646; www.continentaldrifts.uk.com/..Sat 8th PEACE IN THE BALKANS, Stop the War Demo. Meet Embankment 12 noon. Tel 0171 275 0164..Sat 8th HULL RECLAIM THE STREETS. Meet, Pearsons Park, off Beverly Rd. 12 noon...Sat 8 Undercurrants 10 & comedian Mark Thomas at New Theatre Royal, Guildhall Walk, Portsmouth 7pm  £2 ..11th-16th HAGUE APPEAL for PEACE for the abolition of war. International Conference. Tel: 0181 347 6162. www.haguepeace.org...Thurs 13th WORLD STARFISHMAN DAY. Foreshadowed by the Hale-Bopp comet, starfishman left the womb of the ocean and came ashore at Whitby on May 13th '97....Celebrate by doing Starfishmanly things of your own devising, in your own way..Thur 13– Tue 18 Home educators Festival, Work shops and educational activities, Beach, Dorset; 0171 813 5907..Fri 14th National Demo against Live Exports from 9am, Meet Tesco car-park, whitfield. Tel: 01304 613904..Fri14th London Anarchist Forum meets every Friday, 8pm, Conway Hall, 25 Red Lion Square, London WC1R 4RL. Tube Holborn. Various talks and discussions Tel 0181 847 0203 ..Sat 15 London Permaculture Gathering , 11am-7pm, lunch 1.30pm, at the Bowlers Community Nursery, 81 Crouch Hill, London N8. BusesW7, 91, 41, 210. Tube: Archway, Finsbury Park (£5-25 (sliding scale). Tel: 0171 281 3765..Sat 15th FREEDOM FOR OCALAN! FREEDOM FOR KURDISTAN! Demo. Sat 15th May, 1pm, Malet Street WC1. Tel: 0956 155 788...21st –24th Action camp against Highway A20. Nr Lubeck(N.Germany). Protesters travelling from Europe will be reimbursed for 50% of travel expenses(as long as you don't fly). Camp costs between 25 and 40 dm. Vegan/organic food, tree-climbing, canoeing, street theatre, RTS etc. Tel: (+49) 0451/7070646. Email: jupluebeck@t-online.de..Fri 21st Demo at biotech company Zeneca's AGM. Tel: 0161 224 4846..Sat 22 Festival 99 Devonshire Green, Sheffield; 0114 225 4158..22 May – 20th June The Inter-Continental Cararvan will be in town. Around 500 activists from across the globe will be coming to Europe to bring the concerns of the South directly to the hear of the North. Telling us how free trade and economic globalisation is devestating the lives of the poor. Contact the ICC London Welcoming Committee, 39 Thornhill Square, London, N1 1BE  Tel 07970 896736 email icc99uk@hotmail.com..Sat 22nd Citizens Assembly for the Abolition of War, Westminster Central Hall. Tel: 0181 347 6162...Sat 22nd SEX MANIACS BALL and the 6th EROTIC OSCARS. 10pm-4am, The Pleasure Rooms, 604 Highroad Tottenham. Contact Sexual Freedom Coalition 0171 460 1979  www.sfc.org.uk..Sat 22 Stanmer Park Organics  community open day sutainabilty, gardening, music. Bring a picnic 10 am onwards 01273 388673..Sun 23 Moulsecoomb Forest Garden and Wildlife Project (behind Moulsecoomb Railway Station, just off the Lewes Road) Open Day 12 noon till 4 pm 01273 628535..28th-31st BLANDFORD FORUM FESTIVAL, Stour Park, Dorset. Alabama 3 + Zion Train + Headmix + Rory McLeod etc. £5 a day..28th-31st Animal Gathering Festival at Greenacres Sanctuary, Marston Montgomery, Nr Uttoxeter, Derbyshire. Tel: 0171 278 3068

Fri 28 – June 2nd  Alternative to the EU Summit, Cologne  Details from Bundnis Koln 99, KornerstraBe 69, 50823 Koln, Tel 492219520008 email koeln99@gmx.net..Sat 29th EUROPE-WIDE-MARCH. Cologne. Against unemployment, job insecurity, Social Exclusion and racism.Tel: 0191 222 0299. Email: EUROMUK@aol.com...Sat 29th ORGANIC FESTIVAL, Arundel ..Sat 29th CAAT dayschool-planning action against DSEi arms fair(14-17 Sept) 10-5pm, Conway Hall, Red Lion Square, WC1. Tel: 0171 281 0297...Mon 31st KINGSTON GREEN FAIR. Canbury Gardens, Kingston, Surrey. Tel: 0181 974 8883..Mon 31st Anti Bloodsports demo. Surrey County Show, Guilford, 10.30am-5.30pm. Tel:0790 181 4936

## JUNE.......

Tue 1st  LONDON to STONEHENGE WALK begins. Meet Battersea Park Peace Pagoda noon onwards phone Willie X 0171 722 4781..Fri 4th-Sun 6th COVENTRY FESTIVAL..Sat 5th STRAWBERRY FAYRE,Mid Summer Common, Cambridge FREE!..4th-6th LIVING LONDON FESTIVAL, environmental music festie Battersea Park, www.proteusweb.com/gp/..Tues 8th World Oceans Day. Walks, talks, exhibitions and events worldwide. Tel: 0171 924 2355..Tues 8th Protest naked for the right to be naked in public outside 2pm Buckingham Palace. Contact: 208 Foleshill Rd. Coventry, CV1 4JH...Thur 10 Possible Referendum for a ban on genetically modified food. Under the 1972 Local Government Act if 10 local authority electors in a parish vote for a referendum then one has to be called. For a campaign pack ring 01226 762359..Fri 11th National Goldfish Day . For goldfish freaks everywhere, put your best fish forward and boogie on down...Sat 12 National demonstration against Hillgrove cat vivisection farm. Meet 12 noon at Hillgrove, Whitney, Oxfordshire 01386 833846 ..Sat 12th-Sun 13th STOKE NEWINGTON CHURCH STREET FESTIVAL...12TH-20TH STOP THE ARMS TRADE WEEK-An International Week of Action. Contact Campaign Against the Arms Trade (CAAT) Tel: 0171 281 0297 www.gn.apc.org/caat..14th-20th National Vegetarian Week . Vegetarian Society, Tel: 0161 928 0793

### JUNE 18th INTERNATIONAL DAY OF PROTEST AND CARNIVAL

On the first day of the meeting of the G8 Summit in Cologne, Germany a  global day of direct action is being planned, aimed at the heart of the global economy/financial banking districts. Actions are planned to take place in 35  countries across the world. In the UK people are taking their  action to the City of London. Groups including London Animal Action, Campaign Against Arms Trade, Third World First, London Greenpeace/Mclibel and Reclaim The Streets are planning openly advertised action for people to get involved in. Autonomous groups around the are also planning actions to carry out on the day. For info n your local groups contact Reclaim The Streets. A booklet about how the City works and detailed map of the area is also available for a SAE from J18 info, Box E, 111 Magdalen Rd., Oxford, OX4 1RG   www.j18.org

19th –20th LEAMINGTON PEACE FESTIVAL, Warwick (free!) 01926 421830..18th – 27th SPACE 1999-10 Days That Shook The Universe!! A celebration of independent, community-based space exploration including * games of 3 –sided football*All night parties/training for raves in space* Workshops on how to become an autonomous astronaut*Sex in space. The Association of Autonomous Astronauts are keen to hear from those with access to venues, satellites, soundsystems, rocket technology Contact: Space 1999 c/o BM Box 3641, LondonWC1N 3XX. www.deepdisc.com/aaa ...21st-26th Global Week of Action against Quintiles Animal Tests. For info on events tel: 01562 745778. Email: sqat@messages.to..Mon 21st STONEHENGE SUMMER SOLSTICE CELEBRATION!! The exclusion zone has been lifted but in anticipation of a renewal of the old festivities police say their operation will be "adjusted accordingly"  SUNSET 8.49pm at the Stones –BST-..Tues22nd SUNRISE (nearest to solstice) 4.59am at the Stones-BST-    www.geocities.com/soho/9000/ glastone.htm..Fri 25th-Sun 27th GLASTONBURY FESTIVAL, Pilton, Somerset

## JULY........

Fri 2 – Sun 4 Bracknell Festival South Hill Park Tel 01344 484123..Sun 4th FREE FESTIVAL OF GLOBAL RIGHTS 12noon-10pm (Hackney Marshes)..Thur 8- Sun 11 Larmer Tree Music Festival Wilts; £50; 01722 415223 www.larmertree.demon.co.uk..Sat 10th BIG DAY OUT, Milton Keynes..10th-11th T IN THE PARK, Glasgow..15th-17th SEVEN REVELS, Forest of Dean ..17th-18th MUSIC IN THE SQUARE , Portsmouth 01705 357593

Sat 17 Derby Punx Picnick Bass Recreational Ground..Sun 18th ASHTON COURT FREE FESTIVAL, Bristol...Fri 23 – Sun 25 Foothills, Wales..Sat 24th No Animal to Human Transplants Action Day , Jesus Green, Cambridge. Tel:0114 2530020 They want to break the world record for the biggest ever ring-a-roses (over 12,000 people) so come out to play!!..Wed 28th-1st Aug Northern Green Gathering , on an organic farm in West Yorkshire. £30  0113 2249885.. 30th-8th Aug THE 4TH ANARCHIST SUMMERCAMP. Near Hannover, Germany. Tel: 0531/82909. Email: a-camp@gmx.de

## AUGUST.......

1st-21st MOONSHADOW ECLIPSE FAMILY CAMP, Cornwall..6th-8th THE BIG CHILL 'ENCHANTED GARDEN 99', Salisbury Tel: 0181 372 9735; www.bigchill.co.uk..6th-15th SUNSHADOW FESTIVAL, Cornwall www.klasol.demon.co.uk/sve99/sunshadow/ssMain.htm..6th – 12th LIZARD ECLIPSE FESTIVAL, near Plymouth, Devon ..6th-12th MEGADOG SON-OF-A-BEACH FESTIVAL    www.thepulse.co.uk/megadog/index.html..7th-14th CORNISH ECLIPSE STONE FESTIVAL..9th-12th TOTALITY! Newquay Tel: 01637 871999 www.totality.co.uk/..10th-11th ECLIPSE PARTY. + camping for one week. £25 www.splintered.demon.co.uk/eclipse..Wed 11th TOTAL SOLAR ECLIPSE...BOOM SHANKAR!! Who turned the fuckin' lights out..Wed 11 World Earth Healing Day Tel 0181 806 3828 email WEHD@freenet.co.uk..Mon 13th ABBEY PARK FESTIVAL, Leicester ..21st - 22nd V99 Chelmsford  www.gigsandtours.com ..29th-30th NOTTINGHILL HILL CARNIVAL FREE...28th-30th EXODUS FREE FESTIVAL, Luton. Don't miss this one.

## SEPTEMBER.....

14th-17th Demonstrations against the Defence Systems Equipment International, Chertsey and London Docklands arms fair. Campaign Against The Arms Trade 0171 281 0297 . 1/1/00. SATANIC ORGY.Royston Parish Church. Please bring condoms and  a partner Ruth Kettle Project.

## JUST LIKE THE SIXTIES

As SchNEWS went to press, students at Sussex University were still occupying the finance office of their administration building following the threatened expulsion of 89 students over non payment of fees. They said they would remain until their demands were met- that no student would be expelled for non payment and that there would be no repercussions on students involved in the occupation. University management responded by barricading a fire door and cutting off electricity to the occupied part of the building, although they later agreed it was a fire risk and re-connected it.

In Court yesterday morning, a rather senile old judge bored everyone with anecdotes about his involvement in the University choir. He then went on at great length about how much he loved the University before declaring he had no conflict of interest. He also granted the University posession before hearing the defense case, and told to them to be out by 2pm, despite the fact that the wrong papers were served, and he was obviously biased against the students (he refused to call them students, and instead preferred 'undergraduates'). Apparently the University's solicitors used to represent squatters and hippies in the 70s!

Some rather interesting memos from university management about the previous proposed occupations at Sussex in 1994 also surfaced, which showed that the Student Union at the time was in the pockets of management and was told to sabotage the occupation debate. The Union Officers were supposed "to take on the opposition at the EUGM and not be defensive". Nice to know they were sticking up for the interests of students who elected them. The university was also worried that there were 'sleepers' on the staff who would help the students, and that they had links with anarchists from Brighton, and that they were more of a problem than the SWP. How flattering!

* Campaign for Free Education National Conference, Wed May 12, Sheffield Hallam University Union 11am - 5pm Debate + pratical workshops. Contact CFE, PO Box 22615, London, N41 WT email cfe@gn.apc.org

## A BRIDGE TOO FAR

Simon Jones died when he was sent to do highly skilled work in Shoreham docks as a stevedore with no health and safety training. Within two hours he was dead. A year on and despite a high level direct action campaign no-one has been charged with his death.

So on Wednesday (Workers Memorial Day), fifty people including his family, gathered outside the Health and Safety Executive HQ in London to pay their respects with a minute's silence. Health and Safety have done nothing to bring Simon's killers to justice, so people decided to occupy Southwark Bridge for an hour, stopping the traffic by unfurling banners across the street and blowing whistles and shouting. Despite this direct action, when Simon's parents and a few of the group gained access to the director of the Executive, Jenny Bacon, she fobbed them off, telling Simon's aunt to "shush"! This high ranking government official denied receiving 5 letters sent by Simon's mum, and claimed that investigating 1 in 20 serious injuries in workplaces was acceptable due to budget restrictions. Jenny Bacon chose not to respond when asked what chance people would have of having their grievances heard, if they didn't occupy bridges in central London.

Simon Jones Memorial Campaign c/o on the fiddle, PO Box 2600, brighton, E.Sussex BN2 2DX 01273 685913

www. Simonjones.org.uk

## SchNEWS in brief

Cheeky protestors from the No Opencast group have put in a planning application for a 20 acre opencast mine on the site of the **Millenium Dome!** There's gonna be a grand opening ceremony on May 9th 1.30 pm at Westcombe park Station (Charing Cross to Dartford line) Contact 0181 767 3142 ** John Tyndall, the leader of the **British National Party**, has been invited to address the Oxford Union (University Debating Society) on Monday 17th May. Protest to Oxford Union, Frewin Court, Oxford,OX1 3JB Tel(01865) 241353 E-mail:President (Theo Mills): president@oxford-union.org ** MayDay is the offical opening of the **LOFT** (Library of Free Thought)in Penzance. It will be selling anarchist and alternative books, mags, postcards with meeting space. Contact LOFT, PO Box 19, Penzance, TR18 2YP Tel 01736 331236 ** A **'No War but the Class War'** discussion group has been set up in London for people from differing political backgrounds-anarchist, Trotskyist, libertarian Marxist etc., who oppose NATO intervention but want to maintain a socialist or working class perspective. Meet every Wed, 7.30pm, Conway Hall, Red Lion Sq., London WC1. Holborn tube. Email: escape6@hotmail.com **The **Ecstasy.org website,** is being relaunched on Wed Feb 3rd. Hosting the first on-line edition of Nicholas Saunders last book on ecstasy: "Ecstasy Reconsidered"- the most comprehensive and authoritative work on the subject to date. For scientific research-user experiences and the interactive ecstasy testing database surf on into www.ecstacy.org For info. Tel: 01718369404 or email: nicholas@ecstacy.org** **London Anarchist Black Cross,** supporting class struggle prisoners, if you want to fight, inform and organise against the prison system then join 'em at 7.30pm, 1st and 3rd Tues of every month, Red Rose Pub, 129 Seven Sisters rd. N7 (tube Finsbury Park) email: londonABC@hotmail.com**G.M.

## RIOT NOT DIET!

**FREE CAKE!**At the no-diet day celebrations, Thurs 6th May at 4pm in the Pavillion gardens (or Churchill Sq. if it's raining)Bring your bellies and bikinis and let it all hang out..bare your beauty-if you've got it, flaunt it!The diet industry is there to make money out of our insecurities, remember the saying *"you can never be too rich or too thin"?* Well who wants to be a capitalist bastard and waste their life obsessing about their weight? Learn to love your body as it really is. Babes and boyz welcome of all shapes and sizes, WE'LL BE HAVIN'IT LARGE!

## BELT UP

People who said the building of the Newbury Bypass would lead to the opening of greenbelt land had their worse fears confirmed on Wednesday, when planning permission was given to VODAFONE to build a massive new HQ on a greenfield site in the area.

One resident told SchNEWS "Vodaphones attitude to this town has been appalling, nothing less than blackmail, telling residents they would pull out of the town if they did not get planning permission."

Vodaphone refused to contemplate moving to other sites such as vacated MoD site or Greenham Common (which they reckoned was a security risk because of the peace women there - all three of them.)

Funnily enough, Vodaphone were supporters of the pro-bypass campaign.

During the six hour Council meeting it was estimated that the company had earned around half a million pounds.

## BIGGHAM BULLSHIT

*"It is hypocrisy for Sir Robin to accuse Med T.V. of incitement to violence when he is a director of a company selling arms to a security force which tortures and kills it's own people"* Rachel Harford, CAAT.

Sir Robin Biggham, a director of British Aerospace(BAe), would seem to be engaged in a 'serious conflict of interest' or blatant hypocrisy concerning his role as chairman of the Independent Television Commission(ITC). He is apparently unaware of the irony of the ITC decision to revoke the license of the Kurdish satellite station Med T.V. for repeatedly flouting the regulations on incitement to violence and impartiality by sympathising with Turkey's Kurdish separatists. Strange, considering that BA has landed an $18 million contract to start licensed production in Turkey of assault rifles and grenade launchers for the security forces whose reputation for human rights abuses have been repeatedly documented. So the senile old bastard is not prepared to tolerate the use of tv to encourage violence but sees no problem with his company selling arms to a security force which tortures and kills it's own people, an incident in keeping with their long-term tendency to sell arms to repressive regimes. Since the guns will be made locally in Ankara, BAe avoids having to apply for an export license-a handy little scam. The factory in Ankara is now exporting 500 machine guns to the Indonesian Police, friendly types these guys!

BA is also currently trying to buy a Roman Catholic Church in Wharton, Lancashire, so it can improve access to the factory where 16 Hawk jets are being built for Indonesia. BAe's Don MacLean kindly explained to protesters "sometimes you have to leave your conscience at the door" In other words, as long as the cash keeps rolling in they just don't give a shit. Tel: CAAT on 0171 2810297 web-site: www. gn.apc.org/caat

---

Ever wished you could get SchNEWS off the web and print it out so it looks like the real thing? Well now you can. All you need is an internet connection, Web browser, the Acrobat Reader and any old printer. See our web-site for more info.

---

## ...and finally...

Spooky goings-on's at the new HQ for the Intelligence and Security Centre (ISC, an all-services agency established in 1996 to coordinate covert intelligence operations) Apparently the 850-year old Chicksands Priory near Bedford, is haunted by at least nine spirits, including a nun called Rosata who was entombed after being forced to watch her lover's execution. After several sightings, unexplained laughter and moving lights in unoccupied rooms, the MoD deployed surveillance equipment and seismic sensors but drew a blank. Head of the ISC, Brigadier Chris Holten, appreciates the irony of an intelligence agency being haunted by spooks. He believes the apparitions are recordings of "traumatic events imprinted in the fabric of the building". Permission has been obtained for a new investigation involving ISC personnel using high-tech pressure sensors, night vision recorders, infrared video, temperature and movement sensors, to prove Brig. Holten's conviction that there is a "spiritual element to the intelligence business".

## DISCLAIMER....

SchNEWS warns all readers to get their finger out and give the Private Finance Initiative a good kickin' otherwise what's left of our public services will go down the tube.Honest

P.S. Don't forget Reclaim The Streets Party this Saturday. Bus tickets from Brighton Peace Centre

P.P.S. Tune into radio 4A this Sunday 10am onwards 106.6 fm-worth listening to-.

## Subscribe!

Keep SchNEWS FREE! Just send 1st Class stamps (e.g. 20 for next 20 issues) or donations (payable to Justice?) **Ask for "Originals"** if **you can make copies.** Post *free* to all prisoners. SchNEWS, c/o on-the-fiddle, P.O. Box 2600, Brighton, East Sussex, BN2 2DX.

*Tel/Autofax:* +44 (0)1273 685913 *GET IT EVERY WEEK BY E-MAIL:* schnews@brighton.co.uk

# Cannabis Mayday Festival Triumphs

Pic: Ian Hunter

Over ten thousand people gathered in the sunshine on Clapham Common for the hugely successful Mayday Cannabis Festival.

Over 5000 people (police estimate) people took part in the cannabis march from Brixton to Clapham, headed by the Exodus Sound system on a flat bed lorry. The march stopped briefly in Brixton to pay respects to the victims of the Brixton nail bomb before proceeding to Clapham Common. Thousands more headed straight for the Common to hear a multitude of speakers including author and cannabis smuggler Howard Marks and alternative comic-satirist Mark Thomas. A last minute objection to an entertainment licence by local police meant rapid alterations to the scale of the proposed stages and sound systems. However, these readjustments failed to dampen either the spirit or the size of the event. Free party sound systems represented on the day included Oops (drum and bass) from Reading, Exodus (jungle techno and reggae) from Luton, and SQUALL (funky house and drum and bass) and Chrimerea (drum and bass and trance) from London. Continental Drifts also set up out the back of a lorry and presented a number of live acts from its eclectic roster of festival bands. Other attractions included a medical Marijuana Clinic, a hemp fashion expo and the Ecotrip poets.

New home office figures released a couple of days prior to the Festival revealed another rise in the annual conviction rate for cannabis offences. Three quarters of all drug convictions in the UK last year were for Cannabis, with around 10% of the UK prison population presently incarcerated for

Cannabis offences. Using Home Office figures, it is now estimated that nearly a £1 billion a year is spent on legal aid, policing, court costs and prison expenditure as a direct result of Cannabis remaining illegal.

Mayday Cannabis demonstrations and events also took place in 36 cities around the world including New York, Aukland, Sydney and Tel Aviv. Check the Cannabis coalition's web-site at www.schmoo.co.uk/mayday for more info.

> *....A new Britain ... but yet irrefutably ... the same old Britain...*

**"Excuse me Sir, have you dropped something?" Cannabis Mayday, Clapham Common**

**"Tick-a-teenth, Miss?"**

Pics: Ian Hunter

# SMOKE SIGNALS
## Pot debate comes to the boil

SQUALL

Where Do You Want To Grow Today?
---
✓ I Wanna Go Home
  Underground Update
  Features
  Squall Pics
  Frontline Communique
✓ The State Its In
  Squotes
  Resources
  Links
  From Our Correspondence

What a breath of fresh air it was when Alex Salmond, head of the Scottish Nationalist Party, stirred the political stagnancy last year when asked by an interviewer whether he'd ever smoked Cannabis. "Yes," he replied. "But I never exhaled."

Until recently, truthful or even topically humourful comment about drugs has been an endangered species on the political circuit. Besides the odd wry comment from the likes of Salmond, very few politicians have been prepared to utter what the majority refuse to publicly acknowledge; that the UK's tortuously out of touch drug policy is both fallacious and entirely unsuccessful.

The only air circulating amidst this parliamentary stagnancy has been from Paul Flynn, the Labour MP for Newport West, an ardent campaigner for the legalisation of Cannabis and a wider overhaul of the drug policy. Evidently more interested in public health than in career promotion (a rare creature in political circles!), Flynn is to present a private members bill before parliament later this year advocating a radical overhaul of the UK's national drug policy. It has little chance of reaching the statute books without government support, but there's no stopping Flynn's efforts to provoke a more relevant debate. In March he announced he would ask British MPs to support the licensing of Amsterdam style cafes where users can buy and smoke their joints legally.

His familiarity with the issue Europe-wide has led to his selection as a rapporteur to the Council of Europe's Social Policy and Health Committee which is currently examining drug policy in the two European countries it considers to have the most "repressive" drug policies, the UK and Switzerland. There's little doubt that Flynn stands out a mile from the rest of his cowering colleagues who shy in the shadows fearful of the kind of management reprimand which has imprisoned the tongues of intelligent political voices for years.

Until recently this dearth of decent debate has been punctuated only by the odd medical expert or senior police officer who, frustrated by the obvious lack of policy success, have stepped out of line to advocate a different approach to the zero tolerance policy inherited and championed by Uncle Jack Straw and Labour's lackey drugs czar, Keith Hellawell.

And yet seventy six per cent of those imprisoned for drug offences in the UK are incarcerated for Cannabis offences, and according to a recent Europe-wide survey, more people smoke Cannabis in the UK than anywhere else in Europe. So there was little doubt that the pot debate definitely needed a stir and at the end of March it finally got one.

Two years ago, the Police Foundation appointed an eleven strong team of high level academics and social professionals to conduct an independent inquiry into certain aspects of UK drug policy.

The committee - part sponsored by the Princes Trust included a chief constable, an assistant chief constable, a barrister, a headmistress and four professors in Neuropharmacology, Moral Philosophy, Economics and Social Work

Their lengthy investigation included a visit to Amsterdam, a European city much maligned by right-wing hystericists but one which boasts an impressive record on dealing with hard drug abuse. Committee member John Hamilton, Chief Constable of Fife, described Amsterdam as having a "relaxed and unthreatening atmosphere". You

might imagine he'd wish the same of Fife.

When General Barry McCaffrey, the current US drugs czar, castigated Holland for the social consequences of its liberal drug policy the Dutch responded by publishing a series of comparative statistics on their US embassy website. In everyone of them from incidence of drug use in minors to murders related to drug offences, the Dutch fared far better than the US.

McCaffrey muttered a retraction of his accusation when pressed on the subject during a press conference he conducted on a recent UK visit but in the midst of our painfully muted public debate, his retraction went entirely unreported in the mainstream press.

At long last however, the Independent Inquiry into the Misuse of Drugs Act 1971 published its media splashed report on March 28 2000 and prized the gag from the mouth of the debate.

The Inquiry concentrated specifically on the Misuse of Drugs Act 1971 and therefore did not take in all aspects of drug policy. But its recommendations include significant shifts in the legal classification of drugs, the wider implications of which will prove difficult for the Home Office to ignore.

According to the committee's chairperson, Viscountess Runciman: "We have concluded that the most dangerous message of all is the message that all drugs are equally dangerous. When young people know that the advice they are being given is either exaggerated or untrue in relation to less harmful drugs, there is a real risk they will discount everything else they are told."

In response, the report recommends that drugs should be legally reclassified in order to reflect their social impact. That Ecstasy and LSD are not as harmful as Crack and Heroin and therefore should be relegated to Class B status rather than class A. And that Cannabis should be reduced to a Class C drug, with police officer's directed to only fine or caution those found in possession.

The provocative nature of the committee's recommendations compounded a similarly radical report published recently by Cleveland Police. Backed by Cleveland's Chief Constable, Barry Shaw, the report notes: "There is overwhelming evidence to show that the prohibition-based policy in place in this country since 1971 has not been effective in controlling the availability of, or use of, proscribed drugs. If there is indeed a 'war on drugs' it is not being won; drugs are demonstrably cheaper and more easily available than ever before. If prohibition does not work, then either the consequences of this have to be accepted or an alternative approach must be found. The most obvious alternative approach is the legalisation and subsequent regulation of some or all drugs."

However, in the first few days after the publication of the Inquiry report, the Home Office issued flat rejections of its recommendations and chose to ignore altogether the strong suggestions put forward by Cleveland Police.

But then something unusual happened in the land of

Britain; something which Jack Straw's playsafe to the grey galleries could not ignore. The media supported the Inquiry's recommendations to an extent hitherto unwitnessed in the UK. Unbelievable though it may seem, the official newspaper of the right wing old boy network, the Daily Telegraph, published an editorial headlined "An experiment with Cannabis" which called ....wait for it....for cannabis to be legalised!

"People like substances that alter their mood." its editorial observed. "And only strict puritans believe that they should never use any of them. A cup of coffee, a glass of wine or beer, even the odd cigarette are among the legitimate pleasures of life. Are drugs fundamentally different?......The government should draw up plans to legalise cannabis - generally accepted as the least dangerous of the drugs that are widely used - both for its consumption and for its supply."

The Police Review was equally emphatic: "The sizeable community who use soft drugs recreationally...want a change in the law which reflects what is already happening at social gatherings, small and large, every night of the week. It is dismal that this reality, reflected in the report, carries no weight with the government and its disappointing drugs czar, who...appears to be performing a huge U-turn on the more enlightened approach he adopted as a senior police officer."

When the Daily Mail joined both the Telegraph and the Police Review in proposing a wider debate, Jack Straw was left like a beached whale. The following day

" My spy in the Home Office has revealed the truth of Jack Straw's agonising over Pinochet.

'He tortured thousands, Home Secretary,' his advisers told him. 'Serious stuff.' said Jack. 'But he's an old man and it was a long time ago.'

They said, 'He killed hundreds of thousands of people.' 'Nobody's perfect.' said Jack. 'In government you have to take some hard decisions.'

The advisers played their ace. 'We think that here in Britain he took some medicinal cannabis for his back pain'

'That's dreadful,' screamed Jack. 'Pack him off to a Spanish dungeon.'"

he admitted for the first time publicly that there was, after all, a "coherent argument" in favour of the legalisation of cannabis. However without explanation or further discussion he is still electing not to agree with the argument, however coherent or well informed.

Nevertheless, the fact that the traditional right wing media are criticising the government's misplaced puritanism on drugs is a sea-change indeed. Jack Straw, who once ran for student union presidency with the laughable election slogan "Not respectable but respected", looks increasingly isolated from the very media he 's been pandering to in a fervent quest to be indistinguishable from his Tory predecessors.

And what's more his attitude seems to rub off on anyone associated with him. Take the very disappointing drug czar, Keith Hellawell. As a chief constable back in 1994 he observed: "The present policies are not working. We seize more drugs, we arrest more people but when you look at the availability of drugs, the use of drugs, the crime committed because of and through people who use drugs, the violence associated with drugs, it's on the increase. It can't be working."

These days, however, he draws a salary greater the prime minister's and paid for by all of us, and what we get for our money is a man who'll who is prepared to belie his own experience in order to play along with Straw's pitiful ministry. Neither respectable nor respected. And certainly not by his fellow MP, Paul Flynn, whose humourfully astute website at www.paulflynnmp.co.uk makes clear what he thinks of his party colleague at the Home Office:

Pics: Ian Hunter

WAKE UP! IT'S YER LET'S HAVE A LOOK AT YER PASSPORT

# Weekly SchNEWS

Printed and Published in Brighton by *Justice?*

Friday 14th May 1999     http://www.schnews.org.uk/    Issue 211    Free/Donation

# NO ROOM AT THE INN

*The theme of abuse runs through the whole bill"*
Statewatch

As the Kosovan refugee crisis continues, New Labour's draconian plans for asylum seekers are finally out in the open.

Kosovans arriving on our shores can rightly expect decent treatment after the nightmares they have had to endure. They won't have to go through years of aslum-seeking hell to prove they are genuine victims of persecution or locked up in detention centres on arrival because they haven't got the right papers (always an easy one to get the right papers when you're fleeing a conflict or escaping political persecution). They'll get full Income Support payments, be able to take jobs and be free to travel and live wherever they choose in the country. Which is only fair surely.

But woe betide any asylum seeker who arrives in the UK from an obscure country trying to escape an unheard of war or dodgy dictatorship once the Immigration and Asylum Bill becomes law.

Hope Hanlon , Office of the United Nations High Commissioner for Refugees:

*"It is one of the worst Bills ever brought before the House of Commons"* (that's saying something!)

Forget Article 14 of the Universal Declaration of Human Rights (*"Everyone has the right to seek and enjoy asylum"*) Measures outlined in the 138 clauses of the bill include:

* The abolition of welfare benefits for asylum seekers is to be replaced with a voucher system, plus a 'cor blimey what shall I do with a whole' £1 a day cash for adults and 50p per child. This will put asylum seekers 30% below the offical poverty line. Maybe the Home Office have conveniently forgotten evidence from the Refugee Council about the effect of withdrawing cash benefits. Of 200 asylum-seekers recently surveyed, three quarters were utterly penniless and had to walk everywhere, and 60% did not have enough to eat on a daily basis.

* They will have no say in where they can live and instead be dispersed all over the country to "reception zones" , away from relatives, community networks and specialist services.

* Immigration officers will be given powers of arrest without warrant, of breaking into premises, of searching arrested persons both on the street and (including strip-search) in custody, and powers to seize material.

* Lorry drivers who carry illegal entrants will be fined £2,000 per person - including babies. When it was pointed out that many lorries are sealed and impossible to open from the inside, and that many asylum-seekers had died from suffocation, one minister dismissed the accounts as *"tedious"*

* Children of asylum-seekers will be exempt from the provisions of the Children Act.

* Airline liason officers to examine and refuse passengers as they board.

The government reckon they can get away with all this because by 2001 all new asylum cases will be dealt with in six months.

So what about this - the Immigration and Nationality Department that deals with refugees, already have a backlog of 80,000 cases at its headquarters in Croydon and its computers essential for tracking files are in a state of near collapse. Their web-site asks people not to call and claims are currently taking 17 months to process. The staff who are leaving in droves will, if the bill is made law, be asked to deal with the administration of the new voucher system as well. A new computer system, due to be delivered next month, is unlikely to be ready in time. Doesn't exactly inspire confidence now does it.

So SchNEWS asks why is such a draconian bill going through parliament?

This bill will cut costs and make life so unpleasant that others will be deterred from coming. But surely wanting to live in the UK is not a crime? Fleeing repression and war certainly isn't. Yet Britain has adopted the Fortress Europe mentality where every asylum seeker is seen as a bogus criminal. Where refugees are a visible and unwelcome reminder of the precarious balance of the new world order and of the human consequences of International Monetary Fund structural adjustment programmes, of arm sales to repressive regimes and of corrupt aid deals. The politicans pandering to the right wing press reckon that cracking down is seen as a vote winner.

Yet the postive reception that the Kosovar refugees have received from the people of this country shows that when people can see others suffering on our screens rather than

## SchNews
### Book Launch
## HEADMIX COLLECTIVE
### GROUND ZERO
Wednesday 19th May
Bar Centro, Ship St
7 - 11pm £2
Raffle, Video, MegaMash & FAF Decor, Cheap beer

the hysterical shoutings of the tabloid press they can extend a warm welcome.

### THE REALITY

A total of 34,775 persons were kicked out of the UK in 1998 - 668 persons per week - 4 persons per hour.

A 25 year old Kosovan student arrived at Heathrow en route for Canada in February. She was pregnant with her first child and still traumatised by seeing the Serbs destroy her home.Although she was with her husband, she had been forced to leave the rest of her family behind and had no idea whether they were alive .However, the couple had made the mistake of becoming Kosovan refugees before the war with Serbia had made them politically fashionable.

When they were caught at Heathrow using false Greek passports, they said they wished to claim asylum, but  instead were arrested for using false documents in transit, separated and sent to prison. She has just been released from Holloway, where the insanitary conditions made her ill and the isolation made her depressed. Her husband was sent to Wormwood Scrubs where he remains, although he may be released with an electronic tag this month.

* 'Crimes of arrival: immigrants and asylum-seekers in the new Europe' by Frances Webber Essential reading on the European wide criminalisation of asylum seekers. Available from **Statewatch**, PO Box 1516, London N16 OEW Tel 0181 802 1882  www.statewatch.org

**\*National Coalition of Anti-Deportation Campaigns,** 101 Villa Rd., Birmingham, B19 1NH Tel 0121 554 6947  www.ncadc.demon.co.uk/

## SMARTIE-ARSES

The Advertising Standards Authority (ASA) criticised Nestlé on Wednesday for their irresponsible promotion of their milk products in the developing world. The ASA upheld a complaint brought by Baby Milk Action, about a newspaper advert in which Nestlé claimed that it had marketed it's infant formula *"ethically and responsibly"* both before and since the introduction of the international code of the marketing of breast milk substitutes in 1981. After two years of consideration, the ASA ruled that Nestlé's claims *"went too far"*, the ruling cannot be published as Nestlé has lodged an appeal.

The World Health Organisation estimates that more than a million babies die every year from diarrhoea picked up through unhygienic bottle feeding.

For years now, Nestlé have promoted their product in underdeveloped countries, relying heavily on the misconception that 'West is best' to convince mothers that their babies will grow bigger and stronger if they feed them with a western product rather than their own breast milk. Of course, after a short period of bottle feeding a mother's breast milk dries up and another consumer is born. Reversing the decline in breastfeeding could save the lives of 1.5 million infants every year according to United Nations Children's Fund. UNICEF states that in areas with unsafe water, a bottle-fed baby is 25 times more likely to die from diarrhoea than a breastfed one.

Baby milks are over-diluted to make them last longer, while breastmilk is free, safe and best for all babies - but Nestlé know that if they don't get babies hooked on the bottle, they don't do business.

One of their dodgier promotional practices was the use of free supplies which had a significant effect in convincing health workers and mothers to favour artificial milk over breastmilk.

\*\*Nestlé provides information to mothers which promotes bottle feeding and discourages breastfeeding.

\*\*Donates free samples and supplies to health facilities to encourage bottle feeding

\*\*Gives inducements to health workers for promoting its products

\*\*Does not provide clear warnings on labels of the benefits of breastfeeding and dangers of artificial feeding. In some cases the labels are in a language that mothers are unlikely to understand. Nestlé, makes a profit while others count the cost The Baby Milk Action (BMA) group is a small organisation waging a big battle against a powerful multinational - they need your support. For a start, stop consuming Nestlé products and that includes Nescafe. The BMA have information to help and advise you how to protest effectively against these unscrupulous bastards. After dropping sales their worst nightmare is public opinion turning against them so your voice is important and your cash even more - don't buy their products.

Contact the BMA Tel: 01223 464420 Fax: 01223 464417 E-mail: babymilkacti@gn.apc.org Nestle UK Ltd., St George's House, Croydon, Surrey. CR9 1NR.

\* When Marketing Week magazine asked Marjorie Thompson of Saatchi & Saatchi how Nestlé should respond to the bad publicity surrounding its baby food marketing activities. "She suggests the way to counteract the bad publicity is to go on the offensive by using advertising showing the benefits of Nestlé financial contributions to charities.."

DON'T FORGET NATIONAL BREAST-FEEDING WEEK SUN 17TH-21ST MAY. Freephone: 0800 555 777

**HELP!!**-Don't be shy - please come in on a Friday and help with some envelope stuffing -if it doesn't get to our subscribers we don't get any cash -you don't get any SchNEWS!

## SchNEWS in brief

**June 18th benefits: Tues**18th May @ the Cuba 9 -2, funky techno from Cristian Vogel, Counterattack, Da Void, direct action films £2/1 **Thurs 20th May** @ the Volks Tavern 9 - 2, **Mr.Night & Mr .Day**, Blatantly, Touchpaper, DJ tha Funky Ghecko, £2 / £5 tickets for both gigs + SchNews book launch from the Peace Centre.

The A Spire social centre, is a squatted church left empty for over 4 years by Leeds university, now turned into an autonomous zone www.geocities.com/CapitolHill/Parliament/3344 \*\*Could any of the original Weymouth Road Protesters contact Chris on 01270 526 244 asap.\*\* Stammer Organics Open Day Sat 22 May 10am-4pm Bring a picnic.Tel: (01273) 388673\*\* Moulescoomb Forest Garden & Wildlife Project Open Day Sun 23rd May 12 noon 'till 4pm. Visit the weird and wonderful forest garden.The whole site is organic and may soon be designated a Site of Nature Conservation Importance. Tel: Kate (01273) 628535\*\* Anyone lose a a small blue, pink and yellow rucksack on the circle line tube, containing skates and a jumper during the reclaim the streets tube party? It's at the Angel Station lost property. \*\* This Sunday (16) there's an open day for the Native American Educational Trust at Evolution Arts Centre, Silwood Terrace, Brighton 12 noon \*\*

## TARRED TO THE MAX

The construction firm Tarmac has been breaking such different sorts of records-Roy Castle would be proud. They recently scooped four of the government and construction industry's 1999 'Quality in Construction' major awards, including that in the environment category. Which may raise hollow laughs from people in the Bestwood area of Nottinghamshire, if not as hollow as the yawning quarry Tarmac intends to inflict on the forest there. The judges displayed an even more finely honed sense of irony in awarding a Tarmac subsidiary the Safety award, lauding their 'degree of absolute commitment [which] is fantastic', and reflecting the 10(!) awards Tarmac companies have this week received from the Royal Society for the Prevention of Accidents. Now, this ain't going to raise even a hollow laugh (or much else) from any of the 13 Tarmac employees killed at work over the last decade. And that's not just a rogue statistic; to place it in context, note that Tarmac was convicted at that time of more Health and Safety offences than any other UK firm, almost twice as many as the next worst offender. (Let's take a quick glance at the cost benefit analysis: the company received fines of, on average, just over 3 grand for a seriously injured employees, just over 11 grand for a death; while such skimping on H&S considerations may have contributed to their truly fantastic average annual profits of £184 million). That is a serious record. Perhaps just as well they didn't employ Roy Castle, who died before Tarmac could get their hands on him.

## GIVEN A GOOD SEEING TOO

At last eight test sites growing genetically modified oil seed rape got a good kicking last Friday. The action could well have set the commercialisation of genetic oil rape back 12 months. The Genetic Engineering Network (GEN) learned of this unprecedented removal from a group calling themselves "Ambridge Against Genetix". According to GEN this takes the number of sites that have been decontaminated this year to 14. And as the Ambridge crew point out " this is only the start of the summer"

\* A total of 37 genetic sites were destroyed in 1998 according to GEN, PO Box 9656, London, N4 Tel 0181 374 9516 email genetics@gn.apc.org

## Inside SchNEWS

U.S. class struggle anarchist prisoner Harold Thompson is having a rough time at the moment. Due to a corrupt prison librarian official working hand in glove with White Aryan Brotherhood scum, Harold has been brutally assaulted, robbed and placed in segregation for his 'own safety'. Because of his work as prison house lawyer, officials seem to be colluding with white supremacists to halt his good work.If you can please write protesting (civilly) to : Warden Jack Morgan, Turney Centre Industrial Prison, Route 1, Only, Tennessee 37140-9709, USA, in order that Harold might get a transfer avoiding further White Aryan Brotherhood victimisation. You can write to Harold at the same address. Harold H. Thompson #93992.

## BACK WITH A VENGEANCE

The Ministry of Defence have completed the new Trident Submarine at a cost of a mere £1000 million to the taxpayer and in keeping with their general sensitivity they have named their latest toy- - *VENGEANCE*. What kind of minds are at work here? Despite overwhelming opposition-80% of Scots say 'NO' to Trident - all nuclear submarines are kept at Faslane in Scotland.

Meanwhile, as SchNEWS went to press 3 Swedish activists, arrested inside the Marconi Marine shipyard in Barrow-in-Furness, Cumbria in September last year were awaiting the outcome of their trial. They were carrying rope ladders, crowbars and hammers emblazoned with the slogans, "All life is sacred", "Violence ends where love begins" and "For global justice". Their intention - to prevent a serious crime against humanity. For this they were locked up until late January when they were unexpectedly released. After a brief period of freedom they returned to the Barrow shipyard with 20 other activists to ask the workers and security to help continue the disarmament of the Trident. They were nicked again.

Vengeance was moved to Coulport missile depot on April 30th and them last week it went to the Isle of Bute. Seems the MOD are keeping their weapon out of harm's way!

Contact: Trident Ploughshares 2000, 42-46 Bethel St, Norwich, NR2 1NR, Britain.

\* Faslane Peace Camp 01436 820901

\* Time to abolish war - a citizens' assembly Sat 22nd May 11 am Central Hall, Westminister Tickets from Hague Appeal for Peace, 11 Venetia Rd., London, N4 1EJ www.haguepeace.org

**TRAINING DAY**-SchNEWS needs some more hands on deck, so why not come along to our next training day: Wednesday 26th May 12 noon. Limited spaces, so book yer place now.

## ...and finally...

Radioactive boy-scouts may soon be roaming the countryside! The Scout Association, being seriously strapped for cash have accepted a £30,000 sponsorship from British Nuclear Fuels Limited (BNFL). BNFL have invested in this dodgy bit of P.R in an attempt to enhance their image by connecting themselves to the wholesome Kumbya krew. The BNFL logo will be proudly worn by scouts on their proficiency badges. SchNEWS wonders if the badge is for proficiency in nuclear- bomb making? At least this could serve as a method for identifying which scouts have been exposed to the questionable benefits of access to BNFL's laboratories at Sellafield in Cumbria. Alternatively you could just watch to see which of them start to glow in the dark!

## Subscribe!
Keep SchNEWS FREE! Just send 1st Class stamps (e.g. 20 for next 20 issues) or donations (payable to Justice?) **Ask for "Originals"** if you can make copies. Post *free* to all prisoners. SchNEWS, c/o on-the-fiddle, P.O. Box 2600, Brighton, East Sussex, BN2 2DX.
*Tel/Autofax:* +44 (0)1273 685913 *GET IT EVERY WEEK BY E-MAIL:* schnews@brighton.co.uk

The Original and still the best.

NESCAFÉ

At KILLING·BABIES WORLD WIDE

Pic: Alec Smart

**Newbery reunion rally inspect a road full of holes**

# Juxtaposing

*"Ask the good people of Newbury. Having lived in congestion hell for years, the recent opening of the much-maligned by-pass there solved their pollution and congestion problem overnight."*

**Lord Hanson. Sunday Business 18/7/99**

## with

*"It can be seen that there is no consistent pattern of traffic change over the Newbury network as a whole. In many cases local factors are responsible for discrete changes to traffic flows, with the by-pass and pedestrianisation [of Newbury town centre] only having a marginal influence in some cases."*

**West Berkshire Council Report on affects of By-pass published July 1999**

environmental justice

On 28th April (Workers Memorial Day) 50 people shut down Southwark Bridge for an hour to protest against the continued failure of the Health and Safety Executive to bring Simon Jones' killers to justice (SchNEWS 210)

**HUNGOVER? WHO'S IDEA WAS IT TO HOLD A BOOK LAUNCH ON A WEDNESDAY!**

# Weekly SchNEWS

*Printed and Published in Brighton by Justice?*

**Mining out of control**

**Defend lives, lands and homes**

**Friday 21st May 1999**    http://www.schnews.org.uk/    **Issue 212    Free/Donation**

# GOLDFINGERED

*Rio Tinto is the world's biggest profiteer from mineral exploitation. And the majority of these profits are gained at the expense of indigenous land owners who have never given consent to the company's operations"* PARTiZANS

Last Thursday Rio Tinto Zinc (RT), the world's biggest and baddest mining company faced more protests at it's annual general meeting.

The board faced nearly two hours of angry questioning from the floor, as shareholders concerned with their dividends were joined by people, more concerned with the communities and eco-systems across the planet that have been smashed to pieces by the corporation's mining operations. In an at-a-glance quick-fire fact rundown, here's some of their activities that they didn't boast about in their annual report…

• A senior RT exec was one of the chief drafters of an Australian labour law which breaches International Labour Organisation conventions on the rights to organise, collectively bargain, and freely associate.

In West Papua, they've been assisting the military brutally to crush indigenous opposition , where they jointly own one of the world's biggest gold and copper mines.

• Trespassing on Western Shoshone Treaty land in Nevada, US. This gold mine increased production 180% during 1998, and has established itself as the world's lowest cost commercial producer of this (almost) useless metal.

• The recent - and devastating - report on their now obsolete Capper Pas tin smelt on Humberside, England, showed that the plant is a major health and environmental disaster, spewing out an impressive range of poisonous heavy metals for the local kids to play around.

• The lack of consultations with the Wayuu people of Colombia during the recent huge expansion of coal operations in Guajira.

To be fair, the company have acted with with near-perfect consistency, as every time it descends upon another area of wilderness, an ecological nightmare unfolds in its wake. And RT have their green-wash public relations down to a fine art. Like the rest of big business, they see the advantages of talking to environmental groups, as why do battle when you can co-opt the activists? You needn't make any real concessions to the greens, as even a token deal can do so much to foster a green'n'caring image. James Harris, vice-president of PR consultants Hill and Knowlton, put it this way "For corporations, environmental groups offer the opportunity to obtain positive publicity…they also provide credibility, which can be particularly valuable." Stauber and Rampton, who edit PR Watch put it more bluntly - hiring activists is a "crude but effective way to derail potentially meddlesome activists."

In the UK RT are also one of the main providers of information to schools from primary to post-graduate. They even fund two colleges - Atlantic and United World in Wales, while last year they chucked $30 million at charities to make the world a better place (sic).

All of which helps to compensate of course, for the negative publicity that tends to come from systematically polluting the earth and fucking over the locals. Time to hire yerself a credible greenie. Someone like Tom Burke, one time director of Friends of the Earth, who now works for Rio Tinto, helping them pull the wool over the public's eyes. Burke is a well connected man, working for the last 3 environment ministers and setting up the Green Alliance, the people behind Rio Tinto's new forums. These forums are classic examples of greenwash gimmicks - talking shops where groups like Amnesty International, Save The Children Fund and Oxfam help Rio Tinto clean up their image. There seems to be one small oversight at the Forums - no indigenous people whose lands are being destroyed by the company are ever invited.

So do we really need all this gold, copper, and titanium oxide (the stuff that makes toothpaste white)?

In 1998 Rio Tinto had to face one of its biggest-ever financial crises thanks to the fall in virtually all metal prices. But as economists point out prices have been falling for nearly thirty years. Good for consumers as everyone gets cheaper cars, microwaves, fridges etc. But not so good for the miners who face deteriorating conditions.

So will this article get you all scurrying down to the local tin recycling bank? Maybe, but it should be pointed out that the biggest consumers of Rio Tinto's metals is the European armaments industry. Not only are those Hawk jets and missiles a bit tricky to fit in the old recycling bin, the arms connection may help explain why our European leaders might not want to put RT's back up too much.

\* **Rio Tinto Behind The Facade -** report by the International Chemical, Energy and Mineworkers Union £1 postage from PARTiZANS

\* **PARTiZANS**, (who campaign specifically against Rio Tinto) 41A Thornhill Square, London, N1 1BE  Tel 0171 700 6189  email partizans@mole.gn.apc.org

---

Not wanting to miss out on the image-enhancing potential of a few co-opted indigenous people, Rio Tinto Australia has sponsored a new exhibition 'New Directions - Aboriginal Australia and Business'. According to its website, the exhibition presents *"clear signs of a new direction in relationships between the Rio Tinto Group and Aboriginal people based on respect, listening and negotiation for mutual benefit."*

It gets better: apparently *"Rio Tinto has 're-lationships' with Indigenous peoples in many parts of communities along a sometimes uncertain path. There have been misunderstandings and setbacks as each party has learned one another's ways."*

---

" Not a creature on this planet needs a single further ounce of commercially mined gold " PARTiZANS

**GoldBusters**, is a coalition of groups fighting, appropriately, the gold industry, hoping to make the wearing of the sparkling stuff as unattractive as wearing fur. 80% of new gold being mined worldwide is for jewellery - people wearing it are probably unaware of the true costs.

The mining of gold is one of the most environmentally destructive industrial activities, wreaking havoc on indigenous communities on every continent. In dozens of countries mercury-laced tailings, eroded land and acid mine drainage stand as visible and toxic legacies of gold rushes from days gone by.

Unfortunately in the 1990s, the gold mining industry has experienced a boom due to new technologies, principally using cyanide to leech the gold from its parent rock.

The two-pronged campaign is aimed at jewellery consumers, and nations' gold reserves . Depressing its price would lead to the decommissioning of many mines, and the dumping of exploration stocks by investors. For example, 20 gold mines in Australia have been postponed or closed recently because it wasn't cost effective. www.moles.org/projectunderground/

**small bit:** Sorry if you've been e-mailing us, our mail has been down for 2 weeks-we're not ignoring you , we love you really and are on the case sorting it

---

### SchNews Survival Handbook

The new SchNEWS book is out **now** Featuring issues 151-200 plus cartoons, photos, and other articles to help you protest and survive as well as a comprehensive database of over 500 grass-roots organisations.

Yours for £7 (incl. p+p from the usual address. (Cheers to Headmix and everyone for Wednesdays bash- more cabaret party politics fun on the horizon)

---

## NO BAD WOMEN ONLY BAD LAWS

*"These measures will only serve to further criminalise women whose choice of profession is the result of a lack of viable economic alternatives."* Cari Mitchell, English Collection of Prostitutes

The incorrigible Jack Straw is the man behind the master plan to rid Britain of so called 'tartcards' in 'phone boxes and push prostitution back on to the streets. It 's incredible that the Government refuse to acknowledge prostitution as an established industry, regardless of the various scandals involving politicians, exposed over the years. So, are we to surmise that those with power to protect through legislation are content to exploit women surreptitiously but refuse to offer the same women any degree of protection? And now, in the name of 'decency' they intend to destroy one means which the women have found of making their work a little safer.

A spokeswoman from the ECP, told SchNEWS *"The impact will be very serious .Working in premises and advertising in this way enables women to work independently. Some women will be forced out onto the street where it is 10 times more dangerous to work and where women will face increased arrests and hostility from residents. Black and immigrant women will be particularly targeted and vulnerable."* Girls who tout for work using cards operate from flats, places of relative safety where they have control over who they allow on the premises. The Well Woman clinic visits the flats once a fortnight . There are facilities for the girls and the clients to wash, the whole environment is cleaner and better controlled than street prostitution. This is not intended to imply that women working on the street are less aware of the necessity of cleanliness, in fact they have given a lot of leadership to all sex industry workers on the issue of using condoms. In Britain it has been left to the prostitutes themselves to organise their industry and make it as safe and clean as possible. It would seem obvious that if the girls are forced back onto the streets there will be a marked increase in violence and pimp-related crime. Carole, an 'ex-working girl', explained *"I used to work on the streets in the freezing cold and you never know who is going to rob you or rape you. I was so severely raped it traumatised me for nearly six years. There is less chance of someone coming into a flat and doing that."*

The girls  suggest that the cards are allowed to remain with no images. Discreet cards which offer a specialised service without using explicit pictures or language would be preferable to a total ban on 'carding'.

The government has decided against giving BT the power to invoke criminal sanctions for offenders. Instead, local authorities will decide what advertisements should be allowed in 'phoneboxes. B.T announced yesterday that it had cut off all incoming calls to 600 numbers being used by prostitutes which serves to emphasise the lack of rights suffered by these women. SchNews detects a hint of 'double-standards', after all, since when has B.T been so conciencious in clamping down on immoral uses of their phone lines-they don't seem so swift to close down  the 0898 sex lines which bring them  revenue whilst incidentally encouraging the exploitation of women. To quote a spokeswoman for ECP, " *B.T's main objection to women advertising seems to be that BT does not profit from it…..Workers on a prostitution project have also been told by BT that they were prepared to negotiate an advertising fee for their cards."*

If Jack Straw is serious about dealing with prostitution' he needs to address women's poverty. Prostitute's and the people who put up cards for them are struggling to support themselves and their families in the face of poverty, unemployment and cuts in benefits and resources. De-criminalisation of prostitution is essential if these women are to achieve basic human rights and an acceptable level of safety in their work.

•A book about violence against prostitute's can be obtained from Crossroads Womens Centre, PO Box 287, London NW6 5QU. 0171 482 2496

## SchNEWS in brief

**Cambridge Reclaim the Streets.** Sat 12th June @ railway station 1pm Bring your party toyz, banners, strawberries and cream.A coach will be going up on the day from Brighton. Tickets cost £5; available soon from the Peace Centre, Gardner Street ** How about a summer of **mass trespass** for the right to roam? Meet 10.30 am Sun. 30th May at Brighton Station for a 6 mile walk, bring a packed lunch - sorry no dogs. Contact Brighton The Land Is Ours 01273 620815 \*\***Be Tranceformed** – massive five roomed party featuring everything from funk to trance to drum'n'bass at The Drome, Stainer St, London Bridge on Saturday 12th June. It's £10 and all profits go to Guilfin magazine. 0956 250 108 ** ** **Friends and Families of Travellers:** Health and Safety workshops available. 01426 218424 ** **Animal Freedom Gathering**, at The Miners Welfare Recreational Ground, Moira, nr Ashby-de-la-Zouch, 28th-31st May various workshops, transport available 0171 278 3068 \*\*Next demonstration against **Hillgrove** Cat vivisection farm nr Oxford on June 12th, coaches from London as usual 0121 632 6460 \*\***Is Anarchism a Religion?** For a rivetting discussion turn up at Conway hall, 25 red Lion Square, London WC1 on 4th June 8pm. It's organised by the London Anarchist Forum who put on talks same time same place every Friday. List of events ring 0181 847 0203 ** **SchNEWS** is looking for someone to print yer favourite news-sheet every Friday 9 am (yes, the morning). Any reliable people out there interested should ring the office ** Everybody's favourite cheeky geezer **Mark Thomas**(perhaps excepting New Labour bods) has done a documentary about the nasty new Immigration and Asylum Bill (see last weeks SchNEWS). It will be on C4 27th May. Don't know a time yet

## SICK AS A DOG

A week of intensive campaigning against the sport(?) of greyhound racing is happening from May 22nd to 29th. In case you were under the impression that this is a fairly innocent, cruelty free form of amusement, let us put the record straight here…..

* Every year in Britain 30,000 greyhounds that are surplus to the industry are drowned, poisoned, beaten to death, starved, dumped on the streets or impounded and destroyed.

*Greyhound pups are killed if they fail to reach racing standards-1/3 are put to death before they reach a year old.

*Many greyhounds are exported to Spain for exhibition racing. Kennel conditions are appalling with animals  kept locked up 23 hours a day.
*Many exported dogs are used for hunting and coursing. Greyhounds do not have the stamina for this work & many are being hanged (some have been found burned and skinned)as a cheap means of disposal

**Greyhounds naturally live about 14 years but racing dogs generally only live two.

Greyhound action are working to change this appalling situation. As it is not possible to re-home the vast number of greyhounds disposed of every year by the racing industry, the total abolition of greyhound racing seems to be the only real solution. For once SchNews can say "gawd bless America" without a trace of irony as greyhound racing has been illegal in the States since 1993.

Greyhound Action, PO Box 127, Kidderminster, Worcs. DY10 3UZ01562 745778.

+++

## Happy Campers

After loads of hassle from the Foreign & Commonwealth Office, the Inter-Continental Caravan (ICC) have finally got their visas. There are 600 activists in the caravans, from as many countries as you can think of (well, almost), including shed-loads from the Indian subcontinent. They're coming over to bring the concerns of the South (such as those about being fucked over by western companies) directly to the heart of the North. Their visit will coincide with the G8 summit on (wait for it) June 18th' whose date has surely now been etched into all our readers' hearts.

On Friday 28 May, 150 'caravanners' will come to London. There'll be a public meeting, with first-hand accounts from Indian farmers of the REAL effects of  free trade. And its free!! Anarchist Teapot will be doing the catering! What more could you ask for? (well, an end to global capitalism would be nice)\*\*12.00 til 4.30ish at the Friends House, Euston Road (opp Euston station) London NW1. For  info, call 0181 357 8504. Friday 7.30pm, there's a public seminar on the World Trade Organisation and the International Monetary Fund. Oxford House community centre, Derbyshire Street, London E2 (Bethnal Green tube).  And there's more!! Sat 29 May – genetic crop squat with the cara-van crew– meet @ Lincoln Station 10am, or call 07971 755 823 Squall / Strike PARTY Sat. 11-29 Fashion Street. Contact ICC London Committee: 07801 708  4966 / 0171 375 3596. www.stalk.net/caravan.

On June 18th  leaders of the 8 most powerful nations will meet for the G8 summit in Germany. On their agenda will be more economic growth, more free trade and more power for corporations. Some people don't think this is a very good idea – so across the globe on June 18th, people will be organising demonstrations. In the UK there will be a massive carnival in the city of London "replacing the roar of profit and plunder with the sounds and rhythms of party, carnival and pleasure." (SchNews likes the sound of that) Meet 12 noon Liverpool Street Station, London.* If you want posters, flyers, stickers for J18 contact Reclaim the Streets 0171 281 4621 rts@gn.apc.org

* Get yer tickets now for coaches up to London from Brighton now on sale at the Peace Centre, Gardner St. £4.* The Legal Defence & Monitoring Group will watching the cops and offering legal support on J18, but need volunteers. Full training provided, no legal knowledge necessary. Contact LDMG c/o PO Box 2474, London N8, P/F 0181 374 5027.* If you want A Crap Night Out  get to the Free Butt, Sat. 22nd feat. Flannel, Tragic Roundabout, the Borg (famous anarchist tennis players) for yet another bloody J18th benefit.

* Squaring up to the Square Mile – a rough guide to the City of London  For a free copy send a SAE (31p) to June 18 Info, Box E, 111 Magdalen Rd., Oxford, OX4 1RQ

## …and finally…
### WHICH? MERCENARY SPECIAL

Your Third World regime wants to profit from the nation's rich mineral reserves, but first you have to stave off the indigenous populace and others with competing power claims. Who ya gonna call - Tribesmen-and-Peasant-and-Rebel-Army-Busters? I don't think you'll find them in the Yellow Pages! Try reading 'The Privatisation of Violence - New Mercenaries and the State' a new special report by Campaign Against the Arms Trade. See here which of the corporate military firms on the market have delivered the best performance in areas as diverse as Sierra Leone and Bougainville - and which have been rubbish! In a new, easy-to-read format, with loadsa pop pix n' fax.. CAAT: 11 Goodwin St, Finsbury Park, London N4 3HQ. Tel. 0171 281 0297.

**Disclaimer\*** SchNews warns all readers not to prostitute themselves to multinationals as they'll fuck you over and leave you holding the baby. Honest.

# BOYZ IN THE HOOD

The recent Home Office recommendation that all members of the criminal justice system should declare masonic affiliations opened a can of worms in public. Peter Panatone reviews the evidence and the significant rift the issue has caused amongst the British police force.

Weird isn't it? To think that policemen, judges, MPs, council officers and a multitude of other public servants go through such bizarre rituals.

Wearing a shoe on one foot and a slipper on the other, they roll up their trouser leg, bear their chest, are blindfolded and tied with a hangman's noose and, whilst standing on a marble chess board with a dagger pressed to their heart, swear oaths of secrecy, allegiance and mutual aid. And yet this ritual is performed by every one of the 350,000 masons in England and Wales, the 30,000 in Scotland and the estimated six million world-wide.

Such occult practices would normally be easy fodder for tabloid derision but one look at the kind of names known to be Freemasons explains why public criticism has up until now remained so scant. In Britain, aristocratic members of the 'brotherhood' - for they are all men - include the Duke of Edinburgh; the Earl of Cadogan; the Marquess of Northampton and the Duke of Kent. Among the political figures known to be 'on the square' are Willie Whitelaw, Cecil Parkinson and the current head of the Criminal Cases Review Commission, Sir Frederick Crawford.

Whilst a few high profile 'brethren' break cover to perform a public relations role and a few others are 'outed' by tenacious researchers, most Masons in public positions, including those populating the two Masonic lodges thought to operate in the Houses of Parliament, remain clandestine. When author and researcher Martin Short wrote to Willie Whitelaw asking him if he was a Freemason, the ex-Home Secretary replied: "I have never been an active Mason since I entered the House of Commons in 1955." However, the 1987 yearbook for the Grand Lodge of Antient Free and Accepted Masons of Scotland - not publicly available but shown to SQUALL- reveals that he is still an active Freemason and a Scottish representative of Australia's Grand Lodge of New South Wales. The casual ease with which such an influential political figure was prepared to lie about his Masonic affiliations casts further doubt upon Masonic integrity. It is a doubt many see will only be assuaged by enforced public declaration of Masonic membership by all public officials.

According to Sir Maurice Drake, a top ranking Royal Arch Mason and the High Courts' principal libel lawyer before retiring in 1995, the public's concern is misplaced: "It involves play-acting. An outsider might say it is a lot of grown men behaving like children. I can understand that but it is fun. The secrecy was always silly and I think the majority of people think that it is not very important." His fellow judicial Mason, Lord Justice Millet, concords: "It involves a certain amount of learning and performing which is quite fun. We claim to have secrets but they are harmless. There is nothing in the slightest bit sinister."

**Pic: Nick Cobbing**

However, the oaths of secrecy sworn by Freemasons sound anything but innocuous. Upon entering the first level of Masonry, an initiate promises to guard its secrets upon pain of "having my throat cut out by the root and buried in the sand of the sea at low water mark... or the more effective punishment of being branded as a wilfully perjured individual, void of all moral worth." This so-called "harmless play-acting" seems remarkably effective in ensuring secrecy. Even those who have ceased to be Masons refuse to speak of its ceremonies and practices, whilst the very few people with experience of Masonry who have dared to speak to researchers have done so anonymously. There is little doubt that retribution for public disclosure is a real threat in the minds of all those who have ever been initiated.

Commander Michael Higham wriggled in his chair in visible discomfort. In front of a packed press gallery, his pallor grew ever more pale as he sat cornered by questions thrown at him with increasing frustration by members of the Home Affairs Select Committee. As grand secretary to the United Grand Lodge of Freemasonry, the governing body for English and Welsh Masons, he had been requested to provide the committee with the names of Masonic police officers involved with units responsible for several miscarriages of justice. Despite indicating to the committee in November 1997 that the United Grand Lodge would reveal these names, a 50-strong meeting of the Masonic Board of General Purposes had ordered Higham not to reveal them afterall. The miscarriages of justice in question were major ones: the scurrilous ruining of John Stalker, the ex-Chief Constable of Manchester who got too close to the truth in his investigations into the Royal Ulster Constabulary's shoot to kill policy in Northern Ireland; the disgraced West Midlands Serious Crime Squad which, after 30 charges of misconduct, was closed down in 1986, and the discredited police investigation into the Birmingham pub bombings which led to the malicious prosecution and imprisonment of the now pardoned Birmingham Six.

Ex-police officers had made allegations that Freemason officers in the West Midlands Serious Crime Squad had operated a "firm within a firm". Serious allegations of malign Masonic manipulation extended to police officers in the John Stalker affair and to both journalists and police officers implicated in the Birmingham Six scandal. The Home Affairs Select Committee, which had been considering the influence of Freemasonry on the judiciary and police since 1995, wanted to know which of the 161 names under suspicion in these cases were Masons so that it could assess the validity of these allegations. But now, Commander Higham - who once gave a speech asserting "there is very little secret about Freemasonry" - was refusing to comply with one of the most powerful select committees in parliament. "I hope you will accept that is 'no', but not with contempt," he whimpered in his impossible situation as public fall guy for the clandestine Masonic hierarchy.

For a while a constitutional crisis looked on the cards. The Serjeant at Arms issued an order giving the United Grand Lodge 14 days to comply with the request of the Committee or else........ what? No one had ever defied parliament in this way before but now the Freemasons thought themselves powerful enough to try. Both parliament and the press held its breath. Finally, as the deadline approached, a deal was made. The United Grand Lodge agreed to provide Chris Mullin, the Chairman of the Select Committee, with the requested names on condition that only he and the clerk to the

Pic: Nick Cobbing

committee would see them. Not even the other members of the Committee would be allowed to see them and many argued that the necessity to strike a deal at all provided further evidence of the extant political power still wielded by Masons. The hapless Commander Michael Higham, who many view as a relatively harmless Mason occupying a public relations role, informed the Committee that the United Grand Lodge was to retire him early for reasons that he did not know.

The persistent public impression that masonry provides a conduit of perniciously manipulative influence in the police force finally found direct evidence to back up its concerns in the 1960's,

when 12 officers from Scotland Yard's Obscene Publications Squad were jailed for taking bribes from pornographers. All 12 were found to be Freemasons, with one of them, Chief Superintendent Bill Moody, discovered to have helped one of the pornographers to become a fellow Freemason. The integrity of the police force in general took a serious denting from the scandal and non-Masonic police officers weren't keen to take the rap. Public condemnation of freemasonic influence was, however, slow to appear.

In a pamphlet entitled "The Principles of Policing and Guidance for Professional Behaviour" published in April 1985, the then Commissioner of the Metropolitan Police, Sir Kenneth Newman concluded: "The discerning officer will probably consider it wise to forego the prospect of pleasure and social advantage in Freemasonry so as to enjoy the unreserved regard of all those around him. It follows from this that one who is already a Freemason would also be wise to ponder, from time to time, whether he should continue as a Freemason; that it would probably be prudent in the light of the way that our force is striving in these critical days, to present to the public a more open and wholehearted image of itself, to show a greater readiness to be invigilated and to be free of any unnecessary concealment or secrecy." Despite this call, the Manor of St James Lodge No9179 was set up exclusively for Metropolitan Police officers in 1989.

At least two Deputy Assistant Commissioners and 12 commanders, including the heads of the Anti-Terrorist Squad and the head of Scotland Yard's intelligence service, are known to have joined this lodge. The present Commissioner of the Metropolitan Police, Sir Paul Condon, reiterated Sir Kenneth Newman's call with a similar degree of unsuccess: "Because of the public's concern surrounding this issue I would advise my colleagues that it is better that they are not involved in Freemasonry."

Condon is presently being sued by a former metropolitan police officer for several malicious prosecutions brought after a Masonic dispute. Graham Peacock, a police constable for 26 years and a member of Masonic lodges in both London and Surrey, claims to have been victimised after a "bitter dispute" with a fellow Masonic police officer in 1992. Since that time he is alleged to have been maliciously prosecuted on three separate occasions for cannabis cultivation, murder and the illegal possession of firearms. He was acquitted of all these charges but spent time in prison on remand. He also claims that his wife has been phoned up and threatened, and that his cat went missing only to be found dead later with "horrific injuries", thrown in the neighbour's garden. If such exchanges go on between fellow Masonic police officers, what happens to others who have run-ins with Freemason officers? Two Leicester businessmen found out when they decided to have a late night drink at the Goat Moat House Hotel in Blackburn where they were staying in April 1988. Sidney and Shaun Callis (father and son) were unaware they had walked into the 'Ladies night' organised by the Victory Lodge of Blackburn. Two Masonic Lancashire police officers approached the pair and ordered them out of the hotel bar. After refusing to leave, the couple were beaten up and then charged with assault by other Masonic police officers also present. When the two men were released on bail the following morning, they found that the hotel management had seized the Callis' belongings demanding compensation for damage to the bar. The Hotel manager was later found to be a Mason and a member of the Victory Lodge. The Callis' also found that the tyres of their car had been drained of air and the hub caps removed.

When their assault charge reached court the following year, the jury rejected police evidence and acquitted the pair. The Callis' subsequently sued Lancashire Police for malicious prosecution and won £85,000 in compensation. The total pay out, including court costs, came to £170,000. However, the retribution did not stop there. Since 1989, unknown police officers put phoney criminal records for Sidney and Shaun Callis on the police national computer. Another unnamed person wrote to police suggesting that Sidney Callis was responsible for murdering two people, shot dead on the Pembrokeshire Coast in 1989. He was arrested for murder and interrogated at Hinckley Police Station before being released. Leicestershire Police also made efforts to revoke Sidney Callis's 12-bore shotgun licence. As Callis told Private Eye magazine in April: "I've never had so much as a parking fine."

The Home Affairs Select Committee was told that the Victory Lodge in Blackburn, whose members triggered this catalogue of retribution, is a lodge set up for police Masons.

According to Martin Short, author of 'Inside the Brotherhood' and a major testifier before the Home Affairs Select Committee, an estimated 25 per cent of Metropolitan Police officers and 20 per cent of national police officers still belong to Masonic lodges. The United Grand Lodge of England estimate that membership of freemasonry has declined by an estimated 200,000 over the last 30 years. Partly as a result of this diminution of power, more non-masonic public service officials have felt braver about publicly criticising the masonic network's influence on promotion prospects within their profession.

The pace of this dissent in the police force picked up considerably when the powerful Home Affairs Select Committee instigated its inquiry into the influence of Freemasonry on the police and the judiciary in 1995, an event which immediately split the police force in two. Whilst the Police Complaints Authority and the Association of Chief Police Officers called for public declaration, the Police Federation and the Police Superintendents' Association were vehemently against. The rift reached public airing after the 1995 Police Complaints Authority (PCA) annual report called for compulsory public declaration of Masonic membership by all police officers. Its chairman, Sir Leonard Peach, told the Home Affairs Select Committee that the PCA wanted to allay public fears that Masonry was being used to influence the outcome of its investigations.

The Police Superintendents' Association's backlash was remarkable. They told the committee: "Over the past two years our confidence in the impartiality of the PCA has been shaken. Many of our members no longer see the PCA as being truly independent."

Indeed, public confidence in the PCA, whose investigations are predominantly staffed by members of the police force, has never been that strong. As the body responsible for investigating malpractice in the police force, many have pointed out the questionable validity of having the police investigate the police. However, for the Police Superintendent's Association to criticise the PCA's impartiality was unheard of, and provided further indication of the tenacity with which Masonry would fight to avoid public exposure.

The Association of Chief Police Officers (ACPO), which acknowledged to the Committee that between five and ten Chief Constables (out of 43) are Masons, were nevertheless in favour of a declaration of membership in order to restore public confidence. This caused an internal rift within ACPO itself. Paul Whitehouse, ACPO's vice chairman and Chief Constable of Sussex, asserted that "It's the secrecy that is cause for concern", whilst David Wilmott, Chief Constable of Manchester and presumably one of the five to ten Masons in ACPO, called it "an infringement of personal liberty".

The Police Federation, which represents the rank and file of the police service, acknowledged to the committee that "there may well be a significant number" of their members who were Masons and were critical of ACPO's pro-declaration stance: "It is

Pic: Nick Cobbing

for those who allege that Freemasonry does have such harmful consequences to establish a case, and so far such persons or bodies that take this view, have totally failed to furnish such evidence. Rumour and innuendo are not enough to make the case." The paradox of the Federation's position was there for all to see. Which policeman, for instance, could hope to firmly establish any case if the identity of all potential suspects was kept secret from them?

Indeed, the Home Affairs Select Committee received a number of submissions from individual police officers who remained anonymous in the Committee's subsequent report. Whilst six of these submissions were from Masonic policemen insisting their membership had no adverse affect on their professional conduct, ten submissions were from policemen who claimed malign Masonic influence at work. The allegations they cited included suppression of serious criminal and disciplinary allegations, promotion preferment for Freemasons; cheating in promotion exams facilitated by Masonic connections and falsifying blood test results for Freemasons charged with drink driving. A constituent of Chris Mullin's (the current chairman of the Home Affairs Select Committee) wrote to the MP saying: "I am a retired Chief Superintendent who commanded the Commercial Fraud Squad and Complaints and Discipline Department in a big metropolitan force and, as such, I conducted many enquiries in various parts of this country and abroad. I have frequently experienced interference from Masonic sources calculated to impede the progress of an enquiry and do not doubt that improper decisions have been made along the way." Mullin was charged with not revealing any details of his case in order to protect the ex-police officer. From what?

More fearless was PC Kitit Gordhandas, from West Yorkshire Police, who wrote to the Police Review saying: "I feel that Freemasonry stands for white, male, middle-class members working for the advancement of themselves and their fellow Masons."

After a two year enquiry, the Home Affairs Select Committee published their report in 1997: "We believe that nothing so much undermines public confidence in public institutions as the knowledge that some public servants are members of a secret society one of whose aims is mutual self-advancement." The report recommended that "police officers, magistrates, judges and crown prosecutors should be required to register membership of any secret society and that the record should be available publicly."

Home Secretary Jack Straw has acknowledged this recommendation and looks set to insist it covers the entire criminal justice system. Earlier this year, Straw told the House of Commons: "The Freemasons have said they are not a secret society but a society with secrets. I think it is widely accepted that one secret they should not be keeping is who their members are in the criminal justice system."

Exactly how this is to be implemented is not yet known or indeed whether such public declaration might be extended to public servants both national and local. Certainly the clandestine leviathan of Freemasonry still has a multitude of friends in high places and has had to be dragged kicking and screaming to this point. The battle against the malignant opportunities for political and social manipulation offered by the extensive and secret network of Masonic influence is far from over.

# A WHOLE CAN of WORMS

3.5% EXTRA FREE £1.49

**Bilderberg**

BY APPOINTMENT OF THEMSELVES

## SECRET BREW

SINTRA PORTUGAL JUNE 99

**Bilderberg**

Brewing Up A Storm

## SECRET BREW

Where's it made? Who's making it?

It's a badly kept SECRET

WAKE UP! WAKE UP! IT'S YER UNELECTED & UNACCOUNTABLE

# Weekly SchNEWS

*Printed and Published in Brighton by Justice?*

Friday 28th May 1999     http://www.schnews.org.uk/     Issue 213     Free/Donation

# World Domination & Bondage

rich and powerful tastes catered for at www.
**Bilderberg.org**

*"Bilderberg, reputedly the most secretive organisation in the world"* The News, Portugal

The Famous Five. The Brady Bunch. The Red Hand Gang. The Bilderberg Group. What is it about these collectives of spirited youths that make them prone to so many thrilling adventures?

But – hang on a minute - that last one doesn't sound so familiar. Apparently the Bilderberg Group, rather than enriching our cultural lives through the world of children's literature and television, is actually a sinister, and all-too-real, *global power elite*. One moment you're being entertained by the exploits of another group of intrepid youngsters; the next, you're witnessing the continued onset of world corporate dominance. What's going on?

Why not ask staff at the Caesar Park Penha Longa resort in Sintra, Portugal, who from June 2nd to 7th will be playing host to this shadowy group, for its annual meeting. A Portuguese newspaper reporter did, but that all they got from the resort was that an organisation 'wishing for the utmost privacy' would be staying.. And you won't learn much more from the Portuguese authorities, whose military forces are reportedly being deployed to safeguard privacy at the hotel, fully and exclusively booked by the Bilderberg Group for that time.

Another hotel, this time in Osterbeek, Holland, gave the group its name after the latter met there for the first time in 1954. The Bilderberg Group is said to have been established as a secret support wing of NATO as part of its Marshall plan, launched in the 1940s. Since then, its membership has comprised some fairly high-powered figures; not only government ministers, but industrial leaders, royals, press barons and presidents. In 1977 the *Times* described Bilderberg thus; *"a clique of the richest, economically and politically most powerful and influential men in the Western world."*

Their mission? Strategic planning to hasten the pace of globalisation; not only economic, but political – *'the principal feature of Bilderberg is that it seeks one global government'*, reports Portugal's main English language newspaper. Yet they meet entirely in secret,

shun all publicity, and don't disclose their agenda to the public. The Famous Five have just found themselves in the middle of a plot by Orwell.

*"If the Bilderbergers seem more publicity shy than ever, that is, among other reasons, because their proposals, implemented by subservient agencies such as the International Monetary Fund, have caused more mass devastation in recent years than World War II ever did."* Michael Thomas Wall Street investment banker and author.

## READ ALL ABOUT IT

*"The Bilderbergers have been removed from our assignment list years ago by executive order... Our policy seems to be that if the Bilderbergers want to parley in private, leave them alone "* Anthony Holder former UN correspondent for the Economist, now working for the European

*"We are barely aware of the [Bilderbergers'] existence, and we don't report on their activities,"* William Glasgow, 'Business Week.'

*"The Bilderbergers are too powerful and omnipresent to be exposed,"* French broadcaster Thierry de Segonzac

No wonder David Rockefeller congratulated the world's press for keeping "their project" secret for so long!

\* 'Bilderberg Group - The Global Manipulators' by Robert Eringer (Pentacle Books 1980) www.Bilderberg.org

## YOUR NAME'S NOT DOWN, YOU'RE NOT COMING IN...

People who've attended previous Bilderberg parties include . Henry Kissinger, Tony Blair, Gordon Brown (chancellor), David Rockerfeller. Edward Heath (former Conservative PM), Kenneth Clark (former Tory Chancellor), Niall Fitgerald (Executive Unilever), George Soros (international financier), William Hague (charisma-bypass tory boy), Peter Carrington (former chairman of the Board, Christies International PLC) Former Secretary General, NATO), Leon Brittan- Vice President of the European Commission , John Browne (Group Chief Executive, British Petroleum Company plc) , George Robertson Minister for Defence D.Sutherland -(Chairman, Goldman Sachs International)

### SOLAR (SUNNY DELIGHT?)

Energy companies are notoriously resistant to such subversive ideas as generating power from renewable sources, preferring to stick to old favourites like fossil fuels and nuclear power.

To highlight this, activists in America have started generating power from small-scale solar panels and giving it away, a shamelessly anti-commercial practice which is sure to enrage the corporate monsters of the energy industry... The snag is that they're giving it to the national grid itself. Will the leccy companies complain about such disgraceful generosity? Watch this space... For practical info on renewable energy check out www.homepower.com

## ENGLISH HERETICS

English Heritage started work on Wednesday on their latest scheme to trash - sorry, preserve - one of our sacred sites. Holmehenge consists of an 18 foot circle of 54 trees enclosing an inverted oak tree, planted over 4,000 years ago. The tree has been named after the legendary Scandinavian tree Ygdrasil-the tree of life, traditionally considered a portal to the underworld. It marks the end of 'Pedars Way', an ancient walkway, forming a linear triangle with Stonehenge and a group of monuments in Essex. The site would have originally been deep in the forest before the land was claimed by the sea. A local expert in tree circles, Buster, told SchNEWS, *"This sacred site would have been built as a place of burial and sacrifice, the centre of the circle is a magical space, the tree is symbolic of Godspace in traditional beliefs and the ancient word for oak is Dur meaning 'door', derived from gaelic and sanskrit. The name Druid is derived from Dur."* The people who built this monument over 4,000 years ago worked with great precision aligning the four exposed roots to the points of the compass, the site was obviously chosen with equal care for it's sacred significance, the gateway to one side of the tree marking a gateway between the worlds. When English Heritage move the henge it will no longer retain any significance .

English Heritage are concerned that the site will be damaged by erosion, yet when SchNews spoke to local geographer Miss Ellis she assured us " *Due to the alignment of the coast at this point there is a constant build up of sand banks. Also, it is thanks to the sea that the monument has survived for so long, wood does not decay as long as it stays saturated and the tide times on this stretch of the coast ensure that the monument is revealed only rarely and for short periods of time."*

In their preliminary attempts to carbon date the tree E. H. have gouged out a 6 inch wedge passing through the heart of the tree and completely chopping off both the East and West points. This precise incision was made with a chainsaw!!! It seems safe to surmise that their primary criteria has little to do with respect for our ancient heritage so what are they trying to do? Blatantly they're not going to make any money from the henge where it is now, but in a museum on the other hand....there are also rumours that someone is aiming to achieve a Phd through all this, well you can surely see that the furtherance of one man's career is far more important than a sacred henge that has survived for a mere 4,000 years fulfilling the purpose it's makers intended.

Basically, someone should remind British Heretics that our sacred sites are not theirs to mess with. We have not sanctioned their interference any more than they have listened to the pleas of those who want the henge to be left alone. As work is already in progress anyone who wants to experience the Henge should get down to Holme as quick as you can. For info: www.talkingtrees.org.uk E.H 0171 9733000

## Earth Die, But We Still Fight!!!!

Says our Polish Correspondent, One-Day Action 7-8 June in memory of tousends trees cuted by Techocrats, which biulding motorway inside "Mountain St.Anna" in Poland. One year ago was 40 days action against this motorway. Unfortonetly, police and private security broken our bodys but NOT HEARTS !!!. We meet on squat Rozbrat in Poznan - Poland, 6 June about 6 pm. We will play football on motorway, some sit-in, much of fun. Propably will be necessity of using U-locks, chains and another things. (police and private security agency try stop our fun)Please take sleeping bags, candels, black wear and smile. More info akcja@zpw.most.org.pl

## SchNEWS in brief

**Music And Dance (MAD) for Humanity Ltd** are putting on a party Sat 5th June at the Pleasure Rooms in Tottenham, proceeds to humanitarian aid for Kosovan refugees. Including Trance Orbital, Irreverent Ink and ARC-i. Tickets £10/£12 from usual outlets.**Legalize! Streetparty June 5** 10 AM until 22 PM on against the War on Drugs Meet-De Dam Sq. Amsterdam. Live entertainment. FREE!**"Acme TaT Supplies"** have decided to call it a day – but are keen to pass to any sorted people with a list of their suppliers 0113 262 9365 email acme-tat@iname.com **

**The Right to Protest Forum** is setting up an organisation to provide legal observers and legal observer training to defend protestors and demonstrators. Meeting/discussion Weds. 23rd June in the Bertrand Russell Room, Conway Hall, 25 Red Lion Sq, London 0171 727 0590 jb1@netlane.com ** Rally For Socialism, in Birmingham on Mon 7th June with Jeremy Hardy & Mark Thomas 01203 229311 ** Claiming Compensation for Police Misconduct: A Guide to Your Rights booklet available from Irwin Mitchell Solicitors, Sheffield 0114 276 7777/273 9011 ** Get a brand new fridge for £25 from Fridgesavers 0131 554 2532 ** **Reclaim the Streets** preview, a video screening of past Reclaim the Street carnivals, is being shown at 7.30 pm, June 1st, at Portsmouth's Spithead Housing CO-OP meeting room**The Wanstead stretch of the M11 link is the next green space of the capital due for a splash of concrete and tarmac. Shoppers may soon be able to drive over where the Independent Free Area of Wanstonia was and the old chestnut tree, site of the country's first officially recognised tree house. Then again they could park the 'old lady' in a skip and join the No M11 Link Road Campaign which will open with a "music and gathering" event on 7 June. Meet 9.30am George Green, Wanstead **Sunday 13 June **King Arthur** will lead a **MASS TRESPASS** of the proposed Avon Ring Road. Meet at the site 12.00 noon. Bring Banners, Insruments, & Creativity.A Samba Band will accompany the march .Cyclists will set off as groups from either end of the Railway Path. Meet Brassmill lane in Bath and Trinty street in Bristol at 10.30 am. Overnight accommodation available at the camp, bring your sleeping gear. FFI phone 0797-999-0389

## TORY ROADS PROGRAM CAUGHT CLIMBING OUT OF GRAVE

Just when you thought the Torys' roadbuilding progam was dead and buried, it has been seen wandering around Essex, mumbling about smearing the countryside with more sticky black shit.

The Gorse Wood Campaign has been founded in order to bury any hopes New Labour have of reviving the Torys roads policy. During the last week a camp has been set up in woods on route of the proposed new stretch of the A130 between Basildon and Chelmsford . Undoubtedly something needs to be done about the congested state of the present stretch of road; however, a new road is not the answer. The road is being funded through the Private Finance Initiative, the same scheme that brought us the A30 extension. This road, like all roads, will further fragment what is left of our indigenous ecosystems, ie…it will basically be another nail in the coffin of our already destroyed native wilderness by agriculture. Apparently this road could be the beginning of a new London orbital motorway. Just what we need - another ring of death , great!, top one !!, sorted !!!, won-derful !!!!, fantastic!!!!! Top banana. Anyway, if you want to get yourself down there, the site is near the village of Rettendon, between Basildon and Chelmsford . The nearest reference point is Rettendon church; by the time of writing, signs may have been put up to direct folk to the site. Phone the site mobile for more detailed directions, 07957 915977 .

## GET OFF YOUR LAND

"Relocation is a word that does not exist in the Dineh language. To be relocated is to disappear and never be seen again" Pauline Whitesinger, Dineh Elder and relocation resister

The ancestral homeland of the Navajo and Hopi people is being transformed into a "National Sacrifice Area" because of the vast quantities of coal, uranium and natural gas found beneath the homes of these indigenous people. Since 1974 when Congress passed a law to let the Peabody Coal Company opencast the largest coal reserve in North America, over 14,000 Navajo have been pressured into moving, and now just 83 families remain. The United Nations has described the relocation as a serious violation of indigenous peoples' human rights. Many of those left face imminent eviction and constant harassment. Since February families have had livestock impounded (their central food and cash source) by armed Federal agents as well as restricted wood gathering, stopping the building or even repair of homes, destroying wells, capping springs, bulldozing homes and ceremonial structures, and had to put up with F-16 fighter jets flying 100 feet above the ground.

Most of those that have been relocated have been sent to the Sanders, New Mexico, downstream from one of the worst radioactive waste spills in the world, second only to Chernobyl. Since moving there about 25% of the people have died from cancer.

*A few years back when NASA was preparing for the Apollo project, they did some astronaut training on a Navajo Indian reservation. When the Navajo Indians found out about it, they asked if they could send a message to the moon on the Apollo. NASA spindoctors happily agreed (dreaming sweetly about the free propaganda!), and quickly arranged to record a message of an elder. With the recording completed, NASA asked what the message said, the Navajo elder smiled and said nothing. Intrigued, the NASA men played the recording to several Indians in an attempt to find out what the message said, but the Indians would only laugh and refused to translate the elder's message to the moon. Finally, NASA called in an official government translator. He reported that the moon message said, "Watchout for these guys; they've come to steal your land."Black Mesa Indigenous Support, PO Box 23501, Flagstaff, AZ86002, USA www.netmanor.com/unity/unity.

## ...and finally...

"Big Mamma is watching you, kid". In Copenhagen there is a new surveillance facility available to working parents, letting them watch their children and child minders from the office computer. The surveillance cameras will link to parents' workplaces via the internet. This experiment poses a serious threat to the right to privacy for both child and minder. SchNEWS wonders about the effect of constant surveillance on children and on their interaction with one another and their teachers. The experiment has been welcomed enthusiastically by officials and parents and the model will be followed by other institutions as an alternate way of getting a suntan.

**disclaimer**

SchNEWS warns readers not to get into bed with capitalist pigs, coz you'll only regret it in the morning, Honest!

STAY IN BED! PHONE IN SICK ON JUNE 18TH

# Weekly SchNEWS

Printed and Published in Brighton by *Justice?*

**Friday 4th June 1999**  http://www.schnews.org.uk/  **Issue 214**  **Free/Donation**

# Carn'ival, *n. 1. An explosion of freedom involving laughter, mockery, dancing, masquerade and revelry 2. Occupation of the streets in which the symbols and ideals of authority are subverted 3. You cannot watch carnival, you take part.*

*"We will not bow to these people. We have money to make here"* City professional

*"Banks and financial houses being urged by the City of London Police to tighten security"* … *"shadowy organisations"* with plans *"to bring Britain's financial centre to a standstill"* What's going on?

In August last year a call to action was buzzed around the world to any groups and individuals who recognised that, *"the global capitalist system, based on the exploitation of people and the planet for the profit of a few, is at the root of all our social and ecological troubles"*.

June 18th was the day picked for international action - the day when the world's seven most industrialised countries and Russia (G8) will meet in Koln, Germany. On their agenda will be more economic growth, more free trade and more power for corporations(for a low down on why these things are bad read previous SchNEWS #1-213)

Last year the G8 met in May in Birmingham. Their meeting was intended to pass unnoticed and unopposed but across the globe people rose up in opposition. 30 Reclaim the Streets parties took place in over 20 countries, whilst 200,000 protested in Hydrabad, India and 50,000 landless peasants and unemployed workers took to the streets in Brasilia.

This year's party and protests promise to be even bigger and more effective.

From radical ecologists in Zimbabwe, Poland, Israel and Portugal, the Auto-workers in Canada, the North Sumatra Peasant's Union, the Bangladesh Garment Worker's Union, the Fisherfolk's Union in India and the Independant Unionists of Austria, the unemployed of France, indigenous groups fighting oil companies in Nigeria and Peasant groups in Senegal are all gonna take part in the day's events.

Groups involved are based in each continent, so as the Earth spins and the sun rises on June 18th, actions will start in Perth, Sydney and Melbourne, Australia, through Indonesia, India and Bangladesh, moving on to simultaneous actions in Senegal and Nigeria in concert with many European states from Czech Republic to Ireland and Italy to Greece, with June 18th finishing with events in almost 20 U.S. cities together with actions in Brazil, Argentina, Chile, Columbia and Uruguay.

*"The roar of profit and plunder will be replaced by the sounds and rhythms of party and pleasure as a massive carnival of resistance snakes its way through the square mile."* Reclaim The Streets

In the UK people are targeting the City of London, because as a June 18th flyer explains

*"If a road or dam is built or an eco-system destroyed it is because an investment has been made in the City. Whether it's factories closing in Liverpool or sweat-shops opening in Jakarta, it is because the City is making millions from the misery it creates."*

And that's getting the powers that be all hot under the collar. As an article in the The Sunday Telegraph explained, *"City insiders say the police are taking the protest threat seriously and expect to see at least 10,000 demonstrators take to the streets. One insider close to the discussions said that the police are even concerned about reports of a huge surge in the sales of second-hand suits in Oxfam and other Charity shops … the feeling is that the City could face considerable disruption."*

### See ya there!

\* SchNEWS rang up a local OXFAM shop to ask if sales of suits had been soaring. A confused shopworker confessed she hadn't noticed adding "They do make up some silly things those journalists". Meanwhile other City-types reckon the suit-plan is seriously flawed "no banker would be seen dead in an Oxfam suit…everyone in the City dresses in Ermenegildo Zegna chinos". Security men have apparently been told to wrestle to the ground anyone in a moth-eaten suit.

**Here's a quick run down on some of the events taking place in the City on the 18th.**

**7:30am Critical Mass** - Huge cycle action to jam the City streets - bring your bike! Meet West Smithfield, EC1, (near City Thameslink)

**10 am Picket of Reed Employment Agency**, 87 Moorgate, EC2 - resisting "New Deal" harassment of Claimants. Haringey Solidarity Group 0181 374 5027

**10:30am Animal Abuse is as Transnational as Capital** - meet Farringdon tube to demonstrate against the City's role in animal abuse. Tel 0171 278 3068

**11am Anti-McDonalds picket** - meet Liverpool Street McDonalds. Tel 0171 713 1269

**11am Global Chain Reaction** - human chain around Whitehall. Bring banners + whistles.

**12 noon Carnival Against Capital** - a Reclaim the Streets style carnival and parade through the City. Bring things to make music and noise with, radios, food to share, banners etc… Consider dressing as a City worker or a cycle courier. Meet Liverpool Street Station. Tel 0171 281 4621.

**1:30 pm Association of Autonomous Astronauts** - protest against the militarisation of space. Assemble Green Park Tube

**4:00pm Picket of Aroma**, McDonalds brought the Aroma café chain earlier this year. Meet Bishopsgate entrance of Liverpool Street BR Station Tel 0171 713 1269

**7:00pm EuroBunk** - meet at Waterloo International for the 19:27 Eurostar to Brussels, for an overnight stay in Brussels (accommodation provided - bring a sleeping bag), then meet with Belgian and French activists to catch the 08:25 train to Cologne at 10:57 in time for a huge demo against the G8 summit. e-mail: eurobunk01@hotmail.com

**Campaign Against Arms Trade** will be taking action against an arms trade related financial institution. Bring smart clothes and D-locks. Tel 0171 281 0297. They will also be co-ordinating a "Bread Not Bombs" free food distribution on the day. Give them a ring if you wanna help cook.

\* Protest against Vodaphone, the multi-billion pound company who recently managed to twist the arms of (ie bribe) Lib Dem councillors to build a giant HQ on a greenfield site north of the town, close to surprise, surprise, the new bypass. Meet 8 am Newbury train station

.**Accomodation:**If people require crash space call Reclaim The Streets 0171 281 4621 /e-mail rts@gn.apc.org

**Legal info:**If you are arrested on the day call 0171 837 7557. If the line has been blocked call Bindmans and Co. 0171 833 4433. A defendants and witnesses meeting will be held on June 19th in Marchmont Community Center, 62, Marchmont Street, WC1. Nearest tube: Russell Square

Global street Party Glasgow Friday 18th June. Meet 1pm at Kelvinbridge or Kinning Park undergrounds.

\* Squaring up to the Square Mile - a rough guide to the City. Send a SAE (31p) to June 18 info, Box E, 111 Magdalen Rd., Oxford, OX4 1RQ

For more info about actions happening in the UK and the rest of the world visit: **www.j18.org**

\* Transport to the City leaves Brighton 9am on June 18th. Tickets are available from Brighton Peace and Environment Center. £4 each. If people want to guarantee a place in the transport get yer tickets <u>now</u>.

It's strawberries and cream at **Cambridge Reclaim the Streets** Saturday 12 June. meet Cambridge train station, 1pmCoach from Brighton:tickets £5 @ Peace Centre

## CARAVAN CREW

*"I am here to `Kill Monsanto' before it kills families like mine"* **Kumud Chowdhary, Gujarat, India**

About 500 farmers from S.Asia are on a whistle-stop tour of Europe as part of the Inter-Continental Caravan, against globalisation, free trade and corporate rule. For many women, like Kumud, joining the caravan meant leaving their homes, family and village for the first time.

During the tour, they plan to hassle the World Trade Organisation , the European Commission in Brussels and the Organisation for Economic Co-operation and Development in Paris, before converging at the G-8 summit in Cologne, Germany.

Last weekend some of them came to the UK and got involved in a genetic crop-squat in Essex. The site was turned into an organic, permaculture garden with an info centre focusing on the global dangers of genetic engineering.

Lapshanka Upadia, a Caravan delegate rejected claims made by the Nuffield Council that biotech companies have a *"moral imperative"* to experiment with the world's ecosystems in an effort to feed the world. *"The farmers of India can produce more than enough food for the whole country."*

So who are the 'moral' people behind the Nuffield Council's 'independent' report that reckon genetic food will help to feed the world? Er, reputable authorities such as the Department of Trade and Industry and many of the biotech companies. Oh, nearly forgot, Nuffield is also funded partly by Wellcome Trust, strong supporters of biotech research.

* The Caravanners are ending their jaunt of Europe with a Laugh Parade outside the G8 summit on June 18th.
* The Caravan crew were also part of the 35,000 crowd gathered in Cologne last weekend to protest about the EU summit.
* Genetic Engineering, Food, and Our Environment: A Brief Guide by Luke Anderson. £3.95 from Green Books, Totnes, Devon TQ9 6EB www.greenbooks.co.uk
* Another 'shadowy' organisation have published a comprehensive guide for people to find out where all the UK's genetically engineered test sites are. Check out the Friends of the Earth web-site www. foe.co.uk

## NOTHING TO CROW ABOUT

Police surrounded a farm in Bedfordshire last week after a member of the public said that shots had been fired and a gang of youths had been spotted in a field(an ominous combination of circumstances if ever we heard one!) A helicopter using it's 'sky shout' broadcast *"stay where you are. We are armed".* Mr Cooper who owns the land said *" I couldn't believe my eyes. The helicopter was over my house, telling me to stay indoors. Police were crawling everywhere"* The 'shots' came from a crow scarer that Mr Cooper has been using for 30 years. The surprised 'yoofs' were sitting down 'minding their own business'(yeah - and enjoying the natural high of communing with nature no doubt) when armed police surrounded them, barking orders as the helicopter hovered overhead. SchNEWS can just imagine the resulting mild panic - like one of yer more extreme paranoias ain't it!

## THE ELECTORAL KOOL-AID ACID TEST

Following a new rule for the European elections the Green Party are urging voters to indicate their choice using a smiley face symbol 'synonymous with the drug ecstacy'! SchNEWS reckons it will take more than a smiley face to impart a loved-up vibe to the whole elections farce. Apparently almost any sort of drawing including a flying pig is acceptable!

## SchNEWS in (well) brief

What with the publication of CJ Stone's new book '**Last of the Hippies**' are even the organisers of the Earth Spirit festie taking the hint? Dave Morris of McLibel fame was there to give his view of multinationals, then later after a debate about Kosova one man is invited back next time to talk about class struggle! ** Talking of **Kosovo**, there's a public meeting next Wednesday 9th at Cock Tavern, Between Euston and Kings Cross 7.15 pm ** Next Demo against **Hillgrove cat visiection Farm**, Sat. 12th June 12 noon, Dry Lane, Witney, Oxfordshire. 0121 6326460 **Demo/support for 10 arrested in '**mini Reclaim The Streets**', Mon 7th June, 10.30am Manchester Magistrates Court. 0161 226 6814**Save Our World Festival.** Brockwell Park, Lambeth, Sun 20 June Three music stages and an interactive and performance area. Tel: 0171 6400 492_** **Reclaim The Streets Party!** Sat 12 June 1999, Newcastle upon Tyne - Meet Monument Metro or Central station, 1pm Tel 07091135047,

## TIANANMEN : TEN YEARS ON

"It seemed as if (the tank's) gun barrel was within inches of my face. The treads rolled over my legs...and I was dragged for a distance." Fang Zheng's legs were amputated in hospital. Police told him, 'keep quiet' about it but he refused. The Chinese government still denies that anyone was crushed.

Ten years ago today, the Chinese government staged a full scale massacre of peaceful protesters occupying Tiananmen square killing thousands of people, followed by intense repression throughout the country; arresting and beating thousands and throwing many into jail for such heinous crimes as egg-throwing. The carnage and injustice is widely remembered, but what happened to the ordinary folk, the students and workers, who dared to speak out for democracy? Beijing signed a UN covenant last October, raising hopes of a human-rights thaw. Not a chance. Latest events show that there is still zero tolerance of individual expression which may be construed as a threat to Communist Party rule. At least 241Tiananmen prisoners are still incarcerated in squalid conditions in China's prisons experiencing a continued denial by the Chinese government of basic human rights. People who just threw eggs are still serving sentences of up to 20 years. Many others still inside were jailed simply for making speeches, putting up posters, or writing pamphlets. Their sentences range from ten years to life.

Others have been locked up in mental institutions. A Chinese textbook on criminal investigation, published for the police, lists "writing reactionary letters or posters" among symptoms of illness. Most people are unaware of the continuing plight of the dissidents as the majority of cases go unreported and often relatives can't find out where they 're being held. China denies the existence of political prisoners, stating that everyone has been sentenced according to law. This does not account for those sent to the detention camps by " administrative decision" without a trial.Following a depressingly similar pattern the Chinese authorities were in full-on control freak mode yesterday as the nation celebrated the Qing Ming festival in which families honour their dead. Human rights campaigners were detained in a security sweep aimed at preventing protests in the run-up to the 10th anniversary Tiananmen. In Hangzhou, a group of activists were detained by police when they tried to lay flowers for victims of the 1989 massacre, being warned to cease such political(!) activities. The square, in the heart of Beijing, has been fenced off since the end of last year and will remain closed –conveniently – for renovation work until after the June 4 anniversary.

Support the prisoners. Contact Amnesty International 0171 413 5500

## Inside SchNEWS
### June 8th 1994

"While out with my baby daughter (then aged just six weeks) and a family friend, I was attacked by 15 drunken students... hit over the head with a glass bottle, punched, kicked and cut with a knife. I was chased 150 yards and received a number of substantial injuries including a broken nose and cheek, broken ribs, a number of open wounds to my head, face and hands, and cuts and bruises covering my entire body, but in the course of the struggle, to stop myself being stabbed, I managed to gain possession of the knife produced by one of the attackers and five of the students were injured with it. Despite the fact that every single independent witness formed the clear view that I was the person being attacked I was the only person arrested. After spending over a year on remand, and following a trial characterised by... every dirty trick in the book I was convicted on 2 counts of GBH and received a sentence of 12 years imprisonment."

My own 20 odd year history of revolutionary anarchism frequently brought me to the attention of the police. It may be no co-incidence that the Special Branch Detective Inspector involved in my arrest in Dover in 1980 on an explosion charge was in charge of the police station in Sheffield which dealt with my prosecution 14 years later. Following the Pomona Incident(the attack took place outside the Pomona Pub) they really pulled out all the stops to secure my conviction and a lengthy prison sentence."

June 8th is an international day of action in solidarity of Mark. In the UK there will be pickets outside Sheffield Crown Court 12.30 – 2.30 pm and the Star newspaper, York St. 3.30 – 5pm in protest at the papers campaign of lies against Mark.

Public meeting at the SADACAA Centre, 48 The Wicker, Sheffield 7.30 pm speakers include Paddy Hill of the Birmingham 6.

Contact Justice for Mark Barnsley c/o 145-149 Cardigan Rd., Leeds, LS6 iLJ email snide@globalnet.co.uk

Write letters of support (recorded delivery to make sure they get there) Mark Barnsley WA2897, HMP Full Sutton, York, YO41 1PS

## ...and finally...
**"Only those who attempt the impossible will achieve the absurd"**

So say the Association of Autonomous Astronauts, a global network of those who 'want to build their own spaceships and leave this society behind'. And so they're organising the Festival of Independent and Community-Based Space Exploration, in 'London, Earth'. Those of you wondering what community based space exploration is, come to the Intergalactic Conference, where you can hear lectures on 'the everythingisation of stuff' and catch some Extraterrestrial Cinema; play three-sided football; take part in the 'debate of the millennium'- (that's Star Trek vs Babylon 5 of course)and protest against Spaceship Licensing Laws and the militarisation of space. For the practically minded, there's training on how to build your own rocket, star navigation, low level gravity practice and astral projection. If you haven't lost your nut after all this, you'll probably manage it at the All-Night Rave in Space (venue TBA)at the end of the week, which promises to make stumbling around the M25 at 3am look like a walk in the park.Contact: AAA 0181 9859981 web: ourworld.compuserve.com/homepages/infoc

### disclaimer
SchNEWS warns all readers not to stay at work dressed-up in silly costumes but to go and commit carnival sin. Then you will be content. Honest.

# INTERCONTINENTAL CARAVAN

June 99: Representatives of some of the poorest farmers from India and the developing world brought their protest to the City of London as part of the 'Inter Continental Caravan' (ICC). This saw 400 farmers travel through Europe and India protesting against the increase in globalisation and free trade which benefits multi-national companies at the expense of the livelihoods of the poorest people on the land.

# The Intercontinental Caravan ... and us ...

So there was going to be a tour of Third World activists, mainly Indian Farmers, around Europe in June. And we were asked, as the Anarchist Teapot mobile kitchen, to cook for their stay of 4 days in the UK. Fine, we thought, could be interesting...

So we drove an overloaded van to London, to Kingsley Hall where the caravan was to be accomodated.

No one knew what had been planned, so we arranged a get together in the main hall to sort it out. The organisation seemed increasingly flawed...

2 out of 3 coaches were turned away at the border, so there were only 40.

and we had way too much bread and veg.. doh !

SO DO WE KNOW WHAT'S HAPPEN-ING TOMORROW?

WELL, WE'RE DOING BREAK-FAST AT 7AM AND THEN THERE'S THAT CONFERENCE.

SHARK NOISES

heehee

LOOK HE'S AL-READY FLIRTING WITH THE SEXY INDIAN WOMAN.

There was this big conference at the Friends Meeting House the next day and we set up lunch there

LOOK, THEY'RE ALL TAKING SALAD AND CAKE AND PUTTING PEANUT BUTTER OVER EVERYTHING!

ODD

Cause a report had just come out about how Genetic engi-neering is solving all the problems of the Third World, a spontaneous action happened where the farmers occupied the offices of those who commission-ed the report (or something) to say "NO it's fucking us over in fact"

JUST SAY NO TO THE W.T.O.

but we couldn't all join in · Some of us had to Go back and cook dinner..

and after that, we went to the off license (again). The only pub we found in the area had Union Jacks hanging in every window. Not a very inviting place.

On Saturday we went to a squatted Genetics test site.

ANYTHING YOU WANT TO KNOW BEFORE WE GO?

YES.. CAN WE SHOUT SLOGANS?

Only the sikhs and the two Nepalese came along. The rather Grumpy Guje-rats stayed in London.

The coach couldn't Get through the country lanes so we had to walk a bit providing an odd sight in the Essex country-side!

WURST REISEN

..INDUSTRIAL CAPITALISM. CAN YOU TRANSLATE?

One of our lot lectured the sikhs.

It was very sunny and we spent a few hours there in which we made a stew for everyone.

WHAT A COOL BIG PAN!

I BET HE'S SINGING ABOUT BRITISH IMPERIALIST SCUM. FAIR ENOUGH..

blabla bla

The Sikhs sang..

and someone hung our flag from the tripod.

ANARCHIST TEAPOT

It was a nice day out.

— back in London... —

I'M STILL NOT TOO SURE THEY LIKE THE FOOD..

CAN I HAVE A CIGARETTE, TOO?

SURE.

THIS IS MY FIRST CIGARETTE, EVER!

WHAT?

YES, IN MY SOCIETY, IT IS ILLEGAL!

Some 'evening entertainment' was planned for the last night. We had discovered a snooker table upstairs and had been playing and drinking beer, but jumped onto the coach when it finally left to go where-ever the party was.

It was odd.

SO NOW I'D LIKE EVERYONE TO STAND UP AND DO THIS SALT-RITUAL WITH ME..

I'M GOING TO THE TOILET..

ME TOO

ME TOO

THERE HAS TO BE A PUB NEARBY!

I SAY THAT WAY!

WHEN YOU WEREN'T AT THE "PARTY" I KNEW YOU'D BE IN A PUB!

We bumped into a friend which was nice.

and we got very drunk & obnoxious. On the way back the coach did a 'tour' of the city...

AND ON THE LEFT, YOU SEE THE HOUSES OF PARLIAMENT

BURN MOTHER-FUCKER, BURN!

WURST REISEN

The next morning they were off to France...

I GUESS THIS ISN'T THE BEST ADVERTISEMENT FOR THE MOBILE KITCHEN. YES, WE ARE GRUMPY BASTARDS BUT WE ARE UP FOR & ABLE TO TAKE OVER ALL FEEDING ASPECTS OF A RADICAL EVENT.
* BOX B, 21 LITTLE PRESTON STREET, BRIGHTON...

## SQUOTES

"The direct action movement is an organic network of people taking responsibility for their own lives, expressed through local interventions, chaotic global connections and friendships. Reclaim the Streets spontaneously and temporarily emerges from a shared dissatisfaction with the way our lives are run for us, with the rat-race and a society based on exclusion and enclosure, profit and control. As a dis-organisation, RTS is mobile and furtive. It is there when people decide to intervene in public spaces, evoking the utopia of a better society.

What RTS is becoming, where it will go from now, relies on your ideas, your dreams and desires."

*'MAYBE' May 1st, 2000.*

## NEWCASTLE RTS

A car reclaimed and decorated to advertise the Newcastle Reclaim the Streets and the annual Newcastle Green Festival. The RTS, on 12th June, attracted several hundred people to reclaim a central city street for the day. Seven people were arrested.

# NEW DEALS DOWN ON THE FARM

The Exodus Collective of Luton have been making a name for themselves as a movement for people-led social regeneration over the last eight years. Now a multi-ethnic housing estate, on which many of them were born and live, is coming together in a New Deal for Communities partnership which could secure £50 million of government money. Jim Carey and Tim Malyon catch up with the Collective.

## SQUALL

Where Do You Want To Grow Today?
--
I Wanna Go Home
Underground Update
**Features**
Squall Pics
Frontline Communique
The State Its In
Squotes
Resources
Links
From Our Correspondence

"It is ordered that the defendants must not do any of the following acts: holding, causing to be held, organising or permitting the holding of, or participating in, or otherwise assisting in any manner whatsoever, any entertainment, party, concert or other gathering....at any time between 9pm 31 December 1999 and 11am on 3 January 2000 (inclusive)."

Sandwiched between the M1 and the main London to Bedford railway line, the farm was once used as a rubbish tip during its years of dereliction. "You can grow plants that will take the pollutants out of the air and the soil," says long time Exodus member, Arms. "You've gotta extract positives out of negatives. If we can do it here, we can do it anywhere." Arms embodies this principle, having served 9 months for being "pissed and fucking angry" during the Marsh Farm riots. He's now in the forefront of planning for the farm and has built a home with his partner and two children at HAZ Manor.

Constructive planning is also being put into effect at Housing Action Zone (HAZ) Manor, a former derelict old people's home rebuilt by Exodus, initially using money from the dances then by pooling housing benefit. Squatted in 1994 then licensed from Luton Borough Council, HAZ Manor now houses forty people, with a communal creche, workshops and permaculture garden.

Pic: Tim Malyon

So read the message of millennium goodwill sent to three key members of the Exodus Collective by South Bedfordshire District Council. But, with entry prices going through the roof for millennium new year events, Exodus persevered with their annual free party festivities in a disused warehouse near Luton. Thousands of local people danced in the next millennium, without being fleeced.

Most recently a New Deal work placement was being planned for the Manor. Exodus went through an extensive process of certification involving the Employment Service, Luton's Barnfield College, the County Training Group and The Training Network, all of whom supported the idea.

Then on September 18 1999, the Collective took part in an

As regular SQUALL readers will be aware, the Exodus Collective have claimed headlines for reasons far wider than their well attended raves. Throughout their eight year history they have also attracted a reputation for the stance they make on behalf of human rights and community regeneration. Tenants since December 1992, Exodus bought Long Meadow Community Free Farm on the outskirts of Luton in December 1999, all 17 acres. The Collective were loaned £105,000 by Triodos Bank and £50,000 by ICOM, the Industrial Common Ownership Movement, interest to be paid from the housing benefit of those living on the land.

Pic: Ian Hunter

episode of BBC 2's 'Living With The Enemy'. The theme of the programme was cannabis legalisation, which Exodus supports as an essential first step in establishing a realistic national drugs policy. With BBC cameras recording the exchanges, former Chairman of Cambridge University Conservatives, James Hellyer, came to live at HAZ Manor and debate drug issues. He lasted just three days before disappearing to inform local police of the cannabis smoking he'd witnessed. Although Luton Police took no action, on 26 September Bedfordshire Chief Constable Michael O'Byrne used Exodus' position on cannabis to question the Collective's application for "the use of public funds or public resources."

On September 27, the Employment Service's district manager, Dave Sutherland, sent Exodus a letter terminating "plans for providing New Deal Options on sites occupied by the Exodus Collective" because of their "open support for the legalisation of cannabis" and press reports "alleging widespread smoking of cannabis at HAZ Manor." Replying to the ban, Exodus pointed out that there was no smoking in the workplace and "the personal use of marijuana at home by some residents at HAZ Manor does not represent a Health and Safety risk to the project."

A regional Employment Services spokesperson told SQUALL: "Exodus had quite clearly come out as being a group of people that were supporting the legalisation of cannabis...if they're actively promoting and supporting something which the government doesn't agree with, for us to give public money to that organisation to deliver a contract would have been a problem."

The confrontational obstacles were mounting.

Then out of the blue it came. Almost by chance, residents of the Marsh Farm Estate discovered that Government regeneration funding under the New Deal for Communities (NDC) scheme had been earmarked for Luton. An area of between 1000-4000 households would be selected to receive up to £50 million over the next ten years and the criteria for securing the money strongly stressed the visions and decisions should be resident-led.

The estate was an obvious choice, with 31% of its available workforce unemployed (national average 4%) and a recent history of riot and social unrest. On the positive side, twenty two per cent of the 9430 residents come from ethnic minorities although, as rastafarian and long-standing resident, Levi, observes: "I've seen lots of graffiti here, but never racist graffiti."

With Xmas and Millennium celebrations cluttering an already tight deadline, an embryonic umbrella group of Marsh Farm residents and community groups, including local churches, tenants associations, sports societies and the Exodus Collective, went into overdrive to develop the estate's presentation and succeeded in securing the bid.

Now, with a potential £50 million to facilitate their visions, the residents and community groups of Marsh Farm are already coming out with radical proposals which may yet change the face of community regeneration in the UK. One suggestion includes the purchase of a 120,000 sq ft disused industrial warehouse situated in the middle of the estate with a view to converting it into a multifunctional community centre run by the Trust. Also, at the beginning of February, representatives of the Centre for Alternative Technology in Wales visited the estate to conduct a feasibility study into the use of wind turbines and solar panels to provide low cost electricity for estate residents; free for pensioners. "Windpower for the people" trumpeted the local paper.

Having only won the right to bid for the money, Marsh Farm now enters the crucial phase one of the scheme. By April 14, the estate's residents and community groups are required to have established a fully representative Marsh Farm Community Development Trust capable of interfacing with local authorities, business and service providers. It's no small task for an area of some 4000 households, neither formally defined by pre-existing council wards nor previously represented as a whole, working to a tight, some might say ridiculous deadline.

However, using a small part of the £10,000 made available by the NDC for the initial consensus building process, Marsh Farm residents have opened a community office in the old Co-op supermarket which had long stood idle with its grey steel shutters down. This vital component is designed to address a common problem of excluding residents unfamiliar or uncomfortable with formal meetings. To counter such community 'turn-offs', the old Co-op is now a drop-in centre where residents - young and old - can come in their own time to present their visions for their estate's regeneration or to view ideas already under consideration. The people they will be talking with won't be bureaucrats but fellow Marsh Farm residents staffing the office on a voluntary basis. The office is now buzzing with activity.

Exodus plan to transfer Long Meadow Community Free Farm

Pic: Ian Hunter

and HAZ Manor housing schemes to the jurisdiction of the Marsh Farm Community Development Trust. "We're trying to find a way to give it back to the people so that it stays that way for eternity," explained Steve Sovereign, an Exodus Collective member and Long Meadow Farm's representative on the emerging Development Trust. The Collective have already part raised and part attracted £11,000 of separate funding to open a recording studio in a youth club on the estate. Management of the studio will be passed over to the Development Trust once it is up and running.

Meanwhile Lord Andrew Howland is currently negotiating with Exodus over the selection of a suitable piece of his 135,000 acre Bedfordshire estate to be freely loaned for their outdoor raves: "Certainly if someone said to me, do you have a problem dealing with Exodus, I would say we had problems when we didn't talk," Lord Howland told SQUALL. "But they are very easy to talk to, they talk perfectly good sense and I would recommend someone talking to them rather than doing it on a confrontational basis."

It has been a long hard road for Exodus to reach this point. The possibility that they will promptly transfer their hard won assets over to the emerging Marsh Farm Community Development Trust is one which may surprise many. But Exodus support for the new initiative is unequivocal.
"We didn't struggle to take land to make it private to us," affirms Exodus spokesperson, Marsh Farm resident and father of four, Glenn Jenkins. "We've had 'community free' on the name from day one. Long Meadow Community Free Farm will be an autonomous unit serving the estate and owned by the Marsh Farm Community Development Trust. All the early indications are that bottom up, do it ourselves, is gonna work on Marsh Farm. And when it works on Marsh Farm it's gonna glow like a candle in a dark place so other estates can emulate the same way."

Additional information on the Exodus Collective can be found at www.squall.co.uk

Pic: Nick Cobbing

Pic: Ian Hunter

WAKE UP! WAKE UP! WHO'S GOT THE SKINS ?

# Weekly SchNEWS

Printed and Published in Brighton by *Justice?*

**Friday 11th June 1999**  http://www.schnews.org.uk/  **Issue 215  Free/Donation**

# PARTY ANIMALS

*"Sire, I am from the other country. We are bored in the city, there is no longer any Temple of the Sun....And you, forgotten....without music and without geography, no longer setting out for the hacienda where the roots think of the child and where the wine is finished off with fables from an old almanac. Now that's finished. You'll never see the hacienda. It doesn't exist. The hacienda must be built."*
– Formulary for a New Urbanism (1953)

Two weeks in the wake of police impounding the Exodus Collective's soundsystem, which had provided sounds at dozens of their renowned free parties, last weekend just one party rocked the North. The Hacienda, once epicentre of the country's burgeoning new dance culture, revered international music venue, and mecca for those of the chemical generation, was squatted last weekend for one final blow-out bash.

The thousand or so party-goers inside were matched by almost as many again outside, as police moved in at midnight to prevent any more people from gaining entrance to the building, squatted since the previous day. When their cheeky attempt at storming the building was repelled by vigilant party people, the cops went wild outside, randomly batonning anyone who seemed most lively. One particularly excited six and a half foot uniformed officer struck someone straight across the back, before this plain clothes guy cried out *"I'm a copper you idiot!"*

The soundsystem eventually was negotiated out at 8am. Until then overhead, the police helicopter spotlight swept over determined party-heads getting hauled up into windows or shuffling along ledges, and all those still circling the building.

Funny how things turn full circle. The Hacienda, whose name came from an obscure political tract written in the 1950s (quoted above, and, where unattributed, elsewhere in this article) was so-called by the club's original co-owners Factory Records and the band New Order, to echo those no-compromise situationist ideals of untrammelled desire and sensory pleasure.

*"There will be rooms more conducive to dreams than any drug, and houses where one cannot help but love."*

Pioneering in playing imported Chicago house music, in its 1988 heyday the club stood at the heart of the acid house scene, and fresh wave of dance culture - the second 'summer of love'. Venue for Madonna's first UK concert, now for a brief time the Hacienda was the world's most famous club, featuring on the front page of Time magazine. But things fell apart. The profit motive cut in as gangsters sought to control the drug trade; guns and fear, threats of closure. Then the demons took our space: after Factory records spectacularly crashed, the Hacienda closed in '97 as that same profit motive put it in the hands of property developers. The word is they are planning to turn the building into luxury flats. Ever felt the hardcore dance energy rush in a luxury apartment?

Not so luxurious, anyhow, as the Marquess of Tavistock's gaff, holed up as he is in one of Britain's largest stately homes, Wobern Abbey. We might be content to let him fester there for the time being, but that when the Exodus Collective came to put on their last big 'do' on a out-of-the-way bit of his land last May 29, the police turned nasty. After their strategically-planned operation seized the Collective's vehicles and rig at the tail-end of the party, and nicked seven, one senior Bedfordshire officer was unusually honest; *"It is unfortunate that a telephone call from the Marquess of Tavistock receives more attention from high up than a complaint from a member of the general public. But that's the way it goes."*

Exodus continued to receive plenty of attention the following day when, securing the release of their rig from a compound in Leighton Buzzard, they were trailed by two police helicopters and an armed response unit(!), while another helicopter buzzed over Exodus' HAZ Manor. Spokesperson for Exodus, Glenn Jenkins commented *"Once again, improper political pressure on the police at a high level has made them jump like grasshoppers. Previous to this incident, we were in a situation of dialogue, discussion and no confrontation with the police...but when there are dodgy attempts to stop the dances then the consensus of the Exodus Collective and the people who come to the dances is that the frequency of the events should step up."*

"Games are forbidden in the labyrinth."

For what would be the alternative to Exodus' exemplary determination? On the same bank holiday as Exodus got busted, Homeland's 'pay-rave' took place in Hampshire. 17 hours of corporate entertainment, yours for a mere £44 +booking fee (then pints £3 a go; burgers £4). Part-sponsored by the Mean Fiddler, the event's seven dance stages were all sponsored by such dance culture devotees as Ericson mobile phone company, Bud Ice and Strongbow. Meanwhile on the hill outside the triple fencing compound, a blacked out police van carried out surveillance to watch out for any 'dodgy looking geezers.' SchNEWS has learned they had instructions to move in if people hadn't spent enough money in the past hour (OK that last sentence we made up, but you get the picture).

### The hacienda must be built.

\* Anyone who was arrested at the Hacienda party, knows anyone who was or witnessed an arrest, please call the Manchester Hacienda legal hotline - 0161 2266814

\* For a survival guide to free parties (including gems like 'Wherever you party, cleaning up afterwards is essential. Why should we fuck up the countryside for a party - after all, industry and roads do it much more effectively') check out the latest SchNews book. The 260 page Survival Guide includes issues 151 - 200 and a whole lot more. Yours for £7.20 inc p +p from the usual address.

\* Watch out, there's some dodgy pills about!(no, really?!) White, hard gloss finish, domed, with identical obverse & reverse,no logo, no score,some have blue flecks inside, 7mm wide x 4.3mm thick in centre, 3.1mm thick at edge. These contain dangerous amounts of a chemical which has killed 2 people recently in the US: www.ecstasy.org

### Spot the odd one out!

*The army, navy, RAF and royal marines, British Nuclear Fuels, British Aerospace, Defence Evaluation Research Association, Ferranti, Glaxo Wellcome, SchNEWS, John Lewis, McDonald's, Rolls Royce.*

Yep, all of them except SchNEWS are dodgy enterprises who take an active role in killing people, animals and the planet. What's more, they will all be participating in the "Manchester Graduate Recruitment Fair" run by the universities and The Guardian. So, if you're interested in clarifying the options for job-seekers to promote more ethical employment, there'll be a large demo outside the main entrance on Thursday 24 June 9:45am.

\* A recent careers fair in Norwich saw the Huntingdon Life Sciences (vivisectionists extradionaires) stall occupied and the company's propoganda replaced with leaflets explaining the true nature of the company's work.

## MORE PRIVITISATION BY THE BACK DOOR...

*"Council housing was originally championed as a method of providing decent affordable housing to millions of people. Local councils were accountable through elections and could use cheap rates of interest available to local authorities to finance investment programs, squeezing out the profiteers who were making so much money out of people's desperate housing needs".* Defend Council Housing

In March this year New Labour, following in Thatcher's foot-steps announced plans to privatise over 140,000 council houses over the coming year, thus continuing a policy that has seen 250,000 council homes sold over the past 10 years.

Of course, tenants have to be balloted first to see if they want a change in landlord - but unless there is a strong tenants group opposed to the sell-off, aggressive sales techniques such as glossy pamphlets, paid door to door canvassers and the promise of doing up run-down estates puts the pressure on people to switch.

The Tories hated council houses(rents have increased by over 50% in the last ten years). and building came to a standstill. Councils weren't even allowed to spend the money they received from selling their houses! To cap it all in the past 10 years over £8 billion has been taxed from council rents, thus starving councils of the cash to spend on carrying out desperately needed repairs. And whereas housing associations are able to borrow money to invest in decaying stock - local councils can't.

So does it matter who your landlord is? The people behind Defend Council Housing (DCH) obviously think so *'Rents are higher in the private sector and in housing associations and tenants have much less security.* " Even the Housing Corporation - the housing associations' own governing body – have slammed Associations for deteriorating tenant services!

Defend Council Housing are having a National Conference on Saturday 19th June at the Friends Meeting House, Mount St., Manchester City Centre

Contact them at DCH, c/o Haggerston Community Centre, Haggerston Rd., London E8 4JA Tel 0171 254 2312

* Are you concerned about proposals for 4.4 million new homes in England over the next two decades? The fact that all the homes being built in the countryside seem to be executive homes?-Then you need to get along to The Urban Regeneration and Greenfied Environment Network (URGENT)Conference on Sustainable Housing Sunday 10th July 10 am – 9 pm Ruskin College, Walton St., Oxford

Contact URGENT, Box HN,111 Magdalen Rd, Oxford, OX4 1RQ Tel 07000 785202 www.urgent.org.uk

## FREEDOM TO CHOOSE

The Government is telling us that killing people at a distance is sorted behaviour, but deciding to take care of our health isn't. So next time you feel a bit rough and think some herbs used for thousands of years might help, don't bother going down to a health food shop and getting some supplements! As reported in SchNEWS 205, a Govt proposal will attempt to reclassify herbal remedies and vitamin/mineral supplements as *medicines*, potentially putting loads of small businesses out on their collective ears and paving the path to a toxic corporate future. For those balanced individuals whose ears can still hear what's going on there's a March for the Freedom To Choose on Sunday 20th June, 11.45 am from Hyde Park (Cumberland Gate) to Trafalgar Square. Coaches from Brighton leave at 8.30 am from St. Peter's Church, tickets £5. 01273 276648/0171 385 0012. if you feel like some direct action, 22nd June , 6 pm Jubilee Room, Houses of Parliament, Consumers For Health Choice are lobbying 200 MPs at a meeting not open to the public.

## SchNEWS in brief

Gill Emerson, featured in a recent **crap arrest** after being nicked for sitting on a wall during a visit by Prince Charles, beaten up in a cell, given a broken nose, sprayed with CS Gas then charged for criminal damage to a police camcorder, has had her case thrown out of court ** **The Porkbolter** - Worthings premier monthly newssheet - are claiming victory at last months local elections with their Don't Vote campaign. The final score was Pork-bolter 69%, All the political parties 31% "many thanks to all of you who actually got off your back-sides and stayed at home." The Tories now control the town with the backing of just 16.8% of the electorate! For copies of their excellent newsletter send an SAE to PO Box 4144, Worthing, BN14 7NZ www.worthing.eco-action.org/porkbolter** **Naughty students** occupied the National Union of Students HQ this week to demand that they support a campaign for non-payment of tuition fees. An NUS spokesman told SchNEWS they were against students paying tuition fees, but - eh, refused to support students who didn't pay them! This was because it was apparently against the law, (although he couldn't think of which law it was against), and not what students wanted (because they all can't wait to cough up an extra grand a year). Nice to see the NUS is sticking up for students' interests with such clear, well thought out policies. ** On Wednesday 3rd of June a group of activists squatted the building previously known as **Bishopston Community Centre**, in solidarity with the previous community workers who were forced to leave after a long battle with their religious owners. The church want to turn the space into - another church. There's all sorts of activities happening. Tel. 0117 9444401 ** **Party in protest against UCI Cinemas** outside the Empire Cinema Leicester Square, London WC2 on June 18th at 6pm This is the company who want to build the multiscreen shopping car-park nightmare at **Crystal Palace** (SchNEWS 203) ** GM whistle-blower **Dr Pusztai** will be one of the special guests at a debate on GM farm animal feed @The Oxford Union, St Michael Street, Oxford.8.30pm, Mon June 14th Tel: 01865 513224 http://millennium-deabte.org ** **Camden Green Fair** is on Sunday 20th June 12 - 6 pm at Kilburn Grange Park Tel 0171 911 0959 ** ** Brighton Urban Design and Development **(BUDD)** the people who organised the protests against the Sainsburys superstore in Brighton, are holding a public meeting to find out what people want on the station site. It's at St.Peters Memorial Hall, London Rd on Thursday June 17th 7.30 pm Tel 01273 681166 ** There's also a public meeting on the **Fur Trade** on June 18th at the Woodlands Centre, Woodlands Ave., Rustington 7.30 pm ** Haringey Against Privatisation have organised a public meeting about the councils plans to privitise the schools in the area under the **Private Finance Initiative** (SchNEWS 210) It's on Wed. 16th June at the Sixth Form Centre, White Hart Lane Secondary School, N22 7.45 pm Tel 0181 211 0558 ***The London to Stonehenge Walk** will arrive in Winchester on 18th June. If you want to join them on their way to the stones for the solstice call 07979 013795**A GM oil-seed rape trial was destroyed this week by sneaky Wiltshire landowner Capt. Fred Barker. The hunstman was growing the crop for Agrevo with 8 organic farms within a six-mile radius, there's even an organic plot on his own farm. With the Soil Association threatening to revoke his and the surrounding farms' organic growers licenses, legal actions would have flown. If only more farmers opted for an easy life.

## INSIDE SchNEWS SPECIAL

*"The flowers are all dying in the heat. They desperately need help."*

These were the emotional words from Johnathan Aitken's mum as she revealed that she had to sell the story of her son's fall from grace so that she could pay for a water sprinkler system at her house in Ibiza. SchNews is greatly saddened to report the deplorable incarceration of the former Tory hot-shot. The once proud minister who secured arms deals with Saudi royals was given 18 months free accommodation courtesy of HM govt. (will he declare it as an interest?) this week. It all began when he promised to use the sword of truth to expose the terrible lies that the Guardian printed, concerning who paid his hotel bills in Paris. There was just one teensy problem- they were right, so his libel case against them collapsed, and he got done for perverting the course of justice, for amongst other things, getting his teenage daughter to lie to cover for him. So poor little Johnny ended up getting shafted by his own sword. SchNews feel it is wrong to gloat over the man's demise, and are organising an appeal to help raise money for his mum's sprinkler system. You can also write to him at Belmarsh prison, where he is currently residing, but he will soon be moved to Ford Prison. Please send only genuine letters of condolence, and definitely not anything along the lines of, "you deserve everything you got you tory bastard!"

Please donate generously to the Johnathan Aitken golden shower campaign., we may also be organising trips to visit him if there is enough demand.

## Wild in the city

Typical , a bit of wilderness manages to flourish inoffensively in an inner-city park in Liverpool for long enough that even the Council recognise the informal footpath that has become a right of way. Then suddenly it's sold off for development. Who needs owls, foxes, rabbits, pipistrel bats and other wildlife not to mention many different species of trees when you can have two three-storey blocks of luxury flats, a new road and a car park? Determined to make the council think again, local residents have moved into the area occupying the trees. This area has few wild spaces, yet lots of empty buildings and waste land. So why was planning permission given on this site? The Council's own Nature Conservation Strategy states that " *the aim will be to provide the people of Liverpool with a network of wildlife sites throughout the city which are an accessible part of their everyday lives- and provide a living educational facility".* How exactly do they suppose that this planning permission will achieve that aim?

Friends of Princes Park  0403 176 279.

## ...and finally...

Curators at Madame Tussaud's Wax Museum in Sydney, Australia, have had a hard time curbing one of their exhibits' sexual appetites, *'We were finding that every time we went past Bill Clinton, his zipper was undone,"* says manager Vicky Brown. The wax reproductions *"are very accessible, unlike the real President"* she said (that's not what we've heard!) *'People tend to get up close to get their photographs taken."* The wax museum staff has therefore sewn the President's zipper shut. Shame they can't do that to the real thing and maybe sew up his mouth too while they're at it and do us all a real favour!

### disclaimer

SchNEWS mailout crew needed every Friday!

*Subscribe!* —————————————
Keep SchNEWS FREE! Just send 1st Class stamps (e.g. 20 for next 20 issues) or donations payable to Justice?) **Ask for "Originals" if you can make copies.** Post *free* to all prisoners. **SchNEWS, c/o on-the-fiddle, P.O. Box 2600, Brighton, East Sussex, BN2 2DX.**

Tel/Autofax: +44  (0)1273  685913  *GET IT EVERY WEEK BY E-MAIL:* schnews@brighton.co.uk

WAKE UP! WAKE UP! IT'S YER SUITED AND BOOTED

# Weekly SchNEWS

## Printed and Published in Brighton by Justice?

**Friday 18th June 1999**     http://www.schnews.org.uk/     **Issue 216**     **Free/Donation**

# A KICK IN THE BALKANS

"The economy shall function in accordance with free market principles."
Rambouillet accord Feb 99

"There will be a new deal for financial institutions"

These were the words of the UK's Foreign Secretary Robin Cook last week after Nato's 'victory' against Serbia. Where Nato's troops tread, multinational corporations will surely follow in their never ending pursuit of minerals, fossil-fuels and cheap labour.

For the bombing was never a humanitarian mission, but a war not only about Nato expansion, but about resources; it's a resource war which, as former head of the European Commission, Jaques Delors, said will define the 21st Century.

Kosovo is rich in nickel, lead, zinc magnesium, lignite and kaolin. It also has vast forests of wild chestnut, oak and beech all ripe for multinational pickings.

Further afield is the question of oil under the Caspian Sea. As environmental journalist Robert Allen points out *"For some time now the leases for this oil have been up for grabs and the US oil corporations have been desperate to get their hands on them."*

The problem is access. In the winter of 1997, the American oil boys began seriously hassling Washington politicians to loosen the restrictions on doing business in that part of the world. The best route for a pipeline is through Iran, a country which nicknamed the US 'the Great Satan'. Maybe not the best option. An alternative is via the Balkans, but that would require a US military and diplomatic presence to 'stabilise' the region. Enter Nato. On 12 August 1998, the US Senate Republican Policy Committee claimed *"Planning for a US led Nato intervention in Kosovo is now largely in place. The only missing element seems to be an event –with suitably vivid media coverage – that could make the intervention politically saleable…That Clinton is waiting for a 'trigger' in Kosovo is increasingly obvious."*

That trigger was Serbia's failure to sign the "peace accords" drafted at Rambouillet, France in February. The accords would have given a NATO force occupying Kosovo complete and unaccountable political power, immunity from laws, ability to go where they want, when they want, and *"upon simple request"* to be given all telecommunications services completely free. As the author John Pilger commented, *"The peace negotiations were stage-managed, and the Serbs were told: surrender and be occupied, or don't surrender and be destroyed…No government anywhere could accept this "*

**Hey, we won the war!**

SchNews aren't apologists for Serbian atrocities but what about some of 'our boys' antics.

* 1,500 is the number of Yugoslavian soldiers Serbia admit have been killed in the bombing campaign. That's also the number of 'collateral damage', sorry - civilians casualties Nato admit have been killed by their bombs.

* Professor Nikos Katsaros, head of the Union of Greek Chemists reckons *"an ecological catastrophe"* has taken place in Serbia. Nikos Charalambides, of Greenpeace Athens adds *"When pharmaceutical plants, oil refineries, fertiliser depots and transformers are bombed you create the conditions for the production of dioxin."* Dioxin is the industrialised world's most toxic product, a carcinogen that can exist in the atmosphere for up to 50 years, it has been linked to foetal death, immune deficiencies and skin diseases.

* Depleted uranium shells were being used, as they were in Iraq, where the incidence of leukaemia and rare cancers has multiplied seven fold since the 1991 Gulf War. Depleted uranium is also the most likely cause of *"Gulf War Syndrome"*, which has crippled thousands of veterans.

* There's nothing like a war for improving arms sales. On the first day of the bombing shares at British Aerospace rose faster than any other company in the FTSE index. Meanwhile, when President Clinton gave a speech in May refusing to rule out a ground war the Janes Defence Weekly Index shares rose 24 points.

But it is after the conflict that the real arms bonanza begins. Planes unable to fly because of cloud cover, rain and cruise missiles missing targets, will result in a race to supply high-tech more accurate weapons. The B2 Stealth Bomber, can bomb in any weather, even at night, but costs $2 billion a throw so only a few have been built. Post conflict, Clinton has promised to pay for a whole lot more.

* The expansion of Nato' report by the campaign Against the Arms Trade, 11 Goodwin St., Finsbury Park, London, N4 3HQ Tel 0171 281 0297 www.caat.demon.co.uk

## GLOBILISATION BAD FOR YOU SHOCKER

After salmonella in eggs, BSE and the Belgian dioxin scare, the latest threat to our health is, wait for it, the globalised economy. Despite being the favourite project of western governments and businesses, the World Health Organisation and the International Labour Organisation reckon that shifting production to developing countries where it's easier to kill workers without fear of prosecution might, amazingly enough, increase the number of deaths and injuries at work. Work accidents and diseases kill 1.1 m people a year-as many as malaria. In the US alone, occupational deaths and injuries cost $171bn a year, which makes work as costly as cancer. This suggests yet another reason for business' love affair with globalisation - western employees are expensive, what with inconveniences like pensions, national security and work place safety measures. If you poison and maim third world workers, however, it won't cost a penny and there's always more where the last one came from.

## WOTTA LOADA BULL

Under Rio de Janeiro's new arms legislation, pit bull terriers are labelled as *"dangerous weapons"* . Apparently the animals are popular with teenagers, who roam the streets in packs, terrorising the rich. The authorities have banned pit bulls from Rio's streets between 10pm and 5am, thus thwarting the young scamps who will, of course, all be tucked in bed at that time. Pit bull owners have promised a dogged non-compliance campaign.

## STONED AGAIN

This Summer Solstice we truly have something to celebrate when the sun rises over Stonehenge, the Exclusion zone has been lifted for the first time since the Battle of the Beanfield in 1985. Stonehenge has traditionally been a gathering place for people to celebrate the Solstice. From '74 onwards the Stonehenge People's Free Festival grew to be a massive annual event, celebrating the solstice in style until 1985 when the police resorted to violence to stop the party. A shocked ITN reporter who witnessed the scene described it, "*we saw police tactics which seemed to break new ground in the scale and intensity of their violence. We saw police throw hammers, stones and other missiles through the windscreens of advancing vehicles; a woman dragged away by her hair; young men beaten over the head with truncheons as they tried to surrender; police using sledgehammers to smash up the interiors of hippies' coaches.*" Although 420 people were arrested that day, every case was thrown out of court, with the police ending up paying damages. Then, in March this year, Margaret Jones and Richard Lloyd won a historic victory in The House of Lords which allows them and others the right to peaceful protest in the area. In gleeful celebration during the spring equinox, various pagans and druids were joined by the Mutant Dance sound system at the stones where they partied through the night.

This weekend the annual walk by the Free Stonehenge Campaign from London arrives at the Stones where they hope to join up with like-minded individuals for a peaceful party within the exclusion zone. The aim is to play it cool this year 'cos y' know those Wiltshire Police are easily aroused! Superintendent Andy Hollingshead promises to use his powers "vigorously" to stop any free-parties from happening. Hmmm. www.mutant-dance.org.uk

**Solstice:** The sun will set at 8.49pm on Mon 21st and rise at 4.59 am BST on Tues 22nd.

Stonehenge Campaign c/o 99 Torriano Ave., London, NW5 2RX For a copy of their quarterly newsletter send an SAE

* The Last of the Hippies - booklet about Wally Hope, one of the main people who got the Stonehenge Festival going and what happened to him at the hands of the authorities. £1 + SAE from DS4A, Box 8, Colston St., Bristol, BS1 5BB

## GLOOMY WEATHER

While you were out sunbathing, you didn't see a couple of islands disappear did you? SchNEWS asks this because two Pacific islands in Kiribati are gone, disappeared, sunk without a trace, down the plug-hole. This follows record storms and floods across the planet over the last few years. And why? The real reason is that global warming is taking place even faster than scientists previously thought.

Global warming causes the level of the ocean to rise, due largely to increased levels of greenhouse gas emissions (CFCs, carbon dioxide etc). As the overall temperature of this planet is raised, bits of Antarctica break off and melt, there is more evaporation and rainfall then it's goodbye to land masses, leaving people scrambling from their homes for higher ground.

As global warming continues, small low-lying islands will be the first to go, but not the last. A one metre rise in sea level - easily possible within a century - would affect up to 5 million square kilometres - 3% of the planet's land area - including New York, London, Bangkok, not to mention 30% of total cropland. The statistical facts are staggering, we haven't the space or anti-depressants to list 'em all here.

Read the 'Climate Crisis' issue of The Ecologist £3.50 inc.p+p, c/o Cissbury House, Furze View, Five Oaks Road, Slinfold, W.Sussex RH13 7RH 01403 786726.

## SchNEWS in brief

A Danish army officer really got on the tits of his female colleagues when he ordered 500 uniform brassieres - all the same size. When they complained, he resorted to **vital statistics**, claiming the manufacturer had told him a C-cup size 100 bra would fit 90% of Danish women. **The government is preparing to scrap restrictions on huge new supermarkets. By a peculiar coincidence, the news comes days after Wal-Mart, that's the world's biggest retailer to you, took over ASDA. Apparently Tory Blair met Wal-Mart bosses in March, and presumably promised to **bend over backwards** to accommodate them ** Behind a banner reading *Global capital can bank on Global Resistance* around 100 demonstrators occupied two banks, blockaded a third and staged an unauthorised march along Princes Street., Edinburgh, last Saturday. The protests were part of co-ordinated world protests to highlight the links between economic **globalisation,** poverty, and the destruction of the Earth's environment.**Tommy Sheridan,** Scottish Socialist Party MSP, and Ian Page, new Socialist Party Lewisham councillor, are speaking at a Socialist Party rally. Thurs 24th June 7:30pm, Conway Hall, Red Lion Square. Tube: Holborn. ** The new copy of **Green Pepper** is out now with lots of dirt on the European Union and resistance to nasty bureaucrats and greedy corporations. Send £2.50 inc p+p to eyfa, PO Box 94115, 1090 GC Amsterdam, The Netherlands email greenpep@eyfa.org **Brighton Lifeline for Kosova** meeting upstairs at the Hobgoblin, Monday 21st 7:00pm, arranging convoys out to the Balkans. Come along or phone 234 788 ext 234 or 0780 864 3523.

**RIP** . Our thoughts go out to the friends and family of Joseph Glover, one of the survivors of the Hillsborough football disaster (SchNEWS 208). Joseph, a founder member of the Hillsborough Justice Campaign, lost a brother at the ground. He died last month after pushing his friend out of the way of a five-tonne marble load and taking the weight himself.

## NUKEM, COWBOY

These days it can be nearly impossible to get a train where you want to go, so here's a SchNEWS top tip to ease those transport blues...strap a load of nuclear waste to yourself, and watch the rail network open up before you. Well, it works for British Nuclear Fuels Ltd, who transport 50 tons of radioactive waste across the country this way every week, exposing communities miles from nuclear power stations to the delights of radioactive dust and the risks of serious disaster if one of the trains derailed. When BNFL decided to re-route trains through Cricklewood, parking nuclear waste there for fifteen hour periods, the locals were'nt happy. In response, the government ordered an 'independent survey', appointing the appropriately named company, Nukem to carry it out. The report was published on May 4th and according to the transport minister John Reid it proved that the nuclear wagon trains present *'no threat to public health'*. So, who are these defenders of public health and safety? Well, CND have revealed that 'independent' Nukem have nearly £100m of contracts with...BNFL, and both companies own chunks of Urenco, a uranium enrichment firm. Nukem also has a long record of corruption and lying - they're being sued in the US for trying to stitch up Kazakhstan's uranium deposits, and have been done by the German government for bribery, corruption, falsifying documents and illegaly dumping nuclear waste into the north sea. SchNEWS reckons Nukem is doing a great job and calls on all whinging residents and eco-freaks to lay off them and get proper jobs themselves.

Contact: Communities Against Nuclear Trains (at CND) 0171-700-2393

## Not So Natty NATO

Over 300 peace activists from 31 countries took part in a 10-day march from the International Court of Justice in the Hague to NATO HQ in Brussels at the end of last month.

Their aim was to see *'NATO's plans for the use of weapons of mass destruction/crimes against humanity'*, which they said they had 'a right and duty' to see under the Nuremburg principles. These state that every citizen must act to prevent such crimes.

After being received by local politicians and delivering anti-nuclear speeches and flyers in towns and villages along the way, the marchers were refused entry to Brussels by the Mayor. The NATO HQ was sealed with barbed wire, and the notoriously unpleasant Belgian riot police were out in force. NATO allowed 5 representatives into the HQ for talks, but showed them no nuclear plans. Activists then climbed and cut through fences to carry out "citizens' war crime inspections". This did not go down well at the high-security head quarters, with riot police throwing protesters back over the fence, hitting them with batons and firing water cannon. 130 protesters were arrested, though all were later released without charge.

Two days later protestors were back again, making the arrestometer spiral to the dizzy heights of 272. This time one activist managed to get inside the main building and "borrow" a military uniform. Whilst wearing it, he "confiscated" some floppy discs, but lost them again during his subsequent arrest. The events received good media coverage, being reported across the world by CNN, but surprisingly, not in the US.

Contact the Hague Appeal for Peace, 11 Venetia Road, London N4 1EJ, Tel/Fax 0181 347 6162.

## HUNGRY FOR JUSTICE

On the 28th May a Sudanese refugee was murdered during deportation from Frankfurt airport. The police put a motor bike helmet on him, his hands and feet were tied and he was dragged onto the plane where he died from heart failure.

Two weeks ago refugees and their supporters, losing patience with this kind of abuse from Fortress Europe, occupied the Green Party offices in Cologne. Protesters were still on Hunger Strike as the G8 met in Cologne. *'We are not only exposing the racist reality we face in Germany but also the reasons for our flight, the reality of the dictatorships and the fascist regimes that exist in the countries where we came from and how Germany and other G7 countries prop up those regimes to maximise their profits."* International Human Rights Association          00-49-421-5577093 www.humanrights.de/

## ...and finally...

There were a few interesting names on the guestlist at the recent meeting of international baddies, the Bilderberg Group (see SchNEWS 213).The 120 delegates met in Portugal to discuss *'Nato, Genetics, Emerging Markets, and International Financial Architecture'*and how great they all are. If that doesn't get your paranoia flowing, two of the guests were none other than the prince of darkness himself Peter Mandelson, and housewive's favourite environmentalist Jonathan Porrit.

Mandelson is due to make a comeback soon, and with the backing of SPECTRE we're sure that all those nasty rumours about him will be dealt with, and that bodies of rebellious MPs will start turning up in the Thames. Equally worrying was the presence of Porrit's name (see SchNEWS 212 on greenwash and co-opting ecologists). What was Porrit doing there? We shall never know, 'cos of course the Bilderbergers never reveal what was said, and anyway Porrit's PA reckons he hasn't been to Portugal for years. The plot thickens...

**disclaimer: :** SchNews recomends all readers go to free gatherings and stop being such a bunch of merchant bankers. Then you 'll feel relieved. Honest.

## Subscribe!

Keep SchNEWS FREE! Just send 1st Class stamps (e.g. 20 for next 20 issues) or donations (payable to Justice?) **Ask for "Originals"** if you can make copies. Post *free* to all prisoners. **SchNEWS, c/o on-the-fiddle, P.O. Box 2600, Brighton, East Sussex, BN2 2DX.**

*Tel/Autofax :* +44 (0)1273 685913 *GET IT EVERY WEEK BY E-MAIL:* schnews@brighton.co.uk

# THE SCHNEWS GUIDE TO PUTTING ON A BENEFIT GIG...

Your campaign group's skint, but you're game for a laugh and you've decided to put on a benefit gig. You turn up about nine o'clock on the night only to find one of the bands has pulled out, the compere's arguing with the DJ about running orders, the soundman's got the wrong gear, the venue owner's demanding money with menaces and no-one turned up cos someone forgot to sort the advertising out!!! Hopefully this isn't a familiar scenario to y'awl, dear readers, but just to make sure YOUR fundraising extravaganza goes with a bang not a whimper, your hip-to-the-groove-SchNEWS massive brings you... *The SchNEWS Guide To Putting on a Benefit Gig.*

**REQUIRED.** 1 up-for-it posse, 1 phone, a supply of the oft-neglected art of delegation and shitloads of that attitood stuff.....

*STEP ONE - GETTING YOUR ACT TOGETHER...* Bands and DJs are an obvious starting point. Local acts that have just started out will have lots of mates that they'll bring along. But why not have a bit of poetry, caberet, theatre, comedy, circus......? UK readers can check out the Continental Drifts agency (see contacts) for performers on this sort of tip. Most performers are up for doing benefits for free, but the rule of thumb is you stump up for expenses, usually transport. It's a nice touch on the night to chuck in a bit of food and booze too, (the so-called 'rider' - wot no charlie?!!). How about contacting an artist with a large national/international profile, and have a local act for support? Your local library will have a copy of the White Book, a directory of all UK-based artists and agents, in the reference section.

*STEP TWO - FIND A VENUE...* Needs to be co-ordinated with the availability of your acts. You'll need to book one at least two weeks in advance to get publicity sorted. Many places are booked up well in advance, so all round it's good to give yourself plenty of time. You might need to stump up for the hire fee and/or a deposit, (get them to waive it - it's a benefit!!!). Does the fee include the hire of any PA/mics/lighting and technical backup you might need? (See STEP 4, below). If you have access to a place that doesn't have a Public Entertainments License, you won't be able to have more than two performers at any one time. Squatting a venue for a night can be a good plan, (see 'How to have a free party' - SchNEWS Survival Handbook, 1999), but DON'T RELY ON DONATIONS to raise cash!!! Sell booze or food, (a mere trip down the Cash and Carry)!!! Or another way around this is to have a 'private party' in a local hall or wherever, invite only, and sell booze using a raffle system, ie sell raffle tickets that 'mysteriously' allow the holder to win a can of lager!! This keeps things semi-legal, but these methods are skirting the limits of the law, so think about how this will affect your campaign if you're busted or you wind the wrong sort of people up.

*STEP 3 - PUBLICITY...* Flyers, posters, listing guides, local papers, the net, radio, Cable TV..... It could be good to get someone with a bit of experience with computers to get the flyer/poster funky 'n' everything!!! And it's easy to forget little things on the flyer like the time, date, place and the name of your campaign.....Schwoops! Fly posting is good but don't name the venue cos the owner could get into trouble - beware negative publicity. And avoid CCTV - obviously! Finally, word of mouth is all important, so get a buzz going, mention it at campaign meetings, in the pub/khazi/bedroom ...

*STEP 4 - A BLAGGER'S GUIDE TO TECHNICAL STUFF...* Generally speaking, it's best to have someone on side with a bit of the ol' technical knowledge. These sorts of people can be blagged from local music shops or recording studios, especially if you've got a good bill together. Most venues will have a PA system and sound man but you might have to hire them in. Bands may be up for sharing amps, drum kits etc, (the 'backline'), but let them sort it out amongst themselves well in advance. DJs need decks and all the right connector leads!! And the venue may need special insurance if you have certain circus stuff (like fire-eating). IF ANYONE STARTS ON ABOUT MULTICORES, DI'S OR MONITORS, CALL FOR TECHNICAL ASSISTANCE!!!! FAST!!

*STEP 5 - ON THE NIGHT...* Get everyone in as early as possible to set up. Bands soundcheck in the reverse order they're appearing in. Usually everyone will just get on with it as they arrive but it helps to have someone from your posse to co-ordinate things and welcome everyone in. Transport on hand is a good idea, cos things get lunched out and need buying at the last minute. MAKE THE PLACE LOOK BEAUTIFUL!! You're doing some consciousness-raising here, so a decor crew is a good move!! Or what about a video? And don't forget to put campaign related stall/posters/info around the place for easy info access. It also helps to have a right bastard working out the running order and making sure people stick to it. KEEP THOSE EGOS IN CHECK!! Remember, everyone's working for free and may have travelled a long way, so be cheerful and friendly and we're all only human and things can get stressful but it's all OK!!! RIGHT!!!

*STEP SIX - HAVE A RIGHT LAUGH INNIT...* If you've followed the first five steps, then you should be ready to have it large style by now. In between acts it can be a good idea to buy a bottle of something and have a raffle. And this is a party with a purpose, so get one of the acts to give it some on the mic about your campaign! (or get a speaker in, but not too late on, for fuck's sake, cos everyone will be far too lashed.)...

*RIGHT! SNORTED! SEE YOU DOWN THE FRONT!!!!*

# Liverpool St Station

## Before June 18th: Visions

*Thousands of leaflets and stickers were circulated in the run-up to June 18th. These are some of the messages that were put out:*

**Imagine** Financial districts across the world filled not for profit and plunder but with the sounds and rhythms of party and pleasure.
**Imagine** A world where people have control of their lives and communities.
**Imagine** A society based on mutual aid, sharing and the respect of nature.
**Imagine** Taking your desires for reality.
**Imagine** Replacing the existing social order with a free and ecological society based upon mutual aid and voluntary co-operation.

### Involve Yourself

Dream up an amazing action.
Organise local planning meetings or come to the monthly London meetings.
Choose your favourite transnational company, bank or investment fund, find out as much as possible about them - location of HQs etc and prepare fun and games.
Spread the word - print leaflets - talk to people - network.
Take a day off work or go sick on 18/6/99.

### What?

Demonstrations, protests, actions, pickets, stunts, shut-downs, sabotage, leafleting, blockades, games, hacktivism, parties & more.
Simultaneously transforming the city of London and other financial centres across the world.

### Why?

In recognition that the global capitalist system is at the root of our social and ecological troubles.

### When?

18/6/99 - To coincide with the annual meeting of the G8 leaders.

### Who?

A growing alliance of social and environmental movements.
"We are more possible than they can powerfully IMAGINE."[1]

## After June 18th: Reflections

The following is very short excerpts from the *Reflections on June 18th* booklet. To the authors - thank you and sorry if you find your comments wildly out of context. And there is some slight paraphrasing for grammatical reasons. Just remember that these comments were made *after* J18, but *before* the developments of November 30th and beyond.

"…last year, I went to one of the very early J18 meetings. Something that came out very clearly then was the following idea: "This is not another street party. We will even try and avoid using the words 'street party'. Rather, we will be taking the fight against destruction and exploitation directly to the place where much of it is controlled. We will be targeting the Square Mile. Though a carnival did end up being part of the day, I feel the 'targeting the Mile' line carried right through all the J18 publicity and planning. I personally was well aware of the kind of things that might - and did - happen, in the way of such buildings as the LIFFE and banks being damaged and occupied, and accepted - okay hoped! - that this would just as much be part of the day as dancing, boys in sexy frocks, sound systems, and running into old friends. (And) from a personal point of view I am totally chuffed by what happened to the LIFFE and other such places - it will be a cheerful memory for a long time.[2]

## An Activist Ghetto?

The tension between the form of 'activism' in which our political activity appears and its increasingly radical content has only been growing over the last few years. The background of a lot of the people involved in June 18th is of being 'activists' who 'campaign' on an 'issue'. The political progress that has been made in the activist scene over the last few years has resulted in a situation where many people have moved beyond single issue campaigns against specific companies or developments to a rather ill-defined yet nonetheless promising anti-capitalist perspective. Yet although the content of the campaigning activity has altered, the form of activism has not. So instead of taking on Monsanto and going to their headquarters and occupying it, we have now seen beyond the single facet of capital represented by Monsanto and so develop a 'campaign' against capitalism. And where better to go and occupy than what is perceived as being the headquarters of capitalism - the City?
…It seems we have very little idea of what it might actually require to bring down capitalism. As if all it needed was some sort of critical mass of activists occupying offices to be reached and then we'd have a revolution…[3]

The activist role is a self-imposed isolation from all the people we should be connecting to. Taking the role of an activist separates you from the rest of the human race as someone special and different. People tend to think of their own first person plural (who are you referring to when you say 'we'?) as referring to some community of activists, rather than class. For example, for some time now in the activist milieu it has been popular to argue for 'no more single issues' and for the importance of 'making links'. However, many peoples' conception of what this involved was to 'make links' with 'other activists' and other campaign groups. June 18th demonstrated this quite well, the whole idea being to get all the representatives of all the various different causes or issues in one place at one time, voluntarily relegating ourselves to the ghetto of good causes. … (But) part of our difficulty is articulating a sustainable form of resistance outside of activist ghettos, finding forms of engagement which enable others to participate and constructing networks which go beyond those already in place.[4]

## If I Can Dance, It's Not My Revolution

Despite having approximately 10,000 people in the City of London, only a handful of

Pic: John Hodge

# 12pm June 18th 1999

occupations took place on the morning of June 18th, and actions that were taken were generalised in the sense that they were organised in established fashion, CAAT actions involving locking on in banks, Critical Mass etc. Despite the notable attempts to block London Bridge most peoples' involvement was to choose to meet at Liverpool Street and await further instructions, rather than to plan their own autonomous actions.[5]

## Reaching Out To A Wider Range of People

…There are times - such as in the campaign against genetics and in the later stages of the anti-roads movement - when by happy co-incidence we attract genuine popular support. This is bolstered by events which are both radical and genuinely inclusive - such as the rally at Watlington and the crop trashing that followed. It is then, and only then, that our battles are won. …(We need the) sympathies and interests of a wider social base in England and beyond.

But what about all those who either out of dignity or necessity feel they must work for a living, and that they have some stake in the system that we're destroying? For me this is the crux of the issue. The key message is not to the capitalists, it is to us. It says this: 'If you have pretensions towards being a truly revolutionary movement, you must work with the people. You must listen, and not assume that you know best.[6]

## Violence

Smashing windows … piling up rubbish on the street … throwing things at the police … a buzz yes, but none of these things automatically imply the refusal of capitalist wage labour and commodities, the creation of common wealth and the building of world human community. The social revolutionary process we desire will sometimes involve a riot or two on its periphery, but a street riot does not a social revolution make. Nor does proletarian bargaining power come primarily from streetfighting. Proletarian bargaining power comes from collective withdrawal of labour, organising solidarity, sharing free goods in the community... If you lived in a part of the world where street fighting was a daily occurrence you'd soon find that the novelty wears off.[7]

We must be very clear that the media concentration on the "violence" on Friday is a deliberate attempt to discredit our movement and divide us along the line of whether we agree that "violence" is legitimate or not. …Violence was only a minuscule portion of the global J18 project and most J18 manifestations passed off peacefully. I'm glad about that.[8]

…Of course the police were more violent than we were - but that's their job… should we not ignore the fact that violence occurred and seek instead to emphasise the exciting and diverse global movement which seemed to coalesce on June 18th?[9]

## Suggestions For The Future

If we are to hold further mass actions against finance capital they should be explicitly targeted against key nodal points in the network of institutions, corporations, and exchanges which facilitate the current globalisation of neo-liberal capitalism, not at its totality which despite our understandings of the 'spectacle', or the 'military/indus-

trial/entertainment complex' remains an abstract proposition for most people. This could involve a call to stop a particular institution working for a day… by the people whose lives are affected in the everyday by its operation… We could target a different institution every six months … calling for actions against their offices or buildings globally. Instead of dissipating our energies rallying against something so big it disappears, we would be uniquely focused on the points at which their system is weakest. Imagine the police defending a sieged building of a major multinational or finance exchange when for weeks before local groups had distributed information about how it effects the lives of people in the region, before going to take part in the action. The police role as puppets of private capital would be increasingly revealed…

If we could stop them once it could be done again, and if they can be stopped once the utopia of stopping them permanently would appear almost in sight. Imagine five years from now when everyone knows how the City operates because they've seen it sieged, exchange after exchange, bank after bank, institution after institution. Imagine it permanently cut off from the rest of London - its own need for security strangling its operation - whilst its reputation as a key player in the global network of finance is devastated.[10]

How can we decentralise, strengthen and expand our networks? By next year's G8 summit, I don't know if I will be interested in repeating the strategy of targeting the financial centres. Perhaps to encourage greater local organising we should break from having a lot of organising happening in London, instead taking actions where we live all on the same day. Thirty actions across the country … linking local concerns to the global system might have more impact than focussing on the financial centres.[11]

## Mainstream Media Response

We should know very well by now the role we are placed in by the media - regardless of what we actually do. If everyone at J18 had done nothing but dance, we still would have been 'eco-terrorists obstructing mums and kids needing to get to schools & hospitals'… As well as putting effort into using our own alternative media, I am still trying to learn what we can do with the mainstream lot… (but) I will certainly not let the media affect my memory of my real experience of the day, or our own legitimate debate, as if they are something we are, or can be, responsible for.[12]

But what will people think? If they believe the media tell the truth, they'll have a ridiculously inaccurate angle on the day … I feel we have little or no control over that. I would imagine a large proportion of the population take what they read in the papers with a lot of pinches of salt, and they'll get some of the message, possibly, and perhaps think a bit themselves about the day and what it was about. Maybe.[13]

1 excerpts from RTS's 'Black Leaflet' reproduced in Appendix, 2 from Dancing On The Ruins, 3 from Give Up Activism, 4 ibid, 5 from If I Can Dance, It's Not My Revolution, 6 from The Challenge of June 18, 7 from Mustn't Grumble, 8 from Keep It Up, Don't Let Violence Divide Us, 9 from The Challenge of June 18, 10 from Give Up Activism, 11 from Not Just Capitalism Or Globalisation, 12 from Dancing On The Ruins, 13 ibid.

**Water laugh!**

# City of London June 18 1999

**Horsing about!**

**A critical mass of rozzers**

WAKE UP! WAKE UP! IT'S YER SARKY AS YER LIKE

# Weekly SchNEWS

### Printed and Published in Brighton by *Justice?*

**Friday 25th June 1999**    http://www.schnews.org.uk/    **Issue 217/8**

# SUITS YOU, SIR!

*'Booze-fuelled hardcore anarchists turn anti-capitalist protest into orgy of violence'-* Daily Star

It all started *nicely* enough- 500 cyclists staged a Critical Mass blockade of the streets, Lloyds and NatWest banks were occupied and animal rights activists were shouted at an empty building. No-one- least of all the police- could anticipate the mayhem to come.

*'Just heard that the boys at Tullett and Tokyo whose office overlooks London Bridge have been waving their gold cards and shouting 'Wankers' at the eco-warriors going past'-E-mail circulating City*

Liverpool St. Station, 12 noon: Ten thousand ungrateful, work-shy dole-scroungers gathered to bite both the hand that feeds them and the free sandwiches provided to lure them away from consumer Utopia; colour-coded party masks distributed amongst the crowd resulted in four separate columns of protesters winding their way through the city streets to converge on the belly of the beast- The London International Financial Futures and Options Exchange (LIFFE). At this point the Carnival- organised by and for a coalition of nice, peaceful anarchists- was hijacked by the disgraceful, masked-up, beer-swilling, black-clad, cop-hating psychopaths that give anarchy a bad name.

And then the fun *really* began.

*"We're being beseiged by open-toed-sandalled hippy vandals. We have armed our doorman, Bernard, with a shotgun."-*partner at Maclay, Murray and Spens ('The Lawyer')

To the noise of pneumatic drill gabba from a sound-system, a trained Class War hate mob trampled on the bare toes of decent liberal protesters and embarked on a systematic redesign of the urban environment. *'Imagine London with its rivers unearthed and its valleys revealed'* they screamed as CCTV cameras were bagged up, revellers danced in a four-storey fountain of their own urine and the front door of LIFFE was bricked up with breeze blocks and cement hauled in by crack-fuelled chaos junkies. Punk band P.A.I.N.- *at least one member sporting an outrageous mohican haircut-* baited rioters with angry hate music- with added percussion from boots going through the windows of a Mercedes showroom.

*'Five activists are reported to have shaved the head of a besuited City type, while pinning him against Freshfield's wall'-* The Lawyer

Dreadlocked crusties disguised in Oxfam suits stormed their way into the reception of the Liffe building, showering traders- cowering behind piles of photocopied tenners- with fountains of diseased blood as bare feet demolished the plate-glass reception. The masked middle-class mayhem mongers stormed the escalators in pitched battle with salt-of-the-earth Cockney dealers before being squirted back out on the street with champagne cannons.

*'Bankers, traders and stockbrokers are the real working class"* Daily Telegraph editorial

Other demonstrators attacked branches of McDonalds; kamikaze vegans hurled themselves through the windows and bombarded police with frozen burgers, urging customers to eat Edward and Sophie instead. Others covered themselves with ketchup and deceitfully claimed police brutality.

*'Schroeders were attacked by climbing nuts, who attempted to scale the building with ropes and crampons, but were thwarted when traders urinated on their heads'-*E-mail circulating city traders

Thankfully, citizens, such spontaneity is unlikely to happen again. Assistant Chief Constable James Hart of City Police has stated: *'We may, if conditions call for it, be more assertive next time; we'll come in harder, at significant risk to innocent members of the public peaceful protesters and police officers."* Or maybe they'll just ban dissent altogether. Meanwhile…

*'Next Friday will be the International City Day of Action. On this day, we ask you all to don your finest pinstripe, knot the italian silk tie, booted with British brogue, apply your monocles, glue mobile phone to ear and then head off down to Brighton to disrupt as many dreadlocked soap dodging men and women with dogs on string as possible. '-*E-mail circulating City traders (unfortunately everyone in Brighton will be at Glastonbury)

## WHO WERE THE VIOLENT MINORITY?

The actions of a few hundred troublemakers clearly intent on causing mayhem and violence marred what was otherwise a great day out. This small, highly organised group, some of them wearing suits and sporting mobile phones, managed to get into buildings housing major financial institutions. One man who didn't want to be named told SchNews: "They had little or no connection with the thousands of ordinary protesters out on the streets and were clearly intent on causing serious violence. They used computer and comms equipment and were quite aware of what they were doing. We did all we could to stop them but by the end of the day they had killed 11,000 kids. That may sound shocking, but these people are responsible for that, through easily preventable poverty-related diseases, every day . They give protests like the one today a very bad name, because they own the newspapers that print complete crap about what's really going on. It is very important that the public supports our efforts to bring these people to justice".

## SO WHY THE CITY ?

June 18th was the day when the world's seven most industralised countries and Russia (G8) met in Cologne, Germany. On their agenda was more economic growth, more 'free' trade and more power for corporations. (check back issues of SchNEWS to find out why these are bad things)

The city was chosen because it is the place, as Anthony Sampson described in the 'The Midas Touch' where "people buy and sell blips on an electronic screen. They deal with people they never see, they talk to people over the 'phone in rooms that have no windows. They sit and look at screens. It is almost like modern warfare where people sit in bunkers and look at screens and push buttons and make things happen."

It's a place where a small number of people play the world's largest and most risky video game - the money game. But the consequences of this game are very real: human lives, ecosystems, jobs and even entire economies are at the mercy of this reckless system. To the frenzied traders it's might be about just gambling with blips on a screen, but to the Peruvian coffee growers who's just had the value of their crop halved ovenight, the game's for real.

As Business Week once observed "in this new market…billions can flow in or out of an economy in seconds. So powerful has this force of money become that some observers now see the hot-money set becoming a sort of shadow world government." Perhaps one demonstrator put it best *"the damage to property that happened today, is nothing compared to the misery these financial corporations create in their never ending quest for profits."*Are we all ready for a terrorist back-lash?

And now for a lesson on how multi-national companies bribe whole towns. One of the UK's biggest companies, Vodaphone recently got planning permission to build a giant HQ on a greenfield site on the outskirts of Newbury. Vodaphone refused to contemplate moving to other sites such as the vacated MOD site at Greenham Common (which they reckoned was a security risk because of the peace women there - all three of them!), they said to the town, give us permission or we'll pack our bags and go. Vodaphone were also surprisingly enough supporters of the Newbury bypass, which was built, residents were told, to stop traffic congestion and infil development.

* Did you witness, photograph or video an arrest or injury at the J18protests in London? If so please send details (location & time of incident) with your name, address & tel number to Legal Defence & Monitoring Grp, BM Haven, London WC1N 3XX.

* A discussion pamphlet on J 18 to be published soon. Send contributions, analysis, critiques and graphics etc to rts@gn.apc.org  or RTS, PO Box 9656, Ldn N4 4JY,  www.j18.org

# "Our resistance will be as Transnational as capital"

Hey, it's wasn't just about one day "it's about building a movement. From the global to the local it's about taking back control of our lives." Here's a quick round-up of what SchNEWS has heard so far about last Friday…

## AUSTRALIA:

Kim Beazley, Opposition leader, was pied for speaking at an APEC/Global Trade meeting sponsored by Shell. Protestors harassed the Stock Exchange, McDonalds and Australian bank, Westpac who invest in the Jabiluka uranium mine. Elsewhere in **Melbourne**, bells were sounded to wake up the world to Third World Debt problems, a Critical Mass and a Food not Bombs breakfast were held. Protesters blockaded the stock exchange with dead wombats!

## ARGENTINA:

Unfortunately the report we've received is all In Spanish.

## BELARUS:

Picketers from Eco-resistance and Chyrvony Zhond gave out flyers and toilet paper to customers leaving McDonalds. Permission for a large demonstration wasn't granted.

## BRAZIL:

In **Desterro** protesters defaced a city centre clock (built by an 'entertainment' corporation) symbolising the 500 years of "discoverment" (invasion) of Brazil.

## CANADA:

In **Vancouver** a hundred people blockaded the Stock Exchange. In **TORONTO** the RTS was a fun celebration and reminder that public space is for public benefit, though it occurred very much within an imposed framework.

## CZECH REPUBLIC:

350 people met in central Prague, disrupting banks and multinationals despite over a thousand police (probably due to the previous 7000-strong street party with people from the Intercontinental Caravan, where there were 114 arrests.)

## GERMANY:

In **Cologne**, about 95 people were arrested, mainly from the InterContinental Caravan, who have been making peaceful protests thoughout Europe. People were beaten by police outside an art hall and 500 people protested outside the chemical transnational company Bayer in Leverkusen.

The Caravan members came to Cologne for the World Economic Summit to ridicule the Gang of Seven in a Gandhi-style "Laugh Parade", but 250 were prevented by police from entering the city centre. They were surrounded and some arrested, including Vijay JAWANDHIA, president of the Inter-State Co-ordination Committee of Farmers' Organisations, and his wife. Police used brute force, injuring at least two and making racist remarks, this despite an admission that there had been no violence on the side of the Caravan. On Saturday 19/6 estimates of the numbers still in custody ranged from 6 to 30 people.

## ISRAEL:

In **Tel Aviv**, a street carnival was held, and torches lit for the victims of corporate human and animal rights abuse.

## ITALY:

Demonstrators established night-long autonomous zones in the centre of **Bologna**. Similar actions took place in **Milan, Rome, Siena, Florence, Ancona** and **Hamburg**.

## MEXICO:

On June 15, the Electronic Disturbance Theatre staged a **virtual sit-in** and clogged up the Internet pathways to the Mexican Embassy in the UK in protest at the continuing war in Chiapas.

## NETHERLANDS:

**Amsterdam** protesters were not allowed any sound (not even a car radio) or an 8x6m banner. 50 people and lots of press showed up.

## NIGERIA:

A 10 000 strong "carnival of the oppressed," brought Port Harcourt, Nigeria's petroleum capital to a standstill. Many were from the Niger Delta where oil corporations are destroying their environment. Shell and Agip had their offices blockaded and a street named after General Abacha was unofficially re-named after Ken Saro-Wiwa and the old signpost pulled out.

## PAKISTAN:

In Gujrat, Pakistan there was an enthusiastic anti-nuclear procession. The leadership of the trade union association, Apfutu, which had gone underground on the 14th came out masked and veiled and joined the rally despite blockades by a local administration eager to arrest them. Angry protesters broke the police control circle. Women went on hunger strike outside the deputy commissioner's office.

During a protest gathering about 300-400 hundred police commandos arrested several of the leaders. They used baton charges and tear gas on innocent men, women and school children. 50 of the protesters were released on bail, and the rest were shifted to the district jail. A reliable source says they are charged with attempting to damage/harm the territorial integrity of the country. The punishment for this is death. Bail had now been granted to all but about 9 leaders, who are said to have been tortured and beaten.

Neither the defendants not the trade union organisations can raise the money to hire lawyers to defend them in court, but they welcome any donations to the "International Solidarity Funds of APFUTU": title of account: International Solidarity Fund of APFUTU, bank account no : 1180 (U.S. Dollars), 1181 (German marks); Allied Bank of Pakistan Limited, main branch, Chowk Nawabsahib Gujrat (Pakistan).

Supporters may transfer cash direct to the above accounts or send cheques/bank drafts to the union address: All Pakistan Federation of United Trade Unions (APFUTU) Union House, Rang Pura, Sargodha Rd, Gujrat 50700, Pakistan Tel: + 92 4331 28736/26398 Fax: + 92 4331 525302 E-mail: union@grt.space.net.pk

## SPAIN

300 people spent a couple of hours with music, fireworks closing down streets and banks and Lladro's, the richest and most hated speculator in **Valencia**.

In **Madrid** seven days of action in the financial capital came to a head with a Reclaim The Streets smack bang in the commercial centre of the city. Other highlights of the week included 100 people occupying the Madrid Stock Exchange for more than an hour.

In **Barcelona**, two small groups of people closed two main streets in. One of them, in **Sant Andreu Town**, recreated a beach and they give fried potatoes to commuters in cars. 100 people took part in action at the derelict site of a squatted house evicted and demolished by police two years ago, creating an organic vegetable and medicinal garden, with water features.

In **Sant Cugat** (20 km from Barcelona)a bike demonstration of just 13 people managed to close the motorway and get to Barcelona to join the main demonstration. Barcelona's Reclaim The Streets proper took place with up to 700 people dancing until 11pm.

## SWITZERLAND:

In **Zurich**, 300 people occupied a construction site in an area currently being gentrified and held one of "the best parties for years". In **Geneva**, over 50 anarchists washed (!) major banks in the centre and 100 took part in a mobile carnival.

## UK:

In **Lancaster** activists occupied Freshfields, a city law firm which boasts of representing nuclear, aviation, road transport, chemical, mining, asbestos companies, tobacco products and the drinks industry, this was followed by a critical mass.

500 people turned **Glasgow's** George Square into the site of an unofficial party with two sound systems, a critical mass bike ride and one old Ford Fiesta with a J18 RTS registration plate. The Bank of Scotland, the Job Centre, The Army Recruitment Office and Strathclyde Police HQ were targeted as demonstrators marched around the centre for about 2 hours then headed for the park for more partying.

In **Edinburgh** Reed Employment had paint and posters telling them what people thought about their involvement in New Deal plastered all their offices.

## URUGUAY:

The Montevideo June 18th Network occupied the main square of the Old

Town (the financial centre).A trade fair was set up, with themes such as cheap labour, child labour, education, local culture, consumption and communication. Trade unions were also involved. There was also a parade, entering into the Stock Exchange, the Banco de Montevideo and passing in front of the Ministry of Housing and the Environment and McDonalds, where they stayed for a while singing and getting in the way.

## USA:

37 people were arrested after people reclaimed the streets in **New York's** financial centre. For nearly 2 hours, 500 costume clad protesters took over, tying up traffic and rallying in front of the New York Stock Exchange on Wall Street. 2 People were nicked and equipment seized.

**In San Francisco** over 500 people came out to Reclaim the Streets, dancing through the Financial District, stopping outside the corporate headquarters of some of the world's largest and most vile transnational corporations and financial institutions. Stops also occurred at two of the city's giant retail chains.

In **Los Angeles** protesters played cat and mouse with the police as they tried to hold a party, blocking streets despite baton charges. Police were forcing people out of the park by pushing and hitting people with their batons.

More than 100 activists joined in a Carnival Against Capital in frontof a Bank **Boston** in the city's financial district. Hundreds more workers watched, costing the bankers many thousands in lost "productivity." 600 demonstrators organised by Jubilee 2000 in **Washington DC** formed a human chain around the U.S. Treasury Department.

In **Eugene, Oregan**, a parade escalated into violence as police deployed tear gas and arrested 15 people for rioting, a felony, and other charges. Three officers suffered minor injures in the rioting, as did an unknown number of protesters. As many as 200 protesters played cat-and-mouse with police for hours stopping long enough at intersections to disrupt rush-hour traffic and anger drivers, but paraded away when threatened with arrest and tear gas.

Around 50 demonstrators in **Austin, Texas** baracaded both ends of a street and took control of a section of road. The police arrived and arrested three of them.

# PARTY AND PROTEST SUMMER GUIDE

**JULY** Thur 1 onwards **Russian Rainbow Gathering**, near Moscow Tel +7 (812) 3146920 **Fri 2/4** Bracknell Festival £40 Tel: 01344 4241232 **Fri 4 Return To The Source** Open Air Festival, Tel:0181 674 6003 www.rtts.com **Fri 2 - 4 Winchester Hat Fair** Tel: 01962 849841 **Fri 2-3 X72 End of the world** (according to Nostradamous) **free party**, Spain Tel 0034 93 316 5763 **Sat 3 Mardi Gras Gay Pride Festival**, Finsbury Park, London £10/7 **Sun 4 Free Festival of Global Rights** (Hackney Marshes); Tel: 0181 808 9755 CANCELLED **Fri 9/11 Larmer Tree Music Festival** nr. Shaftsbury £50 Tel: 01722 415223 **Fri 9 Education for Sustainable Communities** at Pearce Institute, Govan Rd., Glasgow 3 pm Tel 0141 332 8064 **Sat 10 Conference on sustainable housing** by the Urban Regenration and Greenfield Environment Network (Urgent) Ruskin College, Walton St., Oxford Tel 07000 785202 www.urgent.org.uk **Sat 10 Summer Animal Fair**, Hove Town Hall, E.Sussex 10 am-5 pm organised by Justice and Freedom for Animals, PO Box 2279, Hove, BN3 5BY **Sat 10-11 T in the park**, Kinross, Scotland £58 0115 912 9190 www.tinthepark.com **Sun 11 Ambient Green Picnic**, Shalford Park, Guildford 12 noon - 9 pm Michael Dog/Mandragora + lots more FREE/DONATION Tel 0956 319 692 www.guilfin.org **Sun 11 Demonstration to commemorate the fourth anniversary of the fall of Srebrenica** when 8,000 Bosnian Muslim men and boys were massacred when the UN 'safe area' was allowed to fall to the Bosnian Serb and Yugoslav armies. Tel Women of Srebrenica 0171 465 5312 **Mon 19** The three hunt sabs who were nabbed in December 1997 and charged with Conspiracy to Commit Violent Disorder after a big day out at the Hursley Hambledon foxhunt are finally coming to court. Support them on the first day of the trial, 1:00pm, at Portsmouth Crown Court. Portsmouth 3 Defence Campaign, c/o Box H, 167 Fawcett Rd, Southsea, Hants.**Fri 16 Babymilk Scandel** - London Anarchist Forum, Conway Hall, 25 Red Lion Square, London WC1 (Holborn) 8pm Tel 0181 847 0203 **Fri1 6 - 18 Severn Revels** CANCELLED; Tel: 01452 505384 **Fri 17 - 18 Ashton Court Free Festival**, Bristol : 0117 904 2275 FREE **Fri 17 - 18 Music In The Square**, Portsmouth FREE Tel: 01705 357593;www.btinternet.com/~themagiccat/square/square.html **Sat 17 National Day of Action against Tarmac** contact Earth First! 07971 755823 **Sat 17 Derby Punx Picnic** Bass Recreation Ground, Derby 12 noon onwards + weekend of gigs **Sun 18 Tolpuddle Rally and festival** nr. Dorchester. South West TUC events Tel 0117 965 3394 **Sun 18 NATIONAL GENETICS EVENT**:Stop the farm scale GE trial at Model Farm, Watlington, Oxfordshire rally followed by walk to the site. Meeting place in Watlington tba Contact GEN on 0181 374 9516 www.gene.ch/ * to find out what genetic test crop sites are near you, check out the Friends of the Earth web-site www.foe.co.uk **Mon 19-20 Organic Gardening Weekend** Contact Henry Doubleday Research Association Tel 01203 303517 **Tue 20** - onwards **International anti-nuclear camp** near the Balakovo nuclear plant, one of the most dangerous power stations in Russia. In 1990 protests stopped construction of the second part of the plant. Contact Ecodefense!,Moskovsky Pr 120-34, 236006 Kaliningrad Tel +7 0112 437286 email ecodefense@glasnet.ru **Wed 21 - 25 Buddhafield Festival,** Somerset Tel 0181 677 9564 **Thurs 22 - 29 Annual Congress of the European Civic Forum** Stubbendorf @ Mecklenburg-Vorpommern, Germany Tel +33 (0)4 92731818 email Longomai@karatel.fr **Fri 23 - 25 Foothills Festival**, Wales 01558 823005 **Fri 23 - 25 Womad**, Reading £65 Tel: 0118 939 0930 http://realworld.on.net/womad/ **Fri 23 - 25 Guildford Live**; Tel: 01483 454159 **Fri 23 - 25 Music In The Sun**, Donvalley Grass Bowl Attercliffe, Sheffield £6 Tel: 0114 275 **Sat 24 Tissue! Tissue!** We all fall down! Action against animal to human transplants with an attempt to break world record for largest ring-a-roses (currently 1,197 people) Jesus Green, Cambridge 2 pm sharp Contact Uncaged, 14 Ridgeway Rd., Shefield, S12 2SS Tel 0114 2530020 www.uncaged.co.uk **Sun 27 - Wed 4 Aug** Sprial Women's Camp near Shepton Mallet, Somerset. Pay what you can afford Tel 0181 257 5028 **Weds 28 - 1 Aug Northern Green Gathering**, Pontefract, W.Yorks £30 0113 224 9885 **Wed 28 Protest naked** for the right to be naked in public 2 pm Royal Courts of Justice (Holborn tube) **Wed 28 National Bog Day** 0131 312 7765 **Thur 29 - 1 Aug Greenbelt 99** Cheltenham Racecourse, Cotswolds, £60 0845 845 0021 www.greenbelt.org.uk **Fri 30 - 8 Aug The 4th Anarchist summercamp,** nr.Hannover, Germany Tel 0049 531 82909 **Fri 30 - 1 Aug** Organic Food and Wine Festival at Royal Horticultural Halls, London, SW1 Tel 0181 746 2832 **Sat 31 - 1 Aug Brighton Festival**, Stanmer Park **Sat 31 - 2 Setting up Ecological Communities** course at Stepping Stones Coop, Wales 0870 7332538 **Sat 31 Sexual Freedom Parade** 2pm Soho Sq., London, W1. Sexual Freedom Coalition 0171 460 1979 www.sfc.org.uk

**AUGUST** There's loads of eclipse events in the 'line of totality', all of which will see you seriously out of pocket, so keep your ears to the ground for free events. The police have already promised to use the party-pooping 'five mile exclusion zone' powers contained in the Criminal Justice Act if they think a rave might take place, so use your wits - and respect the land. **Sun 1 Sunsplash 99** www.reggaesunsplash.co.uk **Sun 1-2 Ecotopia** nr. Timisoara, Romania solar eclipse info EYFA, Postbus 94115, 1090 GC Amsterdam, The Netherlands Tel + 31 20 665 7743 **Sun 1 - 15 Moonshadow Eclipse Family Camp**, Cornwall 0181 941 6277 **Sun 1 - 21 Green Futures Eclipse Family Camp** - a snip at £200 01736 788926 **Fri 6 Hiroshima Day Fri 6 - Sat 8 The Big Chill 'Enchanted Garden 99'**, Salisbury £73 Tel: 0181 372 9735 www.bigchill.co.uk **Fri 6 - 13 Zac's Tipi's Total Eclipse Camp** (family friendly) 01558 685682 **Fri 6 - 12 Megadog Essential Total Eclipse FestivaL**, Plymouth £95 Tel:0181 806 6242 www.megadog.net **Fri 6 - 15 Sunshadow Festival**, Torpoint, Cornwall £85 Tel: 01502 230387 www.sunshadow.com **Sat 7 - 12 Eclipse Party**, Cornwall Tel: 0161 860 6472 £25 www.splintered.demon.co.uk/eclipse/ **Sat 7 - 14 Lizard Festival**, Goonhilly Down, Cornwall £125 Tel: 0906 2102376(25pp/m) www.lizard.net **Sat 14 - 17 Cornish Eclipse Stone Festival**, nr.Lostwithiel **Sat 7-8 Organic Gardening** Weekend - Henry Doubleday Research Assocation 01203 303517 **Mon 9 - 16 Solipse**; Tel: 0049 30 440 56263 www.solipse.com **Mon 9 Nagasaki Day Mon 9 - 16 If i had a hammer.**Trident Ploughshares 2000 Disarmament Camp at Coulport Trident missile base, Scotland Tel 01603 611953 www.gn.apc.org/tp2000/ **Tue 10 Prisoner Justice Day** This day has been commemorated in several countries since 1976. This year in the UK the focus is on the notorious Woodhill control unit in Milton Keynes. Opened last year, it consists of 3 units, where prisoners considered too "subversive" to be contained in the mainstream of the prison system can be arbitrarily confined until they "progress" with the behaviour modification programme. More details from Anarchist Black Cross (London), 27 Old Gloucester St., London, WC1N 3XX email londonabc@hotmail.com **Wed 11 Total Solar Eclipse** Devon/Cornwall 11.11 am **Wed 11 Tribal Gathering**, Men-an-Toll, Cornwall FREE **Thur 12 Day of action against the glorious Twelfth** (protest against the start of the grouse shooting season) Hunt Sabs Assocation 01273 622827 **Fri 13 Abbey Park Festival** Leicester Tel: 0116 2673196 **Fri 13-14 Cropredy** (Fairport Convention) Festival, Oxfordshire Tel: 01869 338853 **Sat 14 Brighton Gay Pride** FREE 01273 730562 **Sun 15 National Vegan Festival**, Camden Centre, Bidborough St., London WC1 0181 670 9585 **Sun 15 Smokey Bears Picnic**, 2 pm Southsea Common, Portsmouth FREE **Wed 18 - 23 Earth First!** Summer Gathering in East Anglia. Contact 0113 262 9365 www.eco-action.org/gathering **Sat 21 - 22 V99** Weston Park, Staffs £70 Tel: 01142 554973 **Sat 21 - 22 V99** Chelmsford £70 Tel: 01142 554973; **Mon 23 - 26** second conference of the **People's Global Action against 'free' trade** and the World Trade Organisation.Hosted by the Karnataka State Farmers Association in Bangalore, India. www.agp.org **Tue 24 Aug - 19 Sept Apple** - a story of club culture The Etcetera Theatre (above the Oxford Arms), Camden Town, London NW1 **Fri 27 - 29 Reading Festival** £78 Tel: 0181 961 5490 if you must **Fri 27 - 30 Exodus festival**, Long Meadow Farm, Charlton, Beds FREE 01582 508936 **Sat 28 - 30 Leeds Festival** Tel: 0181 961 5490 www.readingfestival.com/ **Sun 29-30 Notting Hill Carnival**, FREE **Mon 30 Sutton Green Fair**, Carshalton Park, Ruskin Rd., Carshalton, Surrey. 10.30 am - 8 pm 0181 647 7706

**SEPTEMBER** **Fri 3-5 Building Sustainable Economies**, Centre for Alternative Technology/, Machynlleth,SY20 9AZ ATA .co.uk **www.cat.org.uk/** **Sat 11 Norwich Reclaim The Streets** 0793 1308091 **Sat 11 National demo at Wickham Research Laboratories** 12 noon meet in Mill Lane car park Tel 01705 588516 **Tue14-17 Demonstrations against the Defence Systems Equipment International**, Chertsey and London Docklands arms fair. Campaign Against The Arms Trade 0171 281 0297

**OCTOBER** **Sat 16 Anarchist Bookfair**, Conway Hall, Red Lion Square, Holborn, London 0191 2479249 **Mon 18** Marks the **15th anniversary of Veggies catering** company to be celebrated with parties and picnics. The comprehensive Animal Contacts Directory is available for £4/3.50 from Veggies Catering Campaign. Tel: 0115 958 5666 E-mail: veggies@veggies.org.uk A book is to be published, if you've got any submissions should be sent to 180 Mansfield Rd., Nottingham, NG1 3HW **Fri 15 23 Aberdeen Alternative Festival** http://dspace.dial.pipex.com/abfest

**NOVEMBER** **Tue 2 - 4 Shut down the Copex arms and equipment fair** at Sandown Park.This is the place to be if you are a dictactor on the look out for the latest in electro-shock batons or other torture equipment. Campaign Against The Arms Trade, 11 Goodwin St., London, N4 3HQ Tel 0171 281 0297 www.gn.apc.org/caat

**DECEMBER** **Wed 22nd Winter Solstice and Full Moon Sat 1/1/00**.**Satanic orgy** Royston Parish Church. Please bring condoms and a partner **REGULAR; Rebal Alliance** last Weds every mnth 7pm upstairs @ Hobgoblin Pub (next one 30 June) **London Reclaim The Streets** meet every Tuesday 7pm - Cock Tavern pub, Phoenix Road, Euston. Tel 0171 281 4621 rts@gn.apc.org **SQUALL** Crew presents **COMMOTION** every alternate Friday(next one 2nd July)Pembury Tavern, Amhurst Rd., Dalston Lane, London www.squall.co.uk/
London Anarchist Forum meet every Friday 8pm Conway Hall, 25 Red Lion Square, London WC1r (Holborn tube) Tel 0181 847 0203 *
**FOR MORE PARTY & PROTEST INFO CHECK OUT** www.guilfin.org * www.bassdove.demon.co.uk * www.cobaltmagazine.demon.co.uk

## YOU WTO MATE? IT AIN'T ALL OVER?

Unfortunately, global capitalism has obviously managed to survive June 18th and so the process of stripping away what minimal protection the inhabitants and environment of planet Earth currently enjoy continues.

After the big G8 shindig at Cologne, the next date on the calendar of the world's power elite is 29th November, when the 3rd Ministerial Conference of the World Trade Organisation (WTO) will start in Seattle, USA.

Here high ranking representatives of member states will continue shaping what has been called 'the constitution of a single global economy.' Feeling nervous? You should be - that quote was from ex WTO head Renato Ruggiero. Since its birth in 1995 the WTO has, surprise, surprise, become almost entirely dominated by the big economic powers, who have vast technical, political and economic resources deployed to ensure 'negotiations' go their way. Most 'agreements' are dreamed up in small, informal meetings of Western officials, and then forced onto developing nations, whose small, under-resourced and overworked delegations have little chance of getting a word in edgeways.

Even big powers like the EU can feel the wrath of the WTO's unelected globalising maniacs - which is why we are being forced to buy all our bananas from one of Clinton's funders, not just the 70% we already did buy from exploitative US firms in Latin America. Its also why we shall soon be importing US beef pumped full of carcinogenic hormones.

What can we expect from Seattle99? More of the same, of course. The Millennium Round of "negotiations" will focus on amongst other things TRIPs. This one is unfortunately not about acid legalisation, but the sinister stitch-up which allows US agribusiness companies to patent plants that farmers and herbalists have been using for thousands of years, and them charge them for the right to continue using them. So, what are we gonna do about it? As SchNEWS went to press we were awaiting info on the plans for the resistance. We can tell you that there will be a second Inter-Continental Caravan from Latin America, and expect J18 style antics. Watch this space. PGA_Seattle99-subscribe@listbot.com

## *Gaviotas* - a village to reinvent

the world by Alan Weisman (Green Books) This is one of the most amazing, inspiring books you'll ever read. Over the past 30 years, the Gaviotas community have turned parched savannah into a sustainable forest of Eden, despite being surrounded by the violence of Colombia. But this isn't some hippie drop-out commune, Gaviotas have searched and come up with solutions - dreamers who put their words into practice, and for the most part got it right. "Surrounded by a land seen either as empty or plagued with misery, they had forged a way and a peace they believed could prosper long after the last drop of the earth's petroleum was burned away. They were so small, but their hope was great enough to brighten the planet turning beneath them, no matter how much their fellow humans seemed bent on wrecking it."

Order from Green Books Ltd, Foxhole, Dartington, Totness, Devon, TQ9 6EB Tel 01803 863260 www.greenbooks.co.uk . £17.95 Or get yor library to stock it(ISBN 0 930031 95 4)

**RADIO 4A**, July 4th, 106.6 FM, Independence Day special, Analysis on Kosova, June 18th, Britains part in the arms trade + usual mayhem 11am - 7 pm www.indifference.demon.co.uk/radio4a, email radio4a@hotmail.com

---

# CAMP ROUND UP

Want something to do this summer - why not get along to a protest camp?

**GORSE WOOD, ESSEX** A new anti-road camp set up to stop the A170 bypass from Chelmsford to Southend, to be built under the Private Finance Inititive Scheme. Directions -go round the back of All Saints Church in Rettendon, and follow the path round until you come to the camp. 07957 915977

**ARTHURS/CEDARS WOOD** The camps are in National Trust owned woodland, but despite that Manchester airport want the trees chopped cos they might block radar signals. Directions: near Oversley Lodge Farm, Altrincham R., Styal, Wilmslow, Cheshire. Tel 0161 225 4863/07931 931850

Victory! Plans to trash a neglected woodland **HAGBOURNE COPSE** by junction 16 of the M4 have been dropped. The woodland was up for sale and the agents dealing with it just love industrial development. However, after the Rational Trust, threatened direct action, the sale was dropped. Rational Trust, c/o 21 Beaulieu Close, Swindon SN5 8AQ.

**AVON RING ROAD** The Camp to stop 'Bristols answer to the M25' was recently evicted. A fun day and further actions are planned for 28th July. 0797 9990389

**BIRMINGHAM RELIEF ROAD**

The campaign to stop England's first toll motorway continues despite the camp being evicted last Friday. The road will be 27 miles long and will pave the way for greenbelt expansion along its route. A new camp is promised soon. 07931 161761

**FASLANE PEACE CAMP**

Still hassling the Trident nuclear base next door after 16 years! The latest is that there's a massive development under construction on the west bank of Loch Lomond. Trees have been cut down, a long-established swan's nest trashed, 2 lagoons filled in, so a golf course, hotel/lodges can be built. People are badly needed, a camp is planned and there's strong local support. 5th July there's a Reclaim the Loch meet Balloch train Station 11am. 01436 820901

The Anti-Wicca War" is a new book out that covers the 3 years of the **Pressmennan Wood** campaign in Scotland exposing how the bureaucratic process was rigged, and also talks about the importance of ancient woods especially their use in alchemy. The woodland is still under threat despite ancient woodland covering a mere 1% of Scotland - over 300 of the trees are due to be felled in the autumn. To get involved email lothian@burn.ucsd.edu To buy the book send £5 (includes postage) to Potent Productions c/o PO Box 1021,Edinburgh. EH8 9PW

## FREE PARTY GUIDELINES

Despite the best efforts of the authorities, people are still putting on free parties up and down the country. Here's a few do's and don'ts just in case you stumble wide-eyed across one:

* Be prepared to be self-sufficient. Facilities will be minimal.

*Park sensibly, keep site roads clear.

*Be friendly to local residents, ramblers etc. Smile - you're at a free party!

* Bury your shit!

* Don't trash the site - take a bin bag.

* Fires - use dead not live wood (it doesn't burn)

*Make a donation - if someone passes a bucket round, don't be a mean git. It costs money to put on a free event.

* Know your rights - get yourself a BUST CARD, 10p from Release. Advice line 0171 729 9904.

## SchNEWS *SURVIVIAL GUIDE*

If you like this piece of paper you have in your grubby Glastonbury hand, why not get a copy of our all new 260 page book. Includes issues 151-200 +photos, cartoons and other articles to help you survive the new millenium, & comprehensive database of over 500 grassroots organisations. Yours for £7.20 (inc.p+p). Don't forget our other books, **SchNEWS Annual** (issues 101 - 150), **SchNewsround** (issues 51 - 100) Both £5 inc. p+p. Or get all three books for just £15 inc postage

---

# *STONEHENGE*

"Excuse me, Mr.Policeman, why are you in riot gear, guarding a load of old stones."

Down came the fence, and in poured the people, heading for the five thousand year old Stone circle. It was nearly two hours before the Cavalry started clearing people out. Private security swung punches and cops dragged people away while all the time a helicopter with spotlight buzzed nosily overhead. Next from the darkness came the riot cops, dog-handlers and the horses, their heads flashing with red-lights, pushing people back out over the fence.

The next few hours were a surreal stand-off as the sunrise began in earnest. Every now and then someone made a dash for it, there was the obligatory naked protest, while others who had managed to clamber onto the relative safety of the stones were joined by people who had been given tickets by English Heritage. About 500 people had gathered now, watching through the lines of riot cops as the sun began its spectacular sun-rise. With the 4 mile Exclusion Zone recently ruled illegal in the High Court, this was the nearest most people had got in years.

Stonehenge means a lot of different things to a lot of people. To some it is a spiritual home – so imagine if you can, being at a church service, surrounded by riot police who every now and then throw someone out who hasn't got a 'ticket'. To others it has been the scene of so many broken bones, arrests and trashed vehicles as the authorities put their foot down hard on the free festival scene.

The next night people again headed for the Stones, but this time even the ticket-holders were banned by English Heritage. As one veteran put it *"You don't stop the whole football season because of a twenty minute pitch invasion."*

* In 1985 a large convoy of vehicles on their way to Stonehenge were forced into a field and brutally attacked by cops. It has gone down in traveller folklore as the 'Battle of the Beanfield'. For a copy of the video 'Operation Solstice' send £8 inc p+p (cheques made payable to Neil Goodwin) to 37 Nightingale Road, Wanstead, London, E11 2HD. Essential.

* Stonehenge Campaign newsletter Send SAE + donation to 99 Torriano Ave., London, NW5 2RX

* 'Last of the Hippies ' Wally Hope was one of the people who got the StonehengeFestival going in the early 70's, and met with a very suspicious death £1 + SAE from DS4A, Box 8, 82 Colston St., Bristol,BS1

## ONE LUMP OR TWO?

Monsanto's aspartame nutrasweet slowly destroys the nervous system. It is made up of 3 neurotoxins - phenylalanine (20 million people cannot metabolose it); Methonol (wood alcohol, deadly to diabetics). Monsanto fund the American Diabetics Association - funny that)& Aspartic Acid (a substance that rots the brain especially of new born babies) Symptons of aspartame include convulsions, loss of memory, cramps, dizziness, headaches, depression, anxiety attacks -so beware, it may be sugar free but it ain't poison free. Info from Dr.HJ Roberts (diabetics specialist and world expert an aspartame poisoning)

### *...and finally...*

If you think you are too small to make a difference, try sleeping with a mosquito

### disclaimer

SchNEWS warns all readers that if they got a bit carried away in the heat of the day last Friday and forgot to put on a disguise, lay low for a bit. Don't go on any demo's, cut/bleach/perm your hair, grow a beard (ok, maybe not) get some cosmetic surgery (and let's face it some of you ugly-bugs need it, this'll just give you the perfect excuse), then hopefully you won't get your collar felt. Honest.

**Disclaimer PS:** please don't take peoples masks off - if someone's a bit shy and doesn't want to reveal their identity, that's up to then. No-one runs up to you and forces a balaclava over your head now do they?

---

# The STORMING of The CITY

'BOOZE-FUELLED HARDCORE ANARCHISTS TURN ANTI-CAPITALIST PROTEST INTO ORGY OF VIOLENCE' — DAILY STAR

It all started *nicely* enough — 500 cyclists staged a Critical Mass blockade of the streets, Lloyds and NatWest banks were occupied and animal rights activists shouted at an empty building. No-one — least of all the police — could anticipate the mayhem to come.

'JUST HEARD THAT THE BOYS AT TULLETT AND TOKYO WHOSE OFFICE OVERLOOKS LONDON BRIDGE HAVE BEEN WAVING THEIR GOLD CARDS AND SHOUTING 'WANKERS!' AT THE ECO-WARRIORS GOING PAST' — E-MAIL CIRCULATING CITY

Liverpool Street Station, 12 noon: Ten thousand ungrateful work-shy dole-scroungers gathered to bite both the hand that feeds them and the free sandwiches provided to lure them away from consumer Utopia; colour-coded party masks distributed amongst the crowd resulted in four separate columns of protesters winding their way through the city streets to converge on the belly of the beast — The London International Financial Futures and Options Exchange (LIFFE). At this point the Carnival — organised by and for a coalition of nice peaceful anarchists — was hijacked by the disgraceful, masked-up, beer-swilling, black-clad, cop-hating psychopaths that give anarchy a bad name.
And then the fun *really* began.

'WE'RE BEING BESEIGED BY OPEN-TOED-SANDALLED HIPPY VANDALS. WE HAVE ARMED OUR DOORMAN, BERNARD, WITH A SHOT-GUN' — PARTNER AT MACLAY, MURRAY AND SPENS ('THE LAWYER')

FUCK OFF!

DESTROY THE LOT

KILL!   KILL!

666

666

GOSH! MONEY'S UNCOOL

CAPITALISTS ARE SO NAUGHTY

FUCK THE FRENCH

To the noise of pneumatic drill gabba from a sound-system, a trained Class War hate mob trampled on the bare toes of decent liberal protesters and embarked on a systematic redesign of the urban environment. 'IMAGINE LONDON WITH ITS RIVERS UNEARTHED AND ITS VALLEYS REVEALED,' they screamed as CCTV cameras were bagged up, revellers danced in a four-storey fountain of their own urine and the front door of LIFFE was bricked up with breeze blocks and cement hauled in by crack-fuelled chaos junkies. Punk band P.A.I.N. — AT LEAST ONE MEMBER SPORTING AN OUTRAGEOUS MOHICAN HAIRCUT— baited rioters with angry hate music — with added percussion from boots going through the windows of a Mercedes showroom.

'FIVE ACTIVISTS ARE REPORTED TO HAVE SHAVED THE HEAD OF A BESUITED CITY TYPE WHILE PINNING HIM AGAINST FRESHFIELD'S WALL' —'THE LAWYER'

Dreadlocked crusties disguised in Oxfam suits stormed their way into the reception of the LIFFE building, showering traders – cowering behind piles of photocopied tenners – with fountains of diseased blood as bare feet demolished the plate-glass reception. The masked middle-class mayhem mongers stormed the escalators in pitched battle with salt-of-the-earth Cockney dealers before being squirted back out on the street with champagne cannons.

'BANKERS, TRADERS AND STOCKBROKERS ARE THE REAL WORKING CLASS'
—DAILY TELEGRAPH EDITORIAL

Other demonstrators attacked branches of McDonalds; kamikaze vegans hurled themselves through the windows and bombarded police with frozen burgers, urging customers to eat Edward and Sophie instead. Others covered themselves with ketchup and deceitfully claimed police brutality.

666

'SCHROEDER'S WERE ATTACKED BY CLIMBING NUTS WHO ATTEMPTED TO SCALE THE BUILDING WITH ROPES AND CRAMPONS, BUT WERE THWARTED WHEN TRADERS URINATED ON THEIR HEADS'
—E-MAIL CIRCULATING CITY TRADERS

Thankfully, citizens, such spontaneity is unlikely to happen again. Assistant Chief Constable James Hart of City Police has stated 'WE MAY, IF CONDITIONS CALL FOR IT, BE MORE ASSERTIVE NEXT TIME; WE'LL COME IN HARDER, AT SIGNIFICANT RISK TO INNOCENT MEMBERS OF THE PUBLIC, PEACEFUL PROTESTERS AND POLICE OFFICERS.' Or maybe they'll just ban dissent altogether.

ARTWORK PETE LOVEDAY TEXT FROM SCHNEWS

Meanwhile..... 'NEXT FRIDAY WILL BE THE INTERNATIONAL CITY DAY OF ACTION. ON THIS DAY WE ASK YOU ALL TO DON YOUR FINEST PINSTRIPE, KNOT THE ITALIAN SILK TIE, BOOTED WITH BRITISH BROGUE, APPLY YOUR MONOCLE, GLUE MOBILE PHONE TO EAR AND THEN HEAD OFF DOWN TO BRIGHTON TO DISRUPT AS MANY DREADLOCKED SOAP DODGING MEN AND WOMEN WITH DOGS ON STRING AS POSSIBLE.' — E-MAIL CIRCULATING CITY TRADERS (Unfortunately everyone in Brighton will be at Glastonbury!)

## WHO WERE THE VIOLENT MINORITY?

The actions of a few hundred troublemakers clearly intent on causing mayhem and violence marred what was otherwise a great day out. This small highly organised group, some of them wearing suits and sporting mobile phones, managed to get into buildings housing major financial institutions. One man who didn't want to be named told SchNews:

'THEY HAD LITTLE OR NO CONNECTION WITH THE THOUSANDS OF ORDINARY PROTESTERS OUT ON THE STREETS AND WERE CLEARLY INTENT ON CAUSING SERIOUS VIOLENCE. THEY USED COMPUTER AND COMMS EQUIPMENT AND WERE QUITE AWARE OF WHAT THEY WERE DOING.

'WE DID ALL WE COULD TO STOP THEM BUT BY THE END OF THE DAY THEY HAD KILLED 11,000 KIDS.

'THAT MAY SOUND SHOCKING, BUT THESE PEOPLE ARE RESPONSIBLE FOR THAT, THROUGH EASILY PREVENTABLE POVERTY-RELATED DISEASES, EVERY DAY. THEY GIVE PROTESTS LIKE THE ONE TODAY A VERY BAD NAME, BECAUSE THEY OWN THE NEWSPAPERS THAT PRINT COMPLETE CRAP ABOUT WHAT'S REALLY GOING ON.

'IT IS VERY IMPORTANT THAT THE PUBLIC SUPPORTS OUR EFFORTS TO BRING THESE PEOPLE TO JUSTICE.'

A COOL HAND VISIONS STRIP

City high-flyers

"Would you like a merchant bank?"

Bringing planet earth to the commercial world

# Active on the airwaves

Airto Coral catches up with Interference FM, the pirate politico's

SQUALL

Where Do You Want To Grow Today?
--
I Wanna Go Home
Underground Update
Features
Squall Pics
Frontline Communique
The State Its In
Squotes
Resources
Links
From Our Correspondence

Teletext March 1 1998......pirate radio activists make unexpected appearance on airwaves. According to The Times newspaper two days later, the Countryside Alliance had sold 50,000 ear-piece radios to pro-hunting demonstrators gathering for the Countryside March. After paying £2.50 each they were expecting to listen to a day of fox hunting tales on the temporarily licenced March FM. There were angry ripples in the sea of barbour jackets, however, when a clandestine team of pirate radioteers calling themselves Interference FM made their first appearance on the airwaves. Climbing onto a tower block near Hyde Park, five members of the guerilla team crystal-locked their powerful transmitter onto 87.7FM and out-broadcast the hunters with "This is

*Pic - Ian Hunter*

Hunt Saboteurs Broadcasting Association broadcasting to the nation's bigots. Get orf my land." £125,000 worth of ear-piece radios locked to the 87.7 FM frequency were binned as a result.

The next time Interference FM reappeared on the London airwaves was in the following year when the team reassembled to out-broadcast a commercial radio station in the run up to J18. Millenium FM are an advertising based radio station which boasts a 75% ABC 1 audience in the CanaryWharf/Greenwich area of London and broadcasts on 106.8FM. "Millennium FM prides itself in reaching a market with the highest purchasing power and fuels values based on greed and profit," says Chris Winton, one of Interference FM's founder members. "We were only too happy to be taking it out whilst at the same time doing our bizniss." Broadcasting throughout the week on 106.8, Interference wiped over much of Millennium FM, confining them to a small area next to their transmitter in Thamesmead. On June 18 itself, Interference switched to 107.4 to stay one step ahead of Department of Trade and Industry (DTI) detection, and ministry officials took longer than expected to trace their transmitter. During the day Interference FM broadcast a mixture of music, news and direct action adverts, countering the mainstream media's regurgitation of police press statements with live mobile phone reports from people inside the Square Mile. At 5.45pm, DTI officials finally located the transmitter on a tower block in Peckham and smashed it with sledgehammers. "We had been broadcasting for several hours and were due to come off air at 6pm," recalls Tim Larey. "We were all fucked on the final

furlong as we'd been up for two nights getting it all sorted. Then with a quarter of an hour to go the sound went down. We went out on the balcony with the binoculars and could see the silhouettes of the DTI officials pummelling the transmitter on a distant tower block." Using triangulation techniques and maximum resources, it is possible for the DTI to locate a pirate transmitter to within 20 metres of its exact location after only ten minutes of broadcast. By distancing the sound source from the transmitter using microwave links, however, pirate radio stations can avoid easy detection of their studio and therefore avoid personal arrests. During the technical set up on the day of J18, an unusual tower block electrical circuit of 110V threw off Interference FM's microwave link leaving the transmitter broadcasting direct from the sound source. A dangerous situation the team did well to survive. Chris Winton told SQUALL: "We were booming. Despite a few technical hitches we managed to keep it on air for most of the day and, given the radical nature of the station, we were expecting the DTI a lot sooner. Losing the transmitter was not unexpected, we were pleased we were able to maintain it for so long."

Meanwhile, Interference FM reappeared in Bristol a few months later, broadcasting several times in the run up to the Mumia Abu-Jamal demonstrations on October 24. On the day they successfully negotiated a day long broadcast without losing equipment and have broadcast regularly ever since. With the DTI less rabid in provincial towns, Interference FM's Bristol team have avoided any equipment loss, despite the regularity and radical nature of their programming content.

The full Interference team made another reappearance later that year, for the series of actions around N30. Once again the team relocated between several tower blocks during a number of broadcasts in the run up to the day of direct action. On the day itself they remained on air for eight hours until the DTI finally tracked down and destroyed the transmitter at 5pm.

According to the bizarrely wayward Sunday Times Insight team, the anti-capitalist protests in London on Mayday 2000 were to be co-ordinated with pirate radio broadcasts from Interference FM.

On Mayday morning, Interference activists setting up a transmitter on a tower block in south London happened to glance over the railing to see two police cars and a van disgorge several police officers below. They were looking upwards towards the top of the tower block.

"We grabbed our tools and could hear the lift coming up as we walked down and out through the back route," recalls Chris Winton. "We pulled the nonchalant one as we walked out the front door and noticed the coppers on the roof looking down."

This time then, Interference were trailed and temporarily thwarted but with their transmitter intact they intend to step up their operations for future actions. According to Chris Winton: "You can look out for us. When we first started we were replying to the lack of decent radio news media but as we've developed we've realised that the exclusivity of radio licensing is part of the commodification of the airwaves. It is another form of enclosure by capitalism. The media is a war and we're ready for it."

# The revolution will not be emailed

Most British media reports and commentaries on the event of J18 repeatedly declared that the action had been organised on the internet. While the internet was indeed useful, the mainstream media's devotion to exploring it's use by radical groups reflects more the current technological restructuring of the global economy than the reality of the peoples' knowledge of and participation in the event.

Those involved in J18 organising in London for instance, though prone to forgetfulness, were well aware of the elitist connotations of the technology. In addition to website and email use organisers sent out over a thousand action proposal letters in several languages through libertarian and anarchist address lists, printed up a succession of leaflets in runs of 30,000 or more, held and attended regular meetings, conferences and the like, all of which are, contrary to media imposed impression, still crucial to any successful mobilisation or movement. "THE INTERNET IS AN ELITE ORGANISATION; MOST OF THE WORLD HASN'T EVEN MADE A PHONE CALL."

The media ignored this old fashioned organising but any movement serious about confronting inequalities of power and creating free and ecological communities can ill afford to do so. Internet access and use is controlled and dominated by 'the north' and the rich in the north at that. Like various lifestyle choices internet access tends to coincide with how much cash there is in your pocket and with a particular background. We will not 'connect' with the peoples' of 'the south' through internet working; regardless of the Zapatistas mythical laptop communiqués from the Mexican jungle. Nor will we connect with the needs and desires of many people in our own regions through any number of email discussion lists. Why? Because the internationalised market system will increasingly polarise

*Squaring up to the Square Mile*

A rough guide to the City of London

For a copy send an SAE and some stamps to: Squaring Up To The Square Mile, 16B Cherwell St, Oxford, OX4 1BG

For a copy send an SAE and some stamps to: Reclaim the Streets, PO Box 9656, London, N4 4JY.

**reflections**
on june 18

contributions on the politics behind the events that occurred in the city of london on june 18, 1999

**AND CHECK OUT:**
www.agp.org
www.j18.org
www.gn.apc.org/rts

the inequalities of the internet access along class lines and tolerate radical use only to the extent that it doesn't hinder the technology's commercial development.

Even if organising mainly through the internet were possible it wouldn't be desirable. Given the present social system, the internet is to communication what the motor car is to transport; useful for getting you there, or your message from A to B but ultimately an atomiser of social space and a commodified substitute for human association.

We should of course continue to use the internet for information sharing and for initial contact with like minded groups but with awareness of it's market-led trajectory, its limitations and always alongside more involving and humanising activities. For a radical grassroots movement we require the real warmth of human togetherness and the raw 'shout on the street' to make a true social and ecological communications revolution; and it probably won't be emailed.

*Source: Worldwide Resistance Round-up, Peoples Global Action*

# Stonehenge Summer Solstice

Around 200 people clashed with police at Stonehenge after being excluded from the invite only summer solstice ceremony on June 21.

Frustrated at having to watch proceedings from behind barbed wire fences and lines of police, a group of 200 broke away from a thousand strong crowd assembled on Salisbury Plain. Wiltshire Police with riot gear, horses and dogs steamed in an attempt to prevent the group from reaching the 5000 year old monument. Twenty three people were arrested after a section of the barbed wire perimeter fence was torn down around 2am. Twenty of these were detained for aggravated trespass (Criminal Justice and Public Order Act 1994), two for an alleged assault on police and one for a drugs offence. English Heritage, who own the site, had sent out 150 exclusive invites to druids, astrologers and councillors allowing them access to the stone circle for an 'official' solstice ceremony. The ceremony was abandoned following the disturbances.

A High Court decision delivered earlier this year upheld people's right to demonstrate peacefully on the by-ways next to Stonehenge. In the light of this decision Wiltshire Police did not apply for the four mile exclusion zone for the first time since 1985, the year of the infamous Battle of the Beanfield. However they were still intent on keeping those not invited out of the stone-circle itself. Wiltshire Police spokeswoman, Elizabeth Marginson, opined: "There are still people at the stones who have no right to be there."

**The sun illuminates a present day reveller, summoning up the image of an ancestor on the sacred stones.**

Pic: Ivan Coleman

Some meaningful spiritual exchanges around the stones just before sunrise

In the future...

"Did you know that at one point there was a road going straight past here, a tacky tourist shop down there, and they actually brought in the police to stop worshipping here during the summer."

J Hodge

## SQUOTES 30/3/00

"Since "New Labour" was elected, there has been a notable de-politicisation of young people, many of whom tend to think of the prime minister as if he were the well-liked manager of a successful United Kingdom football team, who they admire as spectators without much sense of personal involvement."

*TONY BENN. LABOUR MP.*

## Stop And Search

real news   [Search Us!]

*www.squall.co.uk* already has a huge amount of news, features and comment on-line plus an extensive gallery of pictures. Now it's all searchable too!
Over the coming months we'll be making as much of our archive material available on the web as we can, so a full-on search should never be hassle again!

# www.squall.co.uk

*....An amicable and tolerant Britain ... but yet a Britain that still calls a spade a spade...*

## SQUOTES

"No one prepares you for the horrific effect office work can have on your creativity and civility levels… I had no idea that two years into my job at a leading UK merchant bank I would have no energy, no time for friends.. and no remaining creative impulses (for creativity, read: ability to write a letter, formulate independent opinions, decide what colour to paint my flat)… Initially, my tasks seemed reassuringly structured. I was shown which calculations to make, which font to display the resulting wisdom and which photocopier to use to distribute the end product around the division… Unable to shrug off the insane pace of weekday life, I found myself scowling impatiently at hapless couple enjoying a Sunday stroll ("chop chop, get a MOVE on!")… I confronted the fact that, fundamentally, I don't really care about the fluctuations of the Stock Market… from the day I resigned, I felt like a new woman… I certainly don't mean to imply that gainful employment is wicked or bound to corrupt, but shoving a square peg in a round hole never did anyone any good and achieving a healthy balance between work and time out is more than just a good idea, it is essential."

*From "No Job for a Woman", The Idler, Issue 3*

WAKE UP! WAKE UP! IT'S YER BADLY PHOTOCOPIED

# Weekly SchNEWS

Printed and Published in Brighton by *Justice?*

Friday 9th July 1999     http://www.schnews.org.uk/     Issue 219   Free/Donation

# SALE OF THE CENTURY

If you've been getting all hot under the collar recently waiting for your passport, who have you been pointing the finger of blame at? The government? The new childs passport? Initial teething problems of a new computer system? Perhaps you jumped on the Telegraph bandwagon and blamed the Millennium Bug? Or nodded in agreement with the Times that it is the "*culture of mismanagement…that is still ingrained in parts of the public sector.*" No-one it seems wants to face facts and shake an accusatory digit at big business for making such a monumental cock-up of the passport system.

Welcome to the world of the **Private Finance Initiative** (PFI).

Siemens Business Systems were given the £120m contract to install the passport department's new computer system under the little publicised Initiative, which is essentially privatisation by the back door. The scheme was hatched by the Tories and has – oh, *surprise*-been taken up rather enthusiastically by New Labour. Schools, hospitals, the fire service, you name it, are being touched by the hand of big business(see SchNews 210).

Siemens managed to get the passport contract by promising to make the system: **cheaper** – sacking staff to reduce costs, they've now had to re-employ more people to sort out the backlog; **faster** - waiting time at the two offices with Siemens new system has more than doubled. And more **secure** - in desperation at the backlog 'security procedures' have now been relaxed.

As that blatant anarchist kill-joy publication Computer Weekly pointed out, Siemens' "*reducing staff in anticipation of a new system's introduction is madness.*" But if you think that's bad check out the Immigration and Nationality Department, which makes the Passport Agency look efficient. Here some of the world's most vulnerable people fleeing repression and torture are forced to wait for up to six years for a decision on whether they can stay. In fact things have got so bad at the immigration offices in Croydon that a roomful of unopened letters has started to rot, and staff can no longer even enter the room due to health risks!

But don't panic it's Siemens to the rescue, who have missed both their deadlines, sacked staff and made refugees wait even longer. But

they still made a mint from the 'efficiency gains' they hadn't even made, because they get paid for reducing costs, not improving the service. Nice little earner, this one: the more people you sack and the more chaotic the system becomes, the more you get paid.

Meanwhile over at the National Health Service, that well-known revolutionary organ the British Medical Journal, called the PFI "*perfidious financial idiocy that could destroy the NHS.*" Clearly they haven't understood that the whole point of the PFI is that it allows corporate fatcats to get their claws on some of the last bits of the country they don't already own.

Nearly all the new hospitals being built are funded under the PFI, which means the NHS doesn't get to choose where they will be built, but has to pick up the bill later anyway. And as the 'miracle' of private finance is involved, the treasury doesn't give 'em any more cash to pay, which means... yep, cutting beds, sacking staff and closing hospitals. One PFI scheme alone, at the Edinburgh Royal Infirmary, will mean 900 medical staff getting sacked.

So if you've been fingering your collar in queued annoyance waiting for your passport, are holed up in some dodgy refugee detention centre, or waiting for an operation, don't jump on the Tory Blair bandwagon and blame the public sector for its '*lack of modernisation and reaction to change*'.

---

**WELCOME TO THE PFI EVERYTHING MUST GO SALE**
The basic idea of the PFI is that business stumps up the cash to pay for big capital projects like building a new hospital, then lease it back to the local health authority over a period of time. This saves the tax-payer money. Simple. Except it doesn't, because unfortunately PFI schemes require interest payments some 5% above the rate the Treasury would pay if it borrowed directly. This means for every £1 billion of PFI contracts there is an extra cost to the public sector of £50 million per year.

---

\*\*Ever wished you could get SchNEWS off the web and print it out so it looks like the real thing? Well you can. All you need is an internet connection, web browser, the Acrobat Reader and any old printer. See our website for more details

---

## CRAP ARREST OF THE WEEK
For handing out leaflets! Two people were dishing the dirt in the St.Helen's branch of NatWest Bank, letting customers know about the banks £24.5 million loan to vivisection experts Huntingdon Life Sciences. The two were held overnight and charged with the well known 1361 Justices of the Peace Act (an act so old it actually predates parliament!).

---

## RING OF ROSES
Have you heard the one about the evidence gatherer that forgot to gather any evidence? Or maybe the one about the Ring-of-Steel being replaced by a Ring-of-Roses? The City of London Police have.

In a vain attempt to redeem their sorry little arses for the mass protests that happened on June 18th, the police attempted, to get their grubby mitts on all journalists notes and footage of the day, a right they thought they had under the 1984 Police and Criminal Evidence Act. But The Old Bailey this week said " *Oi,No! You had 9 months to sort out a decent surveillance operation, and polish up the steel.Leave it out!*" The media world feared they would be seen as agents of the police.

21 people have been arrested so far, all for violent disorder. Yet it was the police who showed themselves as 'violent' and 'disordered'. The girl who was run over by the police van has only just come out of hospital where her condition was described as 'critical'.

One person still inside since the day is due in the City of London Magistrates court this Friday. CeeJay (Charles McBride) is being held in Feltham young offenders.If you saw him arrested about 2:15pm on the corner of London Wall and Moorgate (sorry, no description of Ceejay) ring London Defence Monitoring Group 0171 837 7557. Letters of support to Charles Mcbride DC8504, HMYOI Feltham Bedfont Rd Middlesex, TW13 4ND.

If you want to see a copy of June 18th video send £5 + SAE to Undercurrents, 16b Cherwell St., Oxford, OX4 1BG

There will be a defendants only meeting for those nicked on J18 on Sat. 24th July 2 pm Conway Hall,Red Lion Square, London (Holborn tube)

* SchNews has been leaked some interesting internal email memos sent to workers at Natwest. They mention "*nuisance calls…we are unfortunately not able to stop these calls coming in, but should you receive such a call, just hang up the phone*". They then talk about the "*day of action against the financial services sector planned for Friday 18 June. A number of demonstrations and disruptive actions are anticipated…we all need to be vigilant..Threats could manifest themselves in many ways, the most likely being denial of service, virus infection and attempted vandalism of web sites.*" We hope this warms the cockles of our readers, that corporations do take our threats more seriously than they often care to let on.

# DOCK ON

This is a shout to all SchNEWS readers to be glued to a TV this Sunday (11th) to watch 'The Dockers' Channel 4 8pm. The drama was co-written by 14 of the former sacked Liverpool dock workers, Jimmy McGovern of 'Brookside' and 'Cracker' fame and Trainspotting's Irvine Welsh. As you would expect it's all about their 28 month epic dispute against low-pay and casualisation.

SchNEWS finds it rather ironic that the dockers are now getting more press about Sunday's drama than they ever did during the dispute. As one sacked docker told SchNEWS this week *"We're like dead artists, once they've killed you off, people realise what they've lost!"*

Not that the dockers have been idle since the end of the dispute. They've been busy trying to sort out decent training, life long learning and employment opportunities for local people, setting up a workers co-operative *Liverpool Dockers and Stevedores Ltd, Transneeds,* and *The Waterfront Trust.* And they've established the Initiative Factory to bring these and the other myriad of projects to life. With a mission statement like "Work can be, and should be, creative; it should illuminate a life and not dampen it; seen as a liberating and not an incarcerating force; and should release the potential of individuals" the message and actions from the dockers is as relevant as ever. Respect. Initiative Factory, 29 Hope St., Liverpool 1 Tel 0151 207 9111

## SISTERS OF MERCY

Workers across the world are fighting back against bosses and governments for better pay and conditions. For sheer numbers, check out what's happening in Canada. More than 47,000 nurses in Quebec have been striking for nearly two weeks, demanding a wage increase and an improvement to their stressful working conditions.

This despite the Quebec government, having extraordinary powers to deal with "illegal" strikes. They've threatened the nurses with fines, the loss of one year of seniority for every day on strike, and the loss of two days pay for each day on the picket line.

Despite this the strike is holding strong and the nurses have widespread support. During the day in Montreal, nurses' picket lines outside major hospitals are supported almost continuously by passers-by with honking car horns and bike bells. And according to the Order of Nurses, not one complaint has been received from patients.

## GET KETTED OUT

It's the summer of 1549 and a time of uprisings by the dispossessed rural peasantry. Enclosure of common land was leading to starvation, begging was met with whippin', hangin' & mutilation and any help from the Church was forcefully put down. Robert Kett , a landowner seeing the injustice of what was happening to the common folk became leader of a 20,000 strong army, tearing down fences, filling in ditches and returning the land to common ownership. The area was run equitably from under an oak tree in Wymondham for 2 months, and the worst landowners were locked up before defeat by mainly foreign mercenaries at Norwich.

450 years on and this Saturday (10) The Land Is Ours is organising an occupation against the fight against enclosure of public space. Privatisation has seen closures & developments grow drastically in number, local councils selling allotments, schools selling playing fields and access to the countryside denied by Forestry Commission & landowners. Meet 12 noon, Haymarket, Norwich. Bring yer camping gear, instruments, pitchforks, etc. Contact 01603 484412 *Ketts celebration info www.paston.co.uk/commonlot/links.htm

## SchNEWS in brief

**Quote of the Month** *"I can proudly say that on my farm, that employs not only all my family, but also four outside workers, there are no badgers, no rabbits, no mice, no snakes, no lizards, no rodents, and if I could stop the birds flying over I would. My farm produces food, not fluffy little animals. I am a farmer not a zoo keeper."*…Letter to the North Devon Journal from C Roberts, Black Torrington

\*\* Last Friday, two asylum seekers detained in Campsfield Detention Centre decided to give themselves permanent admission to the UK, via a back window in the detention centre. One Russian and one Kosovan, scaled a 18 foot high fence, topped with 3 coils of barbed wire and disappeared into the country-side! \*\***The Heckler** is a splendid new free newsletter from south east London, mixing anarcho politics with real life and a good sense of humour. Urban survival hints and no pompous critiques of dead intellectuals. So get it. Send stamps and/or donation to Red & Black Club, PO Box 17773, London SE84WX Tel 0171 358 1854\*\* **Defend Public Services** Conference 11am-4pm Sat 10th July Mechanics Institute, Princes St. Manchester, six sacked Tameside care workers opposing privatisation, cheap labour, casualisation, corruption, sleaze and all forms of prejudice have invited speakers from trade unions and various care services to assist them in their fight to defend a decent public care service £3/1 Contact Tel:01618618390\*\***Brighton Urban Design & Development (BUDD)**- spearheading opposition to supermarket development on Brighton station site. Meetings every Thurs 7pm; 01273 681166/ 389279 for venue details. Also BUDD Picnic, 1pm July 18 @ Harvest Forestry. Bring food & drink\*\* Support the **Portsmouth Three** demo 19th July 1pm Portsmouth Crown Court, Winston Churchill Ave: 3 sabs on conspiracy charges for mass sab on notoriously violent hunt \*\***Anti-Live Exports** March and Rally: Sat July 17. 11 am, Speakers Corner, Hyde Park.\*\***National Anti-vivisection** demo against Harlan UK & Astra Charnwood, Loughborough 25th July 12noon & every Wednesday tel:01162366450\*\* July is **Gene-Free** month including a Stop the Crop National Rally & GM site visit 18th July 2pm Model Farm nr Watlington 12miles S of Oxford., for details of more actions tel:01813749516 \*\* There's a **Genetically Engineered Free Forests** Action July 14 Oxford, meet 9.30am meet in front of University of Oxford National History Museum Parks Road. T e l : 0 1 7 1 - 5 6 1 - 9 1 4 6 mailto:GEFFcoalition@hotmail.com GEFFcoalition@hotmail.com. And while you're about it, **Smash Genetic Engineering**, meet 12 noon sat 31st July, bring transport w/ full tank of petrol, road map, flags, costumes & disguises. More precise details from the 24th onwards tel:0708 191858\*\***WHAGA** Open Day all day Sat July 10th at Whitehawk Hill Allotments, with free food, bouncy castle and kids entertainment, and loadsa fun and games inc.\*\* The **'Les Tanneries'** social squatted centre in Dijon, France needs you! The former slaughterhouse had stood empty for five years before it was turned into a squatted social centre for the past couple of years. Now the local council want to evict and knock the whole area down - not that they've got any plans to replace the site with. There's a letter of protest to be sent to the local mayor on their web-site www.ville-dijon.fr/contact/index\*Trajic Roundabout and a sound system\*\*Also on Saturday **Kemp Town Carnival**, starting at midday, procession of floats leaving the gala bingo hall at 1pm and then wandering round ending up at the NHS Trust buildings… see ya there! \*\* We thought you like to know that one of the nets premiere on-line casinos is **giving away** $50.00.Checkout www.worldcasino.\*\*www.ville-dijon.fr/contact/index.\*\* Please only send e-news to mailto:schnews@brighton.co.uk schnews@brighton.co.uk, not to the webmaster he's going spare!

## Target Tarmac Big Day Out

17th July, will kick off somewhere in the Midlands & be a big chance to take action against Tarmac's trouncing of our green & pleasant land. Tarmac is the main exponent of corporate greenwash bullshit tactics, placing ads in the nationals advising companies to green themselves for the 21st Century & even running courses on how to pull the green wool over our collective eyes... But we know the dirty truth beneath the slick PR machine. Luckily we're not as stupid as they think…They helped to destroy Twyford Down, they provided the roadstone to the Newbury by-pass, they're trying to bulldoze through what remains of Sherwood Forest, etc. Tel:07971755823

\* There's a Critical Mass bike ride this Sunday (11th) Meet George Green, Wanstead, E11 (near Wanstead tube), 3pm, for a ride on the M11 Link Road for the last time before it turns into a rat run. The M11 Link Road destroyed more than 1,000 homes and already a new Tesco hypermarket, an Asda/Wal-Mart hypermarket, and a 1,000 Millennium Dome car park are planned for the area.Contact STORM 0181 527 9857

## THE NATIONAL TRAVESTY

Protesters who have been living in tree houses in the National Trust owned Arthur's Wood since last summer, occupied the Trust HQ in London on Wednesday. The woodland is situated adjacent to Manchester Airport's controversial Runway 2 and the airport authority want to chop down the trees because they reckon they will block radar signals.The Trust granted a license to the Airport to fell the woods and to evict the campaigners in direct contravention to the Trust Act of 1907 which states' *They shall by all lawful means prevent resist and abate all enclosures and encroachments upon and all attempts to enclose or encroach upon such property or any part thereof...'.* Obviously this decision has nothing to do with the fact that the Airport is a sponsor of nearby Quarry bank Mill ,owned by the National Trust, and apparently used to host conferences for the airport, AMEC and Tarmac.

The protester's recent appeal in the Lords was rejected so eviction could be anytime. The good news is that Wednesdays occupation has resulted in the Trust agreeing to talk with the protesters. And Manchester Airport have had to pull out of their plans to build a massive staff car park on Green Belt land after it was called in for a public inquiry due to the large number of protests.Contact Tel:0161 225 4863/0961-517324

## ...and finally...

Carry On Indulging, everybody: Chocolate Is Good For You- Official. It's rich in many beneficial compounds and minerals, is packed with antioxidants which may reduce the risk of cancer, and as for obesity from scoffing all that luvverly gak- well, there's just no link. Dentists have the cheek to blame it for tooth decay, but that's bollocks too. Not only that, but it also increases athletic performance and improves driving skills. It must be true, cos it says so in a new book, 'Chocolate and Cocoa: Health and Nutrition', from no less an authority than the International Cocoa Research and Education Foundation. "We're just interested in established facts" said Eduard Kouame, one of the book's sponsors. "Researchers are discovering new information about this cherished treat." SchNEWS scorns all readers who may be moved to cynicism by the fact that the authors are employed by Mars and Nestle. Why should that have to mean they're just interested in flogging more Snickers? Unfortunately, Dr Carol King, president of ICREF, lets the side down a bit by mentioning that the Asian market is still 'largely untapped' and that the book might help, er, increase…sales. Oh dear. Time to stop gobbling that sexy Flake and pick up the gun….

*disclaimer..* SchNEWS warns all readers to get someone else to put up their PFI wardrobes!

WAKE UP! WAKE UP! IT'S YER BEEFED UP & BONED

# Weekly SchNEWS

Printed and Published in Brighton by *Justice?*

**Friday 16th July 1999**    http://www.schnews.org.uk/    **Issue 220**    **Free/Donation**

# Raging Hormones

*"It is not unrealistic to regard the World Trade Organisation as representing effective world government for the first time in human history"*

Steven Shrybman, West Coast Environment Law

In the same week that Europe lifted their beef ban on Britain's mad cows, those bully-boys from the World Trade Organisation (WTO) gave America the green light to apply sanctions on the European Union, because of its ban on hormone-treated beef.

A secret panel decided that we Europeans are missing out and want to get our teeth stuck into some meat laced with artificial hormones. Its scientific panel, stuffed with corporate nominees and US officials, reckon the stuff is safe to eat. However, they somehow forgot to test the effects the six injected chemicals have on levels of natural hormones in the body. They also failed to find out what they might do to kids, even though a new study has concluded that one of the hormones is a potent carcinogen placing children at particular risk.

But they, the *Arbitrators* reckon the 11 year old ban has resulted in $128 million a year in lost revenue to the US and Canada.

So how will these two countries get their compensation money? By hitting certain European goods with massive import duties. A list is currently being drawn up which will penalise companies that have nothing to do with the beef trade, effectively triggering job losses and bankruptcy. Once again, the ruling has shown that the WTO is nothing more than *"an international bill of rights for multinational corporations"*.

* Last month environmentalists highlighted WTO plans to speed up the destruction of the worlds remaining forests (SchNEWS 206). The WTO wants amongst other things, a reduction on tariffs for forest products, which even the American Forest and Papers Association have admitted could raise world-wide consumption of wood and paper products by as much as 4 percent. Environmentalists are also worried that logging companies will gain the right to claim damages against any environmental regulations that get in the way of profits. In a joint statement, the groups said *"Our forests don't need more logging...they need stronger protection...The WTO is bad for forests."* Make that 'bad for the planet.'

* Earlier this year the US imposed $191m of sanctions against the EU in a dispute over bananas (SchNEWS 204)

* The US actually got a slap in its corporate face a few weeks back when the international food standards body broke with long established tradition and finally produced a ruling the US didn't like; that BST-treated milk is not the same as ordinary milk. BST is produced from cattle treated with genetically engineered growth hormone, is linked to appalling animal welfare problems and breast and prostate cancer in humans. The US quietly withdrew its attempt to force the EU to import its poisoned produce and the EU won a silent victory

A U.S. court recently ruled that it was illegal for Massachusetts to have a law that penalized firms doing business with Burma. The EU had filed a complaint with, you've guessed it, the WTO. The ruling basically gives the thumbs up for countries to trade with any old dodgy dictator, bugger their human rights record.

*Seattle is the next stop for the WTO. 29th November is the date for the Millennium Round of "negotiations" For details of protests planned:

PGA_Seattle99-subscribe@listbot.com

* A Canadian company is suing the US government for nearly $1 billion in damages after the state of California banned methanol as a petrol additive. The chemical is leaking into water supplies, a potential health hazard, but so what, the company are using the terms under the North American Free Trade Agreement to railroad environmental laws they say are affecting their profits.

* For a low down on the WTO get a copy

of the latest 'Ecologist'. £3.50 inc. p+p from Cissbury House, Furze View, Five Oaks Rd., Slinfold, W.Sussex, RH13 7RH Tel 01403 786726. Or why not take out a yearly subscription on this essential publication. £24/£18 concessions.

## SO JUST WHO ARE THE SHADOWY PEOPLE BEHIND THE WTO?

The WTO was established on January 1st, 1995 and is currently made up of 135 nations (surprise surprise though, it's America who pull the strings with their delegations meeting with multinational corporations before and after every set of negotiations). Their mission statement is the promotion of global free trade. They monitor and settle trade disputes, then set the rules which, if broken by any nation, result in punishments including sanctions. Most importantly, the WTO rules are supreme over the laws of nations, taking power away from local communities and governments and handing it to corporations - sod environment, labour and human rights.

*"(The WTO is) this un-elected body which is taking decisions which then become binding. It's going to take a huge amount of public pressure to remove it, because the avenues aren't there. It's not as if we could have elections and throw them out, it's not as if we have elected representatives that are overseeing their proceedings, it isn't as if we even have an independent judiciary".*

Susan George, author and researcher

## CRITCHLEY BOTTOMS UP

*'I pay tribute to our members, whose strength and dignity is as deep as the spite and stupidity of Critchley.'*

Gasp in shock horror, the longest running industrial dispute in Britain has ended in victory for the workers. A few years back, British Telecom sold their bussiness/factory in Gwent to Critchley Labels, who derecognised the union despite over 70% of its employees being members. 31 people were then sacked in February 1977 for having the bloody cheek to take strike action in February 1997. Dubbed 'the worst employer in Wales', the staff mounted a continuous picket line outside the factory, triggering a collapse in Critchley's UK sales. Eventually the company bowed to pressure and gave £325,000 compensation to be divided amongst the strikers. To cap it all, they have now been offered full-time employment by their old bosses BT. Funny how things come round. The campaign against the company continues, with the newly-formed Critchley Shareholders' Action Group, who plan to attend the company's AGM on 29th of this month. Nice one.

## Reclaim yer Bristols

Last Saturday 350 party people closed off part of the M32 for a few hours for a Reclaim The Streets party. Despite the best efforts of the organisers and lengthy negotiations with the cops to keep things peaceful, the boyz in blue came in heavy handed in full riot force and dogs only an hour after the celebrations commenced. The cops made 20 arrests on the day with 8 appearing in Bristol Magistrates on Monday.

So why the major panic on the part of the forces of law and order? Post June18 hysteria? So it seems, as the Bristol Evening Scare Mongerer dutifully informed its readers that the party was organised in a squat in Stoke Newington and a pub in Hackney (this was news to the Bristol party people!) The paper then surpassed itself in the paranoia stakes by saying " *In previous marches the women and children have been lined up in front while the militant fringe have come up behind armed with poles and sticks. The women and children, who frequently get hurt, are known as cannon fodder' to some extremists".* Amazing the lengths some people will go to to have a bit of a boogie whilst making a statement! Speaking of dirty tactics, the police were ushering people through the police cordon assuring them that they would be allowed to leave the other side only to be trapped by police who would not let them out again. People and children suffering from the heat were forced to remain inside the cordon without water.

If anyone has any film footage or photographic evidence pertaining to events at the street party please contact Kebele, 0117 9399469

*The same evening, over 50 police in 8 riot vans cordoned off the Bishopston Community Centre to foil the evil intention of a planned community dance. Residents at the centre were denied access to their home and other local residents were questioned and obstructed by police. The police justified their actions by quoting section 63 of the Criminal Justice and Public Order Act 1994, a law that applies only to open air dance parties but hey, who cares about the law! Though there was no sound system in the building the police remained until midnight. Another stylish operation in public relations from your friendly neighbourhood bobbys!

*Keeping it in the area, a kilometre length of the most beautiful section of the most famous cycleway in the UK - the Bristol & Bath Railway Path- is due to be closed for destruction at the end of July 99 to make way for the building of the Avon Ring Road - Bristol's version of the M25. STARR campaign , which has been fighting this wanton vandalism, meets every week in Bristol Tel: 0797-999-0389

### WE FUCKING TOLD YOU SO

Guess what? The Newbury by-pass doesn't work. Yes, the little bit of road that cost£125 million, destroyed countryside and converted peaceful old ladies and previously law-abiding Volvo-owners into environmental activists has only succeeded in cutting rush-hour traffic in the town by a piddling 15%. Adrian Foster-Fletcher, spokesman for Newbury Friends of the Earth, has described the scheme as "*an appalling waste of money*". He believes Newbury's traffic problems, barely eased by the bypass, are destined to get worse. Sandleford Park, a new college development and Vodaphone's expansion plans will all lead to an increase in traffic. Lib-Dem Council transport spokesman, David Beckett, admitted the new road has not eased rush hour congestion as much as the Highways Agency promised, hinting that the new road may encourage people to drive who didn't before. He agreed Newbury's traffic problems will soon be back to square one. Still, at least Lib Dem Newbury MP David Randel is pleased. He says the road has been *"the fulfillment of our dreams".*

## KAOS IN KOREA

South Korea used to be *the* showcase economy, a shining example of how great free enterprise and capitalism was. After the Korean war and the split with communist North Korea, the Masters of the Universe set about transforming South Korea into an investor's paradise. Koreans were promised all the riches of Western style consumerism, and so much cash around that they could even afford to be nice to their workers. Growth levels went through the roof and South Korea joined the big league of consumer economies, while North Korea sank into poverty and isolation. And so the whole world witnessed the triumph of capitalism, and everyone imagined the boom would go on forever…

Unfortunately those nice men from the West who designed this miracle economy didn't mention some of the less savoury aspects of joining the consumer capitalist club, and the inevitable crash that hit the Asian Tiger economies two years ago came as a bit of a shock. Unable to cope with the end of innocence, the South Koreans needed to be taught IMF Lesson Number 2 - leaving the boom-time nursery. With fucked up finances, they needed a fat IMF loan ($57 bn), which of course comes with Structural Adjustments - ie sacking people and cutbacks. There ain't no room in the rock 'ard world of free market capitalism for soft little mummies-boy economies, and in their youthful innocence South Koreans had developed a dangerous habit of giving people jobs for life, social security and so on. Keen to show the IMF how tough he could be, President Kim Dae-Jung started cutting services and 'restructuring' firms.

To implement all this you need to deal with any potential trouble makers like unionists, so the Public Security Prosecution Departments (PSPD) was created to supress trade unions. So far this lovely piece of IMF weaponry has nicked 11 union leaders, and 60 striking union members, for resisting the government's restructuring programme. The PSPD's other strategy only came out when its former chief got too pissed one night, and let slip that they had actually encouraged an illegal strike at the national mint, to create an excuse for a savage clampdown on the unions.

All this, and an on-going government corruption scandal, pissed a few people off, and 41,000 workers have gone on strike demanding an end to the IMF's plans and the PSPD's plots. Learning their new game fast, the South Korean government quickly engineered yet another naval 'confrontation' with North Korea to divert international attention, and vowed to hold out against the workers. SchNEWS is confident that with such dirty tricks and military posturing South Korea has proved that its really grown up now, and ready to play with the big boys in the deregulated, de-unionised global market.

## NOT SO POPLAR

Cheeky activists sneaked into a genetically modified tree test site on Monday felling and ringbarking 115 Poplars, that had been growing since 1995. In an anonymous phone call to Genetic Engineering Network the activists said "*Genetic Modification of trees is a mjor threat to the environment and those manipulating the DNA of trees are using powerful but dimly understood technology and show contempt for our planet. They respect only profit for themselves and their shareholders*"

* Smash Genetics action - Saturday 31st July Meet 12 noon in Cambridge. For details of location ring 07808 191858 email smashgenetics@yahooo.com
( bring transport with a full tank of petrol)

Check out the 1999 NORTHERN GREEN GATHERING next Wed 28-1st August, Pontefract, W.Yorks £30 Tel:0113 224 9885 The Northern Permaculture Convergance will be there to put permaculture in the north on the map.

## Inside SchNEWS

*'It is vital that people such as Michal are defended from victimisation by the state.On July 30th we will burn a Czech Flag, symbolising the Czech States' collusion with neo-nazis We call on the Czech prosecution service to immediately drop the charges.'*A spokesperson for the Solidarity Federation, the British Section of the International Workers' Association(IWA)

On Friday 27th November '98 Michal was attacked by neo-Nazis. Convinced that they were aiming to kill him, he shot the leading nazi with his legally held pistol, in self defence, and escaped Michal was arrested and charged with attempted murder. Though released on bail, he still faces up to 15 years inside. None of the neo Nazis have been charged with any offence.

The IWA believe that Michal has been framed for his political activity, in a country where more than one third of police officers are members of neo-fascist organisations. The Czech government is totally failing to deal with incidents of racism and xenophobia. Human Rights groups have warned that neo Nazi violence is now reaching "epidemic proportions" in the Republic, mainly targeted at the Roma Gypsy minority. Direct co-operation between police and neo-nazis is well known.

The address of the Czech Embassy is 25 Kensington Palace Gardens, London W8. Contact: The Solidarity Federation 0181 374 5027 e-mail: da@directa.force9.co.uk Web: www.directa.force9.co.uk

## Stalked

Last month the High Court decided to uphold an appeal by the Crown Prosecution Service against Diane Selvanayagham, who had the cheek to protest against Cornyhaugh fur farm near Newcastle. Diane had originally been acquitted after being charged under the stalking laws for causing the owner of the farm harassment. However two wise judges decided that the actions she was involved in (such as candle-lit vigils and veggie burger stalls), were such a threat to the farmer's safety that they overturned the original decision.

The anti-stalking legislation became law in 1997, but the powers that be seem rather keen to use it against animal rights protestors. They are a lot more serious than civil injunctions that were previously used in such disputes, and can land people who break them with a 5 year prison sentence. There are weekley demos outside the Cornyhaugh fur farm, Contact Northern Animal Rights Coalition PO Box 1JY Newcastle-Upon-Tyne NE99 1JY

## in brief

Workers' Aid have organised a public meeting entitled 'After the Bombing' with speakers from Prishtina and Belgrade. It's on Thursday 22nd July 7 pm Conway Hall, Red Lion Square, London, WC1 (Holborn tube)

## ...and finally...

The new Lord Mayor of Belfast, Unionist 'Big Bad' Bob Stoker, has refused to invite 13 local Sinn Fein councillors to his inaugural lunch(out). However Sinn Fein local councillor Mick Conlon who chairs a sub-committee was phoned by the mayor's office to put together the official menu.

SchNEWS reckons it just shows that not only have the Unionists no ideas for the negotiating table but they have none for the banqueting table either. Perhaps they should bite the bullet and not the prawn cocktail?

### disclaimer

SchNews warns all veggie and vegan readers not to go all mad cow about the word beef in the front page story. Hey, we're not saying eat the stuff, its just a good example of the topsy-turvy free trade for the world we in, Honest!

Many came in fancy dress for the Bristol RTS 10th July

"Will you be paying for that with a card?" GM food action, Bristol

# Totally 'Avon it!

Bristol July 99: Defending the Bishopston Community Centre, Bristol, from the hands of the owners - the Church of England. The Church kicked the local community out in order to open the place up to *their* 'community' - ie redevelopment.

# Stopping Mox Boxes

SQUALL

Where Do You Want To Grow Today?

I Wanna Go Home
Underground Update
Features
Frontline Communique
State It's In
Squall Pics
Squall Events
Squotes
Resources

Japanese Maritime Safety Commandos were briefed to expect terrorists. Instead they were faced with Greenpeace's 'MV Arctic Sunrise' and a team determined not to let British-made nuclear fuel dock in Japan without a fuss. After four weeks at sea, photographer Nick Cobbing jumped into a Greenpeace dinghy for the final cat and mouse. He sent this e-mail via ISDN Sat. phone.

Went to bed last night feeling crap and bored, headache, nothing happening, rumour that it'll maybe kick off at 4AM so set my alarm, had these false alarms before, so don't take it too seriously. woken at 3.30AM by (Dave) the action coordinator, asked to get shit together and be ready to go now, arrive on deck half dressed with cameras dangling.

Greeted by 7-8 coastguard ships and motor-launches surrounding us with searchlights bouncing in all directions through the darkness loads of engine noise and smoke, lights bobing up and down in all directions. Looks and sounds like an eviction only more scary and i'm on a ship, not a rooftop, nowhere to run.

Could see riot police behind shields on the bows of all the nearest boats, shouting inaudible stuff up at us via loud hailer, through the engine noise.

Some of the riot police duck right down, so we see only a row of upright shields with nothing but little eye holes at the top. A few of them are drawing right up close underneath the ship, it's clear that they are trying to stop us from reaching the harbour where it's confirmed that the plutonium ships will dock this morning. Act/coordinator says that me and the video guy are first to go in the water in an inflatable with him driving as we planned, looks like we're gonna get nicked as soon as we hit the water. Suicide mission I think to myself, my mad Aussie cameraman team mate, 'Moose' is jumping up and down with excitement, in his element (this guy usually does war-zone stuff for the beeb). For some reason, i'll never know why, after our inflatable reaches the water we're able to speed away in the right direction without these Japanese SAS-types jumping on us immediately, they just follow at high speed. chasing us around, driving in front of us and blocking our path whenever we try to cut through a gap, meanwhile our other two boats are launched on the other side taking four people with 'No Plut.' flags and stuff towards the Mox/Plut ship that is now approaching the harbour. It's starting to get light, but barely enough of it to take decent pictures, plus the spray and the boat banging up and down and then cornering at speed. This tests me, have never done anything like this before. five of their boats concentrate on us, probably 'cos they can see that we're trying to get cameras to the plu. ships, making it impossible for us to get through their line and reach the action, they come up close as if trying to grab us but don't seem to know how to finish it.

Guys in orange boiler suits and yellow helmets, they hold their hands up and shout at us to stop, looking surprised when we ignore them. This chase continues for a while, we take in one circle of the ship and drop film and video tape into a bucket. That point i thought we 'we're nicked', certain of it, no way we were going to get back to the ship and get hoisted up the 20ft or so to safety, expecting to have five demented Japanese ninjas pull me off any moment, thinking about miso and rice and who i will share my cell with.

Somehow we get back below the Sunrise again and thanks to some nifty boat driving, quick people on the crane and shit loads of luck we get winched to safety. The other two boats had been hoisted up onto the deck too, everybody back in one piece. Then darkroom, chemicals, scanning and transmitting whilst the ship heads back away from the port towards relative safety of international waters, locked in our media container in the hold, expecting the ship to be boarded at any moment, listening for the noises outside. The captain holds it all together keeps cool, despite the radio messages telling him to stop, "Arctic Sunrise!, Arctic Sunrise!, stop now for immediate boarding and inspection" The other TV/Stills crew in the helicopter got pics of the two smaller inflatables that reached the bows of The Pacific Teal with their 'stop plu.' flags as it was moving into the harbour to dock in front of the power station.

Got 2 or 3 reasonable pics in spite of the conditions, a couple of mine and several that the other guy took from the helicopter were sent out, eventually syndicated along with the video via AFP, AP, Reuters. The video footage was something else, can see it all from the air, boats trails crisscrossing through the frame. Everybody here is made up, after so many weeks of sitting around and after all that rough weather. Campaigner is over the moon......Apparently the shots have been used widely in Japan.

Pic: Nick Cobbing

WAKE UP! WAKE UP! IT'S YER BRITISH NUCLEAR FOOLS!

# Weekly SchNEWS

### Printed and Published in Brighton by Justice?

**Friday 23rd July 1999**  http://www.schnews.org.uk/  **Issue 221**  **Free/Donation**

# ☢ SHIP OF FOOLS ☢

*" We are in danger of sparking a whole new arms race around the Pacific rim."* Greenpeace International.

Cumbria… rural England, home to the Lakes, Fells… oh, and British Nuclear Fuels Limited (BNFL). Sellafield, the sprawling nuclear metropolis, with its sordid history of radioactive pollution, on-site fires, and other such niceties, has this week begun a major operation to ship reprocessed nuclear fuel across International waters to Japan.

The nuclear cargo is MOx fuel, mixed oxide rods containing both uranium and plutonium. The rods are heated within the reactor, which produces an ashy film on the outside. This ash is weapons-grade Plutonium. You wouldn't have to be a nuclear physicist to remove it. Pacific Nuclear Transport (PNT) is the company that owns both Pacific Pintail and Pacific Teal, the ships which will be carrying the nuclear cargo. Japan cannot reprocess fuel itself, and therefore, needs European plants to do the dirty work for them, namely Sellafield in Britain and La Hague in France. PNT is owned by BNFL, which is in turn owned by the Government…how cosy ?

The undisclosed route is expected to take two months, even though most countries don't want the ships to pass through their waters. Fourteen Caribbean heads of government are furious that they were not consulted about the route. The fisher folk in South Korea have vowed to blockade the ships en-mass with their boats, fearing the cargo will threaten their safety and livelihoods.

There will be over 400kg of plutonium on board the ships, enough to manufacture 60 nuclear bombs. This is quite worrying for the international community, as Japan has had tight reins on its arsenal of weapons since WW2. As Kevin Dunion, Friends of the Earth, points out, *" As its neighbours watch, Japan is slowly increasing its stockpile of weapons- useable nuclear materials with the blessing of British Nuclear Fuels and our Government."*

In a vain PR attempt, BNFL would like to sever the link between the nuclear industry and the military in the minds of both the public and foreign Governments. Activists clambered onto a crane in the civilian dock at Cherbourg, where the Pacific Teal was to collect it's deadly cargo from the COGEMA plant at Cape de La Hague, Northern France. The goal of the action was to push the ship into the military dock next door, to highlight the link.

This is the first time a shipment of this kind will NOT receive a Naval escort. Instead The Pintail and The Teal have both under-

gone a multi-million pound refit to arm them against military and terrorist threat (oh, and it seems good old-fashioned piracy hasn't been ruled out, either!) Greenpeace state that *"If a government or paramilitary force seizes the cargo it could have a nuclear weapon within three weeks."*

The 30mm canons and other defence weapons on board have made the Pintail and Teal the first armed merchant ships in 50 years. Despite BNFL's claims that the ships are not at risk, the civilian crews sailing them will receive danger money!! The National Union of Marine Aviation and Shipping Officers (NUMAST) asked for a pay increase for the staff and warzone payments if the ship sailed into difficulties!!

The Government have decided to sell off 49% of British Nuclear Fuels to the private sector, making themselves a nice little earner to the tune of £1.5 BILLION! But there's a catch. This will only happen if Sellafield can generate lucrative profits from the successful production and shipping of the controversial MOx fuel. If this week's shipment goes smoothly, there will be another 80 to follow over the next decade.

The last thing BNFL need is bad publicity as it hardly encourages the investors they so desperately need. Greenpeace, old acquaintances of the nuclear industry, set out to pull the rug from under BNFL's feet. Dragging an inflatable white elephant infront of the Pacific Teal to expose the farce of this whole venture, the shipment was delayed for 12 hrs. Not taking too kindly to this 'scary' ordeal, BNFL immediately hauled Greenpeace into court, where they accused the organization of breaching a High Court injunction obtained 3 days before the consignment even left Sellafield. In an obvious attempt to prevent any embarrassing protests, the company tried to ensure Greenpeace kept their distance.

*"As a company, BNFL has no problem with a peaceful and lawful protest. However we would not want to see the safety of the ships' crews, the escort team or the public at large put in*

danger by some irresponsible media stunt," Alastair Thomas, BNFL's head of transport, said in a statement. So plutonium doesn't put anyone's safety in danger, does it Alastair?!!

The outcome in court was that Greenpeace International has had its bank accounts frozen at BNFL's request. The company is claiming £90,275 damages for extra wages they claim they had to pay because of the delay. Also, John Prescott, the deputy prime minister ordered Greenpeace to remove its ships from British waters. This is the first time such an order has been made under the 1995 merchant shipping act. *"Greenpeace will not be strangled in its peaceful efforts to expose the dangerous and dirty nature of the plutonium industry by this financial terrorism. It is an obscene miscarriage of justice that Greenpeace is under attack rather than the French, British and Japanese Gov's, who are conducting a trade in weapons-useable plutonium."*

The Governments' little baby, BNFL are themselves in a state of disarray, breaking their own environmental guidelines and promises. They were in such a rush to escape from Barrow, they even forgot to weld down the hatches

*"If this cargo is allowed to leave, the governments ethical foreign policy will be in tatters. It is not ethical to annually pump millions of litres of radioactive waste into the sea. It is not ethical to impose this dangerous transport on the en route states, threatening the lives and livelihoods of millions of people. It is not ethical to be a world leader in the sale of weapons-useable radioactive material."* Jenny MacKay, Greenpeace.

* A captain in the Russian navy walked free this week after spending 14 months inside for handing footage of sailors dumping radioactive waste into the sea, to a Japanese TV network.. Espionage charges against him were dropped, and he was freed under an amnesty. The Russian authorities tried to hush it all up, but the failed, and he became a local hero, gaining support from monks and women who gave him pizza.

---

## CRAP ARREST OF THE WEEK

For secretly tape recording the police! Michael Hyde was found guilty of violating Massachusetts state wiretap laws, which forbid recording the voice a person without their knowledge. Mr Hyde recorded the police swearing and threatening him with jail. When he brought the tape to the Abington police, he was charged and in court sentenced to six months probation and a $500 fine.

---

*" A report written in 1994 states that a coolant failure at sellafield, lasting for as little as half a day could result in an explosion that would force the evacuation of two million people from Britain and cripple the Irish economy for several decades."* The Ecologist

For excellent, up to the minuite account of the ships, check-out www.greenpeace.org Or call…Cumbrians Opposed to a Radioactive Environment (CORE) ..01229 833 851

---

## MULTI-COLOURED SWAP SHOP

Protestors attending a 'Stop the Crop' rally in Oxfordshire last Sunday, did just that. About 400 hundred people donned bio-hazard suits and de-contaminated (read trashed) one of the UK's largest genetic farm scale trials. The 25 hectares of genetically modified oilseed rape was one of six major GM crop trials currently taking place in the UK. The rape at Model Farm has been modified to tolerate the AgrEvo corporation's '*Liberty*' herbicide, killing all other nearby wildplants dead. Pollen from oil seed rape is also known to travel 2.5 km on the wind, and bees and other insects aren't too clued up on telling the difference, leading it's feared to so called 'superweeds'.

Gene pollution is not the only problem. A recent experiment in the US, revealed that the Monarch butterfly was poisoned by contact with pollen from crops which are modified to contain herbicide. Six people were arrested and the police droned on as per usual about "*a peaceful and enjoyable day for many people has been spoilt by the criminal actions of a few.*" The cops are also threatening to study footage taken by the police helicopter - but with everybody looking the bloody same, SchNEWS wonders have the dirty perverts got x-ray cameras.

* Despite claims by the bio-tech industry that genetic engineering would reduce the use of pesticides, statistics from the US Department of Agriculture from 1997 show that expanded plantings of Roundup Ready soybeans (i.e. soybeans genetically engineered to be tolerant to the herbicide) resulted in a 72% increase in the use of glyphosate.

* Genetic Engineering Network, genetics@gn.apc.org Tel 0181 374 9516

* Campaigners from GenetiX Snowball are at the Royal Courts of Justice, The Strand, London next Wednesday (28th) and need your support. Court starts at 9.30 am Tel 0161 834 0295

## SISTERS OF MERCY PART 2

Black-clad Polish nurses have added their voices to the rising swell of anti-government feeling by blockading central Warsaw for the second time in two weeks. 30,000 nurses and midwives began a hunger strike demanding an increase in their monthly wage of £65 and more stable employment terms. Another 100,000 workers were expected to join them unless the health service receives more money. Warsaw officials insisted that funding should be agreed regionally with health managers, most of whom deny having spare cash. The managers have controlled nurses' salaries since a January reform introduced tough market-led reforms in health, education, adminand social security replacing former communist systems. These moves, reminiscent of the 'free' market truncheon-wielding reforms in eighties Britain, give high earnings for managers while impoverishing ordinary state employees. Doctors, anaesthetists, miners, steelworkers, dockers, farmers and railway staff have staged parallel protests in recent months. Poland's Solidarity-led government, intent on getting its economy in line for early EU membership or bust, has a hard-line response to the protests. Union leaders have warned the government of widespread unrest if they refuse to permit "social dialogue" about its reforms. It seems that the rosy glow of Soviet overthrow has well and truly disappeared, leaving the Poles wondering whatever happened to democracy. Surely loss of freedom to protest and degradation of quality of life should not be the price of joining the West – where, supposedly, we have freedom of speech, and all earn loadsa money to spend in McDonalds?

* Meanwhile over in Quebec, nurses have called off their five week strike while members vote on a deal that will give them a 6% pay-rise and better job security (see Schnews219).

## SchNEWS in brief

Direct Action Works! After 18 days of picketing, 300 striking **Malaysian** workers have won the right to sit down at work. Previously workers at Sanyo Electric in Kuala Lumpur were forced to work in a standing position for 8 hours and 45 minutes every day. www.struggs@mindspring.com ** We got an e-mail this week from someone who was caught reading the Schnews at work by his boss, and got **the sack!** ** The word '**greenwash**' has entered the Oxford Dictionary. It's explained as "*Disinformation disseminated by an organisation so as to present an environmentally responsible public image*". That's bullshitting to you and me** Guildford squatters have been evicted from a squat - so the house can be turned into hostel for the homeless! The eviction took place after squatters offered to pay rent and bills ** **Ecuadorian taxi drivers** have won a 12 day strike over fuel prices when the president gave in to their demands, and froze the price of gas, as he feared there would be a coup d'etat. During the strike, the transport system was gridlocked, and a state of emergency was declared with troops and tanks patrolling the streets of the capital. Ecuador is in the throes of its worst economic crisis saddled with a $16.4 billion foreign debt, made worse by El Nino flood damage and sinking international prices for its key oil and banana exports. Two-thirds of Ecuador's people live below the poverty line ** The Tory block of MEPs in the European parliament looks set to choose Caroline Jackson to head the committee on the environment, despite the fact that she's been on the board of Peugeot UK for 12 years. No conflict of interest there then. ** Don't forget the **Gladstonebury mini-festival** at the Gladstone Pub, Brighton on Sat July 31. Bands, DJs, performers, poets, barbecue + more. £2 all day, in aid of Brighton Lifeline for Kosova. *Contact: 01273 234 788.*

## DEATH IN CHILKA

4 protesters have been killed and thirteen injured at Chilka Lake in India after local villagers destroyed 11 illegal prawn farms. The lake, declared a wetland of international importance is home to dolphins and migratory birds. Despite a Supreme Court judgement saying there should be no shrimp farms within 1000 metres of the lake, large scale industrial shrimp farming gave way to smaller, less scrupulous operators with the support of corrupt local politicians and bureaucrats. After a 24 hour ultimatum was ignored, local villagers moved in. The police subsequently raided the villages, throwing tear gas and beating and shooting. In response there was a mass strike action with fishworkers blocking rail and road links, while in the regional capital Bhurbaneswar shops were closed and vehicles stopped as people made a human wall in the city resulting in *two thousand* arrests!

## YOUR LAND IS THEIRS

The Land Is Ours are trying to use the little known 1965 Commons Registration Act, to get land they are currently occupying turned into a village green. The former hospital site was squatted by the group to commemorate the Kett rebellion of 1549, a time of uprisings by the rural dispossessed over the enclosure of common land. Kett became leader of a 20,000 Norfolk barmy-army, which reclaimed the commons for two months and locked up the worst landowners until they were eventually defeated. Land Is Ours, Box E, 111 Magdalen Rd., Oxford, OX4 1RQ Tel 01865 722016 Site mobile 0961 460171 www.oneworld.org/tlio/

** The villagers of Sunningwell, Oxfordshire are celebrating winning a landmark victory against a housing development. Thanks to a Law Lords ruling, the 10 acre piece of land known as the 'glebe', used as a recreation area for over twenty years, can now be classed as a village green .

## Inside SchNEWS

" *I am convinced the most important drug case in U.S history will take place in Canada on November 1st*" Maury Mason ex- media & PR Greenpeace Canada

Renee Boje is in Canada awaiting extradition to the U.S. This is the story she told SchNews."I was working for Todd McCormick, a medical marijuana advocate, under Proposition 215 which states that patients with a prescription or a doctors recommendation, may cultivate or use marijuana medicinally. Todd was researching how different strains help different illnesses . On July 29, 1997 the Federal Drug Enforcement Agency descended on our group with the aggressiveness of a military attack. The charges against me are conspiracy to cultivate, possession of and intent to distribute marijuana, each count punishable by a mandatory minimum of 10 years to life. I deny these charges in the strongest terms. Three months later, the charges were dropped. While I was visiting Canada and without my knowledge, the charges were reinstated . I was arrested and steps toward my extradition to the US were initiated. In L.A, after my arrest, I was strip searched 15 times in 72 hours, sometimes in front of male guards who made threatening and degrading remarks. So, I am seeking protection through Canada's Refugee Board."

Renee needs your support to get her refugee status in Canada. Cash is essential to fund this important legal battle. For every donation of $25 or more that Renee receives she will send you a cannabis certificate, guaranteed and redeemable against a quarter ounce of organic cannabis flowers as soon as the drug is legalised in Canada.

Renee Boje, P.O. Box 1557 Gibsons, British Columbia, Canada, VON 1VO www.thecompassionclub.org/renee

* It may have passed you by, but in 1993 the (non-psychoactive) cultivation of cannabis was legalised . Eventually hemp could well replace cotton, coal and cattle in terms of providing our fibre, fuel and protein needs. It is not only eco-friendly, requiring neither pesticides or fertilisers, but is also three times as strong as cotton, burns hotter than coal if compressed and is arguably the most nutritious foodstuff in the plant kingdom.

www.thehempcorp.demon.co.uk

## ...and finally...
## Computers 2, People 0

In what seems like a sinister robot plot to throw humans into chaos, faulty computer systems in drinks machines are inundating Australian emergency services with bogus distress calls. Thousands of Sydney vending machines, programmed to call distributors when they run out of sodas, are calling the emergency services 000 number instead! Hundreds of the calls were made to fire, police and ambulance services by the glorified refrigerators, blocking real emergency calls. Perhaps the poor things are lonely, missing their human stock-checkers. A spokeswoman for the 000 service said the problem is getting worse and spreading to other electronic devices! Meanwhile, Toronto had a scary foretaste of millenium plague last week when a small circuit box fire managed to wipe out 170,000 phone lines, most cell phones and cash points. Systems also crashed at the stock exchange, doctors' pagers and much internet and e-mail. Financial traders could only operate by (horror!) talking to each other face-to-face in the street. Building security systems collapsed, including banks, though this was not made public until later to avoid spontaneous outbursts of wealth redistribution.

**disclaimer**....SchNEWS warns all readers that plutonium blondes really do have more fun especially if they're bombshells! Honest.

**WAKE UP! WAKE UP! WE HAVE A CUNNING PLAN MY LORD**

# Weekly SchNEWS

*Printed and Published in Brighton by Justice?*

*I CONSUME, THEREFORE I AM*

**Friday 30th July 1999**     http://www.schnews.org.uk/     **Issue 222   Free/Donation**

# CUNNING STUNT M'LORD

*W*e have always given detailed information, put it into the public domain, about the specific location of trials and experiments…..But you have to ask yourself a question. If small minorities are determined by illegal methods to impose their minority view on the situation by taking pre-meditated reckless action in this way, we may have to reconsider that."

Jack Cunningham, Cabinet Enforcer

**But you have to ask yourself a question, Jack. Are you talking about the protesters or Monsanto?**

In the early hours of Monday morning, a secret Greenpeace action on a 6-acre GM maize test site in Lyng, Norfolk, resulted in a bizarre 'Carry- on meets Monty Python' style scene . Led by the oily Elizabethan noble Lord Melchitt, Norfolk farmer and Executive Director of Greenpeace,  and tooled up with a mechanical mower, 30+ activists barricaded themselves into the test-site field, for a morning of weed-pulling in the dawning  Agro-Evo garden of mutant delights.

Yet after 20 minutes of  faking crop circles, Melchitt and his band of Merry Persons were caught green-handed by the Brigham Brothers. Likened to  the modern day rural Krays, or Phil and Grant Mitchell playing a cameo role in Emmerdale, the 3 brothers lease the field to genetics firm AgrEvo for the  maize trial. The Brighams, long-standing local farmers who boast 4.5 eyes and more than two metres of forehead between them, were swiftly on the scene, crying  "Genetics never did us any harm!"

All 3 brothers started their tractor rampage, ramming the Greenpeace mower and dispersing the gardeners further into the field. Jumping off their tractors, they even chased the activists round and round the field, by which point, over a quarter of the site was trashed.

The action resulted in 28 arrests for theft, criminal damage and vandalism, including Lord Melchett, who alone was denied bail, initial police reports citing Queenie's displeasure. Melchett, however, laid the blame for his detention firmly at the door of  rival fictional toff, Edmund Blackadder. "Thus private parts to the gods are we," he bemoaned to SchNEWS, "They play with us for their sport."

The only one to be kept on remand, Melchett was eventually released after two nights in Norwich nick, with strict bail conditions. The others arrested were bailed to appear before magistrates on 5 August. Nice-one Melch' n'co. ( SchNews has one request, Melch…..drop the 'Lord' title, congratulating a Lord  does nothing for our street cred. )

**GENE POLLUTION**

*"The public has the right to a safe environment and a food chain free from genetic contamination. If the authorities, in this case the government, fail to uphold those rights it is legitimate for others to do so. We took urgent action to defend those public rights."*-Sarah Burton, Greenpeace.

Genetic test crops are fast approaching pollination, where they can cross-contaminate with natural crops; they are 'living pollution', threatening the food chain and the purity of organic crops. As the pollen of rape can travel up to a couple of miles, the concept of short-term 'test sites' is a mutated red herring: Once the pollen takes to the air, we're basically fucked. Quoting Sarah Burton again *"We already know this crop is a threat, so much so that the Swiss government. banned it from open air trials. It is a danger to the food chain and the environment and once the crop has flowered then the contamination is irreversible."*

*A leaked memo from AgrEvo to the Dept. of the Environment estimates genetics farm-scale trials could total 12,350 acres next year. Unless we do something about it (hint)

*AgrEvo has complained that government 'openness' has encouraged this disgraceful outbreak of direct action. It's possible new test farms will be kept secret to ensure 'safety'.

*Rio Grande do Sul, Brazil's southernmost state and second-largest soya grower in Brazil, has declared itself the world's first GM-free zone. Overturning a government decision to hand over the country's soya production to Monsanto, all agricultural secretaries of  Brazils 27 states voted against such GM commercialisation. The reasons, predictably, are primarily economic- but encouraging: Brazilian officials reckon the world demand for GM-free soya makes it a better bet than Frankenstein muck.(so how long till the World Trade Organisation lays its Grim Reaper hands on the state?.....answers on a postcard.)

*More than half the soybeans in the US are now grown with Monsanto's genetically engineered seeds and treated with Roundup herbicide!!

* More info on Genetics and to receive their very fine 'Update'Contact Genetic Engineering Network (GEN) 0181 374 9516 Genetics@gn.apc.org

## SAB VICTORY

Two hunt sabs were celebrating this week after being found not guilty of conspirarcy to commit violent disorder at Portsmouth Crown Court.

Martin Palmer (40) and Nicholas Checketts (39) were two of the 42 hunt sabatours arrested in December 1997 after clashes with the notirously violent Hursley Hambledon Hunt. Those arrested spent up to 36 hours in the cells, and had all their clothes,mobiles and cameras taken. Then for good measure they all had their houses raided. Nice

*The police set up a full time CID incident room operational for over 4 months and involving up to 30 cops. One Hunt Sab explained "The arrests had more to do with evidence gathering for Special Branch, Scotland Yards Public Order Intelligence Unit and Animal Rights National Index." A delighted Martin told SchNEWS to thank everone for the mass of support they received before and after the trial.*

## COR BLIMLEY SQUALLS BACK

Great news SQUALL magazine is back next month. The new A5 16 page monthly 'SQUALL Download' will present the best of the regularly updated On-line SQUALL at www.squall.co.uk. We can look forward to articles on US trade wars, pirate radio, Cuba, the shooting of WPC Yvonne Fletcher, Freemasonry, genetics, cannabis, fast food, CCTV, the Exodus Collective and much more.Subscriptions are £10 for 12 issues with cheques payable to 'SQUALL' sent to SQUALL Download, PO Box 8959,London N19 5HW. As a certain person used to say, if SchNEWS is the tabloid, then SQUALL is yer broadsheet.

### Write to this man!

June 18th prisoner CeeJay McBride is still inside awaiting trial for affray – write to him at Prisoner DC8504, Kestrel Wing, HMYOI&RC Feltham, Bedfont Rd, Feltham, TW13 4ND

### Camps It Up

A new protest camp to resist a proposed housing development of 66 luxury homes on 11 acres of ex-greenbelt land is under construction near Southend. Seeing as the adults in the area weren't doing anything, the camp has been put together by a group of teenagers aged between 14-16. The site's next to a designated wildlife area featuring great-crested newts, badgers, adders, shrews and more. People are desperately needed, as is tat. For directions contact 01702 206181.

## JUNE 18 - THE AFTERMATH

*"The demonstration signals a new era of violent protest which has implications for the whole country and policing at a national level."*

It was the worst disturbance in London since the Poll Tax riots, the City isn't best pleased and everyone agrees the police operation was a total cock-up. So, of course, a report was commissioned, under former Met officer and *'public order expert'* Tony *"whizz-kid"* Speed. In his report Speed admitted that the police were all over the gaff, despite this, the *"gratuitous violence and criminality"* is blamed on, surprise, surprise, the protesters. The City police couldn't cope with their use of high-tech resources such as bikes and packed lunches, especially as their own communications system collapsed under the weight of panicking suits dialling 999 on their mobiles. All this means is that the Met will take over the City police, whose juicy fraud and anti-terrorism briefs it has been eyeing up for ages.

Immediately after the day, the media, police and government line was the usual *"violent minority ruining peaceful protest"* bollocks, but after Jack Straw had spoken to senior coppers, the angle shifted. Basically, grass-roots protesters are being re-branded as *"enemies of democracy."* The Lord Mayor has already described the protesters as *"terrorists"* and when Straw addressed the Commons he admitted that controlling groups *"intent on covert criminal conspiracies is extremely difficult."* This allowed him to hint darkly about using F Branch, the MI5 dept responsible for monitoring and infiltrating subversive groups. Last year it was announced that they were stopping following commies, but would *"continue to be interested in those who pose a serious threat to public order."* The spooks are probably involved already, since the definition of serious crime that MI5 can investigate includes *"conduct by a large number of persons in pursuit of a common purpose".* According to the City Police Commissioner, their intention is not to nick a few people for kicking in McDonalds, but the *"long-term attrition of the groups involved."*

And that's how suddenly a bunch of crusties became the biggest threat since Hitler, inspiring Churchillian statements of defiance. People's Champion Jack "The Last" Straw *again: 'nothing that took place last Friday will remove the City from its pre-eminent position as one of the world's financial centres."*

Of course, there was no mention of why J18 happened, namely the extreme violence inflicted on the planet's people and ecosystems by the deregulated money markets of the City. Straw claimed that *"it appears that the protests were linked in some incoherent way to the G8 summit in Cologne. I fail to understand the direct connection."* There is, according to Straw, *"no excuse whatsoever"* for the £2m of damage done to the City on June 18th - but as *The Ecologist* says, *"perhaps if he took a good look at the wholly deplorable and plainly pre-meditated damage that is being inflicted on the Earth by minority elements of the business community, he might see things in a different light."*

Although only 16 people got nicked on the day, the number has risen to 43 - the latest, a bloke called Thor, found 7 pigs - 2 of them armed - trying to kick his door in. Unfortunately, Lambeth council had just reinforced his door, so when one of the rozzers injured his foot, he let them in, only to be held down while they did his flat over. After being held for 12 hours he was released without charge.

---

**SPOT THE CONTRADICTION**
City Police Commissioner Perry Nove claimed there were two main problems: firstly, the cops didn't know what was going on 'cos the protesters unsportingly refused to tell them; and secondly, they published "significant information" on the internet before the event!

---

## SchNEWS in brief

On the same day Great Western Train's were fined a record £1 1/2 million under the Health and Safety Act, New Labour announced plans to semi privitise air traffic control. There were cheers and congratulations from one side of the house, but silence and attacks from the other. Unfortunately for the transport minister Helen Liddell, the cheers all came from the Tories who thanked her for 'sound capitalist and conservative pratices', while Labour MP's hurled abuse. Safety service being offered up for the profit motive! One MP stormed *"Who knows best? Those who have given us the safest system in the world, or politicians and a bunch of city investors"* ** Respect due to 85 year old Robert Leakey who confronted workmen felling an 85ft sycamore tree prodding them with his umbrella and walking stick and warning *"I'm going to damage your equipment".* He then hit a workman on the shoulder who susequently wrestled him to the ground for possesion of the stick. Mr Leakey was fined £50 for assault ** Read all about it - "The poll-tax rebellion in Haringey" a booklet recording the history of the campaign that brought down Thatcher. £1 + large SAE to Haringey Solidarity Group, PO Box 2474, London, N8 OHW

## SUMMER SOLSTICE 2000

(June 21  2.45 am)

The authorities seem to be getting all steamed up about what might happen at Stonehenge next year.According to the Salisbury Journal a 'reclaim our culture' flyer posted on the internet, is being seen "as possibly a thinly coded invitation for a mass breach of the security cordon". It's so 'thinly coded' SchNews could hardly understand the message - 'Stonehenge 2000 biggest ever free party summer solstice Wednesday June 21st.' The police, who blamed this summers 'invasion' on, yep you've guessed it "a hardcore of troublemakers", reckon next year "the potential for violence and disorder will be incalculable." Which it no doubt will, if the cops turn up in riot gear with dogs, horses and nasty looking batons again. But don't worry, the Journal informs us that "Already a dedicated intelligence team…based in Devizes are monitoring all forms of underground commuincation..to try to stay one step ahead." Basically, the rub is the authorities aren't too pleased with their four mile exclusion zone being ruled illegal, letting all those oiks get near to the stones, even touch them, without paying a bloody penny. 'We need new laws' screams local MP Robert Key because "the police must have adequate powers to prevent a tiny minority runing it for everyone else." Now where has SchNews heard that one before?* There are regular Stonehenge Campaign meetings 2nd Sept and 10th Nov at 99 Torriano Ave, Kentish Town, London NW5 2RX 8 pm (send SAE to same address for their newsletter)

## POLICE LOSE THEIR HALO

Halo, the Brighton Homeless and Lonely Organisation has been offering food, shelter, and a bit of love and care for Brighton's homeless for the past seven years. On Tuesday mid-day they were invaded by 80 riot police citing the 1971 Misuse of Drugs Act. The entire staff and clients were dragged outside, where they were handcuffed and videoed with detailschecked to see if they were wanted for any offences. Sick and mentally ill patients were wrestled to the ground and pinned down while the police passed bottles of water amongst themselves to quench themselves in the scorching mid-day heat. The detainees however weren't allowed a drink.

Out of the 40 people, a mere 5 were found in possession of a few bits of cannabis resin. SchNEWS reckons if the cops raided any pub or club on any average night they would get a lot more of a substantial drug seizure.

Happy B'day Tony "Rebel" Green, Punk's not dead!

## PRISONERS JUSTICE DAY

*"Woodhill remains an environment that engenders psychosis and despair"*John Bowden long term prisoner  As part of International Prisoners' Justice Day, there will a demonstration to close down the notorious Woodhill control unit in Milton Keynes. Opened last year, prisoners considered too *"subversive"* to be contained in the mainstream of the prison system can be arbitarily confined in the units until they *"progress"* with the behaviour modification programme. This 'modification programme' in reality means breaking the spirit of inmates. As Domenyk Noonan a prisoner at Woodhill explained *"Prisoners on A and D wings are treated like animals. They are fed through door hatches, no access to own radios or drawing materials, half hour visits, £2.50 private cash; the cell windows don't open to prevent prisoners talking to one another; 23 hour bang-up, one shower a week. The list is endless."*

In reality the control unit, is merely a big stick to make so-called trouble-some prisoners keep in line.

*"In truth, Woodhill exists as an instrument of fear and political control over long term prisoners, and is specifically intended to isolate and destroy both individual and collective response".* John Bowden.

**Demonstrate**! Saturday 7th August. Meet 1.30 pm at HMP Woodhill, Tattenhoe St., Milton Keynes. Contact London Anarchist Black Cross, 27 Old Gloucester St., London, WC1N 3XX email londonabc@hotmail.com * On Tuesday 10th prisoners from around the country will be taking various forms of action in solidarity with the prisoners at Woodhill, including 24 hour work strikes and hunger strikes. Show your solidarity by phoning and faxing Governor, David Yeomans 01908 501999 fax 01908 505 417. John Gaynor is the man responsible for moving prisoners into the control unit. Tell him what you think by phoning 0171 217 6319/fax 0171 217 6664 protesting at the inhuman conditions.

## ...and finally...

SchNEWS has had to admit that we were wrong about corporations. We had some naïve belief that they were more interested in profits than people. However, we've discovered they **do** care after finding a website sponsored by various corporations that is dedicated to alleviating world hunger. Yes, all you have to do is log on to them, click on the "donate free food" button, and a starving person in the third world will be given a day's supply of food - how caring! Not only that, but you get a free link to the sponsors of the site, who have some lovely products to sell. This week it was all about back pain relief - very useful if you're starving. There's only one problem - you can only do it once a day, or the system may overload! So don't think you can bankrupt these nice corporations by clicking on 1000 times a day (although you could get 1000 friends to do it once a day!). You can do your bit too, by logging on at www.thehungersite.com/index.html

However, the World Health Organisation (WHO) has revealed that between one-third and a half of emergency medical aid shipped to the tent cities of Macedonia and Albania at the height of the Kosovo refugee crisis is useless and will have to be destroyed. Some cynical folk have suggested that the shipments of essential drug supplies (such as lip salve,haemorrhoid ointment, and anti-smoking packs) donated by pharmaceutical companies were done so they could write off their gifts as tax breaks, and were not intended to help the refugees. What a disgrace, as we at SchNEWS now realise that multinationals only have our best interests at heart!

**disclaimer.....**

Schnews warns all readers not to play with their genes otherwise....oh my god everthing's blurring, it's all going dark… Arrrggghhh!!

---

**Stick that in your pipe and smoke it!**

# Doing a bit of gardening

**TOTAL ECLIPSE** of the **SUN**          98%   11·20am

August **11** 1999
Seen from Wolstonbury Hill on
the South Downs, Sussex
Luckily, not obscured by clouds.
But will the chance of a
SOUTH DOWNS NATIONAL PARK
be obscured by bureacracy?

Brighton & Hove

Wolstonbury Hill

Ditchling Beacon

Jack & Jill Windmills

Super 8 Cine Camera

Katri Indian Memorial

Peter Dooze

---

## Squotes

"Big festivals are now covered with advertising which leads people to think it's ours not theirs."
*Sean Pillot de Chenencey, corporate marketing consultant.*
***Sunday Business 19/9/99***

---

**Watching the Eclipse in 3D - Solipse Festival, Hungary**

## WAKE UP! WAKE UP! IT'S YER BLACKED OUT AND MASHED UP

# Weekly SchNEWS

### Printed and Published in Brighton by Justice?

RA GOD OF THE SUN... BRINGER OF SOLAR POWER

**Friday 6th August1999**     http://www.schnews.org.uk/     **Issue 223**     **Free/Donation**

# RURAL PARANOIA

Cornwall is bracing itself for the worst pillaging and raping since the Vikings. Police have issued warnings of a New Age Invasion complete with funny hats and free-love! Landowners have been advised to turn down any requests to camp as *"kindliness can be costly"*, so if some harmless hippie should meander onto their land they ought to block all routes, alert neighbours through the cunning early warning scheme and document all vehicles using photographic and video evidence, noting damage caused to crops or land, so…remember your country code and follow the SchNEWS free-party guidelines, available from our stall at various festivals. Devon and Cornwall Constabulary assure us they are liaising with other *forces*, presumably they mean police forces not spiritual forces.

* If you were planning to check out Sasha and Digweed at 'Totality' you may be amused to hear that licencees will permit camping and liquor but **NO DANCING!** Dancing? That's outrageous, will you debauched bunch of degenerates stop at nothing? So if you're looking for an alternative, SchNEWS has received confirmation from NASA that the place to be to experience totality is Iran-yeah man, the infamous party place where you can expect to be welcomed with open arms by the old Ayatollahs. Forget the balaclavas but all you loose Western women had better remember your veils. Turns out that the South West has a groovie 45%-60% chance of cloud cover which will only enhance the visuals for psychedelic enthusiasts. Cornwall's eclipse co-ordinator (*"move the Moon twenty centimetres to the left, please"*) Gage Williams claims that a little cloud cover will make the eclipse effects more stunning *'Those patiently waiting suddenly saw a circular sharp-edged shadow racing towards them like an express train. There was also the optical illusion where the clouds looked as though they were falling on them."* What was he on?

* The Friends of the Lizard, a crack team of party poopers, and the main opposition group to The Lizard Festival, have said they are investigating every possible avenue to stop the festival despite it already getting a licence. They are organising an around-the-clock photographic and video monitoring team from inside and outside the event . How quaint!

* English Heritage and councils are hypeing their concern about the threat of a Tribal Gathering taking place at Men-an-Tol, near Madron. More than 30,000 acres in Penwith alone have been barricaded to prevent vehicles stopping. Countryside officer, Mike Rosendale claims that in their 4,000 years of existence some of the neolithic sites have never faced such a level of risk. They fail to explain why free party people need to destroy their sacred sites when English Heritage (not to mention industry and roads) do it much more effectively as we have seen through their recent treatment of the Woodhenge at Holme( SchNEWS 213).Makes you wonder whether the real problem is that such gatherings are free, bringing zero revenue to those who like to believe they 'own' these sites. Barriers are also being erected around the Merry Maiden's stones, on Viscount Falmouth's land, and the Boscawen-Un stone circles. Codenamed Operation Obscure, Devon and Cornwall Police have advised landowners to block routes leading to their private land with boulders in an attempt to discourage illicit raves. Anyone who's still bemused by all this Eclipse business check-out www.firstbyteuk.co.uk/eclipse/

## BLINDING PARTY!

So you thought you would be experiencing the eclipse on the chaos of the dance floor, to the sound of your favourite d.j's and bands, grooving with all your friends…..not if you follow the advice of Britain's chief medical oficer of health, Liam Donaldson who recommends the best way to view the eclipse is *"on television"*-well hold on to your party hats, what a crazy guy! His fears about the risks of eye damage are substantiated by the experience of Bob Brown, 35, from Manchester who suffered scarring of the retina during the 1984 partial eclipse. Bob said *"I just glanced up at sun because it looked a bit strange…and carried on waiting for my train"*. Basically, you will fuck your eyes if you look directly at the sun during the eclipse, the eclipse specs work well and welding glass is good too. Film negatives are no good for looking at a permanent thermonuclear explosion, 400 times the size of the moon, 90 million miles away.

## JUST SAY 'NO'!

* Mr A Robbins, of Truro, wrote to his local newspaper asking for the eclipse to be cancelled. He said that now Cornwall is now finally on the national and international map(!), Cornish people should be content with what has already been achieved and not be too greedy. He added: *"Indeed, we might need to move heaven and earth: so be it. We got Objective One status, surely we can do this too. Whatever they do in Devon and the remainder of those European parts, let Cornwall have no eclipse whatever. Cornwall should lead the way!"* Maybe we could all sign a petition and send it to our maker.

# PARTY AND PROTEST

**JULY** 31st Gladstonebury one day festie in aid of Brighton Lifeline for Kosova, bands, performers, DJs, BBQ, kids stuff. 3pm – 1am, £2 Gladstone Pub, Lewes Rd, Brighton. **AUGUST** 1st Sunsplash 99 legendary raggae event www.reggaesunsplash.co.uk 1-2nd Ecotopia nr. Timisoara, Romania solar eclipse info EYFA, Postbus 94115, 1090 GC Amsterdam, The Netherlands Tel + 31 20 665 7743 2-8th European Animal Rights gathering Oslo, Norway www.noahonline.org 1-15 Moonshadow Eclipse Family Camp, Cornwall 0181 941 6277 1–21st Green Futures Eclipse Family Camp – a snip at £200  01736 788926 3rd Hackney Solidarity Group are campaigning against the housing benefit delays since the council housing benefit office was taken over by private firm IT-NET. Public Meeting 6.30pm at The Old Fire Station, Leswin Road, N16. For info. HSG Contact HSG, 136-138 Kingsland High St., London E8 2NS Pager: 07654 513 180. 6th Hiroshima SayIn Preston there will be a vigil at Navy Recruitment Centre, Fishergate Rd. City Centre 3-4pm, followed by an evening of films about nuclear deviance at St. Wilfred's Church Hall, City Centre 7.30 pm *Organised by Bread Not Bombs Ploughshares Support Group. Ciaron 07930-961842 email ciaronx@hotmail.com 6 -8thThe Big Chill 'Enchanted Garden 99', Salisbury £73 Tel: 0181 372 9735    www.bigchill.co.uk 6-13th Zac's Tipi's Total Eclipse Camp (family friendly) 01558 685682 6–12th Megadog Essential Total Eclipse FestivaL, Nr.Plymouth £95 Tel: 0181 806 6242  www.megadog .net 6-15th Sunshadow Festival, Torpoint, Cornwall £85 Tel: 01502 230387   www.sunshadow .com SchNews RECOMMENDED TOP ECLIPSE FESTIVAL! The Lizard Festival, 7-14th August, Goonhilly Down, Cornwall £125  A Celebration of the Spiritual Significance of the Eclipse organised by a crew of idealists who have been involved in the festival scene since the 70's. Lizard are committed to supporting the local economy. The site will be supplied with locally produced food, with not a shitty burger van in sight. Tel: 0906 2102376  www.lizard.net Fri 6–15th Rainbow Circle Astrology and Solar Eclipse Camp, Devon Tel 01452 813505 7–12th Eclipse Party, Cornwall Tel: 0161 860 6472 £25 www.splintered.demon.co.uk/eclipse/ Fri7  Close Down Woodhill Prison Control Unit (part of the **Prisoners' Justice Day** demonstrations, see article) Sat7–15th No One Is Illegal Border Camp – no racism and fortress Europe. The camp will be where the German, Polish and... (cont)

Czech borders meet. Contact Forschungsstelle Flucht und Migration, GneisenaustraBe 2a, D-10961 Berlin www.contrast.org/borders/camp **Critical Mass**. Swansea. This and every first Sat. of the month. Meet 12.15pm @ The University & 12.30pm @ The Guildhall. www.members.tripod.co.uk/swanseacm/ **9-15th Solipse**, solar eclipse festival Ozora, Hungry. Tickets 0171 428 0127 www. solipse.com **7th - 14th** National week of action at **burger bars** across the country. VIVA! 01273 777688 (on the 7th there will be a demo outside Burger King nr. Clocktower 10.30 am) **7th The Animal Jive**. Hillfields Animal Sanctuary, Greenhill, Blackwell, Nr Bromsgrove, Worcs. £2 **7–14th** Cornish Eclipse Stone Festival, nr.Lostwithiel **7/8th Organic Gardening Weekend** – Henry Doubleday Research Assocation 01203 303517 **9th** Nagasaki Day **9–16th If I had a hammer..**Trident Ploughkin House, Morning Lane, E8. Tel: 0181 374 5027 Web: http://home.clara.net/hsg/hhome.html Email: hsg@clara.net **13 Abbey Park Festival** (Leicester); Tel: 0116 2673196 **13-14th** Cropredy (Fairport Convention) Festival, Oxfordshire Tel: 01869 338853 (good if you're into beards) **Sat 14th Brighton Gay Pride FREE and wicked** 01273 730562 **15th** National Vegan Festival,10am-7pm, Camden Centre, Bidborough St., London WC1 0181 670 9585 **15th Smokey Bears Picnic**, 2 pm Southsea Common, Portsmouth FREE! The picnic now in its sixth year, is the largest and most established regular legislation event in the UK challenging the countries ridiculous cannabis laws. **15-13th Natty Gathering** near Lampeter, S.Wales. Exploring practical solutions to sustainable living. Tel: 01273 834995 Email: nattytrust@gn.apc.org Web: www.gn.apc.org/nattytrust **18-23rd Earth First!** Summer Gathering in East Anglia. An opportunity for actvists involved in or interested in environmental direct action to come together to learn new skills and plan campaigns with hundreds of workshops and discussions. Contact 0113 262 9365 www.eco-action.org/gathering **19-20th Festival of the Unknown**, Hackney (of course), London Tel 0181509 3353 **19-23th**, 1999 in Tabor, Czech Republic. Cesta presents 'At Home Abroad' An arts festival whose goal is to explore and collect reflections on adopted cultures from Im/E/Migrants, Refugees, Extra-legal and Resident Aliens, and Others making their homes on foreign soil. CESTA Novakova 387, Tabor 39001, Czech Republic Tel: (420) 361 258 004 e-mail: cesta@mbox.vol.cz http://www.cesta.cz **21st Save the Shamrock Monkeys**. National Demo noon outside Shamrock, at Henfield Road, Small Dole, West Sussex. To offer or request transport call 07020 936956. **21–22st** V99 Weston Park, Staffs £70 Tel: 01142 554973 **21-22 V99** Chelmsford £70 Tel: 01142 554973; **23-26th** second conference of the **People's Global Action** against 'free' trade and the World Trade Organisation.Hosted by the Karnataka State Farmers Association in Bangalore, India. www.agp.org **27–29th** Reading Festival £78 if you must Tel: 0181 961 5490 **27–30th** Exodus festival, Long Meadow Farm, Sundun Rd., Charlton, Beds FREE 01582 508936 **28th Critical Mass Brighton** meet top of Montpelier Cresc, by bottle bank @12pm, **28-30th Leeds Festival** Tel: 0181 961 5490 www.readingfestival.com/ **29-30th** Notting Hill Carnival, FREE **30th Sutton Green Fair**, Carshalton Park, Ruskin Rd., Carshalton, Surrey. 10.30 am - 9 pm 0181 647 7706

**SEPTEMBER** 1-3rd Groundswell's 3rd Annual Self Help Forum FREE! The Ponderosa, Crookesmoor, Sheffield. The only UK wide event for homeless people creating their own solutions. Contact: National Homeless Alliance, 5-15 Cromer St, London, WC1H 8LS Tel: 0171 833 2071 www.oneworld.org/groundswell/ **3-5th Building Sustainable Economies**, Centre for Alternative Technology, Machynlleth, Powys. SY20 9AZ Tel: 01654702400 www.cat.org.uk **3-6th The Land Is Ours Autumn Gathering** @ 'Flying Pig Farm' Nr Stroud, Gloucestershire. (a long-term rural land squat planned straight after the gathering)Tel: 01865 722 016/0585 132080 www.oneworld.org/tlio/ **4th** Human Genetics briefing day, central London. Contact: The Campaign Against Human Genetic Engineering, PO Box 6313, London N16 0DY. Email: cahge@globalnet.co.uk **4th Worthing Green Fair** 12 noon – 11 pm Field of Hope, Beach House Green, Brighton Rd, Worthing seafront 01903 210351 **9 11 year Solar Cycle Festival** at Glastonbury Tor (9/9/99 – how significant) **11-12th CND National Conference**, London 0171 7002393 **18th Demonstration against Hillgrove cat vivisection Farm**. Meet 12 noon. Details-see 31st July- . All-Night Vigil 10pm-7am. **25th** International Rabbit Day! We kid you not. The Rabbit Charity, PO box 23698, London N8 0WS. **7-21st The Colour Of Justice**-The Stephen Lawrence Inquiry U.K Tour. A dramatised reconstruction of key moments in the 6 month murder inquiry. For tour details ring 0171 636 3750 **10-12th Loony Left Weekend** "It's time to stop being sad and start going mad" Three Days to change the world culminating in the loony left football cup Sun 12th starting 11am £15 per team payable to Between the Lines, Box 32 136, Kingsland High St. London E8 2NS Tel: 0171 787 9510 **11th Norwich Reclaim the Streets** party 07931 308091 **11th** National demo at Wickham Animal Research Laboratories 12 noon meet in Mill Lane car park Tel 01705 588516 **12-15th** The American Association of Petroleum Geologists are having their annual shindig at the International Convention Centre in Birmingham with the inspiring title: **'Oil & Gas in the 21st Century-Dawn of the Third Age.'** Highlights include a talk from Sir John Browne (Group Chief Executive, BP/Amoco)on 'Oil, Gas and the Environment.' Nice to know that the environment makes it into the top three priorities of the fossil fuel business. SchNews reckons someone should organise a little reminder that there may not be room in the Third Age for fossil fuels…For more info on the conference, see: http://www.aapg.org/uk99/uk99.html **14-17th** All your top torturers will be at the **Defence Systems Equipment International arms exhibition** in Chertsey. Held on Ministry of Defence land it will be the largest exhibition of its kind ever in the UK with over 20,000 delegates, buyers and officials attending. Unfortunately, despite the taxpayer forking out £1/4 million to host the event the public aren't allowed in. Previous government guests include delegates from such torture-friendly countries as Indonesia, Turkey and Nigeria. Hey what happened to our ethicial arms policy? Campaign Against The Arms Trade will be organising demonstrations throughout the event 11 Goodwin St., Finsbury Park, London, N4 3HQ Tel 0171 281 0297 www.gn.apc.org/caat **23rd Autumn Equinox** BST **24-26th Equinox Party**, Rustlers Valley, The Free State, South Africa. Tel 0027 519333939 www.rustlers.co.za

**OCTOBER** 15-17th 'Gathering Visions Gathering Strength' III, Bringing together people from different movements and communities to explore self organising for radical social change. GVGS III c/o yorkshire CND, 22 Edmunds St, Bradford, BD5 0BH. 07971 302412. www.gvgs3.freeserve.co.uk/' **15 to 23 Aberdeen Alternative Festival** http://dspace.dial.pipex.com/abfest **16th World-wide day of action against McDonalds**. McLibel Support Campaign: 0171 713 1269. Adopt-A-Store Network: 0115 958 5666 **16th Anarchist Bookfair**, Conway Hall, Red Lion Square, Holborn, London 0191 2479249 **17-24th One World Week**. Campaign opportunities on theme of "Re-forming our Futures". P O Box 2555, Reading, RG1 4XW. Ph: 0118 939 4933. email:oneworldweek@gn.apc.org **18th** Marks the 15th anniversary of **Veggies catering company** to be celebrated with parties and picnics. A book is to be published, if you've got any submissions send them to 180 Mansfield Rd., Nottingham, NG1 3HW

**NOVEMBER** 1st Fox Hunt Sabbing Season begins. Contact Hunt Sab Assocation 01273 622827 **27th International No Shop Day.** Contact Enough!One World Centre, 6 Mount St., Manchester, M2 5NS **27th – Seattle, USA** is the place for the next big shindig for the world's power elite. SchNews favourite 'shadowery organisation' **The World Trade Organisation** (see issues 206 & 221) meet to plan the next wave of free trade with their mission to write 'the constitution of a single global economy'. Protests are planned, but details are vague at the momement, but we know International Forum on Globalisation will be having a 'Teach In' on why Globalisation is bad, a few days before also in Seattle. Contact IFG, 155 Pacific Ave, San Francisco, CA 9409 USA, www.ifg.org * "Demystifying the WTO" Booklet available upon request. Contact A SEED, PO Box92066, 1090 AB Amsterdam, Netherlands. Tel: +31 20 668 2236 Web: www.antenna.nl/aseed

**JANUARY 2000** 1st End of the World. We survived Nostradamus Day, but if you believe half the emails SchNEWS get, the end is definitely coming in the form of the Millennium Bug.(see SchNews 191) It's something to do with embedded chips, apparently, so if you've got a potato wedge stuck up yer arse, stock up on baked beans and prepare to spend the new Millennium in a bunker with a bunch of paranoid squaddies back from Kosova to deal with the crisis. On the brighter side maybe it through all the hype why not head (?) along to the **SATANIC ORGY 1/1/00** and start the millenium with a bang!!. Royston Parish Church. Please bring condoms and a partner .

*Subscribe!* PS SchNEWS is having 2 weeks off cos we fucking deserve it!!! so buy us a beer at the eclipse

## WAKE UP! WAKE UP! IT'S YER NO BUDGET ECO-PRANKSTER

# weekly SchNEWS

### Printed and Published in Brighton by *Justice?*

**Friday 20th August 1999**   http://www.schnews.org.uk/   **Issue 224   Free/Donation**

---

# ANARCHY IN THE UK

*'A picture is developing of a cabal of anarchist ringleaders who ally themselves to protest movements and subvert them for their own ends'*

**(Evening Standard, August 11)**

What is it about anarchists that makes everyone love them so much? While the solar eclipse has been looming, their image has been stock fare for news editors and police who have kept them paramount upon the nation's consciousness, with word of their suspected activities on everyone's lips.

*'Anarchist violence erupted at an eclipse site yesterday as police fought to close down an illegal rave'* barked the *Express* on August 11. What has so stirred the blood of this particular tabloid? Apparently, *'Officers believe members of the anarchist group Reclaim the Streets - who played a key role in the riots in London in June - are on the site'*. June 18's memorable day of action against London's financial centre, is still playing on some people's minds. And the trouble seems to be spreading, with:

*'Anarchists 'hijacking' GM food protest groups'*, as proclaims the *Evening Standard* (Aug 11), identifying *'links between organisers of the GM food protests and those responsible for the 18 June action'*. No shit, Sherlock. But the career of those anarchists seems not only to have broadened; now, they're mobile:

*'Some of the most ancient stones in Penwith could be desecrated and vandalised by travelling anarchists prior to next week's total eclipse'* we read in *The Cornishman* (Aug 5). Again, it is *The same groups of anarchists who have recently rioted in central London [who] are on their way to target the Men an Tol stones near Morvah.'* Might they not be tired after infiltrating anti-GM groups and raving all night? Apparently not; as, reports the paper, those wacky anarchists are getting a bit arty: *We believe that they intend to disrupt the eclipse celebrations at the stones....by painting the holed stone white to make it look like a Polo-Mint'*.

Phew! You can see why, in the words of one Cornwall resident reported in *The West Briton*: *'People are scared to go out of their doors. People will protect their property in any way they can. The police seem to have no conception of how scared everyone is out here.'*

On the other hand, the mass action and street carnival that London saw on June 18 was aimed at hurting some of the major financial institutions based in the banking district – hardly a threat to yer average Jo(e), who stands to gain as much 'trickledown' from the selling of futures as did Bob Crachitt. So: from *whence* such terror? If, as the *Evening Standard* claims, *'A picture is developing of a cabal*

*of anarchist ringleaders'* - just who is painting it? The police have recently released to the press a number of stills from CCTV footage of the riot, which, apparently, a crack team of City of London and Metropolitan officers have been busily scrutinising since the day. Their analysis, claim the police in a recent report, points to a number of individuals orchestrating the rioting.

*Police 'have pinpointed six smartly-dressed men as the ringleaders'* babbles the *Sun* of August 10. The *Mail* lets on that *'The ringleaders carried mobile phones and could be seen huddled in corners apparently communicating with each other'*, before offering the predictable revelation that *'a number of rioters drank huge quantities of alcohol and took drugs.'* The *Evening Standard* of the day before adds, darkly: *'One even carried a copy of the Financial Times.'*

If anyone who wore a suit must have been in charge of the riot, you'd better not make too much effort dressing up for Hallowe'en this year, lest you're held responsible for the entire festival. By dint of similar reasoning, the police note that some funds went into hiring the vans and soundsystem for the event, and that someone involved in Reclaim the Streets has a pot of wedge from his rich folks. *Ergo*: he funded the do.

The police seem to be just the kind of people whose salacious minds lap up tabloid sensationalism – and take it literally. You can imagine their team, huddled wide-eyed over monitor screens, whispering to one another like children telling ghost stories around a campfire. Look - there's that *'man in a suit with a mobile phone who called the shots in the City riot'* (*The Independent*). Well, someone at SchNEWS knows someone, whose sister's boyfriend's cousin's uncle plays darts with the person in that photo; and he never actually carried a mobile. These kids seem to convince themselves of more-or-less what they want to believe, before passing down the hot gossip to the public.

For theirs is the same kind of Playschool logic as makes for damn good copy, as amply proven by the quantity of press coverage generated by the police report. The police are by no means innocent of this, when that same report of theirs announces their intent *'to achieve long-term attrition'* against direct action groups. It's an informal conspiracy which is convenient for all sides; the media get some great stories, the police and government to engineer a climate favourable to their ends.

The promise of a new police campaign against grassroots activists

chimes strangely well with a recent Home Office consultation paper, seeking to increase police powers to target *'animal rights, and, to a lesser extent environmental rights activists'*. The key shift here is semantic; at once redefining 'violence' to include 'serious disruption', while loosening the category of 'terrorism' from one purely denoting certain types of violence against **people**, to the US definition of 'serious violence against persons or property, or the threat to use such violence'. The meaning of words is as much a site of struggle as the fields or the streets, as well anyone might remember, who next gets nicked with banner in hand, and labelled 'terrorist'.

Meanwhile, who reports on all the other groups around the world who took action on June 18; the unemployed, the unions, the landless and indigenous groups, who stand to get at least as surely screwed by the free trade policies of the G8 summit which then took place? In fact, there was one dissenting press article, which spoke of June 18 in terms of IMF policy and the *'social and environmental breakdown [which] is occurring across the world'* (*The Guardian* Aug 14). But, you see, we know the author; glance at the name and you'll see an aging ex-superstar comedian from north London. (And the article all, presumably, inspired by literature he gleaned from the info-stalls we did at a benefit gig he put on for us last year).

One other paper, at least, puts forward a calm voice of reason. *'Anarchist fears groundless'*, says the *Cornish Guardian* on August 12, assuring us: 'Fears that troublemakers would descend on Penzance on Monday for an "anarchist jamboree" proved unfounded.'

\*    An Italian national is currently being held after being arrested on June 18. He has limited English, but would appreciate support. Write to: Onofrio Lo Verso, TC3014, HMP Rochester, 1 Ford Road, Rochester, Kent ME1 3SQ

---

# IT'S NO TOKE !

A crack team of Hampshire's finest made over 80 arrests at last Sunday's Smokey Bears Picnic on Southsea Common, Portsmouth. Arrests made on the day included, bongo playing (SchNEWS can't really argue with that one after many sleepless festival nights), growling at a police dog and of course the heinous crime of possessing cannabis. Inspector Kevin Whaller of Hampshire police defended the police action as "positive policing" while Superintendent Martyn Powell, said "the number of arrests justified the large police presence."

However Portsmouth's well known subversive publication "The News" has attacked the police actions in their editorial. *"The actions of the police at this years rally make a mockery of last years decision to ignore drug offences at the same event."* So what brought around this U-turn in police policy? SchNews has tracked down a copy of the literature that inspired Superintendent Powell and his boyz and feel we must warn readers of the true facts about cannabis.

* Marijuana is a drug. A drug which affects the mind. And don't be fooled into thinking that just one toke, sorry, hit - is harmless. Many cases of psychopathology have been reported after a single dose.

* Recently, in quest for bigger thrills, some have injected marijuana directly into the bloodstream

* Many myths regarding marijuana have suggested that the cannabis drug can trigger sexual debauchery. During marijuana intoxication a persons control of his/her mind is loosened, breaks down moral barriers and contributes to immortality.

* Studies have shown that most people who take drugs have a somewhat poorly organised personality to begin with that's why they take drugs.

All the above were taken from *New Facts About Marijuana*. Ambassador College Press, California.

## TURKISH EARTHQUAKE

As the toll continues to rises in Turkey, the blame for many of the earthquake deaths has been put firmly at the feet of dodgy house builders. Aerial t.v. footage shows many apartment blocks which collapsed only metres away from others which remained intact. According to the Architects Chamber of Turkey more than half of all buildings in Turkey disregard construction regulations and are prone to collapse in an earthquake. The builders are often people with political connections who put profit above safety, while corrupt officials look the other way. Metin Munir writing in The Financial Times said *"What building laws there are virtually unenforceable because those who break them are politically too powerful."* 6 years ago a cabinet minister was even fired because he tried to end building trade corruption. Turkey has suffered a deadly earthquake on average every 18 months this century.

## BLOWN AWAY AT THE ECLIPSE

At an eclipse party at Summer Court between Truro and Bodmin attended by 1000+ people, 20 riot cops attempted to shut down one of the 5 sound systems and take it away, while more of their kind sat waiting in vans. The crowd didn't take kindly to this disruption of their fun, and replied with bricks, spades etc. Out came the CS gas, with a woman and her young daughter getting sprayed. After a brief stand-off the press showed up, possibly preventing events escalating even further. Crowd highlights apparently included a woman giving a man a blowjob in front of the old bill, but SchNEWS don't swallow that story.

# SchNEWS in brief

We're sure you've all heard - **Hillgrove cat vivisection farm** has finally been closed down because the owner is retiring (yeah, right) Congratulations all round. Anyone for Shamrock? ** Home Secretary Jack Straw's in trouble after remarks he made on a Birmingham radio show. Commenting after 100 armed police turned up at an Irish **traveller's wedding,** Straw complained *"there has been rather too much toleration of travellers ...travellers seem to think that it's perfectly OK for them to cause mayhem in an area, to go burgling, thieving, breaking into vehicles, defecating in the doorways of firms and so on..."* The matter has now been referred to the police and Comission for Racial Equality. Ever heard of the Stephen Lawrence enquiry, Jack? ** Meanwhile SchNEWS can reveal the reasons for last weekends trouble in Kent between asylum seekers and local residents – a misunderstanding of different traditions. This includes according to one local councillor *'children playing in the street because they believe it's the acceptable way'*, Whatever next! Don't they know roads are for cars ** Maybe they should check out Broughton Road in West Ealing where pedal powered toddlers joined an open air tea party (let's give the more up-beat name of say, *reclaim the streets*). Ealing is one of nine areas that will pilot the "home zone" project, which puts the rights of and their children before cars with 10 mph speed limits, traffic calming measures, whole streets even pedestrianised. The idea comes from the Netherlands, where there are 6,000 home zones. ** A National **Non Payment Collective** has just been launched to help co-ordinate the fight back against tuition fees around the country. A briefing pack will be available soon from nonpayment@onelist.com_. Meanwhile its been estimated that students owe up to £15 million in unpaid fees! ** **Spoilt brat** Charlotte Townsend, reputed to be Britain's second richest woman, has pulled out of an agreement to give Chesil Beach in Dorset to English Nature so it could become a National Nature Reserve. Townsend pulled out of the deal to hand over the 17 mile shingle ridge in protest at Labour plans to ban fox hunting. ** **The farce continues.** Less than 10 months after opening, the much loved Newbury bypass is to be closed for two months to allow the top surface to be replaced. The estimated bill is £2.5 million and will be met by the contractors. **Rob Newman** is doing a benefit gig for Sea Action, at the Komedia Tuesday 31st August. Tickets from the Brighton Peace & Environment Centre, £5-10 (pay what you can afford but remember it's for a good cause) **Last week people dressed as bats swooped down on the Cubana Bar in London, which serves Cuban food and drink. However, Bacardi have paid them £12 000 to only stock their rum, despite the fact that **Bacardi** rum hasn't been produced in Cuba since they were kicked out during the Revolution. For an info-pack on Bacardi's dodginess and their manipulation and support of the US 40 year blockade of Cuba, contact Rock Around the Blockade c/o BCM Box 5909, London WC1N 3XX Tel: 0171 837 1688.**A homeless **'tent city'** has been evicted after just three days by police. The Safe Park for homeless people was Ontario Coalition Against Poverty answer to the citys increasing homeless problem and the police's hard-line against the city poor. A study in January described Toronto's 26,000 homeless as a national crisis. Despite this, the mayor called the park protestors *"professional bums,"* and police officers have been working overtime in recent weeks to purge the city of squeegee kids, panhandler and homeless. e m a i l < o c a p @ t a o . c a > www.welfarewatch.toronto.on.ca/** **Bath Reclaim The Streets** 11th September, meet 12 noon The Circus.

# 121 FINALLY EVICTED

The 121 Centre in Brixton has finally been evicted after 150 riot police backed by an armed squad and helicopter sealed off Railton Rd and adjoining streets before bursting in through the first floor window. Within minutes the 8 occupiers had been removed and the council went about trashing and barricading the building. Lambeth leader Jim Dickson said *"We are systematically clearing up the borough and dealing with the legacy of the past. Our action today sends out a very clear message to the squatters - the council will keep taking action over squatted property until there is none left."*

The Centre, which had been occupied for 18 years is the latest victim in Lambeth Councils plans to gentrify Brixton. Used as an advice centre for squatters as well as a cafe, party venue and printing office, the building will now be auctioned off to line some fat cats pocket.

# OH, THE HOCKLEY-COKEY

Welcome to the topsy turvy world of Hockley near Southend, Essex. North Thames Ltd, who sponsor the Essex Wildlife Trust, want to build 66 luxury homes on land sited next to an important wildlife reserve. The company butter up the local council with some serious financial incentives (between £750 000 and £2 million) and get them to release greenbelt land they last year said would never be built on. The money also helps them forget about their recently published Biodiversity Plan which they said would help defend local wildlife.

A protest camp has now been set up. Respect due to the kids who've sorted it out. The Council reckon it's disgraceful that 10-12 year old kids are camping out (even tho' the average age is actually 14). What should they be doing - sitting at home staring at computer screens?

And there's more - the Southend Relief Road, which is going round Hockley, may link to the A130, site of another protest camp, Gorse Wood at Rettendon, whose crew have been helping out in Hockley. There's a "Save the Woods" march and picnic on Sat. 28th August. For details contact: 0831 678635/01702 206181.

# IN DEEP WATER

The infamous Narmada Dam in India has been raised to 85m, threatening 200,000 people's homes. As part of the Satyaghira (non-violent mass action), protesters refused to leave when water from the dam flooded their valley. Apparently, the *"Satyagrahis were facing the increasing waters while the police were making merry at the higher camp and some indulging in the liquor as it was the "gataari amavaas" ( dirty first-moon day)."* When the police sobered up, 62 protesters were dragged out of their homes, beaten and arrested. For info on Narmada and the other 3,165 dams being built, check out www.ens-news.com

# ...and finally...

A panel of SchNEWS marketing consultants (most of them disaffected ex-Saatchi and Saatchi high-flyers) have been reflecting on how to make anarchists seem more exciting, sexy, more attractive for today's youth. These are just some of their ideas:

* Good old anarchism. As true today as it's always been.

* 'Here's Gail Porter, with some letters from you about *New* Anarchism'

* 'Anarchy – won't dry your Ph balanced like a great taste all your family will love, even with problem hair. That's the Anarchist promise.'

**disclaimer**
SchNEWS warns all readers that like dope, New Labour can induce mild euphoria, a distorted sense of reality, and a tendency to talk crap in a meaningful way. When under the influence, everything takes on added significance despite the fact that nothin's 'appenin.

# Narmada Dam, India

Praying at the half submerged ghats at Maheshwar town, Madhya Pradesh, India, August, 1999

The Narmada Dam development project will build thirty large dams, 135 medium and 3000 small dams along the river, controlling the waters of the Narmada and its tributaries - all at a cost of $11.4 billion.

Anti-dams activists also wish to raise awareness of the environmental impact of dam building. They believe the water and electricity can be provided to Gujarat and other regions through alternative technologies, which will be more socially, economically and environmentally sustainable.

They also argue that the state is using the "emotive power of thirst" to hide its real aim of promoting big business. Suger mills, five star hotels, golf courses and petro-chemical plants are springing up at the mouth of the main canal, attracted by the promise of plentiful water.

Pics: Karen Robinson

Women bathe and pray next to the half submerged temple at Khoteswar, a village on the banks of the Narmada River. The temple was in use until last year but has since been submerged due to a rise in the water level, a direct result of the building of and raising the height of the Sardar Sarovar Dam, India August 1999

Anti-dam activists and tribal women prepare to drown themselves as the monsoon waters rise rapidly, flooding land and homes in Domkhedi village, on the bank of the Narmada river, Maharashtra, India. August 1999.

WAKE UP! WAKE UP! IT'S YER EVER GROWING

# SchNEWS

## Printed and Published in Brighton by Justice?

**Friday 27th August 1999**　　http://www.schnews.org.uk/　　**Issue 225**　　**Free/Donation**

# SEEDY BUSINESS

*"Corporations want to control our food from the seed to the spoon, effectively privatising our future food security. We need to resist them and reclaim our food and our environment back into common ownership."*　　Joyce Hambling
Women's Environmental Network

*"We are seeing an unprecedented consolidation of control of food in the hands of a tiny elite of corporate directors and senior executives."*
John Madeley, UK Food Group

Activists who've been busy de-contaminating genetic crops sites will be rubbing shoulders with yer more traditional allotment growers at an alternative conference next month in Cambridge. The three day event titled 'Seeds of Resistance', will be running counter to another event, same time, same town. The counter-conference is for people to share ideas in the fight against the global agri-business monster and the development of positive alternatives, while blowing a big raspberry at the corporate bastards down the road.

*So just who is down the road?*

A range of sinister lobbying organisations, like the International Seed Federation, the ISTA and various other CLFA's (that's Confusing Four Letter Acronyms...) who are getting together for the World Seed Conference, where the world's biggest seed corporations are meeting to discuss *"the globalisation of the economy, development of new techniques, regulatory evolution(!), and the increasing impact of environmental concerns."* The heavily greenwashed blurb for this corporate shindig notes that *"irrespective of technical merits, promising innovations can prompt suspicion."* No, really?

Just 10 corporations including Du Pont, Monsanto, Novartis, Astria/Zeneca and Aventis now control 32% of the commercial seed market - and the figure is rising all the time. Those very same bio-tech giants that are trying to get us all to eat genetically modified food, have been steadily buying up all your favourite garden seed companies. Because, as Alfonso Romo Garza, owner of one of those corporations'Empressa La Moderna' put it *"Seeds are software. And we have the seeds"*

Over the past hundred years a massive percentage of our food bio-diversity has been lost. In the USA, since the turn of the century, 95% of small family farms have disappeared, and along with them 90% of all fruit and vegetable varieties. On the eve of the new millennium, farming is characterised by massive farms producing crops that are designed to feed massive food processing plants, not people. So should we be worried? Joyce Hambling of the Women's Environmental Network (WEN) clearly thinks so *"Bio-diversity is the key to future food security. We need a broad range of varieties of each kind of crop- one variety might be resistant to a certain pest, another to a certain disease. There are countless examples of whole years' crops of rice, coffee, potatoes, maize and wheat being wiped out because just one variety was grown, yet big business still hasn't learnt."*

As Bob Sherman from the UK's main organic gardening organisation the Henry Doubleday Research Association (HDRA) points out *"The risk of concentrating so much commercial power into the hands of one corporate empire is that we then become subject to the dreams and aspirations of a very few people. Do they care about biodiversity? Not as much, I suspect, as they do about profit."*

Or, as Robert Fraley from Monsanto puts it more bluntly *"What you are seeing is not just a consolidation of seed companies, it's really a consolidation of the entire food chain."* And SchNEWS reckons people should find that hard to swallow.

\* **Seeds of Resistance** runs from 6 - 8th September in Cambridge. More info from WEN, 87 Worship St., London, EC2A 2BE Tel 0171 247 3327 www.gn.apc.org/wen

\*One man who will be attending *both* conferences is the highly respected Pat Mooney, from the Rural Advancement Foundation International. A passionate defender of biodiversity, he has worked for over a decade to make big businesses accountable. Check out RAFI's excellent website www.rafi.org

\*'Hungry for Power – the impact of transnational corporations on food security' is an excellent publication from the UK Food Group, PO Box 100, London, SE1 7RT Tel 0171 523 2369 www.ukfg.org.uk

*Here's some people fighting the global seed-swallowing monster*

There are quite a few seed exchanges around the countries offering unusual or outlawed vegetable seeds. The most well known is the **HDRA Heritage Seed Library**, Ryton Organic Gardens, Coventry, CV8 3LG Tel 01203 303517 www.hdra.org.uk. (send a large SAE and ask for a copy of their catalogue).

From Penzance to Inverness **farmers markets** have mushroomed from just one in 1997 to over eighty. Only local growers and producers can sell their own produce at the market meaning the food is fresh, has little if any packaging and fewer food miles. Check out www.soilassociation.org.

**Common Ground** run a campaign to safeguard and plant new Orchards. Send SAE to PO Box 25309, London, NW5 1ZA Tel 0171 267 2144 www.commonground.org.uk. They've also organised an *'Orchards and Wildlife Conference'* 22/23rd September at English Nature Three Counties Office, Ledbury, Herefordshire. Also look out for *'Apple Day'* events on 21st October. \* **The Permaculture Association** produce an excellent magazine that provides 'solutions for sustainable living' publish an Earth Repair catalogue Hyden House Ltd., The Sustainability Centre, East Moon, Hampshire Tel 01703-823322 www.btinternet.com/~permaculture.uk/ A resource guide including the above organisations and a whole lot more will be available at Seeds of Resistance or get copies from WEN.

## SEEDS OF DOPE!

September is Free Cannabis Month and events have been lined-up and down the country SchNEWS highligs include **Cannabis Prisoners Day.**(9th): National Cannabis Action Conference at Norwich.(10/11) **'Living with the Enemy'** BBC 2,  9pm Watch the shadow conservative minister for the family (he's twenty two and still lives with his mum) freak out about the Exodus Collective (Weds 15th).  **'Healer of the Nations'** march and one day cannabis festival at Stockwood Park, Luton. Organised by the 'Campaign Against Narcotic Abuse Because of Ignorance in Society' (C.A.N.A.B.I.S), (Sat 18th) **Smokey Bears Picnic**, Speakers Corner, Hyde Park, London. High noon onwards. (Sat 25) **Smokey Bears Picnic**, Norwich. Chapelfield Gardens, Norwich. High noon.(Sun 26) **Free Cannabis Month** Info Lines: 0171 637 7467 / 01605 625 780 Listings update www.schmoo.co.uk/ free99.htm **PS** Cannabis Prohibition costs the British tax payers £1 billion a year to enforce

**SchWOOPS** Last week we said 80 arrests were made at the Smokey Bears Picnic in Portsmouth. In fact there were only 30. Okay, so sorry- now leave me alone the fax was all blurred, honest!!

# PULP FRICTION

*"Commercial logging poses by far the greatest danger to frontier forests"* The World Resources Institute

If you think activists in Britain get a hard time then check out the prospects for activists in Mexico. Mexico's vast forest resources came up for grabs when the 1994 North American Free Trade Agreement (NAFTA) removed restrictions on foreign investment in communal land, which contain 80% of the country's forests. Within eighteen months, 15 U.S. logging companies moved in. In May 1995, Boise Cascade joined the party, targeting the state of Guerrero where the local Governor was eventually forced to resign after the state police ambushed and killed 17 small farmers who had protested against logging. When the logging in the Guerrero region started to affect water supplies, local farmers, led by a poor *campesino*, Rodolpho Montiel , set up Ecologistas de la Sierra de Petatln. The activists blocked roads, hijacked trucks, unloaded logs and returned them to the communities. In early 1998, Boise Cascade suspended its contracts. *"An incredible victory for the campesinos against one of the world's largest transnational timber corporations, who was blatantly colluding with a repressive government."* said an American Lands Alliance spokesperson. However, local beneficiaries of Boise started to show up at meetings armed and threatening Rodolpho. Eventually, on May 2nd, Mexican soldiers entered the village, shooting and killing one unarmed campesino. Rodolpho was arrested and subsequently beaten, tortured with electric shock and put in prison. Immediately after Rodolfo's arrest (on trumped up drugs n' guns charges ), Boise Cascade tried to start logging again, but activists once again stopped them. Rodolpho is now in solitary confinement Coyucade Catalan prison, Guerrero.

There is a national campaign in Mexico to free Rodolfo and the other defenders of the forest jailed with him." N*ot only is Rodolfo Montiel innocent, but his being denied adequate medical treatment, food, and water is a violation of his basic human rights and he should be freed immediately."* Sign on to the letter by emailing Pat Rasmussen prasmussen@igc.org Donations to: RodolfoMontiel Defense Fund c/o American Lands Alliance, 726 7th St. SE Washington DC.

**Boise Cascade** are one of the largest US wood companies, who've been busy closing down their sawmills in Idaho, and looking south to where labour is cheap and environmental laws weak. * In Brazil , they are merging with Klabin, , the largest producer of wood pulp products in Latin America, so they can get their hands on over 200,000 hectares of pine and eucalyptus forests. * In Ilque, Chile, Boise intend to produce one million cubic metres of woodchip annually, using native forests. They are currently being sued after they trashed Conchales de Ilque, an archaeological monument. Despite Ilque being a traditional fishing town, Cascade has constructed a port on the town's cleanest bay. Cascade's president kindly reassured locals that the plant would provide Ilque with telephones, jobs and better roads - ample compensation for the loss of their livelihood and environment!

# SchNEWS in brief

This Saturday (28th) it's **on yer bikes Brighton for a Critical Mass.** Fed up of abuse from car drivers, pedestrians and the Evening Anus? Then join the wheels for a leisurely pedal through our town for a picnic lunch somewhere. meet 12 noon, Montpelier Cresc, by the bottle bank. bring fizzy pop and sarnies, dress as fancy as yer like. ** Fancy building some sustainable conomies? Then get along to a Conference at the Centre for Alternative Technology **Sept 3-5th,:** Info: 01654-702400 ATA@cleanslate.force9.co.uk. ** **Worthing Green Fair Sat 4th Sept** Field of Hope, Beach House Green, Worthing Seafront. Music & merriment until 11pm inc. healing garden, café area and stalls including good old SchNEWS so come and buy our books and have a chat. ** **Sept 8th, The Right to Protest Legal Forum Legal Observer Steering Group.** Interested in developing a legal observation group? Then turn up and get involved. Artist's Room, Conway Hall, 25 Red Lion Sq., London. 6.30-8pm. ** **Sat 11th Reclaim the Streets Norwich**, Norfolk, 1pm Bus Station Entrance, Queens Road. "Holding up the Traffic to Liberate the Streets" ** **Sept 11-12th Working Class Politics Conference.** A weekend of ideas and discussion, such as, Solidarity Through Football, Drugs and working class. £3 /£1.50. @ Crown Inn, Bridgewater, Somerset. Info: 01278-450562. ** Sept 12 - 18 **Green Front! (Green Front!)** ACTION CAMP Action week against Trans European Network (TEN's) railfreight 'Betuveline', through the deepest (if that exists!) and greenest part of Holland. e-mail grgroenfr@dds.nl ** **Sept 22nd The Land Is Ours Autumn Gathering 99** at The Reddings (AKA Flying Pig Farm), Stockend Lane, Edge NR. Stroud, Gloucestershire. **Land Occupation after Gathering**. 01865 722016/0961 460171 www.oneworld.org

## PSSTT! WANNA SHOOTER?

Any arms dealers out there should get down to the **Defence Systems & Equipment International** exhibition on September 14 – 17th All paid for by the taxpayer to the tune of £1/ 4 million. Luvverly. The UK is the world's second largest arms exporter and just loves being generous little dictators. Recently 500,000 H&K assault rifles were sold to Turkey to repress the Kurds. While the international community calls for restraint in the increasing violence between Pakistan and India, the Campaign Against Arms Trade (CAAT) has revealed that the UK has been supplying arms to both sides for years. Despite, and contrary, to Robin Cook's ethical foreign policy pledge over 500 arms export licences were signed to India and 128 licences to Pakistan in 'New' Labours first year of power. *"When will this government start to match its rhetoric with actions"* asks Rachel Harford from CAAT *"It is guilty of fuelling the very conflicts and repression it condemns".* The sale of arms to *"developing countries"* also contradicts the government's goal of reducing poverty, by diverting poor countries scarce national resources from luxuries like clean drinking water to necessities like guns.

The exhibition is being held on two sites, Chertsy in Surrey and London Docklands. **CAAT** will be protesting throughout starting with a "peace train" from Waterloo to Virginia Waters's station in Chertsy followed by a march to the gates of the exhibition on the 14th. On the 15th there will be protest at the Docklands site. Campaign Against Arms Trade, 11 Goodwin St., Finsbury Park, London, N4 3HQ Tel 0171 281 0297 www.caat.demon.co.uk

'The Arms Trade, Debt and Development' by Susan Willett available from the above address.

# WHAT A LOAD OF HUNTS !

Making what some felt to be a less-than-convincing bid for a prize in the 'statistician of the year' awards, was wishful-thinking Sam Butler, chair of the Countryside Alliance. When results of a poll commissioned by his organisation showed that 52% of the public strongly supported a ban on foxhunting, with a further 11% 'tending to support' a ban, he was robust in his observation; *'This poll gives the lie to the idea that there is any majority public enthusiasm or support for outlawing hunting'.*

**Anyone for early mornings?**

Those with a better head for elementary maths than Sam may like to get on the case of the beleaguered hunting community, as we once again reach one of the most crucial times of the year for their sport. Cubhunting (now often renamed 'autumn hunting' in PR-aware hunting circles) goes on from late August until November, and trains the new intake of foxhounds by letting them loose on litters of young foxes.

Hunt Saboteurs Association, PO Box 2786, Brighton, BN2 2AX Tel 01273 622827.

**The Countryside Alliance** are planning to march in Bournemouth during the New Labour conference on September 28th! A Carnival Against Bloodsports is also expected to be heading in the same direction. How's that for balanced reporting.

---

Ever wished you could get SchNEWS off the web and print it out so it looks like the *real thing?* You can mate. All you need is an internet connection, web browser, acrobat reader and any old printer. Check out our web site for more info.

---

# ...and finally...

While it's oft been said that Americans lack any sense of irony, the US military have been doing little to explode the idea. The Pentagon is investing in research to develop a cleaner alternative to lead bullets, which, says the spokeswoman for their armament research centre, will be a 'safer bullet with the....same lethality as its lead counterpart'. Of course, she means safer to the *environment*; such that of any of the hundreds of firing ranges the US army has been forced to close due to lead pollution, now leaving them with a clean-up bill of £9 billion (dwarfing the mere $12 million pledged to the green ammunition research). SchNEWS had to charge up its cynicism drive to full power to deal with this one. The new material that promises to save the US military so much money in future is called tungsten, a dense white metal they rejected in the 70's for use in a new generation of armour-piercing shells, when in this instance they found they could save money by using depleted uranium instead. So now American soldiers will be able to fire on teenage conscripts in far-off lands, freed from the crippling guilt that made their fingers quiver at the trigger of a gun loaded with eco-unfriendly lead rounds. On the other hand, as many as one in twenty Iraqi children continue to be born with serious birth defects, thought to be caused by pollution from the uranium-tipped shells UN fired there during the Persian Gulf war.

**disclaimer**

SchNEWS warns all readers that if you've got any budding ideas go sit in a compost bin or flower bed with someone swop seeds& get germinating then you'll be blossoming, honest!!!!

# BANGIN' IN BANGA

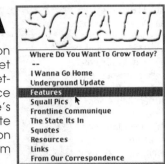

With transnational corporations and the World Trade Organisation becoming ever more strategic in their drive to facilitate market dominance, the official line is "resistance is futile". However, a network of activists has now evolved to help co-ordinate resistance movements across the world. The second conference of People's Global Action took place in Bangalore in the southern Indian state of Karnataka from August 23rd to 26th 1999. Jon Towne reports on the triumphs, tribulations and remarkable encounters resulting from this multinational resistance network.

The hosts for this year's People's Global Action (PGA) encounter were India's mighty Karnataka State Farmers Association; the so-called 'laughing arsonists' renowned for the recent torching of genetically modified test sites (including Monsanto), the dismantling of a local office belonging to seed giant Cargill and the burning down of a KFC outlet in India. Our host's credentials were definitely intact.

The conference was called in the main to plan actions against the looming 'millenium round' talks of the World Trade Organisation in Seattle from November 29th to December 3rd 1999. A meeting which will see the world's most greedy political vampires gathering to carve up more of the planet under the guise of free trade. PGA distinguishes itself from the predominantly reformist NGO agenda on the WTO, by calling for its death, or - as they say in India - 'Kill the WTO before it kills us'.

Springing from the Zapatista-inspired 'Encuentro' held in Spain in 1997, PGA was really christened at a huge, chaotic and fantastically inspiring conference in Geneva in February 1998, where 400 or so activists from a huge variety of movements and backgrounds came together to "turn the fingers of resistance into a fist". It was in Geneva that the key PGA hallmarks (as well as an impressive though overlong manifesto) were formulated. Key amongst these is a rejection of reformist, NGO-style 'top down' approaches to resistance, a call to direct action and a non-hierarchical structure with no office, no employees and no HQ; relying instead on regional 'convenors' who would attempt to facilitate activity in their respective areas. So in Western Europe, Reclaim the Streets in London took on the role of convenor (somewhat reluctantly at first!), eventually mak-

ing more of a go of it but not managing to get a promised 3-language leaflet and video out before the end of its tenure. All convenors have to change at every conference; the other regions are Eastern Europe, Africa, Latin America, North America, South-East Asia and the Pacific Rim (Australasia & the Far East.) [Interest in PGA issues in the Middle East has been hard to tap into, the area being one of the many holes in the latticework of resistance that still needs to be covered.]

An immediate result of the Geneva conference were the world-wide actions which took place in May 1998, with hundreds of thousands on the streets from Hyderabad in India to Brazil, not to mention a Global Street Party which found a home in over 20 countries. In the UK this took the form of a street party at the Bullring in Birmingham during the G8 summit.. And it was the Global Street Party which provided the template for the autonomous delights of June 18th this year, a date many of you may be familiar with.

But back to Bangalore, which was really an attempt to keep the some-would-say faltering global resistance movement on the rails and travelling at a healthy speed. How could it be faltering you may ask, with the successes of May '98

Pic: Jon Towne

and J18 under its belt? Well the problem springs from the lack of real workaday day-in day-out networking and network building both inside and between regions.

While excellent links are being made between, say, the landless peasants struggle in Brazil and campaigners in the UK, the fledgling infrastructure of PGA has almost buckled because of many convenors' inability or lack of desire to play a part in building it. So, for example, the Bangalore conference wasn't as well

Pic: Jon Towne

planned as it could have been because it was left mainly to a valiant though unrepresentative and really quite centralised 'support group'. As has happened often in the last year and a half, the vacuum left by the convenors (who may well have been working their guts out on more localised issues) has been filled by this support group, of 'freelance' activists mainly based in Western Europe. One of the unspoken objectives of the Bangalore conference, then, was to see this support group dwindle in the onrush of convenors' keenness to share the day-to-day workload of the PGA's networking activities. Did we achieve that aim? Well read on and find out.

It is perhaps important to look closely and honestly at some of the problems as well as the successes that PGA has encountered. After all, it would be hard to over-emphasise the importance of this attempt to provide the bare bones of a structure to support what will have to be a constantly growing movement of global resistance against capitalism. The many cultural and other differences of outlook of the various groups involved are perhaps what the movement must struggle most energetically to recognise and respect; coming together physically provides the greatest opportunity to solve many of these problems. The problem is, like Christmas family reunions, they also provide the perfect opportunity for festering conflicts to erupt.

In a conference about a quarter of the size of Geneva, 100 people from over 25 countries as diverse as Nicaragua and Indonesia gathered for the four day conference (six days if you included roundtable discussions, and two weeks including 'exposure trips' to some very inspiring local struggles). Western Europe, South Asia and Latin America were most strongly represented, with Africa and Eastern Europe sadly absent. (The Chikoko Movement of Nigeria, who pulled off a massive demonstration of over 50,000 people on June 18th, had hoped to come but had to pull out at the last minute due to administrative problems in Bangalore.) The general consensus of the group was that while there

had been impressive worldwide actions both in May 1998 and on June 18th earlier this year, these were spectaculars which hadn't been followed up with a concerted bout of global networking and communication. The regional convenors had failed to facilitate a dialogue between themselves or to build a meaningful network of grassroots resistance contacts within their regions. (The new Western European convenors are the Milan 'branch' of the Zapatista solidarity movement 'Ya Basta', based in the very sorted Leoncavallo social/resource centre there. London RTS will be part of a support network of groups in the region who'll attempt to make Ya Basta's job a little less daunting.)

Although many of the meetings were fantastically chaotic and necessarily slowed down by translation into Spanish and two or more Indian languages, the final mood was of a renewed resolve to make this frighteningly important experiment work properly in the coming months and years. One tip especially for all English-speaking activists at these events: having a second language (preferably Spanish or French) really makes border-breaking dialogue a reality, as well as chipping away at our reputation as arrogant linguistic imperialists! Many who went might well argue that the really useful networking stuff took place over plates of coconut curry or late into the night whilst nursing preciously acquired bottles of beer. This rendered the 'plenary' discussions as empty in comparison, with lasting cross-border/ocean relationships being formed informally and fused by friendship. But interminable plenary sessions have their uses. After all, a certain amount of bureaucratic chat had to take place, and it certainly sent a shiver down the spine of this correspondent to hear the angry and eloquent speech to all the gathered tribes of resistance of an Indian activist pledging all in the battle against the hugely destructive Narmada River dam project. The shadow of this extraordinarily inspiring campaign to save local lives and villages not to mention thousands of years of irreplaceable culture from the western TNC-backed dam (the main TNC being

Siemens) was ever-present during the week. Many anti-dam activists were unable to be present because of their promise to stay in their villages even as the water level rose to waist height and threatened to take their lives. Many European activists travelled to the soon-to-be-submerged valley either before or after the conference, some no doubt returning to these shores in the early autumn with a strong desire to act in solidarity with the Adivasis (indigenous people) of the region. Another inspiration was the presence of one of the most active campaigners against GM and globalisation in France. The presence of Rene Riesel, a veteran of Paris 1968 and a prominant campaigner against GM foods and American corporate imperialism in France - gave the whole gathering a real boost.

There were flashpoints during the week, especially when much of the delegation from Nepal threatened to leave the conference over what they saw as unacceptable behaviour from one of the conference organisers, who had been driven - it seems - to distraction by what he regarded as their unacceptabley high-handed attitude to everyone else, (including those from the more 'grassroots' Nepalese groups). Disputes such as these are almost impossible to present accurately, since they are so bound up in cultural mores and the subtle shading of relationships between groups which have yawning political differences even while agreeing that the WTO must die. In this case, on the one hand there was a fear that PGA was being overrun by unrepresentative NGO-style campaigners, and on the other that Western colonialist values were still dominating our new and supposedly mutually co-operative structures. Complicated stuff, especially if you're attempting to facilitate a fair discussion between angry contributors who are unaware that the planned agenda is running three hours behind schedule! This particular flashpoint ended fairly happily with honour intact, but it was touch and go for a while.

Anyway, after a few false starts and sessions lost to rain and wild local folk drummers, a determined desire to get things sorted out emerged, becoming more focussed in direct relation to the diminishing amount of time available. There will be a regular bulletin, customised to suit each region, and a more dynamic, useful and regularly updated website. There was strong support for a move away from elitist e-communication, a view especially vehement in India, where such resources are thin on the ground and only available to those often at the top of steep hierarchies. One issue which became central during the week was that of gender, which many felt had been left out of the previous 4 'hallmarks' and the mammoth manifesto thrashed out in Geneva in February 1998. For this reason a new hallmark was adopted: "We reject all forms and systems of domination and discrimination including, but not limited to, patriarchy, racism and religious fundamentalism of all creeds. We embrace the full dignity of all human beings". This was seen as a crucial step in the battle to disassociate PGA from right-wing anti-globalisation groups threatening to hitch onto our bandwagon. A more outright anti-capitalist thrust was also welcomed, most realising that the WTO et al are simply modern manifestations of the age-old capitalist beast. (There is also a plan for the creation of a new convenor, to be a group working specifically on gender issues.)

What tensions there were often centred around the big differences between autonomous Western activists and those who came representing large social movements, mainly in this case from Latin America (even with the absence of Brazil's Movimento Sem Terra and the Zapatistas.) This correspondent certainly felt an urgent need for the European posse to be more representative of its region (including non-white struggles for example.) The next conference, pencilled in for 2001 in Latin America, will have to make some well-judged and possibly controversial decisions about who attends, otherwise some of the movements many of us see as central to future worldwide resistance will probably stay away. Wherever the conference takes place, there will always be cultural and regional differences to consider, such as the fact that in some areas those who speak at great length deserve respect, while in other areas they would be asked to edit their contributions more brutally. Frequent male domination also needs to be addressed.

But notwithstanding all these problems, the final vibe was pretty positive, with plenty of energy set aside to make November 30th a powerful global day of action (even if the UK contingent warned that their input wouldn't be on the scale of J18.) There was widespread support for decentralised actions a la J18, with more of a thumbs down for centralised affairs like the Inter-Continental Caravan. (Having said that, there are plans for a much smaller North American caravan leading up to Seattle, starting fairly soon.) There was also growing enthusiasm for a big day out on May 1st 2000 in a 'Reclaim Mayday' style. People from Latin America, Sri Lanka, North America and Western Europe all seemed up for it, but obviously the real proof will be in the responses of their groups back home. One final heartening sight: the Vice-President of the Karanataka State Farmer's Association (KRRS) leaving Bangalore for a 12 hour bus ride to a marathon of weddings with only his green plastic PGA wallet containing the SchNEWS Survival Handbook for company.

Held in the very relaxed grounds of a craft museum across the way from a blind school, many evenings ended alongside a nearby lake with bottles of over-empowered Indian 'Knockout' beer, (to the mild annoyance of the KRRS who are in the middle of an anti-alcohol campaign - some of the biggest recent mobilisations for example, women in Nepal and in areas of India, have been dedicated to implementing a prohibition of alcohol, seen as a way of stopping the men abusing the women and drinking away their earnings.) On the last night the lake resounded to an impromptu rewrite of the Diggers anthem 'The World Turned Upside Down', beginning: "In 1999, in Bangalore, a ragged band of jetset activists came to give it some jaw-jaw" and heading rapidly downhill.

So, the PGA: battered but unbowed. If you would like to be a part of making the thing work e-mail: info@agp.org Or email the new Western European convenors at patham@iol.it Or contact the new PGA secretariat: Canadian Union of Postal Workers (CUPW), 377 Bank Street, Ottawa, Ontario, Canada; dbleakney@cupw-sttp.org (There are plans for a UK PGA get-together sometime in October, possibly in London. Contact RTS for more details: 020 7281 4621; rts@gn.apc.org; PO Box 9656, London N4 4JY.)

## The Coke Dude

The following letter (which we have abridged) was sent to school principals in Colorado Springs, US, by the district executive director of 'school leadership'.

Dear Principal,

Here we are in year two of the great Coke contract. I hope your first weeks were successful and that pretty much everything is in place (except staffing, technology, planning time and telephones).

First, the good news: this year's installment from Coke is 'in the house' and checks will be cut for you to pick up in my office this week.

Now the not-so-good news: we must sell 70,000 cases of product (including juices, sodas, waters etc) during the first three years of the contract.

The math on how to achieve this is really quite simple. Last year we had 32,439 students, 3,000 employees and 176 days in the school year. If 35,439 staff and students buy one Coke product every other day for the school year, we will double the required quota.

Here is how we can do it:

1. Allow students to purchase and consume vended products during the day. If sodas are not allowed in the class, consider allowing juices, teas and waters.
2. Locate machines where they are accessible to the students all day. Location, location, location is the key
3. A list of Coke products is enclosed to allow you to select from the entire menu.
4. A calendar of promotional events is enclosed to help you advertise Coke products.

I know this is 'just one more thing from downtown', but the long-term benefits are worth it.

Thanks for all your help.

From: New Internationalist Aug 99

10th August 1999: A digger which was being used to re-build a car park at Newcastle University is re-decorated. Activists proposed that the area be used as a park instead, and that the University encourage the use of sustainable transport rather than cars. The protesters were removed by police.

# Weekly SchNEWS

*Printed and Published in Brighton by Justice?*

**Friday 3rd September 1999**   http://www.schnews.org.uk/   **Issue 226**   **Free/Donation**

# CHILD PAWNS

*"Educashon, Educayshon, Edukeyshun"*
Tony Blair

The school classroom looks set to become the latest scene of popular uprising, if a recent action by pupils in Hackney, east London, is anything to go by. 500 pupils at Kingsland school recently walked out of lessons en masse, in disgust at the government's new plans to open up to business the running of the school. The parents had already voted against the proposal, the local teachers' union were up in arms; but it was the kids who, clearly undeterred by the demise of student radicalism in their university-age siblings, took action by marching into the headmaster's office and seizing control of the tannoy system. The kids at Grange Hill were never so brash.

So what turned this school into such an action zone?

Funnily enough, the government's plan for the school bears the snappy New Labour title of the Education Action Zone (EAZ). The EAZ (now a *'firmly established feature of the education landscape'* beams a government spokesperson) is aimed at schools deemed not up to scratch by the schools inspectorate. Undermining the traditional, more accountable Local Educational Authority, the EAZs set up an 'action forum' to involve business, police, LEAs, school governors, religious, community and other groups. The government has been cooking this one up for a while now, without saying too much of what it was about. Last year they invited bids from those wishing to run the zones, and suddenly things started to become clear.

The government wanted to see *"one zone in the first five which is led and run by a business, and several like this in the programme of 25 zones."* And the bids came pouring in. Zones are to be sponsored by companies like Tate & Lyle, Shell, McDonald's, Yorkshire Water as well as Nord Anglia, Britain's self styled 'market leader' in privatised education. Its shares soared by £1.6m overnight when EAZs were first announced. Nothing for the kids to get het up about? Bids to run zones include a switch to a five term year in Croydon, a 50% increase in the school day in Birmingham, and weekend schooling in Newcastle. Then there are the teachers – for whom the action forums can apply to disregard the statutory guidelines over

their pay and conditions. Meanwhile, the government's planned new elite of Advanced Skills Teachers will be getting up to £40,000 a year. And the advertised post of director of Lambeth action forum's 'Project Steering Group' carries a salary of £50,000.

And there's more: Remember the Private Finance Initiative (PFI) that SchNEWS has been bangin' on about in relation to the NHS? We know obscure-sounding government finance schemes probably don't grab your imagination but check what the PFI will mean for schools.

The government wanted to sort out the £3.2bn backlog of repairs to Britain's school buildings, but as they obviously couldn't actually do it themselves, they offered the rebuilding contracts to private firms. These contracts last for 25 years, which is quite a long time to patch up a few classrooms – but then, that's not what the PFI is all about. Just as with PFI hospitals, the companies get ownership of the site and all the non-teaching services, forcing all staff to reapply for their jobs

If you reckon SchNEWS is being a tad paranoid, check out what's happening in the US, where such schemes are way ahead of us. Edison, a firm which pioneers *"the transformation of the American public education system into a major for-profit industry"*, was founded by Chris Whittle, who also started Channel One, a fantastic scheme in which schools got free use of satellite TVs and videos. The catch was that they had to force kids to watch a 12 minute ad-soaked 'programme' everyday. Pepsi, Reebok and other educationally-helpful firms signed up, and Channel One made $33m in profits in one year. It gets better: corporations have started 'sponsoring' entire towns. Here's an extract from a letter sent to school heads by the director of 'school leadership' of Colorado Springs, which is sponsored by Coca-Cola. *"We must sell 70,000 cases of product during the first three years of the contract…If 35,439 staff and students buy one Coke product every other day, we will double the required quota. Here's how we can do it: 1) Allow students to purchase and consume vended products throughout the day. 2) Locate machines where they are accessible to students all day. Location, location, location.is the key. 3) A list of Coke products is enclosed…."*

and allowing the firm to do what it wants with them. Take Pimlico School, where a certain J Straw was recently removed as chairman of the governors. A private consortium has won a rebuilding and managing contract for 25 years, which gives it £22m of public cash… oh, and a big chunk of hugely valuable land in Westminster, much of which will be flogged off to make luxury housing. The consortium also gets the right to sell computer courses, car parking, and vending machines – all in all, a nice little earner.

All this offers socially-minded corporate fat cats plenty of scope to cream off cash from the public purse. As says the Socialist Teacher's Alliance: *'Business is interested in profits. If it doesn't get them one way – directly by 'productivity' deals or cutting wages – then it will get them another way – through lucrative contracts to provide IT for example….Can you imagine business saying "Oh No we'll pick up the loss and the LEA can take the profit?"'*

Perhaps most sinister is the ability of the EAZs to alter the National Curriculum. The chair of Hackney Council's education committee assures us that this is *'not business taking over schools, it's about helping pupils prepare for the world of work – and I mean proper jobs, not casual jobs.'* Of course those who drafted the McDonald's bid would hasten to agree. Witness the onset of a "vocationalist" agenda, where in the Lambeth bid, *'extended work experience and classes will continue into the holidays.'*

Did Mrs McCluskey see any of this coming? No wonder Sammo turned to smack.

* Trojan Horses – Education Action Zones. The case against the privatisation of Education

50p + A5 SAE from the Socialist Teachers Alliance , 1 Shrubland Rd., Walthamstow, London, E17 7QH

* Check out an article on how the Private Finance Iniative is undermining the NHS www.labournet.org

* New Internationalist mag recently devoted a whole issue to the privitisation of education. Copies from Tower House, Lathkill St., Market Harborough, LE16 www.newint.org/

## ARMS IN THE AIR

*"The turnout shows that fear, violence and intimidation cannot stop the people when they want to have their voice heard".*
Karina Pirelli  UN election official

The East Timorese people, or what's left of them, finally got to vote on independence from Indonesia this week. In what has been described as a hard fought campaign Indonesian backed militiamen have spent the last eight months trying to kill anyone or anything that moved, burnt houses and sent hundreds fleeing to the hills for safety. On the day of voting militiamen managed to close seven polling stations for a few hours while those waiting outside were systematically beaten and killed.

For twenty four years Indonesia has illegally occupied East Timor killing at least 200,000 people, proportionally more than Pol Pot killed in Cambodia. Britain has helped repress the people of East Timor by becoming the biggest supplier of weapons to the Indonesian military (see Schnews issues 78, 125, 133, 145, 153/4, 158, 181 & 198 in fact just buy the books). In 1994 when US Congress voted to ban small arms sales to Indonesia, on grounds of genocide, a spokesperson for the dictatorship said *"no problem we can always turn to Britain."*

In 1997 East Timorese Nobel peace prize winner Bishop Carlos Belo appealed to Tony Blair and Robin Cook *"Please do not sustain any longer conflict which without these* [arms] *sales could never have been pursued in the first place, nor for so long"*. Robin 'The liar' Cook promised the Bish' that Britain would *'speak up'* for the East Timorese; speaking up actually involved secretly approving 64 new arms shipments to Indonesia then using 'commercial confidentiality' to justify ministers' refusals to answer MP's questions.

Before taking office Robin Cook campaigned for an 'ethical foreign policy' even writing *'The current sale of Hawk aircraft to Indonesia is particularly disturbing as the purchasing regime is not only repressive but actually at war"* in the New Statesmen in the late seventies. 22 years later he and the government have the legal power to revoke the licences but remain happy with the Indonesian assurances that the hawk fighters and weapons won't be used in their illegal colony!

If you fancy shaking hands with Indonesia's finest torturers, murderers and bully-boys, get down to the Defence Systems & Equipment International Arms fair. Organised by UK plc, it will be the largest arms exhibition ever held in the country - and big protests are planned.

Contact Campaign Against Arms Trade, 11 Goodwin St, Finsbury Park, London N4 3HQ. Tel 0171 281 0297

email  campaigns@caat.demon.co.uk

*They're 'avin a laugh. A lengthy investigation into the alleged corruption of the former Suharto regime in Indonesia may be called off *"because of the lack of proof"*. Proof! Under Suharto's regime millions perished, while he ran the country dry becoming one of the richest men in the world!

---

## TRAINING DAY

**15th September  12 noon.**

Psssst!! Wanna get involved in your favourite weekly direct action newsheet? (ok, so we're the only one). Then why not come to our next training day? Limited places, so give us a call now and book your place for the experience of a lifetime! Are you good at getting up on a Friday? Coz we need someone to print SchNEWS.

---

## SchNEWS in brief

Charges have been dropped  against 8 women who broke into RAF Fairford and spray painted bombs. Accused of disrupting a *"lawful activity"*, their defence was that under International Law, the NATO bombing of Serbia was itself unlawful. *"The British Government is not prepared to have NATO's illegal bombing campaign scrunitized in a public court of law"* said one of the anti-war protestors ** **Job of the week!** Manchester Airport need a copy writer for a book about the development of its new second runway. (see SchNEWS) To apply tel:0161 489 2700 E. Mail:jeanette.murpy@manairport.co.uk-give 'em hell! ** **No Birmingham Northern Relief Road** Picnic in the Park Hednesfield Rd Nr Brownhills, Sat 11th Sept 1pm. Tel:01922 860514 ** **The Comic Relief UK Grants Travellers Initiative** will provide funding for various traveller-led projects. Find out more by sending an SAE to UK Grants Team, Comic Relief, 74 New Oxford St, London WC1A 1EF by 5th Nov. Tel:0171 436 1122 **Last November **Lufthansa Skychef** , the worlds biggest airline catering company, sacked 270 mainly Asian Transport and General Union workers, after  a lawful one day strike. Even people on sick leave or on holiday got the boot. The workers went on strike after refusing to sign new contracts which would have effectively slashed their wages. Their union have now threatened to withdraw support unless binding arbritration is accepted by the sacked employees. Just like the Liverpool dock dispute, the T&G are trying to sabotage the efforts of these strikers. Demo outside the TUC Conference, the Brighton Centre.Monday September 13th  1 pm

## RED SKY AT NIGHT, MCDONALDS ALIGHT

Rotting fruit poured onto McDonalds forecourt in Martigues; six tonnes of manure dumped in front of Big Muck's doors in Arles; other outlets smashed to bits, blocked by angry farmers armed with shopping trolleys or filled with farm animals running amok. Is this the stuff that eco-protest dreams are made of? Well, yes, but the scenes are currently reality in France, as angry farmers vent their frustration at American tit-for-tat trade sanctions after a recent ruling by the World Trade Organisation (see SchNEWS 220). The ruling gave the US the green light to impose tariffs on millions of pounds worth of EU goods. That's the amount the WTO reckon America has lost because us bloody Europeans refusal to eat Uncle Sam's delicious hormone-treated cancer-forming beef. Unfortunately for the French, some of the countrys' poshest foods have come under the tariff scheme.

As SchNEWS went to press, the leader of the farmers union *'Confederation Paysanne'*, Jose Bove, was waiting to see if he would remain behind bars after he joined an attack a month ago, with 500 others, on a McMac's outlet under construction in the south-western town of Millau. Monsieur Bove raises sheep that supply milk for Roquefort cheese –a cheese that is on the US hitlist. *" I am hostage to global commercialisation"* he explained. Another farmer added *'We are here to defend the right of people to feed themselves with their own food in their own way and against the determination of the United States to impose their way of eating on the whole planet."*

The protests are enjoying widespread public support and are expected to spread. However, they are part of a bigger picture, farmers are also unhappy about low prices, increasing domination of big retail distributors and genetically modified crops.

Meanwhile Noel Kapferer, a professor at a Paris Business School, said the campaign against McDonalds was the first sign of a European rebellion against American imposed cultural uniformity *"today's consumers are rejecting the American way of life."* SchNEWS will drink a bottle of yer finest chateau 'avin it' to that.

---

## The day we went to Banga

The second conference of People's Global Action (PGA) took place last week in Bangalore in the southern Indian state of Karnataka. The hosts were the so-called 'laughing arsonists' the 10 million strong  Karnataka State Farmers'Association, renowned amongst other things for their recent torching of a Monsanto test site. About 100 people from over 25 countries as diverse as Nicaragua and Indonesia gathered for the 4 day conference (6 days if you included roundtable discussions, and 2 weeks including 'exposure trips' to some very inspiring local struggles.) Western Europe, South Asia and Latin America were most strongly represented, with Africa and Eastern Europe sadly absent.

'**Kill WTO before it kills us**' has become a rallying cry in India, and the Conference was called predominantly to plan for actions against the looming meeting of the World Trade Organisation (WTO) in Seattle (November 29th to December 3rd). Here the world's most thirsty free market vampires will gather to carve up more of the planet under the guise of the 'millennial trade round'. The general consensus of the group was that while there had been impressive worldwide actions both in May 1998 and on June 18th earlier this year, these were spectaculars that hadn't been followed up with a concerted bout of global networking and communication.

Although many of the meetings were fantastically chaotic and necessarily  slowed down by translation into Spanish and two or more Indian languages, the final mood was of a renewed resolve to make this frighteningly important experiment work properly in the coming months and years. There will be a regular bulletin, customised to suit each region, and a more dynamic website. There was strong support for a move away from elitist e-communication, that support being especially vehement in India, where such resources are thin on the ground.

Tensions (of which there were many in amongst the abounding global solidarity) were often centred around the big differences between autonomous Western activists and those who came representing large social movements, mainly, in this case,  from Latin America (even with the absence of Brazil's Movimento Sem Terra and the Zapatistas.) But, notwithstanding all these problems, the final vibe was pretty positive, with plenty of energy set aside to make November 30th a powerful global day ofaction. There was also growing enthusiasm for a big day out on May 1st 2000 in a 'Reclaim Mayday' style.

* If you would like to be a part of making the PGA work, check out the (soon-to-be radically face-lifted) website at  www.agp.org

* 'Turn around the WTO' Conference Sunday 26th September 11 am - 5 pm Conway Hall, 25 Red Lion Square, London, WC1R 4LR. To register contact Chris Keene, 90 The Parkway, Canvey Island, Essex, SS8 OAE Tel: 01268 682820 email chris.keene@which.net

---

## ...and finally...

*The old ones are the best !*

Heard the one about the big financial institution that decided to mailshot 2000 of its richest customers?. One of the computer programmers trawled through the companies database, using  an imaginary customer called Richard Bastard. Unfortunately, an error resulted in all 2000 letters sent out being addressed *"Dear Rich Bastard"*. The luckless programmer was shown the door. Poor bastard.

**disclaimer**

SchNEWS warns all kids that if you don't get no education you'll end up working on a newsletter like wot we wrote. Honest

---

to the Indonesian activists who got rid of the dictator and now demonstrate their solidarity with the people of East Timor **Respect**

Graphics: Martin

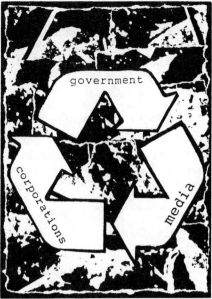

government
corporations
media

## SQUOTES

"The only real way is to take the land from our own government and get rid of the United States of America. We can talk about free trade today, or immigrants tomorrow, but it's pushing little band aids while we die of haemorrhage because of the world system."

***BOBBY, AZTLAN NATION***

*....A Britain that does an honest day's work... but yet a ... cool ... Britain*

# Prisoner Support

## WANT TO SUPPORT PRISONERS BUT DON'T KNOW WHERE TO START...HOW ABOUT BEGINNING WITH A LETTER?

Writing to prisoners is one of the best support techniques that you can give. Those inside really appreciate contact from the outside world as it enables them to keep in touch with what's going on and also lets them know that they're not forgotten. However, there are a few points to bear in mind before you put pen to paper. One of the main problems that puts people off getting involved in supporting prisoners is a feeling of being intimidated about writing to a prisoner for the first time…It is very hard to write a letter to someone you don't know: people find that they don't know what to say, they feel there are things they can't talk about, or think that most prisoners won't be interested in what they have to say. Hopefully these tips will help you.

\* Remember that all letters are opened and read by the prison. So don't write about anything that could get the prisoner or anybody else in trouble or could cause problems for future actions.

\* Make sure that you put your address on the back of the envelope – most prisons will not allow mail to be received that does not have the sender's name and address with it (sending letters recorded delivery *should* make sure your letter gets to the prisoner)

\* Don't make the letter too long. 4 sides of writing paper or two sides of A4 is about the limit.

\* If you can't think of anything to write, a card of postcard will be appreciated just as much.

\* Talk about your life and what you've been doing, prisoners will like to hear about normal life.

\* Say where you heard about them and their case.

## Sending stuff to prisoners

It's best to check with the prison concerned as to what the rules are for sending in books, magazines or anything else as they tend to vary and some may be more lenient than others.

## Visiting prisoners

Remand prisoners are generally entitled to a visit of 15 minutes every day. Convicted prisoners are allowed one visit every two weeks for under 21s and every week for over 21s. These visits can usually last between 30 minutes and two hours. Prisoners will need to send out a visiting order to the people they want to visit. Two people are usually allowed to visit a prisoner at once.

At the end of the day, writing to prisoners is about common sense and using your head. Most are not the mad beasts the tabloids would have us believe, they are ordinary people just like you. Prison is there to isolate people, so keeping the link to the outside world is really important, and receiving mail on the whole is the brightest point of the day for most prisoners.

## SOME USEFUL PRISONER SUPPORT CONTACTS

**(For more info on what they do, check out the yellow pages at the back of the book)**

**Legal Defence and Monitoring Group** BM Haven, London WC1N 3XX tel: 020 8245 2930

**Haven Distribution** supply free books to prisoners. 27 Old Gloucester Street, London WC1N 3XX

**Earth Liberation Prisoners** Cornerstone Resource Centre, 16 Sholebroke Ave, Leeds, LS7 3HB

**Brighton Anarchist Black Cross** c/o Prior House, 6 Tilbury Place, Brighton, BN2 2GY

**CAGE** c/o P.O. Box 68, Oxford OX3 1RH 07931 401962 www.veggies.org/cage

**GM-Free Prisoner Support** Dept. 29, 255 Wilmslow Rd, Manchester M14 5LW tel: 0161 226 6814

**Vegan Prisoners Support Group** P.O. Box 194, Enfield EN1 3HD tel: 020 8292 8325 hvsp@vpsg.freeserve.co.uk

**Women in Prison** 22 Highbury Grove, London N5 2EA 020 7226 5879

# TO TRAMPLE ON US THEY NEED CONCRETE AND CONSENT.

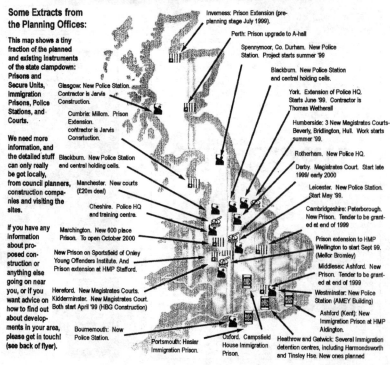

**Some Extracts from the Planning Offices:**

This map shows a tiny fraction of the planned and existing Instruments of the state clampdown: Prisons and Secure Units, Immigration Prisons, Police Stations, and Courts.

We need more information, and the detailed stuff can only really be got locally, from council planners, construction companies and visiting the sites.

If you have any information about proposed construction or anything else going on near you, or if you want advice on how to find out about developments in your area, please get in touch! (see back of flyer).

Glasgow. New Police Station. Contractor is Jarvis Construction.

Cumbria: Millom. Prison Extension. contractor is Jarvis Constuction.

Blackburn. New Police Station and central holding cells.

Manchester. New courts (£20m deal).

Cheshire. Police HQ and training centre.

Marchington. New 600 place Prison. To open October 2000

New Prison on Sportsfield of Onley Young Offenders Institute. And Prison extension at HMP Stafford.

Hereford. New Magistrates Courts. Kidderminster. New Magistrates Court. Both start April '99 (HBG Construction)

Bournemouth. New Police Station.

Portsmouth: Haslar Immigration Prison.

Inverness: Prison Extension (pre-planning stage July 1999).

Perth: Prison upgrade to A-hall

Spennymoor, Co. Durham. New Police Station. Project starts summer '99

Blackburn. New Police Station and central holding cells.

York. Extension of Police HQ. Starts June '99. Contractor is Thomas Wetherall

Humberside: 3 New Magistrates Courts- Beverly, Bridlington, Hull. Work starts summer '99.

Rotherham. New Police HQ.

Derby. Magistrates Court. Start late 1999/ early 2000

Leicester. New Police Station. Start May '99.

Cambridgeshire: Peterborough. New Prison. Tender to be granted at end of 1999

Prison extension to HMP Wellington to start Sept 99. (Mellor Bromley)

Middlesex: Ashford. New Prison. Tender to be granted at end of 1999

Westminster: New Police Station (AMEY Building)

Ashford (Kent): New Immigration Prison at HMP Aldington.

Oxford. Campsfield House Immigration Prison.

Heathrow and Gatwick: Several Immigration detention centres, including Harmondsworth and Tinsley Hse. New ones planned

## WAKE UP! WAKE UP! IT'S YER CHEST BEATIN'

# Weekly SchNEWS

### Printed and Published in Brighton by Justice?

**Friday 10th September 1999**   http://www.schnews.org.uk/   **Issue 227 Free/Donation**

---

# BOTTLE-DEAD

"Over 4,000 babies die every day in poor countries because they're not breastfed. That's not conjecture, it's UNICEF fact."
Baby Milk Action.

"Many people now believe in modern superstitions, these include the use of bottle milk; these are superstitions no less pernicious than the unhealthy folk traditions. But while the wrong traditional ways are superstitions borne out of ignorance, the wrong ' modern' ways are superstitions borne out of greed. And we all know that greed has strong powerful interests"
A former Philippine Health Secretary.

SchNEWS has an old chestnut for you this week. Corporate giants, Nestle would have us believe they're overflowing with 'the milk of human kindness' these days; a response to Baby Milk Action's long-term campaign exposing dodgy dealings in developing countries.

A few months back the company got their wrists slapped and advert banned by the Advertising Standards Authority after claiming they marketed their babymilk *"ethically and responsibly"*. So they turned to advertising gurus Saatchi and Snaatchi who suggested Nestle *"go on the offensive by using advertising showing the benefits of Nestle financial contributions to charities"*. Nestle general manager, Arthur Furer stated, *"It is clear that we have an urgent need to develop an effective counter-propaganda operation".*

With an annual promotion budget of **nearly $8 billion** Nestle has a slight advantage over mothers who produce breastmilk naturally and do not have a fortune to spend promoting the advantages of their 'product'. Their new tactic has been to advertise through publications who are respected for their discerning views (such as the *Big Issue*) and to make self-promoting donations to childrens' charities and the church. The first, presumably to counteract the mental image that the word Nestle conjures up of third world babies dying in their millions after converting from breast to bottle; the latter to persuade the church to chill out on their Nestle boycotting campaign. Nestle have now launched a new range of baby food on the European market. Reliable sources indicate that in the remaining 4 months of this year Nestle's promotion budget of £2 million for their new range exceeds the equivalent expenditure of the two rival brands for the whole year. Plenty of scope for 'nestling' up to the public.

**"A bottle fed child is 25 times more likely to die from diarrhoea than a breast fed child where water is unsafe."**   UNICEF

Just to remind you of the facts, the World Health Organisation (WHO) estimate that more than a million babies die every year as a result of diarrhoea picked up from unhygienic bottle feeding. That's one baby every 30 seconds. Nestle control about 40% of the world baby milk market, aggressively promoting their babymilk products in developing countries, and discouraging breastfeeding. Of course, after a short period of bottle feeding a mother's breastmilk dries up and another consumer is born. They give 'sweeteners' to healthworkers encouraging them to promote their products. They are still 'donating' freebies to health facilities in Gabon, Africa, to encourage the use of their product, despite the Gabon government asking them to stop. In the Philippines, the company have been exposed for hiring graduate nurses as 'health educators' to visit mothers at home and try to convince them to use their products. Ignoring WHO recommendations that complimentary foods only be introduced from 6 months, Nestle market teas labelled for feeding 2 week old infants. They do not always provide clear information and in some cases the labels are in a language that mothers can't understand.

Sickeningly, Nestle have been getting away with this for longer than you would believe possible. As early as 1873, Nestle was exporting its 'milk food' to the colonised world. It's a measure of their power that 126 years on they still see themselves as above the law, and they're 'milking it' for all it's worth. Currently in court in India over their baby food labels, Nestle's reaction is to use their clout to have key sections of the Indian baby food marketing law scrapped. Back in '39 they were exporting

Nestle is the worlds largest food manufacturer, with factories in more than 80 countries and a turnover of $52 billion, taking over £1000 a second. They are also the focus of the worlds longest running consumer boycott (22 years). *"Breaking the boycott is like crossing the world's longest running picket line"* said a pissed off hack. As a final accolade, when the European Parliament start holding public hearings on multinational responsibility and corporate abuses later this year, Nestle are the first company they intend to put in the hotseat.

condensed milk to Singapore and Malaysia as "ideal for delicate infants", though it was banned in Britain for causing rickets and blindness. In a speech that would sadly be as relevant 60 years later, Dr Cecily Williams said *"misguided propaganda on infant feeding should be punished as the most miserable form of sedition; these deaths should be regarded as murder."*

## BREAST FEEDING : SOME FACTS

*"Breastfeeding declined rapidly between 1960-70 as the formula milk market expanded. In Mexico from 100% to 40%, in Chile from 90% to 5% and in Singapore from 80% to 5%"*   UK Food Group.

* In the 50's & 60's, doctors working in the 'developing' world observed that diarrhoea, infections and malnutrition were increasing in babies. This is rare amongst breastfed babies.

* Breastfeeding is vital not only because of the nutrients but because the anti-infective properties protect against disease. * In developing countries, extra food for the mother can cost as little as one tenth of the cost of artificial food for the baby. * Poor people often over-dilute baby milk powder with unsafe water to make it last longer resulting in malnourishment. * Recent research by the British Medical Council found that cow's milk at 26p a pint is just as good for six month old babies as formula milk which costs around £5 for 10 pints.

### BOYCOTT THE BASTARDS

Nescafe, Gold Blend, Rowntree, After Eights, Quality Street, Sarsons seasonings, Perrier, Buxton, Findus, Buitoni, Crosse and Blackwell, Maggi, Branston pickle , Sun-Pat, Shredded Wheat, L'Oreal and Lancome cosmetics, Winalot, Felix and Choosy pet foods and many, more…For a comprehensive list contact **Baby Milk Action**, 23 St Andrews St., Cambridge CB2 3AX Tel: 01223 464420 www.gn.apc.org/babymilk

---

## MARCHING ORDERS

*"The Colombian people and workers have won, but if the government doesn't do it's part, you can expect more action from the Colombian people."* Union leader and very brave man Tarcisio Mora

Seeing as 80% of all trade unionist murdered are Colombian (72 of 'em last year), to call a general strike seems pretty suicidal. Nevertheless, with unemployment at 20%, the economy shagged, and the IMF pushing its beloved 'austerity measures' (ie starvation policy) on the govt, those plucky unionists got together with groups representing indigenous peoples, peasants and debtors, and got 20 million people out on strike last week. The austerity plan contains all the usual neo-liberal shit – cutting wages and worker protection, raising the retirement age, privatisation etc – which the IMF demands in exchange for a $3bn loan, which of course will go on servicing Colombia's $35bn debt.

Demanding all sorts of lefty bollocks like respect for human rights, decent wages and an end to the privatisation programme, the strikers were clearly asking for it. So, naturally, the army and the paramilitary responded in their usual style, planting bombs at human rights organisations' offices, trying to assassinate unionist Domingo Tobar, and shooting a ten year old girl in the head. Unfortunately this didn't stop the strikers bringing the country to a standstill, with massive disruption in all major cities and pitched battles with security forces. With far more style than their paramilitary rivals, the Marxist revolutionary army FARC occupied a hydro plant in support of the strikers, and demanded cheaper leccy for Colombia's poor. After two days, costing $130m each, the govt gave in and promised to meet the unions' demands. Whether they actually will, or just let their paramilitary chums shoot anyone who tries to join the negotiations remians to be seen…

Already a candidate for the most fucked up country in the world, Colombia's been having a particularly tough time of late, with the good ol' US of A wading in with a load of guns and dollars. What with two main Marxist revolutionary armies, armed cocaine cartels, untold far-right paramilitary groups, and a savage national army turning most of the country into a war zone, the obvious thing to do was spend millions of bucks on 'military aid', and prepare for a full scale US invasion under the cover of the War on Drugs. Last year Uncle Sam gave the Colombian govt $289 million in 'security assistance'; gave training in counter-insurgency techniques to the army, which has the worst human rights record in the Americas; and started to build military bases in Colombia and neighbouring countries. It won't be long before arming psychopaths and spraying toxic chemicals on peasants ain't enough, and the defenders of the free world invade, thereby making Colombia safe for democracy, oh, and getting their grubby little mitts on those tasty oil reserves…

### Home In One

On Monday people tee'd off with the House Builders Federation (HBF) obsession with covering the countryside in small boxes, disrupted their annual golf tournament in Chepstow. Members of URGENT and the Land Is Ours erected a low-impact eco-dwelling at the 18th hole A spokesperson commented "It is clear that the HBF and their friends are determined to profit from rapid private development of vast tracts of land whatever the social and environmental costs. The sort of homes we should be building for the future need to be affordable, well-designed and sustainable - not the sort of executive homes for commuters and their cars that are being built all over the countryside." The HBF is the house building lobby group. Their new Chief Executive is Stuart Hill, who rather conveniently the moved from his former post of Chief Executive at the HM Land Registry to take on the job. URGENT, Box HN, 111 Magdalen Rd, Oxford, OX4 1RQ   01865 794800 www.urgent.org.uk/

## SchNEWS in brief

Nice one to **Exodus Collective** for putting on the best and biggest free festival of the year again. SchNEWS crew had a wicked time. Respect! ** Congrat's to **Mike Schwarz** (of Bindman's solicitors) and his partner, who recently gave birth to twins. Hope you're not too busy to keep us all out of prison tho' **After yet more villages were illegally flooded by the **Narmada dam**, youths from the Rewa ke Yuva group got their own back by flooding the offices of the Narmada Valley Development Authority with buckets of water and 'slush.' ** 22 of those charged with conspiracy to cause criminal damage after the Smash Genetic Engineering action in July have had their charges dropped. The rest have had conspiracy charges reduced to aggravated trespass. ** The **Greenham Common** Women's Collective (the 3 remaining activists in a caravan, who recently put off Vodaphone from using the former military base as a site of operations) celebrated the 18th anniversary of the Peace Camp this week. The Collective, who organise actions at nuclear sites nation-wide, are planning a sculpture based on the four elements to commemorate the inspiring actions at the Peace Camp. Tel   01635   269109   or   email: greenhamwpc@hotmail.com ** Naturewise are organising an introductory weekend on **permaculture** in London this month 18th-19th., Call 0171 281 3765 **For all you **millennium bug** enthusiasts out there, check out a one day conference on the Y2K- Nuclear threat. It's at Conway Hall, London, Sat.18th Red Lion Square, London WC1 (Holborn tube) Cost is £10/5 conc.. More details from Paul Swann, Y2K CAN, 14 Beacon Hill, London N7 9LY  Tel:0171-609 7764 email: pswann@easynet.co.uk And now SchNEWS begins the Y2K gumpf column – please send us your favourites: Like rock 'n roll, y2k is also here to stay. I like rock better" ** The **Arts Factory**, a community owned business in South Wales, is showing top box office films free until Christmas. They promise "No charge no catch!" Info 01443 757954 ** Support **Simon Jones** family in their latest step to get justice for Simon - killed by casualisation. The Crown Prosecution Service will be in court defending their decision not to prosecute Euromin or its dodgy manager James Martell for the killing of casual worker Simon Jones in their Shoreham dock last April -Come and hear their interesting arguments. next Friday (17th) High Court, the Strand. 10.30am, www.simonjones.org.uk

### SCHNEWS IS ESSENTIAL COZ:

The largest ever media merger was announced this week when CBS, which owns 15 American TV stations, joined forces with Viacom, who own amongst other things MTV and the Paramount film studios. The new company  will be worth more than $66 billion and combined will have 34 TV stations, a film studio, cable TV and radio networks and book publishing companies. The new chief executive commented "Our future is without limit."

SchNEWS meanwhile comes from a rent-free office near the sea, has no paid staff, relies on subscriptions, donations and the odd benefit to keep going and reaches well over 30,000 people a week. No adverts means we don't have corporations breathing down our neck, so we can print a view of the world you don't find in the mainstream press. So if you think SchNEWS is worthwhile why not come to our next training day on **Wednesday 15th September 12 noon.** We always need new writers, researchers, mail-out crew, tea makers…so book your place now.

**Help!** We need a couple of reliable technically competent people who can come in the office every Friday to put SchNEWS on the web. And for just a few hours in the afternoon yer bit of easy-peasy mail-out helps loads to keep the free info' flowing freely. P.S. anyone got a spare laser printer for us?

## Inside SchNEWS

*"With significant court cases coming up and our confidence increasing all the time the campaign is on a roll."* David Mackenzie campaign member.

** At 1.50am on 29th Aug while you lot were asleep (says who?), two women members of the Trident Ploughshares campaign, Sylvia Boyes & Anne Scholar were arrested after spending two hours in the water trying to swim into the Trident submarine docks in Their plan was to lock on to a sub and use a household hammer to disarm it. All this in water where hypothermia sets in after just 15 minutes exposure, and that's just in the summer. This is the fourth attempt by activists to swim in to the docks in just 11 days and follow a Ploughshares summer camp with 102 arrests being made for disarmament actions against Coulport and Faslane nuclear weapon bases. One woman was arrested for cutting the razor wire but because she was up a ladder the cops couldn't drag her down (oh yeah! only stand and support the ladder. nice one!

** Angie Zelter, Ulla Roder and Ellen Moxley "The Loch Goil Three" appear before Greenock Sheriff Court on 27th September. After spending years lobbying parliament, holding public meetings campaigning that the trident system is ethically unjustified as well as being unlawful in international law they boarded Trident support laboratory in Loch Goil and caused £100,000 worth of damage clumsily throwing computers, printers and fax machines all into the drink oops. Support is needed for these swimming activists with their case starting 10am at Greenock Sheriff Court Trident Ploughshares 2000, 41-48 Bethel St, Norwich Norfolk,  NR2  1NR.  Tel  01603-611953 www.gn.apc.org/tp2000

## ...and finally...

If you receive any unsolicited emails from wide eyed activist females, don't count yourself so popular; it could be our mates at the *Sunday Times* with another lesson in the value of media liaison. While journalist Mark Macaskill came across reasonably enough, emailing activists with an approach to interview them, his colleague took a different tack So, it must now be our turn to take the piss out of super-sleuth journo John Ungoed-Thomas, who sent out a few emails under false names, in the hope of getting back some juicy info for an article.

This is not a personal ad: 'Jo' is just one 'committed environmental and anti corporation activist' apparently now flocking to the ranks of our burgeoning movement, if an email recently received by Friends of the Earth is anything to go by. She wants to know how to get more involved in direct action, having '*really enjoyed*' June 18. Likewise, 'Laura' who eco-columnist George Monbiot of the *Guardian* was privileged to hear from, describes herself as a '*committed anti-corporationist*' and is eager to help in any way she can. Any ideas?

Perhaps Laura and Jo might benefit from a few words of advice from someone more canny in covering their tracks, for both sent emails from addresses leading back to Clouseau-esque Ungoed-Thomas, the master of disguise himself. Hardly for us to take the piss now; he's practically giving it away. Fellow hack Macaskill gets annoyed when even his up-front approaches are snubbed, declaring it '*time people in your movement started taking responsibility for their actions*'. Not when it involves talking to people like you, Mark. But, in keeping with his paper's coverage in the aftermath of June 18, if anyone is sufficiently well-educated, coming from a suitably wealthy background, and feels they may have funded a *drug-fuelled orgy of violence* or acted as a *ring leader* – don't keep quiet, but contact that man of  many  masks  at  <Jonathan.Ungoed-Thomas@sundaytimes.co.uk>

**disclaimer**   SchNEWS warns all readers, it's not hard cheese if multinationals lick their lips at the creaming of profits. It's no use bottling it all up, if it this sort of behaviour gets on yer tits then do an exciting action that the media will lap up. Then you'll feel like the cat who got the cream. Honest

# A FREE MANN AT LAST

The only actual crime Keith Mann committed was to cause £6000 worth of damage to three slaughterhouse lorries and plan to damage a battery farm. However, persuaded that a bag of weed-killer constituted bomb-making equipment, the judge sentenced him to fourteen years in prison as a terrorist. The sentence was eventually commuted to eleven upon appeal. Then, without warning, he was suddenly released in March. In an article written four days into his freedom

Keith Mann describes the surprise................

Some strange things have happened over my years inside but by far and away the strangest was being told it was all over and I was free to go. Just a few weeks earlier the management of Parkhurst had refused point blank to allow me any time out to re-adjust before my full term was served (December '99) on the rather bizarre grounds that - in their opinion - the public wouldn't approve. Meanwhile my application for parole was delayed by a month because the paperwork wasn't complete so would now not be heard until March 9th.

March 22nd: I was sat in the TV room out of the way while my cell was being searched- when I was told by a screw that "subject to the paperwork you're out on Friday". As I wasn't really paying that much attention to him, more expecting a moan about something or other I shouldn't have in my cell, I had to ask him to repeat himself which he did. I told him I was still unconvinced by what I was hearing, so he elaborated saying the parole clerk had phoned with the message but wouldn't be sending the required paperwork until the following day. It was a long wait for that to come. The next day two friends were down to visit, and it was during this time that I was able to get it confirmed for sure that I was indeed going to be getting out on the Friday, by getting a trustworthy screw to phone the parole clerk who also said the paperwork was on the wing waiting for my return. Sure enough by 4pm Tuesday I was certain I was going home. This was the weirdest thing.

For six and a half years I'd coped swimmingly with the passing of the hours, days and weeks but all of a sudden time was standing still. Gate fever is often talked about as the condition prisoners suffer from just prior to their release and I went down with a severe dose - hot flushes, irritable, sleepless nights and no desire for food whatsoever. The news was welcome though. Had I had to run the full term of my sentence I expect I'd have had to 'suffer' this for much longer.

A few of us had our parole hearings on the same day but I was the only one to get a positive result so I was quite a novelty for the next few days. So many people wanted to shake my hand and wish me luck; just as many wanted to get their hands on whatever material things I was going to be leaving behind including my lycra shorts, socks, stereo, tapes, food and phonecards. You also usually have to go through a ritual leaving ceremony like being tied up in a bath of cold water type of thing, but I managed to avoid this and came out unscathed.

Up at 1.45am (bed at midnight) my cell was opened up at 7.45am - the longest night of my life. I went straight in the shower. By 8.30 I was on the way to reception with my things and passed through the C wing exercise yard where

Geoff Sheppard was. We got to say our goodbyes - bit sad that. His next shot at parole is in November but he'll have done his lot in Feb 2000 anyway if he gets a knock back. Twenty minutes later I'd signed out, was given the £40 discharge grant and £5 travel warrant and let out of the gate into the arms of my long suffering girlfriend. We've both enjoyed looking forward to this day and all that follows it, but the Prison Service have gone out of their way to make things as unpleasant as possible by shipping me around the country's prisons, interfering with our visits, both strip searching and assaulting her and even banning her from visiting me for life before changing their little minds...all for what? To make us both stronger and more determined than ever to change the world.

We took the ferry away from the island - that was the discharge grant gone - and good riddance to the place. Since then (I wrote this four days after leaving) I have just been doing 'normal' things and enjoying every moment. The weirdest thing about being free after all those years in prison is the fact that it isn't really weird at all, it's just like it should be, like I haven't been away. I was primed to expect everything to be different, the traffic to be heavier, life too fast, paranoia........not a bit of it. I'm in the best of company, am getting well fed and watered, been on the beach with the dogs and out shopping...all normal and everyday but utterly enjoyable.

We've no real plans just yet but are open to offers. What is certain is the extent of my gratitude to all of you for the support you've given me through my sentence - it's immense. Equally the help you have been when the prisons etc have needed reminding about the service they're supposed to be providing - all this has long term effects for present and future POWs.

I've got some catching up to do and I'm itching to get on with it, albeit at a leisurely pace. I have had the law laid down to me with regard to what I can and cannot do and I really have to be careful what I say and write and can't afford to get arrested....not that I have any desire to because that would see me recalled to finish off the eleven years and I don't need that. I will always have the passion for animal welfare they wanted me to lose so badly; the Parole Board used it as a negative factor a year ago. It isn't something you can switch off as you know...it only gets stronger. In fact it isn't so much a passion for animal welfare as a passion for animal liberation. That's what I want and that's what I'll be working for one way or the other for Animal Liberation.

Keith Mann

# DEATH INC:
## WEAPONS TECHNOLOGY FOR THE THIRD MILLENIUM

The largest ever government backed arms sale on UK soil took place in September 1999, confirming Britain's position as the second biggest arms dealer in the world. Despite rhetorical claims for the human rights high ground, this Government, like those before it, are proving there is no morality when it comes to arms sales. Si Mitchell takes a look at the Government's blighted record and investigates behind the scenes moves to privatise government military research.

The excitement surrounding the Defence Systems Equipment International (DSEi) arms fair is dying down. The shipments of assault rifles, cluster bombs and electric shock batons are winging their way to Angola, Turkey and both sides of the India/Pakistan border dispute. So, once again, the top brass at the Ministry of Defence must turn their attention to a problem that has been cluttering their in-trays for some time now - what to do about DSEi's hosting organisation, DERA.

The Defence Evaluation Research Agency (DERA) is the MoD's research and development arm, designing and testing military equipment for the Government to the tune of £2.1 billion a year. It is DERA's responsiblity to develop new and ever more marketable weapons to maintain Britain's position as the world's second largest arms dealer. Though DERA's future has been under discussion for some years now, unsurprisingly we haven't heard much about it. The proposal on the table since mid 1997 is the creation of a Public Private Partnership (PPP), where a significant part of the agency would be sold into private hands. The exact form of the PPP is undecided, or even whether it will go through at all, though the big arms companies are no doubt salivating at the chance of cornering the largest defence research agency in Europe. And after such a productive year, the bank accounts of British Aerospace, GEC and Lockheed, among others, must be fit to burst.

Britain's expenditure on military research and development (R&D) far outstrips any civil research. In 1995 it took 38.9 per cent of the total government's R&D budget; industrial development receiving 9.6 per cent, health 7.6 per cent and environmental protection just 2.3 per cent. DERA employs 12,000 of the keenest scientific and engineering minds in the country. Plucked from the nation's top universities, their ability was so important to the state that they simply couldn't be left to drift uselessly into medical research or waste their attention on devising ways to revive British industry. No, this elite workforce is given by far and away the best budget in the land and told to invent weapons technology. The numerous defence analysis and testing establishments all over the country include Malvern in Worcestershire, Farnborough in Hampshire, Chertsey in Surrey (where September 99's arms fair was held) and the infamous chemical and biological warfare research station at Porton Down in Hampshire. DERA are keen to promote their technological innovations especially the ones with 'realworld' applications. The Liquid Crystal Diode is a particular favourite, as is Thermal Imaging. Designed to give night vision to military reconnaissance and weapons siting, the same technology is used to search for buried victims following earthquakes. However the reality is that only around ten per cent of DERA's work has a civil purpose. The rest is warfare; the quest for Joseph Heller's fictitious Shhhhh!: "The plane so fast, you can bomb someone even before you decide to do it. Decide today - it's done yesterday." Recently declassified documents are only now beginning to shed some light on the extensive chemical and bio-

logical weapons testing carried out in Britain by Porton Down during the 1950s and 60s. The Chemical Defence and Micro-biological Research Establishments, CDE & MRE (DERA has been renamed more times than the dole) released large quantities of a known carcinogen, Zinc Cadmium Sulphide, over substantial tracts of the population. The tests were designed to map the effects of a potential chemical or biological attack on Britain. Salisbury and Norwich were both subject to 'Air Pollution Trials' that consisted of barium treated ZCS being sprayed over the towns by air and out of the back of Land Rovers. Similar, biological, trials to ascertain the danger from offshore germ attack were carried out, along the Dorset coast, throughout the 1960s. An Anthrax simulant, Bacillus Fubtilus Varniger, was sprayed from a boat in the English Channel to see how far inland it could spread. Communities from Portland and East Lulworth experiencing clusters of birth defects and misscarriage, have called for a public inquiry or the setting up of a parliamentary select committee to look into the effects of the trials. DERA have been accused of breaching the Nuremberg code which outlawed "experimenting on people without informed consent". The MoD have said they will appoint a toxicologist to study what effects the releases may have had, though they are having trouble finding a willing candidate.

Last month, Wiltshire police launched an unconnected investigation into claims that nerve gas was tested on servicemen at Porton Down during the 1950s. At least one soldier is known to have died as a result of exposure to the nerve agent Sarin. Possible charges of corporate manslaughter, assault and administering noxious substances could be brought. Another DERA 'breakthrough' was the Future Infantry Soldier Technology (FIST) project. FIST gained celebrity status when it featured in a Channel Four documentary 'The War Machine' screened in February 1998. In the film an army Brigadier lauded the project as creating the "soldier of the future" and described how useful the technology would be to troops in the Gulf. However during the field trials the helmet mounted screen of the automatic 'Video Aiming System', (which was supposed to replace the need for a soldier to aim his rifle), became invisible, and therefore useless, simply because the sun was shining. And the £20,000, satellite linked, 'Global Positioning System' was unable to detect an 'enemy' in full view only yards away.

"As a navigation aid it made a good ashtray," concluded the field trial manager. So far FIST has cost the taxpayer £7 million, they say they hope to have positive results by 2008.

However the dilemma facing DERA at present is not how it spends its money, but where that money is going to come from. The exact form of the proposed PPP is undecided, or even whether it will go through at all, though both the Government and corporate sector are pushing hard for privatisation. "It will make DERA more vital, commercial and efficient," says DERA's Helen Craven.

DERA's 'Agency' status means it is officially classed as a 'trading fund'. That is they "sell" their research to the MoD and other government departments and are not therefore officially subsidised by the MoD. The ninety per cent of their work carried out for the MoD would most likely continue post sell off, resulting in taxpayers effectively subsidising a private corporation whose sole purpose is to make money for its shareholders from the production of weapons. Opposition has come in various forms. The Pentagon has voiced concerns over joint research carried out between the British and US militaries falling into private hands. The Association of Independent Research Organisations has described the plan as "unworkable". And according to Fiona Draper, from the Institute of Professional Management Specialists (IPMS), DERA's leading trade union, the majority of the Agency's workforce are opposed to PPP. Draper says many of her members, who see themselves working for the public good are uncomfortable about working for someone else's private profit. "DERA has to advise the MoD on the usefulness of equipment. If they themselves are owned by a company who had an interest in manufacturing that equipment, they may no longer be in a position to give totally impartial advice." Draper also points out that, as a public body, DERA is accountable to Parliament and through Parliament to the public. As a private company, this would no longer be the case. (Though there are those that argue that the Parliamentary custom of not questioning military expenditure could hardly be described as accountability.) When asked what control the government could maintain over who owns a private DERA, the MoD's Marcus Deville dismissed the danger of military technology falling into the hands of less than ethical regimes, as the new organisation "would still be subject to Strategic Export Controls". However many arms traders have become quite adept at circumventing these controls, and the growing tide of 'free trade', corporate protecting, legislation such as GATT, NAFTA and the soon to be reappearing Multilateral Agreement on Investment, is likely to mean any Government veto over the dealings of the proposed conglomorate would be little at best.

(It is worth noting here that when SQUALL approached Deville for a press pass for the DSEi arms fair, his response was effectively: Sorry but the exhibition is being run by a private company and we dont have any say over who gets allowed in or not. It appears the MoD claim to 'have control' when it suits them, but 'have none' when it doesn't.)

In his book, 'The Armour-Plated Ostrich - The Hidden Costs of Britain's Addiction to the Arms Business', Tim Webb, who spent 25 years in the arms business, details the need for the diversification of the 'defence' industry: "Education, health, social services and other areas of manufacturing have all suffered as a result of successive British governments' over-indulgence in military hardware." Currently standing at £22 billion a year. Tony Blair with his trusty sidekick George Robertson (UK Defence Secretary and Nato Director General-to-be) have proved to be as hell bent on killing foreigners as any of their predecessors. Yet a poll of Labour MPs taken just after the 1997 general election found them to be s=ix to one in favour of a reduction in defence expenditure. All the same, Chancellor Gordon Brown's threats to pull the plug on the £16 billion Eurofighter project quickly disappeared, and Blair's recent Strategic Defence Review fell foul of the MoD's unparalleled muscle in Whitehall.

(Despite a steady flow of reliable reports, spanning much of the last 24 years, demonstrating British arms were being used domestically in East Timor, only now does Foreign Secretary, Robin Cook, become concerned about a hawk jet sighting over Dili. Though despite the massacre underway in East Timor, the UK Government will still not stand by their election pledge to cease arms sales to the Indonesian regime. 'Sales', it was recently revealed, that were in fact 'gifts' when Indonesia could not afford to pay for the planes.)

Reluctantly Labour did stick by one manifesto commitment. In March 1998 a consultation Green Paper was drawn up proposing the setting up of a Defence Diversification Agency (DDA) whose purpose is intended to reduce Britain's defence dependency by transferring military technology into the civil sector. Webb argues that had steps down this road been taken sooner Britain's manufacturing industry could be in a very different state. One DERA project led to the invention of a flat, wall hung, television screen that could project 3D images. The manufacturing licence went to a Japanese company because there are no British owned TV manufacturers. In its presently proposed state the DDA looks likely to fall well short of expectations. The Government has decided to place the new organisation within DERA. Its £2 million budget, described as "paltry" by CAAT, is the equivalent of 0.0001 per cent of total arms expenditure, . Fiona Draper of IPMS believes a DDA within a privatised DERA would prove totally ineffective: "What incentive would DERA have as a commercial body to pass on knowledge to other firms its in competition with." Any real commitment to diversification must also be questioned while DERA's 'Pathfinder' arm is out and about actively encouraging industry to generate new military ideas for the Agency to work on, and the Defence Export Service Organisation (DESO) are zealously promoting arms sales overseas with their air shows and arms conventions.

In response to the Green Paper, Campaign Against the Arms Trade (CAAT) have called for the DDA to be made independent of both DERA and the MoD, suggesting it could be situated within the DTI. "Any diversification agency within these bodies would be highly influenced by its environment," says CAAT's Rachel Harford. She points out that it was another election pledge to promote diversification and reduce arms exports. So Labour owe it to the British people to disband the DESO and put the money into a more powerful DDA. Webb also thinks, given the right conditions,the DDA has potential. He believes it should be a free-standing agency made up of scientists, businessmen, people from education, industry and defence, with trade unions, government departments, local authorities and the EU all playing a role. While wrangling continues over DERA's privatisation, perhaps the question should not be: How does DERA go forward? But: When does DERA stop doing what it does and set their immense cerebral reserve to some more relevant tasks. Are British people not sick of seeing their schools close, their jobs disappear and their relatives die on hospital waiting lists? Yet the government they elected still think it necessary to pour the majority of the nation's wealth into an industry that is like a dog chasing its own tail. Spending on research into undetectable aircraft is matched by that into planes that can detect anything. Despite the "defence" moniker, the aim is thinking up more effective ways of killing people. No doubt the new DERA will get a more cuddly name.

"Its not easy to persuade people that a tank is useful," says disgruntled, DERA spokeswoman, Helen Craven. No it's not. Yet DERA, along with the rest of Britain's defence industry, seem caught up in NATO's incessant push Eastwards. Britain's generals are still Empire building and it benefits the arms manufacturers to keep the Cold War alive. All the smart money is on the 'Smash it up - Rebuild it' school of economic thought. And with George Robertson at the helm? That'll do nicely - American Express? As author Tim Webb puts it: "Learning nothing from past mistakes of cost overruns and weapons designed for a world that no longer exists, the planners press ahead and the multinational manufacturers start jumping into bed with each other to promote their bids. A few dogs may bark but the armoured caravan moves on."

Protesters picket the Houses Of Parliament, calling on Jack Straw to allow the Spanish authorities to bring General Pinochet to trial...

...but in the meantime murderous regimes still queue up to buy weapons from Britain...

...and luxury country mansions across Surrey prepare rooms for any other dictator when the going gets too tough outside the walls of the palace.

## SQUOTES

"We want to thank you all for these days you've been with us. Seeing you, having you so close, our hearts have grown and we are now better and stronger. We see you and we see people, men and women committed to a struggle, to a cause that's also yours. By coming, you've given us a greater strength that will help us resist better and longer. That's why we want to thank you. I know that maybe you won't understand me, but your being here is so very, very lovely."

*Subcomandante Insurgente Marcos, speaking with representatives of the autonomous municipalities of Chiapas.*

**Learn to love the bomb.**

**Vote Labour.**

**Graffiti about French nuclear testing in the South Pacific, stencilled June 18th 1999**

WAKE UP! WAKE UP! IT'S YER BIT OF ARMLESS FUN

# Weekly SchNEWS

### Printed and Published in Brighton by Justice?

**Friday 17th Sept 1999**    http://www.schnews.org.uk/    **Issue 228  Free/Donation**

# Guns 'Я' Us

*'We obviously don't talk about burnt bodies and smashed bones. It tends to put the clients off their vol-au-vents'* - **missile salesman**

*Inside:* decked in pinstripes or uniforms and shiny regalia, 20,000 or so arms-industry delegates, beating the Christmas rush. Not a place to take yer mum shopping – and an invite a tad harder to obtain than a copy of the Argos catalogue.

*Outside:* the characteristic peace movement mixed-bag of Quakers, troskyist paper sellers, direct action types, and the odd backbench MP. And more than a few police. At least as many combat fatigues as were inside the exhibition, and more running around and scrambling across obstacles than on the Krypton Factor assult course.

**SUPERSTAR DSEi - *HERE WE GO!***

Welcome to Defence Systems and Equipment International (DSEi) - the UK's biggest bombs n' guns emporium. Taking place simultaneously in on MoD land near Chertsey, Surrey and at London's Docklands, don't shop around for your military-industrial hardware - just come to and peruse our collection.

And so thousands of participants came from across the globe, representing regimes as far apart as Algeria, China and Saudi Arabia. They rolled up into Chertsey into a grey expanse that looked as muddy as the car parks at a wet Glastonbury - and just as miserable - before herding into the field of marquees. But the projectiles advertised on these stalls would be dangerous to juggle with, the pipes here too full of high-grade aircraft fuel to try to smoke, and the chemicals unlikely to make anyone feel the rush come. The hippies weren't invited to this one.

Still, they rushed there anyway and things kicked off at the exhibition, where several hundred activists flanked the main entrance, at intervals flinging themselves in front of the oncoming coachloads. The tailbacks quickly built up as the anti-arms trade boys and girls crawled beneath the vehicles or sat in the road; chanting Buddhists all the while banging out a rhythmic backdrop to the fun and games. Meanwhile, on the river in East London, amphibious activists harried the six or more state-of-the-art warships, their in-something-of-a-state dinghy tearing along only slightly faster than it let in the Thames. (The ropy old motor, though, shall stall no more: butter-fingered police, after confiscating the vessel, let the engine slip into the bosom of the water. A replacement is coming courtesy of an apologetic constabulary – oops).

Back in rainy Chertsey, police had had to close the main approach route to traffic, giving throngs of dripping wet arms dealers a chance to get to know the lovely Chobham road. Traipsing on foot the mile or more stretch down to the fair's entrance, many apparently suffered collateral damage* to their dignity. One delegate, displaying an IQ similar to that of the average subscriber to *Guns n' Ammo* magazine, took a moment to lunge at a protester with a poorly-aimed umbrella. Some who arrived by train had a better time; not, however, those on the Tuesday morning service held up for the best part of an hour, after a female activist locked on to a carriage at the last station but one from the exhibition site. Chatting on the platform was a pleasure, as the extended stop provided unrivalled access to the considerable number of arms buyers and sellers aboard the train. As too, were the catering staff contracted by the exhibition. *'We'll spit in their food!'* they promised, expressing the same dim view of their arms-trading carriage-fellows as most of the other passengers.

---

**Dear Murderous Bastard,**
You Are Cordially Invited to An Opportunity to Purchase Some of the World's Finest Instruments of Torture & Death.
Set in the Heart of the Beautiful Surrey Countryside, the Defence Systems and Equipment International Offers you the chance to choose from a wide range of Missiles, Attack Aircraft and Internal Repression Equipment, all in the Unrivalled Peace and Security that only the Ministry of Defence can offer.  RSVP MoD

---

Then there were those who got inside…. stowing away in one of the delegates' coaches, one power-dressed woman protester passed unnoticed in the exhibition for several minutes before getting kicked out with some of the industry literature she'd managed to glean. Others ran the gauntlet of forest terrain and barbed perimeter fence, creeping through the undergrowth like soldiers before scaling the double-fencing of the inner-compound.

Then yesterday evening, the target was a Park Lane hotel (don't flash your YHA membership card in this place) where many of the arms industry movers and shakers went to enjoy a banquet. There, one hotel security guard went and punched a guy who had climbed the hotel gate to drape a banner, giving him, nonetheless, rather less injury than, say, the Kurds in eastern Turkey, trade unionists in Kenya, or any of those lucky others at the receiving end of some of that shiny new military hardware.

***collateral damage**, a Gulf War euphemism meaning human casualties, as used by many of the 'peacekeeping enthusiasts' attending DSEi. - SchNEWS VocabWatch

## "WHAT IF WE HAD AN ARMS FAIR & EVERYONE CAME?"

Among the MoD's guests are the following delightful governments.... **Saudi Arabia:** A savagely repressive fundamentalist regime, that according to Amnesty, *'collects arms like others collect Rolls Royces.'* **Israel:** Subject of innumerable UN condemnations for the occupation of Lebanon, ethnic cleansing in the Occupied Territories, including 20 unlawful killings this year, and recently found guilty by its own high court of torturing prisoners. **Syria:** Systematic human rights abuse and repression of political opponents. **Algeria:** Military dictatorship responsible for 100,000 deaths since cancelling the 1992 elections.

Such is the generosity of Britain, we even help such states pay for their weapons, thanks to the Export Credit Guarantees Dept. ECGD has the British tax payer cough up for recipient country that spend more than they can afford, so allowing exporters to trade with 'high-risk'states that no true capitalist would touch. Naturally, this is used largely for UK plc's favourite export, arms – meaning that we pay for dodgy regimes to get nasty weaponry for free, and the merchants of death to make a killing. And the best bit is that it all gets counted as 'aid'.

The Department of Trade and Industry (DTI) admitted in Parliament this year that export credits were covering the sale of arms to Indonesia worth £691 million. The DTI has also rescheduled £200 million in debt repayments from the beleaguered Indonesian economy so that arms deals could continue.

Sadly, due to a few domestic problems (*not* 'cos the UK govt withdrew their invitation, which still stands), Indonesia was unable to attend the DSEi. Fortunately though, the Defence Export Services Organisation, has a permanent bargain-basement store in Jakarta their stated aim: to raise Britain's arms sales to Indonesia tenfold, to £3bn by 2007. Don't forget - even when countries are officiously banned from importing British arms, UK companies can still arrange arms transfers as long as they don't pass directly through Britain. And helpfully, the govt trains military officers from foreign armies - including the Indonesian special forces.

### You missed the DSEi arms fair?

No-one goes away empty-handed. Two more: Armed Forces Communication and Electronics Association (AFCEA) This one's already been driven out of Belgium, (*politically and ethically undesirable* said their parliament) but is coming to the Renaissance Hotel near Heathrow airport, from October 27-29.

Soon after, the nortorious Contingency and Operational Procurement Exhibition (COPEX) takes place at Sandown Park Racecourse in Surrey, November 2-4.

Both these snappily-titled events provide plenty of opportunity to go play with the bastards. Campaign Against Arms Trade: 0171 281 0297

## Inside SchNEWS

Mumia Abu-Jamal is an African-American journalist, awarded the prestigious Peabody Award for Radio Journalism at 26, elected president of the Philadelphia chapter of the Association of Black Journalists, who has been on death row for the past sixteen years charged with the murder of a cop. As a teenager Mumia was a member of the Black Panther Party and his work found him on the 'key agitators index' of the FBI. Because of his outspoken views Mumia was finding it increasingly difficult to make ends meet supporting his wife and children and so took a job driving a taxi. Whilst cabbying he saw a cop beating a black man with his torch. He was shot running to the scene by an officer while another lay mortally wounded nearby. After being beaten by police he underwent intensive surgery, before being charged with murder. Meanwhile, he'd also been highlighting the states escalating harassment of the radical black ecological group MOVE, and its attempts to crush it, eventually leading to the bombing of their homes and the imprisonment and death of most of its members. As one magazine states *"It is impossible to avoid the conclusion that the authorities considered eliminating Mumias reportage an urgent priority."*

There isn't space to go into the details of the trial but in December '97 an international tribunal of 23 prominent jurists convened in Philadelphia, to consider testimony by 'selected witnesses' and look into the evidence. The panel took just 2 hours to return a unanimous verdict that the US government had violated four human rights conventions during and after the trial.

Mumia's work was dubbed "the voice of the voiceless" Now it's our turn to pull out all the stops to make sure he is not executed. Last time, in 1995, worldwide protests stopped his death- let's do it again. The next six months are a critical period in the battle for a new trial because Mumia's certiorari petition is before the U.S. Supreme Court. Unless the Court rules in his favour, which we certainly can't count on - then, by the end of October, Mumia's lawyers must file their habeas corpus appeal in the Federal Courts. This filing for habeas will initiate the final rounds of the legal battle. Remember this is urgent - once the death warrant is signed he has just 30–90 days to live

What's at stake is both Mumia's future- the future of one of the most inspiring and fearless voices of the oppressed today and the future of the disgusting US Penal system. The US government has not dared to carry out the legal execution of a prominent Black revolutionary since the days of slavery. To let them get away with such an act now would send a chilling message to the rest of the world. We must not allow this to happen! Mumia's case underscores *"the criminalization of Black men, the suppression of dissent, the expanded death penalty, the gutting of defendants' rights, and the whole political atmosphere that is based on blame and repression".*

September 19-25 is Mumia awareness week.

Contact Mumia Must Live! BM Haven, London WC1N 3XX email mumia@coolnetuk.com, www. mumia.org

Send protest letters to: Governor Tom Ridge, Main Capital Building, Room 225, Harrisburg, PA 17120, fax +001 717 783 4429.

Letters of support; Mumia Abu-Jamal, S.C.I. Greene, 1040 East R Fuman Highway, Waynesburg, PA, Philadelphia 15370-8090.

There's a meeting at the Brighton Unemployed Workers Centre, 4 Crestway Parade, The Crestway, Hollingdean this Sunday (19th) 7pm to organise local support.

## SchNEWS in brief

Get along to the **Free The World Bike Ride** on September 22nd DAY, for a pedal powered tour of London. *"Along with reclaiming London streets on this 'car free day', we will be visiting various dodgy institutions and businesses to express opposition to the destructive system of global capitalism."* Meet 12 noon at Speakers Corner. The tour will end with a picnic held somewhere inappropriate – so bring food and drink. Contact London Greenpeace, 5 Caledonian Road, N1 9DX. Tel: 0171 713 1269 ** Did you **witness any arrests** at the last Manchester Reclaim the Streets or the squatted Hacienda Party in June? (See SchNEWS 215) Tel 0161 226 6814 ** *"We are of the united opinion that the loss of these antiquities would constitute little less than a national disaster."* Letter to the Times 1975. Planning permissions granted nearly half a century ago allowing the obliteration of a large part of south-west **Dartmoor** to make way for a "super-quarry" and huge waste tips could soon become reality. Much of the ground has yet to be systematically surveyed and it is likely that the monuments currently recorded represent only a fraction of the existing archaeological remains. http://easywebb.easynet.co.uk/aburnham/pers/dquarry.htm Contact Dartmoor Preservation Association, China Clay Campaign, Old Duchy hotel, FREEPOST (PY687), Yelverton, PL20 6ZZ. ** "We are at a turning point in our history. We are on the verge of a new adventure in planetary consciousness". So writes one of the contributors to **'Creating Harmony**: Conflict Resolution in Community' (ed. Hildur Jackson). After a long summer of partying (oh yeah, and protesting), SchNEWS isn't too sure that consciousness is necessary, but for those who do this book might take 'em to a higher level. The book is a varied manual of cooperative living in community experiments written by participants from the 60's onwards. Available from Permanent Publications, Tel:01730-823311email: hello@permaculture.co.uk**

The South African cabinet approved a £3.2 billion deal with major European arms manufacturers to buy ships, submarines, fighters and helicopters, money that is needed to help the country's crumbling public & social services. Meanwhile, whilst the government is busy challenging allegations of corruption, the country has just endured it's biggest ever strike. The President is accused of using hard line tactics against his public sector workers, to impress foreign governments and investors about his "Tight(Assed) Fiscal Policy"! Although they dont seem so tight when buying arms!

## From our Finnish Correspondent

"We had a demonstration in 3-motorwaybuilding-site...Engineers were aggressive, they shouted how "stupid" we are. The top road builder screamed to workers that "machines must move to the other place and you can drive OVER activists if they are in the front of! We were in the front and I gripped in the front of machine my legs under the machine and machine went on!

This was the first time the demonstration wasn't told to police before and it was illegal. After forcing machines we went to the top office of 3-roadbuilding site in Iittala to shout to the leaders. They came out and went away with their big cars, but I called to the leader of this project and he said that he's ready to speak with us. He was ready also before but I hated him so much that I refused to speak with him. Now the engineers said in newspapers that every motorway-resistors in Finland are invited to come to the Iittala to drink coffee, hah hah. And they said that they'll explain us that environment has been taken into consideration in motorwaybuilding, hah!!!! Of course we'll go there but we discuss only that the WHOLE motorwaybuilding must STOP!!"

Contact Aroniinnkatu 5A8, 13500 Hdmeenlinna, Finland. Tel + 358-40-7452057. e-mail: pajuojaa@hmltol.hamkk.fi

## BURMESE YEARS!

17 years imprisonment for possessing pro-democracy fliers was justice Burmese style for James Mawdsley last week. Access to the British Consul was refused, causing suspicion of torture. On the 9/9/99 Pro-democracy demonstrators in Pegu City and Thatone handed out leaflets. Londoner Rachel Godwyn was among 500 demonstrators arrested (for singing a revolutionary song) last week. She now faces 7 years in prison. Demos in solidarity around the world included the Burmese Embassy in London being redecorated, losing its military flag and gaining butterflies and flowers. The Burmese embassy in Australia being stormed by several hundred students and there were large demo's in front of the Burmeses Embassy's in Bangkok, Thailand, and in the USA outside the UN Building, In Nottingham action was taken against electronics firm GEC (sprayed GET OUT OF BURMA), Midland Bank & Daewoo car showrooms (glued up) and Total petrol stations (padlocked during rush hour). Nottingham Earth First! also picketed several Travel Agencies to highlight our ability to directly boycott Burma as ethical tourists. Before Rachel Godwyn left, she made a plea to Tony Blair to end investment in Burma which is ruled by a military dictatorship guilty of ethnic cleansing, forced labour and the disappearances and torture of pro-democracy activists.

Meanwhile 3 year old, Thaint Wunna Khin has become the world's youngest prisoner of conscience, after being arrested by Military Intelligence for helping to plan a march earlier this year! Amnesty International said *"Locking up a young child -effectively holding her hostage to force her father out of hiding - exposes the extent of the Burmese government's ruthlessness in trying to stamp out political dissent."*

Burma Action Group, Bickerton House, 25-27 Bickerton Rd, London N19 5JT. www.freeburmacoalition.org

## PARTNERS IN CRIME

'Partnership' was Prime Minister Tory Blair's buzzword at the TUC Conference in Brighton this week. (mentioned nine times).

*"Business and employees…are not two nations divided. That's old style thinking. That's the thinking of the past."* According to Blair *"The partnership message is spreading "* so here's a few examples:

270 workers at LUFTHANSA SKYCHEF sacked for going on a one day strike over flexible working practices.

Workers at KRUPP CAMFORD PRESSING in Llanelli, Wales threatened with redundancies unless they accept pay cuts of up to £60 a week. Last year the company made a profit of £1.7 million.

New Labour's buddies GRANADA are still refusing to re-employ the Hillingdon Hospital workers who were sacked four years ago for refusing to accept worse pay and conditions. An industrial tribunal told Granada to pull their finger out, so far the company have refused.

## ...and finally...

SchNEWS had to laugh about Sir Ken Jackson, General Secretary of the AEEU union, who told the TUC it should scrap its annual Conference and hold a joint gathering every other year with the bosses union, the Confederation of British Industry. The man also came up with the cunning plan of a strike-free Britain. " Workers want to work, they don't want to strike " he rattled. Maybe he should have said it a bit louder. The very next day hundreds of Ford workers staged a 24 hour strike over pay allowances. A free copy of SchNEWS to any reader who correctly guesses what union the Ford workers are members off.

### disclaimer

SchNEWS warns all readers not to have candy floss arms fayres in the back garden, as loads of dodgy dealers will only turn up and you'll have to dodgem like the bullets.

---

## *Subscribe!*

Keep SchNEWS FREE! Just send 1st Class stamps (e.g. 20 for next 20 issues) or donations (payable to Justice?) **Ask for "Originals"** if **you can make copies.** Post *free* to all prisoners. SchNEWS, c/o on-the-fiddle, P.O. Box 2600, Brighton, East Sussex, BN2 2DX.

*Tel/Autofax:* +44 (0)1273 685913 *GET IT EVERY WEEK BY E-MAIL:* schnews@brighton.co.uk

# SUN, SALSA & SOCIALISMO

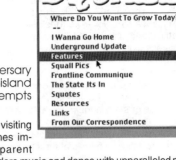

**SQUALL**

Where Do You Want To Grow Today?

--
I Wanna Go Home
Underground Update
Features
Squall Pics
Frontline Communique
The State Its In
Squotes
Resources
Links
From Our Correspondence

Fresh from spending a month in Cuba during the 40th anniversary of their revolution, Jim Carey reports back on an audacious island throbbing with a passion for culture, whilst fending off US attempts to destroy its successful alternative to capitalism

"Fuck the revolution," said the black marketeer striding back to his doorway haunt in Havana. Having had his whispered offer of illicit cigars refused, he'd spotted the Rock Around the Blockade T-shirt and realised we were in Cuba for reasons other than the usual tourist quest for sun, sand, sea, sex and cigars.

The irony stood apparent. Just over forty years ago, an afro-cuban such as himself might well have been living in a shack on the outskirts of Havana with little access to decent sanitation, employment, medical care, education or social respect. Photographs of the period displayed in Havana's Museum of the Revolution depict scenes of poverty and destitution more reminiscent of third world charity appeals; a far cry from both present day Cuba and the well dressed black-marketeer who sneered before us so dismissive of the political changes in his own third world country.

Appropriately, the quote written on the back of my duty-free rolling tobacco advised: "Travel the world, talk to everyone". And so, over the course of a one month journey round Cuba, I did just that. From passionate defenders of the revolutionary principle to Nike-obsessed youth gagging for a slice of capitalist excitement. Contrary to what I had read in the British press about Cuba, no-one seemed the least bit afraid to speak to their mind, regardless of their political perspective. Lesson One: Forget everything you've read in the media about Cuba. The cold war lives on in bizarre propaganda.

So, as one of the very few countries left in the world still actively exploring a political alternative to the American way of doing things, the investigative journey was always destined to be the education.

Our first mission in Cuba was a musical one. Myself and a fellow DJ from the SQUALL Sound System travelled with a fifteen strong brigade of young British people from Rock Around the Blockade, a pro-Cuban activist group based in the UK. Back in 1995, Rock Around the Blockade asked Cuba's Union de Jovenes Communista (Union of Young Communists) what could be done specifically to help Cuban youth. Rather surprisingly for an island short of certain basic necessities, they replied with a request for a sound

system. Upon visiting Cuba it becomes immediately apparent why; Cubans adore music and dance with unparalleled passion. Everywhere you go on the island you'll find a tatty speaker wired up to some tin-box of a radio or tape recorder, spilling copious quantities of salsa, merengue, disco, nueva trova, hip-hop, rumba and latin pop. From factories, farmhouses, apartments and the street.....from dawn til dusk and well beyond.

Pic: El Seed

Largely due to the US economic blockade of the island, enforced since 1961 with a vigour one EU official recently described as "obsessive", musical equipment ranks amidst a multitude of material and medical necessities difficult for the Cubans to obtain. And yet for a community powerfully connected by dance, and for a youth needing to dance as hard as it works, sound systems are a social medicine. And that's where Rock Around the Blockade stepped in for its third visit - on the fortieth anniversary of the Cuban revolution - to give the 36,000 people of Fomento a sound system to keep and a party to remember.

Whilst fulfilling our mission, the Brigade were given a two week tour of the Sancti Spriritus province in which Fomento is situated, as an introduction to the history of the Cuban revolution and the socialist infrastructure developed to deploy its ideals of 'people before profits'.

Facilitated by our hosts, the Union de Jovenes Communista, our brigade of political inquisitors expended its volley of awkward questions in schools, hospitals, clinics, farms, discos, cultural centres and at a multitude of sites of revolutionary significance. We also spent Christmas Day picking coffee alongside Cuban volunteers in the plantations of Sancti Spiritus and spoke to members of the local population who'd participated in the revolution. We were left in little doubt that the region which afforded us such formidable hospitality was passionately steeped both in the history and the present day reality of this most unusual of revolutions.

Exactly forty years ago this year, the Cuban Rebel Army commanded by Fidel Castro Ruz succeeded against all odds in throwing out the corrupt US-backed dictatorship which had seized power in Cuba following a coup d'etat eight years previously. Also removed from the island were the Mafia who, with the dictatorship's continuing complicity, had run Havana's numerous clubs, casinos and brothels since the late twenties. Shortly after the revolution out also went the American companies and landowners who'd controlled 90 per cent of Cuba's land and industry, followed by multi-millionaire corporate Cubans like the Bacardi family.

The grand headquarters building of the Bacardi rum empire - the Edificio Bacardi - had stood just an ingratiated stones throw from the presidential palace in Havana. In a scene irresistibly symbolic of the revolution's reappropriation of resources, the Edificio was swathed in scaffolding as we visited the capital; its cracked marble walls under repair ready for state use. Bacardi's rum producing factories, capable of distilling some of the island's vast acreage of sugar cane into 'ron de Cuba', have now passed into the hands of the state run Havana Club. Cuba's preferred choice of social lubricant is now cheaply available to those who bring their own container to the dispensary. Despite this, the number of drunks on the streets of Havana was significantly less than those visible in London.

Although arriving in Cuba without any taste for rum whatsoever, my 'appointments with Ron' grew ever more frequent. Mystically, my staggered Spanish dramatically improved after a few dashes of the hot stuff, and long nocturnal hours of animated conversation ensued.

Despite still dominating the world's rum market from its relocated base in the United States, Bacardi pour millions of dollars into funding anti-Castro groups. The corporation's lawyers even helped draft the infamous US legislation, the Helms Burton Act, which penalises any company from any country in the world which has trade associations with Cuba.

In order to enact the social principles of the revolution and protect the country from continuing American attempts to bring the island back in line, Castro declared the socialist nature of the new Cuban government in 1961. The subsequent reappropriation of Cuba's resources is now apparent throughout the island. Cuba's grand Spanish colonial architecture, previously occupied by the white and rich, is now inhabited by everyday folk; black, white and all shades in between. Glancing through an open front door in the municipality of Trinidad de Cuba I saw an old lady in a nylon dress swaying back and forth on an ornate wooden rocking chair, chuffing contentedly on a cigar beneath a crystal chandelier.

The Villa Conchita, a splendiferous piece of architectural grandeur we visited in the central municipality of Sancti Spiritus, had been owned by a multi-millionaire childless couple until the day they fled the revolution. Complete with much of its original furniture and ornamentation, the Villa Conchita now lends its opulence as home to 12 orphans and the impressive 11 care-workers who look after them. For a year or so after the victory of the revolutionary forces, the new government tried to continue a relationship with multinational companies operating on the island. However, when big oil companies began refusing to provide the island with oil in protest over its new brand of socialism, Castro's government decided that enough was enough and kicked them all out and nationalised the lot. Black and white film footage of the period shows Cuban citizen's kicking Esso and Shell logo's from the roofs of their former buildings.

Behind the Campismo chalets which provided home to both our brigade and a regularly reinforced contingent of large green frogs, looms the Escambray mountains. It was from here that Column Eight of the Rebel Army commanded by Ernesto Che Guevara conducted the successful and suprisingly rapid take over of the strategically important central regions of Cuba. In a battle Fidel Castro thought would take at least three months, the 300 rebel soldiers of Column Eight took just three days to defeat over 5000 government troops entrenched in the city of Santa Clara. Following this decisive rebel victory, the dictatorship of Fulgencio Batista collapsed as he fled the country with a sackful of loot stolen from the state coffers. Eight days later, the rebel army entered Havana triumphant.

It is not possible to exaggerate the reverence with which Che Guevara's memory is held in Cuba. Everyday in schools right across the island, Cuban children repeat: "We aspire to be like Che", as a mantra to self-improvement. Pictures, medallions, statues and memorials to the Argentine-born freedom fighter can be found on hill tops and roadsides, in shady groves and adorning the walls of private homes, schools and hospitals.

What was especially surprising was that even the minority of people who expressed dissatisfaction with Cuba's revolutionary government still loved Che. When I asked one such person whether the incessant reverence shown to Guevara ever got on his nerves, the answer was an emphatic 'no'. "Even when he was a commander in the army and a minister in the government, he drew an ordinary soldiers wage," he said. "And even when he was both of these he still occupied his free time doing huge amounts of voluntary work in the plantations and factories despite his chronic asthma. Everybody feels he belonged to the people."

The huge statue of Che in Santa Clara, towering above the interred remains of several key revolutionaries including Guevara himself, is made of bronze donated by ordinary Cuban people. Given the sparsity of material resource in Cuba, the statue stands as a monument to the Cuban people's brimming admiration of his example and legacy. But, although Guevara is the most memorialised of the revolutionaries, statues and images of his ever smiling comrade Camilo Cienfuego are also profuse, whilst factories, hospitals and street names pay respect to other revolutionaries including female warriors like Celia Sanchez and Tania. Those revolutionaries still alive today are not celebrated in this way. As part of the revolutionary government's stated principle of avoiding the cult of political personality, there are relatively few images of Fidel Castro in public places.

When told that two movies about the life of Che Guevara were currently in production in United States, the Cubans we spoke to expressed concern. Normally they love US action flicks plucked from satellite and shown without the necessity for royalty payments; we met passionate communists who were able to recall every scene from films like Silence of the Lambs, Pulp Fiction, The Godfather and Once Upon a Time in America. But the prospect of a Hollywood spin on Che Guevara's life story was not greeted with much excitement. It was upon the orders of the CIA that Che Guevara was executed without trial in Bolivia in 1967, his remains only finally negotiated back to Cuba in 1997.

Perhaps the one and only passion which Che Guevera shared with the rich capitalists of Hollywood was his love affair with Cuban cigars. At one stage in his life, Guevara's doctor insisted that he give up smoking to help him cope better with the chronic asthma he had suffered throughout his life. Guevara reluctantly agreed to hold it down to one a day but saw to it that his cigar box contained only 12 inchers.

According to the Cuban tobacco farmers we spoke to, it is the island's perfect combination of soil and weather which ensures its reputation for producing the world's best tobacco. Fulfilling last year's increased export target of 80 million cigars, Cuba's renowned Havanas provide one of the key sources of international revenue necessary to ensure the continuation of Cuba's steady economic growth over the last five years.

Although officially unobtainable in the United States due to the economic blockade, Bill Clinton was still forced to deny rumours that the infamous Lewinsky blow-job cigar was in fact Cuban. The smuggling of Cuban cigars into the US mostly via Mexico has increased eight fold over recent years. Fidel Castro, on the other hand, is unlikely to suffer similar accusations. Long associated with the global image of the contented Cuban cigar chuffer, he actually gave up smoking a couple of years ago citing it as an unhealthy example to set before young Cubans. Given that he'd smoked cigars everyday for the majority of his life, his sudden abstention at age 71 was impressive.

Another source of both revenue and international representation are the increasing number of Cuban artists travelling abroad to perform in countries like Japan, Mexico, Europe, Canada and even the United States. According to, Fernando Leon Jacamino from the organisation responsible for the development of Cuban culture (SAIZ), there are now more Cuban bands performing abroad than at any time in the country's history, with Europe currently providing the most frequented destination. Schools of music in Cuba provide a free education in the combined disciplines of afro-Cuban, jazz and classical styles. As a legacy of musical exchanges with the former Soviet Union there are still Russian professors teaching classical techniques in the music schools of Havana.

As a result of both state support for culture and the long celebrated confluence of African, European and even some Asian musical styles, the unique quality of musicianship cultivated inside Cuba - the country that gave the world salsa, rumba, cha-cha-cha, latin jazz and mambo - is extraordinarily high and of international renown.

Despite the full deployment of bureaucratic obstacles put before Cuban musicians entering the US, it is still possible for Cuban bands signed up to an economically powerful record company to perform in the US. Anancys Saxon, the woman specifically responsible for music with the SAIZ organisation, told us that with Hispanic people now the biggest ethnic group in the United States, the market demand for Cuban music there is strong. When La Charanga Habenera, one of Cuba's top salsa outfits, was finally allowed into the US to perform as a support band, the audience response was rapturous. The headline salsa act, Peter Conde, simply refused to go on; not out of political objection but through awed respect for the quality of the Cuban's musicianship.

These stories were fully corroborated as we sat in an small cafe just outside Havana. With just two British DJs for an audience, Son del Barrio set up in the corner and proceeded to pour out tune after tune of the most sublime yet fiery acoustic music I'd ever heard in my many years of watching live music.

The largest source of international revenue going into the Cuban economy these days, however, comes from an industry the revolutionary government had deliberately avoided developing. Tourism.

With the United States persuading all but a handful of countries to comply with its economic blockade, Cuba had been left with no option but to rely on the Soviet Union as its principle trading partner. Following the sudden collapse of the USSR at the end of the eighties, Cuba faced its greatest economic crisis since the triumph of the revolution. Previous to this crisis, Cuba had resisted the temptation to exploit the island's obvious potential as a tourist hot spot largely due to the prospective social problems which would accompany an influx of rich holidaymakers onto an island with an average wage of $10 a month.

In the socialist aftermath of the revolution all homelessness, unemployment and starvation had been entirely eradicated from what - I had to constantly remind myself - is classified as a third world country. A free education system had taken Cuba's literacy rate up to a first world standard significantly higher than the US, whilst its health care system increased the number of doctors on the island and dramatically decreased the infant mortality rate, (Cuba has four times as many doctors per capita as the UK, sends more doctors to help out abroad than the entire World Health Organisation and fosters an internationally renowned reputation for medical research). These statistics are formidable for any country but for an island officially classed as third world and under economic attack from the US, they are simply staggering.

However, with the 85 per cent collapse in trade, and the 50 per cent crash in oil resources which occurred subsequent to the break up of the Soviet Union, this entire social infrastructure stood on the brink of destruction. Whilst the Cuban government declared a Special Period of rationing, anti-Castro groups in the US backed with money from Bacardi stepped up their efforts to instigate dissent on the island.

The capitalist world, and particularly the United States, drummed its fingers on the desk waiting for the revolution's imminent demise. It never came. The fact that not one single hospital, school, day care centre or orphanage closed down in Cuba as a result of this crisis stands as a formidable testament to an extraordinary feat of economic juggling. Principle to this survival, was the Cuban government's decision to develop what has now become one of the fastest growing tourist industries in the world.

*****

I didn't notice it at first as I lay on my bed lost in thought. But eventually my eyes fell in disbelief on an all too familiar logo graffitied in biro on the chipboard base of the campismo bunk above me. "Oh no, not here as well," I cried aloud. "Not Nike".

Over the course of the next four weeks it would prove to be a common sight. Scrawled on walls, sewed onto baseball caps, stickered in windscreens and even barbered in the hair of a dog I tripped over in Havana. Some Cubans even used marker pens to write Nike on ordinary white T-shirts.

Part of the explanation for this fashion fad can immediately be ascribed to Nike's world marketing strategy. Despite being a corporation run by white American businessmen, they made a decision early on to use black sports stars like Michael Jordan the American basketball player and Ronaldo the Brazilian footballer, to endorse their products. The Cubans, half of whom are black, love sport with the same passion they devote to both music and revolution. Although Nike products, if you can get hold of them in Cuba, are hugely expensive - the youth of the country are clearly attracted by the lure of the logo through exposure to international sporting events and to music videos featuring artists covered with Nike ticks.

Further exposure comes from the copious quantities of logoed tourists flooding into Cuba. At this point I have to admit to being one of them. The only footwear I took to Cuba happened to a pair of Nike trainers I 'd scored for a tenna from a Red Cross shop in London; discarded, I was to discover later, because an air pocket in both the right and left shoe had burst. No amount of logo-gouging with a pen knife could remove the ident, so my feet became the embarrassing target of envious young gazes, although there were a few sniggers whenever I squelched down echoing hallways.

A remarkable number of Cubans in Havana, having received dollars from exiled family members living in the US or from dealings with tourists, possess clothes with well known brand names. Among those most prevalent are Nike, Adidas, Fils, Calvin Klein and Tommy Hilfiger.

On my second packet of duty-free rolling tobacco I found another quote: "You can tell a nation's ideals by looking at its adverts".

Whilst Cuban communist propaganda bangs on about homelessness, racism, education and health, US capitalist propaganda bangs on about alluring products you're not hip without. The Cuban negro who'd offered us the illicit cigars outside the factory - the one who'd said 'fuck the revolution' - the one whose parents probably lived in a pre-revolutionary shithole - was covered head to toe in logoed sports gear. Despite western media assertions about Cuba, I was left in little doubt which of the two forms of propaganda was the more incessant and insidious, and therefore which of the two nation's ideals I felt more worthy.

I gleaned another insight into the nature of the fashion fad when I saw the receptionist at the Union de Jovenes Communista (UJC) headquatres in central Havana wearing an Operation Desert Storm sweat-shirt complete with a picture of an American F1-11! "To her it's just English writing with an action picture on it," explained an English- speaking UJC worker I asked.

The detrimental effects of Cuba's development of tourism can be most keenly observed in the capital, Havana, and I was fortunate for having started my investigative journey in the Cuban countryside. The incredible hospitality and revolutionary fervour displayed by the Cuban campesinos gave me a context with which to view the capital's preoccupation with the dollar. Particularly that displayed by Havana's youth.

If a Cuban citizen had been caught with dollars in the eighties they would be questioned by police about black market activities. The government had resisted the use of a currency belonging to its arch enemy and ordinary Cubans weren't supposed to break the line. However, with the advent of tourist dollars, the recent condoning of certain small businesses associated with tourism, and the increasing number of dollars sent into the country from relatives and friends abroad, the authorities changed their position. There are now currency exchanges booths on most streets and Cubans, as well as tourists, can go into the numerous Tiendas dollar shops to purchase products not available in peso shops.

As a result there are now three exchangeable currencies in the country. The first is Peso Cubano ($1=20 pesos) used almost exclusively by Cuban nationals to buy food, clothing, cigarettes and other products and services at extremely cheap prices. The second is dollars used by tourists and some Cuban nationals to buy a far greater range of products at very expensive prices. The third is an unusual form of currency called the national tourist peso, directly exchangeable with dollars ($1=1 peso tourismo); an attempt to maintain some form of national Cuban currency with the equivalent value to the dollar, ready for the time when Cu-

ba's reluctant use of US currency will cease. Whilst I was still in Havana, Fidel Castro held a joint press conference with Belgium's visiting foreign minister, to reveal that the Euro will replace the US dollar as Cuba's international exchange currency as soon as it proves itself strong enough.

At present, a Cuban stands to make the equivalent of one months average wage simply through a single black market transaction of cigars, drugs or prostitutes. It is tourists who provide the market; both are on the increase.

It is a clear indication of the continuing support for the ideals and social benefits of the revolution that the vast majority of the population resist such large temptations. For those that don't, stringent new laws are imminent. I watched live TV coverage of a stern Fidel Castro informing the National Revolutionary Police during their 40th anniversary conference, that pimps, drug sellers and thieves would now be receiving 20 to 30 year prison sentences. (Prostitutes - unless they are repeat offenders - are sent to a reform centre where attempts are made to provide them with further education and employment skills before returning them to their communities).

What equipment they do have, the Cubans keep operational with a tenacity which mocks our materialist throwaway culture. The original 1950's Pontiacs, Buicks and Plymouths still to be found in working order on just about every street in Cuba are kept on the road by masterful feats of do-it-yourself engineering. Likewise the sound systems. If a speaker breaks in Cuba, the solenoid is rewired by hand with copper wire!

The result of this tenacity is not only measurable in terms of the resources they keep operational, it is also measurable in the Cubans approach to problem solving. Cuba's success in surviving the US blockade, the staggering 85 per cent overnight collapse in trade following the breakdown of the Soviet Union, the consistent and often hysterical CIA efforts to get rid of Castro, the longest drought in the island's history and several hurricanes are at least due in part to the Cuban's remarkable ingenuity. It has also been achieved by encouraging foreign investment, allowing certain small businesses to operate and encouraging tourism. In one of his many marathon speeches, Castro recently said that the further evolution of socialism in Cuba had been suspended whilst measures to ensure the survival of the Cuban economy are deployed.

The Cuban people are sure a new leader is ready to take the presidential seat in the event of Castro's retirement or death. The postulated selections of those I posed the question to coalesced around Carlos Lago - the general Secretary of the Cuban Communist Party and the man who suggested that Cuba should use its tourism as a weapon in the battle for principled economic survival. "Like Fidel", said one, "Lago has the multi-skilled open mind necessary to be president".

For all those with any interest in socially orientated politics, Cuba is a unique and invigorating example. I hadn't really known just how much it would prove to be so until I left the british media behind and actually went and visited the place.

I venture further to suggest that such a study would breath life into any cynical or jaded socialist who feels defeated, outdated or hopeless.

Perhaps this is real reason why the recurrent McCarthyites of the United States find such a small island, population 11 million, such an ideological threat. Their system works for them very well indeed.

## WAKE UP! WAKE UP! IT'S YER DOWN THE PAN

# Weekly SchNEWS

### Printed and Published in Brighton by Justice?

**Friday 24 September 1999**   http://www.schnews.org.uk/   **Issue 229   Free/Donation**

# END OF THE WORLD OFFICIAL

*'The continued poverty of the majority of the planet's inhabitants and excessive consumption by the minority are the two major causes of environmental degradation. The present course is unsustainable and postponing action is no longer an option.'*

Land degradation, rainforest destruction, species extinction - are we going to find the planet dies of all this before depression at the thought of it drives us all to suicide? Not necessarily, says the UN Environment Program in a handy new report on the state of the Earth's natural environment, entitled *Global Environment Outlook 2000.* But the report identifies world water shortage, destruction of coral reefs and global warming as full-scale emergencies, as well as identifying a new threat - nitrogen pollution.

Hold on to your hats - we were so stirred by the urgency of this major new UN report, we cancelled our annual SchNEWS staff whaling trip. So, is it possible to encapsulate next millenium's prospects for the whole of humanity and the global environment into one media-friendly soundbite? Apparently not, the UN would have us believe. GEO 2000 amounts to perhaps the most thorough-going, wide-ranging and (it says) authoritative stocktake ever of the state of the Earth's natural environment - but don't drop it on your foot.

More dense than David Bellamy's beard, this weighty tome is based on contributions from UN agencies, 850 individuals and more than 30 environmental institutes institutes - all of whom, we trust, faithfully use recycled toilet roll. In terms sometimes as dry as Brazil's growing desert, it reads as a roll-call of the world's top emergent ecological nightmares:

*Hose-pipe bans will be the least of our worries as the water cycle fails to cope with demand.

*City-dwellers are choking as urban air pollution is reaching crisis dimensions, especially in the megacities of the southern hemisphereland degradation has reduced fertility and agricultural potential.

*More than half the world's coral reefs are threatened by human activities.

*With global warming upon us, things are hotting up - 1998 was the hottest year on record, and extreme weather events had left 3 million people dead in the last five years.

*Many marine fisheries have been grossly over-exploited.

*The planet's species are still being wiped out; one quarter of the world's mammal species are now at significant risk of extinction.

Cheer up! We're assured that the report was not sponsored by the makers of prozac. In fact, the report's author's are at great pains to take a balanced tone - stressing the successes to date of environmental policy, and that further change is achievable. So will it be enough to use a CFC-free fridge in which to store your giant panda steaks?

Not quite. As excessive consumtion in rich countries is one of the main causes of environmental degradation, 'A tenfold reduction in resource consumption in the industrialized countries is a necessary long-term target", the report says, cutting boldly to the chase. That's radical stuff; though the report takes a carefully non-combative tone, saying; 'Ideally, such measures must simultaneously maintain the living standards of the wealthy, [as well as] upgrade the living standards of the disadvantaged'. Hmn.

The UN - that idealists' graveyard - may have greater resources of optimism to draw on than political power. Still, Klaus Töpfer, the executive director of the UNEP holds it *'essential to force multinational companies to be accountable for their actions'.* Yet while the US continues to punish French local industry, waging a trade war on behalf of the multinational corporate players it champions, it has been forgetting to keep up with its contributions to UN funding . For the real power lies elsewhere: though sadly, corporate boardrooms and governement trade departments are not so easy to catch a glimpse of as the GEO 2000 report, even if the latter lists some of their effects on the rest of us. Such is the nature of global power elites.

Fortunately, GEO 2000 finds further cause for optimism a bit closer to the ground, lauding the *"public....now much more concerned about environmental issues. Popular movements in many countries are forcing authorities to make changes."* As those in France attacking McD's in opposition the US trade sanctions know well. So what if we can't all be so determined in our resistance?....Pass the Prozac.

*SchNews fave mag, **The Ecologist** 01403 786 726 sgc@mag-subs.demon.co.uk*

## JACKSON'S FIVERS

SchNEWS can't resist having another pop at Sir Ken Jackson, top dog at the AEEU engineering union, who told the TUC last week his workers didn't want to strike - they want to work...so Ford workers from the AEEU prompltly went on strike. On Tuesday it got even better, with a 24 hour unoffical walk-out at the Millennium Dome, the Royal Opera House, the Jubilee Line extension plus sites in Liverpool, Glasgow, Edinburgh, Manchester, Newcastle, Hull and Sandwich in Kent. Sir Ken told workers they could except no pay rises - and anyway some of them where earning a fortune already. We wonder if he let them know his annual pay is over £62,000 a year - plus car, mobile phone and £15,000 bridging loan thrown in for good measure.

## LET THEM EAT CAKE

The council of the Nord Pas de Calais region have some quaint old traditions for dealing with debtors - if you can't pay yer taxes, or even for your kids' school meals, the bailiffs pin the details of your poverty outside the town hall, and then come round and nick yer furniture. These medieval-style repomen work for the tax office, which has wide powers to dish out fines and repossessions for any debts. Interestingly, as a hangover from France's more leftie past, the tax office also has powers to reschedule or even cancel debts, though they haven't used these much of late, preferring to send out the bailiffs to reinforce social exclusion in the world's fourth richest nation. In April this year 40 activists occupied the St Omer council offices, duped two bailiffs into entering the building, and then held them hostage while their victims related the effects of repossessions on their lives.Things have got pretty bad in St Omer: when an unemployed family recently failed to pay their £50 telly license, the diligent tax office spent £1000 sending the goon squad 'round to their gaff. This time, however, they were welcomed by members of AC and ADEPA, local direct action groups, who dully stopped them carting off the familly's possessions. Naturally, five of them were nicked and are up on trial on Oct 19 - send letters/faxes of support to: ADEPA, 29 Rue Gambetta, 62500, St Omer, France. Fax: 0033-321-886789.

# "SHOOT THE FUCKER"

On 23 September 1996, Diarmuid O'Neill was shot and killed by cops in house in West London. As he lay bleeding to death a cop stood on his head and then dragged him down two flights of steps out of the house, leaving him on the ground outside and denying him life saving medical treatment for ½ an hour. Not surprisingly Diarmuid died. Initial media coverage claimed there had been a gun battle in a house that was being used as a bomb factory and an "IRA suspect " had been shot. The mainstream press had a field day, The Daily Mirror's headline, which carried a picture of the bloody steps, was "Don't cry for him. He was going to blow up the Channel Tunnel Tomorrow." The Met Police enthusiastically supported all this misinformation, until they conceded that Diarmuid O'Neill was unarmed, no weapons or explosives were found in the house and the only shots fired were by the cops. So what happened then? Lets start with the briefing just before the raid, when cops were shown a film of the aftermath of the Canary Wharf bombing and a video of an alleged cache of weapons. They were whipped into frenzy, given guns, CS gas and then let loose in the house in Hammersmith. A transcript of the surveillance tape of the raid reveals that the police fired massive quantities of CS gas into the house (so much so that four days after the killing forensic cops still had to wear gas masks), all the men inside the house had surrendered and Diarmuid was struggling to open a door when he was initially shot. As Diarmuid lay bleeding on the floor one of the cops can be heard clearly to order an officer to "shoot the fucker", which he duly obeyed. No wonder the cops preferred the media version of events that day.

The shooting was referred to the Police Complaints Authority (PCA) who then took 2 ½ years to complete their inquiry and then a further 6 months for the Crown Prosecution Service (CPS) to conclude that despite police lying about the events of that day there is insufficient evidence to prosecute! The O'Neill family and the Justice for Diarmuid O'Neill campaign are in disbelief that the PCA & CPS have reached this decision despite a post-mortem clearly showing "that Diarmuid was shot when he was seen and known to be unarmed repeatedly" and are calling for Jack Straw to set up an Independent public enquiry. Help change Jack Straws mind by faxing him direct on 0171-273-2190 or for more info; Justice for Diarmuid O'Neill Campaign, BM Box D. O'Neill, London WC1 3XX justicedoneill@btintrnet.com Tel; 0181 749 2588/ 0411 784 110

## COPS CATCH NAKED FUNGUS

Zoe "Fungus" Weir decided to strip against the Strip at Cedar's Wood, a protest camp at the construction site of Manchester Airport's second runway. Zoe took off all her clothes (save her boots) and attached her head to a treehouse with a bicycle lock. Zoe's action delayed the eviction of the camp by five hours, and three bailiffs had to climb the tree and cut the lock with hydraulic cutters. The runway's completion is now 18 months behind schedule due to wet weather, the protests, and mysterious breakages of construction equipment. The woods are National Trust land, that are facing the chop because they apparently interfere with radar transmission. As SchNEWS went to press the second protest camp at nearby Arthur's Wood still has approximatley 40 people in treetops and tunnels. The protesters anticipate eviction in the next few days, and are asking for supporters to come up for the weekend and for a solidarity action on Monday morning. They also need food and climbing gear. Call Vanessa at 0797 480 3732.

## Subscribe!

Keep SchNEWS FREE! Just send 1st Class stamps (e.g. 20 for next 20 issues) or donations (payable to Justice?) **Ask for "Originals"** if you can make copies. Post *free* to all prisoners. **SchNEWS**, c/o on-the-fiddle, P.O. Box 2600, Brighton, East Sussex, BN2 2DX.
*Tel/Autofax:* +44 (0)1273 685913 *GET IT EVERY WEEK BY E-MAIL:* schnews@brighton.co.uk

# SchNEWS in brief

After 2 **asylum seekers** were seriously hurt trying to bust out of Campsfield Detention Centre, Group 4 guards told detainees that their injuries would "stop others escaping." Maybe if a Group 4 guard was horribly maimed it would stop other psychos from joining the firm…** Don't forget **Anti-McDonald's Day** happening all over the globe on Saturday October 16th. For leaflets contact McLibel Support Campaign: Tel 0171 713 1269. www.mcspotlight.org. For the Birmingham event - meet 12 noon outside M&S in the High St. 0961 810 356.** **Disabled Action Network** will be demonstrating outside the Royal National Hospital, Bedford Way, London (nearest tube Euston) on 27 and 28th Sept as part of the 'Free our People' campaign. They want to stop disabled people being sent to nursing homes and institutions, and instead be able to live in the community with adequate support. Meet each day outside the hospital 9.30 am ** **Campaign Against the Arms Trade** is celebrating its 25th anniversary with a party at Union Chapel, Compton Terrace, London N1 (Angel Tube). Guests include comedian Mark Thomas, John Pilger, Jeremy Hardy and lots more. It's on Saturday 9th October, doors open 7.30 pm £10/7.50 conc. More details and tickets in advance 0171 281 0297 ** Talking of **Mark Thomas**, he's got a new show on Channel 4 every Tuesday 11.05 pm. Essential. ** SchNEWS' **favourite mass-murderer Gen Pinochet** is back in court on Sept 27 - meet 10am at Bow St magistrates to let him know what you think of him, or 7-9pm Parliament Sq every Tues & Thurs to find out what's going on. Contact: Chile Cmte Against Impunity 0171-261-9578.** Protest against the genocide of Arizona's **Navajo** Indians, forced off their land to make way for coal mining and 'resettled' in the world's 2nd most radioactive site (after Chernobyl…). Meet 12 noon Oct 2nd outside US Embassy, Grosvenor Sq.**

---

## THE REBEL ALLIANCE

Brighton's forum for direct action groups meets upstairs at The Hobgoblin, London Rd, Wednesday 29th Sept, 7pm. PLUS Screening of June 18 film.

---

# LUMBERHACKS LOG-ON

Among the various horrors on the agenda for the Seattle WTO bash, is the Global Free Logging Agreement - a plot to scrap all controls on the environmental disaster that is the logging industry. Logging companies really aren't very nice to people either - just ask any of the 'displaced'indigenous peoples of the Amazon, or for that matter, greenies in Canada. Activists in British Columbia have been camping out in the woods trying to stop the Interfor logging co from destroying the local rainforests - so the firm sent around 100 psychotic lumberjacks who burnt down the peace camp, smashed all the equipment, and attacked the 7 protestors there, hospitalising 3 of them. Clearly, the Free Logging Agreement needs attention, so come along to Seattle for the festi. *Contact: No to WTO 2343 NW 100th Seattle WA 98177 USA www.tradewatch.org or ssoriano@igc.org*

* Nasty logging company Boise Cascade (see SchNEWS 225) haS been banned from any further logging of the Boise Forest. OK, so the case was brought by the Idaho Sportsmans Congress, which was worried about "severely reduced hunting and fishing opportunities." After the ruling, ISC boss Ron Mitchell said "sporting folks of Idaho can breathe a sigh of relief." OK, the wildlife is probably less chuffed, but then, as Hunter Ron sez, *"The real issue is, should we allow private corporations like Boise Cascade to continue trashing our public forests at taxpayer expense?"*

# Inside SchNEWS

John Bowden is a life-sentence prisoner who, since his conviction in the early 1980s, has campaigned vociferously for the rights of all prisoners. In the early 1990s he was one of the main organisers of a series of radical debates at Long Lartin. He has also been involved in direct action protests of many kinds, including a workstrike at Perth prison and a high-profile seige at Parkhurst . John is currently in the segregation unit at Long Lartin prison. On 6 September, John joined another prisoner who was already on dirty protest. He and between two and four others have been on it ever since, and is now on hunger strike as well. The water in the cells has been turned off. There have been no routine visits by doctors, Boards of Visitors or governors. John has been repeatedly threatened by prison officers and is denied sleep by them hammering on his door and turning the lights on and off. He has no access to the telephone and none of his letters are being sent out, although letters do appear to reach him. All supporters of prisoners' rights reading this are therefore urged to send cards andmessages of solidarity to *John Bowden B41173, HMP Long Lartin, South Littleton, Evasham, Worcs, WR11 5 TZ.* **Send letters of protest to the governor at the same address or fax them on 01386 832834. Or tel: 01386 830101.**

## more briefs

Any **pregnant mums** will be pleased to hear of Green Baby, a new Islington shop with a wide range of green kiddie stuff, including "everything to take the millennium baby sustainably into the next century, from real nappies, to organic toys" and, no doubt, tie-dye babygrows and junior yogurt-weaving kits.…** If you're worried about **fluoride** in the water coming to a town near you, get along to a public meeting on Wed 6th October 8pm at Willesden Library, 95 High Rd., Willesden Green Tel 0181 902 5949

## ...and finally...

This weeks Greenwash Award goes to… By using solar energy to drive the petrol pumps in 15 new service stations, BP/Amoco recently received an award (not for irony, but the Millennium Products award). After buying up many alternative energy companies, the oil giant is now the worlds largest investor in solar power. The Centre for Alternative Energy told SchNews , 'we can't imagine the global and political agendas involved in their (BP's) investment in solar energy'. Neither can we. Interestingly, last year, worldwide revenues from oil and gas producing activities fell by 24% (to $124.6bn) so you might naively assume these companies are switching their focus to sustainable energy. Er, not quite - capital spending on oil exploration and development in the same year increased by 5% (to $83bn) making the money invested in buying up a few (or even several) sustainable energy companies look like small beer. The burning (oil) question is - will BP/Amoco endanger the price of a barrel of oil by bringing in competing sustainable energy sources that are environmentally friendly, or keep them suppressed until oil is less abundant and profitable? Just ask the government, who recently approved oil contracts for developments off St Kilda- Britains only natural World Heritage Site, 100 miles off the Scottish coast, ranked alongside the Galapagos Island and the Great Barrier Reef. St Kilda's marine life is one of the most diverse ecosystems known whilst puffins, fulmars and gannets are among around a million breeding seebirds nesting in the island's cliffs. We're anticipating another greenwash award after they stick a duck-pond on top of the oil rig. **disclaimer**

SELECTIVE VIEWS ~ the Art of Delusion @ Peter Poole @ April 2000

**Bristol, 1999**

# REEFER GLADNESS

**SQUALL**

Where Do You Want To Grow Today?
--
I Wanna Go Home
Underground Update
**Features**
Squall Pics
Frontline Communique
The State Its In
Squotes
Resources
Links
From Our Correspondence

A recent MORI poll suggested that 80 per cent of the British population now want a more relaxed approach to cannabis. Not so surprising considering that the UK now has the highest incidence of cannabis use in Europe. With an immanent report from the Police Foundation recommending the 'depenalisation' of Cannabis use, here's a taster of some of the recent flurry of comment and revelation...

**BILL CLINTON** may pretend he never inhaled but a new book on the life of his deputy, Al Gore, reveals that Clinton's sidekick and possible replacement as US president, used to chuff like a trooper. Gore's old friend and colleague, John Warnecke, says that he and Gore, "smoked regularly, as buddies. Marijuana, hash. I was his regular supplier. I didn't deal dope, just gave it to him. We smoked more than once, more than a few times, we smoked a lot. We smoked in his car, in his house, we smoked in his parents' house. We smoked at weekends. We smoked a lot."

**WHEN ALEX SALMOND**, head of the Scottish Nationalists, was asked whether he'd ever smoked cannabis, he replied: "Yes but I never exhaled."

**AS A CABINET MINISTER** whose portfolio includes national drugs policy, Mo Mowlam had every reason to tow the official line on cannabis. Respect due then for her admission that not only did she smoke Marijuana when she was a student but that she had inhaled too! "I never cancel anything in or anything out," replied Mo Mowlam when asked about the possibility of a decriminalisation of Cannabis use.

**BBC NEWSREADER, JOHN HUMPHREYS**, When asked about his own past, replied: "None of your business, in short. I can't quite see why we should be excited as to whether somebody puffed on a spliff at the age of 20 or not. I'd be slightly surprised if most students hadn't. In fact I'd probably treat with a certain scepticism any 40 or 50-year-old who'd been to university and said they'd never so much as had a puff on a spliff."

**A SURVEY OF THE 81 MPS** who joined the House of Commons in 1997, revealed that 22 of them had tried illegal drugs. David Prior, now Tory deputy chairman said: "I associate my experience with drugs - soft ones - not with Mick Jagger or Aldous Huxley, but with passing my law degree and working in a bank. You can wear a pinstripe suit and be utterly conventional and still roll a joint."

**PUBLICIST MAX CLIFFORD** didn't see what the fuss was about either: "I know people that take it. I know politicians that use it so what? To a lot of people it's a form of relaxation and if you are under tremendous pressure, if you find something that doesn't harm you or anybody else then good luck to you. Most of the people I've represented took cannabis."

**KEITH HELLAWELL**, Tony Blair's faltering drug czar, finally came out of his useless closet to assert that maybe Cannabis is not as bad as Jack Straw makes out: "By far the greater proportion of arrests are for cannabis and I am looking for a change on that the hidden truth about drugs in Britain is that we need to discriminate between different drugs and the relative harm caused and then talk openly about the difference we can make. The focus is going to be on the drugs that cause the major harm."

**SOME DRUGS** which cause a "greater harm" than cannabis were testified to by Dr George Ventners, chairman of the British Medical Association's Scottish committee for public health medicine: "We want to encourage debate on this issue and should examine the evidence that has existed for a long time, rather than people leaping to prejudice. There is much more damage done by smoking and alcohol than by cannabis."

**FOR THE FIRST TIME A SERVING POLICE CHIEF** has been brazen enough to tout the decriminalisation issue in public. In a report published recently by Cleveland Constabulary and endorsed by their chief constable, Barry Shaw, it says: "There is overwhelming evidence to show that the prohibition-based policy in place in this country since 1971 has not been effective in controlling the availability of, or use of, prescribed drugs. If there is indeed a 'war on drugs' it is not being won; drugs are demonstrably cheaper and more easily available than ever before. If prohibition does not work, then either the consequences of this have to be accepted or an alternative approach must be found. The most obvious alternative approach is the legalisation and subsequent regulation of some or all drugs." The report also notes that the illegal nature of the drugs trade causes further unnecessary risks to drug users because of uncertainty over quality and purity.

**RECENT HOME OFFICE** figures reveal a record high of 128,000 people arrested for drugs in 1998; a 13% rise on the previous year. This sharp increase includes a 30% increase in heroin, a 32% increase in cocaine and a 36% increase in crack. Despite the dramatic increases in hard drug arrests, 76% of all arrests were for cannabis.

**A REPORT BY THE POLICE FOUNDATION** part sponsored by the Princes' Trust is expected to recommend that cannabis be 'depenalised' when published in March. The Prince of Wales has invited Mo Mowlam and Keith Hellawell to speak at a conference about the subject.

**ACCORDING TO THE US DRUG ENFORCEMENT AGENCY,** the UK is now exporting marijuana. In a report prepared recently by US intelligence officers monitoring the European drugs trade, Britain's emergence as a marijuana exporting country builds on the UK's growing reputation in the drugs world for growing superior weed.

**ACCORDING TO THE EU MONITORING CENTRE FOR DRUGS,** 40 million European citizens have smoked Cannabis.

*....A green and pleasant Britain ... but yet ... a hard and at times distinctly grey Britain...*

# The VEGEBERG Conspiracy

SECRET PLANS MADE OVER THE INTERNET?

BLAH BLAH BLAH BLAH BLAH BLAH B

TAPPED TELEPHONE CONVERSATIONS?

COVERT TRIPS BY BUS AND BIKE?

AS STORIES UNFOLD IN TABLOID PAPERS OF AN UNDERGROUND CONSPIRACY INTENT ON OVERTHROWING CAPITALISM WE ASK...

WHO ARE THESE PEOPLE AND WHAT ARE THEY DOING?

KNOCK KNOCK KNOCK KNOCK

Er hi - what can I do for you?

Hello - I'm a reporter for the **Sunday Shite** and I heard that there was going to be a meeting here today. I would like to do a story.

Milk, sugar? Sorry the cup's got no handle

Ooh I hope I'm not overdressed to visit people like this

There's no meeting tonight but you're welcome to come in and have a cup of tea

Nice ...er...place you've got here.

So what were you hoping to find here then?

The VEGEBERG??!!

Well. I was really wanting to find someone willing to talk to me about the VEGEBERG actually.

## WAKE UP! WAKE UP! IT'S YER CHROMOSOME DAMAGED

# Weekly SchNEWS

### Printed and Published in Brighton by Justice?

**Friday October 1st 1999**    http://www.schnews.org.uk/    **Issue 230**   **Free/Donation**

# NO WOMB FOR MISTAKE

*"Soon it will be a sin of parents to have a child that carries the heavy burden of genetic disease. We are entering a world where we need to consider the quality of our children"* Robert Edwards, eugenicist

A conference of the Galton Institute, formerly known as the Eugenics Society, was rudely interrupted two weeks ago by protesters concerned at the rascist and genocidal tendencies of the Institute's members. Actvists from People Against Eugenics stormed the lecture hall and demanded that the conference be abandoned. As they emerged, ruffled, outside, one protester was reported to have said; *"ever notice how eugenicists always look genetically least diverse?"* The somewhat disgruntled chairman, Dr John Timson called the protestors *"fascists preventing us speaking and I hope none of them are British because I'd hate to have to share a nationality with them"*. Funny of him to complain of 'fascism', when eugenics is basically a strand of fascist thought, manifested in science. Particularly unsavoury examples of the noble science include the Nazi holocaust, in which 6 million Jews were murdered, plus thousands of gypsies, homosexuals and others labelled 'inferior'. Or how about the Swedish government's eugenics experiments which lasted 40 years and led to at least 62,000 people being sterilised to prevent genetic 'defects' from being passed on. They operated on people of mixed race, low intelligence and the physically defective, as well as people classed as rebellious, promiscuous or simply people whose views conflicted with those of the state. As Aldous Huxley said, eugenics can be used to control those with *"dangerous thoughts about the social system"* who *"infect others with their discontent."* So watch it.

SchNEWS wasn't surprised to hear that Prof Glayde 'Pretty Boy' Whitney, a speaker at the conference (whose genetically pure good looks are sought after by fashion-conscious parents everywhere), wrote the foreward to a book by David Duke, former leader of the Ku Klux Klan. When questioned about this link, Whitney denied he is racist but said, *"Duke is the only American politician who is prepared to face the issues: genetics, race and crime"*. The link between race and crime was further illuminated at the conference by another stunningly clever and open minded specimen of the master race, Prof Richard 'Einstein' Lynn: *"blacks have a lower IQ than whites and part of the reason for this is genetic."* He has also said, *" blacks have high levels of testosterone that makes males aggressive and this probably contributes to their high crime rate"*.

You may laugh at such blatantly racist crap, but these people have a disturbing amount of respect and influence. In '57 the Eugenics Society decided to branch out into 'crypto-eugenics', working through other organisations to achieve eugenic goals. The Society set up the International Planned Parenthood Federation, now the major world birth/population control agency. The Family Planning Association is it's UK affiliate. Meanwhile, another participant of the conference, Cedric Carter, stressed that efforts should be made to encourage *"the most ignorant"* and *"least gifted groups"* in society to use family planning. Sound familiar?

Theories that this dissatisfaction with the rest of humanity and urge to 'cleanse' those around them are themselves products of an undesirable rogue gene, remain unproven. But it seems that eugenecists may have found a back-door route to public acceptance, through the old chestnut of parental concern. Every parent wants the best for their child - if that means selecting the sex, IQ and physical characteristics of your baby, is that so bad? The tricky thing is drawing the ethical boundary: where 'choice' slips into an abuse of human rights. Eugenecists most disturbing success to date has been the attempt to eliminate disability by the (typically compassionate) approach of eliminating the disabled. While it is not yet possible to select the best overall genetic makeup for your child, individual eugenics is being practised on the disabled. The only way to 'prevent' Down's syndrome, for example, is to prevent people with Down's from being born. Under pressure from doctors 90% of women abort their Down's syndrome babies. The success of the pre-natal testing program is measured not in terms of information given to mothers but rather in terms of the number of children with handicaps who are not born.

Plastic surgery was originally developed to enhance peoples' health, but the consumer market soon grasped the commercial possibilities and it is now used mostly for cosmetic purposes. The same thing may well happen with 'individual eugenics,' creating a new dimension of consumerism with the public being bombarded with incentives to buy the best genetic modifications on the market for their foetus. Of course, only those with enough cash would be able to afford such advantages which would compound the rich-poor divide. SchNEWS has been unable to confirm that the gene for right-wing stupidity has been identified, but there is hope that rich parents will be able to ensure that their designer babies don't grow up to be eugenicists.

Unfortunately, eugenics is unlikely to be put to such good uses: *all* experiments with eugenics and sterilisation so far have been focused on poor minorities and those who might present a threat to the state. That means activists would be in the firing line, road protesters would definately be given the snip and as for the SchNEWS crew.....we just hope those bastards never find out where we live.

For more on eugenics and genetic engineering, check *Genethics News* PO Box 6313, London N16 0DY

Email: genethicsnews@compuserve.com or http://ourworld.comouserve.com/homepages/genethicsnews/blank.htm

## CLASS WAR

In Montreal, students have been protesting over the lack of extra-curricular activities - because teachers are on a work-to-rule. More than 1,000 students walked out of classes last week and their "disorganized" demonstration, is getting the cops all hot under the collar. "We cannot tolerate this spontaneous action" bemoaned one officer "It's important to note that these demonstrations are spontaneous and disorganized, and this worries us. We want school directors to take responsibility, and to tell the students to stay in their classrooms. What they are doing poses a danger for themselves, drivers and for pedestrians.

This week 270 pupils aged from 12 to 15 were arrested by riot cops for disorderly conduct.

* In the same city, university students demonstrating and asking for budget surpluses to be spent on education, attacked the Montreal stock market. "The stock exchange is a symbol of capitalism and the business class who ask the government to make cuts," said one studenbt. 18 people were arrested.

*MEANWHILE IN BRITAIN.....*

Kick off the student protest season in Oxford! Demo against tuition fees at 2pm Sun 10th October, at Balliol College. For transport, or for the new Campaign for Free Education campaign pack Contact CFE at PO Box 22615, London N4 1WT. Tel: 0958 556 756 http://members.xoom.com/nus_cfe/

## HORSING AROUND

The City of London mounted police branch was facing closure, but thankfully a generous bank has stepped forward to save it. HSBC holdings will 'sponsor' the pigs on horses, in return for getting its logo on the horseboxes and saddlecloths worn on ceremonial occasions. The 126 year old horse unit will now be free to ponce around the Square Mile looking like tits and trample protestors again, until their new corporate masters decide that rozzers on horseback are totally fucking useless and pull the plug...or untill the Met takes over the whole incompetent force. A police spokesperson commented "Hong Kong & Shanghai Corp's financial package will provide the glue to keep the service running & cost-effective while we stick to beating crime and people we don't like."

## BANG, BANG, YOU'RE NICKED

Earth First! activists Judi Bari and Darryl Cherney have finally been allowed to begin their lawsuit against the FBI and the Oakland Police Department (OPD) for false arrest, illegal search and seizure and wrongfully associating EF! with violent action. On May 24th 1990 a motion triggered pipe bomb exploded underneath Judi Bari's car seat as she drove through Oakland disabling her until she died in 1997. So when Oakland's finest showed up, they promptly arrested her for carrying a bomb! The Appeals Court now recognises that the FBI, who had the activists under surveillance, wrongfully claimed the bomb had been in view in the back seat (ie they were carrying a detonated motion-detecting bomb in a car… not recommended!) and that the blast hole was directly under the drivers seat. The court ruled that the police did "inhibit Bari and Cherney's First Amendment activities, and that they entered a conspiracy to further this goal." This included lying to the media, monitoring EF! prior to the bombing, and acting "in close co-operation with [FBI] conspirators'" while obtaining search warrants for their homes. The FBI knew about death threats towards Judi Bari, a non-violent campaigner against notoriously aggressive logging companies in the Redwoods, yet she was arrested for the bomb that was meant to kill her. Contact: Redwood Summer Justice Project, Tanya Brannan (707) 887-0262, http://www.monitor

## SchNEWS in brief

**Do or Die** Issue 8 is not so much a zine as a phone directory sized eco-action journal stuffed with in-depth articles and analysis on the June 18th demonstrations, bio-diversity, pirates, beavers (not that kind!), football…plus extensive reviews and contacts. Essential reading. £5 (in UK), £6 (else where). c/o 6 Tilbury Place, Brighton, E.Sussex, BN2 2GY ** **Remember the 30's?** Us neither - but after reading our history we do know that unemployed workers were at the forefront of direct action against capital and the starvation it caused. Find out more and see what we can learn from earlier struggles. Brighton Against Benefit Cuts video and discussion - 5pm, Sun 10 Oct at the Unemployed Workers Centre, 4 Crestway Parade, Hollingdean, 01273 540 717 And a date for yer diary: Friday 10 December is gonna be an international day of action against workfare and other such nasty measures. ** Remember that big bit of land next to Brighton Station? Well, Sainsbury's are still trying to turn it into a megastore, and Brighton Urban Design & Development are still trying to stop em, and get the site used usefully. **BUDD** are holding a meeting to discuss the plans at 7:30, Oct 7 at St Peter's Hall, London Road. The next day, the community (that's us) are going be consulted about the plans at a "Community Planning Event", so it's important to sort out what we want first.**After a battering from the cops the week before, **Stockholm Reclaim the City** held a demo against police violence last Saturday. Media presence was enormous and policing minimal. Chanting "No Police on Our Streets", over 1500 people marched to the scene of the previous week's events. Many bystanders joined the demonstration or showed support. The day ended peacefully with a party of over 2000 people. ** **End the fur trade** by 2000 - if you can spare an hour or several to join the intensive midweek and Sat demos outside London's remaining fur shops. Fur picket tel 0786 762 7491 or London Animal Action Office 0171 278 3068 ** Brighton and Hove World Development Movement group is staging a public debate on "**Can GM crops feed the Third World?**" Hove Town Hall 6th October 7.30pm.**There's a **Save The Shamrock Monkeys** march and rally in Horsham Park (near the Park Recreation Centre) on Sat 9th Oct 12 noon Tel 07020 936956. There's also a phone and fax campaign aimed at the monkey prison Tel 01903 879191/fax 01903 812532 ** **Plain Wordz** is an 'anti authoritarian pro working class' independent distributor of books, leaflets, etc. For a catalogue send an SAE to PO Box 381, Huddersfield, HD1 3XX ** Congrats to the **The Shoreham Protestor** newsletter 100 issues old. The fortnightly animal rights newsletter is available for 30p + SAE 7 Stoneham Rd., Hove, BN3 5HJ** **Keep The Tube Public** are having a free festival in Trafalgar Square on Sat.9th October 12 noon - 4 pm More details about the campaign Tel: 0181 981 8065, or www.catp. infomen.co.uk**Hockley road protest camp** in Essex needs more people - and they're having an open day. Prospective parents come along Oct 2nd or 9th. Tel: 0831 717 815.

## *SCHNEWS QUIZ*

Q.What do British Nuclear Fuels Limited, British Association of Shooting and Conservation, British Bankers Association, Countryside Alliance, Lockheed Martin, Nestle, Quarry Products, Society of British Aerospace Companies ('as the aerospace industry national trade association the society has a powerful policy making influence in the politicial arena') and Bell Pottinger (Monsanto's PR company) et al have in common?

A.They're all employing ex Tories, now going clothcap in hand begging for govt shekels at the new-stylee Labour Party Conference this week.

## Inside SchNEWS

SCHNEWS GETS SERIOUS - J18 WARNING

Photos of 170 people police want to arrest for the June 18th City of London demonstrations have been circulated to 42 police forces around the country. As a result people have already been arrested. Some of those nicked have been shown photos of themselves on the day and thought it best to admit the picture was of them, if this happens to you **refuse** to identify yourself. It is the responsibility of the police to prove it's you and not somebody who looks similar. If you are arrested contact a solicitor (Moss and Co 0171 240 6350 or Bindmans 0171 833 444). If you think the police may be interested in you get rid of clothing you wore on the day, change your appearance, possibly leave the country for a while. Otherwise keep a low profile. If you have photos of the day burn them. City police are sending squads to demos to identify and arrest people. Do not go if you think you may be wanted for something serious. Good Luck!

*Onofrio LoVerso, an Italian, received a 12 month sentence for violent disorder at J18 on 29/9/99. He is currently being held at: TC 3014, HMP-YOI, Remand centre, Bedfont Rd Feltham Middlesex, TW13 4ND.

## *...and finally...*

Book of the New Deal Testament:
And the messiah spake: "The Class War is dead". And his flock waved and cheered.
But maybe, O Great One, you should tell that to:

• Hotel, bar and conference staff. Non unionised, low payed workers some not even getting the minimum wage, hardly acknowledged by the delegates who are obviously too busy to whisper a hello or thank-you.

• 16,000 class-less members of the Countryside Alliance (and some fascists spotted in the crowd for good measure) whose Horse and Hounds placards screamed that they have the right to kill foxes. 15,000 police (!) from seven forces* keep them and the 400 anti-hunt supporters apart. But guess which way the bank of surveillance cameras are pointing?

• The landowners who are furious over the creation of two new National Parks, or that class-free organisation, the Scottish Landowners Federation, who are doing their nut over plans to give people greater access to land and a right to buy for local communities when estates are put on sale. The Fed, which represents 3,500 landowners, said it could cost up to £20m annually to provide 'infrastructure, maintenance and public education' needed to ensure the "well managed" rights of access urged in the bill.

Yes, the class war is dead. We are all equal. Citizens. Together. As one. Party and nation joined in the same cause for the same purpose: to set our people free. (Or at least free to be forced to do crap McDead end jobs on the New Deal).

* Gosh, how much does that many cops cost? Doesn't matter because... under the provisions of the Criminal Justice Act, there is no ceiling on police costs at party conferences. So that's alright then.

### disclaimer

SchNWES warns all readears that there's nothing like an early morning dip in the gene pool. Honest

WAKE UP! WAKE UP! IT'S YER UNCLEAR SCIENTIST

# SchNEWS

### Printed and Published in Brighton by Justice?

"Harris, there's no excuse for this industrial pollution, so I want you to find one."

**Friday October 8th 1999**　　http://www.schnews.org.uk/　　**Issue 231　Free/Donation**

# EAT MY ISOTOPES

*"There are a lot of long faces around here...It lends strength to the argument of the industry's opponents, who say nuclear power is inherently unsafe and should be phased out."*
International Atomic Energy Agency Conference participant.

The nuclear disaster in Japan last Thursday could have come straight out of *The Simpsons*. Evil Mr.Burn's type bosses suspected of using a shadow instruction manual which encouraged workers to cut corners, and a bungling Homer-style supervisor who apparently told police that seven times the permitted uranium was used because he wanted to 'go home early'.(hmmm food).

But Japan's worst atomic explosion since Nagasaki is no joke for the workers and 300,000 residents living in a 10 km radius of the plant who were told to stay indoors and shut all doors and windows.

## "D'OH"

The plant operator, JCO, has been accused of failing to give decent safety training to workers, and had no back-up emergency plans. The Tokaimura site was already the scene of Japan's worst nuclear accident two years ago, when another private firm let a fire in a reprocessing plant get out of control, due to inadequate safety systems. Do we detect a pattern here?

Of course, such terrible things could never happen here, could they? British Nuclear Fuels Ltd (BNFL)* and the UK Atomic Energy Authority have been quick to reassure us that *"in-depth safety procedures ensure that chain reactions do not start accidently."* Would they be the same procedures that allowed BNFL to fake 68 test results for MOx fuel shipped to Japan this summer, and forge 22 safety checks on the next shipment? (See SchNEWS 221) Or the procedures that were found to have 146 safety flaws at Scotland's Dounreay plant alone?

The main cause of these flaws was identified as....yep, lack of control of private contractors: so, reassuringly, the UK government now plans to flog off more of the nuclear industry to Mr Burns & Co.

The International Atomic Energy Authority, with a fine sense of irony, described the accident as *"a huge psychological blow"* Presumably the psychological effects of recivimg 4000 times the 'safe' radiation are fairly serious. Not serious enough,

however, to deter the Japanese govt, which has always said nuclear power is the only option for a "resource poor nation". SchNEWS was a little suprised to learn that Japan considers itself 'resource poor', especially as it has enormous potential for wind and wave generated power seeing as it's an island part surrounded by the Pacific. In fact, the Centre for Alternative Technology (CAT) told SchNEWS that ever since the Climate Summit in the Japanese city of Kyoto in Dec. 97, the Centre has had loads of interest from the Japanese. A former director of CAT was a key-note speaker in the city of Sendai; The 14,000 inhabitants of a World Heritage Site, are looking at finding out how they can produce zero emissions, while a recent half hour documentary on CAT was recently shown on prime time TV.

## ITCHY 'N' SCRATCHY

It seems everyone's into alternatives, except the government and nuclear companies. SchNEWS would never suggest that the Japanese military, who have been carefully limited since WWII, rather like having tons of weapons-grade nuclear material lying around, but one thing is certain: as long as they want the possibility of death and deformity, UK plc will keep giving it to 'em.
* BNFL told a House of Commons committee last year that it was hoping for between £2 billion - £4 billion worth of business from Japan, and depends on future orders to keep its Thorp reprocessing plant going.
Centre for Alternative Technology, Machynlleth, Powys, SY20 9AZ  Tel 01654 702400 www.cat.org.uk/

---

**SCHNEWS STUDENT TRAINING DAY**
OK, so for our last student training day we put the wrong date in SchNEWS, had it on the same day as Freshers Fayre and locked the SchNEWS we were gonna hand out in someone's bedroom. We need some help!So come along on Wednesday 20th October at 12 noon and see how it's all done. Call to book yer place now.
* Wanna keep fit?  We need someone reliable to drop SchNEWS round town at various pubs and cafes every Friday afternoon.

---

## CRAP ARREST OF THE WEEK

For carrying a portrait of the New York City mayor!

So, ok it was one showing 'zero tolerance' Giuliani wide-eyed and grimacing with a large piece of dung attached to his forehead. And the man holding the painting was Robert Lederman, President of the First Amendment rights group, outside the Brooklyn Museum of Art where there's been a big stink over the Sensations exhibition. This is the 40th time Robert has been falsely arrested since Mayor Giuliani was sworn into office. He has never been found guilty on any charge.

Seems like Giuliani doesn't like being portrayed as a shit-head.

## THE PRICE OF LIFE

*"We do not scrimp on spending money where it is necessary to deal with safety on the railways."*
Great Western Trains

After the Clapham crash, there was a lot of talk about the Automatic Train Protection system, which would have prevented the accident, oh, and the Southall and Paddington crashes. After privatisation the new rail companies' "cost benefit analyses" calculated that each (preventable) train death would cost them £2.76m, and each life saved through ATP would cost £14m, so ATP wasn't good value.

P.S. Last year the rail operators got £1.2 billion in govt subsidies, and made £1.6 billion profit. Railtrack made a profit of £442 million.Train drivers start at £8 an hour - guess who'll get the blame.

## AN APPLE A DAY

Biting into another tasteless supermarket apple, you'd  never guess that over the centuries Britain has bred up to 6,000 varieties of the fruit, and that thanks to the climate can grow the best apples in the world (SchNEWS come's over all patriotic like). To celebrate this, Common Ground is holding the 10th Apple Day at Covent Garden's old apple market.

Unfortunately old orchards are being grubbed up like they're going out of fashion. Until the 1950s almost  every farm had one, but in the the last 30 years the total orchard area has declined by two thirds - that's 150,000 acres gone. As Common Ground point out "Our culture is diminished as the local varieties, the recipes, cider, songs, stories, knowledge of planting, grafting and pruning, wassailing ('avin a piss-up - SchNEWS vocabwatch) and a great richness of wildlife are lost"

But it's not all bad news - in 10yrs 100 Community Orchards have been created. Apple Day is 21st October - for a list of events in your area send SAE to Common Ground, PO Box 25309, London, NW5 1ZA Tel 0171 267 2144 www.commonground. org.uk/appledayevents

# INDIGENOUS PEOPLES DAY OF ACTION OCT 12th

" Our armed path is not against skin colour but against the colour of money"
Zapatista proverb

### MEXICO

On January 1st 1994 - the first day of the North American Free Trade Agreement (NAFTA), people from the Chiapas region of Mexico calling themselves the Zapatista's, rose up against their government and the policies of corporate free trade. They have been fighting ever since and have called for a day of action on October 12th - the day after Columbus 'discovered the America's'.

In the last few months the Mexican army has occupied key towns and the Zapatista's army bases in an attempt to cut off the rebels from the outside world. As links are being made between the Zapatistas, the radical electrical workers union and striking students, the Mexican govt and the international investment community is starting to get jumpy. They're squeezing the rebels enclave with an extensive road building programme, which is violently defended by the army. The roads will serve as army access to Zapatistan strongholds in the forests and as a propaganda weapon for the govt, who claim they're bringing 'development' to the poor Indian region. Standing between the multinationals and their profits are a group of indigenous peoples whose cry of Ya Basta!, (enough is enough!), inspires millions around the globe.

Contact:'Zapatista Update' newsletter Box 19, 82 Colston St, Bristol BS1 5BB, Email kebele@marsbard.com. www.ezln.org, or www.mexicosolidarity.org.

### COLUMBIA

On September 21st Columbia granted a permit for U.S company Occidental Petroleum to begin exploratory drilling on the indigenous U'wa people's sacred ancestral homelands. The U'wa have denounced this decision as cultural and environmental genocide, and it will push them closer to their last resort - committing mass suicide. The U'wa have stood their ground despite intimidation, assault and murder of three of their supporters. We need to show Occidental and the Colombian government that activists around the world will stand with the U'wa. Contact: www.RAN.ORG email rags@ran.org. or Nativenews@mLists.net.

### VENEZUELA

Calling themselves "Rainbow Warriors," the Pemon Indians from Venezuela's Amazon area knocked down an electricity tower and blocked a key highway linking the country to Brazil to protest construction of a high-voltage power line in Canaima National Park, which will permanently damage the fragile park and Indian communities. The Pemon have promised to knock down one tower a day until they reach an agreement with the authorities. For more info: gholz85@yahoo.com or forest-americas@igc.org

### PERU

Mobil are about to decide whether to drill for natural gas in the isolated Candamo Valley. Mobil found the gas in one of the most unspoiled and biodiverse valleys left in the Amazon, and has until the end of February to do more exploration before deciding whether it'll release its claim on the valley - or go for future destructive 'development'. "I think it is one of the most pristine ecosystems around," says biologist Carol Mitchell. Daniel Winitzky, who made a film on the Candamo says "what is so incredible about this situation is that the decision is in the hands of a multinational corporation,". Info: gholz85@yahoo.com

For more on indigenous struggles write to Dark Night Field Notes, PO Box 3629, Chicago, Il 60690-3629 email: darknight@igc.apc.org (Send £6/$10 for a sample issue.)

## *Subscribe!*

## "JUST LEAVE US ALONE PLEASE"

Solidarity actions with the indigenous people of West Papua (also known as Irian Jaya) took place around the UK on Monday, targetting companies involved in exploiting the country's massive natural resources. Around Britain, the offices of Rio Tinto, ARCO (US oil co), British Gas were occupied, and three people got nicked. West Papua has been occupied by Indonesia since 1963 where it has unleashed one of the least known genocides of the 20th Century. Massacres, rape, torture, disappearances, the seizure of land - the usual. Result? Perhaps a sixth of the population (300,000 people) killed.

See the latest Do or Die zine. OPM Support Group, c/o 43 Gardner Street,BN1 1UN, www.eco-action.org/opm/

## SchNEWS in brief

It's that time of the year again - the annual **Anarchist Bookfair** is taking place on Sat 16th October at Conway Hall, Red Lion Sq,WC1, (Holborn tube) 10am till late with loads of stalls in the main foyer plus debates, meetings and video screenings throughout the day. For a copy of the programme send an SAE to 84b Whitechapel High St., London, E1 Tel 0181 533 6936 www. freespace. virgin.net/anarchist bookfair ** Well known festie burger crew **VEGGIES** will be celebrating their 15th Anniversary on Monday 18th October. Catch them at the bookfair on the Saturday, have a picnic with them in Nottingham on Sunday, followed by another party at their HQ The Rainbow Centre on Monday. Ring 0115 958 5666 or email: party@veggies.org.uk ** Following the recent High Court decision to grant a judicial review over the killing at work of **Simon Jones** (See SchNEWS 182), the Memorial Campaign are having a meeting on Tuesday 12th October 8pm at the London Unity Pub, Islingword Rd., Brighton ** The second **Big Brother Awards** (See SchNEWS189) takes place at the London School of Economics on the 18th of this month. If you'd like an invite email simon@privacy.org or give SchNEWS a ring and we'll see if we can get you on the guest list mate. ** **Permaculture** conference at the Centre for Alternative Technology on Oct 29-31, Contact: steve.jones@cat.org.uk or 01654 702400...** Procure the latest in warfare technology at the **AFCEA arms fair** 27th - 29th Oct, now at the Renaissance Hotel, Heathrow, after Belgium booted 'em out for being "politically and ethically undesirable" . Details of actions from Campaign Against Arms Trade 0171 281 0297 ** Transport will be going from Brighton to the House of Lords next Monday (11th) where the **Welfare Reform Bill** is being discussed. Ring 01273 540717 to book your place ** **Anti-Fascist Action** are having an afternoon of discussion and film, including the recent 'Up to their knees in Fenian blood', at the Lux Cinema, 2-4 Hoxton Square, London, N1 6NU. 2.30-6pm 10th Oct ** **If Cloning is the Answer, What was the Question?** We're not sure either- so get this well informed briefing paper from: The CornerHouse, PO Box 3137, Station Road, Sturminster, Newton, Dorset, DT10 1YJ or cornerhouse@gn.apc.org ** There's a benefit gig for Mordechai Vanunu, the imprisoned Israeli anti nuke activist ( in solidarity confinement for the past twelve and a half years) on 23rd Oct at Conway Hall, London Tickets £8/4, contact the campaign to book Tel. 0171 378 9324, or email campaignq@vanunu.freeserve.co.uk ** **Gathering Visions, Gathering Strength III** takes place on 15-17th October in Hebden Bridge, West Yorkshire, and is a chance to make links and share campaigning skills for non violent direct action Tel 07971 302412 ** Apparently the **dog unit** of the Essex Police, recently on trial for cruelty to dogs, is looking for sponsorship for a new van, if you can help, ring 01245 223 616 **

## J18th - THE SAGA CONTINUES

Seen the mugshots in the Daily Mail? Checked out the City of Londons 'rogues gallery' web-site? Well, this is a warning to any mischevious readers out there thinking of ringing up the SHOP-A-THUG hotline from a call box with wrong information. You'd be wasting police time, and that is a criminal offence you know, unlike working in the City and fucking over the planet and its inhabitants to make a fast buck. Hotline 0207 601 2222 www.cityoflondon.gov.uk

---

### Y2K BOLLOCKS OF THE WEEK

SchNEWS usually has a no-poetry policy, but this one 'Y2K is coming' by Russell D. Hoffman brought tears to our eyes.

"Y2K is coming of that you can be sure, and the tune that some are humming is "we haven't found a cure".

"Lies may come and lies may go, but the truth remains forever, Y2K could be quite a show — and it's more certain than the weather.

" Low Level Radiation kills as well as does the big stuff. Anyone who says different fills You with useless lies and kids' stuff."

Sorry readers, that's enough.

---

### SMOKEY BANDIT

The May Day Cannabis Festival at Clapham Common, part of a global event that took place in 38 cities and was enjoyed by over 15,000 people and held peacefully with no arrests, no sound level violations and no complaints from local residents. Despite this, organiser Shane Collins is being prosecuted for the heinous crime of permitting dancing and music (without license) and may receive 6 months in prison and a £20,000 fine. Shane told SchNEWS, "Lambeth is wasting Council Taxpayers' money to prosecute me for arranging for the community to have a good time. These proceedings are an attempt to criminalise low key music and dancing at community events and I believe that it is possibly politically motivated." He will be pleading not guilty at Lambeth Town Hall, Brixton at 2.00pm on 5/11/99. To join the petition or give funds to support his defence, send to: International Cannabis Coalition, c/o Green Party, 1A Waterlow Rd, London, N19 5 NJ

## *...and finally...*

**Sometimes it DOES take a Rocket Scientist**

You all know the story about pesky birds that keep colluding with aircraft, well Scientists at NASA have come up with a cunning plan. They built a gun specifically to launch dead chickens at the windshields of airliners, military jets and the space shuttle, all travelling at maximum velocity, to test the strength of the windshields.

British engineers heard about the gun and were eager to test it on the windshields of their new high speed trains. Arrangements were made, and a gun was sent to the British engineers. When the gun was fired, the engineers stood shocked as the chicken hurtled out of the barrel, crashed into the shatterproof shield, smashed it to smithereens, blasted through the control console, snapped the engineer's backrest in two and embedded itself in the back wall of the cabin, like an arrow shot from a bow.

The horrified Britons sent NASA the disastrous results of the experiment, along with the designs of the windshield, and begged the US scientists for suggestions. NASA responded with a one-line memo: "Defrost the chicken."

### disclaimer
Schnews warns all nuclear scientists if they`re gonna put it about with their uranium rods behind closed lead-lined doors they'll be glowing.Honest.

# INDIGENOUS PEOPLES' DAY OF ACTION
## October 12th, 1999

**Movemento Sim Terra (Landless Movement) - Brazil**

Graphic: Martin

## Struggle continues in West Papua

In 1963 Indonesia annexed West Papua- a beautiful land of mountains and jungle with over 200 indigenous cultures. The military marched in guns blazing and the multinational mining and logging companies followed soon after. Ever since the tribes have waged armed resistance against the indonesian army and the exploitation and ecological destruction they defend. Since the occupation began a sixth of the population (300,000) have been killed. Despite the genocide the resistance continues.

Since the elections last year the Jakarta based politicians have been trying to project the caring democratic image. But as the elite stage press conferences in Java, the army are still shooting the demonstrators in West Papua. In the most recent incident in December, hundreds were injured and three were killed at a flag raising attended by thousands. Scattered units of the Liberation Army of the Free West Papua Movement (OPM/TPM) remain in the jungle. On October 4th the offices of the three corporations active in W.Papua were occupied across Britain. The following quote is taken from the communique of thanks sent from the OPM:

"The struggle to free West Papua is not to take away one government and replace it with a new government. We do not want to administer ourselves the capitalist 'profit-making'. It is the struggle between modern society and tribal people. We have a common enemy, we need to work together, throughout the world to make it disappear from this planet. We can only make it happen if we are united. The unity of all people in this world will make it happen. Yi Wa O!"

For more information or to get a copy of the 'West Papua Action Update' contact: OPM SG, c/o 43 Gardner St, Brighton, BN1 1UN, or visit: http//www.eco-action.org/opm/
*Source: Worldwide Resistance Round-up, Peoples Global Action*

## SQUOTES

"We are not a market; first and foremost we are a people"

*La Falda Declaration, South American Chemical and Paper Industry workers*

## UNAM Support Demo: Mexico's Biggest in 12 Years

More than 100,000 people demonstrated in Mexico City on February 9th to demand the liberation of students arrested when police regained control of the country's main campus closed by a nine month strike.

The demonstration, which included students, parents of the detainees, trade unions and leftist groups, was the largest in twelve years in Mexico, and came at the height of campaigning for July 2 presidential elections. Chanting "freedom, freedom" the demonstrators demanded the release of the 85 students still held since police took control of the UNAM's main campus on Sunday. They held up banners pledging to continue their strike even though they lost control of the National Autonomous University of Mexico (UNSM), Latin America's largest university, which they had blockaded for more than nine months. The demonstrators also chanted slogans calling for an end of the Institutional Ruling Party (PRI)'s 70-year hold on power. Chants of "not a vote for the PRI" echoed across the historic city centre as more than 100,000 people- some estimates put the number at 150,000 people- converged on the central Zocalo square.

Zapatista leader sub-commandante Marcos denounced what he described as the jailing of "hundreds of young students in clear violation of the law, common sense and reason." "No one can talk of democracy in this country, as long as students fill the jails." He said.

**We are everywhere! Solidaridad con los estudiantes de la UNAM! Hasta la victoria!**
*Source: Worldwide Resistance Round-up, Peoples Global Action*

# INDOAMNESIA

SQUALL

Where Do You Want To Grow Today?
--
I Wanna Go Home
Underground Update
Features
Squall Pics
Frontline Communique
✓ The State Its In
Squotes
Resources
Links
From Our Correspondence

One December day in 1975, US President Gerald Ford and his secretary of state Henry Kissinger flew out of Indonesia just as the latest bloodbath began. According to Philip Liechty, the CIA's desk officer in Jakarta at the time: "They came and gave Suharto the green light. The invasion was delayed two days so they could get the hell out. We were ordered to give the Indonesian military everything they wanted. I saw all the hard intelligence; the place was a free-fire zone. Women and children were herded into school buildings that were set alight...and all because we didn't want some little country being neutral or leftist at the United Nations."

As a result of America's McCarthyite whims, over 200,000 East Timorese were massacred in the Indonesian government's attempt to subjugate the independent nation-sate. Ever since the CIA helped Suharto assume the presidency of Indonesia in 1967, death, torture and oppression became the norm. Stepping in to facilitate this 'norm' came the United Kingdom - the second largest arms seller in the world - keen to soak up the lucrative arms deals.

David Owen sanctioned the first British Aerospace (BAe) Hawk jet sales to Indonesia back in 1978 worth £500 million and so began an era which would see UK arms companies sell £billions of military equipment to Suharto's regime; the UK government sometimes even loaning the regime money to make the purchases. The rhetoric coming out of the UK government since 1978 was that arms sales to Indonesia were only sanctioned on condition they were not to be used for internal oppression. What farcical obfuscation this now appears given the Indonesian army's backing of the armed militias which rampaged East Timor. Indeed, although the national media in the UK would have us believe Indonesia has only recently turned bad, this long running farce has been clumsily stomping the boards of international theatre for decades. In the grossest indication so far that Robin Cook's "human rights at the forefront of foreign policy" line was insidious nonsense the moment it was uttered, the Labour government have continued arms sales to Indonesia. Between May 1997 and May 1998, the UK Labour Government approved 64 export licenses for military equipment to Indonesia. One week before UN forces went into East Timor in September '99, there were still three BAe Hawk jets on their way to Indonesia. Throughout the entire Labour administration, Indonesian military officials have accepted invitations to attend government backed arms fairs on British soil. Indeed they were due to attend the last Defence Systems Equipment International arms fair on MoD land in September before the British government suggested at the 11th hour they shouldn't come for PR reasons.

Can the present government claim they did not know until recently that British military equipment was being used to massacre, torture and oppress? The answer is clearly 'No'. Back in 1994 when Robin Cook was still trying to impress his credentials on the British political scene, he told parliament that BAe Hawk jets had been "observed on bombing runs in East Timor in most years since 1984". These words now come back to haunt the Foreign Secretary. For Cook has excused the Labour government's continued sale of arms to Indonesia on the basis that they were honouring contracts signed by the previous Tory administration. Honour? If Cook's 1994 assertion was true, the terms of the arms contract with Indonesia had already been broken and, if he had any genuine compunction to match reality with ethical rhetoric, he would have prevented further arms deliveries on the basis that Indonesia were breaking the terms of the contract. However, amnesia proved his preferred choice of action.

Earlier this year Foreign Office minister, Derek Fatchett supported his master's voice thus: "Robin Cook launched a constructive partnership on human rights with the Indonesian government in Jakarta in August 1997, including a number of initiatives on police training..."

Embarrassingly for the foreign office, Indonesian police violently quelled a public demonstration in Jakarta at the end of September 1999, when students took to the streets to protest over a new law passed in Indonesia allowing the government to suspend civil liberties if they deemed it necessary. Using riot control vehicles supplied by Alvis UK and water cannon supplied by Tactica UK, Indonesian police shot dead three students and beat thousands of others.

Even the British judicial system has long acknowledged Indonesia's culpability in internal oppression. In 1996, four female activists were acquited in a Liverpool court of causing £1.5 million of damage to a BAe Hawk jet bound for Indonesia, on the basis that smashing up its cockpit with hammers could be considered a small crime necessary to prevent a greater one. It was an extraordinary legal precedent. But still the UK government took no notice. Still, troops belonging to Indonesia's notorious Kopassus special forces were receiving counter-insurgency training from a Surrey-based company with the full knowledge of the UK government. It has now been proved beyond all doubt that the Kopassus forces provided direct military support to the right-wing militia which have recently raised East Timor to the ground.

National newspapers are treating the issue as if we have only just acquired the evidence proving the Indonesian government and military to be oppressive and corrupt. The strength of evidence proves that a selective blind eye has been turned to a bloody genocide. The moral authority cited by the UK as its reason for bombing Kossovo lies scattered in tatters........rather like East Timor itself and the bodies of its men, women and children blown asunder with British weapons.

With a characteristically understated tone, Amnesty International's annual audit of British foreign policy, published at the end of September, expressed what has been bloodily apparent for years: "The Department of Trade and Industry in particular is not meeting its responsibility to promote trade in a manner which is not harmful to human rights."

Graphic: Martin

... and this is the real stuff. Get your baby drinking this as soon as you can ....

John Hodge

## October 12th, 1999
## KPMG Office Bristol:

**Local activists celebrate America Discovery Day with an office occupation of KPMG - accountants to Nestle, BAe Systems, Tarmac, AstraZeneca. The action was in solidarity with the Zapatistas in Chiapas, Mexico, who, amongst other things, are resisting Nestle's move onto their land to grow coffee. Later the activists moved up to the Nestles Coffee Shop in the Galleries Shopping Centre, handed out leaflets, ranted at shoppers and generally caused a disruption.**

**Graffiti**

Polyp

Pic: Ben

WAKE UP! WAKE UP! IT'S YER PEEPING TOM

# Weekly SchNEWS

### Printed and Published in Brighton by Justice?

**Friday 15th October 1999**   http://www.schnews.org.uk/   **Issue 232   Free/Donation**

# RANCID CAMERA

*"The time has come to remind the villains that we are there. Use the cameras to search the street for likely looking individuals...zoom in and out, look for faces, potential suspects, potential victims, move the camera around from time to time to let them know you're alert."*
-Police Memo to Camera Operators.

The camera never lies. Maybe not, but according to a new study into the rising tide of surveillance in the UK - camera operators, police, politicians and the media lie as regularly about CCTV as Clinton under oath.

*'The Maximum Surveillance Society -The rise of CCTV'* shows how CCTV evidence is being suppressed and distorted by those in charge of the UK's Big Brother spy camera technology.

## WATCH OUT!

Based on 600 hours of research from CCTV monitoring rooms, findings showed 'suspect targets' most likely to be filmed were *"disproportionately young, male, black and working class."* Black men were twice as likely to be filmed as white men, women were often tracked by camera operators for the 'titillation factor,' and if you wear a puffa, designer trainers and drive a flash car - more likely than not- you've been framed.

Several instances of CCTV operators turning a blind eye to some of the worst scenes of 'Police, Camera, Actual Bodily Harm' were also recorded. One off duty copper was also filmed coming out of a night-club, shouting racist crap at three black men. When a fight broke out, 20 uniformed cops arrived and arrested two of the men, presumably letting their mate head off for his kebab. The footage was deleted and the police officer responsible never prosecuted.

Other reported incidents included an operator zooming in and catching a police officer *"punching a young man inside a police van."* On another a man and woman were tracked from the moment they left a night-club, identified as 'suspects' and later picked up and arrested for 'breach of the peace' when the woman stopped for a piss in a doorway. In both cases the camera operators either missed the record button or were busy looking for bra straps through the monitor.

But it's not just the camera operators and police that are busy fuzzing the picture. The first investigation in '95 by the Home Office, was based on information taken from the police, local authorities and private security companies. In Birmingham, the report said, crime levels were up 3 times from when CCTV was first installed. So to avoid embarrassment, when Home Secretary Howard announced a £15 million package for city centre CCTV in November 1995, he censored the Birmingham chapter and released the report in the media 'low' between Xmas and New Year.

## VIEWER'S CHOICE

New Labour's track record on distorting the digital picture is equally impressive. A 2 year study commissioned by the Home Office released on July 15th demonstrated that CCTV does not reduce crime. The research showed that, in Glasgow, crime had increased by 9% over the first year, and also risen in Wales. Yet those findings - virtually unreported in the national press - did not stop Home Secretary Jack Straw announcing a £170 million package for installing CCTV systems over the next 3 years - enough for 40,000 cameras.

There are over 500,000 CCTV cameras in operation in the U.K. today, and the surveillance industry is worth £2 billion a year. When no one is watching the watchers, who can say where this CCTV footage goes? At a rape trial in Nottingham earlier this year the suspect was cleared after the defence council discovered a tape which proved the man's innocence. The police had not disclosed the footage as evidence (Guardian 15/7/99).

Local councils are using CCTV to put entire residential neighbourhoods under surveillance, with the footage collected as evidence to prosecute and evict 'anti-social elements.' In Hull, private detectives were hired by the local council to install covert cameras inside the home of a suspected drug dealer on the Bransholme Estate. The edited highlights were eventually shown in court and the person evicted. In Newcastle's West End estate there are 15 'vandalproof' spy cameras monitored by a single 'dedicated' police operation room. And in Wolverhampton, education budgets for books have instead been splashed out on a flash 16-strong camera network to watch out for evil crack dealers in the playground.

While the UK is fast moving towards the 'Maximum Surveillance Society' the technology remains vulnerable to human error. Tapes are accidentally erased, networks fail and shit happens. Under the 1998 UK Data Protection Act, everyone has a right to access data and digital images that is held on them - be it bank records CCTV footage for the cost of a tenner. So if you think you`ve been recorded on CCTV by some pervy policeman without your permission then it might be worth looking into. "The Maximum Surveillance Soci ety" - Norris and Armstrong, Berg publishers, 1999. UK Data Protection Registrar, Wycliffe House, Water Lane, Wilmslow, Cheshire , SK9 5AF. Web site HTTP://www.hmso.gov.uk/acts/acts1998/19980029.htm

Privacy International, PO Box 3157, Brighton, BN2 2SS. Web Site HTTP://www.privacy.org

## GLOBAL ECHELON DAY

October 21st. Cyber hacktivists are calling on people to send an email containing 50 subversive words and jam the global surveillance system ECHELON which routinely trawls the airwaves and telephone networks for 'subversive' keywords. So kill Clinton`s semtex dealing terrorist organisation... HTTP://www.wodip.opole.pl/~laslo/Echelon-links.html

## STUDENT TRAINING DAY

Fancy joining SchNEWS's biscuit eating crew? We're having a student training day next Weds (20th) 12 noon at Justice? HQ. Give us a call to sign up for this truly great opportunity.

* Help! Got some spare time on a Friday afternoon? We need someone to drop SchNEWS off round town, and people to help with mail out.

We also need people to help out going through our emails on a Monday - we had 350 messages this week. Aren't we a popular square-eyed bunch..

**So the message is - we need help!!**

## Y2K BOLLOCKS OF THE WEEK

SchNEWS hit by millenium bug shocker.

Not content with bombarding us with endless emails about the end of the world, Y2K 'enthusiasts' managed to bring down SchNEWS e-mail system this week by sending us loads of pictures about the millenium bug. Can someone please tell us what the fuck a picture of the millenium bug looks like?

# RICKY REEL R.I.P.

On 14th October '97 20 year old Lakhvinder (Ricky) Reel and 3 friends were attacked and racially abused in Kingston. Terrified they fled the scene. That was the last time Ricky was seen alive. A week later his body was found in the Thames near the scene of the attack.Despite immediately reporting the attack, no action was taken by for a week, during which time the family organised search parties and interviewed witnesses. When the police search was carried out it took only 7 minutes to locate Ricky's body. That evening, before the post mortem was completed, the police concluded that there was no need to carry out a seperate investigation. As a result Ricky's death remains a mystery.

The police's conclusion, that Ricky died instantly having slipped into the river while urinating has not changed despite serious concerns voiced by an independent pathologist. After a second post-mortem, he asked how Ricky fell into the water backwards while urinating; that he didn't die instantly and could have attempted to swim.

Once again it was left to a bereaved family to set up a campaign to persuade the authorities to carry out a detailed investigation and find answers to the following questions ; why were the police so slow to respond, why wasn't the racial incident investigated immediately and properly and why did it take until last week for a TV appeal?

The family and campaign have not given up hope. Yesterday a candlelit vigil took place near where Ricky's body was found, and on Oct 20th parliament are debating Ricky's case and the family's rights to access the police report. The following day the family are hopefully giving a petition to Jack Straw at 11am and holding a vigil outside the Commons from 12-1pm to commemorate the anniversary of the discovery of his body.

The inquest starts on Nov 1st at Fulham Coroners Court, despite the family requesting the case be heard in Hammersmith.

**Justice for Ricky Reel Campaign, c/o Southall Monitoring Group, Unity, PO Box 304, Southall, Middlesex, UB2 5YR. Tel. 0181 843 2333. Donations to the campaign are desperately needed.**

## DRIVEN MAD

The Consumer Association have made a promise to lower the price of cars, saying that motorists are being overcharged. But what about the hidden costs motorists get away with ?

In 1996 3,598 people were killed, 48,071 seriously injured and 320,302 slightly injured on the roads, using up around 10% of the country's hospital resources. According to the British Lung Foundation, pollution related health problems cost the country £11 billion a year. The overall bill from road transport (air pollution, congestion, accidents, road damage and global warming) costs between a trival £45.9 to £52.9 billion. Surprisingly road users only pay a third of these costs. As Transport 2000 point out ,"The private car is responsible for a limited range of benefits for a limited section of the community, and almost entirely responsible for the costs borne by the whole community."

## SchNEWS in brief

"Free For All" is the new play by the **Banner Theatre** who have somehow managed make the governments dodgy Private Finance Iniative **(see SchNEWS 210/219)** entertaining. It's based on extensive video and audio recordings with people who fought to set up the NHS interwoven with satirical sketches, songs and video projections. It'll cost you £600 + petrol to book, if you're interested ring 0121 440 0460 ** This Saturday is international **anti McDonalds Day**. In Brighton there will be a picket outside the Western Rd branch from 12.30 pm ** Workers in Turkey honoured the appearance of a government Minister at the offical opening of an animal hospital in Izmir on **World Animal Day** by sacrificng a ram and calf ** **Morgenmuffel** is a cute little zine full of excellent cartoons and little stories like Isy's cravings for cake and sex. Send some stamps + sae to Box B, 21 Little Preston St., Brighton, BN1 2HQ ** Faster than a speeding bullet, as invisible as x-rays, perhaps a little more detectible than an undercover cop, **microwave weaponry** won't cook yer food and make it taste horrible, no it'll fry yer brain and leave you scared and slightly soggy. Protest peacefully at the House of Commons, 12 pm Tues 19th Oct ** **CND** have organised demonstrations on Saturday 30th October against shipments of nuclear waste from Germany. Transport is going from Brighton. Tickets from the Peace Centre ** Last Sunday over 600 students from across the country gathered in Oxford to launch this year's fees non-payment campaign. Campaign for Free Education PO Box 22615, London N4 1WT. Tel: 0958 556 756 http://members.xoom.com/nus_cfe/

### ON THE EDGE

The Caraquan environmental group, who recently stopped a new Tescos supermarket outside Wellington in Somerset being built, need to hear from anyone who wants to play a benefit gig to help them raise cash to fight against the councils next venture. An initial impact study on local trade in the town was carried out by Debenham Thorpe (who work for Tescos and unsurprisingly found in favour of the scheme) was later found to contain major mistakes. An independant report found that "there was no need for an edge of town supermarket at all." However, the council have since announced that they were much more interested all along in a new development of houses shops and a northern bypass on the other side of Wellington. Contact Caraquan 01823 665592

## HAPPY SHOPPER

Students in America held demonstrations at Wal-Mart stores (the supermarket chain that has just bought ASDA) last week after hearing of the sweatshop working conditions
Sacked workers from El Salvador toured U.S. universities last week, telling students about the conditions they have to endure making Wal-Mart's Kathie Lee labels. 15 - 20 hour days, poverty wages and people fainting at work because of the heat. When workers tried to change these conditions, they were fired, black-listed, and their lives threatened.
* 'Managing the Wal- Mart Effect' a half-day conference about all about the companies corporate culture like driving costs out of the system and bascially trying to take over the supermarket world. Only £450 + VAT - designed to keep protestors away perhaps? Thursday 18th November at the Millennium Britannia Hotel, Grosvenor Square, London W1 Tel 020 7247 0367
* The last issue of Ethical Consumer carried a two page article about Wal-Mart. Copies from Unit 21, 41 Old Birley St., Manchester, M15 5RF
* Out of town supermarkets trying to muscle in your area, check out www.sprawl-busters.com/

## Inside SchNEWS
### MUMIA'S DEATH WARRANT SIGNED

After 16 years on death row, African-American journalist and activist Mumia Abu-Jamal(see SchNEWS 228)'s death warrant has been signed and the date for his execution set for December 2nd. A stay of execution is expected to be granted in a few days, however the worldwide protests that prevented Mumia's death in 1995 must be repeated. Protests are planned across the U.S (contact www.mumia.org or www.freemumia.org). Over here there's a Mumia Must Live! meeting at the Anarchist Bookfair this Saturday at 1pm. Contact Mumia Must Live! BM Haven, London WC1N 3XX email mumia@callnetuk.com web www.callnetuk.com/home/mumiaining

## APEING SUCCESS

New Zealand's Parliament created a world first last week by passing the Animal Welfare Act. The Act bans the use of all great apes in research, testing, or teaching "unless such use is in the best interests of the non-human hominid" or its species. There are five great ape species: chimpanzees, bonobos, gorillas, orangutans, and humans, and all are in the same genetic family.The recognition is based on scientific evidence that the nonhuman great apes share not only our genes but also basic human mental traits, such as self-awareness, intelligence and other forms of mental insight, complex communications and social systems, and even the ability to master some human language skills.
The Great Ape Project , P.O. Box 19492, Portland, OR 97280-0492 GAP@envirolink.org
* A man who received a baboon liver in an experimental transplant became infected with a herpes virus from the animal and later died. The patient,a 35 year-old HIV sufferer, was cured of the virus after being treated with drugs but eventually died of his liver disease. Scientists from the University of Pittsburgh said the evidence that animal diseases could be passed on to humans through transplants placed a major obstacle in the way of future operations. Dan from Uncaged told SchNEWS "It re-inforces our view that going ahead with animal to human transplants would be like playing Russian roulette with the entire human population."
'The Science and Ethics of Xenotransplantation' £6 from Uncaged, 14 Ridgeway Rd., Sheffield, S12 2SS Tel 0114 2530020 www.uncaged.co.uk

## ...and finally...
### Conkerete jungles

Look out kids! Those nasty corporations are after yer conkers. A shadowy organisation known only as ActionAid is attempting to patent conkers under dodgy trade laws which allow companies to patent life forms. The application entitled "Conk 1" is thankfully just a joke but as Isabel McCrea from ActionAid points out, "it highlights the ease with which new regulations on patenting life forms can be used to deprive people of rights they have always taken for granted. Having the potential to charge school kids for playing conkers in the UK is just the thin end of the wedge. Already companies are taking out patents on food crops such as basmati rice, despite the fact that basmati has been grown across Asia for hundreds of years, and has been developed by farming practice through generations. Patenting natural resources is wrong. It is 'biopiracy'. In the Third World it will make poor farmers even poorer if they have to pay royalties."
* The 'patents for life' regulation is due to be discussed at next month's World Trade Organisation summit in Seattle. More on the summit very soon readers.

### disclaimer
SchNEWS warns all paranoids to stop looking behind their shoulders, cos you're making the rest of us nervous!! that's for real

*Subscribe!* _____
Keep SchNEWS FREE! Just send 1st Class stamps (e.g. 20 for next 20 issues) or donations (payable to Justice?) **Ask for "Originals" if you can make copies.** Post *free* to all prisoners. **SchNEWS, c/o on-the-fiddle, P.O. Box 2600, Brighton, East Sussex, BN2 2DX.**
*Tel/Autofax:* +44 (0)1273 685913 *GET IT EVERY WEEK BY E-MAIL:* schnews@brighton.co.uk

## VEGGIES

### 15 YEARS OF RIOTOUS CAMPAIGN CATERING

*"YOU KNOW YOU'VE MADE IT AS A RADICAL CO-OP WHEN THE POLICE INFILTRATE YOUR BIRTHDAY PARTY!"*

**See 'Crap Arrest' SchNEWS 233**

## Squotes

"The reason Japanese people are so short and have yellow skin is because they have eaten nothing but fish and rice for two thousand years - if we eat McDonald's hamburgers and potatoes for a thousand years we will become taller, our skin become white and our hair blonde."

***Den Fujita, President of McDonald's Japan.***

The new Superstore ~ a wolf in sheep's clothing?

WAKE UP! WAKE UP! IT' SLEEPLESS IN SEATTLE!

# Weekly SchNEWS

**Printed and Published in Brighton by Justice?**

HUMANITERRORISM

WE DELIVER

**Friday 22nd October 1999**     http://www.schnews.org.uk/     **Issue 233     Free/Donation**

# Oi, WTO... NO!!

*"As humanity speeds towards ecological disaster, the World Trade Organisation has its foot on the accelerator. "* Tony Juniper, Friends of the Earth.

Anybody out there in SchNEWS land got a soft spot for forests, marine creatures, endangered species or clean air? You have? Then start a f\*\*king museum. If you've a soft spot for exploited, downtrodden, penniless, starving peasants however- don't worry: there'll soon be plenty more...

Yes, folks- the 3rd Ministerial Conference of the World Trade Organisation (WTO) is taking place in Seattle, USA, from 29th November to 3rd December. A low-profile global fat-cattery of unelected, unaccountable trade bureaucrats from 135 countries, the WTO meets annually to try and remove those little niggles standing in the way of uninhibited free trade-like laws protecting environment, health, human rights and working conditions. Current fuhrer is one Michael Moore- although fat, speccy and bearded he is, alas, not 'the American answer to Mark Thomas'. He's Australian, for starters.

*"Defence of local and national interests should be a democratic right. But nations' ability to reflect cultural, economic and environmental uniqueness is increasingly under attack from the WTO."-Tony Juniper, FoE*

Top objective this year will be the 'Millenium Round' (MR), the new round of far-reaching trade negotiations aiming to further 'liberalise' the global economy. Not just the latest crap idea to feature the word 'Millenium', the MR is also the latest in a series of developments which represent the most serious changes in global capitalism for many years. Under the existing regime, if a country believes its companies' trading interests are being "unfairly" discriminated against- by environmental laws, for instance, or sanctions against an oppressive regime- it can file a complaint to the WTO. This can result in the 'offending' countries being ordered to change their laws, or get fined and sanctioned; the WTO has already forced the EU to take un-PC US bananas and hormone-pumped beef (see SchNEWS 204/220).

*"If the WTO had been around in the 1980's, Nelson Mandela would probably still be in prison"*- Chris Keene, Anti-Globalisation Network

**And now it's gonna get worse...**

1st World governments and trans-national corporations are looking to the MR negotiations to further open up the free market. This would mean incorporating into the regime an agreement very similar to the infamous MAI treaty ( *see ScNEWS 141 and loads more..*),

supposedly defeated earlier this year. They also seek to 'expand' WTO agreements on agriculture- a main cause of misery for small farmers worldwide-, to eliminate food security policies, to concentrate production in the hands of agribusiness and force GM technologies on an unwilling world. Oh, and they want to expand 'intellectual property' rights, too- which forces countries to give private patent rights over lifeforms to the corporations.

**YER SchNEWS GUIDE TO WHO'S GETTING SCREWED**

We've already mentioned penniless banana growers and people who don't want a stomachful of growth hormones. What else? Here's a brief selection...

*"WTO rules are undermining 7 of the worlds' most important environmental treaties"*

World Wide Fund for Nature

**Farewell, Flipper!** Last year, a WTO dispute panel ruled against the US Marine Mammal Protection Act, which banned the import of tuna from countries whose fleets use fishing methods that kill dolphins. Congress weakened the Act, and unsound tuna is now in US shops again.

**So long, Shellfish!** The US Endangered Species Act banned shrimp imports from countries that do not use devices designed to keep endangered sea turtles out of shrimp nets. In 1995, four nations challenged this law, claiming that it violated the rules of the WTO. Last October, the WTO ruled against the US ban on unsafe shrimp imports. The US government is now considering weakening the Endangered Species Act to comply with the WTO's ruling.

**Bye bye, Burmese!** In 1996, the state of Massachusetts, appalled at Burma's human rights record, passed a law to discourage state government purchases from companies doing business there. The EU and Japan, egged on by guilty multinationals who were losing business, have challenged the law at the WTO.

**Clear Off, Clean Air!** On behalf of its oil industry, Venezuela went to the WTO about the US Clean Air Act, which unreasonably demands clean gasoline. This was biased against foreign producers and was thus a 'barrier to trade'. The WTO agreed, and in 1997 the US was forced to rewrite its pollution rules.

(And if they do all that to the USA, think what they'll do to everyone else)

**Farewell, Forests!** Eagerly expected is a Global Free Logging Agreement; proposed by the USA, this calls for the elimination of import taxes on forest products, which means increased consumption and accelerated destruction of already endangered forests and a new mahogany table for the SchNEWS office. So it's not *all* bad...

Concerned? Fear not, people. The world is in safe hands:

*"...any interference with free trade and the open markets is anti-environment to begin with. Economic progress and wealth creation are what clean up the environment and minimise pollution..."*-Jack Kemp, Competitive Enterprise Institute, writing in the FT

SchNEWS does NOT recommend readers who disagree with Mr Kemp to join in our 'Millenium Round'-up, where WTO delegates are herded into a field to 'debate' with an AK47...

**THE FORCES OF RESISTANCE.**

Opposition to the WTO is growing. A mass action is planned in Seattle on November 30th. For information and updates about the November 30th preparations around the world, etc. contact: www.n30.org

**EVERYTHING YOU WANNA KNOW ABOUT THE WTO**: Get yerself a copy of 'Demystifying the WTO', an easy-to-read A4 booklet. Contact ASEED Tel + 31 20 6682236 **aseed@antenna.nl**

# NATIVE STATE

Actions called on by the Zapatistas for Indigenous Day, the 12th Oct, to protest at the actions of transnationals - the new conquistadors - against indigenous peoples in Chiapas and other parts of Mexico. The offices of accountants KPMG in Bristol were targeted for their involvement with Nestle who are one of the main investors in Chiapas. The newly opened Nestle café in Bristol was blockaded and leaflets were handed out. In York and Newcastle Nestle factories were targeted. In London a demonstration was held in front of the US Embassy where one speaker accused the US government of helping the Mexican army set up paramilitary groups that are operating in Chiapas - "Bill Clinton, you have blood on your hands". e-mail: chiapaslink@yahoo.com. On the same day solidarity events were held to demand that the Colombian government and Occidental Petroleum cancel their plans to drill for oil on the sacred ancestral homelands of the U'wa people. Protestors targeted all ten Colombian consulates in the US and other events took place in Prague, Dublin, Madrid, Amsterdam, Geneva, Toronto, Vancouver, Santiago Chile, Bogota and in the Narmada Valley in India where communities fighting against the Narmada mega-dam project held a 24 hour vigil and sent a message of solidarity. www.ran.org or contact Patrick at rags@ran.org,.

* Colombia is going through a grave institutional, political and social crisis - and the good 'ole USA wants to send in the military to sort out the mess. US officials have visited Ecuador, Peru, Argentina, Bolivia, Venezuela and Panama promoting the formation of a multinational force to intervene including the installation of radar systems in different parts of the country, increased financial support to the Armed Forces and military bases on the frontiers of Colombia's neighbouring countries. There will be a picket next Friday (29) outside the US Embassy 24 Grosvenor Square, London W1A 4-7pm Contact: Collective Against the North American Invasion of Colombia c/o 36 Vauxhall Street, London SE11

# MUMIA MUST LIVE

A national rally to protest against the signing of the death warrant against Mumia Abu-Jamal is to take place in Trafalgar Square, London on November 6th (2pm). Mumia a radical black journalist, community activist and revolutionary prisoner has been on death row for the past 18 years convicted of the murder of Philadelphia cop. Despite dodgy prosecution evidence, witness intimidation and an ongoing campaign by the right-wing Fraternal Order of Policemen (of which the trial judge, Albert Sabo, was a member) Mumia has continually been denied the opportunity for a retrial. In 1995 international action stopped him being executed .This year on his birthday in April, ten's of thousands of people in both Philadelphia and San Francisco marched for Mumia. He is due to be executed by lethal injection on Dec 2nd. Once again a show of worldwide solidarity could save him.

Next Mumia Must Live! organsing meeting Thursday 28 October at Conway Hall, Holborn at 7:30pm mumia@callnetuk.com www.callnetuk.com/home/mumia/

# REBEL ALLIANCE

It's happy first birthday to Brighton's direct action forum on Wednesday 27th October 7:30pm upstairs at the Hobgoblin Pub, Londno Rd. Food and music will be provided.

# "CITY ANARCHISTS STOCKPILE ARMS"

## FANTASY WORLD

"ANARCHISTS are stockpiling illegal weapons worth thousands of pounds for a planned riot in the City of London on November 30. In two separate transactions in the past six weeks, at least 34 containers of CS gas and four stun guns capable of delivering a 50,000-volt electric shock were purchased by Reclaim the Streets - one of the groups that wrecked property worth £2m in the June 18 "carnival against global capitalism". The weapons...were imported f rom France and sold by a gang of nightclub doormen working in the Euston and Camden Town areas."

**DRIVE A WEDGE BETWEEN PROTESTORS** " The revelation is certain to outrage many of the anarchists' sympathisers, who support the cause but do not approve of the increasingly violent tactics used by groups such as Reclaim the Streets and Earth First!. This is the first evidence of dangerous weapons being stockpiled for campaigns."

**SCARE THE PUBLIC AND GIVE THE POLICE THE RIGHT TO GO IN HARD**

"Detective Chief Inspector Kieron Sharp of City police, who is heading the investigation into the June 18 riot, said he was concerned but not surprised by the purchases. 'This is a new and dangerous trend and we are taking it very seriously...They are obviously getting ready for a big one... It fits in with the way these groups are becoming increasingly militant."

**WHILE WE'RE AT IT, HOW ABOUT NEW TERRORISM LAWS TO HELP LOCK UP THESE ECO-PROTESTORS**

" Last month The Sunday Times revealed that the November protest is planned to mirror the riot that occurred on June 18 targetting banks and other financial institutions in the City. Anarchist groups, including Reclaim the Streets and Earth First, have been in contact with their American counterparts to launch a simultaneous campaign on November 30, making it one of the biggest militant protests ever organised. The date has been chosen to coincide with the meeting of the World Trade Organisation in Seattle."

This masterpiece was in last weeks Sunday-Times. Subtitles by SchNEWS

* Help! **Legal Defence and Monitoring Group** are desperately in need of a hand with monitoring June 18th court hearings and help with fundraising/donations. LDMG,BM Haven,London WC1N 3XX. Tel:0171 837 7557.

* One June 18th prisoner who could do with some letters of support, is Sean Brown BP5610, Huntercobe HMYOI, Howard Nutfield, Henley on Thames, Oxon, R69 5FB

* **Pete Loveday**, the creator of the legendary Russel comics has done a cartoon version of SchNEWS account of June 18th. Send the office an SAE for a copy. Send us A4 SAE + 40p as well and your get **Reflections** a booklet on June 18th.

* **MAYDAY 2000** - a festival of anarchist ideas and actions April 28th - May 1st. More details from BM MayDay, London, WC1N 3XX mayday 2000-subscribe@egroups.com www.freespeech.org/mayday2k

# SchNEWS in brief

Saturday the 30th is a Day of Action again **Huntingdon Death Sciences**. This evil company was recently saved by NatWest Bank wh lent them £24.5 million when major clients pulle out following an expose revealing an horrendou record of animal abuse. Video evidence showe monkeys being thrown into cages and staff sha ing and punching beagles. Meet from 10am NatWest, Emmanuel St, Cambridge. Evening vig will follow at the labs. Tel. 01223 476596 ** **Moulsecoomb Forest Garden** and Wildli Project are having a kids' Halloween Party (31s with story-telling, face-painting, a bonfire an pumpkin soup Ring Kate on 01273 628535 to te them you're coming. ** The UK's so-called be selling policing magazine (how many are there **Police Review** has recently featured a couple o articles entitled *Winning the Eco-war* revealing ne strategies for policing environmental protests. In portant reading – you can see a copy by sending a sae to SchNEWS. **If you saw Mark Thomas o the box this week and wants an in depth analys on that Export Credit Guarantee scam – then ge *Snouts in the Trough* available from The Corne House.01258 473795 or e-mail <cornerhouse( gn.apc.org> to obtain a copy.** More arms fai than you can shake a stick at - next on is **COPE** at Sandown Park Racecourse, Surrey on 2nd to 4 Nov. More details from Campaign Against Arm Trade 0171 281 4369 and on 5th Nov you ar invited to **TORCH TRIDENT**, transport from all round Britain will take you to Falsane Nav base north of Glasgow, home of Faslane Peac Camp 01436 820901** Are you bursting wit ideas? even if you've only got one, you can pro mote it at the **FROME IDEAS FAIR** on Sat 6t Nov, at the Cheese and Grain centre 01373 45542 ** **RAISE YOUR BANNERS FESTIVAL** o Political Song will be held at several venues i Sheffield for a week from 12th Nov. contact RY at PO Box 44, Sheffield, S4 7RN, 0114 249 518 or www.ryb.org.uk** *'Our schools are not for sa* public meeting about the **Private Financ Iniative** scheme in Hackney. Monday 1st Novem ber @ White Hart Lane School, 7.45 pm ** Th **Right To Protest** Forum meet 1st Thurs of ever month (next meeting 4th November) at Conwa Hall, 25 Red Lion Square, London (Holborn tube Tel 0171 727 0590 email jb1@netlane.com

# CHINESE JUNK

The Queens gracious hospitality of the Chinese president Jiang Zemin is motivated entirely by UK plc's greed. Prudential has recently been granted an insurance licence, BP Amoco want to build a petrochemical plant and are among a diverse line of grovelling British companies awaiting the deregulation of Chinese industry and finance in anticipation of WTO membership. Free Tibet Campaign, 1 Rosoman Place, London EC1R 0JY. Tel 0207 833 9958 www.freetibet.org

# ...and finally...

Get all fired up for the start of the Hunt Sabbin season (1st Nov) with a raunchy calendar that ex poses members of the Sir Watkin Williams-Wynn Hunt (phooar). Don't buy too many though, 'co all proceeds go to those bloodthirsty scoundrels a Countryside Alliance, who need all the light relie they can get after an independent research proje on the rural economy trashed their exaggerated jo loss claims if hunting is banned."To help bury thes bawdy sadists, ring 01273 622827 and leave a con tact number. **disclaimer**

SchNEWS warns all readers having sleeple nights worrying about J18 to just settle down wi a nice cuppa Tibetan butter chai- it does wonde for flagging spirits. Honest.

# Costing An Arm and A Leg - The AFCEA Arms Fair

Pic: Richie Andrew

The Armed Forces Communication & Electronics Association (AFCEA) Arms Fair held at the Renaissance Hotel, London Heathrow from the 27th - 29th October didn't go without disruptions by anti-arms trade campaigners. While the Belgian parliament deemed the exhibition "politically and ethically undesirable in the European Union", the British Government continues to suffer no such pangs of conscience and continues to play host to human rights abusing companies including BAe and Racal Communications. Britain does a roaring trade in arms to torturing states such as Turkey. (Shame the picture isn't in colour - it's a bloodbath!)

Pic: Anna

**Faslane Peace Camp:**
Monitoring the naval base and the Trident nuclear submarine programme.
Tel: 01426 820901.

# Torch Trident for Guy Fawkes

Faslane Peace Camp, 6th November: Two activists scaled the razor wire at Coulport at 3 a.m. on Saturday and proceeded to the nuclear warhead storage area, where they were discovered cutting the inner fence.

At 8 a.m. state of the art protesting tactics left police confounded as both entrances to the Faslane base were simultaneously blocked .

At the South Gate experienced protesters erected a scaffold tripod, one activist remaining on his metal perch for five hours before he was forced down by extreme cold.

Meanwhile at the North Gate, protesters crawled beneath a coach and D-locked themselves to it, preventing workers from entering the base for 90 minutes. Overall, nine protesters were arrested and released without charge. One of them - "Fungus" - had recently been pulled naked from up a tree at the Manchester Arthur's Wood eviction - a case of activists spreading themselves around!

# TRIDENT COMPUTERS GO OVERBOARD IN LOCH GOIL

SQUALL
Where Do You Want To Grow Today?

I Wanna Go Home
Underground Update
Features
Frontline Communique
State It's In
Squall Pics
Squall Events
Squotes
Resources

Establishing an extraordinary legal precedent, three female Trident Plough-shares activists were recently acquitted by Greenock Sheriff's Court of caus-ing criminal damage to a laboratory at Faslane nuclear naval base. After a four and half week trial, the Sheriff ruled that the three women had been justified in dismantling the laboratory after arguing that Britain's nuclear arsenal was illegal under International law. Writing whilst on remand at Cornton Vale Prison, Ellen Moxley, tells the story of how the three women, calling themselves the Pheasant's Union, lobbed the contents of the Faslane laboratory into Loch Gail and hung around waiting to be arrested.

......Over eight months in the planning, the Pheasants' Union action finally took place on June 8th in brilliant weather on Loch Goil. Ellen Moxley, Ulla Roder and Angie Zelter were really nerv-ous. During the previous two rec-onnoitres, there had been a lot of police boat/car presence; our small battery operated angle grinder had died; the unreliable inflatable dinghy had a dicey engine. Yet it turned into the perfect action. Ulla was at the spot 4 hours before the start time and phoned with the message: "Beautiful weather." Then the boat, Angie and Ellen arrived in a rented van.

We launched on time (7 p.m.), and in spite of some heart-stop-ping moments with the engine, soon arrived at "Maytime" -the large floating laboratory complex which tests the sonar signals from Trident. We know now that the Chinese Defence Department can track Trident's movements through geo-magnetic fluctuations and the labo-ratory on Maytime is more essential than ever to Trident's operation.

We had tools with us to open padlocks but fortunately we didn't have to use them for that. One window into the labo-ratory was able to be unbolted and in a flash Angie squeezed through. Ellen and Ulla hung a huge black banner, saying: "TP 2000: STOP NUCLEAR DEATH RESEARCH/D.E.R.A.= DEADLY EFFICIENT RESEARCH FOR ANNIHILATION". Helen Steven's beautiful banner had rainbow people push-ing Trident into the sunlight and said: "BRINGING CRIME INTO THE LIGHT". Banners made by other Horties said: "CONSTRUCTIVE DECONSTRUCTION" and "TP 2000 OP-POSES RESEARCH FOR GENOCIDE".

Angie and Ulla handed Ellen load after load of computers, printers, monitors, fax machines, telephones, computer disks, papers, manuals etc. Everything went overboard into the drink! Inside the laboratory there was an almost impen-etrable cage which housed the mechanism for the model submarine which is used for many of the tests. Angie cut her way in and destroyed (by cutting the electric wires and hammering the circuit boards) the three control panels for the winch and model submarine. Ulla found a sign saying "MOD No Mooring, No Boarding" and propped it up beside the cage! We carefully cleaned up the lot, arranged on the table our police statement, video, Tridenting -it handbook and several photos of Hiroshima, Nagasaki and the victims -a good finale to our housework.

Having exhausted the possibilities in the laboratory, we three went up on top of the barge and tried getting into the control room for the vessel. It was protected by hardened

perspex/glass. We tried glass cutter, hammer and cold chis-els, and a drill with several bits and almost got through. Above the control room we cut the aerial antenna and superglued/liquid-metalled the moving parts of an outside winch. We then settled down for a picnic. "Newt", a move-able platform , was a few hundred yards away and we thought we might inspect that with a life-raft (as our own boat was now beyond use and we had untied it in the hope it might wash ashore and be retrieved by our supporters). We let down one life-raft which opened in a spectacular manner. We were unsure whether it was right side up, or if it had paddles inside. So we released the second one which fell into the water, its capsule still intact.

By this time 3 hours had gone by and the internal radio started hailing us. We did not want to be caught ineptly trying to control a life-raft halfway to Newt so we agreed to be satis-fied with the disarmament work already accomplished. It was an excellent time to have done this work, for the laboratory was between experiments. Before damage was done to any component we made sure the power was off.

When the police arrived they were friendly, having had previous experience talking to TP 2000== people.Throwing out these components felt to Ellen as if she were getting rid of the building blocks of oppression: Trident; the "free " mar-ket; the exploitation of children; unbridled militarism; the all-prevailing violence of society; third world debt. This was an amazingly liberating experience. The fact that we three are now on remand for 110 days and will face a protracted trial, we hope with a jury, is a small price to pay for having actually disarmed a Trident- related facility.We send our best wishes to all our fellow pledgers and look forward to reading of their experiences disarming Trident.
***Together we can change the system!***

WAKE UP! WAKE UP! IT'S YER SMASHIN

# Weekly SchNEWS

*Printed and Published in Brighton by Justice?*

**Friday 29th October 1999**    http://www.schnews.org.uk/    **Issue 234**    **Free/Donation**

# TRIDENT TESTED

*"Nuclear weapons have always been perceived as unlawful. Although the defence policy is official, it is not legal. For the last 50 years, the British government and judiciary have refused to look at the legal facts. They have basically said if it is official, it must be lawful."*

**Angie Zelter**

What with the Filthy French and their dirty beef in the press this week, you might- as we did- have missed a little trifle in the news: Britain's Nukes are Illegal! Last Wednesday in Greenock, Scotland, three anti-nuke Ploughshares 2000 women- Angie Zelter, Ellen Moxley and Ulla Roder- were acquitted of malicious damage and of nicking a life raft, after Sherriff Margarett Gimblett ruled that under international law they were right to 'disarm' the research barge 'Maytime' in June this year.

Expert witness Francis Boyle, a top Prof. of International Law, convinced the judge that simply possessing Trident made a nation guilty of 'threatening genocide'- an act forbidden by international conventions, such as the Nuremburg Principles (drawn up in the wake of the holocaust) and an International Court of Justice ruling in 1996, which declared *all* nukes illegal. According to the judge the three were therefore not committing a crime but were acting to *prevent* crimes taking place- and after a four and a half week trial she directed the jury that under Scottish law they should be acquitted.

*"I have the highest respect for these CND women, but I myself am not a CND supporter: I am totally apolitical. I am rather worried about my job after this. I certainly won't be expecting a mention in the Queen's Honours list."*

Sheriff Margaret Gimblett.

On June 8th, the women set off in a leaky dinghy and boarded the 'Maytime', part of the Defence Evaluation and Research Agency (DERA) at Faslane Naval Base, Argyll. Armed only with a hammer and screwdriver, they started to chuck computers and lab equipment overboard and expected to have about ten minutes before getting nicked. They ended up being in there for three and a half hours- and had time for a picnic before the MOD Plod arrived!

*"The police pretended not to be embarrassed, but I'm sure they must have been"* Ellen Moxley.

In court, Bargemaster Iain *'I ain't been nobbled, honest'* McPhee was pressed by Advocate John Mayer to explain the function of the barge and its links with the Trident submarines. McPhee was so hesitant and evasive a witness that Mayer stated: *"This is not cross-examination, this is dentistry."*

Eventually McPhee admitted that the barge conducted important acoustic research for the MOD, that the research related to the operation of Trident submarines, and that the action of the women had some effect on the ability of the research station to proceed with its work. Nice one!

It's a double whammy for Angie- she was one of four Ploughshares activists acquitted two years ago after trashing British-built 'Hawk' planes bound for Indonesia, where they would have been used, as the court agreed, in genocide against East Timor (see SchNEWS 84).

Naturally, the State is not happy with such conclusions and will be launching an appeal about the Maytime case. This won't affect the women, but it could affect any other 'have-a-go-heroes' foolish enough to try to stop the annihilation of millions. After all, as Shadow Conservative Defence Secretary Iain Duncan Smith points out,

*"The judgment is quite absurd. What these women have done is immensely dangerous. In damaging our nuclear deterrent, they do nothing but help other regimes who have the intention of harming the citizens of the UK."*

Like the bloody Frogs and their mucky beef, eh Iain? Get yer finger on that button!!

\*Trident Ploughshares 2000, 41-48 Bethal St., Norwich, Norfolk, NR2 1NR Tel 01603 611953

\*Scottish CND website (Especially useful on Trident) http://ds.dial.pipex.com/cndscot/

\*The latest edition of the Ecologist is devoted entirely to the nuclear industry. £3. 0171 351 3578 www.gn.apc.org/ecologist

\* **Aldermaston Womens' Peace Campaign** have repeated their call for the Atomic Weapons Establishment - which builds Trident warheads- to be closed down after the Greenock judgement and revelations about appalling safety levels. Apparently it's been 'perilously close' to disaster in the past few months. There's a peace camp outside Aldermaston 12-14 Nov. Tel 01222 396563

## DID YOU KNOW?

The UK spends £4 million a day on nuclear weapons

\* **Kvaerner-John Brown (UK)** is bidding to be part of a consortium to build the Akkuyu nuclear plant in Turkey- right in the middle of a well-known earthquake zone. The Turkish govt. seems keen to ignore reports that environmental and human catastrophe is 'inevitable', but then, the Canadians are stumping up the cash and the Turks get weapons-grade plutonium, so who can blame them? Kvaerner just need Blair and co. to grant something called 'export credit insurance' and the deal is on. This must be stopped! Contact Kurdistan Solidarity Committee Trade Union Group 0171 250 1315

\*Following on from Railtrack, don't forget that the next "safety is our number one priority, honest guv" privatisation is...**British Nuclear Fuels Limited**! Sleep well, readers...

## DYNAMITE

Two people who absailed down into a quarry, just in time to stop a meadow being blasted by dynamite have had the charges of aggravated trespass thrown out of court. The two protestors we're part of the campaign to stop part of Ashton Court Park being dug up by a quarrying firm (See SchNEWS183). The judge ruled that as protestors were still underground fighting the quarry expansion, the protestors actions were excusable under the rather obscure eighteenth century Explosive Substances Act.

## DAM BUSTERS

The Solidari@s con Itoiz (SI) and Narmada Valley UK solidarity group scaled the London Eye on Monday protesting against dam-building projects in Spain and India. Two Basque protestors stayed on the wheel for a day and a night, sleeping in tents at the wheel's apex, 145 metres high! The protestors targeted London's £35m prestige millennium bollocks project for it's prominent "banality", and dismissed it pithily as a "fatuous spectacle". Martin Erreafrom Solidari@ said, *"the wheel is a really good example of the waste of money in Western society while other people are being displaced and becoming homeless because of projects like these dams."*

The Itoiz reservoir has been under construction since 1993. Two of the region of Navarra's presidents from the time of the dam's building are currently in prison, interestingly, for *"bribery, theft from the community, and illegal commissions."* A Committee created in response to the project found that it was totally illegal, would flood 9 villages and result in great ecological damage. It threatens two valleys that have a very special microclimate, a thriving habitat for many animals and some of Europe's rarest plants. The Spanish courts condemned the project but unfortunately this did not stop construction and the European courts subsequently supported the dam. SI was set up as a result of this defeat and resolved on direct action. In 1996, 8 activists armed with circular saws cut six 15cm diameter steel cables that were essential to construction on the dam. Work had to be halted for 9 months but the protestors are now facing **five** year jail terms.

In India protesters claim that the Narmada Dam project will leave more than a million people homeless. The project dates back 40 years and has been resisted since work began 15 years ago. About fifteen villagers and activists have been standing in the waist deep waters confronting the submergence of their village. Similar protests and fasts are happening over the area and are being broken up by the police. Narmada UK concluded "The people of the Narmada Valley have resolved to drown, rather than move from their land."

* Activists from Solidari@s con Itoiz will be Brighton next Monday 1ST November, upstairs Hobgoblin Pub, London Rd. 7pm.
NarmadaUK@yahoo.com.
SI: www.solidariosconitoiz.org.uk.

## MAD-HOUSES

On Tuesday last week the protest camp in Hockley, Essex (see SchNEWS 224) was served with a possession order and on Friday security with cherry pickers moved in to clear tree houses. Developers want to build houses by a nature reserve - spending £150,000 on relocating up to 2000 great-crested newts. This despite a similar relocation in Peterborough ending in the deaths of 10,000 of this rare species.

This Monday a fella from Cornwall who owns some of the land Countryside Residential plan to build on appeared. He hadn't been consulted, and offered the protestors the use of his land for a year for 1p! Weird goings on recently include £11,000 worth of damage by militant badgers, a security guard stapling his finger to a piece of wood, a druid mate of King Arthur's showing up and staying, and the replacement with a teddy bear of a local councillor who failed to turn up at a local meeting.

People are needed. Contact C.A.S.H (Campaign Against Silly Houses): 0831 717815/ 01702 206353 www.angelfire.com/mt/GBH

*Subscribe!*

## SchNEWS in brief

The International Monetary Fund (**IMF**) is facing its first lawsuit after being taken to court by a group of South Korean unions over its policies *"which inflicted a huge damage on the Korean people"*. It's the first time the IMF has been faced with a damages suit filed by labour unions in the countries to which it has provided bailout funds ** 'Whose Agenda? Development, Democracy and the **World Trade Organisation'** takes place on Monday 8th November 6 - 8 pm at the House of Commons, 7 Millbank SW1, organised by OXFAM. Hey, even the WTO are turning up 0171 931 9330 ** **Operation Century** is a detailed report about Essex police's covert operation to nail the people who carried out the Rettendon triple murders. Police tactics included terrifying people into spilling the beans by posing as an IRA hit-squad! For a copy send £3 inc p+p cheques payable to Ian Cameron, 10 Knox Court, Studley Rd., London, SW4 6SA ** **TAT** news covers various travellers issues. It's produced by the Community Law Partnership Solicitors, 3rd Floor, Ruskin Chambers, 191 Corporation St., Birmingham, B4 6RP Tel 0121 685 8595. They've also got a 24 hour emergency eviction hotline 0468 316 755 ** **SQUALL** in print form is back - not that the magazine ever went away on the internet. Issue One of the new handy sized download version is now available. Send them some stamps *and* an SAE to P.O. Box 8959, London, N19 5HW www.squall.co.uk ** **Green Left** is to hold its annual forum this year in Bristol under the theme of "Town and Country - our common future." Among the topics to be discussed are low environmental impact design and lifestyles, transport and access issues, GMOs & the future of organic agriculture/permaculture, as well as local planning issues such as new housing developments. It's at Central Friends' Meeting House, River Street, Bristol. 10.30 am - 4.00 p.m. To book a place ring 01823 321304.** **Platform 6** is a new non-profit making community centre now open in Southampton at 6 Onslow Road. Ring 07980 051929 email platform6@angelfire.com ** There's a screening of **Undercurrents** 10 - the alternative news video - at the Ray Tindle Centre, 40 Upper Gardner St., Brighton next Wednesday (3rd Nov) 7.30 pm. Just £1 entrance - popcorn available ** There's a national demonstration outside the Newchurch **Guinea Pig Farm** on Sunday 7th November. At least 10,000 guinea pigs are hidden behind sheds behind Darley Oaks dairy farm to be sold to the vivisection industry. Meet 12 noon Newchurch Village, Staffordshire (A515) **This Halloween Radio 4A broadcasts free speech on the Brighton airwaves on 106.6 FM from 10 a.m till dawn the next morning**

*VEGETABLE OF THE WEEK*

Protestors living on site to stop the Chelmsford to Southend bypass have won second prize in a best **tomato** competition in the local village horticultural show. The prize patch is due to be trashed by another road funded by the government's Private Finance Initiative scheme (See SchNEWS 219). The green-fingered campaigners also came second in the flower arranging section - by putting some sunflowers in a smelly old para' boot! (ok so there was only three entries). They are asking for solidarity actions against the developers Laing. Contact Gorse Wood Campaign 07957 915977

## SLAPPERS

Next month five women from the GenetiX Snowball campaign along with their press officer will be back in court fighting for their right - to go to court! In September last year the six were Slapp'ed * by Monsanto, in what has been dubbed the most "wide ranging injunctions ever seen in British law." (See SchNEWS 184) In April a Judge decided that the six had the right to a full trial. Something Monsanto obviously don't want as a lengthy trial will highlight the dangers of GM technology. So it's back to the High Court for an appeal.

Confused? Well get yerself down to the Royal Courts of Justice, Strand, London on November 8/9th. 9.30 am. It's essential to ring 0161 834 0295 from 5th November just to make sure the dates haven't changed.

GenetiX Snowball Campaign, One World Centre, 6 Mount St., Manchester, M2 5NS www.gn.apc.org/pmhp/gs

**SchNEWS VOCAB WATCH** SLAPP'S are Strategic Lawsuits Against Public Participation, and are a common weapon frequently used by American companies to silence their critics.

## MORE FOUL PLAY

Two Catholic under-11 footie teams have been the latest target from those brave loyalists in Belfast. Last weekend the referee spotted nails on the pitch just before kick-off, a sweep of the pitch uncovering 400 razor sharp masonary nails in the ground that had been planted to injure the mostly nine and ten year olds. The two Catholic sides have to play in a loyalist area as the council has not provided adequate grounds in Nationalist areas. As An Phoblacht points out "Sectarianism in local football is rife with many teams forced to play in loyalist areas being subjected to abuse on a regular basis." * First Minister David Trimble has announced at a 'Peace and Tourism' conference in Glasgow that he wants Orange Order Parades to be marketed as tourist attractions. His idea is to promote the parades as folk festivals! Is this the sort of folk festival where witch-burning, Klu Klux Klan lynching and Spanish Inquisition style debating are part of the programme?

## ON THE HOUSE

In May Conservative Westminster Council unveiled a new hotline for residents to inform on benefit cheats. Within hours a call came in that led, last month, to a successful prosecution and a three month jail sentence for a fraudster who had falsely claimed £9,449 in a housing benefit. The cheat? Richard Stirling-Gibb - a Westminster councillor.
(shamelessly stolen from *Private Eye*; we knew our readers would love it.) ***...and finally...***

A 21-year-old Welsh engineering student is recovering in a South African hospital after his buttock baring antics went horribly wrong. The unnamed man (*"He has requested that we do not give out any further information,"* said a hospital spokeswoman) was returning from a sightseeing trip to Stellenbosch when he got the idea to "moon" drivers on the highway out the back of the bus he was riding. He dropped his pants and pressed his buttocks against the back window. The window, unfortunately was also an emergency exit and swung right open. He tumbled out, landing on the highway with his trousers around his ankles, and skidded along the highway in front of astonished motorists. He was listed in a "serious condition" with "severe abrasions and blood loss," but is expected to recover.    Stolen from Agitprop www.igc.apc.org/laborart      **disclaimer**

SchNEWS hopes all our readers are having a smashing time.

Keep SchNEWS FREE! Just send 1st Class stamps (e.g. 20 for next 20 issues) or donations (payable to Justice?) **Ask for "Originals"** if **you can make copies.** Post *free* to all prisoners. **SchNEWS, c/o on-the-fiddle, P.O. Box 2600, Brighton, East Sussex, BN2 2DX.**
*Tel/Autofax:* +44 (0)1273 685913  *GET IT EVERY WEEK BY E-MAIL:* schnews@brighton.co.uk

**WAKE UP! WAKE UP! IT'S YER SPARKLIN'**

# Weekly SchNEWS

*Printed and Published in Brighton by Justice?*

**Friday 5th November 1999**   http://www.schnews.org.uk/   **Issue 235   Free/Donation**

# ON THE IRAQ!!

*"Whatever its political effectiveness, the success or failure of which is for others to judge, the sanctions regime has clearly had serious onsequences for the ordinary Iraqi population, forcing many into poverty, destroying human dignity and taking lives."* 1998 World Disasters Report.

How best to celebrate a birthday? With a spot of hypocrisy and a wee sip of genocide UN stylee. SchNEWS congratulates the UN on the 10th anniversary of the adoption of the UN Convention on the Human Rights of the Child, the most signed-up-to piece of international law in history, designed to ensure that "there is a place at the table for all the world's children" (Clinton). (Only 2 states never signed it.... Somalia and the US). But the UN has broken its promise to Iraqi children, and SchNEWS has iced the words "Imperialist Scum" on the UN`s birthday cake. According to UNICEF, up to six thousand children die each month as a direct result of the UN imposed sanctions and 32% of children under 5 are chronically malnourished.

### WHOSE WAR IS IT ANYWAY?

*"Sanctions are amongst the most powerful and lethal weapons in our armoury."* Madeleine Albright, US Secretary of State

Even worse than conventional warfare, economic sanctions hit the people harder than governments, and in Iraq they have created a humanitarian disaster. Yet in May 98 the foreign office attempted to contradict hard facts, arguing that *"The government has every sympathy for the people of Iraq. Sanctions are aimed at the Iraqi regime and not at them"*. But UNICEF estimate that if the blockade continues 1.5 million more children will suffer malnutrition and unchecked illnesses. *"It is clear that children are bearing the brunt of current economic hardship...they must be protected from the impact of sanctions. Otherwise they will continue to suffer, and that we cannot accept."* Heffinck, UNICEF rep. Baghdad.

The sanctions imposed on Iraq are the most draconian ones ever imposed by the UN. The UN sanctions committee (based in New York) has the power to veto any materials from going to Iraq, and can include anything not deemed "essential". The list of banned items reads as both tragic and ridiculous: syringes, chlorine for treating water, isotopes that can diagnose and treat cancers (particularly in demand since depleted uranium was used against Iraq in the Gulf War, raising cancers by 10 fold and causing babies to be born without eyes, limbs,genitalia, and with their organs on the outside of their bodies), ambulances, cassettes and CDs, toys (a necessary component of all nuclear arsenals), wheel-barrows (the most malicious of weapons), shoes and polish, ash trays, beads, Vaseline, saucers, mirrors, ink, swimming costumes, rulers, soap, hearing aids, children's clothes, balls, hair pins...

Before the sanctions Iraq had the best national health service in Arab Middle East, 93% of the population had access to a hospital. Now children are suffering and dying from preventable and curable diseases due to a massive lack of medical supplies. $360m. of drugs were imported annually before 1990, in 1996 a mere $13m. were imported. A visiting child psychologist reported that some children no longer play games, because they remindedthem of the dead friends they used to play with.

The UN imposed the punitive sanctions in 1990, initially to get Iraq out of Kuwait, whilst they are now linked to the inspection and monitoring of Iraq's weapons. Last Dec. the US and Britain launched Operation Desert Fox to punish Iraq's repeated non-compliance with the UN arms inspection, and the almost daily bombing has not ended, despite more than 10,000 death toll. Amongst the devastation water and sanitation systems were destroyed, the sanctions prohibit the import of equipment to repair the damaged infrastructure. Before the embargo 90% Iraqi's had access to safe drinking water, now only 50% have.

And while the UN plays Good West, Bad East it is worth remembering who supplied Iraq its weapons (during the Kurdish massacre that the sanctions were originally about and before the Gulf war). The US, Britain, Germany and France all have blood on their hands, and it was German companies that sold Iraq materials for nuclear and chemical weapons.

Smell a rat? It seems that the real issue cannot be disarmament. According to former arms inspector, Ritter, *"what has been disarmed is a very high percentage-over 90%"* In 1997 Albright stated that the sanctions would stay until Saddam goes.

The sanctions serve to contain Iraq not only militarily, but also economically. The crux of the matter is that the UN, acting as proxy for the US and its allies, wants to control potential revenue from Iraq oil sales, impoverish Iraq and force a dependency on foreign imports. The UN's Special Commission (UNSCOM), set up in 1991 to monitor Iraq's disclosure and disarmament of its weapons of mass destruction, turned out to be a cover for US and British spies. It has been expelled from the UN, so sanctions continue with Iraq uninspected and thus the incident sheds light on the West's real concerns. From the horse's mouth indeed, Ritter (one of UNSCOM's key arms inspectors) resigned *"when it became clear that the US and Butler, Director of UNSCOM, were manipulating inspections as a vehicle for maintaining economic sanctions, instead of disarmament. I could not be part of that."*

In 1996 UNSCOM destroyed a veterinary medicines factory, claiming it was producing

---

## CRAP ARREST OF THE WEEK

**For dishing out free food!** People from Food Not Bombs keep getting arrested for handing out free food and drink to the low-income and homeless. 2 were nicked for giving out bagels and juice at UN Plaza in San Francisco. At least 50 heavily armed cops arrived as they tucked in and violently arrested many munchers, confiscating the remaining food. Since the US Dept. of Agriculture reckon that nearly 25 million Americans are so poor they don't get enough food, it's crazy that Food Not Bombs have had over 1000 arrests for sharing hundreds of thousands of veggie meals since 1988. SF Food Not Bombs, P.O. Box 40485 San Francisco, CA 94140 USA www.foodnotbombs.org

---

chemical weapons, that was supplying vaccines cheaply or free to the rest of the Middle East, and so undercutting the multinationals........It's a stinking rat indeed. Dennis Halliday, former UN Humanitarian co-ordinator for Iraq, also resigned in disillusionment saying *"we are in the process of destroying an entire society...it is illegal and immoral."*

### Everything's Albright?

Albright, as US ambassador to the UN in 1996, was asked *"half a million children are said to have died, that's more children than died in Hiroshima. Is the price worth it?"* She replied *"I think this is a very hard choice, but the price-we think the price is worth it."* Would it be worth it if our own kids were starved and bombed because the UN wanted to overthrow New Labour?

*Voices in the Wilderness, an anti-sanctions activist group, state "we can no longer remain party to this slaughter", and challenge the sanctions by delivering medical supplies and text books to Iraq. Set up in the US in 1996 and the UK in 1998 they break the embargo by delivering goods without applying for export licences despite the risk of prosecution

More info.* 'Sanctions on Iraq: background, consequences and strategies' conference13-14 Nov. in Cambridge, contact Campaign Against Sanctions onIraq c/o Seb Wills, Clare College, Cambridge, CB2 1TL (to book send £20/£10 conc.http://welcome.to/casi *Voices in the Wilderness www.nonviolence.org.vitw email:voices@viwuk.freeserve.co.uk tel.0181444 1605, 12 Trinity Rd, London, N2 8JJ. www.peace-action.org . They will be talking in Brighton on 11th November 7.30pm The Exhibition Room, Brighton College of Technology, Pelham St.

* Septmber's issue of New Internationalist was all about Iraq. Copies from Tower House, Larkhill St., Market Harborough, LE16 9EF www.newint.org/*"The Scourging of Iraq, Sanctions, Law andNatural Justice" by Geoff Simons (Macmillan 1998)*"Sanctioning Saddam: The Politics of Intervention" Sarah Graham-Brown (IB Tauris 1999)

## On The Job

You've probably heard all the fuss about the changes to Invalidity Benefit in the Welfare Reform Bill, but here's a few other juicy titbits the buzzword addicts at the DSS want to lay on you:

'**Employment Zones**': a designation for areas like Brighton with high unemployment where claimants will be 'farmed out' to private sector companies like Reed or Manpower, who'll reap profits from hassling claimants into crap jobs.

'**Personal Capability Assessment**': an even stricter 'All Work Test'. Intended to save £780m from Incapacity Benefit and severe disablement allowance by making the tests more rigorous and putting pressure on people too ill to work to find jobs.

'**Trailblazers**': seems the New Deal hasn't been too efficient 'cos most bosses saw many Dealers as 'unemployables'. Hence 'Trailblazers'- four weeks of intensive training to improve those sloppy 'behavioural skills'.

'**ONE- Single Work Focussed Gateway**': the all-new one-stop-shop for benefits. All yer benefits will soon be dealt with in one building! No more traipsing from dole queue to housing office! Trouble is, whatever benefit you're claiming for, the first question will be "Want a £3.60 job in Sainsburys? If not, why not?"

'**Leisure Ratio Assessment**': a new test to determine the percentage of yer giro you manage to set aside for drugs, drink and having fun. Those with more than 0.5% are earmarked for 'Trailblazers'; those with more than 4% are shot. NB-only one of the above is a joke.

For full details of the Reform Bill, how it affects you and what you can do about it get issue 7 of Where's My Giro?, From Brighton Against Benefit Cuts, 4 Crestway Parade, Hollingdean, Brighton BN17BL www.muwc.demon.co.uk/

## Keep Yer Fur On

A national week of action against the fur trade is scheduled for Nov 13- 20th, coinciding with the 'killing season' in Britain's mink farms. The London Day of Action is on the 13th; meet Trafalgar Sq. 11am. London Animal Action (LAA) Tel. 0171 278 3068. LAA is also keeping up a campaign to close down Zwirn's furriers- one of the few remaining in London. Barry Zwirn took out an injunction against activists who had maintained a solid picket outside his Mayfair shop for weeks. Customers dwindled almost to nothing, while legal costs for Zwirn were over £17,000! *'They have made our lives a misery'* wails Barry; perhaps you'd like to phone and tell him what you think of his bloody business, too: 0171 629 2747. Zwirn's solicitors (Kingsley Napley, Knights Quarter, 14 St Johns Lane, London EC1M4AJ) are compelled by law to send a copy of the injunction to anyone who asks for it. Expensive - it's 50 pages long and *very* heavy!!

*The Ministry of Agriculture has announced plans to force fur farmers to increase security in the wake of Animal Liberation Front mink releases; trouble is, security is so expensive most farms could be forced out of business. The ministry suggests security guards, fence sensors, infra-red and CCTV; installment costs could be as much as £156,000 and yearly running costs up to £260,000.

*Horse & Hound, scummy bible of the hunt set, has a freephone number! You know what to do... 0800 316 5450

## SchNEWS in brief

Support is desperately needed at the ongoing inquest on the death of **Ricky Reel** (see SchNEWS 232). Contact the campaign c/o Southall Monitoring Group, Unity, PO Box 304, Southall, Middlesex, UB2 5YR. Tel.0181 843 2333. ** **Women Speak Out** Weekend gathering for women interested or involved in activism, London 19th-21st Nov. Tel. 01422 844932 or send SAE to 5 Barkers Terrace, Hebden Bridge, West Yorkshire, Hx7 6AQ. ** **Advisory Service for Squatters** need new volunteers urgently. Tel. 0171 359 8814 ** Benefit for the **Nicaragua Solidarity Campaign**, Gran Baile de Calaveras (day of the dead party) Music, food and bar. Conway Hall, Red Lion Square. Tel. 0171 272 9619. Fri 19th Nov. 7.30 - Midnight. Tax £7 / 3.50 concs. ** **Fighting Indonesia in the Forest** - a talk by a West Papuan tribesman. Wed 10th Nov. 7.30 pm upstairs at the Hobgoblin Pub, London Road, Brighton. ** **Prisoners Day of Rememberance**, Bobby Sands/ James Connolly Annual commemoration. Sun 14th Nov. McNamara Hall, Camden Irish Centre, Murray St./Camden sq., London NW5. 12.30pm, Entry £1 inc. social. (For more info ring the Wolfe Tone Society on 0181 442 8778.) ** Benefit for **Thespionage**, featuring Halo, DJ Cakeboy, Films, Bar, SchNEWS Stall Fri 12th of Nov. 7pm. Upstairs Hobgoblin. £2.50/£2.

## Failed Its Test

The Arthur Daleys of this world will be rubbing their hands in glee at this week's announcement that Siemans Business Systems have been named as the preferred bidder to computerise the MOT testing scheme in a bid to stamp out fraud.

Siemans you might remember are the same people who caused chaos in the passport agency earlier this year with their new computer system (see SchNEWS 219). Last month the company got a massive slap on the wrists in a scathing report from the National Audit Office, the taxpayer got a bill of £13 million and the cost of passports may rise to £29 to cover the costs.

Then Siemans did the same thing at the Immigration and Nationality Directorate, where once again their computer wizardry left the whole place in more of a mess than it was already (some feat).

So surely the last thing you'd expect is Siemans to get another govt contract. Er...apparently not. And once again it's the Private Finance Initiative (privitisation by the back door to you and me) to big business' rescue.

## MARK BARNSLEY

On November 15th, Mark Barnsley will have spent 2,000 days in prison for the crime of defending himself against attackers.

While out walking with his baby daughter (then just 6 weeks old) and a family friend, he was attacked by a gang of 15 drunken students. Despite his injuries and the views of every single independant witness, it was Mark who was convicted of wounding the students and given a 12 year prison sentence.

November 15th is a Day of Autonomous Action in support of Mark. For ideas of how you can help send an SAE to Justice for Mark Barnsley, c/o 145-149 Cardigan Rd., Leeds, LS6 1LJ email barnsleycampaign@hotmail.com Support to Mark Barnsley, WA2897, HMP Full Sutton, York, YO41 1PS (send letters recorded delivery and enclose a few stamps).

### SCHNEWS NEEDS SOME HELP

Calling all writers! We need **you** Weds and Thurs. Wanna put SchNEWS on the web Friday mornings? Cathy Come Home - we'd love yer laser printer (or anyone else's). Got an external modem for a PC - we can swap it for an internal one.

## Inside SchNEWS

39 year old Robert Thaxton has been given 7 year and four months prison sentence afte throwing a small rock that hit a copper durin rioting in Eugene, on June 18th.

June 18th was an international day of actio against capitalism (see SchNEWS 217/8). I Eugene a parade escalated into violence as cop deployed tear gas and arrested people for rio ing. Even the local paper described the sen tence as "surprisingly stiff" but police and pros ecutors said it was a *"clear signal that viole social protest won't be tolerated."* But as on resident pointed out *"The riot in Eugene th day was sparked by police harassment of th poor community and anarchists."*

Take the example of the harassment of the pa ents of a 15-year-old anarchist, suspected of tak ing part in direct action against Nike. They wer held on their floor with guns pointed at the bac of their heads for 3 hours while the polic searched their house and confiscated materials

* Robert now plans to appeal. SchNEW hasn't got an address, so send letters of sup port/cash to the Defence Fund, PO Box 11331 Eugene, OR, 97440, USA. www.ainfos.ca/org

* Seattle City Council seem to be getting little nervous over next month's demonstration against the World Trade Organisation (se SchNEWS 233). Under the Noise Ordinanc law which was passed last week, a copper ca give you a caution if you make a noise that ca be heard 50 feet away. 3 cautions and you fac six months in gaol!

## Jah Victory!

This week Luton's Exodus Collective wer served with an eviction notice to leave Lon Meadow Farm, a formerly derelict site that the were granted a tenancy on seven years ago b the then Department of Transport (the owner of the land). Exodus are a grassroots collectiv working on 'social inclusion programs', doing free dance parties and putting the money bac into their community. Police oppression and at tempted stitch-ups have dogged their path. Las year Exodus bought the farm, paying a deposit Since then bureaucratic hassles and misinfor mation have been used to try and scupper them This led to the signing of the eviction order Two of the Collective passed on accurate in formation to Lord Whitty at the Department o the Environment, Transport, and the Regions He'd been lied to, and cancelled the evictio order. Sale contracts have now been signed an exchanged. SchNEWS wishes them well for th future. www.squall.co.uk www.exodus.sos.freeuk.com/

## ...and finally...

Eisuke Arai is a Japanese debt collector wh has obviously been watching too much Mont Python. The former employee of Nichiere tol a man whose company had gone to the wall t sell his kidney and eyeball to help pay off loan. He allegedly told the failed businessmar his kidney was worth around £17,500 and hi eyeball a bit less. He added *" You have two don't you? Many of our borrowers have onl one kidney... I want you to sell your heart as well but if you do that you'll die. So I'll bea with you if you sell everything up to that"*. Po lice are now investigating, while the presiden of Nichiei said it was a blow to a sector eage to escape it's "loan shark" reputation. How any one can come to such a conclusion with th average interest rate payment of over 20% i beyond SchNEWS.

**disclaimer**
SchNEWS warns all readers not to make a career of it. Hard work never hurt us. Honest

## Subscribe!

Keep SchNEWS FREE! Just send 1st Class stamps (e.g. 20 for next 20 issues) or donations (payable to Justice?) **Ask for "Originals" if you can make copies.** Post *free* to all prisoners. **SchNEWS, c/o on-the-fiddle, P.O. Box 2600, Brighton, East Sussex, BN2 2DX.**
  Tel/Autofax: +44 (0)1273 685913 *GET IT EVERY WEEK BY E-MAIL:* schnews@brighton.co.uk

# Sea Action and the arms fair : Sept. 99.

One day, our chums do hear
An arms' fair is drawing near

~ ALEC SMART

Murder methods sold for profit
"Ah, hah," they think, "we'd like to stop it"

Where Britain will be selling weapons
To nice peace-loving friendly nations

Countries such as Indonesia
Need to protect their poor dictators

Jets & bombs & guns galore
Stop naughty farmers in East Timor

Our heroes have a plan-of-action
Halt warships entering London docklands!

*Our leaders claim they're ethical*
*But with the truth they're economical*

*When the Thames begins to rise*
*Our chums launch upon the tide*

*But too soon police boats have surrounded*
*Sea Action's mission is confounded*

*Then, yo, ho, ho, lo and behold -*
*It seems someone's gone overboard!*

*Splish and splash and plop for sure*
*Into the drink there are two more!*

*But all too soon the fun is over*
*Our chums handcuffed upon the shore*

WAKE UP! WAKE UP! IT'S YER FISHMONGERIN'

# Weekly SchNEWS

*Printed and Published in Brighton by Justice?*

**Friday 12th November 1999**    http://www.schnews.org.uk/    **Issue 236**    **Free/Donation**

# WHALE OF A TIME

*"This is a massive blow for a government whose policy on fossil fuels is in a mess. On the one hand at an international summit on climate change they are agreeing measures to reduce our use of fossil fuels, while on the other hand defending their policy of new oil exploration in the High Court."*

Peter Melchett, Greenpeace

**It's a piscine\* piss-up for the Crustacean Crew in the North Sea this week joining the Whale Massive in sticking two fins up to marauding oil companies**. In a High Court case brought by Greenpeace, Justice Kay last Friday overruled the Blair Junta, deciding that the interests of Britains' dolphins, whales and deep water coral reefs should be accorded higher priority than those of oil exploration.

The case centred on the government's cunning idea that the European Union's environmental laws need only apply to 'territorial waters' within 12 miles of the coast and not the whole 200 mile 'exclusive economic zone' over which it claims mineral rights. Handy, Tony- but Judge Kay reckons it's illegal. Which means in future, oil exploration in the north-east Atlantic, which severely damages the fragile reefs (more biodiverse than rainforests) and traumatises marine life, will be severely nobbled- *and* conservation areas created.

The judge told the court that Greenpeace's case- that marine mammals can be harmed by oil industry activity- was *"substantially uncontradicted"* by government and oil industry evidence. Already, the ruling has ballsed up the latest round of oil licensing, and oil companies operating in Britain's oilfields are facing long delays and vastly increased costs. Nice one!

**BUT**- this glorious news has been overshadowed by the revelation that the world is fucked. Yup, we're doomed. On Friday, as dolphins danced with wasted whales and crabs caned it, the UN Conference on Climate Change in Bonn was being presented with computer predictions from climate experts at the Hadley Centre. Apparently, the world's climate is heating up far faster than predicted- far too fast for natural systems to adapt. Temperatures by the end of next century are likely to be 8C higher than in 1850- before industrial pollution had taken effect.

Most of the Amazon rainforest will die off, releasing millions of extra tons of carbon dioxide- the 'greenhouse' gas that traps the sun's heat. This will also lead to many more 'extreme' weather events- like Hurricane Mitch and the cyclone in India.

While Britain's delegates no doubt bang on about how much they're doing to reduce our contribution to climate damage, SchNEWS wonders if they can explain why they're so intent on tracking down new reserves of fossil fuels- like in the north-east Atlantic, off the coast of St. Kilda (Britain's only natural world heritage site)- even though we've already found *four times* as much coal, gas and oil as we can afford to burn. For what it's worth, the Royal Commission for Environmental Pollution is aiming to publish by Xmas its investigation into the implications of phasing out fossil fuels. The investigation- in the pipeline for a year- has drilled everyone from Greenpeace to the UK Offshore Oil Association, though the government, not suprisingly, has been less than co-operative. Exxon wouldn't answer questions, BP reckon technology will sort it all out and Shell say oil and gas just ain't the problem- it's *coal*.

Seems SchNEWS's fave bastards Shell are trying to flog off their worldwide coal interests, and are touting the sell-off as *"rationalisation of the portfolio"* and *"part of the necessary upgrading of the group's performance to bring Shell to the position of top performer"* .

According to insiders, the real motive for the sale is that the company is acutely aware of how the coal industry will suffer in a more climate-regulated world. But keep it quiet- it might put off potential purchasers, like Rio Tinto and Anglo-American. What if they heard sHELL exec Mark Moody Stuart: *"All of the estimated resources of conventional oil and gas could be consumed without raising atmospheric carbon concentrations above the limits suggested by even pessimistic observers. The real problem is the very much larger resources of carbon intensive coal."*

If Shell are right and coal *is* the problem, shouldn't they just hang onto their reserves and ensure they're never dug up? Responsibility? Oh, come on now...this is Business

\*SchNEWS VOCABWATCH: for all you fishystines, piscine = fishy

## CRAP ARREST OF THE WEEK

**FOR SLEEPING !** Someone got nicked at Faslane Peace Camp last weekend despite being in bed. The arrest followed a weekend of anti-trident protests which left MOD officials shamefaced and confused. Workers were prevented from entering for two hours as protesters D-locked themselves under vehicles at the North gate and simultaneously blocked the South gate with a tripod. Protesters also compromised security at the base as two activists scaled the razor wire at 3am. They were discovered cutting the inner fence to the nuclear warhead storage area as an impromptu missile attack sent fireworks exploding over the base.Eleven people were arrested and six released without charge.
Faslane Peace Camp 01436 820 901.

**FOR WALKING!** Two people who just happened to be walking past an office occupation of COPEX, (the nice people who organise arms fairs) were bundled into the back of a van by panicking coppers and taken to the local nick!

**FOR SLEEP-WALKING!** A resident of Salisbury was nicked after being found wandering naked around Stonehenge.
Ok,we come clean we made the last one up.

\*Shell was forced from last weekend to shut down its Oil Flow Station at Bonny Port in Nigeria cos of 'persistent community unrest'! Seems in recent months oil flow has been disrupted by locals demanding compensation, social amenities and jobs from the company. With a loss of 100,000 barrels of oil a day, the problems follow similar ones at the company's Forcados terminal.

\* We kid you not - Lego and Shell have developed a miniature solar panel that will power Lego models apparently to *"teach children the science behind renewable energy."*

\*A press release put out at the end of Offshore Europe, the annual piss up for the Euro Oil Industry, spelt out the exciting new plans: companies operating in the North Sea are cordially invited to share their expertise with Darwin, Oz- "the new Aberdeen" in carving up the oil fields of the Timor Sea. As if the Timorese ain't got enough problems...

### Wanna know more?

**The Ecologist** has a special issue packed full of cheery facts about climate change. 0171 351 3578 www.gn.apc.org/ecologist

For alternatives to all this fossil-fuel horror:
**Centre for Alternative Technology**, Machynlleth, Powys, SY20 9AZ Tel.01654 702400. www.cat.org.uk

**'Solar Energy**: from Perennial Promise to Competitive Alternative': for a copy of Greenpeace's briefing on this report tel. 0171 865 2556/7 www.greenpeace.org.uk

**Energy Saving** Trust Info booklets: 0345 277200

## THE COR BLIMLEY COLUMN

Did you know? Group sponsors of the recent high-tech arms fair at Heathrow were CISCO Systems, the people who worked on the Net Aid charity extravaganza. Net Aid's mission statement reads : *"NetAid is a long-term effort to build a community of conscience dedicated to providing basic needs: food, shelter, legal protection, human rights and health care. NetAid artists and sponsors are committed to focusing public and political attention on the needs of the world's poorest citizens and to building an online community that is dedicated to change. Join us."*

So people did, last week occupying their offices and singing bad versions (are there any good ones?) of D.I.S.C.O subtley changed to C.I.S.C.O.

* Surprise, surprise! A report published last week shows that Britain continues to sell weapons to countries with poor human rights records. Nearly £2 billion worth of weapons were exported last year to countries such as Indonesia, Turkey, China, Bahrain, Algeria and Saudi Arabia.

## SWEDISH BOMB-SHELL

Bjorn Soderberg of the Syndicalist trade union in Sweden, was shot dead on his doorstep by nazis on 12th Oct. Neo-nazi groups in Sweden are responsible for violent attacks on immigrants, socialists, gays and the disabled; Bjorn managed to upset them by exposing Robert Westerlund, a top nazi who had infiltrated to a prominent position in the main shop workers union, who later left after being threatened with expulsion. On the morning of 23rd Oct, a bomb exploded in the syndicalist union offices in Gavle, presumably to frighten people from attending demonstrations paying tribute to Bjorn and affirming action against nazism, fascism and racism that had been arranged for that day. It didn't seem to put anyone off though - several thousand people participated in the small town of Gavle, 20,000 turned up in Stockholm to listen to speakers and an anarcho-feminist choir, 6,000 marched through Gutenburg and thousands of others showed solidarity in over 20 cities throughout Sweden. For anti-fascist support contact: ksvensson@motkraft.net

## BAD ATTITUDE

The world just got a lot more dangerous as the American Senate gave the thumbs up to continued nuclear escalation by refusing to sign the Comprehensive Test Ban Treaty. More than thirty American Nobel prizewinners criticised the decision claiming there is no need to explode nukes to test their safety as there is adequate technology for the job. Moreover these scientists understand that any tin pot govt can build fission weapons like the one that destroyed Hiroshima, but since the fifties, these have been outmoded by fusion 'hydrogen' bombs, some 750 times more powerful; these are incredibly difficult to build and will always require repeated testing until you've got it right, so by ditching the CTBT, the US is allowing more countries to build or refine some seriously dangerous weapons. The reasons for their decision range from Republican scepticism of arms control to hatred for Clinton who has been pushing for them to sign. But more likely is commercial interests in weapons investment, as Senator John Warner said, "Many of the nuclear systems...are simply not suited to the subtle, and perhaps more difficult task of deterring rogue states...such weapons do not exist today in the US arsenal". Whatever the reasons, this Catch 22 can only profit the arms trade and jeopardise the safety and peace of the world.

---

# SchNEWS 5th BIRTHDAY PARTY

## Thursday 18th November

All yer usual SchNEWS comedy, performance, films, DJ's and special guest stars.
@ New Madeira Hotel, Marine Parade, Brighton
8 pm - 2 am   £3/4
Tickets from Peace Centre, New Kensington Pub & Klik Klik Whirly Beep Beep Records

---

## SchNEWS in brief

The inquest into the death of **Ricky Reel** (see SchNEWS 232) this week reached an open verdict. Campaigners told SchNEWS that the family had all along claimed that the death of Ricky, who was found dead in the Thames hours after being abused by rascists, was just an accident. ** The police are furious, spitting mad, weally angry cos a woman who was seriously hurt during the **June 18th** City of London shin-dig has had her charges dropped. The 19 year old student was seriously injured by a police van driving into the crowd at high speed. The police wanted her nicked for possession of a lock-knife. And what about criminal damage to a police vehicle for good measure eh? .*A little menace tells us that the police finally returned the **Reclaim The Streets** Sound System they "borrowed" after June 18th. Nice one! ** Witnesses needed urgent. Did anyone see **dockers** supporters being assualted in the back of police vans just after the first anniversary dock dispute in Liverpool, September 1996 by everbody's favourite the Operational Support Division. Then ring Kieran Dunne 0151 236 1944 email info@mail.liv-unison.uk.co ** There's a Crop Protection (**pesticide**) exhibition in Brighton on 16-18th Nov at the Metropole Hotel, with loads of dodgy coporate sponsors and speakers including someone from SchNEWS favourite company Monsanto. Check out their site at www.bcpc.org. and get down there! ** The **Green guide to Xmas** is out now,for an organic, natural and gm-free xmas.£4.99 + 92p p&p to Green Guide Publishing Limited, 271 Upper Street, Islington, London N1 2NU or call 0207 354 2709.The Green Guide for London is also available at £5.99 + 92p p&p ** **Tick a Teenth** a play by Paul Light is making a return for all those who forgot it was on last time! Komedia, Gardner St, Brighton, Sun 21st & Mon 22nd 8pm, 01273 647100. ** Next summer two men plan to walk from John O'Groats to Lands End to raise money for Bury unemployed Centre and *"celebrate 1,000 years of working class diversity, culture, resitance and development"*. If you can sponsor them contact The Jogle Project, c.o Bury Unemplohyed Centre, 12 Tithebarn St., Bury, tel 0161 797 4326 ** **Platform 6**, 6 Onslow Rd, Southampton, is a non profit making squatted centre including a cafe, an arts workshop, a library, a jamming place, a chill out space,a non commercial cinema, a meeting of minds. More is planned, and a list of empty properties in Southampton will shortly be available. Nice one! 07980 051929 platform6@angelfire.com

---

## FISHY PIGS

Good news from the High Court last week, when three Law Lords ruled police 'fishing expeditions' illegal. But that's not the same as the 'sport' involving rods, maggots and sitting around for hours in the rain just to boast about how big the one-that-got-away was down the pub later. This is the sort of 'fishing' the police carry out after you've been nicked. The sort of fishing animal rights protestors have to put up with when they come back from a few cheerful hours in the cell to find the police carted off anything they can get their hands on for examination. Not just yer diaries and phone books, but everything from computers, videos, posters, clothes, food and the contents of your shed (weedkiller and sugar gets cops' hearts racing).

The police can still have a good rummage in your dirty knickers drawer, but thanks to the ruling unless you give them permission they can only take down/away they know will be relevant to any court case.

The Law Lords pointed to the European Convention of human rights and said the govt may now have to consider legislation to balance the right to privacy with the right to investigation.

## TRICK OR TREAT

**Goblins** were out in Saanich, Canada this Halloween, trashing about 1000 trees and seedlings. The trees in a forestry centre owned by Western Forest Productions were forests for GE research to replace temperate rainforests. The "Genetix Goblins" called for an immediate end to 'Frankenscience'. Meanwhile, Reclaim the Genes said it was responsible for destroying 500 evergreen saplings at Silvagen Inc.'s research site at the University of B.C. last week. Getting in on the act this week, The World Wide Fund for Nature published a report that reveals more than 115 trails on GE trees have taken place since 1988 without *"proper controls or research into the effects on the environment"*. GE modification trials on trees mean that soon we can look foward to silent forests, devoid of insects, flowers and birds! The idea is to grow trees that will grow rapidly, resist rot and defy insect attacks. The trees would then be sprayed from planes to kill all life around them! Seventy of the trails are currently being run in the US with a further 5 in the UK. Those bastards at sHELL are currently behind two of these trails genetically mutating eucalyptus trees in **Kent** to improve growth rates and herbicide tolerance. Astra Zeneca did have a site in Bracknell, Berkshire but naughty activists sneaked in and cut them their poplars down! (SchNews 220) For info on past GE actions www.tao.ca/~ban/ar.htm.

## ...and finally...

A bizarre group calling themselves "Friends of the Stone" are apparently behind the 'napalming' of the Men an Tol and Lanyon Quoit stone circles in Cornwall on Bonfire Night. In a letter to the local newspaper, The Cornishman, the group which has caused serious damage wrote

*" For centuries now the meaning of these great monuments has been minsconstrued and wrongly passed down through the generations of now uneducated people. You do not deserve the heritage these monuments hold and therefore we intend to act further. By this time next week, Men-an-Tol will be gone. It shall be set up again, correctly aligned with pertinent sacred stones, in my back garden. We now have over 100 followers and this will be a shrine to us and only us. Lanyon Quoit will be destroyed. Better rubble on the ground than a fake prophet, misunderstood and minconstrued by thousands of non-believers."*

### disclaimer
SchNEWS warns all readers we'll put a smile on yer fishface, and then we'll have you over a barrel or it's down the hatch into Davey Jones Locker. Me hearties (pirate version of honest!)

---

## Subscribe!

Keep SchNEWS FREE! Just send 1st Class stamps (e.g. 20 for next 20 issues) or donations (payable to Justice?) **Ask for "Originals"** if you can make copies. Post *free* to all prisoners. **SchNEWS, c/o on-the-fiddle, P.O. Box 2600, Brighton, East Sussex, BN2 2DX.**
*Tel/Autofax:* +44 (0)1273 685913   *GET IT EVERY WEEK BY E-MAIL:* schnews@brighton.co.uk

**WAKE UP! WAKE UP! IT'S YER FIVE YEARS OLD TODAY!**

# Weekly SchNEWS

*Printed and Published in Brighton by Justice?*

**Thurs 18th November 1999**   http://www.schnews.org.uk/   **Issue 237   Free/Donation**

# DRAG QUEEN'S TERROR

"Animal rights, and to a lesser extent environmental rights activists have mounted, and continue to pursue, persistent, and destructive campaigns. While the level of terrorist activity by such groups is lower than that of some of the terrorist groups in Northern Ireland there is nothing to indicate that the threat they pose will go away."

Home Office consultation paper.

Yesterday's Queens Speech confirmed what SchNEWS has going on about over the past few months, when a new Prevention of Terrorism Act was announced. The bill introduces a new definition of terrorism: **"the use of serious violence against persons or property, or the threat to use such violence to intimidate or coerce the government, the public or any section of the public for political, religious or ideological ends."**

Oi! you, pulling up that genetically modified test site, you're now a terrorist!

This definition comes from America's Federal Bureau of Investigation and will give sweeping new powers allowing the police and security services to target all those pesky protestors that have been getting in the way of big business making a nice profit.

It will also cover foreign-based groups and dissidents living in Britain, giving police and customs officers powers to seize bank accounts and other assets of suspected terrorists. Would that have mean't people in this country supporting the ANC during its armed struggle against apartheid would have been targetted?

Ironically, the new measures are more or less identical to the 1974 Prevention of Terrorism Act emergency legislation, introduced in Northern Ireland, and whose powers were described as "unprecedented in peace time." How ironic that the government announce these brand spanking new sticks to beat protestors with on the same day as the apparent breakthough in the Good Friday agreement.

SchNEWS, celebrating its **fifth birthday** today, would never take the opportunity to be all smug and say we told you so but... (See SchNEWS 224 and continuing hysteria about June 18th). With the definition of terrorism now so broad maybe it's time to drop all this direct action nonsense and instead sit at home, watch TV and go on endless shopping sprees....then we will all feel content. Honest.

Twenty Seven new bills yesterday, not all of them bad, but here's a few SchNEWS readers might find interesting.:

### TRANSPORT

When the New Labour shadow transport secretary complained that the Tories had dreamt up a crazy new scheme to sell off air traffic control he thundered "Our air is not for sale!" Er, it is now.

### MANDATORY DRUG TESTING

If you find yourself the wrong side of the law, then the police will have the right to carry out compulsory drug tests.

### FREEDOM OF INFORMATION

The bill that is anything but.

### POST OFFICE

Rule changes which many fear are the first stages of privitisation.

### CRIMINAL JUSTICE

Includes the end of the right of trial by jury for some people.

### ELECTRONIC COMMUNICATIONS

At the moment e-mailers can keep their correspondence private by using software which encypts or scrambles messages into secret codes. But if the government get their way people could recieve a 2 year prison sentence for refusing to hand over their private 'key'.

## MAD AXEMAN

People are needed desperately to help save the remains of ancient forest - Pressmennan Wood, near Edinburgh- from the chop. SchNEWS has learnt that this ancient forest - around 13,000 years old - is being logged again, "for the excellent reason of equipping stately homes with nice-looking timber." The activists say that a single woodcutter has a contract to cut down 369 trees - he's already felled 160 but the rest can still be saved.

A camp has been set up and more people are needed. Tel: 07771 771240.

## CRAP ARREST OF THE WEEK

**For going home:** Michele Naa-Obed was arrested at the Jonah House Community in Baltimore in June for "leaving the district of Minnesota without permission and associating with felons"and given the maximum 12 months prison sentence. You see Michele had recently spent 18 months in gaol after disarming a fast-attack submarine and part of her parole was that she couldn't return to the house where she lived! While awaiting trial for the new heinous crime of living back home, Michele refused bail conditions which said she should avoid public protest, public speaking, live at a residence approved by the court and associate only with law-abiding persons!

As the Virginia Pilot magazine points out "It's amazing how we become more like the countries we criticise, and worse yet, put sanctions on, because of their abuse of human rights."

## NO BUDGET DAY

New Labour reckon yesterdays Queen's Speech was all about "enterprise and fairness" but there were lots of sticks to bash those who don't want to play the game.

Coupled with last weeks tight-fisted budget, the boot is really being put into those lazy ne'er do wells who refuse to take dead-end low-paid jobs.

It's the end of the "something for nothing" culture (unless your a big business fiddling your tax like Rupert Murdoch ) with a new benefits regime that "will be far tougher than people think" with the New Deal for everyone and anyone suspected of fiddling made to sign on daily.

As one commentator summed up "we are moving towards American workfare system, where not taking a job is not an option."

\* If you want to find out more about all these nasty new benefit changes send an SAE for the latest copy of 'Where's My Giro'. Brighton Against Benefit Cuts, 4 Crestway Parade, Hollingdean, Brighton, BN1 7BL

# DROP TILL YOU SHOP

"The plain fact is that we are starving people, not deliberately in the sense that we want them to die, but willfully in the sense that we prefer their death to our own inconvenience." Victor Gollancz

As SchNEWS went to press there were just 6 no-shopping days left until the 6th International No-Shop Day on Saturday 27th November.

The Ad-hoc Ad-heckling hit squad will strike in Manchester plus many other cities and towns. All will see sights such as bemused alien tourists and shop free zones. As this day of action is well established, instead of coordinated stunts, everyone is being invited to poke their tongue out at commercialism or a finger in the eye of the absurd excess of throwaway, consumerist culture. So either participate, or participate by not participating.

Adbusters magazine is available from book shops and www.adbusters.org and Enough, the Anti-Consumerism Campaign can be contacted at One World Centre, 6 Mount St., Manchester M2 5NS or www.enviroweb.org/enviroissues/enough

## SEEING IS BELIEVING

Footie fans beware; PVI tells us they are "spearheading an assault on European Soccer". Did this threat come from an obscure Dutch football team heralding the return of the glory days of football hooliganism? Alas no, it is scarier than that! PVI is an American advertising company peddling new ways of getting you to buy more shitty products. Virtual Advertising gets products and logos right inside telly programmes, the USA is lapping it up and it'll soon be coming to a screen near you. By digitally attaching images to scenes before broadcasting. Companies like PVI can create adverts that are, in the words of PVI boss Dennis Wilkinson, "embedded in the magic of the show." So for a match broadcast in both Turkey and England, the sidings, team strips and even the pitch itself could show different brands in each country, even each region, allowing the ultimate in consumer targeting. It doesn't stop at sports advertising – sitcoms and soaps are full of characters 'unrealistically' using no-name shampoos, consuming unbranded drinks and passing anonymous shops, which PVI can easily change to Lor*al, P**si or Mac***alds. In fact, every episode of yer favourite soap contains thousands of potential sites for 'brand placement' so they can get you watching ads even when you think you're safe from commercial crap – or as Dennis Wilkinson puts it "From tremendous virtual spectacles to subtle product placements that you barely notice, PVI provides the magic. Viewers are being impacted by virtual advertising." And they'll never even know it.

* Spy TV: Just Who is the Digital TV Revolution Overthrowing? edited David Burke (ISBN: 1 899866 25 6) £5.00 www.whitedot.org "What is all the fuss about interactive TV? Interactive means that when you act, someone at the other end is keeping track, of what you watch, of what you buy online, of your tastes." This book tells you what it will really mean, and how to fight back.

**Shamrock Ltd** are the largest providers of monkeys for vivisection, if you are outraged that up to 300 intelligent, social animals are caged inside windowless sheds and subjected to a barrage of painful tests before being sold to vivisection labs, then come to the national demonstration at 12 noon on 28th Nov. in Small Dole, West Sussex. Save the Shamrock Monkeys, P.O. Box 3090 Brighton, BN1 3QU  Tel 07020 936956

# SchNEWS in brief

There's a **Winter Solstice** gathering (21st December) at St Catherines Hill, Twyford Down, Winchester.Bring friends, mead and cake, music merriment and magic, camping tat. Needed: yurts/ domes, good weather, Tarmac director for pagan sacrifice... Contact tel 01248 750539/ email sop04a@bangor.ac.uk _** Late shout for the **West Country Activist Gathering,** a weekend of direct action workshops, 19th-21st Nov at Calstock Village Hall, Calstock, Cornwall. Tel: 01822 833457 or WCA99@hotmail.com ** **Corporate Watch** has a brand new spanky autumn issue out now.  Issue 9 looks inside the heads of corporate men and women, as well as specials on genetics and the Wal-Mart supermarket empire. £3.50 inc. postage from 16b Cherwell St., Oxford, OX4 1BG ** This year marks the 25th anniversary of **National Tree Week**, which takes place from 24th Nov to 5th Dec. Great - except its sponsored by those well known lovers of the environment ESSO. Contact The Tree Council, 51 Catherine Place, London, SW1E 6DY or www.treecouncil.org.uk** Ibogaine is apparently a 'revolutionary medical treatment for drug, alcohol and nicotine **addiction',** and a speakers tour (including a Dr.Mash!) has been organised in the UK to blow its trumpet. For a list of dates ring 0171 287 2828 ** Medha Patkar from the **Narmada Dam** protests in India will be speaking next Friday (26th)at G2 SOHAS, Russel Square, London, WC1  Tel 07974 125411 email narmadauk@yahoo.

# HORROR HOUSE

While Europe last week celebrated the tenth anniversary of the end of the Berlin Wall, asylum seekers to Europe might have something to say about the new wall being built around 'Fortress Europe'. Across Europe countries are closing borders and clamping down on refugees. Campsfield 'House' is an Immigration Detention Centre. It is run for profit by Group 4, and supervised by the Home Office. 200 people are held inside Campsfield, most are political refugees fleeing danger, torture and death. They are penned in behind a twenty-foot high, razor wire topped fence. Throughout the centre there are surveillance cameras and relatives wishing to visit are searched before passing through five secure doors. This is a high security prison! There are no procedures for detainees to make complaints. This means when they protest they can suddenly find themselves arbitrarily transferred to HM/private prison without appeal - a threat used to maintain order. Despite this a rooftop demonstration took place at the weekend by about 15 refugees complaining about their lengthy detentions (one has been in Campsfield 15 months)

A big demonstration will be held on the 6th anniversary of the opening of Campsfield - the 27th of November. These asylum seekers are isolated from the world and worn down to accept voluntary deportation. Let them hear that there are people on the outside on their side! Meet 11:00 am, Carfax Tower, Central Oxford, or 12 noon at Campsfield House.

Contact Campaign to Close Campsfield c/o 111 Magdalen Rd., Oxford, OX1  Tel 01865 557282 www.users.ox.ac.uk/~asylum

* The Home Office have applied for planning permission to convert Oakington army barracks near Cambridge into a detention centre to gaol 400 asylum seekers.

* A network of groups have got together to take direct action against prison building in the UK As they point out "The British state sends more people to prison than any other in Europe and its getting worse." To find out more contact CAGE, c/o 180-188 Mansfield Rd., Notts, NG1 3HW cage@veggies.org.uk

# WOT THE WTO!

"If they [NGO's] are allowed to hijack the World Trade Organisation talks, it will be a dangerous precedent that every government and every global company will regret long after the protests in Seattle."

Business Week magazine

SchNEWS has banged on about the World Trade Organisation (WTO) enough recently (see issue 233), so let's cut the crap and just say that they're an unelected and unaccountable shadowy organisation - effectively the new world govt for multinational corporations.And their next round of free-trade madness takes place in Seattle, USA from 29th November to 3rd December.

30th November has been picked for the big day of protest when tens of thousands of people will converge on **Seattle** and transform it into a festival of resistance. www.agitprop.org/ artandrevolution/wto

On the same day in **London** Reclaim the Streets and the Strike Support Group have organised a Reclaim The Railways speakers and music evening between 5 - 7 pm to oppose tube privatisation. The govt want to sell of tube lines to Railtrack – a company more concerned about its £1m a day profits,(fattened by more govt dosh than when the railways were publically owned)than about preventing accidents like Paddington and Southall.

In **Cardiff**, there's a Street Party-bring an instrument and dress regal. Meet Band Stand, Queens St. 12 noon.

**Up North,** there's a Doing It Up North action. Bring a sleeping bag and head for the 1 in 12 Club, 21-23 Albion St., Bradford. Tel  01422 844710

* The Seattle Noise Ordinance where you could be nicked for shouting to loud has apparently been vetoed at the last minute by the mayor, who said "Grunge put this city on the map - we don't want to do anything that might damage that" - so presumably the police will leave us all alone if we turn up in ripped jeans, Nirvana T-shirts and teenage sulks.

* China this week came one step nearer to joining the WTO, a deal President Clinton said was "good for the United States, good for China, good for the world economy." (Nothing to do with China being the worlds largest 'untapped' market for consumerables) Leaving aside China's dodgy human records, it won't be so good for all the Chinese people. "The cost will be defined mainly by unemployment. The number of people out of work is bound to surge" said one researcher at Beijing's Academy of Sciences. A flood of cheaper agricultural imports could also risk devastating the country's rural economy which supports 900 million .

# ...and finally...

If you haven't got yer boss a Xmas prezzie yet, don't start fretting cos the Class War 2000 calendar should be right up your street. Anarchic photos and historical dates galore such as 15th April. In 1912 Titanic sinks. More children from 3rd class perish than men in 1st class, 1st Feb. In 1973 Australia – prisoners riot at Bathurst jail, burning it to the ground, 14th Nov. In 1948 London - after a difficult birth due to the size of the baby's ears, Prince Charles is born.

Cheques for £5.50 to 'London Class War' at LCW, P.O. Box 467, London E8 3QX.

**disclaimer**

SchNEWS warns all readers not to get the ridicolous idea to start a weekly newsletter unless (summer) you like sitting in an office when everyone else is on the beach (winter) like sitting in a cold office when everone is in the pub.

WAKE UP! WAKE UP! IT'S YER NOT LYING ARCH

# Weekly SchNEWS

Printed and Published in Brighton by Justice?

Friday 26 NOVEMBER 1999    http://www.schnews.org.uk/    Issue238    Free/Donation

# AGGRO-CHEMICALS

It was around midnight the 2nd December 1984, when a poisonous gas cloud enveloped the hundreds of shanties and huts surrounding a pesticide plant in the central Indian city of Bhopal. As the deadly cloud slowly drifted in the cool night air, sleeping residents awoke, coughing, choking, and rubbing painfully stinging eyes. By the time the gas cleared at dawn, thousands were dead and injured; ranking it alongside Chernobyl as the world's worst industrial disaster, or as one commentator put it "the Hiroshima of the Chemical industry."

The deadly gas had leaked from the nearby Union Carbide factory, built in Bhopal in 1969 to produce pesticides as part of India's Green Revolution, which promised to increase the productivity of crops and feed the country's poor - but once again only fed the profits of the multinationals.

It could have been any poor country desperate to attract multinationals at any cost. As Jamie Cassels, author of 'Lessons From Bhopal', wrote: *"Developing countries confer upon multi-national corporation's a competitive advantage because they offer low-cost labor, access to markets, and lower operating costs. Once there, companies have little incentive to minimize environmental and human risks. Lax environmental and safety regulation, inadequate capital investment in safety equipment, and poor communications between companies and governments compound the problem"*

Carbide's safety standards at the Bhopal plant were well below those of a near-identical factory it owned in West Virginia, USA. In fact, safety standards had been deteriorating and ignored for years. Even a report by the company's own US safety team commented on "a serious potential for sizeable releases of toxic materials...due to equipment failure, operating problems or maintenance problems"

But it's not just the company that should shoulder the blame. What little environmental laws there were, were ignored by the state of Madhya Pradesh and an Indian government afraid of frightening off big business.

When the victims protested, their cries were often met with violence. Thousands were arrested, some on trumped up charges such as attempted murder or violation of the Offical

Secrets Act. One health clinic was raided, with police confiscating medical records and arresting six volunteer doctors. After 15 years most victims remain uncompensated. Meanwhile, according to 'The Lancet', victims suffering from serious health problems are being misdiagnosed or ignored by local doctors, while Union Carbide claim the pesticide is merely a "mild throat and ear irritant"!

The disaster gave rise to the world's largest lawsuit that dragged on for more than seven years. In the end the company received a slap on the wrist fine of just $470 million showing just whose interests the Indian government really serve.

## WE ALL LIVE IN BHOPAL

As one Bhopal activist put it *"Bhopal is not something unfortunate that is only happening to the people of a central Indian city. It is happening everywhere around the world. The routine poisoning of living systems that accompanies the storage, transport, production, consumption and waste treatment of hazardous chemicals are part of our industrial society. The silent and slow Bhopals that are happening in everyday life often go unnoticed and are seldom resisted."*

Bhopal has become a symbol of the way corporations treat humans and the environment. Or as author Ward Churchill puts it: *"Union Carbide's success in avoiding prosecution*

> In 1992 the official death toll for Bhopal stood at over 4,000. However, according to one senior UNICEF offical it could have been as high as 10,000. In addition, 30,000 to 40,000 people were maimed and seriously injured, and 200,000 were otherwise affected through minor injury, death of a family member, and economic and social dislocation.

*underscores the present reality that transnational companies are lawless monsters roaming the earth."*

* Greenpeace's ship the 'Rainbow Warrior' is currently on a two-year "toxic freeAsia" tour and will be visiting India next month to highlight the plight of the victims of Bhopal disaster. * This year Dow Chemicals bought Union Carbide for £7.2 billion to create the world's second largest chemicals producer * A report published by the National Toxic Campaign

## CRAP ARREST OF THE WEEK

For spreading peace and love.

Two girls in Canterbury who'd cheered up locals for ages by chalking 'fluffy' directives around town urging folks to *'choose love'*, *'just be'* and *'listen to the colour of your dreams'* found themselves being forced to *'choose law'* by the unamused, spiky hands of the local Plods who, as always, find it easy to *'just be'* misanthropic, humourless tossers. Backing the cops up were the local McDonalds, who supplied brushes and water so the girls could be forced to scrub off their positive vibes. To add insult to injury, local rag 'The Kent Messenger' printed up mug shots of the girls three days after the event with the caption 'Have You Seen These Men?'...

and the International Council on Public Affairs, showed that even after the disaster Carbide continued to be "a major discharger of toxic substances into the environment, and a major generator of hazardous waste'. In 1988, the company generated more than 300 million pounds of such waste - an increase of 70 million compared with 1987"

## BRIEF ENCOUNTER

Marks and Sparks were caught with their trousers down at the opening of their new Manchester store on Thursday by Super-heroes armed with the biggest pair of pants in the city- and we don't mean the Gallaghers. The Underwear Ubermenschen* unfurled a four-metre pair of shreds and then attempted to pull down all the tasteful trolleys on display in the store. *"Y, Oh Y, **Our** Y-fronts?"* panted perplexed employees, before cottoning on after a briefing from the heroes, who included SuperPants and Captain Y-Fronts. For they were from 'Superheroes Against GM Pants', sniffing out stains in M&S's 'organic' gusset: the use of genetically-modified cotton in their otherwise graceful grits**. *"GM cotton is undesirable for superheroes and the public alike. It's below the belt and should be removed without delay"* said a spokeshero. *"M&S have taken many steps to take GM out of their food and animal feed, but this policy is inconsistent if they continue to sell GM cotton."*

Don't get yer knickers in a twist, but GM cotton is the product of SchNEWS faves Monsanto and is bred to be herbicide and pest resistant. It has all the inherent risks of gene transfer and increased pesticide usage of other GM crops- and it does nothing to prevent skidmarks, either.

Watch for further actions! More info:0161 224 4846 **SchNews vocab watch**: * Supermen. Honest. Ask Nietzsche ** Pants. Honest. Ask Viz

# POWER ADDICTS

"A clique of the richest, economically and politically most powerful and influential men in the Western world [who] meet secretly to plan events that later appear just to happen"- The Times

Heard all about the 'leaked' minutes from the last meeting of conspiracy-faves the Bilderberg Group? How Russia was given carte blanche to bomb Chechnya, and all the rest? Well you can read the leaked documents IN FULL on the SchNEWS website (Most of the 'surfers' visiting our site since we put the Bilderberg thing on it have been US security agencies and multi-national companies. True!)

# POWER DRUNKS

Ever wondered how you get to be a Bilderberger? Well, there's a kindergarten where you'll learn all you need to know. The British American Project for the Successor Generation (BAP) was set up by Ronnie Reagan, Rupert Murdoch and Sir James Goldsmith in 1985 for the elite of up 'n' coming thirtysomethings from both sides of the Atlantic to be nurtured in the 'special relationship' existing between the two nations. Past members Peter Mandelson and George Robertson have both recently spoken at Bilderberg. BAP has just held its 14th annual shindig (described by ex-member Jeremy Paxman as 'four days of beer') in Harrogate, with this years' theme 'Making Culture Count'. No Tracy Emin here, of course, just Saatchi & Saatchi execs and the like discussing art's role in the global marketplace and in the words of Alison Holmes, chair of the executive committee: *"It's all been quite mad, sorting out the world's problems and drinking too much"*. Quite. BAP emerged in response to worries about the anti-nuke, anti-American drift of the Labour Party in the early '80's and the current co-ordinator is all-round bad egg Lord Carrington, ex-NATO chief and chair of the Bilderbergers for 9 years. Sounds dodgy? Never! As Alison Holmes told a Big Issue journalist: *"Bilderwhat? I've never heard of that in all my life."*

# BLAIR WITCH

Cherie Blair went hungry last week after students from the Non Payment Campaign occupied the restaurant at Sussex Uni and cancelled the Chancellor's Society Banquet where Cherie was booked to give a speech. The Uni Chancellor, Lord 'Dickie' Attenborough, displaying shock and horror when told of the Uni administration's coersive tactics towards non-payers, sympathised with the occupiers and expressed support for the cause of Free Education. Despite this 'understanding', the Uni administration is still threatening criminal and disciplinary proceedings against students: there are now 50 refusing or unable to pay the £1025 tuition fees at Sussex.

This action was inspired by the recent occupation at Oxford Uni where buildings where occupied by 200 students from 12th-16th Nov. Their demands were similar to those at Sussex, including an end to the 'residency' requirements which prevents those who have not paid from obtaining their degrees, an end to fee collection by the university and no penalisation of non payers. They encourage others to organise similar action in support of the students everywhere who cannot or will not pay their fees so they can build up the momentum and spread the campaign in the run up to the NUS Demonstration on the 25th. Info: Campaign for Free Education PO Box 22615, London N4 1WT. / Tel: 0958 556 756 http://members.xoom.com/nus_cfe/ Sussex Non-Payment Campaign, Falmer House, University of Sussex, Falmer, Brighton BN1 8DN or e-mail susxnonpay@hotmail.com.

# SchNEWS in brief

**The next **Aldermaston Women's Peace Camp** is on Friday Dec 10th (evening) to Sunday 14th (noon) sian@aldercamp.freeserve.co.uk** Happy first birthday to **OXYACETYLENE**, a free newsletter about actions and campaigns mainly in the Oxford area. Visit www.oxford-city.demon.co.uk/oxyace/' or send stamps and/or cheques to Box G, 111 Magdalen Road, Oxford, OX4 1RQ ** Get digging through the skips and recycle yer old (or new) junk to create an exhibition for the **Cultures of Resistance** celebration of creativity art exhibition from 12th-17th Dec at a squatted venue soon to be revealed. Contact rachred57@hotmail.com or 0958 765151 before 5th Dec to contribute.** The **Housmans Peace Diary 2000** is now on sale containing an up to date world directory of 2000 peace, environment and human rights organisations, international peace days and more. Send £6.95 plus another £4 if you want to sponsor a diary sent free to third world campaigners to Housmans, 5 Caledonian Rd, London, N1 9DX, UK ** Don't breed or buy while stray pets die – then **National Day of Awareness Against the Pet Trade** Sat 4th Dec, for peaceful demos and leafleting outside pet dealers contact; PO Box 233, Liverpool, L69 7 LF or 0151 228 3730.** A **West Papuan** tribesman fighting Indonesian occupation will be addressing the Worthing Eco-Action meeting on Dec 7th. Meetings are held on the first Tuesday of every month upstairs at 42 Marine Parade 7pm, but as they remind us if you're the kind of person who does what you're told you're going to want to stay away! www.worthing.eco-action.org or PO Box 4144, Worthing, BN14 7 NZ **Reclaim the Railways** in opposition to tube privatisation on November 30th in London. Meet Euston Sta. 5pm. Transport from Brighton leaves 2.30pm, Corn Exchange, tickets £3/£5 from Peace Centre **Shutdown Citibank:** worlds' largest holder of student debt, backed by Japanese loansharks who steal clients' organs to pay off their debts. Shut 'em down as part of the international protest at the WTO. 12 noon, 30 Nov, Lewisham. Out of the station and look up!!**Anti-Nato Picket** organised November 30th to welcome Jamie Shea and George Robertson (spokesman and new head of NATO respectively) who are arriving by river for a 'celebratory meal' in their honour at the Royal Naval College, Greenwich SE10. Meet 6.30pm.**

## IT'S GOOD TO STRIKE!

For the first time in 13 years, British Telecom workers kicked off a series of one day strikes, which began on 22nd Nov. BT staff are walking out from call centres across the UK in protest over the low wages, agency casualisation, battery hen working conditions and constant phone monitoring by management. Despite the fact the company earned over £4.3 billion over 1998, and awarded it's fat cat boss Peter Bonfield with an annual pay rise of £1 million, BT continue to employ the majority of it's staff from agencies like Manpower and Blue Arrow - with no contract, no sick pay, and no job security. Call centre workers, over 70% of whom are recruited from agencies, are electronically logged for Call Handling Times (CHT), and monitored by snooping bosses, who are instructed to sack them if they do not meet 'customer service' performance targets. In June this year 120 workers were sacked from their jobs at the Directory Inquiry call centre in Stirling due to '*regrettable advancements in technology*'. As one ex worker described it, working at BT '*is like contracting a microchip tumour of the brain*". Fact sheet: send SAE to: BT - Black Technology, PO Box 3157, Brighton, BN2 2SS.

Communication Workers Union, 150 The Broadway, Wimbledon, London, SW19 1RX

# COPS IN RUBBER SHOCKER

Right that's enough of the funnies- this is serious.Why do coppers in Durham and West Mercia Police forces need Rubber Bullets? Looking for a new war to fight? Not just content with introducing a new definition of the Prevention of Terrorism Act (see SchNEWS 237) the government is slowly arming the Police Forces of Britain with Baton guns that fire "solid four inch long polyurethane rubber rounds"- rubber bullets to you and me. Don't be fooled by the name, rubber bullets are killers; so far they've killed 14 people in Northern Ireland, 7 of them children. A recent report by the Belfast based Committee on the Administration of Justice warned that the use of rubber baton guns in Northern Ireland "appeare[d] to have become a weapon of first resort" and that the current guidelines for their use were "much too weak" and often ignored.But don't worry cos the police describe rubber bullets as "non-lethal" and promise only to use them in "pre-planned operations…" and only as a last resort, like CS gas. Er... since October '98, when it was launched onto the streets, CS gas has been used more than 10,000 times with the Plod receiving hundreds of complaints- such as that against South Wales coppers, who spayed and incapacitated a man as he broke into his own home.

*"There's a tendency for it to be used to ensure an easy arrest, and that's worrying - if I'm a middle-aged officer who is a bit worried about his abilities to handle a situation, the temptation is to pull out the CS spray and use it at an early stage so that I don't have any trouble"*-Peter Moorhouse, chairman, Police Complaints Authority

So giving coppers who can't handle situations baton guns and rubber bullets makes perfect sense then? More info: Committee on the Administration of Justice Tel 01232 232394 fax 01232 246706. also Statewatch (vol.8 no. 5),
PO Box 1516, London, N16 OEW

# ...and finally...
## CITY TRADERS IN DESTRUCTION ORGY

A Hotel had to be evacuated after a late night party decended into chaos and ended in a suspected arson attack reports the Southern Daily Echo. Sixty guests were evacuated from £180 a-night Careys Manor Hotel, Brockenhurst when a blaze began after furniture was placed on a log fire in the residents lounge. Damage alleged to have occured during a party by 11 City traders on a two-day visit to the New Forest. Det Sgt Steve Davies said, "They had just had dinner with plenty of alcohol and began playing a game of indoor cricket." {as you do!} Police said the hotel faces a bill of up to £20K due to damages A police spokesman said "It would appear the blaze began in the residents lounge after a private party got out of hand."

The trip was organised by London based Intercapital whose managing director Paul Newman was reported as saying, "They are just a bunch of boys who got drunk. It was high jinks and a case of boys behaving badly. We will sit down and talk to them and they will pay the repair bill themselves." {just stick it on the Gold card gov} Two of the group arrested on suspicion of arson but released on police bail until January.

### disclaimer

SchNEWS warns all world domination conspirators if they eat a Cheesey Bildeberger BAP they'll get gas in the pants. Then they won't be content. Honest!

# Subscribe!_____
Keep SchNEWS FREE! Just send 1st Class stamps (e.g. 20 for next 20 issues) or donations (payable to Justice?) **Ask for "Originals"** if you can make copies. Post *free* to all prisoners. SchNEWS, c/o on-the-fiddle, P.O. Box 2600, Brighton, East Sussex, BN2 2DX.
Tel/Autofax : +44 (0)1273 685913 *GET IT EVERY WEEK BY E-MAIL:* schnews@brighton.co.uk

# SELECT COMMITTEE SLAMS SECRET AUTHORITY

The Home Affairs Select Committee has strongly criticised the United Grand Lodge of Freemansonry for being unco-operative with a parliamentary examination on the influence of masonry on public life.

In its 2nd report, published in May 1999, the Committee states: "We particularly regret that it was only possible for this Committee to obtain the co-operation of the Grand Lodge by compulsion. We did not do so lightly, but only after being faced with months of prevarication and obfuscation."

The Select Committee had asked the United Grand Lodge - representing 350,000 exclusively male UK freemasons - to provide a list of its members involved in infamous cases of corruption including that involving the West Midlands Serious Crime Squad (disbanded 1989). According to the Committee's 2nd report published in May: "The West Midlands Crime Squad was arguably the most complained about unit in what was the most complained about police force in the country." However, when Committee chairman, Chris Mullins MP provided the Grand Lodge with a list of those involved, the Grand Lodge dragged its heals on confirming their masonic status. The Committee report notes: "We regret that it has taken the Grand Lodge five attempts to arrive at a definitive - if it is definitive - list of masons in the Serious Crime Squad." Doubts over the accuracy of the Grand Lodge's reluctantly given information were further excacerbated when the Committee discovered that one of the names not confirmed by the United Lodge was subsequently discovered by the Committee's chairman to be a mason.

The Select Committee's first report, published in 1997, called for a publicly available register of all masons working in the police and judicial system. Home Secretary, Jack Straw, accepted the Committee's recommendation but only confirmed a vountary declaration scheme which has since proven to be a farce. Ernie Hanrahan, head of the Police Federation representing rank and file police officers, has already publicly urged his members not to co-operate.

From the scant compliance with voluntary questionaires, the Select Committee estimates that between 5-10% of professional judiciary (judges etc), 5-20% of magistrates, and as much as 48% of the Crown Prosecution Service are masons. There are no breakdowns for the police as yet.

The Select Committee report concludes: "Progress has been slow, particularly with the police........We call on the government to speed up the process of establishing the registers of masonic status among the police and other parts of the criminal justice system, and to announce a firm timetable for completion of the exercise...... Additionally the names of all those who have failed to indicate whether or not they are masons should be published; such persons should not be allowed to exempt themselves entirely from the process simply by declining to co-operate."

Responding to indications from Jack Straw that the final register of names might be limited in its public accessiblity, the Select Committee also states: "In the absence of any compelling reason to the contrary, we support full public access....

Finally we look foward to the extension of such disclosure into other areas of public life such as local authorities and Parliament."

Full background investigative articles on Freemasonry and the Home Affairs Select Committee investigation are available in the SQUALL website features section.

## Squotes

"It's not everyone who's been given a golfing lesson by the President of the United States! I certainly had the best instuctor I could possibly have."
**Tony Blair (The Daily Telegraph 19/5/98)**

"So I told him how to hold the club, how to stand, how to swing…"
**President Clinton *on* Tony Blair (The Daily Telegraph 19/5/98)**

....A fair Britain ... but ... unavoidably ... a merciless Britain ...

# SUNDAY MORNING PLEASURES...

RING!

GET UP! WE HAVE TO GO!

COFFEE

WHY would anybody get up at 6 on a Sunday morning? WHY? Well, what if you're a really hardcore social revolutionary and the best way of building revolution is doing a stall at your local car boot sale?

ONWARD, COMRADES!

It's FREEZING I HATE this my fingers will FALL off, my BACK HURTS from lugging turgid anarchist BOOKS I HATE everyone —MOAN—

everyone else has a car...

REMEMBER TO STAY IN THE LINE.

I CAN FEEL MY HANDS! YEAH!

I'M GOING TO GET MYSELF A HOT CHOCOLATE!

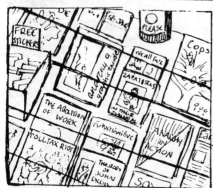

FREE STICKERS

We sell cheap anarcho books and pamphlets, and hand out free info.

↙TOP TIP: ! bits of elastic fastened over the table stops stuff blowing away!

I WANT TO LISTEN TO ABBA!

OH! SOCIETY OF THE SPECTACLE!

Of course, you get a few nutters

or just people who, uh, have slightly misunderstood

but you meet lots of interesting people, too..

last Sunday, a busking santa stood next to us.

sometimes, it is really rewarding (and sometimes, we make lots of **dosh** as well)

and at 1 o'clock, we pack up, go back home and SLEEP.

ISY 98

## SQUOTES

"The time for the war of the powerful to speak has passed; we will let it speak no more. It is now the time for the peace to speak, that we all deserve and need, peace with justice and dignity."

*Clandestine Indigenous Revolutionary Committee-EZLN General Command, Mexico*

BRANDS ARE FOR CATTLE

www.subvertise.org

WAKE UP! WAKE UP! IT'S YER US VERSUS U.S.

# SchNEWS

### Printed and Published in Brighton by Justice?

**Friday 3rd December 1999**   http://www.schnews.org.uk/   **Issue 239   Free/Donation**

# SEATTLE'S A GAS

"I came here to get arrested – let's get back out there tomorrow" Dan, protestor, Tuesday night

"My Trade Minister went to Seattle and all I got was this import quota" T-Shirt for sale, downtown Seattle

"Whose Streets? Our Streets!" Everyone!

Thousands of people are marching on Capitol Hill; the police are at a loss, their most vicious tactics ineffective against the masses gathered in the streets. The alliance of workers, environmentalists, students, human rights activists, anarchists, in fact everyone from the Church of the Underground Elvis to the Wobblies is rock solid. Hundreds of arrested protestors have cut their plastic handcuffs with nail clippers, barricaded themselves in the buses used to take them to the nick and are refusing to even give their names....yes, the SchNEWS team is in Seattle for what was gonna be a nice quiet winter holiday, and seems to have stumbled on America's biggest protest in decades.

As SchNEWS went to press downtown Seattle was still in chaos: riot police in armoured cars (called Peacemakers!) sped through the battle zone lobbing tear gas at anyone in the streets, while protestors still held many parts of the city centre, effectively shutting down the city for a second day running. A state of emergency has been declared; Martial Law is in force; a curfew declared every night between 7 and dawn in the centre of town *and* residential areas. The National Guard are on every street corner arresting anyone, riot cops still loosing tear gas at a peaceful student demos we write. For those Poll Tax/June 18th veterans who reckon they can handle the odd copper, riot police here are better armed than the average Storm Trooper, and the policy seems to be gas first, beatings and arrests later. On Wednesday afternoon a spontaneous march on Bill Clinton's hotel by the Steelworkers and hundreds of protestors was broken up by a constant tear gas barrage, gassing hundreds of shoppers, passers-by and people driving home. TOP TEAR GAS TIPS: Although we're not sure about toothpaste under the eyes, SchNEWS can confirm that vinegar on a scarf does help you breathe more easily.

SchNEWS has been bangin' on about the World Trade Organisation (WTO) for a while (see SchNEWS 233, 190), but now as US Senator Pat Hayden says, "Yesterday no-one knew what the WTO was. Today the whole of America knows it as a household word, and they know it is bad."

Media attention focussed on the violence, but as one protestor said, "I don't think it's right to hurt someone, but property destruction is not violence." SchNEWS favourites like McDonalds, and the Bank of America lost their windows, while shops were pillaged.

Seattle is a pretty laid-back city, considering the amount of coffee consumed, so this was the first time the National Guard has been in action in modern times. An example of the hypocrisy which characterises American politics - in a country where you can buy rifles over the counter, the mayor announced that having a gas mask is illegal!

The WTO is a shadowy organisation that for the past five years has been busy dismantling labour and environmental laws under the guise of 'free trade' (see SchNEWS 220, 204, 187). Effectively this amounts to world domination by multinational corporations, fronted by national govts, with surprise, surprise the good ol' U.S of A running the show. Seattle is the location for thrashing out new agreements, and activists have been arriving for over a week to show their opposition. The aim of the protests was to shut down the meetings - and shut them down they did, with Tuesday's opening ceremony delayed, then finally abandoned as delegates were stopped from entering the Conference centre. Thousands laid siege, blocking the streets in the face of tear gas, pepper spray, concussion grenades, and rubber bullets.

Many have been injured, protestors and delegates alike complaining about the cops' reckless and enthusiastic use of weapons. The crowds were later joined by a 40,000 strong union crowd, worried that the WTO will mean even greater job losses, worse working conditions, lower pay, less job security and greater profits for bosses. Students and schoolchildren walked out, and taxi-drivers with their own grievances went on strike, as buses were under siege round the Western Hotel in a situation reminiscent of Custer's last stand.

By Wednesday the protests were smaller, any-

one daring to raise their voice facing arrest and being shipped off to a naval base. The pre-conference hype had been immense, making Seattle the world's most clued-up city on the WTO. Everyone had an opinion, most unfavourable. One garage attendant told SchNEWS the WTO was "a global conspiracy to make us all eat poison shit."

An aircraft flew over on Sunday spelling out 'People Not Profit'; a 4-page spoof section of the Seattle Post Intelligencer was slipped into thousands of the papers. You could buy t-shirts, caps, and a whole range of other merchandise - even the local strip joint was getting in on the act. Seattle has become a wealthy city, symbol of a 'revitalised economy' and home to Microsoft and Boeing. All this despite a massive homeless problem, the same poverty found in any American city and new laws recently passed to sweep the poor off the streets. As one local paper asked, "Is Seattle nuts?" As Texas DJ and former senator Jim Hightower put it, "they got the fat cats, we got the alley cats." Preparations for the arrival of the WTO included a federal grant *and a stash of hidden medication in the event of a major biological or chemical attack*!

This was the 2nd time Clinton had flown into mass protests over the WTO, last May in Geneva, he saw 5,000 protestors, when cars were torched, offices occupied and trashed, etc (see SchNEWS 168). Clinton's hopes of ending his presidency on a high note, making up for last year's indiscretions and showing the U.S's command of international affairs has gone up in smoke. Last year the WTO were complaining about a low press profile, now it probably wishes it could crawl back into its murky world of secret tribunals and hope the protests go away.

## ANTI-WTO CRAZY

On 25 Nov. 5000 French farmers with their sheep, ducks and goats, feasted on regional products under the Eiffel tower in protest at the impact of trade liberalisation. On Tuesday, 800 miners clashed with cops, ransacking a tax office and burning cars in 2 towns in eastern France.

The more random 'Spackparade' in Berlin left police confused as protesters waved mock banners demanding more order, more security and 'wealth for eels' (a pun on wealth for all).

In Iceland anti-American protests targetted a military base and embassy demanding "Yanks Out" (a promise still unkept since WW2).

At the home of the WTO in Geneva, a city of only 300,000 managed to produce 5,000 protestors made up of farmers and city-dwellers, expressing their solidarity with the struggle against globalisation; the farmers gathering at the UN building and the city folk marching on the international banking district.

Food Not Bombs served up in Prague, and supermarkets were leafletted.

On the 24th in India, 300 scaled the fence of the World Bank building, covering it with posters, grafitti, cow shit and mud, while others sang slogans and traditional songs at the gate.

In London over 1000 gathered outside Euston Station in support of rail and tube workers, and for a privatised and safe rail network. Speeches were made, drums banged, and people partied (despite the dull presence of Socialist Wanker Parasites). Everything was peaceful until the rally had ended and some protestors charged the cops in the return of rabid riot ravers ruckus. A police van was set alight and protestors and lots of heavy-handed cops pushed each other around. Arrests were made, capitalism was mentioned, people went home. And remember folks: you're not obliged to say anything to the cops or have your picture taken! Earlier in the day there were protests in Trafalgar Sq about asbestos, and outside Citibank, about student fees.

In Leeds city centre, around 50 protestors (and yet more SWP sads) were faced by over 300 cops. In the face of these daft odds, people wandered around, handed out leaflets outside scummy companies, and generally had a laff.

A disused garage and an old Toll House, soon to be "luxury flats" have been squatted in Totnes, South Devon to draw local people's attention to the WTO. In Cardiff a procession marched through the centre of town. In Halifax a Nestle factory was occupied and a banner dropped outside; 16 were arrested.

## HUNTINGDON DEATH SCIENCES

The good folk who brought you the closure of Hillgrove cat farm are now set to bring you the demise of vivisectors Huntingdon Life Sciences. The labs, in Cambridgeshire, will be targeted by 'avin' it mass protests until they close. Stop Huntingdon Animal Cruelty Campaign promise the biggest actions yet. HLS holds 70,000 animals at one time and was seriously undermined by campaigners a couple of years back before being bailed out by Nat West. The first national demo is set for Dec 11: details/leaflets/etc 0121 632 6460. Last Sunday's demo against **Shamrock Monkey Farm** in Sussex saw activists blockading Brighton town centre while the riot squad and EG units waited on a country lane 20 miles away. Nice One!! Save The Shamrock Monkeys PO Box 3090, Brighton BN1 3QU tel: 0702 093 6956

## *Subscribe!*

## SchNEWS in brief

Check out **www.geocities.com/newburybypass** for a huge archive about yer favourite road ** 2 hospitals are being closed to make way for a **Private Finance Initiative** (see SchNEWS 210/219) 'superhospital' with losses of beds and jobs. Demo. on Sat 11th Dec, 11 a.m, Selly Oak Hospital: details c/o B'ham TUC, The Union Club, 723 Pershore Rd, Selly Park, Birmingham ** **meals without squeals?** this vegan recipe book for just £2.80 is right up yer street, from VIVA!, 12 Queens Square, Brighton ** **9 Ladies** need your help! Stanton Moor, the Nine Ladies Stone Circle and related areas of the Peak District are in serious danger if the application to re-open two dormant quarries is accepted. Tel 01332 663031 ** Got a **spare video camera**? A Brighton activist heading to Arizona to document the forced relocation of Navajo Indians desperately needs video equipment. Contact SchNEWS office ** Don't know what to get the folk this **Christmas**? Check out Green Books, AK Distribution and Pluto Press catalogues. Green Books 01803 863260 www.greenbooks.co.uk; AK Distribution 0131 555 5165; Pluto Press 0181 348 2724 www.plutobooks.com ** Ethical Xmas pressies? check out the **Fair Trade Fair** at Kensington Olympia 2, 10th - 12th Dec. More info P.O. Box 1001, London SE24 9NL www.globalpartnership.org *

## Car Sick

This week, John Prescott incurred the wrath of car-lovers with his proposals for higher fuel duty and city road tolls. Even Scum readers demanded a series of one-day car drivers' strikes to show John that they won't be pushed around - so now brave 'Two Jags' announces the money raised is to be spent on more *roads* rather than public transport. Yep, folks...time to dust down Swampy and prise him out of his Armani 'cos 37 bypasses and motorways are planned over the next 7 years. And of course, there's also the Fat Hypocrite's sell-off of London Underground, although he's ousted Railtrack from this process, but privitization goes on nonetheless, including a widely criticised plan to remove air traffic control from the public sector. Overcrowding, high fares, delays and accidents are all a result of shareholders' concern for profits rather than people. But before you unpack yer climbing harness, get a copy of *Statewatch*. Cops are calling for new legislation to combat road protestors. In an interview in Police Review, Chief Constable Stephen Green calls for new laws and police powers to deal with non-violent protest and a change in definition, 'upping' road protest from public order to terrorism!! Statewatch: P.O Box 1516, London

## SchNEWS AGGRO GUIDE: Mayday 2000

*MayDay 2000*, a 4-day gathering to be held across London from 28 Apr. - 1st May 2000. Conceived at the Bradford '98 conference and born at the June 18th action. Plans include workshops, speakers, into-the-night discussions, stalls, a bookfair, film festival, art exhibition, footie tournament, tours of revolutionary London, a MASSIVE Critical Mass bike ride, plans for a permanent social centre, top gigs, parties, a May Queen event with a twist, maypoles, mayhem and a MASS ACTION in London on Monday May 1st to celebrate "our diverse struggles against capitalism, exploitation and the destruction of the planet." Any offers of help organising the festivities are welcome, as are donations.MayDay 2000 BM MayDay London WC1N 3XX Email enquiries to : mayday2k@email.com Discussion group: mayday2000-subscribe@egroups.com www.freespeech.org/mayday2k

## Inside SchNEWS

While you're all out 'avin it over the winter hols, spare a thought for those locked down and send a card, or better still a letter. It's important to support those who are serving time for trying to make the world a better place, and contact with the outside world can really make someone's day. Don't forget it could be you... Here's a list to start you off, for more info on letter-writing and prisoner support contact London ABC, 27 Old Gloucester St, London WC1N 3XX londonabc@hotmail.com

Harold H. Thompson, #93992, N.W.C.C, Site 1, Route 1, Box 660, Tiptonville, Tenn. 38079, USA

Edward Mark Williams, P15135, E Wing, HMP Wormwood Scrubs, Du Cane Rd, London W12 0AE

Mark Barnsley, WA2897, HMP Full Sutton, York YO41 1PS

Burley William, 097234 - A1 - P110GW, Box 221, Raiford, FLA 32083, USA

Hannah Thompson, CF 4997 - 01.20, HMP Eastwood Park, Falfield, nr. Wootten-Under-Edge, Glos GL12 8DS

Andrew Kerry, HMP Swaleside, Eastchurch, Kent ME12 4AX

Pablo Locke, MM2797, HMP Kingston, Milton Rd, Portsmouth, Hants PO3 6AS

Richard Gilbert, DP4786, Houseblock 3, HMP Belmarsh, Western Way, Thamesmead, London SE28 OEB

Will Hudson, HG0089, D Wing, HM Prison Blundeston, Lowestoft, Suffolk NR32 5BG

John Bowden, B41173, HMP Long Lartin, South Littleton, Evesham, Worcs WR11 5TZ

Tim Pockett, JW1522, HMP Littlehey, Perry, Huntingdon, Cambs PE18 OSR

Raphael Rowe, HMP Kingston, Milton Rd, Portsmouth PO3 6AS

** And another prisoner's being held in relation to June 18th. Letters of support: Darren Sole CW 9599, HMP Wandsworth, P.O. Box 757, Heathfield Rd, London SW18 3HF

## ...and finally...

After years avoiding anything more strenuous than rushing to the shops for a pack of biscuits, SchNEWS was very surprised by the results of a survey into people's attitudes to work published in the Financial Times this week. We're not sure who was interviewed or if they come from the same planet as we do, but here's some of the 'statistics' that had us running to get on the sick:

* 10% said they go to work because they enjoy it

* 2% go to work for the company of others
* 79% are 'very' or 'fairly satisfied' with their job
* 89% would seek work at once if made unemployed
* Managers are rated as 'very good' or 'quite good' by a staggering 78%

And the survey said, "Are you out of your fucking minds?" On the basis of the above, some employees are too unimaginative to think of anything better to do, have no mates outside the workplace, and love being ordered about by power-crazed nutters. The results might surprise those who continue to endure shit working conditions, get paid virtually fuck-all, and are on a one-way fast-track route to old age with no pensions.

**disclaimer**

# Nov 30th over 'ere

## Mock Trial For Shell

*Activists conduct a mock trial of Shell Oil and the Nigerian - Government outside Bow Magistrates Court, London on November 30 1999.* The action, one of a series which took place around London on the day, highlighted the complicity of Shell and the Nigerian government in an environmentally and community devastating quest for oil in the Niger delta.

### Squotes

"The collapse of the Global marketplace would be a traumatic event with unimaginable consequences. Yet I find it easier to imagine than the continuance of the present regime."

*George Soros, financial speculator.*

**Activists in Bristol devise an impromtu Game Show where the World Trade Organisation defeats ordinary citizens to win control of the globe. Spin that Wheel of Misfortune!**

# november 30th a day of action

The World Trade Organisation was meeting in Seattle, USA. People all across the world were planning actions and demonstrations against this, exploitation and capitalism. In London, a rally was called, and the cops decided that after June 18th, they needed to turn up in force.

About 1000 met up at Euston station 'round 5pm

EUSTON

SOLIDARITY WITH THE TUBE WORKERS BLABLA

SLOGAN JOIN OUR PARTY

ATION LS LISM LS

JUSTISTISE JOINER

PRIVATISATION KILLS BLABLABLA

newspapers were talking about a riot.

SO WHEN IS THIS GONNA KICKOFF THEN?

bla bla

PE

Daily Turd

RIOT PLANNED

Our reporter Edwin Wonkle-Smyth reveals conspiricy to wreak havoc on Nove 30th in London!

only 20p

but really it was just supposed to be a rally against rail privatisation

Anarchists stock-piling weapons for November 30th riot

WOMAN EATS HER BABY!

But when the speeches were finished everyone just piled out onto the street

OOH-THERE'S MILLIONS OF COPS...

SLOGA SLOG SLOG

LS CAPITALISM KILLS

Some people got hold of a transport police van

ARE YOU SURE THIS IS A PIG VAN?

YEAH IT'S GOT A LIGHT ON THE TOP!

there was a fair bit of chaos

FUCK THE PIGS!

HUH HUH

DUH!!! missed again...

Some drunk climbed on top and took 10 minutes to kick off the light

# CRASH, BANG, WALLOP, WOT A PICTURE

SQUALL

Where Do You Want To Grow Today?
--
I Wanna Go Home
Underground Update
Features
Squall Pics
✓ Frontline Communique
The State Its In
Squotes
Resources
Links
From Our Correspondence

Eyewitnesses at the N30 anti-capitalist demonstration at Euston Station report that one individual in particular sparked violence before rapidly leaving the scene. Anthony Fielding saw first hand how the trouble started and his testimony makes for a sobering read.

It was a good turn out, for a cold winter's evening. The Carnival Against Capitalism part 2. On the same day as the World Trade Organisation held its big meeting in Seattle, a large public meeting outside Euston station voiced dissent against global corporate control. People from all walks of life were there. At 5 pm, there was the initial influx of protesters, drumming and dancing, good vibes, a party atmosphere. Sometime around 6 pm, the speakers started. The positive vibes continued, but some hecklers were shouting various remarks. Most of the crowd ignored this. After the speakers had finished, we were treated to a song, and then back to the drumming. Some of the crowd dispersed.

I took a walk around to soak up some positive vibes, and noticed a man wearing a hood and scarf round his face, kicking and shouting at three regular policemen. They shrugged it off, and were not provoked. As his violence increased, so the policemen defended themselves, but without force. I have seen police brutality many times, but this was the model of restraint. It was obvious that his actions were to provoke a response, and in turn, an excuse for a ruck. I shouted at him to stop, getting in the middle of it; either one of us could have walked away, without police interference. I thought that the majority of people in the area would have agreed with me; that this was just one guy, with a problem, and nothing more. But within 60 seconds, the police were moving away, and a charge of protesters were coming at them, spurred on by this guy's cries of "come on then".

group of "anarchists" or "hardcore trouble makers", to give them their media friendly titles. It was no surprise that the burning van was front page news.

Multi-national companies, the target of the protest, try to discredit activists who take direct action against them, as "thugs" or "terrorists". These same companies influence the majority of people in this country every day, through the newspapers and television stations they control. Many people base their opinions and decisions upon information received from these sources. If there is a riot at a protest, all that is reported and remembered is the riot. As it is obvious that violence at a protest, redirects attention away from the protest itself, then could we not conclude, that the people responsible for starting this and other riots, are doing so to lessen the impact of the direct action itself? It's possible that these people who start and maintain riots, are not sympathetic to the efforts of the particular pressure groups who are involved in the protest. I was there at the very start of the trouble. I saw one lone man kicking and shouting at passive police officers who were not being threatening in any way. They were unarmed, and not fighting back after having been attacked by this one lone man. Due to the crowd's automatic association of "them" and "us", the police were rushed by the crowd. The

The masked man who started the whole thing off, dipped out of the crowd, before reaching the police at the other end and left the scene. The riot had started, and took its usual course. A van was left in the area of the protest and the bait was taken. Some people tried to persuade the "mob" to leave it alone. Most people stood silent. There were cameras everywhere. Only the rioters and the curious remained. The van was smashed up and set alight and as the fumes overtook the area, I noticed a group of riot police appearing on the left. It looked like a good time to leave. I headed into the small park-like area and got out on the far side. I heard from a friend who didn't get out, that the riot police did "snatch and grab" missions into the crowd later for specific people caught on camera.

If the rioters thought they could achieve anything positive by fighting the police, their energy was misplaced. All that was achieved by starting a riot was to create a story, with pictures, discrediting the protesters, their efforts, and the issues. There is a lot of good footage to discredit the protest, when a van is set alight by a

Pic: Snaps Picazo

**Here's that gratuitous burning van pic anyway**

imagery of violence against the police force, coupled with the cries of "come on then", led an otherwise peaceful gathering into an unprovoked attack on the police. Let's not forget that there were more than enough riot police, with full body armour, shields, batons and a strategic advantage. With the area of the protest surrounded, they too were just waiting for the excuse to fight. In a combustible atmosphere such as this all you need is the spark, to set off the flames. But who would want to turn a party into a riot? The police in Seattle were seen to be out of hand, because they were fighting a predominanltly peaceful gathering. The police in Euston, on the other hand, were seen to be "dealing with a situation". The rioters handed them the excuse they needed, to legally beat the shit out of anyone in the area. During the worst of the fighting, I stood under a tree a good distance from the action, where I remained still and silent. This was, it seemed,

too much provocation for some of the riot police, who came and battered me around the body, whilst insisting that I "fuck off". I wondered to myself, "where do they want me to fuck off to?", as people were being attacked by the police for trying to leave the area!

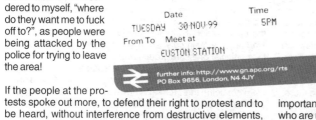

| Class | Action type | Valid |
|-------|-------------|-------|
| STRUGGLE | RECLAIM THE RAILWAYS | NOW |

| Date | | Time |
|------|--|------|
| TUESDAY | 30-NOV-99 | 5PM |

From To   Meet at
EUSTON STATION

further info: http://www.gn.apc.org/rts
PO Box 9656, London, N4 4JY

If the people at the protests spoke out more, to defend their right to protest and to be heard, without interference from destructive elements, then the pressure would be in favour of peaceful protest. It

is interesting to note that everytime the rioters stopped, the drummers started, and everytime the rioters started again, the drummers stopped. There is a difference between civil disobedience and violence directed against symbols of authority. Fighting police and burning vehicles directs attention away from the objective of the protest. It also helps the Government to pass new laws to deal with "public order".

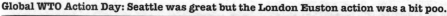

Penalty: misery
If you fail to prevent the privatisation of your public services.

further info: http://www.gn.apc.org/rts
PO Box 9656, London, N4 4JY

There are going to be more laws passed to constrict our already limited "freedom", justified to the media attentive public with film footage of June 18 and November 30 showing only the fighting and the burning vehicles. The more violence there is the stronger support there will be for extra police powers and more public order laws. The most effective weapon, is information. At present, it looks like the majority of people are still waiting for the "truth" (whatever that may be), to be delivered to their homes, in easy to digest forms, through newspapers and television. Whilst this is far from ideal, it is the way it is; and when protests turn into riots, it turns peoples attention away from the issues at hand and alienates the very people we need to support us! The corporate interests have no worries in the propaganda war, as long as the so called "hardcore", keep feeding the media mind control machine with enough ammunition to effectively neutralise our voice. The most important people to reach, are those who don't protest, those who are unaware of the issues, and those who are part of the corporate political system, including the police.

**Global WTO Action Day: Seattle was great but the London Euston action was a bit poo.**

Pic: Snaps Picazo

# K.O. THE WTO

**Where Do You Want To Grow Today?**
--
I Wanna Go Home
Underground Update
**Features**
Squall Pics
Frontline Communique
The State Its In
Squotes
Resources
Links
From Our Correspondence

With the World Trade Organisation still reeling after the recent protests and failed trade negotiations in Seattle, Si Mitchell finds out why the world is suddenly taking a stance against the WTO and its stealthy ambitions.

"There are 25 million milk producing animals in Mongolia, but in the city market places you can only buy German butter. Similarly last year Britain exported 47 million kilograms of butter to Europe while importing 43 million kilograms from the same countries. Here in Devon, New Zealand butter is a quarter of the price of local butter. It's insane."

Founder of the Dartington based International Society for Ecology and Culture (ISEC), Helena Norberg Hodge, is unimpressed by well travelled dairy produce. To coincide with the World Trade Organisation's Seattle conference at the end of the month, ISEC's parent body, the International Forum on Globalisation, is holding its own 'teach-ins' to alert people to the need to reverse the global economy, messianically being pursued by corporate bosses and politicians alike. In his document 'Small is Beautful, Big is Subsidised', ISEC's US programmes director Stephen Gorelick, argues that the efficiencies of scale, at the heart of global trade, are a fallacy. "Governments are encouraging growth at every level. This is costing people their jobs, and breaks down the community fabric that depends on healthy local economies; they are eroding democracy and widening the gap between rich and poor and irreparably damaging ecosystems and human health across the planet." From education, to aid, to infrastructure, the quest for growth is insidious. From Bodmin to Bangalore we are told that local customs and knowledge are inferior to the glossy prosperity fed to us by Western media. While people in the poorer south are goaded to be like those in the affluent north, northerners are made to feel 'greedy', and responsible for the plight of those in the south.

"It's more complex than that," says Norberg Hodge. "We need a shift in direction towards localising economic activity to strike a balance between international trade and production at home."

This is not about people in colder climates going without bananas, but about doing away with the unnecessary intensive, mass scale, production and transportation of goods, and the petrochemical pollution that entails. A recent study in Germany, found the ingredients of a single tub of yoghurt had travelled 1,000 km from four different countries. In Arkansas the US government are stumping up $90 million to build an airport that will handle poultry-carrying 747s with the aim of opening up Japan as "a boom market for US fresh chicken imports". Somerfield supermarkets transport Cornish Cauliflowers to the north of England to be wrapped in cellophane to be brought back to the West country for sale.

In 1970 there were over 100,000 dairy farms in Britain. That figure has been halved and small farms are continuing to disappear at the rate of 100 a month. The biggest ten per cent of farms now account for half the UK output. Gorelick says: "Export led agriculture usually demands large scale monocultural plantations, industrial scale machinery, and heavy chemical inputs; but it does not require many farmers, and a large portion of the agricultural labour force is left redundant." Britain has shed 88,000 rural jobs in the last ten years. Despite this, governments continue to oil the wheels of growth. Fossil fuel and nuclear power plants, megadams, motorway networks and airports are of little use to small traders. Treaties and regulations implemented by the WTO and EU may benefit multinational cross border businesses, but they regularly penalise the local traders, whose plight is inaccurately touted alongside that of the megacorps in media calls for 'trade freedom'.

It is unfortunate that it took the jingoism, unleashed in the latest siege of the Anglo-French trade war, for people to consciously connect export led trade and the decimation of Britain's farming industry. If it wasn't for the corporate quest for maximum payback from minimum outlay we may not be living in dread of hormone injected US beef, GM food, vanishing forests or melting ice caps.

"I think our biggest enemy is narrow focus, more than conscious evil intention," says Norberg Hodge, referring to the blinkered arguments that surround poverty and pollution. "The government and corporate elite are so fixated with growth that they refuse to contemplate alternatives." She goes on to criticise some environmentalists and some of the leading NGOs - who see globalisation as part of the solution - for refusing to see the link between aid projects and the destruction of local economies and culture. The previously self sufficient people of Ladakh in northern India are being encouraged to grow flowers for export to Holland. Many like them, forced by indebted governments courting international monetary aid, have their lands turned into production lines for the richer nations. Microcredit systems of small loans promoted by The World Bank shackle previously stable, though less cash intensive, economies to the notoriously corrupt and unstable speculative currency market. The cash crop system has no need for the majority of rural people who flock to the cities to compete for jobs that don't exist.

What money is left in communities is soon sucked out. "Studies indicate that of the money spent in a typical McDonalds, nearly 75 per cent leaves the local economy," says Gorelick. A DETR report in 1998 found new UK superstores to be taking up to half the trade of local food retailers, while the National Retail Planning Forum calculated each new store caused a net loss of 276 jobs as local traders cut back or closed.

However pressure can be brought on the politicians, companies and self styled international trade police such as the WTO. People all over the world are rejecting the monoculture. Buy local campaigns, community banks, tool lending libraries, ecovillages, LETS schemes, community supported agriculture and farmers markets are all on the increase.

Dave Lang, a livestock farmer from South Gloucestershire, was on the brink of bankruptcy when he joined a farmers market. He now trades in 20 small town markets a month all within forty miles of his farm. "The public can talk to the actual producer (a stipulation for stall holders) and find out how the crop was grown or what the animal was fed on, they can even come down to the farm to see," says Lang. "People are amazed by what's in season and have lost touch with what food tastes like." Unlike McDonalds, 100 per cent of the money spent at a farmers market goes into the local economy.

There are over 40,000 members in Britain's expanding network of 450 Local Exchange Trading Schemes (LETS). Participants receive credits for their contributions which are traded for services from other members. Babysitters trade with language teachers, and therapists with hairdressers. "It's not just for those that can't afford it. It's about taking things into your own hands, uniting communities and building up old and new skills," says Rae Orr from Letslink UK. As they act outside of the mainstream economy LETS trading does not register on conventional prosperity scales.

Kalle Lasn, editor of Adbusters magazine, says that the corporations driving this global economy, are merely doing what we programmed them to do. He suggests that each shareholder should be liable for 'collateral damage' to bystanders or environmental harm. "If you reap the rewards when the going is good, why shouldn't you be held responsible for that company when it becomes criminally liable." He feels that fewer shares would be traded and the worst offending companies would collapse. "Instead of simply choosing the biggest cash cows, potential shareholders would carefully investigate the backgrounds of the companies they were about to sink their money into. They would think twice about buying into Philip Morris or Monsanto.

"We must rewrite the rules of incorporation in such a way that a company caught repeatedly and wilfully dumping toxic wastes, damaging watersheds, violating anti-pollution laws, harming employees, customers or the people living near its factories, engaging in price fixing, defrauding its customers, or keeping vital information secret, automatically has its charter revoked, its assets sold off and the money funnelled into a superfund for its victims."

Company bashing legislation is unlikely, hampered not least by the 'revolving door' between government post and boardroom seat. Transport Secretary Steven Norris now heads the Road Hauliers Association and GM retailer Lord Sainsbury chairs the select committee scrutinising GM crops. This is no new phenomenon. In 1953 General Motors president, Charles Wilson, was appointed US defense secretary. "What's good for General Motors is good for the United States," he said before pushing a 41,000 mile interstate highway system past Congress as a 'national security' measure. (In the 1920s the same company along with Standard Oil and Fyrestone Tyres was found guilty of buying up and systematically destroying the street-car systems of over eighty US cities. Each company was fined a laughable $5,000 and car dependency was born.) Economist and author of 'When Corporations Rule the World', David Korten, likens global capitalism to a cancer in the world economy. "Curing the capitalist cancer to restore democracy, the market and our human rights and freedoms will require virtually eliminating the institution of the limited-liability for-profit public corporation." He told SQUALL: "We need radical campaign finance reform to get big money and corrupt politicians out of politics. An immediate agenda is to stop the WTO from negotiating new agreements that further weaken democracy and speed environmental and social breakdown. The WTO should be closed, while we establish mechanisms under the United Nations to regulate transnational finance, and trade."

There have been small victories. In May 1998 the New York City Attorney General revoked the charters for Tobacco Research and the Tobacco Institute, on the grounds that they are tobacco-funded fronts that serve "as propaganda arms of the industry". While last year the people of Arcata California voted to "ensure democratic control of all corporations conducting business within the city." Recent events in the Microsoft saga suggest that even the ridiculous wealth of Bill Gates may not guarantee his stranglehold on PC system software. All farmer Dave Lang asks for is "a level playing field" to compete with artificially cheap mass-produced imports.

Helena Norberg Hodge believes we must reconnect with our immediate environment. She says region specific education is fundamental to this, not ignoring other cultures, but being more aware of our own. Using local produce does help the local economy, it requires less energy, packaging, preservation and transport and enables those in other communities to look to meeting their own needs with their own resources. "We need a shift in the balance between international trade and production at home. We need to move away from the 'teenage boy culture' that demands mobility, independence and a fear of growing old." Wolfgang Sachs, project director at Germany's Wuppertal Institute for Climate, Environment and Energy told SQUALL that it is not about bringing Southern developing cultures 'up' to our level of lifestyle and consumption, but about reconfiguring our own 'developed' societies to consume and impact less. "We need enthusiasm, competence and passion, a different kind of imagination. Things are happening but they are drops in an ocean. But even drops can change the colour of the water." The message is simple. Think global, act local.

# SEATTLE
# 30th
# November
# 1999

"It's raining fat cats and dogs of war" - delegates getting escorted into the WTO meetings.

SQUALL
Where Do You Want To Grow Today?
--
I Wanna Go Home
✓ Underground Update
Features
Squall Pics
Frontline Communique
The State Its In
Squotes
Resources
Links
From Our Correspondence

**Tear gas used by Seattle Police was found to contain carcinogens.**

# CANCER SPRAY

Seattle Police responsible for gassing demonstrators opposing the World Trade Organisation Ministerial conference in November have admitted using a cancer causing chemical against the peaceful protesters. Seattle Police Department 'Material Safety Data Sheets', recently obtained by the Washington Toxins Coalition under the US Public Disclosure Act (the equivalent of the Freedom of Information Act we haven't got), reported that the tear gas used during the week of November 28 1999, was mixed half and half with the solvent methylene chloride.

Methylene chloride, used industrially in paint stripper, is classified as a Category 1 carcinogen by the UK Health and Safety Commission. The American National Library of Medicine's Toxnet website lists symptoms of exposure to the chemical as: "Lethargy, mental confusion, headache, tingling of the limbs, acoustical and optical delusions, and kidney damage, increase risk of spontaneous abortion, coma and death."

Russell Sparks, a student from Bellingham, Washington who was tear gassed on December 1 told SQUALL: " I felt like I was on fire. A middle aged man near me passed out, eyes open, shaking, dry heaving, twitching at the shoulders. I tried to help but my eyes were burning."

Article Two of the Chemical Weapons Convention specifically excludes chemicals used in domestic situations, making it legal for governments to chemically quell riots as they see fit.

A Seattle Police spokesman told SQUALL that aside from their handguns, "all the weapons carried by the police are non lethal". Further comment has been suspended until completion of an internal review of the week's operations. Leon Eski who travelled from Sussex to oppose the WTO, said: "I was gassed and sprayed at least four times totally unprovoked. After

I got home I was short of breath for a week or more, experienced pains in my kidneys and developed mouth ulcers."

Dr Ray Jones, an Open University toxicologist, said: "Methylene chloride will go through the skin quickly and into the blood stream. It is very soluble in fat. Many carcinogens don't take effect for ten, twenty or thirty years, by which time it would be impossible to trace the cause." Jones added that the body would metabolise the chemical into formaldehyde - an even more toxic category three carcinogen. "Spraying methylene chloride onto someone is very irresponsible," he said.

Def-Tec, the Wyoming based company which produced many of the chemical weapons used in Seattle, denied its products had any safety problems. The Seattle Police Department (SPD) received serious criticism over its handling of the protests. Residents of the city's Capitol Hill district complained of gas choking them in their homes. One woman was reported to have miscarried her baby, and SPD Chief Norm Stamper resigned.

An activist tries out his latest footwear

DON'T BOTHER

Child Labour

Profits

NIKE

Police and business go hand in glove- a Nike logo on the Seattle cops' gloves

All pics: Nick Cobbing

# BATTLE FOR SEATTLE
## Wooden bullets and butt plugs on Capital Hill

After spending the afternoon gassing and concussion-bombing union marches, commuters and shoppers in the downtown area, the stormtroopers of Seattle unleashed their most demented attack on the city's bohemian/gay district, Capitol Hill, around midnight on Wednesday December 1st.

Faceless, numberless riot police and national guardsmen shot repeated volleys of two-inch diameter wooden bullets (similar sized rubber bullets were referred to as butt-plugs by protesters), plastic (marble like) pellets, stun grenades, tear gas and pepper spray at a crowd of around 1500 residents and anti-WTO protesters.

"My neighbourhood is under siege by police," said Nikki Reed, a Capitol Hill resident. "There's tear gas in my apartment and a helicopter buzzing my home."

Residents, old and young, had come out to see why the police felt it necessary to set up a 250 officer defence line at the intersection of 11th and Pine. Ex-councillor, Brian Durdowski, took vote canvassing to extremes as he stood besuited in the thick of smoke and missiles, tears pouring down his face saying: "I will not let the police hurt you." The words 'stable door' and 'bolted' sprang to mind. The protesters filled Pine Street and were congregating at the Pine and Broadway crossroads. Despite claiming to 'maintain the downtown curfew zone', the police lines were on the uptown side of the crowd. (Doh!!) When they charged they were in fact pushing people back towards the no go area. Vans of cops were carrying out drive by, indiscriminate, pepper-spraying on Broadway (Think of Stoke Newington Church Street with homeboys). Despite spending three hours of lunacy firing at protesters, the cops never really tried to drive them from the streets.

*AN ORDNANCE MAKING IT ILLEGAL TO CARRY GAS MASKS IN THE CITY HAD BEEN PASSED THAT AFTERNOON. (BUT EVERY COP WORE ONE)*

Cylindrical wooden and rubber bullets were fired at the crowd, gashing wounds on faces and leaving welts on legs and bodies. The thunderflash of exploding stun grenades echoed around the buildings as tear gas cannisters bounced among the protesters (This gas was stronger than the stuff used during tuesday daytime - when vast numbers of press were present - twenty four hours later I can still feel it clogging my chest and have quite intense lower back pains as my kidneys try to eject the poisons). An ordnance making it illegal to carry gas masks in the city had been passed that afternoon (but every cop wore one).
.......protesters scattered, unable to breathe or see, crying out for water.... others helped collapsed casualties by splashing the toxins from their eyes.

Police chief Norm Stamper commended his officerS' "restraint". The only restraint shown that night was by the beseiged residents. The weeks of workshops, non-violence training and arrest solidarity carried out by the Direct Action Network at their 420 Denny Street Studios were being taken to uncomprehending literal extremes. I only saw one missile thrown back at the police lines. Calls of non violence were met by gunfire.

*"I DON'T GIVE A SHIT WHERE YOU COME FROM BUDDY.....BURN THE FUCKING FLAG!"*

Multinational outlets of KFC and Chevron (think Niger Delta and Ogoni massacres) in the area both escaped any damage - the 'non violent protest' crew were still trying to act within the law even when the police had long since rejected legislative restriction or morality. Mayor, Paul Schell, creating a martial law situation, had suspended the constitution within the city.
.One UK protester who asked if any US citizens present would be offended if he torched the stars and stripes was told: "I don' give a shit where ya come from buddy. Burn the fucking flag."
A few took the opportunity of the police-led chaos to do some pocket shopping: "Hey young thugs. Lets go loot the fucking Texaco - they're the fucking KKK."
The morning's attack on the steelworkers' march into the cordoned off downtown area, led the entire workforce of America's west coast dockers to walk out of work in solidarity with the treatment of their union brothers.
Evening demos attracted more arrests and indiscriminate gassing. A planned anti-gentrification action planned for the Belltown district was literally bombed out of existence.

Pic: Nick Cobbing

WAKE UP! WAKE UP! IT'S YER CHUFFED TO BITS !

# SchNEWS

### Printed and Published in Brighton by Justice?

Fri. 10th December 1999    http://www.schnews.org.uk/    **Issue 240    Free/Donation**

THIS IS ANOTHER BENEFIT THAT COMES WITH THE W.T.O. - A POLICE STATE!

# BARE BREASTS & RUBBER BULLETS

*"They never knew what hit them. They had assumed it would be business as usual, the way it had been for decades. Rich men gather, meet, decide the fate of the world, then return home to amass more wealth. It's the way it's always been. Until Seattle."*
Michael Moore, U.S comedian (not director general of the WTO)

" *The very fact that the World Trade Organisation is global headline news is a sign of our power, for the high priests of capital fully expected their summit to be convened in the usual frat\* boy secrecy. We have done our part to help blow away both their cover and their aura of invincibility. Never again will the economists and technocrats be able to decide the fate of the world...in anonymous tranquility."*

The Aggressive Panhandlers\*\*
*"They are worried about a few windows being smashed. They should come and see the violence being done to our communities in the name of liberalisation of trade."* A Philippino leader

As the gas cleared over Seattle after another uneasy stand-off with the black clad robocops, word on the street last Friday was that the talks had collapsed. There would be no millennium round agreement by the World Trade Organisation (WTO). The people on the streets had won a stunning victory.

**And what a victory it was.** Who would have thought, even a year ago, that sixty thousand people would turn to greet delegates of the World Trade Organisation. Who'd have thought that trade unionists would be marching with environmentalists - people dressed as turtles marching with sacked steelworkers, the topless lesbian avengers mingling with farmers. Churchgoers with the anarchist blackblock.

The mass protests helped focus worldwide attention on what the WTO really stands for - and it crumbled under the pressure.

Forget all their talk about 'free trade', the WTO is nothing more than a nasty little organisation fighting for the rights of multinational organisations to dismantle every country's labour and environmental laws (see inside for more details).

Groups like SchNEWS have been shouting from the rooftops for ages about this,

but no one seemed really bothered cos let's face it economics is hardly the sexiest subject in the universe. But last week's event changed all that, with seven days of protest that shook the corporate world.

*"It is important to acknowledge the fact that we made history this week. No amount of corporate spin doctoring or liberal hand wringing can diminish this reality."* The Aggressive Panhandlers

## WHERE'S THE ORGANISATION ?

"My mother's a member of the Women's Institute and they organise their fetes better than this." U.K Trade Minister Steven Byers who went to the WTO and got hit with pepper spray for his trouble.

It started quietly enough on the **Sunday** with a few hundred people demonstrating outside The Gap over the sweatshop conditions workers have to endure to produce the company's clothes. Then on the **Monday** there was a demonstration by the turtle posse pointing out how the WTO had ruled America's Endangered Species Act illegal. Later, French national hero Jose Bove, who recently demolished McDonalds, demonstrated outside his favourite store as a protest against U.S sanctions on French cheese. Things were hotting up. The last thing the U.S President must have expected was to be flying into a city under a state of emergency with the National Guard on the streets?

*"If you were alive, the police gassed you. People coming back from work, kids, women, everyone. People would go out of their houses to see what was happening because these tear gas guns sound like a cannon - and they would get gassed."*

Eyewitness account from Jim Desyllas
**Tuesday** morning and already thousands are on the streets blocking roads and stopping delegates from getting into the WTO Conference centre. The opening ceremony is abandoned and talks delayed for more than five hours.

Around 10 a.m we have a taste of what's to come as riot cops, with 3 foot clubs & dressed like Darth Vader, start spraying CS gas into the faces of people peacefully blocking the roads. One man commented, "When the gas masks came out we knew they were planning to use pepper spray on the people sitting down. The crowd was pleading with them.

We locked legs and arms and I pulled a bandana over my face, covering my mouth and eyes. People began screaming in pain. I felt a blow from a club, the cops were beating people as well. A police officer pulled my hand away from my face and pepper-sprayed me in the eyes. The rest of the crowd pulled people to safety and began washing their eyes with a solution of baking soda and water to counter the effects of the blinding pepper spray."

By mid-day 30,000 trade unionists joined the demonstrations, "I'm not a trade barrier" reads the marching turtles' banner; giant puppets weave their way down the streets, superheroes slide round corners, cloaks flying, a group of Father Christmases march along waving at the crowd, doubling over with laughter, "WTO? Ho, ho, ho." A Reclaim The Streets sound system blasts out funk, rappers rhyming "WTO, it's gotta go". SchNEWS meet Mexican, Indian and French farmers, Tibetan refugees, steelworkers, striking cabbies, anti logging and deforestation protesters, all experts on the WTO, its power and its direct repercussions on their lives. These people are no random mob, they have gathered from all over the world to be heard and no matter how many issues are at stake here they speak with one voice, united in their opposition to an institution which has no respect for the ordinary people of the world. They are calling for an end to sweatshops, to child labour and the erosion of environmental laws and the third world debt. These people are well informed, well organised and determined.

As one Labour correspondent put it, *"Ten years ago, who would have thought that Teamsters and kids in dreadlocks would be marching together, let alone under the banner of 'fair trade'?* "I never got on with environmentalists until I realised we were all fighting for the same thing," said Dan Petrowski, a Michigan steelworker who was made redundant four months ago. Still, what did that matter to the police who lost patience with the crowd spraying them with jets of gas like water cannons again and again?

SCHNEWS US-UK VOCAB WATCH
\* Frat - fraternity, secret student society.
\*\* P a n h a n d l e r s - b e g g a r s

**SPECIAL SCHNEWS REPORT ON SEVEN DAYS THAT SHOOK THE CORPORATE WORLD**

Meanwhile, groups of anarchists went shopping. McDonalds, Niketown, Gap, Starbucks and the American Bank all had their windows smashed. One man from the UK told SchNEWS, *"Even as a pacifist I was pleased. No-one was hurt. It seemed trivial in comparison to the scenes I had witnessed earlier. This wasn't violence against people it was violence against the property of some of the world's most hated multinationals."*

As early evening approached with the crowds remaining on the streets, and the Clinton adminsistration leaning on the mayor to do something quick, the National Guard were called out for the first time in Seattle in modern times. A no-protest zone and a 12 hour curfew placed in the downtown area - the first time since the second world war. This seemed to be the signal for the robo-cops to unleash an arsenal of weapons against anyone who got in their way for the next 24 hours. SchNEWS is used to a bit of argy-bargy with the police but this was something else.

## BUTT-PLUGGIN' IN THE USA

"Hey! Check it out - these motherfuckers are firing butt-plugs at us," called out one grinning member of the crowd brandishing a two by four inch rubber bullet.

As night drew in the forces of darkness began pushing people into the the city's bohemian/gay district, the Capitol Hill residential area. This was way out of the no-protest zone, and it infuriated locals who came out of the streets in their hundreds. Seattle Gay News takes up the story. "Numerous accounts from witnesses all describe excessive force by police who appeared to have no real reason to be on Capitol Hill. The area is outside of the curfew and no-protest zones. One resident told us, "I haven't been marching, but when the cops turn your neighbourhood into a war zone, it's time to get involved."

WEDNESDAY *"The intolerance of democratic dissent, which is a hallmark of dictatorship was unleashed in full force."* Vandana Shiva, director of Research Foundation New Delhi.

Early morning and the mass arrests begin. If yesterday's show of force by the authorities was meant to scare people from demonstrating then they were mistaken. Thousands of people are regrouping at a steelworkers rally. People grow restless at the speeches and start leaving for the no-protest zone. "Whose streets? Our streets" everyone chants. One man explained to SchNEWS what happened next, *"Eventually we were pushed onto the main road with shoppers, protesters, cars, buses. They're not going to gas us here, are they? I thought. A second later an explosion followed by a barrage of plastic bullets, gas, pepper spray, concussion grenades. Mental. People sitting in their cars were gassed, people leaving work. Everyone."*

The police say they are using non-lethal weapons but one man reports listening to a local radion station when a man calls in weeping - his wife had been attacked by the police while leaving work and they lost their child - she was 4 months pregnant. A doctor blamed this on the gas.

It's getting scary, the town centre is emptying of people as the curfew approaches. The police are roaming around everywhere, kitted-out in the most bizzare Stormtrooper meets Ninja Turtle outfits and riding everything from bicycles to a huge tank-like thing, inappropriately named the 'Peacekeeper'. If you aren't falling head over heels with laughter, your legs are being shot out from under you by rubber bullets!

Still, if it's scary for the demonstrators at least the WTO delegates aren't having much fun. One New Zealand delegate confides in us that there is confusion inside the conference, and in the evening everyone is holed up in their hotels unable to leave.

## THURSDAY

Residents and students march, chanting, from Capitol Hill to join a farmers rally, "Ain't no power like the power of the people 'cos the power of the people don't stop". Thousands then march towards the County Jail where hundreds of protestors are being held, most not giving even their names. The jail is surrounded by people holding hands. A temporary autonomous zone is established as people keep vigil, sleeping, eating, making music and speeches demanding the release of our brothers and sistas. A party evolves outside the jail as people drum, sing, juggle and dance, chanting "This is what democracy looks like". At the windows we can see the silhouettes of prisoners arms waving as they dance in solidarity.

## FRIDAY EVENING

These people just don't give up. A couple of hundred have gathered at the Westin Hotel to support some people who have d-locked themselves to the hotel's entrance.

It's here that SchNEWS hears the news - the talks have collapsed. There will be no millennium round. It doesn't quite sink in.

Inside the Conference centre, the delegates from the poorer countries complained that they were being sidelined, while the world's elite held secret 'green room discussions'. Most of the world's poorest countries have neither the capacity nor the means to implement even the previous round of talks which finished five years ago, let alone take on board a whole new round of negotiations, and couldn't even afford to have a permanent representative in Geneva where the rolling talks are held. (30 countries couldn't even afford to send delegates to Seattle!).

One high-level U.S. journalist said, "The talks failed because of the protests. They failed because of the chaos. They failed because Clinton pushed the labour working group. And they failed because the Southern hemisphere rebelled." The U.S. labour movement forced the Clinton Administration to ensure a working group on labour, which would, in particular, seek to eliminate all global child labour and encourage unionisation. Clinton's speech served to enhance the irony when the Mayor of Seattle declared a "no protest zone" around the Niketown and Nordstrom department stores but encouraged people to keep shopping there. The citizens of Seattle were free to shop for merchandise made in sweatshops, they just couldn't complain about

## WE WON YOU BASTARDS

*" We want a new millennium based on economic democracry, not economic totalitarianism. The future is possible for humans and other species only if the principles of competition, organised greed, commodification of all life, monocultures, monopolies and centralised global corporate control of our daily lives enshrined in the WTO are replaced by the principles of protection of people and nature, the obligation of giving and sharing diversity, and the decentralisation and self-organisation enshrined in our diverse cultures and national constitutions."* Vandana Shiva

What SchNEWS did see last week was how the thin veil of democracy so easily falls away when those in power are really threatened. That the Chief of Police has since resigned gives some indication of how out of control the robo-cops were.

**But what was far more important was that ordinary people made history last week. The thousands of diverse groups that had come together to challenge the corporate power that is taking over our world. And for a week at least, we won.**

## ACTS OF SOLIDARITY

* The Longshore and Warehouse Union shut down the Port of Seattle and dozens of ports along the West Coast.

* Seattle taxi-drivers chose November 30th to strike over worsening pay and conditions. When SchNEWS asked one taxi-driver about Starbucks he told us us, "I don't drink there - they're capatalist bastards." And what if other taxi-drivers break the strike? "They'll get shot buddy!" Just like English cabbies eh?

* The Firebrigade Union refused to turn their fire hoses upon the protesters despite repeated requests from the police.

* One delivery boy handed over his pizzas to the demonstrators outside the Westin Hotel, rather than give them to the right-wing talk radio station presenters who had ordered them.

## SOME OF THE BEST BANNERS

'If you think the WTO is bad you should hear about capitalism'; 'Eat pussy, not cows' (that one courtesy of the Lesbian Avengers).

'WTO - practice safe trade' (on a massive green condom made of 30 foods)

## WTO LUCKY DIP

After riots in Geneva and Seattle SchNEWS asks what city will be the lucky winners for the

## SO THIS IS FREE TRADE?

Many western multi-nationals hop and skip between the North and South, relocating to discourage unionisation or to keep wages low. Nike first started to manufacture its trainers in Taiwan and South Korea. When workers attempted to organise for better wages in the 1970's, Nike pulled out and started production in the Peoples Republic of China and Vietnam, where the workers can be paid 19 cents or less an hour to produce $100 trainers.

# WORLD TYRANNY ORDER

*"The rules set by the secretive WTO violate principles of human rights and ecological survival. They violate rules of justice and sustainability. They are rules of warfare against the people and the planet. Changing these rules is the most important democratic and human rights struggle of our times. It is a matter of survival."* Vandana Shiva, Director of the Research Foundation for Science and Ecology

The World Trade Organization isn't familiar to most people, but it should be. It is, essentially, our unelected global government. Again and again we hear homage to the 'free market'. 'Liberalisation' is the mantra of global decision making, Reduce government rules and the free market will bring about economic growth which benefits us all, we are promised.

But reality is very different. For most of the world, we are anything but free. The giant multinationals are concentrating power and wealth at an alarming rate. Just one man, **Bill Gates, has as much money as 450 million of the world's poorest people.** The WTO has become the vehicle for liberalisation, with the multinationals at the wheel. It has the power to punish governments who 'interfere' with free trade, leaving the field wide open for multinationals in pursuit of profit.

## WHAT'S THE SCORE, CORPORATE WHORE?

The WTO came into existence on the 1st January 1995 promising the world enormous economic gains. Instead its rulings have produced a "race to the bottom" in labour, social and environmental laws. Since it was created, every environmental, health or safety policy it has had to rule on, has been deemed an illegal trade barrier.

In fact the very threat of being taken to the WTO court has made countries water down legislation . And who makes these rulings? The majority of the tribunals are made up of men that meet in secret in Geneva, relying on documents never made public and on anonymous "experts" to make decisions and issue reports that the public cannot see until the hearing, There is no appeal procedure. Once a tribunal has declared a country's law WTO illegal, the country must change its law or facetradesanctions.

Developing countries generally do not have the money and expertise either to bring cases to the WTO or defend themselves before the WTO, thus enabling powerful companies and countries to flex their muscles, make threats and generally act like bully boys.

*"In its short five years of existence, the WTO has had wide-ranging impacts on jobs, wages and livelihoods and on international and domestic environmental, health and food safety laws as well as economic development, human rights, global trade and investment. These impacts have not been systematically studied nor have they been well covered in the press. As a consequence, most people around the globe lack an awareness that their lives, livelihoods, food and environment - indeed, their very futures - are being shaped by a powerful new institution."* Vandana Shiva
Public Citizen

### DON'T BELIEVE US?

*"Free trade is not leading to freedom; it is leading to slavery. Diverse life forms are being enslaved through patents on life, farmers are being enslaved into hi-tech slavery, and countries are being enslaved into debt and dependence and destruction of their domestic economies."*
Vandana Shiva

---

Here are just some of the lesser known examples in the WTO's 'Race To The Bottom'

### U.S. Weakens Clean Air Act

The first attack on environmental laws came just a few months after the WTO was introduced. Venezuela challenged a US Clean Air Act regulation that required gas refiners to produce cleaner petrol. Venuzuela claimed it was biased against foreign refiners who could not meet the high standards. Despite getting no-where by lobbying Congress or by appealing through the state courts, the usual democratic and judicial systems, they finally went to the newly established, unelected, unaccountable WTO.
A WTO panel ruled against the US law as it was a barrier to Venuzuelan trade, allowing countries to now export dirty petrol which results in ozone depletion, smog, health problems, etc.

### Child labour

In WTO rulings, there is no discrimination (good so far..) between products on the basis of *where* or *how* they are produced ( Oh..) It is the final product to be traded that counts, at the minimum possible cost, rather than the conditions under which the product is made. Child labour, forced labour and sweat-shops all help to bring the cost of trading down and keep the WTO bully-boys happy.

### Voluntary eco-labelling could be illegal

Eco-labelling is a hot and sweaty subject in the WTO, with many far reaching consequences if they ever reach a final verdict. Labelling gives a consumer choice between ethical and non ethical products. It doesn't mean that companies must abide by certain ecologically sound standards, rather it is an incentive for certain companies to make their products more appealing to the ethical consumer. The WTO is pushing to forbid such distinctions as it discriminates products on the basis of where and how particular goods are made ( see 'child labour example'), which is WTO illegal. The choice for ethical consumption therefore becomes a barrier to trade. In the case of "dolphin safe" labelling on tuna in the US, despite much publicity over the issue, fisherfolk are still allowed to use the large nets that kill dolphins, and use the dolphin safe labels, as long as they return to shore claiming that no dolphins were caught in their net.

### GMO labelling is WTO-illegal

Likewise, potentially damaging foodstuffs are not allowed to be distinguished from definitely safe alternatives. Hazards such as allergies to hidden ingredients, and the ethical choices of vegetarians and religious believers are entirely overlooked . US delegates are hell bent on protecting industry at any costs. This is despite polls showing 93% of Americans favour labelling of gmo products.

### WTO limits access to medicines in poor nations

Patents are the ultimate in corporate ownership, giving pharmaceutical companies exclusive rights on particular medication, taking control of local markets and resources. After 7 years of US pressure and threats, Thailand finally gave in and amended its 1992 Patent law by disbanding their Pharmaceutical Review Board (PRB), which controlled medical prices in the country, as it went against WTO rules.

### Infant Formula Law weakened

Guatamala passed a law, based on the World Health Organisation (WHO) code, restricting the *promotion* of infant baby milk formula over breast milk for infants. This included banning packaging and advertising that may mislead illiterate parents into associating the formula with the good health

---

of their child. This infuriated Gerber Foods, multinational baby food manufacturers, whose trademark depicts a fat healthy baby. Gerber threatened Guatamala with WTO action under its Trademark Protection laws. The mere threat of WTO action was taken seriously by the Guatamalan Government who subsequently changed their law in favour of Gerber! Milk substitutes have been responsible for the deaths of 1.5 million infants a year according to UNICEF.

### Small business over megastores

The WTO pampers to the needs of multinational companies rather than small localised businesses. Many of the trading rules implemented actually work adversely for smaller companies; chartering banks in foreign countries, relocating factories, acquiring foreign firms and global marketing campaigns.

### Burmese dictatorship law challenged

Massachusetts stopped contracts with companies that have links with Burma, a nation renowned for human rights abuses through its military regime. This action protects the tax-payer from supporting the dictatorship. Yet by considering human rights issues, the WTO claims that Burma is at a disadvantage. Military dictatorship is, after all, irrelevant to trade (Hmmm..).

### CANADA GROVELLING TO WTO

Canada has been one of the leading advocates in asking other nations to rethink their environmental laws in accordance with WTO standards. Canada is intent on selling off its old growth forests and natural resources, reducing their own environmental protection budgets by more than 40%, in the drive for economic profit. Canada is concerned over the EU's decision to restrict both the consumption of seal pelts and the purchases of furs from animals trapped in inhumane ways. Canada wants to continue and spread the sales of seal skins and wild animal furs trapped in the north. Canadian lumber industries are also concerned at some European countries' decisions to restrict purchases of wood and paper products that are clear cut or come from old growth forests. Canadian industries are challenging these environmental decisions using the under WTO to try to force the countries to buy Canada's wood and paper clear cut from their last old growth forests.
Canadian agricultural officials are also using the WTO to challenge the US food and school lunch vouchers system. If the vouchers are defined as "domestic agricultural subsidies" then the whole welfare system may be come under the tyrannical boot of the WTO.
And don't forget Asbestos-the French have banned the substance.So Canada, one of the world's largest exporters of the lovely substance cried out for their trade chums in the WTO to sort out the French. Canada has claimed that even if the ban doesn't violate any WTO rules, then they are at least eligible for compensation as it impairs the expected trade benefits promised to them in the last Round of WTO negotiations.

**According to the United Nations, in almost all developing countries that have undertaken rapid trade liberalisation, wage inequality has increased, most often in the context of declining industrial employment of unskilled workers and large absolute falls in their real wages, in the order of 20-30% in Latin American countries.**

# WHAT HAPPENED IN JAIL

Up to 600 people were arrested herded onto buses and taken to a nearby naval base. Most refused to get off the buses after being denied solicitors and went for over 13 hours without food or water. The next day people were taken to the County jail where many were tortured. One man Bistro said he was denied phone calls for 50 hours and had his glasses removed which were never returned to him. He was in leg irons and handcuffs for fourteen hours. During the tear gassing session downtown (the day before he was arrested), he decided to lie down until the police had run past him. When he thought they had run past, he lifted his hat off his face, and at that moment two officers held him down, took out canisters of tear gas, unscrewed the tops, and then poured the tear gas directly into his eyes. The medics who treated him were afraid that he would suffer permanent eye damage and poured water into his eyes for two hours. But this was nothing compared to what he and 47 other prisoners experienced in the downtown jail. Prisoners were attacked by "henchmen" who locked the protesters together in a circle with handcuffs and leg irons. The prisoners were then separated. Bistro witnessed guards spinning men with dreadlocks around in circles above the ground by their hair. "The guards continued to assert that [they had developed] a new science and that there will never be a wound." Then he related this 'new science', which was a form of torture that involved bending the arm back and twisting the fingers.

## EYE WITNESS REPORT

"There was an old lady there. She had gone downtown by bus to buy something, This lady was in her 70s and I saw her trying to run, but she couldn't breathe. She was in shock. I carried her to a building entryway. She was gasping, terrified. She had been in Germany, and it was like she was having flashbacks. The tear gas sounds like gunfire and there were helicopters overhead, sirens, cops on horses, everything. So anyway there I was with her in this building and she wanted to go to the hospital but there was tear gas everywhere and I was afraid if I tried to move her she'd be gassed again. I went to this line of cops and begged - I mean begged - these riot police

to help her. They ignored me. They shot rubber bullets from four feet away into the face of a guy next to me, broke all his front teeth. I want to emphasise, these protesters were NOT violent people. They were the most non-violent people I have ever seen. Even when I was screaming at the cop, this girl came up to me and said, "Do not scream. This is non-violent." These people were too much to believe. They must meditate all the time."

## EYEWITNESS REPORT

"The local news stations were reporting on the broken windows of businesses and not the broken bones of protesters. They reported on things like 'police fatigue.' Which I assume is when your arms get tired after you beat people for hours. They talked - and continue to talk about - the extreme 'restraint, open mindedness, and gentleness' displayed by police."

## VIOLENCE BY THE NUMBERS

Estimated number of people shot with rubber bullets by police: 500 +

Estimated number of people shot with rubber bullets by protesters: 0

Estimated number of people gassed and pepper-sprayed by police: 1,000 - 3,000

Estimated number of people gassed and pepper-sprayed by protestors: 0

**Essential website**
**www.indymedia.org**

## *Subscribe!*

# AND IT WASN'T JUST SEATTLE

**UK London: Euston station:** Readers probably know the score. 2000 demonstrators turned up to protest against the privitisation of the underground. An unmarked cop van was overturned who then took over half an hour and several attempts to set the van on fire! Finally the van caught and was surrounded by around 30 photographers, at which moment police decided to clear the station . Lots of good media-riot shots, and - well SchNEWS is not one to get all conspiratoral and paranoid but the very next day the papers are full of stuff about the new Prevention of Terrorism Act (if you're interested in this campaign email news@bigissue.com ) The Construction Safety Campaign held a demonstration outside the **Canadian Embassy,** because Canada are presently trying to get the WTO to overturn a decision to ban asbestos.

The **Lewisham** branch of Citibank was picketed by students. The bank is one of the major holders of student loan debt. This follows the global trend to underfund and privatise services, such as education, as part of the expansion of free trade with student grants being scrapped in favour of personal loans. **Covent Garden** magistrates court: The President of Nigeria, and Shell were put on trial by Nigerian exiles and British environmental activists. President Obasanjo, and Mark Moody-Stuart (of Royal-Dutch/Shell) faced a people's court to answer a number of charges relating to human rights abuses and environmental devastation in the Niger Delta. Unfortunately this was only street theatre and not the real thing.In **Leeds** city centre, around 50 protesters were faced by over 300 while they handed leaflets outside scummy companies. .In **Halifax** a Nestle factory was occupied and a banner dropped outside.A procession marched through the centre of **Cardiff** calling for the WTO to be scrapped.A disused garage and an old toll house, soon to be "luxury flats" were squatted in **Totnes, South Devon.**

**Holland: Amsterdam:** Wot no plane ticket? No problem, 100 cheeky Dutch activists turned up at Schipol Airport where official WTO sponsors Lufthansa, Northwest Airways and United Airlines had planes going to Seattle. Unable to blag tickets for this year's party in Seattle the protesters held a sit down in the check-in hall.

**Italy: Padua:** A peaceful demo in front of the genetics Exhibition "Bionova" attended by the top managers of GMO companies was attacked by the police. **Milan:** A group of 'White Coveralls' occupied a McDonald's, locking themselves on the building front and hanging enormous banners denouncing neo-liberism and its effects.**Rome:** Another group of White Coveralls occupied the HQ of the "National Committee for Biosafety", hanging banners against GMOs and the WTO.

**Germany: Berlin:** A parade was held in the city with demonstrators carrying banners with mock slogans and banners demanding more order, more security and 'wealth for eels' (a pun on 'wealth for all') confusing the local police who busied themselves protecting luxurious restaurants and expensive shops. **France:** Altogether 80,000 people joined protests across the country. **Paris:** 20,000 gathered to express a range of complaints, for example some made the link between the WTO and Mumia Abu Jamal, the black activist currently facing the death sentence in the U.S. The week before 5,000 French farmers with their sheep, ducks and goats feasted on regional products under the Eiffel Tower. **Toulouse:** Small groups invaded the main commercial street of the town with a sound-system and hung big anti-WTO signs on Christmas decorations with long sticks as subversive Father Christmases were busy giving capitalist rotten fruits to passer-by. **Dijon:** 40 activists occupied the Dijon Industry and Business Institute and a bank agency in the financial district. While 10 of them wearing D.I.Y "Enslaved By Money?" shirts where block-

ing off the entrances of the two buildings using D-locks and arm-tubes, other groups threw fake blood and money on the pavements, glued posters on the walls and shops around, put up banners, played loud metallic drums, screamed in megaphones, gave out free tea, coffee and flyers about capitalism, anarchism and sustainable D.I.Y alternatives.800 miners clashed with cops , ransacking a tax office and burning cars in 2 towns in eastern France.

**Iceland:** Anti-american protests targetted a military base and the U.S embassy demanding "Yanks out" (a promise still unkept since WWII).

**Czech Republic: Prague:** Food Not Bombs served up, and supermarkets were leafletted.

**Turkey:**The Working Group of Turkey Against the MAI (that's the ill-fated Multinational Agreement On Investment, folks) and Globalisation held a nine day 3,500 km march from Nov. 22nd-30th against the WTO and global capitalism. In Bergama, there were protests against the Eurogold Corporation, which plans to operate a gold mine there using cyanide-based extraction methods and against seplanned thermal and nuclear power plants.

**Switzerland:Geneva:** At the home of the WTO, 5,000 people demonstrated, farmers gathered at the UN building and city folk marching on the international banking district. Meanwhile, electricity was cut at the WTO HQ for 2 hours.

**India:Bangalore:** Several thousand farmers from the district of Kamataka gathered to protest at the central train station before headeding towards Mahatma Gandhi's statue. At the end of the demo they issued a 'Quit India' notice to Monsanto, telling them to leave the country or face direct action. Another notice was issued to the Indian Institute of Science, which has permitted Monsanto to do its research work in its premises.**Anjar (Narmada Valley):** A demonstration with bullock-carts took place, with more than 1000 people from around 60 villages participating in a colourful procession.New Delhi: 500 participated in a 3-day Dharna (sit-in) at Raj Ghat, where Mahatma Gandhi's ashes are buried, to protest against a proposed dam in Maheshwar. The following day 11,000 protest postcards were delivered to the German embassy while a demo took place outside asking them to pull out of the project. Later a statue symbolising the WTO was burned at Raj Ghat, and the 500 activists committed themselves to Gandhi's vision of a self-reliant, sustainable, solidarity-based India composed of village republics. The week before, 300 scaled the fence of the World Bank building, covering it with posters, grafitti, cow shit and mud, while others sang slogans and traditional songs at the gate.The **Philippines:Manila:** 8,000 union members and activists attended rallies in front of the US Embassy and near the Presidential palace to protest Philippine membership of the WTO.

**Central Philippines:** Thousands attended rallies against the 1995 Mining Act, which allows 100 percent foreign equity in local projects but has been challenged by tribespeople who say natural resources are a heritage that should not be exploited by overseas companies. There were actions in loads more countries but we don't know what they were. So there! * There's a meeting to discuss further tactics in the light of the failure of the Seattle WTO Ministerial meeting on Sat 15 Jan, 2pm Conway Hall, Red Lion Square, London WC1.

## *...and finally...*

After the protests comes a shopping plea *"Downtown merchants say the best way to help now is to shop"* reports the Seattle Post-Intelligencer*"Boy, it they want to help us, come down and shop,"*

**disclaimer** May the force be with you, readers. And we don't mean the fucking police force

Cor blimley:- last week SchNEWS said we want a safe and privitised railway system. We meant nationalised.

Keep SchNEWS FREE! Send 1st Class stamps (e.g. 20 for next 20 issues) or donations (payable to Justice?) Ask for "Originals" if you can make copies. Post *free* to all prisoners. SchNEWS, c/o on-the-fiddle, P.O. Box 2600, Brighton, East Sussex, BN2 2DX.

*Tel/Autofax* : +44 (0)1273 685913 *GET IT EVERY WEEK BY E-MAIL:* schnews@brighton.co.uk

## WAKE UP! WAKE UP! END OF THE 20TH CENTURY FOR YER

# Weekly SchNEWS

### Printed and Published in Brighton by Justice?

**17th December, 1999**   http://www.schnews.org.uk/   **Issue 241   Free/Donation**

# More S&M than M&S

"It is no exaggeration to say that this decision will have the most disastrous impact on the UK textile industry for more than half a century.... they are guilty of an act of cold-blooded betrayal"
Des Farrell, National Secretary GMB Union.

Marks and Sparks, that good old fashioned British institution, whose carrier bags once boasted that they sold only British-made goods have now ditched that sales ploy in a desperate bid to placate angry shareholders who have seen their cash go down the pan.

M&S's overpriced and sub standard clothing has been blamed for their staggering 43% fall in profits this year. In a bid to recoup these losses they have resorted to the new trendy fashion (popularised by GAP) of employing child labor to churn out the same old tat. Their recent run of "bad luck" has also seen M&S plummet from 11th to 151st in the most admired companies poll revealed in this months "Managment Today" (see back page).

M&S said they would use "aggression and determination not seen before" in a bid to restore those oh-so important profit margins. All mouth and no trousers? These lot are all crappy trousers and no morals. The threatened aggression was demonstrated last month when they cancelled contracts with British textile firms in favour of buying clothes manufactured in dodgy foreign back-street sweatshops making 4,000 workers, mainly women, jobless & cashless in time for Christmas! (goodwill to all men and the seasonal tinkle ofcash registers-consumer heaven) Not so cheering for Santa's little helpers in Indonesia working for for less than 50p for a 10-hour day.  With 1 in 4 of the UK's 300,000 textile workers employed solely in making goods for M&S, more redundancies are expected in the New Year pushing the number up to at least 8,000. Can't you just hear their hot toddy glasses clinking as the company directors congratulate themselves on their business prowess, and tough shit to the trusty employees of yesteryear.

"M&S say their customers don't care where their clothes are made" says Des Farrell of the General Municipal Boilermakers, who will be demonstrating on British highstreets in the run up to Xmas in a desperate bid to mobilise consumer power to save these workers jobs.

Stella Rimmington, ex boss of MI5 has been hired to track down a new director for the corporation using all her secret service skills. Ms Rimmingtons appointment comes complete with security worthy of the frosty spy catcher. SchNEWS was informed by M&S that they were not prepared to answer questions over the phone but would send a glossy greenwashed propoganda pamphlet to interested parties. We're still waiting!!! It has proved easier to find info about the highly secretive Bilderberg group than good old M&S.(For more info on the Bilderberg group see the SchNEWS web site.) Presumably their investigations into this interested party have revealed an unhealthy preocupation with parties of the techno variety.

Indonesian trade union and labour rights advisers have pulled-up M&S on switching their production to the Indonesian textile industry and investing in clothing produced by grossly underpaid child labourers. They have revealed that working conditions in the factories M&S patronise are so bad that employees are developing chronic health problems made worse by living in slum conditions as a result of their shitty wages.

So, to be a happie shopper, next time you're in M&S check the label b4 you buy, and remember folks, don't get palmed off with all that sweatshop bollox, let them know you've had enough of our high street stores putting profits before people, we ain't buying it any longer. Keep the Xmas stress levels down by buying your pressies from ethically-sound shops who are members of British Fair Trade Shops Or better still, don't bother shopping at all.

## DOWN THE PAN 2

The Teigngrace campaign has had its second and final victory this week. In brief the open cast mine company,Watts, Blake and Bearne (WBB) dig up beautiful stretches of land to mine for white china clay which is then exported to Germany to make toilets. The Germans were shitting faster than the company could find clay, so they decided to extend their quarry, which meant redirecting two rivers, trashing old orchards and digging up badger sets. A camp was set up in the summer of '97 to call for a public enquiry, which they got.

Two years later the villagers of Teigngrace have just won the public enquiry! WBB are to pay £100,000 in costs to both the Teigngrace Parish Council and the Devon Wildlife Trust. The land is now in the pipeline to become a SSSI (Site of Special Scientific Interest) Nice- One! ps. SchNews would like to note that plans on how to build compost toilets are now available in German from all recommended retail outlets.

**SchNEWS FAREWELL MESSAGE FOR THE MILLENNIUM**
SchNEWS is having a three week winter break cos we deserve it. Unless the Millennium Bug nutters were right and civilisation collapses, the next issue will be out on **7th January 2000**. Now, if you're looking for a New Years resolution why not help SchNEWS out next year. Although it's only two bits of A4 and therefore obviously isn't much work at all (honest), somehow it miraculously comes out most weeks. But we can always do with more people getting involved. So, why not come along to our next Training Day on 12th January... Ring to book your place now.
* If you bought raffle ticket numbers 5, 32 or 60 at our birthday bash and want to claim your prize give the office a ring quick sharp.

# BIG UP BIG BUSINESS

After the collapse of of the World Trade Organisation talks in Seattle (see last weeks SchNEWS) the Financial Times has been whinging on that people are increasingly seeing big business in a bad light. So SchNEWS would like to repair some of that damage by reporting on the "Oscar's of the British business world." At the beginning of this festive month Tesco scooped the award, given by Management Today, for the most admired company for a record breaking three consecutive years, while Sir John Browne of BP Amoco won Britain's most admired Chief Executive.

**TESCOS** out of town shopping centres –get 3 green-sites destroyed for the price of 2!

**BP AMOCO** Top-dog polluters of land, sea & air with dodgy connections to the Colombian military

**Runners-up include SchNEWS faves like**

**VODAPHONE** Who backed the Newbury By-pass, then got permission to build a massive new HQ in greenbelt land beside it, after bribing Newbury Council that they'd leave if they didn't get their own way.

**GRANADA GROUP** As the Public Sector Privitisation Unit told SchNEWS "Even though Granada are on the low pay commission, they actually fought hard to keep the minimum wage as low as possible." Cos we all know pay keeps yer profits higher.

**UNILEVER** You might not have heard of these people but they are one of the worlds biggest food and household goods corporations and they've got their dirty little fingers in every pie from tea plantations (they own 20% of the tea-market) to animal testing. They're also big on human rights – which is why they lobbied the World Trade Organisation (remember them?) to get them to overturn a Massachusett's law which refused to award public contracts to companies that do business with Burma.

**ASTRA-ZENECA** We have this lovely company to thank for the first introduction of commercial gm novel foods to Europe, in the form of tomatoe puree.

SchNews just can't see why big business are having such a hard time and so would like all our readers to use this the season of goodwill as an opportunity to love thy corporate neighbour and spend, spend, spend making sure they've got enough capital for the next millennium.

\* According to some estimates, the value of City Christmas bonuses could exceed £1 billion to be shared out amongst a few thousand how-do-they-manage-living-on-the- breadline stock-brokers, investment bankers and the like. Again we ask our readers to spare a thought for them this Yuletide.

Or maybe take out a subscription to Corporate Watch magazine, 16b Cherwell St., Oxford, OX4 1BG www.corporatewatch.org. Send an SAE for a copy of their resources list with all the dirt on the oil industry, supermarkets, genetics etc.

\* \*Is somebody taking the piss - this year's American Business Ethic award was on its way to McDonalds when the whistle was blown by an animal rights group that McDonalds mistreat their animals before killing them and sticking them in buns.

Business Ethics magazine reckoned the company deserved the gold-star award for its "excellence in environmental management" such as recycling. (SchNEWS points out, if people ate off proper plates with knives and forks in the first place, then there wouldn't be a problem with recycling.) The magazine added, "We see you as a giant that is trying to step carefully." Pass the recycled sick bag.

## SchNEWS in brief

**French firefighters**, some of them wearing gasmasks, clashed with police by the Eiffel Tower this week, tearing down protective barriers and throwing stones and bottles injuring 53 coppers. Rather ironically, the police used water cannons on the firefighters who want earlier retirement and their job's officially considered a "risky profession", which would provide them with extra benefits.**

There's a **Winter Solstice** Celebration and Full Moon Party at Catherines Hill, Twyford Down, Wincester. (Dec 21/22). They need yurts/domes to stay warm and cosy and a Tarmac director for a pagan sacrifice. Bring booze and cake! Tel 01248 75039 email sop04@bangor.ac.uk ** **Primal seeds** "exists to challenge corporate domination of the global seed supply." www.primalseeds.org **
**Spiral**, is a new womens centre in a environmentally-welcoming squat at 402 QueensBridge Rd, Dalston E8, free entry. For info 01712542227 or Email-ROSTENKA@Netscapeonline.com **

**Leonard Peltier**, the imprisoned Indian leader who has been languashing in an American jails for the past 23 years has just written a book, 'Prison Writings: My Life Is My Sun Dance' published by St. Martin's Press. ** A new camp has been set up to defend **Stanton Moor** in the Derbyshire part of the peak district. The site is under threat from a proposed quarry development that recieved planning permission in 1952 - permission that would never be approved if it went up for planning now. The camp has good local support, especially since the quarry company has been threatening villagers with violence, including a local shop for having a stop the quarry petition! Tel 07977748436. HTTP:/pages.zoom.co.uk/~nineladies

## NARMADA OFFICES RANSACKED

The Save The Narmada River campaign office in Gujerat, India, has been ransacked, and an activist threatened at knife-point, by pro-dam vigilantes. The campaign is fighting against the destruction of their valley against a series of large dams that is already displacing hundreds of tribal folk from their ancestral land. The issue is sensitive in Gujerat as many people have been duped by the widespread propaganda of the State Government who, needless to say, have vested interests in the proposed Narmada dams.

Six men stormed the building .The one activist in at the time was beaten up, held at gun and knife point, and told to leave Gujarat or face dire consequences. Documents were burnt, the computer was destroyed, and money was stolen. The office has been receiving threatening calls since October, warning the protesters that they will be killed if they do not leave the state.

For an excellent lowdown on the campaign, read For The Greater Common Good by Arandhati Roy.

For more info contact narmadauk@yahoo.com

## GLEN OF THE COMEDOWNS

Last week, the supreme court rejected an appeal by environmentalists who have been trying to stop the building of a £20million dual carriageway through the Glen of the Downs.

The Glen is a beautiful broad leafed forest between the Sugar Loaf mountains in north county Wicklow. Wicklow County Council widening and expanding the Arklow-Dublin road, linking Larne with Paris. The men and machines are bludgeoning miles of oak, beach and hazel, and aim to cut down 2000 trees. The Glen of the Downs was proposed as a Special Area of Conservation (SAC) by Dúchas, the Irish Government's heritage service, and should enjoy the protection of European Law. However, bureaucratic bullshit came to the rescue of the forces of environmental destruction as officials took 4 years too long to send a list of SAC sites to the EU, prompting them to threaten withholding Structural Funds from Ireland.

Eviction of the longest Irish road protest started on 10th December, and despite lock-ons and people up trees, some trees were felled because there weren't enough people to defend the whole site, so ring the number below and get yerselves down there.

What with roads being a much more eco friendly method of transport than trains, as part of the National Development Plan, the National Roads Authority received £4.8 billion, while the public train system received nothing. Ireland, long famed for its unbelievable traffic jam and congestion caused by the fast pace of modern life, may soon breathe a sigh of relief. According to the National Road Authority, "there will never be another traffic jam in Ireland. Congestion can become an unpleasant memory for the people of Ireland." Just like the trees and habitat they nurture. Directions etc from Dublin Friends of the Earth: 0035 31497 3773/373 or website www.emc23.tp/glen/news.htm

**Urgent:** Hockley Protest camp in Essex, set up to prevent 66 luxury houses being built on greenbelt land, is being evicted too. People desperately needed. Tel: 08381 717815 for directions and info.

## FOOD GRAB

Last week the Chateau Champlain hotel in Montreal, was invaded by the "Commando-bouffe" who 'reappropriated' buffet food and brought it outside to a 100 + waiting support demo. People then marched along a street chanting slogans, eating and giving food to beggers and street people. The bouff commented "These food-grab actions are done during the Christmas season, when we hear all this crap about helping the poor and homeless. The poor should just help themselves, which is what they did today."

## ...and finally...

Looking for a Christmas present for a loved one whose feeling all paranoid about their job security. SchNEWS may have just the answer to push them over the edge, and make 'em have a thoroughly miserable Yuletide.

"How to Dismiss Staff" is the catchy title from the Employers Institute that has apparently been selling like hot-pants and has been a godsend to some employers already. "We needed to dismiss Tim or face disaster. This book showed us how." This is a practical, step-by-step guide for employers to give their workers the heave-ho quickly and efficiently on issues such as lateness and having a life, without having to cough up  unfair dismissal damages.

### disclaimer

SchNEWS warns all readers not to attend any illegal gatherings or take part in any illegal activities. Always stay underneath the mistletoe. In fact just stay in, watch the Queen's speech and go on endless present opening sprees filling your lives and homes with endless consumer crap....then you'll feel content. Honest!

## Subscribe!

Keep SchNEWS FREE! Send 1st Class stamps (e.g. 20 for next 20 issues) or donations (payable to Justice?) Ask for "Originals" if you can make copies. Post free to all prisoners. SchNEWS, c/o on-the-fiddle, P.O. Box 2600, Brighton, East Sussex, BN2 2DX.
Tel/Autofax : +44 (0)1273 685913   GET IT EVERY WEEK BY E-MAIL: schnews@brighton.co.uk

# 2:30am, Jan 1, 2000 AD,
## Newcastle upon Tyne, England

Whilst the official millennium events celebrated UK plc, underground free parties were still deemed unacceptable. Phil Rigby reports from Newcastle on the riot squads new year present to the geordie ravers.

**SQUALL**

**Where Do You Want To Grow Today?**

--
I Wanna Go Home
Underground Update
Features
Squall Pics
✓ Frontline Communique
The State Its In
Squotes
Resources
Links
From Our Correspondence

Newcastle is buzzing as thousands of revellers take to the streets to celebrate the dawn of the new millennium. A council organised event on the Quayside has just ended and hundreds of partygoers are looking for where to go next. On the outskirts of town, an 'illegal' rave has been building up to its climax. The venue for this party is an old disused railway workshop, the very building in which Stephenson first built his 'Rocket'. A good 400 people are dancing and partying, everything is fine.

A collective of approximately 25 people had spent the previous 3 days preparing the building to make it safe and usable. Fire exits were available and well marked, fire extinguishers had been bought and placed at every exit, Stewards equipped with torches and walkie-talkies were positioned around the venue. Even safety lighting had been installed especially for the event. There was a first aid team organised and water was freely available, but the police weren't to know any of this.

A patrol car had discovered the party, and called for assistance. A full police riot and crowd control unit was already on standby, and was dispatched to the scene of the 'crime'. AT LEAST 30 police officers with batons and dogs stormed the building, stopped the music, and herded the bewildered dancers off the dancefloor and out into the street.

With a few hundred people now objecting quite strongly to having their New Millennium celebrations ended in such a fashion, the police started to get nervous. When it became clear that some of the party people were going to get 'nasty' by shouting and, in some cases, swearing, the police decided to employ riot control tactics, forming a wall of officers to sweep down the street, with dog handlers in front, driving the crowd down a tunnel underneath the Central Station. This too, was found to be slightly distasteful by the crowd, who objected more strongly than ever. This unwillingness to co-operate now really upset some of the officers in the front line. With adrenalin pumping, they enthusiastically administered some real 'justice' to the closest of the group and set dogs onto the people who were just out of reach. One lucky young girl in her early twenties, about 5ft4inch in height and eight stone in weight, fell on the ground as she tried to run away, and found herself fighting off both the teeth of a psyched-up alsation, and the fists of a 14 stone police officer. The majority of the crowd dispersed quickly now, visibly shocked by the 'style' of policing on display. Several arrests were made, and one person who was dragged off in cuffs (after being arrested for suggesting an officer

was 'way over the top and should pick on someone his own size') now alleges he was assaulted by his arresting officer once taken to the police station. (He wasn't actually charged with an offence.) He is now looking to press charges.

Is this the way to punish people for dancing in an unauthorised venue ? Does partying in the wrong place really warrant violence and intimidation? We think not.

The party was organised by a collective called 'Rabble Alliance' . The idea was to have a free alternative to celebrate the New Year without £100 tickets and £4 pints. The rules of the event, clearly on display around the building stated :"Respect the venue and leave it in a better state than you found it. Don't disturb the neighbours. Look after each other. No drug dealing."

*Frontline Communique's arrive direct from correspondents and are presented without SQUALL edits.*

> ...A power hungry Britain ... but at the same time a RUTHLESS and HARD Britain.

J Hodge

**Download an animation of this from www.squall.co.uk**

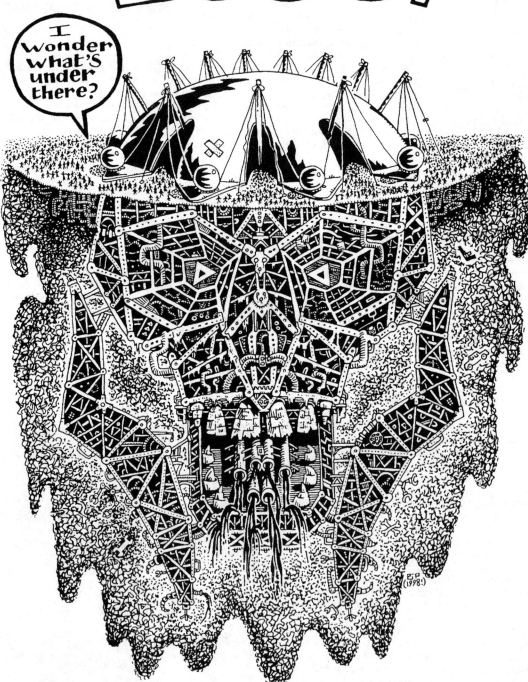

WAKE UP! WAKE UP! IT'S YER TERROR-BILL

# Weekly SchNEWS

*Printed and Published in Brighton by Justice?*

**Friday 7th January 2000**   http://www.schnews.org.uk/   **Issue 242   Free/Donation**

# STATE OF TERROR

Are you digging a tunnel to prevent a road from being built through your neighbourhood? Have you pulled up a few Genetically modified crops from your local test site? Maybe you spoke at a meeting where a member of the Animal Liberation Front, for example, also spoke? Well I'm afraid to tell you that you are soon to be deemed a TERRORIST!

The government are starting to realise that protests are not going away, that people are getting more advanced and organised by using such new technology as telephones and the internet! To combat the outrageous behaviour of people meeting up in public spaces and discussing issues, the government have introduced the glorious, updated, newly improved…. Terrorism Bill!!

Terrorism, in it's hot off the press state, is now "the use of serious violence against persons or property, or the threat to use such violence to intimidate or coerce the Government, the public or any section of the public for political, religious or ideological ends."

This new Bill, which is being fast-tracked through parliament, is targeting environmental groups, animal rights protestors and anyone who shows a social or moral conscience.

If you intended to destroy GM crops coz they are contaminating your local organic farm, you will have less rights than a person who was involved in deliberate assault and robbery. Basically, you will be classed the same legally as the Soho nail bomber!

## FIT THE BILL ?

At present, the only organisations listed are those associated with Northern Ireland. But the Bill gives the police or government the power to add to this list. Reclaim The Streets, Earth First!, Animal Liberation Front have all hit the headlines recently as leading persistent and destructive campaigns against property . By demonising a group, organisation, or sector of a community, you can legitimise a treatment of them that is seen as 'fair punishment' by the general public. This is exactly what happened with Northern Ireland, the coal miners, the anti-poll tax demonstrators, etc.

Under Clause 3 of the new legislation, it will become an offence just to be connected with the new definition of 'terrorists'. If direct action organisations are being targeted as potential terrorists, then it is only a short step to 'proscription'. Once an organisation has been proscribed 'terrorist', it will become a criminal offence to belong to that organisation, to openly support it, or to speak out at a meeting where members of that organisation were also speaking. The Bill

is scare-mongering people against joining organisations, regardless of whether or not they personally take part in criminal activity.

In fact, you won't even have to be directly involved with the organisation. The Incitement clauses of the Bill (clauses 57-59)would make it an offence to support by words alone an armed struggle in a country outside the UK. Those supporting such struggles as the Zapatistas in Mexico, or the Tamil Tigers of Sri Lanka, will be under investigation.

Under the same clauses, there is a danger that refugees who have fled from repressive regimes to this country will become a legitimate target of the police merely because they support the overthrow of that regime.

CLAUSE 38/39 states that the police will be able to arrest, without a warrant, anyone they reasonably suspect as being a 'terrorist'. You won't have to actually have done anything.The powers of stop and search will be extended to include strip searches without a warrant, and failure to comply will result in a three month sentence.

As well as this, new rights are being given to the armed forces with regards to searching premises if they have reasonable suspicion of the property containing munitions and 'wireless transmitter or scanner'. Does this mean that we could be listening to Pirate Radio Terrorism FM? Or that John Peel and Jimmy Saville were once terrorists in their early radio career days? The wording of the Bill is ambiguous and open to misuse thru' misinterpretation.

Clause 18 states that it will be an offence not to report any knowledge of 'terrorist activity'. This has far-reaching implications for investigative journalists who could face up to five years in jail for not grassing people up.

## HISTORY OF THIS BILL

The Bill is going through its Parliamentary stages at an alarming rate, and looks set to become law sometime this autumn.It will replace both the Prevention of Terrorism Act of 1974, and the Northern Ireland Act of 1973. These two Acts have led to some of the worst human rights abuses in this country over the last 25 years, contributed to miscarriages of justice and have led to the unnecessary detention of thousands of innocent people, mainly Irish. This new Bill blatantly ignores the European Convention of Human Rights.

The original Prevention of Terrorism (Temporary Provisions) Act was rushed through Parliament in 1977 in record time - first presented to Parliament on a Wednesday it was law by Friday morning. Not a single Labour MP voted against it.

Despite what the government said at the time, the

PTA was never meant to convict people or prevent bombings - it was introduced to prevent the Irish community in Britain from expressing its support for a united Ireland. Less that 7% of the more than 5,000, mainly Irish, people arrested under the PTA in Britain in its first seven years were charged with any offence at all, although many were detained for days without charge.

The PTA has been widely used to expel innocent Irish people from Britain and prevent Irish republicans from speaking in Britain - In 1982 Sinn Fein's Gerry Adams and Martin McGuiness were both banned from entering Britain to speak. The Act has also been used to remove prominent opposition figures during 'difficult' times for the government - the week before the death of hunger striker Bobby Sands, 30 leading republicans were arrested under the PTA, subject to 'extended detentions', then released without charge.

If you think SchNEWS is getting its knickers in a twist for nothing then here's an example of the PTA working in Ireland.

Bernard O'Connor, a teacher from Eniskillen, was arrested under the PTA in 1977. His first interrogation session in Belfast lasted for over three hours. He was forced to stand on his toes, bend his knees and hold his hands out in front of him and was hit in the face when his heels touched the ground or he lost balance. Every time he denied taking part in bombings and shootings he was hit again. That afternoon, three detectives tried to get him to admit lesser charges to avoid 35 years in jail. Then at night the brutality really started. He was stripped naked, beaten up and forced to do press ups continually. His underpants were placed over his head and he was threatened with being choked. He was then threatened with being handed over to the death squads of the Ulster Volunteer Force. These interrogations continued until he was released without charge on Monday night.

**Want to know more???** * **Liberty,** 21 Tabard Street, London, SE1 4LA. Tel;0171 403 1904, **\*discussion list** ralph@blagged.freeserve.co.uk www.blagged.freeserve.co.uk/law.htm

**\*Brighton Against Benefit Cuts** January 11th, upstairs at The George Beard Pub, 7:30pm, Gloucester Road, Brighton, to plan for a large gathering on Sat, 11th March.

* **Manchester EF!** Mon 24th January, 7:30pm, One World Centre, Manchester. Michelle 0161 442 8635 or Chris 01942 513 792

**\*Cultures of Persistance Squat,** (see in Brief) 13th January, 7:30pm, to discuss a strategy to mobilise against the Bill.

## DEALING IN COMPASSION

Ruth Wyner and John Brock are not heroin dealers. The police admit they have never been involved in dealing. But that didn't stop a judge sending Ruth and John down for 5 and 4 years. Their offence? They supposedly allowed the use and supply of drugs on the premises of Wintercomfort, a drop-in centre for homeless people in Cambridge, (some of whom are drug users). As Director and Assistant Director, Ruth and John had banned people who were suspected of dealing and were monitoring the use of the toilets to try and stop people using drugs there.However,they refused to hand over lists of suspected dealers to the police.

Ruth and John were charged under the Misuse of Drugs Act (1971). Judge Haworth explained, "If the defendants were unwilling to use any reasonable means that were readily available to them to prevent the prohibited activity, then they were permitting the act." Of course, there is a massive gulf between the legal interpretation of 'reasonable means' and the point of view of people providing a service for the homeless. By law, if you fail to close down your project when other measures are ineffective you are permitting the prohibited activity. Also, by law, sharing, swapping or giving constitutes supply, so 2 people sharing a spliff is the same as large scale smack dealing on your premises. This case has some grim implications for homeless facilities. In fact, this ruling could apply to any institution where some people may use drugs; schools, for example, or pubs and clubs. Will headteachers risk imprisonment if dealing is found to take place on school premises? The only answer seems to be body-searching people on entrance to homeless centres, and how would you feel if you were searched every time you went home at night? Chances are, you'd stop going home.

This law effectively criminalises all homeless workers who work with drug users. We need some constructive progress such as establishing links between homeless centres and drugs rehab centres; the ruling only serves to further exclude some of the most marginalised people in our society. For an information pack contact Release 0171 729 5255 www.release-incl.demon.co.uk Letters of support to Ruth Wyner, EH6524 HM Highpoint, Stadishall, Newmarket, Suffolk GB8 9YG & John Brock, 3M 4946, HM Bedford, St Loyes St. MK40 18G.

## BUTTERFLY TOUCHES EARTH

After living in an ancient redwood she called "Luna" for the past two years, Julia ``Butterfly'' Hill came back to Earth just before Christmas. Julia was part of the Headwaters campaign to stop one of the last remaining redwood forests in America being clearcut (see SchNEWS 195). She came down after reaching an agreement with the company. Her supporters have pledged to pay $50,000 to Pacific Lumber to make up for lost logging revenue, while the company agreed to spare Hill's redwood and a 2.9-acre buffer zone around it. The company will donate the $50,000 to Humboldt State University for forestry studies. Well ain't that just swell.

www.enviroweb.org/headwaters-ef/

## SchNEWS in brief

The end of an era. The **Greenham Common Women's** Peace Camp has ended. A council approved sculpture will be erected on the site to commemorate 18 years of campaigning for nuclear disarmament.**

SchNEWS readers will be shedding tears over the sacking of Nick Hudson, editor of the **Dover Express**. Unfortunately it wasn't for his paper's continued racist rantings about asylum seekers ("While labour luvvies dribble...we are left with the backdraft of a nation's human sewage and no cash to wash it down the drain") -that didn't earn him the boot but an article attacking Hoverspeed did. ** One for yer diary: 'Anonymity: the use of pseudonyms and initials in anarchist discourse and **the tyranny of box numbers'.** It's part of the regular Friday meetings of the London Anarchist Forum at Conway Hall, 25 Red Lion Square, London (nearest tube Holborn) 8pm. More details 0181 847 0203 ** Support those arrested for the alleged involvement in the **Smash Genetics** action last year, when an AgrEvo maze test site in Lincolnshire was destroyed. Trial begins on 18th January at Lincoln magistrates Court. Contact GEN 0181 374 9516 ** Carry on squatting! After 'Cultures of Resistance', they're back with **CULTURES OF PERSISTANCE!** From 10th-16th January 2000 at 168 Tower Bridge Road, London. Including an art exhibition on The City...its drawbacks and some positive solutions. If you want to use the space contact rachred57@hotmail.com or ring 0958 765 151 ** **The Earth First! Winter moot** is in Oxford on 28-30th January. More details send SAE to c/o URGENT, Box HN, 111 Magdalen Rd., Oxford, OX41RQ emailwintermoot@yahoo.com**Feeling marginalised by the orthodox anarchist left?! Well if you're a 'druid, odinist, folk autonomist' or part of the 'hermeticist anarchist underground' then pop along to the **Anarchist Heretics Fair,** they offer a chance to discover the unknown and alternative side of anarchy. For info ring 0181 459 5520 or e-mail hermet@synarc.freeserve.co.uk ** **Bloody Sunday** national demo, Sat 22nd January. Meet 12 noon @ Whitehall Place, London. For info. Tel 0181 4428778, e-mail ICNwork@aol.co.uk ** Support **Gill Emerson**, come along to Canterbury Crown Court, Chaucer Road at 10am on Thurs 13th January to show your solidarity at the appeal trial. Gill was arrested during the National Front march in Dover last Jan. Fighting fascism is no crime. ** The **Haringey Solidarity Group** are having a crisis meeting next Monday (10th) to discuss the future of the group. If you care about it's future get along to the Wood Green Labour Club, Stuart Crescent, N22 8pm

---

### SCHNEWS TRAINING DAY

Wednesday 12th January 12 noon
We need people to get involved with SchNEWS so why not make a belated New Year's resolution and help out ? Ring office for more details (oh, and we lost *all* our ansaphone messages over Xmas).
* Have you got a spare PC ? SchNEWS will give it a loving home.
* After helping the homeless for 25 years, the excellent Advisory Service for Squatters are looking for some new recruits. Want to make a difference? Ring 0171 359 8814

---

## Talking of terrorists...

Sixteen people are up on conspirarcy charges after - wait for it, around 50 people entered the Nestle factory in Halifax and climbed on the roof and up a chimney to unfurl banners such as 'People and Planet Before Profit'. The action was in protest at the meeting of the World Trade Organisation in Seattle (see SchNEWS 240), the police reckon it had more to do with a desire to do some burglary. Because you often see burgalars in groups of 50 in broad daylight, with banners and leaflets marching into coporate offices. Their next court appearance is on Tuesday 22 February, 2000. Halifax Magistrates Court, Harrison Road, Halifax, 9.30am onwards, and they are asking for people to turn up outside for support. Contact The Nestle 16, 10 Broughton Street, Hebden Bridge, West Yorkshire, HX7 8JY Tel 01422 844710
* 'After Seattle - What next?' Meeting Saturday 15th January Conway Hall, Red Lion Sq., London WC1 (nearest tube Holborn) 2pm - 5pm. Speakers will include Barry Coates, Director of the World Development Movement, and activists from the Nestle action.

## Meeja Ho Massive

Over in the States, corporate media whores ABC NewsOne, CBS Newspath and Fox News Edge have merged their info sources. This means that although the 3 companies will still be competing to forcefeed soundbite bullshit to those canny Yanks, the news they have access to will be essentially the same spin-doctored bollocks.

## ...and finally...

SchNEWs scribe in millenium crap arrest shocker!! For proclaiming the end of the world!

This gag didn't go down to well with everyone on New Years Eve at the Golden Gate of Jerusalem. In absence of any doomsday prophets, our man decided to act the part before the eagerly expectant media circus "And when the seven seals are broken open on the day of judgement, and the seven angels blow their trumpets - when the third angel blows her bugle...." (this rant lifted directly from the film Naked - film buffs take note). They say that in comedy timing is everything. Lead balloons go down faster at certain times, and in certain climates. The holy city is one such climate. The international journalists were all besides themselves with joy; the Israeli police less so.

The bendy man was released without charge, but the police did ask why he had a dress, holy bible, half a bottle of vodka and some necro * cards in his bag.
* These cards are similar to kidney donor cards except they say 'I support sexual liberation . I want to help others experiment sexually after my death. I request that after my death
A) My body be used for any type of secual activity B) gay only  c) straight only  d) I do not wish my body to be dismembered or disfigured during necrophiliac sex (you get the picture)

**disclaimer**
Schnews asks what are all the Y2K nutters doing with all their spare time these days? Answers on a postcard not necessary. Honest.

# Cambridge Two

## HM Highpoint, Stradishall, Newmarket, Suffolk 17/02/00

Ruth Wyner (Director) and John Brock (Manager) were jailed for five and four years respectively in 1999 for failing to tell police that drug dealing was going on in the homeless drop-in centre where they worked. It took police five months of undercover operations, including hidden cameras, to determine the extent of the problem but the judge ruled that, although they were not involved in the drug dealing, Wyner and Brock should have known about it and told police. The staggering sentences meted out to the two social workers has dire implications for UK social workers.

In a short message sent from their cells Wyner and Brock talk of their shock at the sentences and of prison life. The farce of the case was further exacerbated when Ruth Wyner was asked to help with confidential counselling in the prison where she is incarcerated. Her letter to Home Secretary, Jack Straw, follow on from their short messages.

### Prisoner EH6324 Ruth Wyner wrote (17/02/00):

"The shock subsided after two or three weeks, during which other inmates were very kind, and helped me a lot. It is a sobering situation, one in which you have to use all your strength to stay intact.

An irony for me is that at Highpoint there is a Listeners scheme in which local Samaritans are training inmates to help their fellows to limit the pain of this situation. I have been accepted on the training scheme and during the first session, the importance of complete confidentiality was emphasized. For everything, I venture, even drugs? They insist this has to be so, saying that otherwise Listeners could not gain the trust of those they seek to help. The irony is bittersweet: it was to a considerable extent by upholding confidentiality that I got into this situation in the first place.

I am enormously proud of my family, overwhelmed, greatly lifted and deeply humbled by the energy and commitment people have given to the campaign and by the many letters and cards I have received. They are a great help. The ongoing support for Wintercomfort is a great joy to me, the staff and volunteers are loyal and dedicated, a wonderful bunch of people. My thanks to all."

*Ruth Wyner EH 6524, HM Highpoint, Stradishall, Newmarket, Suffolk CB8 9YG*

### Prisoner EM4946 John Brock wrote in Jan 2000:

"A brief description of how I feel, what life is like for me at the moment and my thoughts in the case/ campaign.

Disbelief at the charge, shock at the Judge's summing up and jury's verdict, devastation at the sentence, depression, fear and bewilderment at being locked in prison.

Missing my wife and family more than I can express.

I am not a natural crusader in righting life's wrongs but more of a reluctant individual thrown into what is rapidly becoming a national issue. I will, however, defend my innocence and vehemently refute suggestions that I or my staff team knowingly turned a blind eye to anything.

I have always been open and honest about the problems and how we tackled them.

Prison life is impossible to describe. Suffice to say that my fellow inmates treat me fairly and those prison officers I have contact with act in a professional and thoughtful manner.

I am truly humbled by the level of support and outrage

**Protestors calling for justice for Cambridge Two, 25th March, London**

Pics: Richie Andrews

expressed by many either directly to me or through the action group."

John Brock EM4946, HM Highpoint, Stradishall, Newmarket, Suffolk CB8 9YG

**Ruth Wyner's letter to the Home Secretary** 12.2.00:

Dear Home Secretary,

I wish to report to you the fact that Class A and B drugs are being supplied at this prison, where I am currently being held, as well as at other prisons.

As Director of the Cambridge charity Wintercomfort, "Number One" as it were, I was convicted for allowing drugs supply of which I was not specifically aware. I therefore feel it is my duty, in order to ensure the safety of the Home secretary, to make you aware of this supply as you are, of course, the "Number One" in regard to prison management.

After all, I do not want to see you doing a 5-year stretch as I am. This is my first offence.

I was charged under Section 8 of the Misuse of Drugs Act. At court, my judge directed that my co-defendant and I were guilty if we "were unwilling to use any reasonable means that were readily available .. to prevent the prohibited activity." Furthermore, Judge Haworth directed that if there was a failure to implement these means effectively then the offence was also committed.

These reasonable means included, according to the judge, closure of the project. The failure to adopt such a measure if other measures to stop the activity had failed would, Judge Haworth said, indicate an unwillingness to use a "reasonable" step and as such be evidence of permitting drug supply.

You may also wish to note that in questions to Paul Boateng, M.P. in the House of Commons on 31.1.00 (nos. 164-7 inc.), Peter Bottomley M.P. was informed that in 1999 there were 17,789 positive drug tests in prisons and 13,409 proven cases of unauthorised uses of a controlled drug in prison. Over the same period, 823 visitors were arrested for bringing drugs into prisons.

In my case, Wintercomfort banned those caught dealing or using illicit drugs at its day centre. But there was additional dealing that was caught on a secret police surveillance camera, of which we were not specifically aware.

We were, however, said in court to "know" because we had discussed our concerns about drug use at the project with, among others, the police.

The similarities are striking: the prison service has caught some dealers but clearly not the majority of people dealing on prison premises, visitors or inmates.

Your methods are clearly ineffective. As you live under the same laws as I do, I believe you are liable to arrest. Or would you like me to perform a citizen's arrest on the governor here?

I look forward to your reply.

Yours sincerely
Ruth Wyner

(copies to Anne Campbell MP for Cambridge, Peter Bottomley MP. Shelley & Co, solicitors, Alex Masters, Chairman of the Cambridge 2 Campaign).

Pic: Sophie

**BOCM Pauls,** a company which manufactures more animal feed than any other company in the UK and allegedly uses GM ingredients in most of its products, was targeted by Newcastle-based genetics group GeneNo! for an action on the 14th of December. The company's cattle feed mill at Chilton Industrial Estate, County Durham was 'visited' by a number of cows - two of which scaled two large grain silos and dropped a banner reading "NO GM Animal Feeds".

No one was arrested and later a letter was faxed to the Chief Executive at the Head Office in Ipswich explaining the reasons for the action.

BOCM Pauls is allegedly one of the companies involved in the contaminated animal feed scandal which led to the BSE crisis.

# RAISING TERROR

**SQUALL**

Where Do You Want To Grow Today?
--
I Wanna Go Home
Underground Update
**Features**
Squall Pics
Frontline Communique
The State Its In
Squotes
Resources
Links
From Our Correspondence

The Terrorism Bill currently racing through parliament with barely a smatter of mainstream dissent looks set to be one of the most liberty-corrosive pieces of legislation for decades. Si Mitchell examines the implications of Jack Straw's latest attempt to remove the last of our residual rights to protest.

*Article 19, Universal Declaration of Human Rights 1948. - Everyone has the right to freedom of opinion and expression; this includes freedom to hold opinions without interference and to seek, receive and impart information and ideas through any media regardless of frontiers.*

*Terrorism Bill 2000. - (1) A person commits an offence if - (a) he collects or makes a record of information of a kind likely to be useful to a person committing or preparing an act of terrorism [as defined by the state] , or (b) he possesses a document or record containing information of that kind.*

"Somehow the threat to the stability of the state has given way to threats to the corporate estate. That will be the basis for the new definition of terrorism. That is a desperately dangerous path to go down."

Alan Simpson is one of the few British politicians to be genuinely shaken by Jack Straw's introduction of the most overtly political law and order legislation since Hitler's proscription of the Jews.

The 2000 Terrorism Bill, currently whistling through the House of Commons and likely to be law by Autumn, has generated little in the way of Parliamentary outcry (unlike its 1974 predecessor, The Prevention of Terrorism Act) despite proposing to outlaw various fundamental democratic rights, including the right to possess or pass on information.

The Bill is text book divide and rule stuff that will criminalise dissent and marginalise dissenters by threatening their wider support base with unlimited fines and lengthy jail sentences.

Home Secretary Jack Straw has given terrorism "a more modern definition" to combat "both the current and future terrorist threat". All this and new "special" powers for the police breaching existing British and international law.

### Moving the Goal Posts:

Taking their lead from the popular press, who liberally label anyone not overjoyed with creeping global destruction as eco-terrorists, New Labour have redefined terrorism as: "The use or threat, for the purpose of advancing a political, religious or ideological cause, of action which a) involves serious violence against any person or property, b) endangers the life of any person, or c) creates a serious risk to the health or safety of the public or a section of the public.

Simon Hughes MP was a lone voice trying to secure amendments during the Bill's committee stage: "The Bill changes the definition of terrorism as understood by the man or woman in the street." Hughes refers to the Oxford Dictionary description of: "The use of violence and intimidation in the pursuit of political aims."

The bones of the new definition are taken from the FBI's own anti terror legislation where property takes precedence over democracy. Both government and big business have made no secret of how much the cost of direct action irks them.

**WEARING AN ITEM OF CLOTHING OR DISPLAYING AN ARTICLE TO AROUSE REASONABLE SUSPICION THAT HE/SHE IS A MEMBER OR SUPPORTER OF A PROSCRIBED ORGANISATION" COULD LEAD TO ARREST AND A TEN YEAR SENTENCE AND UNLIMITED FINE.**

Barrister, Ralph Smyth, currently working at the Council of Europe's Division of Public & International Law, was one of the first to criticise the Bill. "The differentiation between those taking action for moral reasons and those doing so for naked greed is illogical and shows how the obsession with the invisible hand of the market has clouded the minds of those responsible for the Bill," he says. Adding, on a more positive note: "Perhaps some creative activists could argue that multinationals are endangering the public's safety with their bio-tech products for the advancement of neoliberal ideology."

Though the state and its agents are liable under the domestic provisions of the bill, the chances of a successful prosecution are slim, and they are still exempt for any overseas incitement. Propaganda watcher, Noam Chomsky, explains the guiding principle on how the state defines terrorism: "Their terror is terror, and the flimsiest evidence suffices to denounce it and to exact retribution; our terror, even if far more extreme, is merely statecraft, and therefore does not enter into the discussion of the plague of the modern age [terrorism]."

### Parliament - An act of terror

Straw's own logic may go some way to explaining the proposals. "If we look back over the past 25 years, we can see that the [anti-terrorism] powers have been used proportionately," he says, without reference to the Guildford Four, the Birmingham Six or the 98 per cent of people detained under the existing Prevention of Terrorism Act who were innocent of any crime. He claims that there are "adequate non-violent means for expressing opposition and dissent". Smyth points out that the 'life endangering' and 'health and safety' aspects of the Bill could be used to prosecute activists building fortifications at protest sites, that would be seen as posing risks both to themselves and their bailiffs.

However, it is likely that animal rights activists will be the first domestic dissenters to be pursued under the Bill (being closest to what the public perceives as terrorism). The consultation document which preceded this Bill explicitly noted some of the activity which the bill intended to prevent: "Animal and environmental rights activists: high cost of damage from attacks on abbatoirs, laboratories, breeders, hunts, butchers, chemists, doctors, vets, furriers, restaurants, supermarkets and other shops."

Not wishing to appear extreme, Straw claimed that the activities of Greenpeace would not be classed as terrorism. However the environmental group's involvement in pulling up GM crops would fall foul of this law.

The authorities' inability to understand non-hierarchical organisation (and their inability to get conspiracy charges to stick) has generated a clause aimed at anyone "directing" an activist organisation. 'Organisation' is defined as any group of people meeting to discuss a potentially 'terrorist' act and 'directing' can be at any level (booking a room? facilitating a meeting?). The maximum sentence is life imprisonment.

**THE MERE THREAT OF BECOMING INCRIMINATED BY ACCEPTING CORRESPONDENCE OR LITERATURE FROM ANY CAMPAIGNING GROUP MAY WELL BE ENOUGH TO MAKE POTENTIAL 'LIBERAL' SUPPORTERS DELIBERATELY AVOID BECOMING INFORMED."**

According to Smyth: "A combination of dirty tricks, provoking of riots and slick media manipulation will be used to divide the radicals from the liberals." Dirty tricks in the form of propaganda, damning press articles and incitement, played a major roll in Northern Ireland, against the striking miners and are becoming increasingly prevalent against Reclaim The Streets and anti GM activists. (see RTS press complaint about Sunday Times arms allegation. UNDEGROUND UPDATE)

Under the 'possession for terrorist purposes' and 'collection of information' clauses anyone accused of having information "likely to be useful" to someone preparing a terrorist act will have to prove either they didn't have it or that they had reasonable excuse to possess it. Failing to do so could mean a sentence of ten years. The Corporate Watchers' Address Book or the Genetix Snowball Handbook have been cited, by the Bill's opponents, as prime examples of incriminating literature, and campaigning journalists are likely to be targeted with these clauses. (Journalists will also be hit by the 'duty to disclose information' clause which obliges them to hand over any information they come across in a professional capacity as well as acting as a potential gag, this is likely to make activists less keen to talk to the press, leaving an information vacuum, no doubt to be filled by government spin.)

The mere threat of becoming incriminated by accepting correspondence or literature from any campaigning group may well be enough to make potential 'liberal' supporters deliberately avoid becoming informed. As every despot knows, fear is the greatest censor of ideas.

Straw's desire to "tackle fundraising and support networks" by scaring people away from activities they are entitled to do in a democracy is open to challenge under the 1998 Human Rights Act (HRA). The HRA will incorporate the European Convention on Human Rights (ECHR) into UK law. By introducing contradictory legislation, the government may be leaving it up to the judges, who will set the legal precedents, to see which is more important democracy or control.

Civil rights group, Liberty, have identified several potential violations of the ECHR, including new police powers to arrest on suspicion (the return of the discredited 'sus' laws - exposed as being little more than intimidation and information gathering exercises). The government had also intended to apply for an opt-out (derogation) of the ECHR to be able to hold people without charge for an extended period of seven days, though has since thought better of it. It is the introduction of new police powers that Jack Straw says is the main purpose of the Bill. He claims they are not designed to be used where actions "turn ugly". Though one of the more lasting memories (in the mainstream psyche) surrounding the J18, City of London, protests is the repeated description of 'planned' and 'orchestrated' violence.

Other "special powers" include permission to search without a warrant, where a suspect must then give an explanation for anything found (another reversal of the burden of proof), and the ability to declare a cordon around a designated area for up to 28 days (long enough for an eviction?) and demand anyone inside it to leave.

Once a campaigning group's name has been sufficiently blackened, in the eyes of the public, the Home Secretary will be able to proscribe (ban) them. It would become an offence not only to be a member of a banned group, but to organise or address a meeting, where a member of it speaks. Not only support, but encouraging support (for example saying it should not be banned), would become an offence.

**"IF YOU'VE BEEN INVOLVED IN ANY CAMPAIGN THEY START USING ANTI-TERRORIST POWERS AGAINST, YOU WOULD NOT BE BEING AT ALL PARANOID TO EXPECT A VISIT FROM THE POLICE AND A FREE TRIP DOWN THE STATION."**

Though a Proscribed Organisations Appeal Committee (POAC) will be set up under the Bill, the appeal will only be along the lines of Judicial Review where the legality, but not the merits, of the decision to proscribe can be challenged. The POAC will meet in secret and need not disclose its reasons for dismissing an appeal. You get a hearing. But not a fair hearing.

Under this section of the Bill "wearing an item of clothing or displaying an article to arouse reasonable suspicion that he/she is a member or supporter of a proscribed organisation" could lead to arrest and a ten year sentence and unlimited fine.

If the Home Secretary sees fit to ban the ALF, will everyone in vegan shoes be arrested? If he bans RTS, will all stilt walkers get collars felt? (Might need the flying squad for that one.) The banning of a hardline Islamic group could lead to some serious compromising of the police's already questionable impartiality.

As the 'terrorism' under the Bill can occur in the UK or overseas, anyone involved in solidarity with movements from abroad may find themselves prosecuted (particularly under pressure from foreign governments that Britain may be trying to keep sweet). Critics are already listing Ghandi, Mandela and Jesus Christ as historical figures you would not have wanted to have been caught supporting. Today, campaigning for the liberation of Tibet may go unpunished. But will backing less 'comfortable' causes such as Palestinians fighting for recognition in the West Bank, or opposing Western sanctions against Libya be as readily overlooked.

Ralph Smyth says: "If you've been involved in any campaign they start using anti-terrorist powers against, you would not be being at all paranoid to expect a visit from the police and a free trip down the station." Though opposition to the Bill is growing, it is unlikely to be blocked or receive significant amendments (several have been proposed including bringing the Bill into line with the ECHR and removing the reverse proof burdens and the references to property). Smyth believes how much they will use this Act will depend on how much society consents to its use. Yet, like the Criminal Justice and Public Order Act 1994, it is likely the powers will not be used for some time and then be slowly brought in to play.

Italy has recently reintroduced terrorist legislation from the 1970s against activists, jailing three for sabotaging an Alpine building site for high speed trains (two have subsequently committed suicide, the third got 6 years 8 months). The Italian state prosecutor explained the thinking behind the prosecutions: "It was not so much the nature of their crimes, but for the popular consensus which they create in a potentially explosive situation." Terrorists, it would seem, are those who carry out the will of the people. In Britain the more cynical commentators are suggesting that this Bill has little to do with any potential terrorist threat and more to do with silencing dissenting voices that are beginning to muster some serious support. Blair is still reeling from the embarrassment of going against the wishes of 70 per cent of the population over GM foods.

The final article of the Universal Declaration says that no state can "perform any act aimed at the destruction of any of the rights set forth herein [the Declaration]". Straw says his Bill is "simply protecting democracy". Though the establishment's historians probably won't record it, those that defy the 2000 Terrorism Bill may well go down as the real protectors of democracy.

To keep up to date with the passage of the Bill and opposition to it check:
http://www.blagged.freeserve.co.uk/terrorbill/index.htm
To keep up to date with the passage of the Bill and opposition to it check:
http://www.blagged.freeserve.co.uk/terrorbill/index.htm
Text of UK Government Terrorism Bill -
http://www.publications.parliament.uk/pa/cm199900/cmbills/063/2000063.htm
Home Office Terrorism Bill web page:
http://www.homeoffice.gov.uk/oicd/terrbill.htm
The best way of being kept up to date with the campaign is to subscribe to the email list. You can do this by accessing the web page at -
http://tb_campaign.listbot.com/
Liberty - http://www.liberty-human-rights.org.uk/
Contact the Home Office to protest against this legislation
http://www.homeoffice.gov.uk/webwork/contact.htm
FFI on Italian anti terror measures vs activists:
asilosquat@tiscalinet.it

# SOME SIMPLE QUESTIONS Mr Straw

K.evans

ONE OF THESE INSPIRES TERROR IN PEOPLE, MR STRAW, CAN YOU TELL WHICH?

YES OF COURSE! THE ONE ON THE RIGHT IS A TERRORIST.

**TERRORISM ACT 2000:** 1 (1) In this Act "terrorism" means the use, or threat, for the purpose of advancing a political, religious or ideological cause, of action which:
(a) involves serious violence against any person **or property.**

NOW, TAKE YOUR TIME MR STRAW, ONE OF THESE PEOPLE IS SCARED, WHICH ONE COULD IT BE?

HERE'S A CLUE:

**PREVENTION OF TERRORISM ACT 2000:**

1 (1) In this Act "terrorism" means the use, or threat for the purpose of advancing a political, religious or ideological cause, of action which:

(b) endangers the life of **any** person.

AH, YES THE SECURITY GUARD ON THE GROUND MUST BE PETRIFIED OF THAT WOMAN UP THERE ON THAT BRANCH.

HEY, BY ENDANGERING HER OWN LIFE THERE, SHE SURE HAS ME SCARED

THE TERRORISM ACT 2000 IS EXPRESSLY DESIGNED TO INCLUDE PEOPLE WHO DON'T ADVOCATE VIOLENCE AGAINST ANYONE AND WHO DON'T CARRY GUNS. IT ALSO AFFECTS PEOPLE FIGHTING IN OTHER COUNTRIES FOR THEIR FREEDOM FROM OPPRESSIVE DICTATORS OR GENOCIDAL REGIMES

GIVE IT A BIT OF POLITICAL SPIN

MR STRAW...

Clever, isn't it?

TERRORISM ACT ~ 2000 ~

1.-(1) In this Act "terrorism" means the use or threat, for the purpose of advancing a political, religious or ideological cause, of action which—

(a) involves serious violence against any person or property

(b) endangers the life of any person, or

(c) creates a serious risk to the health and safety of the public or a section of the public.

(2) In subsection (1)-

(a) "action" includes action outside the United Kingdom

(b) a reference to persons or property is a reference to any person, or to property, wherever situated, and

(c) a reference to the public includes a reference to the public of a country other than the United Kingdom

HUMAN RIGHTS RECORD

... AND ALL THESE PEOPLE BECOME **TERRORISTS!**

# SO **WHAT'S IN STORE?**

LET US FOLLOW THE THEORETICAL CASE OF ROSEMARY MORLEY, BIRDWATCHER, WHO HAS BEEN MONITORING THE EFFECT OF CHEMICAL SPILLS FROM THE LOCAL TOXICO FACTORY ON HER LOCAL BEACH. AFTER A SERIES OF SUCCESSFUL PROSECUTIONS RESULT IN ONLY INEFFECTUAL FINES, SHE FORMS THE GROUP 'FRIENDS OF NETHERTHONG BAY' WITH THE AIM OF TAKING ACCOUNTABLE NON-VIOLENT DIRECT ACTION AGAINST THE CORPORATION

Rosemary Morley in happier times

'Paul' (Ayo) Adedeji leaving mission school aged 12 - this is the only known photograph

OR, IN A DIFFERENT LEAGUE ~ WHAT ABOUT AYO ADEDEJI WHO HAS SEEN HIS TRIBAL PEOPLE SUFFER ENSLAVEMENT, STERILISATION, MASSACRE + ULTIMATELY DISPOSSESSION. WITH HIS CHARISMATIC PREACHING ON THE CITY STREETS, HE FINDS HIMSELF THE LEADER OF A CROSS CULTURAL RESISTANCE DETERMINED TO FIGHT BACK...

ROSEMARY MORLEY SETS OUT LATE ONE NIGHT WITH CONSIDERABLE QUANTITIES OF STEEL MESH AND WATER-PROOF CEMENT... SHE SUCCESSFULLY BLOCKS TOXICO'S OUTFLOW PIPE AND IMMEDIATELY TELEPHONES THE LOCAL POLICE STATION TO INFORM THEM OF THE CRIME.

terribly sorry to trouble you P.C. Hynes...

SHE IS IMPRISONED, AND SENTENCED IN DUE COURSE

Well, Miss Morely, were your crime motivated by simple GREED, REVENGE or misguided PASSION I would be happy to recommend a sentence of weeks. But it appears that you have an IDEOLOGICAL JUSTIFICATION for your actions. This clearly meets the terms of "serious violence against property" under the Prevention of Terrorism Act, and as such I shall sentence you to a much longer term.

...Flooding at the Toxico plant... blah blah ...damage to the value of £60,000... blah...

I did it for the birds

APPALLED AT THE SEVERITY OF THE DAMAGE (FRESH FROM LUNCH WITH THE TOXICO MANAGING DIRECTOR) THE SECRETARY OF STATE DECIDES TO **BAN** 'FRIENDS OF NETHERTHONG BAY' AS A TERRORIST ORGANISATION

love your policies, Jack

THE NETHERTHONGIANS MOUNT A LEGAL CHALLENGE, BUT THE MEMBERS OF THE APPEALS COMMISSION (WHO MAY OR MAY NOT BE MAJOR TOXICO SHAREHOLDERS) EXCLUDE THEM AND THEIR LAWYERS FROM THE APPEAL HEARING. THE COMMISSION UPHOLDS THE BAN, WITHOUT GIVING A REASON WHY.

FRIENDS OF THE BAY

WE'RE HERE TO SAVE THE BAY

Are you members of 'Friends of Netherthong Bay?'

Indeed we are.

I'm afraid I'm going to have to ask you all to come with me.

ALL THE MEMBERS OF THE GROUP ARE CONVICTED OF "membership offences" AND ARE SENTENCED TO TEN YEARS IN PRISON.

ROSEMARY MORLEY, GUILTY OF "directing" THEIR ACTIVITIES, GETS LIFE.

AYO ADEDEJI LIVES FAR AWAY IN A COUNTRY WHERE HUMAN RIGHTS ABUSES ARE COMMONPLACE. THINGS LIKE THAT COULD NEVER HAPPEN HERE.

AYO ADEDEJI DIES IN PRISON FROM HIS WOUNDS. HIS WIFE AND SONS ARE SHOT BY MASKED GUNMEN. HIS DAUGHTER FLEES TO ENGLAND WHERE AFTER ONLY 14 MONTHS IN DETENTION, HER CLAIM FOR ASYLUM IS ALLOWED.

DALAPO ADEDEJI VOWS TO CONTINUE HER FATHER'S STRUGGLE.

Goodness, yes, I see that last year your country bought nearly the entire U.K. export of electric shock batons

**UNFORTUNATELY** THE UK GOVERNMENT PROVES UNWILLING TO UPSET THEIR VALUABLE TRADE PARTNER. DALAPO'S ORGANISATION IS BANNED.

We've got some smashing new legislation to deal with things like that. I'll talk to Jack.

See you at the arms fair then?

Offences Membership .11.—
Directing (BANNED)
(1) A person commits an offence if he belongs or professes to belong to a proscribed organisation.
(2) It is a defence for a person charged under subsection (1) to **prove**
(a) that the organisation was not proscribed on the last...occasion on which he became a member... and
(b) that he has not taken part in the activities of the organisation at any time while it was proscribed.
(3) A person guilty of an offence under this section shall be liable—
(a) ... to imprisonment for a term not exceeding **ten** years...

Directing Terrorist Organisation
56.— (1) A person commits an offence if he directs, at any level, the activities of an organisation which is concerned in the commission of acts of terrorism.
(2) A person guilty of an offence under this section is liable on conviction to imprisonment for **life.**

**INTERESTINGLY** MEMBERSHIP OFFENCES UNDER THE NEW ACT INCLUDE A CLAUSE OF 'NEGATIVE PROOF'. THIS MEANS THAT ALTHOUGH DALAPO WAS WILLING TO RENOUNCE HER POLITICAL BELIEFS IN ORDER TO AVOID JAIL, SHE WAS IN EFFECT GUILTY UNTIL **PROVEN** INNOCENT, AND HAD TO **PROVE** TO THE COURT THAT SHE HAD NO FURTHER CONTACT WITH THE "TERRORIST" ORGANISATION. SHE FAILED.

NOW, GIVEN THAT:

1. (3) In this Act... action taken for the purposes of terrorism includes ... action taken for the benefit of a proscribed [banned] organisation.

~SO, AS THE NUMBER OF SYMPATHISERS WITH OUR HEROES GROWS, SO A GREATER AND GREATER PROPORTION OF THE POPULATION BECOME **TERRORISTS.** AND THEREFORE, WHEN A SPONTANEOUS DEMONSTRATION OCCURS A WEEK LATER, AND THE POLICE DECIDE TO EXERCISE THEIR NEW POWER OF DECLARING A 'CORDON' AROUND THE PROTESTORS TO DISPERSE THEM, THEY DO IT WITH THE SOLE AIM OF ERADICATING THE **EVIL** OF **TERRORISM** IN OUR MIDST. LOOK~

Cordons Cordoned Areas. 33.-

(2) A designation may be made only if the person making it considers it expedient for the purposes of a terrorist investigation.

NOT BECAUSE IT'S A USEFUL TOOL FOR SUPRESSING THE RIGHT TO FREE ASSEMBLY. NOT THAT, AT ALL.

33.- (4) ...the demarcation of the cordoned area [shall be made]
(a) by means of tape marked with the word "police", **or**
(b) in such other manner as a constable considers appropriate.

Police powers 36.- (1) A constable in uniform may-
(a) order a person in a cordoned area to leave it immediately;
(b) order a person to leave premises which are wholly or partly in or adjacent to a cordoned area;
BLAH BLAH... removal of a vehicle ... movement of a vehicle... prohibit or restrict access to a cordoned area by pedestrians or vehicles...
(2) A person commits an offence if he fails to comply with an order...
BLAH BLAH (4)... liable on summary conviction to -
(a) imprisonment for a term not exceeding three months...

AND HERE'S THAT NEGATIVE PROOF CLAUSE AGAIN:
(3) It is a defence for a person charged ... to **prove** he had reasonable excuse for his failure [to comply]
LOVELY!

THE FRIENDS OF NETHERTHONG BAY CONTINUES TO FUNCTION IN ORDER TO PAY COURT COSTS, PROVIDE PRISONER SUPPORT AND, UNWISELY, IN ACCORDANCE WITH ROSEMARY MORLEY'S STATEMENT FROM HER PRISON CELL...

We shall not rest in our attacks on Toxico until each fluffy, downy chick that hatches in Netherthong Bay can grow free, unpolluted, strong and fly, fly, fly, fly...

...SILLY REALLY BECAUSE SECTIONS 14 + 15 OF THE T.A. HAVE SOMETHING TO SAY ABOUT BANNED ORGANIS~ATIONS ATTEMPTING TO RAISE FUNDS...

*Terrorist Property* 14 (1) In this Act "terrorist property"... includes] **any** resources of a proscribed organisation...

*Offences Fundraising.* **15.** ~ (1) A person commits an offence if he —

(a) invites another to provide money or... property

(2)(a) receives money or other property

(3)(a)...provides money or other property...

Help save the seagulls.

AND SO THE EARLY SUPERMARKET COLLECTIONS WERE RATHER UNSUCCESSFUL.

SECTIONS 17 + 18 CRIMINAL~ISE MORE SECRETIVE ARRANGEMENTS TOO.
*Funding Arrangements.* **17.** A person commits an offence if he ... enters into... an arrangement ... YAWN and money or other property is made available...
*Money Laundering.* **18...** YAWN YAWN BLAH... conceal~ment... transfer to nominees, or (d)... any other way

AND THEN SECTION 16 GIVES THE WHOLE FUNDS/PROPERTY THING A NICE CATCH~ALL:
*Possession* **16.** (2) A person commits an offence if he—
(a) possesses money or other property, and
(b) **intends** that it should be used... for the purposes of terrorism.

5 YEARS IN JAIL

I could give some money to the Adedeji Campaign

but I'm a bit skint at the moment.

NO LONGER LIABLE TO 5 YEARS IN JAIL

Maybe when my student loan comes through.

AHA! QUICK LOCK HER UP!

NOW CHECK OUT THE DEFINITION OF "PROPERTY" GIVEN IN SECTION 120 OF THE ACT:
120. "property" includes property wherever situated and whether real or personal, heritable or moveable, and things in action and other intang~ible or incorporeal property.
SUDDENLY **EVERYTHING** TO DO WITH THE NETHERTHONGIANS AND THE ADEDEJI CAMPAIGN BECOM~ES INCREDIBLY **HOT.**

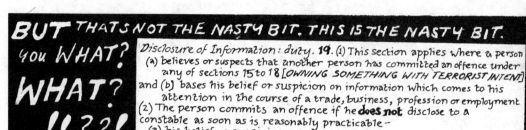

BUT STILL RANDOM, SPORADIC ATTACKS OCCUR ON TOXICO INSTALLATIONS.
ABROAD, THE ADEDEJI RESISTANCE MOVEMENT GOES FROM STRENGTH TO STRENGTH

# TERRORISTS COULD BE ANYWHERE

SOME ARE EASY TO SPOT:

13.—(1) A person in a public place commits an offence if he
(a) wears an item of clothing or;
(b) wears, carries or displays an article,
in such a way or circumstances as to arouse reasonable suspicion that he is a member or supporter of a proscribed organisation.

(3)... imprisonment for a term not exceeding six months
SERIOUSLY, THIS REALLY IS U.K. LAW.

BUT ONCE THESE FOOLHARDY TYPES HAVE BEEN ROUNDED UP, THE POLICE REALLY HAVE TO EXTEND THEIR POWERS. THE ASSISTANT CHIEF CONSTABLE OF WEST YORKSHIRE DECLARES A STOP + SEARCH AREA AROUND NETHERTHONG BAY, WHERE COPS ARE AUTHORISED TO SEARCH VEHICLES, DRIVERS PASSENGERS, PEDESTRIANS + ANYTHING THEY ARE CARRYING (SECTION 42)

OK – let's see who we stopped this week. My God man! Do any of these look particularly like environmental activists to you? Let's hope the CRE don't hear about this!

It's OK Sarge, we're covered.

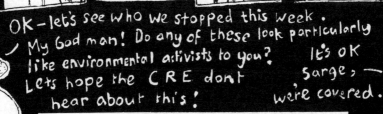

Exercise of power 45.—(1) The power conferred by an authorisation under section 42 (1) or (2)
(a) may be exercised only for the purpose of searching for articles of a kind which could be used in connection with terrorism and
(b) may be exercised whether or not the constable has grounds for suspecting the presence of articles of that kind.

NOW IT'S TIME FOR THE POLICE TO USE MORE NEW POWERS TO AMASS LOW LEVEL INTELLIGENCE ON THE ENTIRE UK POPULATION

I fink we're in need of some low level intelligence constable.

Right oh Sarge

THIS IS WHERE YOU SHOULD GET WORRIED. BASICALLY, YOU DON'T HAVE TO BE A MEMBER OF A BANNED ORGANISATION FOR THE POLICE TO INVESTIGATE YOU. YOU DON'T HAVE TO HAVE COMMITTED ANY CRIMINAL OFFENCE, OR INTEND TO. THE POLICE CAN INVESTIGATE ANYWAY, IN CASE YOU **MIGHT** BE DOING SOMETHING THAT **SHOULD** BE BANNED.

[THIS IS SECTION **32** IF YOU WANT TO LOOK IT UP ~ ALL THESE QUOTES ARE GETTING BORING]

The line's very crackly

DEAR SUE I GOT YOUR EMAIL...

She's coming out Sarge

AND IF THEY REALLY WANT TO DIG THE DIRT, THEY CAN COME INTO YOUR HOME TO FIND SOMETHING TO ARREST YOU FOR...

Warrant for a terrorist investigation

SAVE THE SEAGULL

What about these boltcroppers Mrs Grundlethorn?

I don't know anything about them, young man

I'm afraid you're going to have to do better than that.

What are THESE Mrs Grundlethorn?

Er, they're ordinary household pliers Constable. I wouldn't do anything harmful with them

PROVE IT Mrs Grundlethorn

**...ANYTHING THAT COULD BE USED BY A TERRORIST!**
*Possession for Terrorist Purposes.* **57** - (1) A person commits an offence if he possesses an article in circumstances which give rise to a reasonable suspicion that his possession is for a purpose connected with the commission, preparation or instigation of an act of terrorism...

...(2) It is a defence... to **prove** his possession of the article was not... connected with the commission, preparation or instigation of acts of terrorism.

(3)...If it is proved that an article –

(a) was on any premises at the same time as the accused ...the court may assume that the accused possessed the article, unless he **proves** that he did not know of its presence on the premises or that he had no control over it.

**[SCARY BIT]**

*Collection of Information.* **58** -(1) A person commits an offence if –
(a) he collects or makes a record of information of a kind likely to be useful to a person committing or preparing an act of terrorism, or
(b) he possesses a document or record containing information of that kind.

**SO** ⌄

Ah! I see that you've made a note of the PLACE and TIME where your local M.P. holds his surgery. We've got you now, oh-so-innocent-seeming granny. You're looking at a **TEN YEAR STRETCH IN PORRIDGE**

QUAKER OATS

YOU MAY NOT ADVOCATE ANY KIND OF IDEOLOGICALLY MOTIVATED ACTIVISM. YOU MAY NOT LEND YOUR SUPPORT TO THOSE WHO DO...

**BUT DO YOU POSSESS INFORMATION THAT A TERRORIST MIGHT FIND USEFUL?**
A PHONE BOOK? AN ELECTRONICS MANUAL? A GUIDE TO LAW, OR HUMAN RIGHTS?

HANG ON! WHAT ABOUT THIS CARTOON!? WHAT ABOUT THAT THEN? HUH?!! HUH?

BLAM!

[unfortunately this cartoon appears to have exploded under the pressure of its own paranoia]

DON'T WORRY, IT WON'T HAPPEN LIKE THAT. THE GOVERNMENT WON'T IMMEDIATELY BAN EVERY POLITICAL ACTIVIST WHO DAMAGES PROPERTY. THAT WOULD RISK A HUGE BACKLASH.
IT'S O.K., THE SECRETARY OF STATE WON'T BAN ANY GROUPS AT ALL, UNTIL HE WANTS TO...

AND THEN PEOPLE WILL BE ARRESTED, AND THEY WILL BE HELD WITHOUT CHARGE, QUESTIONED, HELD QUESTIONED, HELD FOR **SEVEN DAYS** WITHOUT CHARGE...

...MEASURED (BY FORCE) PHOTOGRAPHED (BY FORCE), SWABBED, SAMPLED, FINGER-PRINTED, (BY FORCE)

... QUESTIONED, QUESTIONED...

SOME OF THE PEOPLE WILL BE DENIED ACCESS TO A SOLICITOR FOR TWO DAYS,* AND NO-ONE WILL BE INFORMED WHERE THEY ARE.* AND SOME CHILDREN WILL BE ARRESTED, AND THEIR PARENTS WON'T BE TOLD FOR TWO DAYS,* AND THEN SOMETIMES THEY'LL ONLY BE ALLOWED TO SEE EACH OTHER "in the presence of a uniformed officer not below the rank of inspector. [Schedule 8.19.-(1)]

* Schedule 8.19-(3) [when] it is in the interests of the investigation or prevention of crime, or of the apprehension, prosecution or conviction of offenders

MR STRAW, I DON'T CARE IF SOME SENIOR POLICE OFFICER DECIDES THAT IT'S IN THE INTERESTS OF CRIME PREVENTION, I DON'T SEE HOW YOU CAN JUSTIFY THAT.

IF A PERSON COMMITS MURDER OR CRIMINAL DAMAGE, MR STRAW, THE ORDINARY CRIMINAL LAW CAN DEAL WITH IT. SO WHY CREATE ADDITIONAL OFFENCES, OF SPEAKING, THINKING (INTENT), POSSESSING INFORMATION, WEARING CLOTHES? YOU'VE ACQUIRED THE POWER TO CRUSH POLITICAL DISSENT MR STRAW. WHY DO YOU NEED IT? SHOULD I TRUST YOU NOT TO MISUSE IT? THIS MAKES ME SCARED, MR STRAW. IT MAKES ME TERRIFIED.

Translated from Cantonese:

"Did you know that these shoes sell in America for more money than my house cost?"

"What a rip-off eh. They're CRAP!!"

John Hodge

## WAKE UP! WAKE UP! IT'S YER ARBEIT MACHT FREIHEIT !

# Weekly SchNEWS

### FUCK ALL FOR THE UNEMPLOYED

#### Printed and Published in Brighton by Justice?

**Fri 14th January 2000**    http://www.schnews.org.uk/    **Issue 243**    **Free/Donation**

# WELCOME TO THE
# PROFIT ZONE

"Of course there is some commercial return, our shareholders would be unhappy if we ran this as a voluntary programme"

Kevin Faulkner, company secretary Manpower Services UK

"If you're over 25 and have been signing on for the past 2 years in Brighton you're no longer covered by the welfare state"

Public Commercial Union (PCU) rep.

Blink and you might have missed it, but come April three private companies will be running parts of the UK's Employment Service. If you live in Brighton, Plymouth, Southwark, Brent, Glasgow, Tower Hamlets (Working Links), Haringey, Newham, Liverpool, Sefton (Reed) or Birmingham (Pertemps), are over 25 and have been signing on for at least a year * then welcome to the "employment zone."

In Brighton a 'new' company called Working Links – made up of the Employment Service, Ernst and Young and Manpower Services will be running the zone. SchNEWS spoke to a member of the Job Centre's Union PCS to ask just what all this zone business was about.

"Employment Zones are a good idea in theory – all these different pots of money for training, dole etc will be put in one lump to say ok what do you want to do with it –with less emphasis on getting a crap job and more on decent training. However, it soon became apparent that that wasn't actually what was going to happen. Advisers will be the ones who make decisions on how a client's pot of money is spent."

And these private companies are in it for profit. Decent training costs a lot of money while forcing someone into a crap, unsubsidised job costs nothing. And if the company can find you a job, it gets to keep the pot of money. Your client adviser will also have all the powers under the Job Seekers Allowance to force people into any job. Refuse a job and your benefits will be stopped.

"Look what's happened with the New Deal in Hackney which Reed have been running. Their results have been very poor but despite that they're getting more and more work. Manpower are in it for the money – what else are they there for? All this bollocks about a new way forward, a lot more flexibility for the unemployed, it's exactly what Reed said, and it didn't happen It's just been like a cattle ranch there with people being sent to any old crap job."

Manpower have been sniffing around the job centres for years, and now their dreams have come true. As the PCS rep told SchNEWS " It's basically privatisation. A foot in the door for private companies who will no doubt want to expand into other areas of the employment service."

* varies in each area

## ALL YOU EVER WANTED TO KNOW ABOUT EMPLOYMENT AGENCIES, BUT WERE AFRAID TO ASK.

**MANPOWER** is now the largest employer in the world, finding people 1.4 million temporary jobs in 1997, and their last annual report revealed earnings of $10.5 billion worldwide. It already has a New Deal contract in Wales, where it came a stunning eighth out of 11 in the area for getting people into work. It has also earned itself lots of brownie points from the government by sponsoring the 'work-zone' in the Millennium Dome. Manpower had the job of recruiting strike-breakers when British Airways was facing strikes in 1997.

They are also the biggest employers of call centre staff in the UK - 25,000.

One disgruntled ex-employee told SchNEWS " Manpower is like an employment corporate cattle market for companies like BT. Labour is cheap, flexible and temporary - with no employment or union rights. Manpower have an office in every BT call centre in the country, and re-cycle staff on a week by week basis. Every week there is a new batch of automated voice robots for BT's telephone networks. Talk about job insecurity – I've seen Manpower staff thrown out of the building for arriving at work five minutes late, accidently cutting a customer off, or phoning in sick."

**ERNST AND YOUNG** are an accountancy firm that did a report on privitising the Employment Service. Hey presto – they become part of the 'team' that is getting work from privitisation!

**REED** Their boss is Alec Reed who likes to bung New Labour the odd £100,000, which is loose change when your family fortune is around £50 million. The firm have demonstrated the power of profit-led solutions by coming up with the country's fourth worse rate (19.6%) for getting "new dealers" from welfare to work. Reed did create one job, however, for Labour's Lord Tom Sawyer who got on the board of Reed Executive.

**PERTEMPS** meanwhile recently had their wrists slapped by the Advertising Standards Authority and had to change its brochure in which it claimed to be "the acknowledged market leader in both the temporary and permanent employment sectors...and the largest independent in the country." Pertemps is only the 11th largest employment agency by turnover, and only 5 per cent of this is generated by getting people permanent jobs.

\* The audit commission recently revealed that 383 councillors and officials have been caught fiddling the housing benefit system, getting away with an average of £2,200 in fraudulent claims!

\* The minimum 'how-the-bloody-hell-are-you-meant-to-live-on-that' wage is set to stay at the penny-pinching rate of £3.60 an hour for at least another year.

\* Scruffy job-seekers who refuse to get their dirty little fingers out and take jobs will face losing benefit, the government announced this week. It's all part of the New Deal ten point plan to clamp down on the hardcore of the long-term unemployed. The ten points include literacy and numeracy tests, compulsory two week presentation lessons 'to ensure young jobseekers can present themselves well to employers', and job coaches (?). The overhaul, on the second anniversary of New Deal, follows complaints from employers that 'a lack of basic skills and a negative attitude in job interviews' is holding people back.

**Brighton Against Benefit Cuts** produce a bi-monthly newsletter, 'Where's My Giro?' available for an SAE from 4 Crestway Parade, Hollingdean, Brighton, BN1 7BL www.muwc.demon.co.uk/

## CRAP ARREST OF THE WEEK

**For throwing a piece of mud**

Andy Wasley received a three month sentence for violent disorder last November for the dangerous crime of throwing mud! He was arrested after a demo at Hillgrove Farm, breeders of hundreds of cats for experimentation, which has now closed down.

The Chief Constable of Oxfordshire had complained to the Lord Chancellor that not enough people were receiving custodial sentences, and so Andy began a three month sentence at HMP Birmingham, even though the only evidence of this crime was some video footage of him bending down! He's since been released on the tagging system

\* Now that Hillgrove's gone, let's help Shamrock Farm monkey prison go the same way. National demo Sunday 30th January, ring 07020 936956 for transport.

# EXTERMINATE!

'The World Economic Forum is an independent, impartial, non profit foundation which acts in the spirit of entrepreneurship in the global public interest to further public interest to further economic growth and social progress'. World Economic Forum.

Yet again, unaccountable, un-elected, representatives from the corporate world of industry, political leaders, media moguls, and academics will sit behind closed doors to discuss the future of the global economy and the fate of the planet and it's people, in what has been coined, 'The Summit of Summits'.

The 30th meeting of the annual World Economic Forum (WEF) will be held from January 27th to February 1st, in the winter resort of Davos, Switzerland. The 2,000 self-proclaimed "Global Leaders" have chosen the theme for this meeting as 'New Beginnings: Making a Difference', or in laymans terms, 'New Exploitations: Making a Profit.'

When it was founded in 1971,the WEF was just a boring old management seminar. Now it has become one of the most important "think tanks" of the global economy. After the failure of the Millenium Round in Seattle (SchNEWS 240) the meeting in Davos will have a special significance. The WEF could once again come to the rescue. In the eighties, WEF provided the backbone to the Uruguay Round of the General Agreement on Tariffs and Trade, the nasty negotiations that led to the founding of the World Trade Organization, the global institution we all love to hate!

The WEF web-site boasts: 'We are moving from a world of territorial states to a world of different layers of authority…The Foundation Members of the World Economic Forum are the 1000 foremost global companies in the world today…One of our new "initiatives" is the Centre for the Global Agenda. This new orientation also encompasses our Centre for Regional Strategies, which will provide our members with privileged opportunities to have an impact on policy making in the worlds most important regions'.

But is this not just another arm of corporate control, bypassing and over-riding existing legislation and policies that often have an environmental, ecological and generally humane backbone, to make way for bigger corporate profits?

Demos are planned for the 29th January. Meet Davos train station 3 pm. Check out the WEF website www.weforum.org/

## DANCING AT FESTIVAL HORROR

Shane Collins,last years May Day pro-cannabis carnival organiser at Clapham Common,has been summoned to appear in court for the most hideous of crimes, having too much fun.Apparently 30-40 people out of 15,000 were dancing without a license-BASTARDS! Despite no complaints from the local residents, Lambeth Council have decided to bring this undesireable to justice. Shane is to appear at Balham Magistrates on Thursday 20th January 1pm 217 Balham High Rd.,SW17. He could face a fine of £20,000 or 6 months inside.For further info ring 0181-671-5936

## Remember Jill Phipps?

Jill Phipps was killed on 1st February 1995, crushed to death by a lorry carrying veal calves to Coventry airport. She was part of the campaign to stop the live export trade, in which week old calves are exported to France or Holland where they are reared in the appalling conditions necessary to produce white veal.There's a vigil to remember Jill on Sunday 30th January. Meet outside M Yates & Sons, opposite Manor Inn pub, Fridythorpe on the A166 York to Bridlington Road.  Tel 01482 899580

## SchNEWS in brief

Keith Campbell one of the creators of "**Dolly the sheep"** is giving an illustrated talk at the Gardner Arts Centre, University of Sussex on Monday the 24 January at 7pm, touting his book "The Second Creation". ** Cornerhouse have a new pamphlet out entitlted "How not to Reduce **Plutonium** Stocks" full of all the info you need on the dangers of nuclear reactors. Available from PO Box 3137, Station Road, Sturminster Newton, Dorset, DT10 1YJ. ** **Foxhunters** everywhere may be set to hang up their red coats and don green ones in a move that they believe will make them less objectionable to the general public! ** The Hull Schnews fan club tells us that there is a new autonomous centre called **MAFIA**, standing for Music, Arts, Food, Info and Action. Find them at the Old Balti House in Springbank or contact Hull Mafia @hotmail.com.** More good news from Dover! Nick Hudson, editor of the **Dover Express** has not only been sacked, but also slapped! Apparently Nick got involved in a heated debate at a party as to whether rascists should be allowed to dance to reggae music!** There's an all London march against racist police frame-up and murder on Saturday 22nd January. Meet 12 noon at Wood Green Common (Wood Green tube) then march to Tottenham Police Station ** After the **Seattle** hangover, there will be a public meeting with videos and speakers on Thurs 3rd Feb at 8pm at St Stephens Church Hall, Chessingham Road, Lewisham.** Oh vicious **Zapatistas**! Members of the revolutionary Mexican Zapatista Air Force, have attacked the Federal Army Encampment with paper aeroplanes carrying messages such as "Soldiers, we know that poverty has made you sell your lives and souls." ** **Pedal powered** PA's,children's pedal generators and recycled computer parts will be on display at the Campaign for Real Events,4th Pedal Power Convention,Sunday 30th January 12.00 till 6pm R.I.S.C. 35-39 London Street Reading.Cafe Open - and it's free **. Don't scoff yer **budgies**!The State Duma of Russia, the lower house of Parliament,has passed an animal rights Bill banning people from eating their pets.Their children have no such protection.

## CAMP CALL OUT

People are needed to defend mature oak trees and network of tunnels at **Gorse wood**, near Chelmsford, Essex, threatened by the building of a six lane bypass, 800 houses and a golf course. The camp, currently under the threat of eviction, is behind Rettendon church on the A130 between Chelmsford and Basildon. Plenty of sleeping space, bring useful tat. Site mobile 07957 915977

* Latest news from the camp in Essex where they are trying to stop Countryside Residential (North Thames Ltd, based in Basildon) from trashing a wildlife rich area between ancient woodlands for 66 luxury houses. The site contains endangered species such as great crested newts and is being cleared even though the legal agreements with Rochford District Council have yet to be signed. Interestingly no one seems to be able to get hold of the local police officer responsible for enforcing the Wildlife Protection Act ... and it turns out Countryside Residential have been funding the Essex Wildlife Trust.

As SchNEWS went to press contractors are clearing the land around the camp and have cut into Section 6 (squatted) land. Extra people desperately needed to help stop the clearance. They are also calling on groups up and down the country to protest at Countryside Residential estates being built around the country.
Contact: 0831-717815/01702-206353.

## HAMMERED

On February 1st 1999, Two members of the Aldermaston Women's Trash Trident affinity group swam through water in Barrow-in-Furness to cause damage and disarm specially designed radar equipment on the fourth Trident submarine.  Rosie and Rachel are charged with committing £100,000 of damage. That's a mere 7.5 percent of the staggering  cost of the Millenium Dome. Can we take a hammer to that?  Their trial begins on 24th January at Lancaster Crown Court. Get there and show them some support. This is an important trial, as Rosie and Rachel will be defending themselves, using both moral arguments and international law about nuclear weapons.

* Meanwhile... On Valentine's Day a day-long blockade of Faslane Naval Base is planned by Ploughshares and other anti-nuclear groups. Ring Brighton Peace Centre for transport details and spread some peace and love amongst the MOD! Trident Ploughshares: 01603 611953 or visit their Website on **http://www.gn.apc.org/tp2000/**

## TIME-PEACE

Meanwhile The National Peace Council is launching a "peace clock" to measure our progress towards the eventual abolition of war. The project was inspired by the 'bulletin of atomic scientists' back in 1945 when they began publishing a 'doomsday clock ' on the cover of their journal to show how close the world was to a nuclear holocaust. The hands of the peace clock will move forward and back at indications such as the number of countries signing key international treaties. The hands have been set at one hour to midnight, as we at the eleventh hour on our way to a world without war?

* For an epic millennium read, forget War and Peace, read 'Bloody Hell' by Dan Hallock. It tells the true story of the military machine with accounts from veterans of every major war this century revealing some of the horror. Tel Plough Publishing House, 08000180799 www.WARisHELL.com.

* Keep up to date with the latest information on the peace movement with the new magainzine from the new National Peace Council magazine 'Peace Movement'. For details ring the NPC 02076099666.

## ...and finally...

"We are no longer prawns of the government we are now prawns in our own right," says the **P**eople's **R**epublic of **A**shurst **W**ood **N**ation **S**tate (Prawns.) The East Sussex hamlet has declared independence from the UK and erected a series of border posts and demanded "foreigners" obtain visas for entry - "your UK passport means nothing here", SchNEWS was told by a spokesman.Their declaration of independence reads in part, "The formerly oppressed and unjustly taxed peoples are and of right ought to be free and independent, that they are absolved from all allegiance to the state of Great Britain." A letter was sent to HM Queen with no reply, though interested anarchists have been phoning from the continent, and a visiting TV crew from Russia invited King Prawn Mark over there! In 979 King Ethelred was thought to have died in the Village after waking up on the funeral pyre just before it was lit, and he granted them immunity from taxation.

www.ashdownforest.co.uk

### disclaimer

## Subscribe! _ _ _ _ _ _ _ _ _ _ _ _ _ _ _ _ _

Keep SchNEWS FREE! Send 1st Class stamps (e.g. 20 for next 20 issues) or donations (payable to Justice?) Ask for "Originals" if you can make copies. Post *free* to all prisoners. SchNEWS, c/o on-the-fiddle, P.O. Box 2600, Brighton, East Sussex, BN2 2DX.
*Tel/Autofax* : +44 (0)1273 685913    *GET IT EVERY WEEK BY E-MAIL*: schnews@brighton.co.uk

## Gorse Wood protest camp, Essex

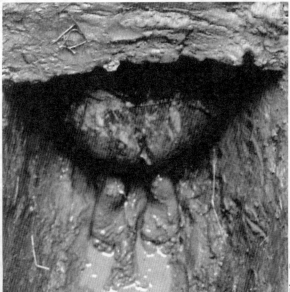

Pics: Ben

**Ferretting around in the tunnel at Gorse Wood.**

---

# SQUOTES 06/03/00

"I must have seen more than 500 very sick patients who are hyper-sensitive to electromagnitsm and lots more who are more moderately affected. Just as our bodies have evolved to respond to light, sound or heat, they have evolved to respond to the earth's magnetic field. The increasing number of man-made fields [mobiles/VDU's etc] is creating an electromagnetic smog which interferes with this and which I believe is very damaging to us all in the long term."

*DR JEAN MUNRO.*

FIXING THE PLUMBING AT OUR LOCAL AUTONOMOUS SQUAT CENTRE ALSO INVOLVED SAVING THE WHALE.

Pic: Dave Mirzoeff

**The disco at the Holtsfield low-impact Chalet Community, Gower, Wales.**

# GAIA'S SLAP - ATMOSFEAR IN THE 21st CENTURY

For years the world's big polluters poured scorn on the existance of global warming. But with sixty one British meteorological records broken over the last 20 years, climate change and global warming are now an officially acknowledged cause for major concern. In an extensive new investigation, Neil Goodwin unearths the raw truths which compromise our planets' future habitability.

**SQUALL**

**Where Do You Want To Grow Today?**
--
I Wanna Go Home
Underground Update
Features
Squall Pics
Frontline Communique
The State Its In
Squotes
Resources
Links
From Our Correspondence

Red sky at night, so the saying goes, is a shepherd's delight. But ask any gardener or farmer and they'll probably tell you that the ancient folklore which has underlined our expectations of the Great British weather for centuries is looking increasingly dodgy.

In fact over the last twenty years, 61 major meteorological records, from warmest November to wettest June, highest temperature to fastest wind, have been broken in the UK. How many times do we overhear conversations about late frosts and early blooms, or the discovery of another exotic insect hiking across a British windowsill?

The world is now experiencing the early symptoms of climate change, a process which is set to transform the world's weather beyond all recognition during the next century, and one that will severely test the human race's ability to adapt and survive. The Met Office has predicted an increase in Britain's average temperature of up to 3*C by the end of the next century, and a sea level rise of between 2 and 10 centimetres.

"It doesn't seem that much of a difference when you compare it to day to day weather variability," says Prof. Phil Jones, from the Climate Research Unit. "But our estimates of how cold it was during the last Ice Age - that it was about somewhere between 5-6¡ C colder than today, means we're talking about a rise that will have occurred between 1900 and 2100 of about nearly 3¡ C, which is half way to an Ice Age but in the opposite direction."

Natural disasters are increasing at a terrifying rate, both here and abroad. In 1998 the world suffered more than twice as much environmental damage as during the entire decade of the 1980's, at a cost of £142.4 billion. According to the Worldwatch Institute, 54 countries suffered from floods and 45 from severe drought.

The polar ice caps, which are particularly sensitive to global climate change, are melting at an alarming rate. In Antarctica, which has experienced a rapid temperature rise of 2.5¡ C over the last 50 years, the ice shelf

known as Larson A has already collapsed into the sea, while huge cracks have begun to appear in Larson B. Almost 2,000 square miles of Antarctica's south eastern tip has melted throughout the past year, and an iceberg larger than London is currently drifting towards the Argentinean coast.

Like its European neighbours, Britain has experienced its fair share of floods, droughts, coastal erosion and gales. The total cost of weather claims in Britain for 1998 was £663 million, with some sections of the Midlands being hit by severe flooding three times. Last year began with the worst floods to hit North Yorkshire in 68 years, and continued to throw up extraordinary natural anomalies such as invasions of jellyfish, and plankton blooms the size of Cornwall.

Throughout the past ten years Britain has endured four out of five of the hottest years ever recorded over a 330-year period. Scientists from the University of East Anglia have observed that this warmer weather has radically altered the migratory habits of birds such as swallows. Trees are coming into leaf much earlier and increasing numbers of 'alien' insects and spiders have colonised southern England. Huge numbers of termites in north Devon have been feeding on timber causing havoc to homes, whilst the rotund, black and brown spider (one of the 'False Widow' spiders), a bite from which can cause considerable pain, has also made an appearance.

## WOE ZONE

### Massive ozone hole observed over the Arctic.

An international group of scientists measuring the earth's Ozone layer have recorded a two third decrease in the earth's Ozone layer over the Arctic. Caused by man made pollution, the losses mean that the Ozone layer over Europe - which protects the earth from the sun's ultraviolet radiation will be thinner over the next few weeks leading to more of the kind of global warming which has been breaking up both Arctic and Antarctic iceshelves. The most dramatic ozone depletion occurs over the Antarctic, where British scientists observed a hole the size of the US and as deep as Everest in 1985. The latest ozone depletions come as a result of man made pollution nearly forty years ago and is sounding alarm bells for the future.

Even the Great British cod'n'chips is under threat. A 4¡ C rise in winter North Sea temperatures during the past six years has disrupted the breeding patterns of cod and whiting, causing stocks to plummet and prompting the EU to slash catch quotas for 2000. At the same time, exotic species such as red mullet, octopus and even Great White sharks have started to inhabit British waters.

Far from lending our climate a pleasant Mediterranean feel - a misconception based on the prediction that Southern England will become frost-free by the end of the next century - some scientists are warning that climate change could plunge Northern Europe into a mini Ice Age. Melt water from the Arctic could, they say, weaken and eventually shut down the Gulf Stream which draws up warm salty water from the tropics. A testament to the present effectiveness of the Gulf Stream in warming British waters comes from the fact that Britain shares the same latitude, but mercifully not the same icy winters, as Newfoundland on the Canadian coast.

The idea of Global cooling may seem decidedly unhelpful to those of us still grappling with the concept of Global warming, but whatever its final manifestation, climate change is set to transform every aspect of British life, from how we travel to what we wear, from where we live to what we eat. Business as usual, the politicians are now saying, will not be an option.

"I would say that we are being hit by five related issues," says Sir Crispin Tickell, the government's advisor on the environment. "The first is human population increase, which, in spite of figures starting to come down in certain places, is a major hazard. The second is degradation of land surfaces. The third is shortages of water and the pollution of water. The fourth is the destruction of biodiversity, so that we no longer have the natural services that we have hitherto enjoyed for free. And the last is climate change'"

Despite the best efforts of a tiny but noisy band of climate sceptics, such as Richard North and Dennis Avery, who continue to muddy the waters, the Government now accept 'the very real threat' that climate change will represent in the 21st Century and has begun to face up to what it describes as "difficult choices".

Last October, the Environment Agency, which estimates that 1.3 million British homes are currently at risk from flooding, launched a £2million flood awareness campaign called FloodLine. Speaking at the launch was the Rev. Graham St. John, who was one of ten thousand people affected by Britain's most devastating flood which hit Northampton in 1998, killing two people and destroying 2,500 homes and businesses.

THE GREENHOUSE EFFECT

GOSH, I WONDER WHY WE'RE GETTING THIS WEIRD WEATHER?

"What can you say to the couple I was only speaking to last week?" he asked the assembled media. "Aged 80, they'd spent eight and half-hours perched on top of their kitchen work surfaces waiting to be rescued. She was sitting on the cooker. Her husband was sitting there with his legs dangling in sewerage-strewn freezing cold water. There was no escape from it."

The Government has also initiated a number of studies into the effects of climate change on a regional basis across all sectors. These include Wales, Cornwall, Scotland, East Anglia, the Northwest, and the Southeast. As their findings emerge, our understanding of the extent to which climate change will transform Britain during the coming century will become more sophisticated.

The North West became the first region in Europe to complete such a study. It recognised that climate change is already a fact of life. Sea levels at Liverpool, it said, have been rising by 1 cm per decade and average temperatures have been increasing consistently since the 1960s. It pinpointed potential benefits from 'global warming' such as lower winter heating bills and higher incomes from tourism ('cafe society'), as well as detrimental effects such as coastal erosion ("managed retreat is a serious policy option, but will be controversial"), the increased likelihood of flood and storm damage, and a possible future difficulty in obtaining re-insurance cover. It underlined "the very real need to prepare for an uncertain future as climate change continues."

A £25 million government ad campaign was launched to encourage us to 'do our bit' by car sharing, recycling household waste, and taking a shower instead of a bath. In stark contrast to the scare tactics employed by the Tories over Aids awareness, New Labour's approach seems to be to tickle us into a more responsible attitude towards the environment. In one ad a woman careers down stairs on a death slide and proceeds to turn down her central heating.

In March 1999, the Chancellor Gordon Brown announced Britain's greenest budget, with 17 measures designed to tackle our over-dependency on the car, a major source of carbon dioxide and an essential nut to crack if Britain is to meet its target of a 20 per cent reduction in CO2 emissions by 2010.

Of these measures, the introduction of a six per cent road fuel duty has proved the most controversial, whipping up the full fury of the Road Haulage Association, and bringing hundreds of blockading lorry drivers onto the streets of London, their banners proclaiming 'PRESCOTT - AS YOU SCUBA DIVE, UK HAULIERS DIVE INTO THE RED!' (a reference to the Deputy Prime Minister's recent inspection of dying coral reefs), and 'GREEDY, GREEDY, GREEDY 2 JAGS' (a dig at Prescott's taste for Ministerial privilege).

Eight months on, however, Greenpeace blew a hole in the government's green credentials when it won a High Court action against them and ten oil companies over their failure to protect whales, dolphins and other marine species from the impacts of oil exploration on the Atlantic Frontier.

"We exposed the contradiction at the heart of Government policy," says Peter Melchett, Executive Director of Greenpeace UK. "Their environmental policy says we should cut down the use of fossil fuels to protect the climate and wildlife, while their energy policy tells the fossil fuel industry to go and dig as much oil as they can regardless of the consequences."

In October 1999 the Met Office issued a grave prediction that if the international community fails to curb greenhouse gas emissions large parts of South America and southern

Africa could lose their tropical forests by the 2080's. Eighty million people, they say, could be flooded each year due to rising sea levels, and some three billion people could suffer from increased water stress.

However, according to Peter Bunyard, author of 'Gaia in Action: Science of the Living Earth': "The radiative thermodynamic physics of the greenhouse effect [The what?! - Ed.] are such as to cause a long delay between the emissions of carbon dioxide into the atmosphere and the time when the effects on the climate actually manifest themselves. Hence, the CO2 that society emits into the atmosphere today will only act on the climate 50 to 80 years in the future. Conversely, the climatic changes that we are experiencing today are occurring in response to the CO2 we emitted during the Second World War." Therefore, measures to prevent severe ongoing climatic disruption cannot be taken soon enough.

American cars and industry currently belch out 25% of the greenhouse gasses which cause climate change, yet American society only amounts to four per cent of the world's population. Perhaps it's no surprise therefore, to learn that the US government is most resistant to international agreements designed to limit the level of greenhouse gas emissions.

So, as the world wakes up to the realities of climate change, a key question emerges: Do the politicians of the rich North have the will to risk political suicide by forcing their populations to curb lifestyles based on selfishness and greed?

"The Age of Consumerism has lead us to Climate Change," observes Sir Sonny Ramphel, the former Commonwealth Secretary General. "To roll back the dangers, we have got to undo some of the worst aspects of consumerism. And that means a change in lifestyles. The politicians who, in democratic societies, go to the polls promising the moon and the stars, conscious that they cannot fulfil them, are not about to turn around and say 'What I promise you is less of the same'. Until we develop the moral stature at the political level to the people of the rich world, we really will not be facing up to the challenges of Climate Change.'

Like Sir Sonny Ramphel, Dr. Mick Kelly, from the Climate Research Unit, senses the need for "a new kind of politician - a politician that's concerned about the next generation. How our children will fair as we move into the 21st Century."

But as society moves beyond a purely preventative approach to climate change, and steps up the process of actually dealing with the symptoms, there is, he recognises, the potential for an entirely new set of political challenges. "The challenge now is can we actually protect the whole population, even though that may prove very costly?

Do we have to take difficult decisions about levels of protection which may mean that we leave some people exposed simply because it would cost too much to provide them with an absolute level of protection? So these are questions we have to address."

No one can accurately predict the socio-economic effects of climate change. However, as Hurricane Mitch, the Orissa cyclone, and, more recently, the Mozambique floods have so ruthlessly demonstrated, many thousands will undoubtedly lose their homes and lives. Whole countries could become uninhabitable. Once again, food shortages could exacerbate an array of historical tensions and resentments. Water wars, environmental refugees, and the spread of diseases such as malaria and dengue fever could cripple entire continents.

So what, if anything, is your average person supposed to make of it all? Given the extent to which the debate around climate change has largely been conducted above our heads with liberal sprinklings of scientific gobbledegook - not a lot, says Charlie Kronick, from the Climate Action Network.

"If any global issue has been dogged by the democratic deficit, it's climate change. People you don't know, are telling you things you don't understand, about a problem you can't be sure you have, and instructing you to do things (like drive less or use less energy) that you feel that you can't achieve.
It is soul destroying, dis-empowering and has encouraged a complete opt out on the part of the public."

He continues: "Climate change as an issue has been dominated by the experts, whether from government, the scientific establishment or environment groups. To have any relevance beyond this ghetto, it will need to register within real communities, with real people, who are willing to make real change happen."

*For a fuller version of this article which includes statistics on major climactic events in the UK since 1980, log on to the features page at www.squall.co.uk*

---

# THAWS FOR THOUGHT

### *Global warming produces record breaking iceberg*

One of the largest icebergs ever recorded has broken away from the Ross Ice Shelf in Antarctica. The iceberg is over 183 miles long and 22 miles wide, covering an area the size of East Anglia. It is the latest Antarctic breakaway thought to be occurring because of global warming.

WAKE UP! WAKE UP! IT'S YER KURDISH-DAM *

# SchNEWS

### Printed and Published in Brighton by Justice?

**21st January 2000**     http://www.schnews.org.uk/    **Issue 244   Free/Donation**

THE DAM WILL NOT BE BUILT

# TURKISH DELIGHT

**"The prime minister is backing a project that would be a disaster for the environment, a tragedy for local people, and a threat to peace."**

Tony Juniper, Friends of the Earth

SchNEWS ain't having a Turkish ** but the planned Ilisu Dam, in South-East Turkey could well be "the biggest corruption scandal in western Europe" (George Monbiot). **The hydro-electric dam will flood 52 Kurdish villages and 15 towns.** One of these is Hasankeyf, one of the most ancient settlements in the world. It is the only town in the region to survive the middle ages, protected so tightly by planning laws that hotels are not even allowed to be built for the hoards of visiting tourists. The Kurds regard this city as their cultural heartland and see this project as a political tool to continue to ethnically cleanse them from Turkey. One angry Kurd commented "By destroying Hasankeyf, they hope to eliminate our history". About 16,000 Kurds are expected to lose their homes and land without compensation, and another 20,000 will have their lives disrupted. At least 19 Kurdish villages in the reservoir area have already been cleared at gunpoint and then burnt. Disagreeing with the dam's construction has been outlawed. Surprise, surprise, there is no resettlement package for the dispossessed.

There is also the added fear that Turkey will have the means to cut off the water supply to Syria and Iraq once the dam is built. This issue has already been identified as a potential cause of war in the region. Boutros Boutros-Ghali, former secretary-general of the UN has stated that, "The next war in the Middle East will be fought over water, not politics."

Top cabinet ministers, including Robin Cook, Stephen Byers and fat controller John Prescott, have advised against the dam. Even those environmentally challenged people at the World Bank are refusing to have anything to do with the project. The Bank admits that the plan violates the UN Convention drawn up to prevent border disputes and wars between states that share water resources. If it violates World Bank 'ethical' policy (?!), just who is prepared to get involved...and why?!

## Balfour Beatty and Tony Blair...come on down!!!

Balfour Beatty have become the New chums of the Labour crew. One of its executives was seconded to the Dept of Trade and Industry's "innovation unit", while Sir Malcolm Bates, architect of the Private Finance Initiative (see SchNEWS 219), and one of Blair's heroes, was chosen as the ideal man to chair London Transport. Until his appointment, he was a director of BICC - the parent company of Balfour Beatty. Oooh.. what nasty tangled webs they weave!

Who's Balfour Beatty? They are the lovely company that built roads like the A30 in Devon. They also played a part in the Pergau Dam fiasco in Malaysia, which never worked but gave the government the opportunity to sell the Malaysians arms.

As for Tony Blair's involvement... issues such as Turkey's desire to become part of the European Union, and the fear of losing money gained by extensive arms sales to a Nato ally were clearly too pressing for him to risk upsetting the Turkish Government. Don't worry about the 20,000 people set to have their lives disrupted, Tony, we're sure they'll manage somehow!

In order for the Ilisu dam to comply with European Law, the government needed to provide an environmental assessment of the dam. The documents revealed the devastating environmental impact of the dam and the expected human rights violations. But all this now means nothing as the final environmental assessment report will be prepared by none other than... Balfour Beatty!!

---

**WE DON'T BYATT MR WIMP**

Thames Water, has decided in its wisdom to cut 1,000 jobs over the next five years. Welsh Water 600 jobs. Severn-Trent Water 1,100 jobs. Are they skint or bastards? Apparently the latter. This all arose due to regulators asking for bill reductions. One, namely Mr Byatt, known affectionately in the trade as "water wimp" violently responded by speaking through a spokesman saying "There is nothing we can do" Water wanker! No wonder Ofwat employed him. Poverty stricken Welsh Water make £35 profit on every £100 bill.

---

Feeling outraged at these projects? Did you realise that you have, and will be, actually helping to fund them? Welcome to the world of the Export Credit Guarantee Department.

This is a cheeky little scam that provides insurance for companies operating abroad. If the host country doesn't pay, the agency, meaning the taxpayers, foot the bill. The Department then uses its muscle, backed by the govt, to force the reluctant country to reimburse it with interest effectively acting as a global debt collector for British corporations.

The Department kindly refuses to take social, human or environmental rights into account preferring to leave it up to the host country. George Monbiot has described them as, "the biggest threat to sustainability and social justice on earth...It pursues it's money with ruthless determination, even when the debts were incurred for projects crawling with corporate corruption It is responsible for 95% of the debt owed by Southern countries to the British Government."

Want to hear more? This nasty, secretive little lot is at present backing two nuclear power plants in China and supported the Nathpa Dam in India. And it gets worse! British Aerospace's sale of 40 Hawk jets to Indonesia was insured by the Department.

### DAMNED STUPID

Another controversial dam is the one on the Narmada River in India, turning the valley into a series of reservoirs. It will affect the lives of 25 million people who live in the valley, and will submerge and destroy 4,000 square kilometres of deciduous woodland. The Narmada Bachao Andolan (Save Narmada Movement) have been fighting against the proposed dams for the past 14 years. Arundhati Roy, the Booker Prize winning author who was arrested last week for her part in the anti-dam demonstrations, describes the effects of such developments in her book 'The Greater Common Good', "Big Dams are obsolete...They're undemocratic...There was a time when Big Dams moved men to poetry. Not any longer. All over the world there is a movement growing against Big Dams".

## SchNews Vocab Watch

* **Kurdish-Dam** is *not* Cockney Rhyming Slang for Kurdistan. Kurdistan is the area Kurdish people have inhabited for over 4,000 yrs. It was carved up by French & British colonialists in a 1923 treaty after the collapse of the Ottoman empire to become parts of Iran, Iraq, Syria and Turkey.

** **Turkish-Bath** – Cockney Rhyming Slang for Laugh

* **Kurdistan Solidarity Committee Trade Union Group**, Tel: 0171 250 1317

## Occidental Damage

"We will in no way sell our Mother Earth, to do so would be to give up our work of collaborating with the spirits to protect the heart of the world, which sustains and gives life to the rest of the universe, it would be to go against our own origins, and those of all existence."

Statement of the U'wa People, August 1998.

The U'wa of the Colombian cloud forest are in a life-and-death struggle to protect their traditional culture and sacred homeland from Occidental (Oxy) Petroleum's proposed oil drill site. 200 of the U'wa people are occupying the drilling site and thousands more will join them at any sign of activity. The U'wa's opposition to the oil project is so strong that they have vowed to commit collective suicide if Occidental Petroleum and the Colombian government proceed with the project on their ancestral lands. Throughout Colombia, oil is linked with violence and terror.

The U'wa people's struggle exploded into the public arena last March with the murders in Colombia of three American indigenous rights activists. One of them Terence Freitas was a founder of the U'wa Defense Working Group and had devoted the last two years of his life to supporting the tribe in their campaign to stop Occidental's oil project.

"...we ask that our brothers and sisters from other races and cultures unite in the struggle that we are undertaking...we believe that this struggle has to become a global crusade to defend life." - Statement of the U'wa people

One of Occidental's largest shareholders is Boston-based financial giant Fidelity Investments. Fidelity have been given a deadline of the 1st March to either convince Occidental to cancel the project or show that they will not invest in genocide. Ironically, Fidelity's slogan is, "We help you invest responsibly."

There's a day of action on 3rd February. Further info: www.ran.org.

## FISTFUL OF DOLLARS

The capital of Ecuador has been brought to a standstill by thousands of indigenous locals who are protesting against the worsening economic situation in the country. The local currency, the sucre has collapsed from being worth 7000 to the dollar, to over 25,000 and many previously owned state companies have been privatized in the pursuit of more profit. Indigenous people make up over a fifth of the population of Ecuador, but are among the most impoverished and repressed sections of society. The President of Ecuador also recently announced the 'dollarisation' of Ecuador's economy, meaning that the dollar would replace the sucre.

This was the final straw for millions who were fed up with the country's neo-liberal policies, and lack of real democracy. So they formed the confederation of the indigenous nationalities of Ecuador –CONAIE. This operates as an alternative people's parliament and believes in decentralizing power to the country's 21 regions. Mass protests are bringing the country to a standstill, with protestors blocking roads and teaming up with striking oil workers to try and cut off the country's fuel supplies. Over 45,000 cops and troops have been mobilized to confront the protestors in the capital, but the Indians are refusing to leave or to negotiate with the president, who they don't consider to be president anyway!

Info is still sketchy about just what is going on at the moment, but check out www.coli_uni-sb.de/~pietsch/kosovo/

## SchNEWS in brief

Lorenzo Kom'boa Ervin, a former **Black Panther** who has previously been imprisoned for his struggle for the Black community, is coming to the UK as part of the MayDay 2000 Festival. He plans to do a tour speaking of his life, struggles and beliefs. If anyone is interested in arranging a venue or putting Lorenzo up during his stay, contact MayDay 2000, London WC1N 3XX, Tel: 020 8374 5027 ** There will be a public meeting entitled "**People and Protest**" discussing the war against capitalism with a slant on the Seattle protests. It's at 8pm on Thursday 3rd February at Middle Street Primary School Hall, Middle Street, Brighton.** The Museum of London is holding an unusually radical exhibition called "**Message to the Mayor**: Don't Sterilise our City". It plans to draw the Mayoral candidates' attentions to issues regarding the state of the city including 'Keep Our Capital Messy'. It runs from 11th Jan to 20th Feb. Tel: 0171 814 5500 ** An inquest into the murder of **Diarmuid O'Neill**, shot and killed by the Metropolitan Police during a raid on his home on 23rd September 1996, begins at Kingston Crown Court on Jan 31st. Justice for Diarmuid O'Neill Campaign, BM Box D. O'Neill, London WC1N 3XX.** The **Smash Genetix** 20, who were in court this week for a proposed three week trial over alledgedly trashing an AgrEvo GM maize site last year, were out of court after 1 1/2 days! After a plea bargain, 11 were bound over to keep the peace for twelve months. The remaining nine received either one year conditional discharges, or £200 fines. ** There's a meeting against the **Terrorism Bill** Conway Hall, Red Lion Square, Holborn, 26th January, 6:30pm ** Campaign Against Arms Trade women's network are meeting on Saturday 29th 2-5 pm at Conway Hall, Red Lion Square, Holborn to plan an event for **International Women's Day** in March Tel 0171 281 4369

## GET OFF THE 28 BUS!

Outrage! are calling for a boycott of all Stagecoach bus and train services, after the companies chairman Brian Souter gave more than £500,000 through his charitable foundation to the Scottish Schoolboards Association. The money will fund a T.V. and advertising campaign against the repeal of section 28 in Scotland – the law which prevents schools and teachers promoting homosexuality.

Brian Souter's a lovely bloke: New Labour supporter, committed Christian, and rampant capitalist who has made his millions by buying up bus and rail systems as they become privitised, with operations in China, Brazil, U.S., Canada, and New Zealand.

An example of just how the firm made it's millions can be seen in Darlington, where a Monopolies and Mergers Commission report called their activities "predatory, deplorable and against the public interest". The 90-year-old municipal Darlington Transport found that its drivers were poached and Stagecoach arrived two minutes earlier at bus stops offering free trips. Darlington Transport went bust, Stagecoach raised the fares and cashed in.

Since then they've been the subject of 8 other reports from Monopolies & Mergers and 24 inquiries by the Office of Fair Trading.

Repeal of section 28 is supported by organisations like the Children First and Childline and most of MPs in the new Scottish parliament. But a spokesman for the Souter Foundation reckons that "this is about democracy." And moral decency perhaps as well? Something Souter and his Stagecoach cronies know all about.

## PARTY ALL WEEK LONG!

It's been a good week to boogie, first we heard the government was gonna be gracious enough to allow us to dance on Sundays. The Home Office Minister responsible for relaxing the 200 year old Sunday Observance Act, obviously has the funk saying, "If people want a bit of Sunday night fever, that's fine with me." Better news was to come when Shane Collins, organiser of the May Day Cannabis Festival at Clapham Common, faced getting on down with a 6 months prison sentence and a £20,000 fine because people danced at last year's event without a license. On Thursday Shane was found not guilty and awarded court costs of two travelcards.(It's estimated Lambeth Council spent £12,000). He'll probably still be celebrating on the 6th May when the next 'Smokey Bear' festival will be held at Kennington Park.

* Boo! This years Ambient Picnic in Guildford has been cancelled by the Guildford Philharmonic (they have a concert the night before the Picnic and the Ambient organisers share the staging costs). Apparently, last year the Philharmonic went over-budget, and so have decided to have a "tribute-band" gig instead on the Sunday to pay off the debt.

## CLIFF'S DYING FLAME

Plans for a Flame of Hope, lit by Sir Cliff Richard, that was to last all year to remind the people of Birmingham of Jesus Christ quickly burnt out when the beacon went out after just a couple of weeks because someone had forgotten to order enough gas! Prior to lighting the flame on New Year's Eve, an excited Cliff said "It's great to know that...a Flame of Hope will burn throughout the Millennium year." When SchNEWS spoke with Cliff this week, he told us, "The Church will always be full of gas, even if the bottle isn't.' Never mind, Cliff, you could always take a match to 'Millennium Prayer' instead!

## Davos Station

The city of **Davos** has announced that it won't tolerate planned protests during the week in which the **World Economic Forum** will meet at the Swiss winter resort (see Schnews 243.) Thousands of policemen, private security guards and military will transform this little place in the swiss mountains into a high security area. Anti-WTO-Koordination, a group based in Bern, has announced its protest "against this decision which is a clear violation of our civil rights." Demos are still planned for 29 January. Meet at Davos train station at 3 pm. www.reitschule.ch/reitschule/anti-wto or e-mail them at fantasia39@hotmail.com.

## ...and finally...
## Fucking Tourists

Tourists are causing a lot of anxiety - and are costing money - to a tiny village where signs keep disappearing. What do the signs read? "Welcome to Fucking, Austria."

Pronounced "fooking," the little hamlet of Fucking is named after the man who founded the village in the 6th century. His name? Focko.

The town sign has been stolen seven times in the last few months. With signs costing several hundred dollars apiece, much of the tiny town's budget is being spent replacing the signs, says Siegfried Hoeppel, the Mayor of Fucking. He went on to express his hope that further thefts will be avoided through the use of increased concrete and ... bigger screws.

**disclaimer**

## Subscribe!

Keep SchNEWS FREE! Send 1st Class stamps (e.g. 20 for next 20 issues) or donations (payable to Justice?) Ask for "Originals" if you can make copies. Post *free* to all prisoners. SchNEWS, c/o on-the-fiddle, P.O. Box 2600, Brighton, East Sussex, BN2 2DX.

Tel/Autofax : +44 (0)1273 685913 *GET IT EVERY WEEK BY E-MAIL:* schnews@brighton.co.uk

WAKE UP! WAKE UP! IT'S YER GENES ARE UNDER ATTACK

# Weekly SchNEWS

*Printed and Published in Brighton by Justice?*

**FRI 28TH JA0NUARY 2000**  http://www.schnews.org.uk/ **Issue 245  Free/Donation**

# TRIPS, D.N.A. & ORGASMS

"Right now, the US is supporting a loophole so large that ship-loads of genetically engineered grain could go through there."
Sarah Newport, Friends of the Earth

Surprise, surprise! The first major international trade talks since the Seattle debacle look set to fall apart, just like the stomachs of the poor bastards eating the crap..

Representatives of 150 nations began talks in Montreal on Monday in another attempt to come to an agreement which would regulate trade in Genetically Modified foods. However, the U.S. and four other nations in the so-called Miami "Mice" Group, Canada, Australia, Argentina, Chile and Uruguay – basically the world's biggest grain exporters - plus their lobbying mates from the Global Industry Coalition representing 2,200 biotech companies worldwide, are once again trying to put the boot into any agreement

The European ministers arrived at the talks on Wednesday, except for the French minister who thought there was more chance on him dining on British beef than this bunch of G.M. freaks coming to a consensus. One U.S. official put it more bluntly: "It would be a miracle if we succeed in hammering out an agreement." Meanwhile, the Italian minister, contrary to popular belief did not surrender when he saw the protesters, but was in fact at home with the flu.

## PIE THE GM GUY!

Proponents of biotechnology were holding a news conference to extol the virtues of genetically altered food when a pie-wielding protester found his mark. "Down with biotechnology!" the assailant shouted. "We have to eat those foods — not you!" Joyce Groote, the receiver of this well aimed flan stated "at least it was to my taste" Unlike the shite he throws at us.

In London banners bearing the slogan 'Gene dictators - the world is watching' were hung outside Canada House, with the area being symbolically sealed with biohazard tape by protesters in decontamination suits. Anti-GM activists around the globe also joined the demonstrations this week, with a march in Montreal and actions as far afield as South Korea and Australia.

With massive pressures from consumers European Union ministers are pushing for clear labelling on foods. They are part of the 'like-minded' group (many of whom

are 'third world' countries) representing over a hundred nations, who are arguing for the right to be informed of and refuse to import genetically modified foods, seeds and other GM products. The US reckon not only will this break 'free trade' rules but will cost them billions of dollars just to seperate GM and non GM food. Our genetically modified hearts bleed.

And if an agreement is signed? Well, the US could once again use the strong arm tactics of the World Trade Organisation (WTO) to say that the agreement was a barrier to trade. The stakes are high with the bio-technology industry worth billions, and the US complaining that it is already losing £120 million annually because of the European Unions resistance to GM foods. But force feeding us all frankenstein fodder will not go down well with the public, and will make the WTO, still shaky after the kicking it got in Seattle (see SchNEWS 240) about as popular as a socialist at a New Labour Conference

* Look out for the Trade Related International Property rights talks in Geneva, in February. TRIPS (not as fun as they sound) give the multinationals the right to patent life. They're already selling living organisms and robbing indigenous people of their DNA. Watch out for protests in Geneva. Hooray!

* Genetic Engineering Network (GEN),PO Box 9656, London N4 4JY,Tel 0208 374 9516 www.geneticsaction.org.uk/protocol

* 'Animal feed and genetic engineering' available for 40p SAE to Corporate Watch, 16b Cherwell St., Oxford, OX4 1BG www.corporatewatch.org

## MIAMI MICE

"The Biosafety talks have been stalled for too long…if the Miami Group wants to remain isolated, so be it. The rest of the world cannot be their hostage forever".    Benny Haerlin,Greenpeace

At the international trade talks in Seattle an attempt was made to form a "biotech working group" within the World Trade Organisation. This would mean that trade in genetically modified organisms would fall under WTO regulations. Luckily for people who eat food, this motion was defeated. If no protocol agreement is reached in Montreal by Saturday, talks will continue in Nairobi in May – a less friendly atmosphere for U.S. based multinationals.

## WOT A RELIEF!

Midland Expressway Limited (MEL), the company behind the Birmingham Northern Relief Road, are in a little financial strife thanks to a long public enquiry and the occupation of the site by protesters. After a 3 year delay the cost of the road has doubled, and now MEL is being relieved by a shortlist of eight of yer favourite banks. MEL are looking for a little spare change from the banks, somewhere in the region of £700million, to make sure the road goes ahead. As Birmingham Friends of the Earth points out " Investment into this road is the achilies heel for the Highways Agency and the Department of the Environment."

* The **HOCKLEY** protest camp in Essex, set up to prevent 66 luxury houses being built on greenbelt land, are in court today (Friday) and expecting eviction within the next 2 weeks. Legal aid for an appeal has been mysteriously withdrawn, but a friendly local lawyer has offered his services for free. Tel 0831 717815 or check out www.angelfire.com/mt/GBH

* Clearance work has started on the **Glen of the Downs** protest site near Dublin. The nature reserve is being destroyed so a road can be widened to a dual carriageway. People needed now. www.emc23.tp/glen

# REVOLTIN' STUDENTS

Students at School of Oriental and African Studies (SOAS) in London went into occupation this Tuesday in defence of over 30 tuition fee non payers who are threatened with disciplinary action. The occupiers took over the college's management offices on the 1st floor to demand that the college does not expel non payers, that they refuse to collect fees and that they lobby the Government for their abolition. SOAS management continually winge about how they're not responsible for tuition fees, and students should lobby the government. However the head of SOAS, Tim Lankester has considerable influence in government circles, since he has been an executive director to the World Bank and IMF, and was permanent secretary at the Dept for Education for a while.

Management decided to evacuate all 5 floors of the SOAS building. They even shut down the college's telephone and internet system as well for a while, so no-one on campus could use their e-mail! Management claim that this was done under Health and Safety law, but it is more likely to be a tactic to try and turn students and staff against the occupiers. However, the lecturers' union said that closing down the building amounted to a lock-out under trade union law, and contested it. Some sympathetic lecturers have even been holding lectures in the occupied building. Management agreed to reopen most of the building on Thursday morning, but the floors above and below the occupied corridor are still locked. They also agreed to meet the occupiers to negotiate, but they are still up for eviction in the High Court this Friday, and could be evicted at any time after.

* Campaign for free Education, PO Box 22615 London. N4 1WT   Tel 0958 556 756 cfe@gn.apc.org,

## BLAIR WITCH-HUNT

SchNEWS readers may remember that last November 40+ students from Sussex University stopped Cherie Blair coming to a posh Uni dinner. She was supposed to talk about increasing access for women to enter higher education, but the Sussex Non-Payment Campaign saw this as complete hypocrisy when it was her husband's government that had abolished grants and brought in fees during the last two years. They occupied the dining room where the dinner was to take place and eventually the dinner was cancelled. The University weren't best pleased, and in retaliation are now victimising some of the students who were there. Seven are to be disciplined and 3 of these are to be done for breaking and entering. On top of this the Uni have also sent the cops round to people's homes. This victimisation and harassment is a political move to break the Non-Payment Campaign. These students need your support now.

* Sussex Non-Payment Campaign, Falmer House, University of Sussex, Falmer, Brighton BN1 8DN or susxnonpay@hotmail.com.

## VIVISECTORS SHOPPED

The Shopworkers Union, UDSAW, this week announced that it was withdrawing it's investments in Huntingdon Life Sciences. Huntingdon vivisect dogs, cats and monkeys among other animals and were secretly filmed by Channel 4 showing workers punching and beating Beagle puppies. Apparently the union was not aware of the involvement which came from Labour's staff pension fund. * National Demo against HLS on Sat 12th Feb. Phone 0121 632 6460 for transport and more details.

# SchNEWS in brief

**Riotous Assembly** is a forum for direct action campaigners in Manchester to meet each other. Their next meeting Tuesday 1st February, 7:30pm, Yard Theatre, 41, Old Birley Street, Hulme (opposite the Junction Pub)This month's short discussion is "World Trade Organisation / Seattle - What Next? www.snet.co.uk/ef/ ** On the same lines in the Capital, is the **London Underground**. Next meeting Friday 4th February at the Arsenal Tavern, Blackstock Road, London, N4 (Finsbury Park Tube). With cheap food and music from 9pm and a suggested donation of £2. And if you're in Brighton, then check out the Rebel Alliance. Next meeting Sunday February 6th at Brighton Unemployed Centre, 6 Tilbury Place 6pm (turn left past Hectors Pub up very steep Carlton Hill) ** A demonstration has been called in London to oppose the Russian war in **Chechny** on Saturday 5 February . The march starts at 12 noon at Tothill Street (behind WestminsterHall, Tubes: St James's Park) Tel 0171 207 3997 ** **Showcase for Kosova** Headmix Collective, story telling and films. Sunday 30th, 5pm-10:30pm, The Gloucester, Brighton. Free food before 7pm!. + SEATTLE FILM ** There's a **The Land Is Ours** Winter Gathering at the Exodus Collective Manor Road (the A6), Nr Luton on the18th - 20th February. Sleeping space avaliable, bring a mat and money (£1 charge for each meal). Tel 0181 357 8504 www.oneworld.org/tlio ** **Peace 2000** aims to "promote a culture of Nonviolence for the New Millennium". For a diary of events ring 01273 620125.** On 1st Feb there will be a talk and video showing about Shamrock monkey farm, followed by a discussion of the Terroism Bill. Contact Worthing eco-action, PO Box 4144, BN14 7NZ. ** Protesters took Pie-rect action against Dolly the Sheep's father this week.While promoting his new book, The Second Creation, Keith Campbell was planted a lovely fresh pie in the face, while being told to 'fuck his sheep'. ** Congrats to **Chumbawumba's** Alice Nutter and Keir on the birth of baby Mae.

## Inside SchNEWS

Two more people have been sent down for June 18, and would all love to receive your witty scriblings: Jeff Booker , DN 7071, and Stuart Tokham, DN 7072, both at HMP Brixton, Jebb Avenue, London, SW2 5XF. Jeff got 21 months for violent disorder, while Stuart received 12 months.

**\*URGENT WITNESS APPEAL** - Danny Penman is a sympathetic journalist, who has covered such issues as the M11 campaign. He was visciously attacked and hospitalised by the police in Euston, November 30th. You can Call Danny on 0850 751575. *If there are any witnesses from **J18**, or **Euston** that may help someones case, call:Legal Defence Monitoring Group 0171 837 7557

## SPUD-U-LIKE

Fed up with the choice of potatoes in your local greengrocers? Want to get your hands on an *International Kidney* or a *Yukon Gold*?. Then why not get along to Ryton Organic Gardens on the 5th and 6th February for the 7th National Potato Days. On offer for spud lovers will be seeds and tubers from 120 varieties of potatoes. The event organised by the Henry Doubleday Research Association(HDRA) who are keen to increase the number of potato varieties avaliable, will also include talks, gardening advice and cookery demonstrations. Entrance is £3, or free to HDRA members. More information: 024 7630 8211. www.hdra.org.uk

# DEATH IN CUSTODY

"The Home Office has confirmed that, early on the morning of Monday 24th January, a 49 year old asylum seeker from Lithuania, committed suicide in Harmondsworth Detention centre".

Figures announced by the Commons Public Accounts Committee, reveal that 71,000 asylum seekers entered Britain last year, a 55% increase from 1998. Downing Street blames the confict in Kosovo for the significant rise, MPs criticise the Home Office for not doing enough whilst Barbara Roche, the immigration minister claims that the problem is under control! BUT WHAT ABOUT THE REFUGEES??? Welcome to the lovely world of refugee detention!

Yes, the Government's answer is to lock asylum seekers up in Detention Centres and prisons whilst they wait for their cases to be heard. One of these places is HMP Rochester where refugees make up almost half the prison population. A report compiled by Sir David Ramsbotham the chief inspector of prisons, showed the appalling treatment that the asylum seekers receive. The denial of basic rights, and disregard for regulations was revealed to be commonplace. Refugees are given no opportunity to work and earn money, being forced to survive on the generous amount of £2.50 a week. Prison guidelines are issued to them only in English, despite the majority being unable to speak the language. The list goes on..no visits, no right to exercise, no choice of menu, no access to the gym or library...

So what's being done about it??? Surprise, surprise...not a great deal. Prison officials admit that Embassies are not informed of the refugees' detention. Even more worrying is the confirmation that the Immigration and Nationality Directorate has "no recognised imput into the treatment of detainees". So there we have it, Great Britain, what a wonderful place to be a refugee! Hardly suprising that one took his own life, is it?

* National Coalition of Anti-Deportation Campaigns, 110 Hamstead Road, Birmingham, B20 2QS. Tel 0121 554 6947.

# ...and finally...

"I don't like doing this" Judge Leahy told defendant Kenneth Saasta while pronouncing sentence, "because cocaine dealing carries a mandatory prison sentence. But after looking at all the evidence, I'm gonna have to let you off with community service, because you're so goddam fat you'd break the jail."The prosecuting attorney begged the judge not to impose a custodial sentence: "Saasta weighs more than 47 stone and there isn't a jail in the state that can hold him. We have to prise him through the cell doors. The night he was arrested, he demolished all the bunks in the police cells by lying down on them, and smashed three toilets simply by sitting on them. No prison uniforms will fit him, he can't stand for more than 5 minutes but chairs collapse when he sits on them, and because of this problem with constant diarrhoea, we have to hose everywhere he's been. The jail would need to buy reinforced beds, chairs and toilets and worse, he's so fat he can't even cut his own toenails or wipe himself in the bathroom,. Someone has to do it for him and the sheriff's department is threatening strike action if Saasta is sent to jail." Judge Leahy also ordered that Saasta be tagged with an electronic monitoring device, but this was overuled when it was discovered that none of the devices were large enough to fit round his ankles.Stolen from Merseyfin, who nicked it themselves from San Jose Mercury News

**disclaimer**
SchNEWS warns all gen'ies not to grant any wishes to profit mad crazy genetic scientists. Honest!

***Subscribe!***
Keep SchNEWS FREE! Send 1st Class stamps (e.g. 20 for next 20 issues) or donations (payable to Justice?) Ask for "Originals" if you can make copies. Post *free* to all prisoners. SchNEWS, c/o on-the-fiddle, P.O. Box 2600, Brighton, East Sussex, BN2 2DX.
*Tel/Autofax* : +44 (0)1273 685913   *GET IT EVERY WEEK BY E-MAIL:* schnews@brighton.co.uk

WAKE UP! WAKE UP! WE'RE NOT LICKED YET

# Weekly SchNEWS

Printed and Published in Brighton by Justice?

**Friday 4th February 2000**   http://www.schnews.org.uk/   **Issue 246   Free/Donation**

# POSTMAN SPLAT

> "We are fundamentally a benefits post office, this decision will close me down, and the knock on effect will be devastating to the local community."
> Rod, Sub Postmaster, Brighton

"The government talks a lot about social exclusion and you don't get much more excluded than living in a village without any services."

David Mundell, Member of the Scottish Parliament

**A new Post Office Bill announced in parliament last week could lead to the closure of thousands of sub post offices, thanks to a decision to pay state benefits directly into bank accounts.**

The government's own figures show that nearly 8,000 of the 19,000 Post Offices in Britain are at least 40% reliant on income from dealing with benefits. The switch could sound the death knell to thousands.

SchNEWS visited our local sub post office in Sutherland Road which like the majority are small and independently owned. While we were there chatting to Pheme and Rod, about 20 people popped in - one person paid some bills, a couple bought stamps, the rest were all there to cash their benefits. But it is more than just a post office, it is a focal point for the community. Each person that came in was greeted by name, came to chat and exchange news, to ask advice or help in filling out forms. Sutherland Road postie also serves a large area where there is just one grocery store, a newsagents and a pub. All these undoubtedly benefit from people cashing pensions or unemployed cheques nearby.

The decision to use the new system will save the government around £400 million a year - if you don't take into account the loss of some 30,000 counter jobs and the knock on affect to local communities and the fact that even the government admit they might have to spend money subsidising post offices to keep them open.

New Labour has even admitted that the country needs to maintain a wide network of post offices, which is obviously why it has let around 200 sub post offices close every year since it has been in office.

Of course it's convenient for some people to get benefits paid into their bank account - but what if you're poor, old and frail; there's no bank in your village, you don't have a car, and the bus service is non-existent?

While 60% of parishes still have post offices, only 5% have bank or building society branches – and the situation is set to get a lot worse. Even a new report from the British Bankers Association admitted that the elderly, people with mobility disabilities and women with young children faced difficulties getting to their nearest bank. 4,000 branches have closed since 1990, and the Campaign for Community Banking Services forecast that another one thousand communities will be "bankless" in the next five years.

So what's the answer. Well as Colin Baker, General Secretary of the National Federation of Sub-postmasters said, "The Government could build on sub post offices' ...making it the place to get information, check documents, pay for government services and find out about what you are entitled to."

And while SchNEWS would never be cynical about government policy, all European Union mail services face a radical shake up in readiness for 'liberalisation' of the European postal market in 2003. That's privitisation to you and me.

## Up Yer Privates!

New Labour are busy privatising everything – they just dress it up in fancy jargon to try to pull the wool over our eyes. But no more! Yer nosy-parker SchNEWS has decided to start a regular column, so if you know about dodgy Private Finance Initiative Schemes, Best Value nonsense, or whatever else let us know.

## CRAP ARREST OF THE WEEK
### DJ GETS KNICKERED

A Brighton DJ, who wishes to remain anonymous, was arrested this week for being in possession of a pair of stolen Y Fronts. He rang SchNews and panted "How can I afford underwear on DJ's wages?" He is now looking for a brief to cover his case. * Keep sending SchNEWS yer crap arrests!

## BIG MAC IN KIDS TAKEAWAY

"Head teachers are the key to the whole system-in the same way that a chief executive can be at a well-run company." Tony Blair

The biggest high-profile privatisation of education is happening in the same secondary schools  Blair rejected for his own children. He obviously didn't realise that a super hero of a company, a pioneer of specialist needs education, a company that has worked in developing countries, is an organisation so ethically minded it provides school inspectors to Ofsted. (This is quite ironic considering this same bunch of hypocritical spell checkers must not fail its Ofsted inspection in any of its schools.)

So, who are they you may well ask.

Step forward Cambridge Education Associates, part of the Mott MacDonald Group, not to be confused with Ronald McDonald (one wears a clown's suit). Their vested interest in children's education became apparent at the McLibel Trial, where the Corporations Head of marketing from Chicago stated "Children were virgin ground as far as marketing is concerned". In the same way, C.E.A. obviously see the children of Tony Blair's former home of Islington as a developing market.

Estelle Morris, the School Standards Minister, managed to put parents' minds at rest by declaring "There will be no change of signs outside their children's schools". That's a bloody relief! We thought they would have gargantuan signs reading "CHILD EXPLOITATION TAKING PLACE HERE"

When SchNEWS asked Brian Oakley Smith, the Managing Director of C.E.A. a simple question -"What are you getting out of this?" the flustered reply was "We care." Yeah right! And I'm a pony's uncle. He then squeaked "We only get £600,000 a year, the other 15 million we just manage". Say what! C.E.A stand to loose £75,000 on each target it misses. That is of course if their own inspectors fail them. Mr Oakley was quick to point out "That's if the children don't reach their targets" It's the kid's fault already.

Old McDonald had a farm now he's got your kids.

Now, what is Mott MacDonald's interest in children's education? If we look at their past record we can see how relevant it is, for instance they educated people at the Newbury By Pass; Twyford Down; road building in Indonesia; rebuilding Kosovo; various dam projects and a military hospital in Malaysia. Oh! Nearly forgot, there has also been a rumour they were involved in the Baghdad By Pass. Very educational. Their Head office by the way is in Croydon, snuggled in next to SchNEWS's old friends Nestle. How sweet!

## Diary of Adrian Molesworth

February 6th is the 15th anniversary of the eviction of the "Rainbow Village" at Molesworth, Cambridgeshire. The site was a proposed second base for 64 American cruise missiles. Under the cover of darkness on 6th February 1985, a convoy containing 1,500 Royal engineers, 600 MoD police and 1,000 civil Police descended on the village to evict 150 peace campers. The eviction took 5 months to plan, and was the largest peacetime mobilisation of troops in this country. Those protesters that refused to move their homes had to stand by and watch as their caravans were bulldozed off site. At 10am when the eviction was nearly over, Tarzan (Michael Heseltine) himself appeared from his helicopter wearing an army combat jacket and was quoted as saying he was "Deeply concerned for the children of the village". In order to keep the protesters out a £3million security fence was constructed. Unfortunately, with the ending of the 'Cold War' only a few missiles ever reached the base before it was redundant. A permanent peace garden is being maintained at the base, for more details contact Cambridge CND 01480 475284

## POSITIVE AGREEMENT?

Don't believe everything you read - even in SchNEWS! It appears that we may have been too cynical in last week's issue, when we doubted whether the Montreal talks on genetic food would reach any positive outcome. However, it seems miracles do happen as 130 government delegations came to an agreement..hey presto..the Cartagena Protocol was born!

In plain English this means that big nasty genetic companies have to tell governments what they are up to when they try to introduce their suspect wares. Imports will also be subject to new guidelines, with warning labels being introduced for GM products. And finally, ministers got rid of a clause that would have given big businesses unrivalled power courtesy of the World Trade Organisation (WTO)!

Sounding too good to be true? Maybe SchNEWS may have been right to be a little scathing. On closer inspection, it appears that labels on GM food only have to say "may contain" GMOs, and in fact the US companies can still go the WTO, if they believe that 'free trade' rules are being broken. Confused? How do you think we feel writing this stuff.

## ANARCHY ON THE ALPS

The hills were alive with the sound of protest in the small ski resort of Davos, Switzerland last week, when the World Economic Forum held their annual conference. 1,000 chief executives of the world's largest companies and 30 heads of government gathered to pat themselves on the back about the joys of globalisation. Does this sound familiar? Yes, the WEF is not much different to the World Trade Organisation who we all know and love, and, like the Seattle Conference, the WEF met opposition. Swiss police, backed by Army units and reinforced by officers from Germany, responded to snowball throwing protestors by using metal grilled land cruisers, guns and tear gas. Just a bit over the top? Of course not! We wouldn't want anything to happen to those 1,000 executives now, would we? Where would the world be without them?!? * "After five days in Davos he understands that the masters of the markets know as little about the likely movements of the global economy as the waiters supplying them with plum brandy and cheese fondue" Lewis Lapham, "The Agony of Mammon" (Verso, 98). Don't be put off by the title!

## SchNEWS in brief

Sat 5th Feb the University of East London are running a 'Political Activism and Social Movements' Day School, a free one-day event aiming to bring activists and academics together. Including speakers from Exodus, Genetix Snowball, and Amnesty International, it takes place at University of East London, Docklands campus (nearest station Cyprus Station , Docklands light railway). Maps and further details etc at the UEL website www.uel.ac.uk/ ** **May Day open meeting** Sat 5th February to discuss action possibilities for May Day. At University of London Union, Malet Street, 1-5pm ** And to raise funds for May Day, there's a benefit "evening of music and comedy with Atilla the Stockbroker, the Doleclaimer's Robb Johnson, and North London Anarcho Syndicalist Choir", Sat 19th February the Arsenal Tavern, Blackstock Road (Nearest tube Finsbury Park) 7.30 'till late £4/£2. ** **Refugees at One World Week**: Sunday 4th February Sir David Ramsbotham, Chief Inspector of Prisons will be speaking at the One World Week Fair, 2-4 pm Wadham College, Oxford. What a good opportunity for people to raise issues about the new practices at Campsfield... http:// users.ox.ac.uk/~asylum ** **Another Chumbawumba Baby!** Belated congratulations Danbert on the arrival of twins, Carson and Stella. Shall we make births, deaths and marriages a regular feature? ** **Direct action by the deaf!** Members of Parents Against Childhood Experimentation were set to take direct action last night (Thurs) at a talk at the Royal Society of Medicine about hearing implants for young children. "We do not want our children to be turned into Frankenstein monsters" said a spokesperson.** In a rare burst of honesty **The World Bank** has admitted it's crap - its failure to implement policies is fucking up old forests and the poor. So you heard it from them first then, eh! ** SOAS students occupying their school's officeswere evicted at 5.30 am Saturday morning, but over 250 students at UCL went into occupation on Wednesday to protest against tuition fees. Contact the Campaign For Free Education on PO Box 22615 London N1 1WT ** **Radio 4A** takes to the skies of brighton again on Sunday 13th Feb, from noon till the next day on 106.4FM, with its usual mix of speech-based programming, this time sharing the airwaves with other top broadcasters.

## STOP THE SANCTIONS

Voices in the Wilderness, a campaign group for the people of Iraq, is planning a day of action at the UN on 14th Feb to highlight the ongoing humanitarian crisis. In case you'd forgotten, airstrikes by the US and UK are still wreaking havoc across Iraq, with one US jet managing to hit a primary school last November, injuring schoolchildren. Just to make you feel even better, this war is costing you, the taxpayer, an estimated £1m a week! Added to the constant bombardment are the economic santions imposed upon Iraq in 1990, which have led to around 227,000 deaths in young children owing to the imposed poverty and social ruin.

Voices in the wilderness is urging people to send postcards to Robin Cook, the Foreign Secretary, asking him to help lift the sanctions. This is planned alongside the day of action on 14 Feb. Voices in the Wilderness UK, 16b Cherwell Street, Oxford, OX4 1BG 01865 243232. And if you're in Brighton on 29th Feb, there's a talk on the Iraq sanctions at The Auditorium, Brighthelm Centre, North Road at 7.30pm.

## Inside SchNEWS

There were riots in Turin on Monday after Silvano Pellissero was given 6 years and 8 months in prison. His crime? According to the state prosecuter, Tatangelo, "Pellissero and those like him are dangerous for the democratic state, not so much for the nature of their crimes, but for the popular consensus which they create in a potentially explosive social situation."

3 people, Silvano, Soledad Maria Rosas and Edoardo Massari were the scapegoats of a continued crackdown by the Italian authorities on people labelled as 'terrorists'. Despite no evidence they were accused of being involved in the Grey Wolves, a so-called eco-terrorist group which allegedly 'sabotaged' a building site for high speed trains in the Northern Italian Alps.

The Italian state used special 'terrorism laws' to keep the three in prison despite lack of evidence against them. This led to first Edoardo, then Sole a month later to commit suicide (knowing the reputation of the Italian police in causing 'accidental deaths of anarchists' some people seriously question these suicides).

The terrorist laws were introduced in the 1970's, against a background of armed militant left wing activism. These laws are now being used, for example, against people for simply belonging to an activist group, and a special police force similar to the secret services, deal entirely with political activists. As one Italian activist explained to SchNEWS "If you are involved in direct action even to the most minimal extent you are followed and spied on night and day; but what is most detrimental of this 'terrorism legacy' is the public image given to us.What the media calls us, this is what people see us: people are now scared of those who fight on the same side, popular support is no longer part of us, such laws have thrown the entire population against us."

Show solidarity! Protest in front of the Italian Embassy, Wednesday 23rd February ( Bond Street tube) email: silosquat@tiscalinet.it

**IN THE UK , The Terrorism Bill** (See SchNews 242), as predicted, is being rushed through the various Parliamentary stages at high speed. It is now likely to become law by April.But this isn't stopping groups around the country from making some noise. See website for events around the cointry: www.blagged.freeserve.co.uk/law.htm or join the on-line discussion list: tb-campaigns@listbot.com or phone 01273 298192 for latest updates.

## ...and finally...

When yer public popularity drops, perhaps a name change is in order. Hence after a nuclear accident Windscale changed its name to Sellafield (must be up for another name change soon); The Special Patrol Group changed its name to Teritorial Support Group (after the death of Blair Peach); British Aerospace changed its name to BAE Systems after it brought up the military wing of GEC Marconi. Compulsory Competitive Tendering, where Councils have to buy the cheapest most crappy services, is now Best Value in New Labour speak. Now the latest cosmetic change is everyone's favourite chemical company Monsanto, who are to be known as Pharmacia and Searle and Upjohn, strangely the despised gene bending soya splicing section is still being known as Monsanto. Monsanto have in the past also been known as Globalstrike, Flextrex, Pantalone, Solutia and Flexsys.

**disclaimer**
SchNEWS apologises to all readers. This week's disclaimer got lost in the post. Honest

## Subscribe! ▬▬▬▬▬▬▬▬▬▬

**DRRINGG DRRINGG! PRESS 3 FOR THIS WEEK'S**

# Weekly SchNEWS

*Printed and Published in Brighton by Justice?*

**A RESPECT AT WORK ZONE**

**Friday 11th February**    http://www.schnews.org.uk/    **Issue 247**   **Free/Donation**

# RINGPEACE

"You feel like you are on a galley boat – being watched, answering calls every 30 seconds, monitored and told off if there are mistakes"

Dougie Rafferty, (ex) Excell call centre worker

"I feel absolutely knackered like a total zombie, can't be bothered speaking to anyone, I go home and I just want to sleep"

Anonymous Excell call centre worker

They've been described as the "modern day sweatshops" with "battery hen" working conditions. Yet one in fifty people now work in the them. Welcome to the world of the Call Centre.

SchNEWS is used to hearing about dodgy companies but Arizona-based multinational Excell multimedia LLC really takes the biscuit. They run two call centres in Glasgow employing more than 600 operators who deal with things like directory enquiries and 999. Starting their jobs on a pocket bulging £9,000 a year, company documents show that the company aim for operators to be on the phone for 97% of the time. This means staff must answer the phone twice a minute for over seven hours a day, ask the manager for a drink of water, and make up lost time at the end of a shift if they spend too much time in the loo. And all the time closely monitored.

When Channel 4 spilled the beans on this bunch of dodgy bastards, they uncovered one story of a man who had an epileptic fit while at work and was taken to hospital after cutting his head. When his pay slip came through, the company had deducted three hours for the time he spent in the hospital! This then had a knock on affect on his attendance record, costing him more than two hundred quid in lost wages.

Of course the firm don't take criticism lying down and sacked Dougie Rafferty, and have threatened one woman member of staff with "facial mapping" to prove that she was not the anonymous employee who dared to criticise them on TV!

But surely with the new Trade Union laws Call Centres and the like aren't gonna get away with acting like latter day scrooges? Under the law if enough staff get together and want to join a union then employees have an obligation to recognise them. There's just one small snag. As one former Excell manager pointed out, thanks to massive turnover in staff, it's unlikely that there'll ever be the numbers needed to come to any agreement. And while people try to organise or speak out against their work conditions, they'll just be shown the door. In other words, "don't call us we'll call you."

## Bunch of BT Balls...

British Telecom is the third largest company in the UK (after BP Amoco and Glaxo Wellcome) and the fifth largest telecommunication company in the world. Its last annual report in 1998 revealed £4.3 billion in profits, or £136 a second, and they have operations in over 230 countries from Indonesia to Eastern Europe.

Chief Executive Sir Peter Bonfield earns £2.53 million pounds a year, a pay rise of over £1 million. SchNEWS wonders how he manages.

In June 1999, 120 workers were sacked from their jobs at the Directory Inquiries call centre in Stirling due to "regrettable advancements in technology" (Daily Record 6/7/99). The following week Glasgow telemarketing phone -=operators had their commission rates slashed from £4.50 an hour to £2.50 to boost profits and attract more business investment.

BT recruits the majority of its staff from employment agencies like Manpower and Blue Arrow. With a flexible workforce, no contracts, sick pay or holiday pay, BT is a New Labour model of corporate modernity - putting profit before employment rights.

All BT telephone operators and Customer Service Advisors are monitored and timed for the amount of calls taken in a shift. If employees do not meet Call Handling Time targets of one call every 180 seconds, then they are disciplined, refused overtime, and in some cases sacked. Calls are routinely recorded and listened to from a remote call centre in Coventry, where if an employee is caught swearing or hanging up they are immediately sacked and escorted from the building.

\* Got a gripe against call centres – then why not share your story with SchNEWS?

## CRAP ARREST OF THE WEEK

For smiling! At the last Shamrock monkey farm demo a lost-it cop was pointing people out for the snatch squads. One bloke wound him up by standing around doing nothing more sinister and life-threatening than grinning. Not for long - "Grab him!"

At the same demo someone was jumped by the goons (not the funny ones) and thrown to the ground, resulting in a shattered hip. He's still waiting to see if he'll need a hip replacement.

## UP YER PRIVATES: PUSEY SAYS ME-OW

The company who took over when the passport agency was privatised have been told by MPs to stop pussy-footing around.

Siemens Business Services, the company at the heart of the passport fiasco which led to thousands of people having their holidays ruined last summer, have announced a 33% rise in the cost of a passport – due to their cock-ups. The rise includes the cost of handing out umbrellas and luncheon vouchers to people queueing in the pissing rain waiting for their passports.

The agency was privatised under the Private Finance Initiative, a dodgy scheme which has been grasped enthusiastically by Blair's grateful dead (see SchNEWS 219). Passport costs have now risen from £21 to £28. Thanks a poxy lot! The new director of this company, Gary Pusey, who sneaked in though the back cat flap and seems intent on milking us dry, has obviously pulled a few strokes in his time. He purred "the company had already had £1.4 billion worth of public sector contracts - two of which, the passport agency and immigration directorate, were in the dog house." OK! he didn't say dog house.

Poor old Sir David Omand, who only gets paid a measly £100,000 a year as permanent secretary at the Home Office, told MPs the rise will go towards recuperating some of the £12.6m lost in last summer's fiasco. However, Home Secretary Mr Jack "the pancake" Straw, not normally known for his involvement in catastrophes, insisted the increase was to fund the agency's £25m a year modernisation programme. Maybe he'd picked up his son's wacky backy that morning or was it Mo Mowlam's?

## Master Bates

While we're on the subject of privatised goon shows, (SchNEWS 246 Big Mac in Kids Takeaway) we should mention Rams Episcopal school in Hackney, London. 3% of schools are judged by inspectors to be failing pupils, so it's quite ironic that Rams Episcopal, the first school taken over by a private company, is to be closed and reopened under a new name due to it being judged as… failing. The teachers are now doing a thousand lines "we are not failing tossers".

## BEACH-BUMMER

" The affair raises issues of economic imperialism. Want to chop down a mountain in Yosemite? Not at any price. Want to destroy a beach in Maya Bay? That'll be $100,000 dollars plus deposit, whilst the leading man pockets $20 million thank you very much"

Maya Bay International Alliance

Ever wondered what a tropical paradise looks like? Rupurt Murder's new 20th Century Fox film "The Beach", directed by Andrew Macdonald and Danny Boyle, obviously didn't. They were slightly confused as far as the word 'paradise' was concerned, and thought it meant bulldozing beaches, pulling up indigenous trees and single-handedly helping to destroy an ecosystem.This lot make the Benidorm lager louts look like Noddy in the land of Oz.

The usual fee for filming in a Thai National park is 1,000 baht, about $26, but as Fox films handed over $108,000 which they termed a donation and an additional deposit of 5 million baht, it was hardly a surprise they received the green light.

This holiday romance took place at Maya Bay, Ko Phi Phi Thailand. However, on visiting this area of National Park they discovered it was not their definition of utopia, so, against the wishes of local people the film makers chose to change the paradise into Hell by removing vital dune plants and introducing palm trees. MacDonald then had the audacity to state "everything is tiptop on Phi Phi Leh" even though the last monsoon washed his make shift beach away.

Local people are now asking people to boycott the film, and on Wednesday at the film premier in Leicester Square, activists from the Campaign for Ethical Filmmaking gatecrashed proceedings. Donning Leonardo DiCaprio masks, they were waved through police lines, under the cover of a stretched limo and alighted to the screams of thousands of waiting fans! Screams turned to laughter, though, as one penguin-suited activist held aloft a Golden Bulldozer Award.

To add insult to injury, Leonardo DiCaprio is hosting the Earth day celebrations in April on, you've guessed it - sustainable living.

SchNEWS suggests that instead of watching the film you read the original book by Alex Garland. www.uq.edu.au/~pggredde/

## ESSEX EVICTIONS

As SchNEWS went to press, the protest camp at Gorse Wood, was being evicted. In case you've forgotten, large areas of meadowland, woodland and the environmentally sensitive Curry Hill are set to be destroyed to make way for the A130 link road. This is no country lane we're talking about here, the proposed road is to be a six lane motorway.

The road is being financed by the private finance iniative, and is sponsored by Countryroute plc which is a consortium of roadbuilders Laing and other contractors.

Help is urgently needed, so ring 02082 994241 or mobile 07957 915977 for more info, and get involved!

P.S - Can anyone tell us if this road is set to be part of the Trans-European Network?

* The protest camp at Hockley is to be evicted any day now  Campaigners are trying to stop 66 luxury homes being built (SchNEWS 243). Security have now arrived and surrounded the site, and the waiting protestors could do with more help. Arriving activists are advised to ring the camp mobile before arriving. Contact 01702 206353 or site mobile 0831 717815 for more info. www.angelfire.com/mt/GBH

*Subscribe!*

## SchNEWS in brief

Stop Press!! The first action against the British **Terrorism Bill** is in solidarity with an Italian anarchist who got 6 years and 8 months, under special terrorism laws, for allegedly sabotaging a building site, despite no evidence (SchNEWS 246). Meet 12 noon, outside the Italian Embassy (Bond Street Tube), Sat 19th Feb (changed from the 23rd). Asilosquat@tiscalinet.it ** Meeting to discuss the **Terrorism** Bill, Thurs 17th Feb at 6.30pm at the Bridge Hotel, Newcastle Upon Tyne. Contact Box 1TA, Newcastle Upon Tyne, NE99 1TA. ** Demo against the far-right Freedom Party outside the **Austrian Embassy** on Sat, 19th February. 6:30pm outside Austrian Embassy, Belgrave Square, London (Hyde Park Corner tube). ** **Protest Songs**, an open mike night of protest songs against the Terrorism Bill. Wednesday 16th Feb, The Gladstone, Brighton. Call Sarah 01273 231374 if you are interested in playing ** Has anyone out there got photos of **Travellers' New Year's Parties in Europe** for inclusion in our next annual? If so send 'em to SchNEWS with yer name and address on the back if you want them returned, also write down where they were taken ** Anyone in Brighton who is **fluent in French and English** (!) and can spare some time to do some translating, give SchNEWS a call, we'd really appreciate your help ** ** The **Nestle 16** (SchNEWS 242) are up in court on Feb 22nd at Halifax Magistrates Court, Harrison Road, Halifax at 9.30am. A demo and solidarity actions are planned. Tel: 01268 682820

■ ■ ■ ■ ■ ■ ■ ■ ■ ■ ■ ■ ■ ■ ■ ■ ■ ■
■ If you want some **full frontal naked radio**, ■
■tune into 106.5 FM in Brighton this Sunday ■
■for Radio 4A                                              ■
■ ■ ■ ■ ■ ■ ■ ■ ■ ■ ■ ■ ■ ■ ■ ■ ■ ■

## Bus Outing

Passengers on the number 15 Stagecoach bus in London this week took a ride with a difference when the bus suddenly met a woman holding a banner, ordering the vehicle to 'Stop in the name of Love!'. As the bus drew to a halt, members of the Lesbian Avengers group commenced their mission – hanging banners stating 'Repeal Section 28', distributing leaflets to the passengers and painting the bus bright pink!

Lesbian Avengers, 0181 374 9885

## U'wa Misses

On February 3rd the U'wa tribe in Colombia's call for international support was answered by people around the world, as one of Occidental Petroleum (Oxy) biggest shareholder's Fidelity Investments was targetted in 34 cities across the globe.

The U'wa tribe of Colombia have been fighting against Oxy extracting oil from their land for a few years. Even Shell pulled out of the project citing human rights concerns. In Colombia oil brings militarisation and environmental destruction.Since November 1999 over 250 people have been occupying a proposed oil drilling site (SchNEWS 244). On 19th January thousands of Columbian miltary invaded U'wa territory and evicted the tribe from the test site.

Meanwhile Fidelity have hardly done their PR any favours by announing that they invests in "companies with the highest likelihood of stock-price appreciation.... Our portfolio managers are not trained to make investment decisions in order to fulfill social or political objectives." Meanwhile Oxy are trying to silence critics by requesting a temporary restraining order against groups supporting the U'wa.

## Inside SchNEWS

City Police spotters nabbed **Kuldip Bajwa** while demonstrating outside the Labour party conference in Bournemouth due to his likeness to someone caught on video hitting a police riot shield with a placard pole at June 18. Judge Barthurst Norman said too much leniency had previously been shown to J18 reprobates and sentenced Kuldip to a full 21 months for violent disorder. Letters of support to: Kuldip Bajwa, DN 7230, HMP Jebb Ave., Brixton, London, SW2 5XF.

**Jeff Booker,** sentenced to 18 months for the J18 protests, has been moved. His new address is HMP Elmley, Church Road, Eastchurch, Sheerness, Kent ME12 4AX. Prison number DN7071.

**Saptal Ram** has now been in jail for fourteen years, for defending himself against a violent racist attack in a Birmingham restaurant. Whilst in prison, he has been subjected to strip-searches and beatings. On Monday 28th Feb, his family are due to meet with Paul Boateng, the Minister for prisons, to demand that Saptal be released immediately. There will be a vigil of support on the same day outside the Home Office, Queen Anne's Gate, London SW1 beginning at 9.30am.

Free Saptal Ram, PO Box 23139, London SE1 IZU. www.ncadc.demon.co.uk/saptal.html

## ...and finally...

The World Trade Organisation's (WTO) last utterance was its wish to be more open. And where could be more open than a diminutive Middle East enclave clinging on to the edge of that famous democratic state, Saudi Arabia, opposite Iran and run by a monarchy with a population of just 540,000. Qatar of course. Their embassy told a startled SchNEWS, "Qatar expressed a wish to hold a meeting;  our chances are good."

After full on riots greeted their last two Conferences in Geneva and Seattle, it seems that out of the 135 member countries of the WTO, nobody wanted to bite the (rubber) bullet and invite those global racketeers to their shores. So the WTO must have thought it was the multinationals' answer to winning the lottery when Qatar, after fighting off stiff competition from absolutely no one, invited them to hold the next big trade talks in 2001 in the middle of an Arabian desert in the capital Doha. The only people who are "over the moon" about this gathering are the all dressed in black, scarf clad anarchists,who feel quite confident about blending in.

Still, readers, you've got a bit of time to think of a good excuse to get through customs - but you'll need to find someone who lives there. If that's too much, SchNEWS recommends that protestors and soundsystems can leg it over the hills of Afghanistan, sneak though Iran then swim across The Gulf, or maybe just cut across Saudia Arabia. Dress as an Arab-looking tourist and you're laughing.

Next time you're surfing the web, why not do your bit to uphold society and give the Seattle Police Department a hand in bringing to justice those naughty anarchists who brought terror to Seattle during the WTO protests. Yes, the Seattle Police Intelligence Division has a lovely website full of colourful pictures of protestors wreaking havoc, and is divided into categories such as 'arson', 'property damage' and 'assaults'. If you fancy having a look, then check out this ridiculously long website www.pan.ci.seattle.wa.us/seattle/spd/wto/spdwtosuspecthome.htm

### disclaimer

SchNEWS warns all readers that your disclaimer is currently unobtainable and engaged on another line. Please try later.

# THE HILLS HAVE EARS

## SQUALL

Where Do You Want To Grow Today?
--
I Wanna Go Home
Underground Update
**Features**
Squall Pics
Frontline Communique
The State Its In
Squotes
Resources
Links
From Our Correspondence

Menwith Hill is a little piece of the USA in Britain, a listening post monitoring the telecommunications traffic of Europe. It is rapidly expanding, unaccountable (even to parliament) and no-one is able to get any answers. Ally Fogg reports, additional material by Gibby Zobel.

Take a short walk west from the A59 near Harrogate, North Yorkshire, across a designated site of Outstanding Natural Beauty, and you could be forgiven for thinking you had found a set from Space 1999. Twenty seven vast white golfballs up to 60 metres in diameter, satellite dishes and a host of towering aerial masts line the horizon. If a little bird were to tell you what was going on inside, you might feel you had walked into the middle of George Orwell's nightmares. The fibre-optic cables running under your feet carry 32,000 telephone lines, and the space-age hardware before your eyes monitors transmissions from land and mobile telephones, radios, faxes, satellite communications and cyberspace. It is capable of intercepting two million telephone calls every hour. Its targets are military, political, commercial, industrial and domestic. This is not science fiction. It is Menwith Hill spy station.

Officially titled 'RAF Menwith Hill', the largest regional intelligence station on Earth is in fact run by, and for, the US National Security Agency (NSA). There are 1,200 American staff and 600 British staff on site. It operates in close tandem with GCHQ at Cheltenham, but GCHQ has no automatic access to the intelligence gathered at Menwith Hill. All domestic and international telephone calls in Britain pass through Menwith Hill, allowing US officers to spy on any British citizen without a warrant. Information collected on political activists, for example, can then be passed on to MI5, Special Branch or Scotland Yard.

Despite the end of the Cold War, the NSA continues to have a budget of $10 billion per year. It spends $1 million per minute spying on the communications of the UK, France and Germany. The US 'acquired' 562 acres of Yorkshire moorland in 1956 in a secret arrangement with the British government. The arrangement was never approved by the British Parliament. A 21-year tenure was agreed, and renewed in 1976 for a further 21 years, again in secret and without parliamentary approval. Despite the expiry of this tenure , the base continues to expand. Since the arrangements between the UK and US governments which allow Menwith Hill to operate are secret, nobody knows on what legal grounds Menwith Hill now functions. The rapid expansion of the base has required planning applications, in 1985 there were four radomes (golfballs), now there are 27. However Harrogate Council has no power to refuse permission or impose conditions.

The reasons for Menwith Hill's very existence give an important insight into the 'special relationship' between the UK and USA. In a court case last year, former Cabinet Minister Tony Benn MP testified that Britain is under contract to the US to buy nuclear weapons on the condition that bases like Menwith are allowed to operate from here and provided that the US has access to all British intelligence operations. The role of Menwith Hill in a military context is undeniable, it won an award from the NSA as "Sta-

tion of the Year"in 1991 for its role in the Gulf War. The use of this technology for commercial espionage is no less controversial. American companies, notably arms dealers Loral Space Systems Incorporated and Lockheed Aerospace, sell much of the spy equipment to the NSA and they are both involved in arms sales to third-world countries. Menwith Hill gains information that would be highly useful to them. In the same testimony, Tony Benn told the court that it was "inconceivable"that the intelligence collected at Menwith Hill would not be used for commercial advantage. Even the NSA's own website admits that its work includes "monitoring the development of new technology"around the world.

Benn is one of a small band of MPs who have attempted to impose some form of parliamentary accountablity on Menwith Hill. In his last speech to the House before his untimely death in 1994, Bob Cryer gave a blistering attack on the station, and the fudging of Ministerial replies on the subject. He described how the then Minister of State for the Armed Forces (Nicholas Soames) had said there is parliamentary accountability for Menwith Hill, while the Minister for Public Transport (Stephen Norris) found

**Action at Menwith Hill 4th March**

Big Brother is watching you

Pic: Sophie

the station so secret that while he was a minister at the Department of Defence he thought it was a railway station! Max Madden MP asked questions between 1986 and 1997. Norman Baker, Lib-Dem MP for Lewes, has asked dozens of parliamentary questions about Menwith Hill and related issues since entering the house in May 97. "I'm a believer in freedom of information," he told Squall. "I don't like the way Menwith Hill is shrouded in secrecy, and I'm not convinced that what happens there is for the good of this country. Most of us assume the cold war is over, so the question must be what are they using it for? One of the assumptions must be that it is being used for industrial espionage."

The standard ministerial reply to almost any question on the subject is: "The use of Menwith Hill by the United States Department of Defence is subject to confidential arrangements between the United Kingdom and the United States Government."

Recently the US and UK Governments have been embarassed by an EC report from the Science and Technology Office of Assessment which stated that "within Europe all e-mail, telephone and fax communications are routinely intercepted by the United States National Security Agency transferring all target information from the European mainland via the strategic hub of London then by satellite to Fort Meade in Maryland via the crucial hub at Menwith Hill". The report confirmed that this included diplomatic, economic, and political communications, monitored through a massive US global spy web, mainly at Menwith Hill. European business leaders are believed to be less than delighted at the confirmation that their commercial confidentiality is routinely breached by an arm of the US Government.

Not surprisingly, those who have worked the hardest to highlight the scandal of Menwith Hill have not been political representatives or disgruntled business leaders, but a dedicated collection of peace campaigners. There have been campaigns to stop Menwith Hill since it began in 1952. Groups now involved include the WoMenwith Hill Women's Peace Camp, Yorkshire CND and the Campaign for the Accountability of American Bases (CAAB). The peace camp has been sitting in a lay-by on the A59 since 1994. There have been literally hundreds of trespasses at the station over many years. Activists have been arrested, assaulted, imprisoned and injuncted, but refuse to give up. British MoD Police are used to protect the base, paid for with American money. In a typical example of the lengths to which the authorities have gone in attempting to quell these activists, the second military land byelaws were passed in the summer of 1997, forbidding trespass onto the base. The first set of byelaws had been declared invalid in 1993. The first two activists to be arrested under the byelaw, Helen John and Anne Lee, were acquitted by a judge at York Crown Court in October. He ruled that since 70 per cent of the land covered by the law was used for grazing sheep, it could not be considered primarily of 'military use'. Less than a week later, activists Lindis Percy and Anni Rainbow were arrested under the same byelaw which had just been ruled invalid. They had been removing byelaw notices.

In February Lindis Percy, who has had an injuction since 1991 banning her from the area around Menwith Hill with the exception of two public footpaths, was arrested for removing one of these signs from the side of one of the footpaths. "They deliberately moved the bylaw notices three feet to 'protect' the signs from protestors! The intent was entrapment. They say the notices are off the footpath, I say they are still on it. So by reading the notices you have to get so close you are, in their eyes, committing a criminal offence. The MoD Police appeared out of nowhere and arrested me."

**Action at Menwith Hill 4th March**

Pic: Sophie

It has been alleged that she had nine injunctions banning her from the base, but claims she was entitled to use the footpath. Lindis has been a thorn in the side of the US military in the UK for many years. She has taken out civil and criminal actions against the US Government for assault and false imprisonment at a number of US bases. The Americans cited diplomatic immunity and the cases failed. The criminal action is now being considered at the European Court. Last year she served more than two months of a nine-month sentence in Holloway, and was released after intervention from the Official Solicitor when her health was compromised after she was subjected to involuntary stripsearches. "I firmly believe that out of bad things, good things will come,"she told Squall, "and that people can make a difference, when we know what we are doing is right... My family know this is important work and accept that the arrests and court cases is what is going to be. Of course there have been problems and they used to get very angry, but I think it is sorted out now.

"This crazy zany world of secrecy, collusion and deceit is bizarre - I still work as a health visitor in Bradford which keeps me sane. They want you to give up - but the more they try and silence me the stronger I get."

It has recently been confirmed that there are plans for the continued expansion of Menwith Hill until at least 2005. The physical expansion shall enable it to house the technology to transmit and receive communications and full-spectrum photographic images from military satellites, allowing the US military to see and hear what is going on, on literally any inch of the planet. It will also be able to control laser weapons which could be fired anywhere to an accuracy of six feet. The space probe Cassini, launched last autumn with 72 lb of plutonium on board, was directly connected to the need to fuel these weapons in space. There is every reason to believe that it will continue to grow well beyond 2005, and who knows what technology it will house by then. Big Brother is not just watching you, he's getting bigger all the time.

EVERYTIME BNFL DOES ANOTHER

GReeNWaSH

BRITISH NUCLEAR FIASCO LTD

EVERYTHING TURNS

FLORESCENT GREEN

British Nuclear Fiasco Ltd

"I tawt I taw a fat-cat"

## Boycotting 'The Beach'

**Friday 11th February: More than a dozen protesters brought the remains of the beach to Warner Village Cinema, Newcastle. Sand, trees and the sea - plus an image of Leonardo di Caprio - were deposited at the entrance by environmentalists in beach gear, in order to highlight the environmental destruction caused to Maya Bay, Thailand, during filming of 'The Beach' which began its general release that day.**

## SchQUFACT

The USA alone, with only 6% of the world's population, consumes 30% of its resources.

ENVIRONMENTALLY UNSOUND LOAD

# Glen of the Downs

**Ireland's longest running road protest camp**
**(See SchNEWS 241)**

FIGHT THE FUND

DROP THE DEBT

CELEBRATE THE TRIUMPH OF THE
**GLOBAL CAPITALIST ECONOMY**
WITH THESE FINELY CRAFTED
'INCOME DISTRIBUTION'
SOUVENIR CHAMPAGNE GLASSES

RICHEST FIFTH — 82.7% OF THE WORLD'S WEALTH

EACH HORIZONTAL BAND REPRESENTS AN EQUAL FIFTH OF THE GLOBAL POPULATION ARRANGED IN ORDER OF INCOME

11.7%

2.3%

1.9%

POOREST FIFTH — 1.4% OF THE WORLD'S WEALTH

Polyp

WAKE UP! WAKE UP! IT'S YER DEBT-RIDDEN

# Weekly SchNEWS

FREEZEWORLD plc

— globe, schmobe

### Printed and Published in Brighton by Justice?

**Friday 18th February 2000**   **http://www.schnews.org.uk/**   **Issue 248   Free/Donation**

# "FRIENDS OF THE POOR"

**"One Filipino child is said to die every hour, in a country where more than half the national budget is given over to paying just the interest on World Bank and IMF loans."** John Pilger, 'Hidden Agendas'.

The outgoing head of the International Monetary Fund (IMF) became the latest victim to be pied last Sunday. In a farewell speech at a meeting of the United Nations Conference on Trade and Development (UNCTAD)in Bangkok,Michel Camdessus' claim that the IMF "are best friends of the poor" was clearly too much for one outraged person, who pied him full in the face. Splat!

And SchNEWS can reveal that the pie in the face is nothing compared to the global protests being planned when the IMF next meets at Washington DC in April!

So why all the fuss? What's the IMF? Read on for your quick economics lesson...

In 1944, 44 nations met in the New England village of Bretton Woods to construct a new framework of stability and national sovereignty for the post-war economy. This little gathering gave birth to three beautiful offspring... The IMF, the World Bank and the WTO (which at that time was called the General Agreement on Tariffs and Trade or GATT). Frederic F.Clairmont, in 'The Rise and Fall of Economic Liberalism' described the Bretton Woods creation as "a lethal totalitarian blueprint for the carve up of world markets". The IMF, in its infancy, was set up to maintain currency stability and develop world trade, but as it grew up it got bigger and badder. In the 1970s, the Organisation of Oil Producing Countries (OPEC) shoved large amounts of money in western banks which the banks then loaned out to developing countries. When governments began to run into trouble with the repayments, the IMF and World Bank hastily stepped in to bail out the private banks. The transfer of private debt into public liability was therefore complete - the third world debt crisis had begun! In order that third world governments rescheduled their debts and received new loans, the IMF imposed certain conditions, conditions called 'structural adjustments'.

## Structurally adjusted...

Countries whose economies are going down the pan can receive loans from the IMF in return for a bit of 'adjustment'. Adjustment, to the IMF, means de-regulation of industry, cutbacks in public services and subsistence farming abandoned to cash crops. In short, the economic direction of the country is planned, monitored and controlled by the IMF in Washington. Lovely! Or as John Pilger put it,"the surrender of sovereignty, and without a gunboat in sight." Any Governments that refuse to comply are cast into financial darkness and refused further loans.

> In 1997, the foreign debt of 'developing countries' was $2 trillion. Put another way this is $400 for every man, woman and child, whilst the average income in these countries is less than a dollar a day. Meanwhile... net nurd Bill Gates is worth over $60 billion; more than $1.5 trillion changes hands on the global currency market each day; the World's richest 200 people are worth more than $1 trillion!!!

## The IMF: Working wonders worldwide...

**Chile** was the first lucky recipient of the IMF's restructuring revolution under Augosto Pinochet's regime. This resulted in industries being dismantled and the majority of Chileans being plunged into poverty. At the end of this programme, Chile's debt was higher than it was at the start. Surely this was a failure? Oh no, the IMF were proud of the results!

The reign of ruin spread to **Africa,** the poorest continent in the world where more money is spent of debt repayments than on healthcare. What a lovely target...the IMF rubbed its hands with joy as they took over the management of the economies, increasing debt by 400%. In the city of Lusaka in **Zambia**, four out of every five people are unemployed and half of the newly privatised companies are bankrupt. **Nicaragua**

is equally fortunate, structural adjustments have moved the economic burden from the rich to the poor. Living standards have declined and many state workers face a bleak future owing to the privitisation of almost everything.

Dictators, unsurprisingly, are very good at applying IMF policies, and so have been very successful at receiving loans. Very often this money has not reached the poor who suffer most through the subsequent debt. In the **Philipines**, the late Ferdinand Marcos managed to build up a wealth of $10 billion thanks to International Aid. On his departure, the IMF refused to cancel repayment and simply moved the burden to the Filipino government who had to raise taxes and end rice subsidies. In **Brazil** there is no record for 80% of the amount borrowed by the former military dictatorship.

* The IMF's program extends to complimenting dodgy regimes, which maybe accounts for their recent praise of New Labour's chancellor, Gordon Brown.

* A small group of protesters, disguised with West Papuan tribal masks, greeted the Indonesian President and 100 of his corporate cronies this week, throwing pies and fake blood and blocking the entrance to a business seminar. The Indonesians were here to chat to 400 delegates from British industry.

**DIARY DATES**

* April 16-17 are the dates for the 'mobilisation for global justice', with actions planned when the IMF next meet in Washington DC, and simultaneously in countries across the world. * There also a proposal for a Global Day of Action during the annual ministerial meeting of the IMF in Prague, in September.

* For a good in depth analysis of the global economy get this months issue of the New Internationalist. Tel 01858 439616 or www.newint.org

## Chemical Terrorism

"I was ordered to go into a brick room and take off my gas mask for 3-4 minutes. I then ran out tears streaming from my face and I felt awful." Anonymous ex-serviceman from WWII

Shocking evidence is emerging from scientists investigating chemical gases carried out by the Ministry of Defence in "Demoralising Experiments". The International Scientific Environmental Research Network (I.S.E.R.N) told SchNEWS, "We were digging into the controversial topic of Gulf War Syndrome when we made an astonishing discovery."

I.S.E.R.N started investigating ex-servicemen and found that men who were in the army as far back as 1945 suffered illnesses related to chemical damage to the brain. When the ex-serviceman above asked why the M.O.D had gassed him, he was told it was an experiment "to see if I could carry out orders while demoralised." An I.S.E.R.N spokesman told us, "this soldier was subjected to a concoction of chemicals, which attacked the limbic region of his brain, which controls mood and memory. Hence the demoralising effect. When tested we discovered he had chemicals in his blood from 55 years ago! Furthermore, his children have developed an illness known as Multiple Chemical Sensitivity and they have allergies to everyday chemicals such as perfume, paint, tobacco smoke, household cleaners, car fumes etc. This illness is caused by chemical damage to the limbic region of the brain." What a coincidence!

This is the thin end of the wedge. Evidence suggests up to 2 million people in the UK may be ill due to the M.O.D's use and creation of toxic chemicals. Illnesses range from Spina Bifida, Asthma, Arthritis, Alzheimers, thyroid disorders, Eczema, Dyslexia, Anaemia, Allergies, to hormonal disorders such as PMT, sleep disorders, mood swings, memory problems, the list just goes on…

I.S.E.R.N intend to carry on their research and need ex-servicemen to come forward with information, which will be treated in confidence. Contact: isern2000@hotmail.com or by post c/o SchNEWS

## SANTA CLAUSE

"To remove Clause 28 without replacing it with alternative protective legislation is irresponsible, leaving children without any statutory protection from homosexual campaigning." Keep the Clause, anti gay campaigners.

In Scotland, Media House has handed over £500,000, to this bunch of paranoid arseholes, who seem to possess the combined intellect of a dead pilchard. "Keep the Clause," in their quest for spreading hateful rhetoric have made the slight mistake in advertising a new Freepost in the Daily Record and have been bombarded with empty envelopes, old beer mats, telephone books, and it was a rumoured, a paving slab. Of course SchNEWS is not the kind of publication that would print such an address which is Keep the Clause, Freepost SCO 5219, Perth PH2 8BR. Meanwhile Stagecoach boss Brian Souter, is also a keen supporter of the clause, and gave £500,000 to the Scottish Schoolboards Association to help them rant on about how our kids need protecting. What these gallant pioneers of child protection neglected to disclose however, was that when Stagecoach took over South West Trains, one of their first decisions was to close the work's nursery. This left Carol Moya, who was employed as a rail operator, having her contract terminated due to her being unable to find childcare !

## SchNEWS in brief

**March 8th** is **International Women's Day**. Women all over the world will be taking part in a Global Strike, calling for fairer wages for women, a total change in the priorities of the world's budget, and recognition of women's work both paid and unpaid. The strike has been called by the National Women's Council of Ireland, and the International Wages For Housework Campaign. Contact Crossroads Women's Centre, 0171 482 2496 or http://womenstrike8m.server101.com**Two people from the **Protest Naked For The Right To Be Naked In Public** campaign are up for, yes, indecent exposure at Birmingham Crown Court on the 25th Feb. They reckon the 1847 law is outdated and should be scrapped. After stripping off at such tightly dressed places as the Royal Courts of Justice, the campaign plans to protest naked at New Scotland Yard on July 15th. 01203 222076 www.geocities.com/thehumanmind/**Campaign Against Arms Trade** National Student Gathering, including evening entertainment from Mark Thomas and Seize the Day, Sat 11th March, London. Tickets £7 including vegan meal. Info: 020 7281 0297.**Leicester Prevent the Terrorism Act** are having a day of action to highlight the new bill (SchNews 242), Meet on Sat Feb 26th at the Clocktower, Leicester city centre, 12 noon.**There's a benefit for the **Southdowns Hunt Sabs** this Sat 19th at The Freebutt, Albion Street, Brighton. It starts at 8pm and features ska/dub/punk group Inner Terrestials + support.** **Pedal Power!** A critical mass cycling event is planned for 26th Feb. Meet at Markeaton car park derby at 1.30pm to ride to the city centre.**Canadian Pacific Coastal Airlines** recently barred a member of Greenpeace from boarding one of their planes because it regards Greenpeace as a "quasi-terrorist organisation". ** **West Country Activist** has been revamped as Action South West, and they are looking for people to re-subscribe. Send donations, spare stationary, stories, or office equipment to Box 80 Greenleaf, 82 Colston St. Bristol, BS1 5BB, tel. 07931 268966, e-mail wca99@hotmail.com

## SEED OF DESTRUCTION

Want to hear about yet more genetically modified madness? The government has announced plans to introduce the first genetically modified seed onto the National Seed List. This list dictates exactly which potatoes and peas get to make it onto our plates. A herbicide-tolerant maize fodder, made by Aventis, could be placed on the list by the end of this month, and would give the corporation the right to sell and grow their mutant produce. To add further insult, MAFF is seeking to remove peoples' right to object to products placed on the Seed List. More info contact Friends of the Earth 0171 490 1555 www.foe.co.uk/camps/foodbio/seedlist/.

For an ethical alternative for your allotment, contact the Heritage Seed Library who have around 700 types of vegetables which are ex-National Seed List owing to their not being commercially viable. The aim of the library is to keep these poor unwanted seeds alive and well, and it is run on a non-profit basis. Tel 01203 303517

* Week of protest against genetic foods 1-10 April, www.RESISTANCE isFERTILE.com

## LIFE IN THE FASLANE

The Valentine's Day demo at the Faslane Naval Base, home of the Trident nuclear submarines, resulted in 179 arrests – the largest arrest of the New Millennium! Around 400 anti-nuclear protestors descended on the base and blocked the main entrances in an attempt to prevent employees reaching their workplace. They managed to close down the main road for four and a half hours! A spokesperson from the base gave his opinion, "The workforce is sick and tired of these people trying to stop us earning a living".Those arrested may be charged with minor criminal damage. For more info contact Trident Ploughshares on 01603 611953 or visit www.gn.apc.org/tp2000/

* Visit Faslane Peace Camp, 81d Shandon, Helensburgh, Argyll and Bute, Scotland, G84 8NT Tel 01436 820901

Also on Valentine's Day...86 people were arrested at the US mission to the UN, and 3 at the US embassy in London in a protest to highlight the ongoing economic sanctions on Iraq. A second member of the UN team in Iraq has quit in protest against sanctions.

There's a talk on Iraq titled **'Death of a Nation?'** featuring a speaker from Voices in the Wildernest, taking place in Brighton on Tues. 29th Feb at the Brighthelm Centre, North Rd, 7.30 pm. And on March 6th, there's a documentary by John Pilger on the same issue. ITV, 9.30pm

* Voices in the Wilderness, 16b Cherwell St, Oxford OX4 1BG, 01865 243232. .

## FU'CANAL

Campaigners in Oxford are trying to stop Berkeley Homes evicting voles and lizards and building £350,000 worth of 'socially useful' housing alongside the canal. Slogans appear every night and are whitewashed by contractors each day. Anarchist rules football has been played, watched by an audience of 4 police for 2 hours. In a separate incident Laing Homes have demolished the wall of a listed bridge and are now in trouble with the Council. They are also in trouble with the fire brigade for blocking access to the industrial estate with a JCB where they were burning demolition waste and being unable to find the keys. Check out http://freespace.virgin.net/art.2000/OxfordCanal

## ...and finally...

Dig this!What do you get if you tear up 8.5 miles of countryside, trashing 358 acres of land containing three special sites of scientific interest, 10,000 trees, two civil war battle sites and then concrete the bloody lot? In the illogical, road fanatical Blighty, believe it or not,you win an award.Environment wrecking, hard core terrorists, Mott MacDonald, the organisation responsible for this solid achievement, won the Concrete Society's Millennium Award. As they have spread the stuff over half of China, Hong Kong and Malaysia, to name but a few, it's no wonder. In fact, the only place they haven't is a park in southern Mongolia which they don't know about yet. SchNews have concrete evidence that these stone hearted tree killers were the Newbury Bypass overall winners.We had to grit our teeth when we heard they also took away the civil engineering category and were awarded a certificate of excellence.This is obviously going to pave the way for other multinational lovelies to grace our land.

**disclaimer**

SchNEWS warns all readers to structurally adjust their Section 28 on leaving the bathroom.Honest

*Subscribe!* _____

Keep SchNEWS FREE! Send 1st Class stamps (e.g. 20 for next 20 issues) or donations (payable to Justice?) Ask for "Originals" if you can make copies. Post *free* to all prisoners. SchNEWS, c/o on-the-fiddle, P.O. Box 2600, Brighton, East Sussex, BN2 2DX.

*Tel/Autofax :* +44 (0)1273 685913  *GET IT EVERY WEEK BY E-MAIL:* schnews@brighton.co.uk

## WAKE UP! WAKE UP! IT'S YER SIZE DON'T MATTER

# Weekly SchNEWS

### Printed and Published in Brighton by Justice?

**Friday 25th February 2000**     http://www.schnews.org.uk/     **Issue 249    Free/Donation**

# NANO NANO

"What is possible and what is bananas is hard to judge at present, but from our experience every bone in our bodies says this technology will happen because of the similarities with the bio-tech industry."

**- Pat Mooney, Rural Advancement Foundation International (RAFI)**

Smaller than the SchNEWS bank account, nanotechnology is set to be the next big thing in the manipulation of reality since biotechnology. Who says? The American Assocation for the Advancement of Science who had their Annual General Meeting last week, and believe that machines made up of a few atoms could be possible in a few years time.

After the dazzling and life-affirming science that led from the discovery of the atom to the atom bomb, from DNA to Frankenfoods, SchNEWS readers will excuse us for not jumping up and down with excitement at this next big leap forward.

So what is nanotechnology? And why aren't we digging in the SchNEWS biscuit tin for our long lost microscope in anticipation?

A nanometre is a billionth of a metre. If you put 50 million nanos side by side they'd be the width of a human hair. Where biotechnology manipulated genes to alter what was there already, nanotechnology can build pretty much anything atom by atom, or alter existing structures. Which could mean much faster and smaller computers that assemble themselves, or manipulating the atomic structure of objects so they that may even be turned into something else. As Pat Mooney puts it, "You could have a household microwave which you simply pop the garbage into and out pops - well another microwave if you want. Or a hamburger, a piece of furniture, TV set, anything!"

As is the case with a lot of science, whether the new research gets used for everyone's benefit depends on who controls it and what their motives are. Nanotech could be used for microsurgery, since it would be a lot easier to inject surgical robots to perform operations rather than cutting people open, or for recycling waste into something useful. However, on a darker note, the U.S has already developed a spy plane the size of a pound coin that can fly up to 1000 feet at 40 mph, with built-in sensors, and it is only a matter of time until ones smaller than the eye can detect will be invented. How can you prevent yourself being monitored, if you don't even know it's happening?

Governments are taking the technology seriously. Following the Japanese lead in investment, the U.S gov't's National Nanotechnology Initiative (N.N.I.) has been given a proposed budget of $500 million dollars for next year, but as Pat Mooney notes, "We don't know what is being spent by the Department of Energy or Dept of Defence, but it's considerably more than that." Research is accelerating fast, and we are no more than a few years away from nanomachines. Last year researchers in the U.S built a motor from just 78 atoms, small enough to fit in a cop's brain (okay, that's not what they used it for, cops are VERY clever really).

Now call us cynical but we at SchNEWS are a little concerned. Control of research and funding is already in the tiny hands of national governments and corporations. Among those funding the N.N.I., are the U.S Department of Defence, and NASA, and the current corporate leader of nanotech research is IBM, an early backer of the Multilateral Agreement on Investment (SchNEWS 141) which threatened to strip away the worlds labour and environmental laws. If nanotech follows the same pattern as biotech, then we can look forward to companies like Monsanto moving in to try and get a stranglehold on the nanotech market, as they have tried on the agricultural markets with their GM products. If they start patenting this research as they are doing with GM products, then you could find that you will only be allowed to use such technology if you pay them a hefty fee. Pat Mooney: "When I discuss it, it's like talking about bio-technology in the 70s – people asking how could it be possible. They say we're crazy. But at RAFI we reckon that bio-technology will not be with us much longer. We are in a transition towards nano-technology if you look at where the money is being spent on research around the world."

---

**TERROR TUBBIES BENEFIT NIGHT**
**THIS SUNDAY 27TH FEB**
To raise awareness of the Government's proposed Terrorism Bill
@ The Gloucester, with P.A.I.N., Tragic Roundabout and Mark Leveller
5pm-10.30 Free food B4  7pm
£3.50/£2.50 concs.

---

## CRAP ARREST OF THE WEEK

For having dirty sheets! A couple had their house searched by Manchester cops and were locked in police cells for seven hours (while their three young kids were left unsupervised at home) for the alleged theft of a bed sheet from a Road Chef hotel. They had put the sheet in a laundry bag and left it outside for collection after one of her children had spilled a drink on it. The next day hotel staff found the missing sheet.

Maybe we're being a bit too pessimistic about all this fiddling around with atoms, and it will turn out to bring nothing but good for humanity. After all the nanobots in Star Trek are sometimes mischievous, but basically cute little robots who help out the crew of the Enterprise from time to time. However, does anyone remember what happened the first time scientists started playing round with the atom?

Check out www.rafi.org in mid-March for more info.

## OFF THEIR STED!

What do you reckon the Government does to a school which has exam results 27% above the national average? Praise them? No, tries to close them down!!

Summerhill in Suffolk is an independent progressive school founded in 1921 by A.S.Neill, a teacher and revolutionary. He created a community free from authoritarian rule, in which pupils' personal interests and development have priority. Children have a direct say in the running of the school through weekly meetings. The school's ideals have influenced educational theories and political thinking worldwide. However, not everyone is enthusiastic. The Education Authorities equate 'the pursuit of freedom' with 'the pursuit of idleness', and they can't handle the non-compulsory lesson attendance policy. Despite having only 58 pupils, Summerhill is the most inspected school in Britain. Last May's OFSTED inspection led to them being served with a Statutory Order of Complaint. The order required changes including compulsory attendance of lessons and stricter discipline. Failure to comply may lead to closure. Summerhill believe that these measures go against the fundamental principles on which the school is founded. An appeal has been lodged with the Independent Schools Tribunal, it's hearing will take place over 8 days, from 20th March. Please show your support for Summerhill in it's fight against closure. As Zoe Readhead, Principal, said "If Summerhill is closed it would simply be another nail in the coffin of anything that's different." Save Summerhill Campaign, Summerhill, Leiston, Suffolk IP16 4HY. 01728 830 540. www.s-hill.demon.co.uk

## IT'S A SIN

In December 1991 a woman was held captive at knife-point and raped. Her attacker took obscene photographs, asking his victim to smile for the camera. He attempted to force pills down her throat. He took the number of her car to further intimidate her. When she started to receive threatening phone calls, terrified for the safety of her two children, she went to the police. But a policewoman advised her to drop the case. A year later the same man committed an almost identical attack at the same premises. Christopher Davies was arrested, the case was forwarded to the Crown Prosecution Service (CPS) who decided not to prosecute.

Why? The two women are prostitutes, so the courts deem them "not credible". Forget preconceptions - of these two women one was saving to buy an electric wheelchair for her disabled husband, the other was funding her degree. The English Collective of Prostitutes estimate at least 70% of prostitutes are mothers, mostly single, struggling to support their families in the face of benefit cuts and low wages.

Prostitute women, being criminalised, are very vulnerable to violence and are forced onto the streets by laws which say that women working from the same premises constitutes a brothel despite the fact that working on the streets is ten times more dangerous than working indoors. Men who attack prostitute women are hardly ever arrested; only one in twelve women who is raped reports it to the police; only one tenth of recorded rapes result in a conviction.

Though prostitutes' clients include police, lawyers, judges and MP's, it is the women who are considered corrupt, not the men who use them. If the police neglect to investigate a crime because the victim was 'only' a prostitute then all women are vulnerable to attack from the rapist who remains free. In the case of the Yorkshire Ripper the prosecuting Attorney General Sir Michael Havers said of the Ripper's victims, "some were prostitutes, but perhaps the saddest part of this case is that some were not. The last six attacks were on totally respectable women."

When a sex worker secures the prosecution of her attacker the next hurdle is the Criminal Injuries Compensation Authority who are likely to refuse compensation on the grounds that the victim's job puts her at risk by choice. But, as Harry Cohen MP wrote to the Board, "If it is regarded that their profession is by nature a dangerous one then the logic of your argument breaks down. On that basis you would refuse compensation to policemen and their families who have been the victims of crime."

When the CPS decided not to prosecute, the ECP helped them to bring the first ever private prosecution for rape in an English court. Their case made legal history when 3 years later, Christopher Davies was convicted.

Recommended reading: 'Some Mother's Daughter' from Crossroads Womens Centre, P.O. Box 287, London NW6 5QU Tel 0171 482 2496

## KEEP IT UP

Last Friday a Laing building site in Surrey was occupied in solidarity with protestors who are fighting eviction at the Gorsewood road protest camp in Essex. Grateful workers enjoyed a break from building a massive complex for Pfizer - the makers of viagra. Maybe that's why people found it so easy to get up a massive crane to unfurl a banner saying 'more roads! Don't even try it!' Laing were targeted as they are part of the consortium that is building the six lane motorway through the Essex countryside. 20 days into the eviction and 5 people are still down the tunnels. Gorse Wood 07957 915977

## SchNEWS in brief

You can always rely on the Tories to come up with the **odd gem**, and David Shaw, the prospective parliamentary candidate for Kingston and Surbiton doesn't disappoint: "I think it's no coincidence that Mo Mowlam had a brain tumour *and* smoked cannabis in her youth"! ** SchNEWS would never gloat, but felt we should share the **Evening Anus'** apology to demonstrators who went to Shamrock Monkey Farm the other week and were branded, amongst other things, "terrorists". The Anus grovelled "...we let you down with our lopsided and half-hearted reporting of the protest and the ugly clashes with police.. Equally we condemn police brutality against anyone in the same way we condemn extremists... We strive for fair play. Yes, we let readers down this once, but don't leap to the conclusion it was because we are biased. Quite simply, we slipped from our normal standards." ** Next **Shamrock** Demo: Noon, 12th March. Tel 07020 936956 e-mail shamrockmonkeys@yahoo.com ** Join satirist Mark Thomas for the real **"Star Wars"** on Saturday 4th March at the U.S-run Menwith Hill Spy Base, near Harrogate, Yorkshire. Noon-4pm www.gn.apc.org/cndyorks/m4 ** Think Bacardi's Cuban cool? Find out the truth at a **Boycott Bacardi**, Smash the Cuban Blockade Dayschool on Sat 11th March 11am - 5 pm at Marchmont Centre, Marchmont Street, London WC1 £5/£2. Contact FRFI BCM, Box 5909, London, WC1N 3XX Tel 0171 837 1688 ** Housing benefit privitised. **Refuse collectors** next? On Tuesday 7th March there's a demonstration against the privitisation of Sheffield's public services, meet 12.30 pm outside the town hall. ** The **Socialist Alliance** are holding a National Campaigns and Activists Conference on Sat. 25th March in Leicester. The aim? "How to link direct action more closely with socialist and green campaigning. 0116 244 0956 leicesterradical@hotmail.com ** The **Nestle 16**, who were arrested last November on charges of 'conspiracy to commit burglary' after dropping a banner outside the Nestle factory in Halifax (SchNEWS 242), have funnily enough had their charges dropped! ** Campaigners will be protesting outside 30 UCI cinemas this Saturday (26th) to highlight the company's destruction of **Crystal Palace park**. Meanwhile, Bromley Council, not content with giving planning permission to UCI to carve up the Grade II listed park with a planned 20 screen multiplex cinema and huge roof-top carpark, now want to cut down another 200 trees. The Council want to clear 'historically inaccurate trees' that don't look primeval enough to make way for a dinosaur area! www.crystal.dircon.co.uk

## JOLLY HOCKLEY STICKS

The campaign against housing development is hotting-up in Essex. At Hockley, protesters are awaiting the results of a court case brought by the developers to quash the protesters' injunction which is stopping the company from entering the land which remains sectioned off. Campaigners are trying to stop 66 luxury homes being built. The site is still under siege by the developers' hired security using violent intimidation tactics, protesters are imprisoned on site with only a trickle of supplies being allowed in. Last Saturday locals stormed the barricades and a few managed to get through the fence to join the protesters. A new camp has been established at Ashingdon on Golden Cross road - 20 mins from the Hockley camp - on 5 acres of the 7 acre site that is due to be developed by Wilcon Homes. Residents have registered the site as a public open space. More people are desperately needed. Tel 0831 717815-Hockley or 07833 191951-Ashingdon. www.thisisessex.com.au

## Inside SchNEWS

Saturday 4th March is an international day of solidarity with death row prisoner Mumia Abu Jamal. Ex-Black Panther member and award winning journalist Mumia has been on death row for the past 16 years after he was found guilty of killing a policeman in a rigged trial that violated 4 human rights conventions. For a full list of events taking place all over the U.K contact mumia@callnetuk.com

## U'wa Update

The peaceful occupation by 450 U'wa people protecting their tribal lands from oil exploration (SchNEWS 244) has been attacked by the Colombian Police and Army resulting in the deaths of three children and the disappearance of 11 others. Rural workers throughout the region began a three day general strike on February 15th in response to the police brutality. The children apparently drowned after the soldiers and anti-riot police used tear gas, bulldozers and riot sticks to charge the blockade, forcing the U'wa to jump into the fast flowing Cubujón River. There will be another Global Day of Action for the U'wa on March 9th, details www.ran.org, e-mail organize@ran.org

## Glen Sent Down

13 Glen of the Downs campaigners were imprisoned last Friday after refusing to promise the High Court not to interfere with Wicklow County Council. The Council are constructing a £20 million dual-carriageway through the Glen, a beautiful broad leaf forest which unfortunately just happens to be in the way of the European Union's grand scheme to expand the road network. Mr Justice Barr said that if the protestors wanted to be "made martyrs of and carted off to prison" he would oblige them! The unlucky 13 were taken off to Mountjoy Prison where they will remain until they comply with the High Court. Those jailed were due in the High Court today, but as SchNEWS went to press we we're still waiting for the outcome. www.emc23.tp/glen/news.htm or Dublin FoE 0035 31497 3773.

## CASUAL KILLERS

Simon Jones was killed in 1998 on his first day at work at Shoreham Harbour. He was doing one of the most dangerous jobs in the country with no health and safety training, and was killed when his head was crushed by the grab of a crane (SchNEWS 182). There will be a judicial review into the failure of the Crown Prosecution Service to prosecute those responsible for Simon's death at 10am, 16th March at the High Court in the Strand, London. An overnight vigil will take place starting at 8pm, 15th March. There's also a benefit featuring comedians Mark Thomas, Jo Brand and Rob Newman and a short video about the campaign on 10th March at Hove Town Hall. Get yer tickets fast! c/o the SchNEWS www.simonjones.org.uk

## ...and finally...

SchNEWs congratulates the Labour Party on one hundred glorious years. Jorg Haider, the leader of Austria's far right Freedom Party, got the congratulations in first claiming that him and Blair share "amazing similarities" except that Blair's immigration laws are "more extreme". Like Tory Blair he is committed to finding a "new sense of community", and "both parties stand up for the weak and underprivileged". Mr Haider also draws parallels between both parties' employment policies. Perhaps they should change their name to Neo-Labour.

**nano-disclaimer**
SchNEWS warns all actors with small parts not to make a drama out of a crisis. (That's about the size of it!).

WAKE UP! WAKE UP! COR BLIMLEY WE'VE REACHED 250!

# the Weekly SchNEWS

**Printed and Published in Brighton by Justice?**

Friday 3rd March 2000    http://www.schnews.org.uk/    Issue 250    Free/Donation

# STRIKE IT LUCKY!

"She meets March 8th with her face erased and her name hidden. With her come thousands of women. More and more arrive. Dozens, hundreds, thousands, millions of women who remember all over the world that there is much to be done and remember that there is still much to fight for. It appears that that thing called dignity is contagious". A Zapatista woman's statement about International Women's Day.

Women and girls do two thirds of the world's work, for only 5% of the world's income, women's average full time weekly earnings are 72% of men's (Office of National Stats 1998), and a report in Red magazine (Jan 2000) stated that two thirds of women working full time do most of the housework.

March 8th is International Women's Day and women all over the world are hanging up their pinnies, turning off their disk drives and taking to the streets. Since March 8th 1907, when the women garment makers of New York went on strike for a living wage and a 10-hour day, the date has been earmarked to inspire women worldwide in their fight for their rights.

The National Women's Council of Ireland have called this year's strike, and it's gone global. Anne Neale from Crossroads Women's Centre reckons that the strike "could be very disruptive. When a similar action took place in Iceland in 1975, factories would not function and everything shut down". Cynthia Enloe in her book "Bananas, Beaches and Bases" argues that "if secretaries went out on strike, foreign affairs might grind to a standstill". Without women's work the world economy would fall to its knees. Kingston Raging Grannies ask "Can you imagine what would happen if all the women stopped work…at Wal-Mart or McDonalds?".

**WHAT DO WOMEN WANT?**

The global women's movement is a diverse tapestry. Some are calling for the abolition of 3rd world debt, 'cos it's really women that are owed billions for centuries of work, or for clean drinking water, affordable housing, safety from violence, fair wages, and increased benefits for carers and mothers

Women are striking to demand a change in the priorities of the global economy. According to the United Nations $9billion of the world's budget goes on health and nutrition, $6bn on water and sanitation, $4bn on education and $538bn on military budgets. This spending reflects the attitudes of the people who pull the purse strings, attitudes that consider arms to be more important than welfare. As the floodgates open for multinational corporations to enter developing countries women are forced into low paid work with poor conditions.

**And for the boys...** Men are supporting the women's strike. Payday Men's Network said, "Like women, we want to work less and have more money. We too want our unwaged work recognised and paid with money, time, resources, land, peace and rights. And we know that as long as women work too much, even more than men, their pay and conditions are the standard for men". The network have men ready to strike on the day, other are making donations to the strike fund, or committing themselves to do all the domestic chores and childcare for the day.

**"At the beginning was the deed."**

Rosa Luxemburg, Revolutionary Socialist, 1871-1919.

Women have a strong tradition of resistance; from taking up arms in the Zapatista struggle, to the Chipko women in India hugging trees, from the Greenham Common women, to the mum who asks for childcare provision in her workplace, from the suffragettes on hunger strike, to the 1917 Russian women factory worker's strike that started the revolution. In the UK women have made their presence felt actively enough to worry Detective Chief Inspector Kieron Sharp, the copper leading the inquiry into City of London protests on June 18, who panicked that "women are playing a greater role in this kind of subversive activity than you would normally find in criminal activity".

Black women, mothers, lesbians, asylum seekers, sex workers, pensioners, students, women with disabilities, waged and non-waged women, and loads more are holding actions from demos to a day's strike around the globe. So if you fancy making a stand why not make a partner take over household or childcare duties for the day, walkout with your colleagues at work or at college. Undercurrents are keen to film yer fun, contact them on 01865 203662 or underc@gn.apc.org

Here's what women are up to in over 30 countries from Albania to Rwanda...

**LONDON**: Women are invited to a Day of Celebration and Protest, with films and performances by women singers, dancers and poets from around the world. Full wheelchair access, childcare, and refreshments. 1pm-11pm, Union Chapel, Compton Avenue, Islington, N1 (Highbury & Islington tube). Women working in the red light area of Soho are considering stopping work and hanging banners outside their working flats saying SOHO ON STRIKE to protest about their lack of recognition. Picket the Dept. of Trade and Industry, Kingsgate House (next to Clinton card shop, Victoria or St James Park tubes). Trafalgar Square will be leafleted, and Crossroads Women's centre will be touring the city with their loud speaker system. **ASHTON-UNDER-LYNE:** Tameside women will be invited into a Strike Marquee

in Market Square for a glass of champers and to list their own strike demands. **GREATER MANCHESTER** - 0161 344 0758. **LIVERPOOL** - contact the Black Sisters about their Open Day 0151 709 8162!. **KEIGHLEY**-check out the Women's Centre for alternative therapy sessions all day 01535 681316.

**INDIA** Women will do no housework or other work in the villages of Madhya Pradesh; thousands will march in Raipur, Ragard, and Mahasmund. Deputations led by Chhattisgarh Women's Organisation will go to Bhopal to meet officials and to Delhi to lobby the government Chief Minister, pressing demands to end violence and poverty. **IRELAND** The Women Count Network will be striking in various ways, and along with the National Women's Council is pressing for a national paid holiday on 1st Feb. (St Brigid's Day), "A DAY OFF - because we're worth it!" to value women's work. Women's unwaged work is the largest industry in Ireland, estimated to be worth at least £314bn a year. **BURKINO FASO** Rural women are Striking to Exist, demanding money for birth certificates and identity cards which most can't afford. **PHILIPPINES** Community groups will lobby the president to issue a Presidential Proclamation making 8th March a paid holiday; parties and picnics are happening all day, and there'll be a "No Shopping Day" to protest against the consumer industry's profits at women's expense. **MEXICO** Daughters of the Corn Women's Collective are holding a strike day with a public meeting, debate and celebration in Mexico City. **TRINIDAD AND TOBAGO** The National Union of Domestic Employees will lead a women's march and rally in the capital city. **NIGERIA** The Grassroots Women Foundation is demanding that 8th March be declared a national public holiday and that breastfeeding working mothers be paid a special allowance. **USA** Demonstrations and parties in several major cities planned by US Wages for Housework. The Welfare Warriors (Wisconsin) are presenting women's Bills to Bill Clinton on 8th March, stating what welfare they're owed for the work he steals, and other cities will hold parties with the slogan "If you don't pay us for our work, we'd rather party instead!"

More info… Crossroads Women's Centre 0171-482-2496 womenstrike8m@server101.com

# YA BASTA!

**"It is better to die fighting than from hunger"** Major Ana Maria, EZLN

Over the past year, two dates stand out as defining moments of global resistance against global capitalism: June 18th and November 30th. Events which the world's press could not ignore; events which showed that not everyone was happy with the neo-liberal* agenda being forced down our throats.

The press like to talk about this 'globalisation of protest' as if it's something new, but what about the international movement against America's war in Vietnam? The mass solidarity against South African apartheid? Hey, some people are even using the Internet to co-ordinate protests across the globe (This reminds SchNEWS of when the cops were getting all hot under the collar because 'new age travellers' were using mobile phones to organise free parties!).

But where did this new movement come from? Where is its inspiration? A good starting point is the Zapatista uprising which came to the world's attention on January 1st, 1994. On the same day the North American Free Trade Agreement (NAFTA) was signed, four towns in the Chiapas region of Mexico were taken over by the Zapatista Army of National Liberation (EZLN), and the news was quickly broadcast around the world via the Internet.

SchNEWS recently spoke to someone just returned from Chiapas.

**Q: CAN YOU GIVE US A BRIEF HISTORY?**

A: The Zapitista's chose 1st January 1994 to occupy four major towns in the state of Chiapas to coincide with the introduction of NAFTA. They only held them for two or three days before the Mexican army chased them back into the jungle, but they'd made their point by then! The Zapatista resistance has been going on ever since.

**Q: SO 1994 WAS THE ZAPATISTAS' ANNOUNCEMENT TO THE WORLD THAT THEY MEAN'T BUSINESS AS WELL AS TWO FINGERS TO THE NAFTA AGREEMENT?**

A: Yeah. I think there had been fights with the army the year before, but the army had decided to not pursue them because the government was trying to negotiate this NAFTA deal. The government were really keen not to show there was a guerrilla war in any part of Mexico so they kept it quiet.

**Q: SO IT'S A SORT OF LOW INTENSITY WAR?**

A: Oh yeah, it's definitely a war but not one where many people are getting killed at the moment; and even though we don't hear much about the Zapatistas at the moment, the movement is as strong as ever, even in the face of 70,000 Mexican troops constantly surrounding them.

**Q: HOW DO THE ZAPATISTAS ORGANISE?**

A: The Zapatista's control 35 autonomous municipalities, and each municipal-ity covers a huge area with thousands of people in it. The scale of the area is something people don't appreciate.

Each municipality is named after an important revolutionary event or person. So you have the 1st January, or April 10th when Zapata was assassinated. Or Flores Magon, who was a Mexican anarchist, and Pancho Villa, who was once an ally of Zapata.

What is important is that the Zapatista's have broken away from the old guerrilla style of organising where the central committee tells you what to do.

Instead each village in the municipalities has it's own assembly to run it's own affairs. For example, some communities have decided on completely communal ownership of the land, while others have a mixed system with common and individual land. Each village sends a delegate to the Clandestine Indigenous Revolutionary Committee, where important military decisions can only be made after all the communities have been consulted.

For example during the San Andres Peace Accords, when the Zapatistas talked to the gov't, every single community was consulted, and these debates can go on for days - they talk it out, till everyone who wants to say something has said it, and then some kind of consensus is made. We were in one community where they had called a congress to decide the education structure for the whole of the municipality and the meeting lasted two days!

**Q: TELL US ABOUT THE LAND OCCUPATIONS**

A: I think the mainland takeovers started around 1995. Just three landlords used to control the municipality we were in. The landowners had passed land to each other for generations, until they were kicked out, and the area put under Zapatista control.

Before, in many places instead of being paid wages, the Indians were given credit for the landowners shop where everything was priced really high so reinforcing their poverty.

Many communities have debated what to do with the old landowners houses because no Zapatistas will live in them. Some have been used as warehouses, some have been demolished. In one community they took down a house brick by brick when they heard the landlord and his heavies we're coming back. They sent him a Christmas card with a picture of where the house once stood and said don't bother - there's nothing to come back to!

**Q: WHAT IS THE STANDARD OF LIVING?**

A: They are dirt poor, they haven't got any money, but they haven't got anyone to tell them what to do now. They always come out with "we have dignity". Their standard of living probably hasn't changed that much since the uprising, but at least now they are farming the land for themselves.

**Q: WHAT'S THE ATMOSPHERE THERE LIKE?**

A: Schizophrenic! You get the feeling from some that they can take on the whole world, but at the same time army planes are flying really low every day, there's troop carriers and police helicopters, military bases next to some municipalities - it all causes a certain desperation.

What the army and police do, is come into some communities on the pretext of looking for someone. It's always the women who are there, with these big sticks and little babies on their backs, fighting them off. A Mexican general recently complained that he didn't join the army to fight women and children!

**Q: TELL US ABOUT THE ROLE OF WOMEN**

A: My experience was that the women are tough as hell. They take part in the command structures of EZLN, for example the occupation of San Cristobal was directed by women. One third of the army are women. When I was in San Cristobal there was this huge women's march against militarisation in Chiapas.

Women insisted on alcohol being banned in the whole of the Zapatista controlled region. Landowners used to make sure the Indians got addicted to alcohol, which got them into so much debt until they were basically slaves. If they tried to leave they would be shot or punished, so this alcohol thing was a really useful form of control and it had an effect on the women as there

---

## A (VERY) BRIEF HISTORY OF MEXICO

The Institutional Party of the Revolution is the longest-running political dynasty on the planet, and has been in power in Mexico since 1929!

In the early eighties Mexico defaulted on its debts, causing a worldwide crisis. In came the International Monetary Fund, offering cash but with the usual 'structually adjusted' strings attached. These strings meant that Mexico had to flog off virtually every state owned business. However, after a brief recovery, the Mexican stock market crashed in 1994, causing the local currency, the peso to be devalued. This neo-liberal miracle culminated in the signing of the North American Free Trade Agreement, with the Mexican President being praised as champion of "liberal reform who had brought economic stability and social [sic] justice to Mexico". Unfortunately for the President, the Zapatistas disagreed, and began their uprising, which continues to this day.

was a lot more domestic violence then.

Now, each community has got a little jail big enough for one or two people and if any of the men turn up pissed they just stick them in the jail for the night. And it works, people don't drink.

Another example of the influence of women is the story of one guy who organises clean water projects for the communities. He put a proposal to the men in one village and said for the water project to work, it would take a lot of hard work; three weeks of solid digging a four mile trench from the mountain to the village. The men decided not to bother, and let the women continue to go down to the river and bring water back in buckets. However, when he went back to the village a week later, he was approached and told by one of the elders, that the women had had a meeting and told the men in no uncertain terms that they were gonna dig the pipeline!

However, in the assemblies there is still a hierarchy and it is still often the men who do the talking; the women's revolution has happened, but it's not all the way there yet by any means.

**Q: DO YOU THINK THE UNITED STATES SEES THE ZAPATISTAS AS A THREAT?**

A: Yeah, definitely. The US use the excuse of the war on drugs to arm the Mexican army and most of that weaponry is being used against the Zapatistas. And of course the US is worried because the Zapatistas are setting an example in not accepting poverty and injustice. The Americans spent millions destroying guerrilla movements in El Salvador, Guatemala and of course Nicaragua. And now a whole new rebellion has happened in Mexico, a country the US has always had a high level of control over.

The region is also rich in oil. The Mexican government wants to get its hands on it, but this revolutionary movement is in its way, so at some point there is gonna be a conflict . There is also huge bio-diversity in the forests, and the American bio-tech companies want to get into the jungle and start copywriting the genetic codes.

**Q: HOW IMPORTANT DO YOU THINK THE INTERNET HAS BEEN TO THE STRUGGLE?**

A: I had this vision of them all tapping away on their computers in the jungle and that was rubbish - most communities don't even have electricity. It is Zapatista supporters in Mexico City and America who have been invaluable in terms of getting the message out and creating a public mood where the Mexican government feels it can't intervene because it would be too controversial.

**Q: HOW IMPORTANT DO YOU THINK IT IS THAT PEOPLE LIKE YOURSELVES GO ABROAD AND VISIT AND SHOW SOLIDARITY WITH THE ZAPATISTAS?**

A: To be honest in terms of material support, the most useful thing that could happen, is some solidarity movement in America to try and stop the weaponry getting to the Mexican army. In the absence of that, it's a morale booster. We went over as a football team, and every community

we visited we had to get up on stage and introduce ourselves, say where we are from - they're all like 'where's Europe?' However, if their grasp of geography isn't very good, they are politicised and they understand why we are there.

**Q: HOW IMPORTANT DO YOU THINK THE ZAPITISTA STRUGGLE IS FOR INSPIRING PEOPLE?**

A: With the collapse of 'communism' there was gloating about the triumph of capitalism. If you want to get rid of the way the world is now being run, you've got to have some kind of idea about what the new world will be like, and the Zapatista's are vital because they are not only saying it, they've actually done it. They're running the municipalities communally, they're organising their own education projects, their own water projects, have their own army, they're reaching out to the other indigenous people of Mexico – it's inspirational.

**Recommended reading:** Zapatista! Documents of the New Mexican Revolution (Autonomedia, New York '95)
Rebellion from the Roots by John Ross (Common Courage '95)
Zapatista! Re-inventing Revolution in Mexico by John Holloway (Pluto Press '99)
**C h e c k o u t :** http://www.eco.utexas.edu:80/Homepages/Faculty/Cleaver/chiapas95.html
**Contact:** Chiapas Link, Box 79, 82 Colston Street, Bristol. Chiapaslink@yahoo.com

### *SCHNEWS VOCAB WATCH*
**NEO-LIBERAL:**
Initially associated with that romantic duo, Reagan and Thatcher, neo-liberalism has been the dominant economic theory for the past two decades.

Supporters of neo-liberalism talk of 'free market' policies that encourage private enterprise, consumer choice and personal initiative, and use these arguments to justify everything from lowering taxes on the wealthy, to dismantling education and social welfare programmes and scrapping environmental regulations.

These well thought out conscientious, economic policies, have resulted in ...a massive increase in social and economic inequality, a marked increase in severe deprivation for the poorest nations, a disastrous global environment and unstable global economy – but, and here's the key to it's popularity with its supporters, an unprecedented bonanza for the wealthy.

When these pioneers of righteousness, are presented with some of the rather large downside, they claim that the spoils of the good life will invariably spread to the broad mass of the population - as long as the neo-liberal policies that exacerbated these problems in the first place are not interfered with! Or as Robert McChesney put it "at their most eloquent, proponents of neo-liberalism sound as if they are doing poor people, the environment and everybody else a tremendous service as they enact policies on behalf of the wealthy few."

Worse still, the neo-liberal zealots loudest message is that humanity has hit the jackpot and there is no alternative to the status quo.

## IT'S YER SCHNEWS BLOW BY BLOW ACCOUNT OF GLOBAL RESISTANCE

**Jan 94:** The Zapatistas rise up with the signing of NAFTA (SchNEWS 174/5 and SchNEWS 200 for effects of NAFTA in Mexico)
**Sept 96:** The First Intergalactic Encuentro for Humanity and Against Neo-Liberalism, in Mexico
**July 97:** The second Encuentro in Spain (SchNEWS 128)
**Feb 98:** Geneva people's movements from around the globe met and form the People's Global Action against "Free" Trade and theWorld Trade Organisation (SchNEWS 156)
**May 98:** Street parties in 40 countries across the globe to protest against the G8 meeting in Birmingham (SchNEWS 168)
**June 18th 99:** Carnival against capitalism in the City of London , and actions in 27 other countries around the world (SchNEWS 217/218)
**Aug 99:** Peoples Global Action Meeting in Bangalore, India. (SchNEWS 226)
**Nov 30th 99:** Battle of Seattle: The World Trade Organisation's talks are de-railed by mass protests, with solidarity actions across the world (SchNEWS 240)

### GLOBAL DATES FOR YER DIARY
**April 16/17 Mobilisation for Global Justice**. There will be week long series of events in Washington, with workshops and training on the global economy, ending with a massive rally at the International Monetary Fund's (IMF) headquarters on Sunday April 16. Simultaneous events are planned in other countries. www.a16.org
**MayDay 2000 April 29 – May 1st**
A four day gathering featuring
Workshops, bookfair, film festival, art exhibition, footie tournament, tours of revolutionairy London, Critical Mass bike ride, plans for a permanent social centre, music, parties, May Queen event with a twist...
Maypoles, mayhem and a MASS ACTION in London on Monday May 1st to "celebrate our diverse struggles against capitalism, exploitation and the destruction of the planet."
MayDay 2000, BM MayDay, London, WC1N 3XX
www.freespeech.org/mayday2k
Part of the international call for action by People's Global Action on 1ST May
**September, Prague**:
Global Day of Action against the IMF annual meeting: www.destroyimf.org

A WORLD TO WIN

# KOSOVO'S WOMEN

March 2000 marks one year since NATO began it's bombardment of Serbia in response to the ethnic 'cleansing' of Albanians in Kosovo. Far from abating the crisis, Nato's campaign not only subjected civilians to the violence, it perpetuated the forced evacuation of thousands of Kosovans. In June, after an agreement of sorts was reached, NATO withdrew and its peacekeeping forces K-For and the United Nations Administraion were introduced to the ravaged province. So what's changed one year on?...evidence of human rights abuses is still rife, with Albanians and Serbs engaged in a vicious circle of endless retaliation attacks. Among the countless organisations that are at working to instill some sense of security into the humanitarian disaster, are those that are specific to women's needs. As well as enduring the systematic torture meted out indiscriminately to the ethnic Albanians, women have had to endure the added trauma of rape and other sexual abuses.

Medica is an organisation born out of the conflict in Bosnia, who now run the successful Medica Women's Therapy Centre in central Bosnia which has so far helped over 20,000 women since 1993. Bosnian women are now involved in an emergency initiative in Kosovo, undertaking the training of Albanian and Kosovan female psychologists, nurses and doctors in what they term "appropriate, gender-sensitive, medical and psycho-social responses to rape and other forms of war trauma."

Among Medica's aims are: the documentation of women's rights violations to bring about prosecutions; the establishment of a mobile clinic to reach those refugees scattered across rural areas; the establishment of six tent-clinics in Albanian refugee camps.

Medica's principles have a clear woman-to woman focus: "Women who have been systematically abused need care in the first instant from women; they may be respected and their stories believed."

Medica,
P.O. Box 9560, London NW5 2WF. 0171 482 5670. c.cockburn@ktown.demon.co.uk

## YOU'RE NEVER TOO OLD

Have you ever worried that perhaps you're too old to be a feminist? Well panic no longer, the Older Feminists Network could be for you!

Launched in 1982 out of the Spare Rib women's magazine collective, this group has been going strong ever since. It's aims are to challenge the stereotypes of older women, to mobilise their skills and provide support and information. "We felt that the larger Women's Liberation Movement was not giving sufficient attention and value to older women" said a spokeswoman.

The group hold day long events on the second Saturday of each month, which include general meetings, discussions and two workshops. Here's just some of the topics covered in these workshops...widowhood, motherhood, self-defence, sexuality, public transport, social status, health...and many more. As well as all this, there's a bi-monthly newsletter containing stories, articles, photos, campaigns and letters to name just a few.

Meetings are held at the Millman Street Community Centre, 50 Millman Street, London WC1 on the 2nd Sunday of each month from 11am-5pm. Older Feminists Network, c/o 54 Gordon Road, London N3 1EP, 0208 346 1900

## SchNEWS in brief

Need information? Interested in getting active? Want to get help of any sort? Here's your quick run down of what to do and where to go... **BRIGHTON:** ** **Women's Refuge**. Safe accommodation for women who are victims of domestic abuse. 01273 622822 ** **Rape Crisis Helpline**, 01273 203773 ** **Stopover Residential Project**. Safe accommodation for women aged 16-21 suffering domestic abuse. 01273 603775 ** **Women's Writing Group.** Opportunity for women to write poetry, stories, articles, or anything you want to really! They meet every Tuesday at Brighton Women's Centre, Basement, Brighthelm Centre, North Road, Brighton 7.30-9.30pm. 01273 240044 ** **Queenspark Women's Writing Group**, space for women to do creative and autobiographical writing. Every Thursday 10-12 am, 49 Grand Parade, Brighton. Annual membership fee of £10/5. 01273 505642 ** **Women's Yoga** at the Youth Centre, Whitehawk Road. Thursdays 10.30-12pm. £2 ** **Women's Rugby** at Hove Park every Saturday 7.30-9pm. ** **Adventure Unlimited** offers women only outdoor activities and camps for those of you who are feeling fit! 01273 681058 ** **Mosaic**. Black and Mixed Race Community Group that meets at Community Base, 113-115 Queens Road, Brighton, 01273 234017 ** **Akwaaba Black and Ethnic Minority Support and Information.** St. Gabriel's Family Centre, 8 Wellington Road, Brighton, 01273 325039 ** **Lesbian Drop-in**. Fridays 12-4pm at Brighton and Hove Lesbian and Gay Community Centre. 113-117 Queens Road, 01273 234005 ** **Young Mothers Support Group**. Organisation for mothers up to age 19. Contact Tracy Holder or Sara Downing, Morley Street Family Centre, Brighton, 01273 295858 ** **Oasis Women's Drug Project**, 22 Richmond Place, BN2 2NA, 01273 696970 ** **Threshold**, women's mental health initiative holding groups, sessions and counselling. ** And last but by no means least, there's the **Brighton Women's Centre** where you can find practically everything you could ever want. They offer counselling, legal advice, a creche, pregnancy testing and drop-in sessions. Basement, Brighthelm Centre, North Road, Brighton BN1 1YD. www.btnwomen.u-net.com 01273 749567 **AND ELSEWHERE: ** Training for Women.** Courses in furniture making, plumbing, electrical installation, carpentry etc for women out of work for over 6 months. Childcare available and no course fees. Also allowances for materials and clothing. Northbrook College, Broadwater Road, Worthing. 01903 606002 ** **Women Returning to Study.** Women only college offering certificates to higher education. Residential and day study available. Hilcroft College, Southbank, Surbiton. 0181 399 2688

## CAAT'S EYES

In case you didn't know, the Campaign Against the Arms Trade (CAAT) now has a women's network. It was set up in September 1999 and raises awareness of the specific traumas encountered by women during conflict. "Women and children make up the majority of the world's refugees, struggling to survive when families, homes and livelihoods have been lost.

There's a free Women's Information Pack available. And an action planned in London for International Women's Day. Contact June at CAAT, 11 Goodwin Street, Finsbury Park, London N4 3HQ 0171 281 1297

## Let's Haggle

If you fancy some revolutionary feminist activity, join the HAGs! Don't be scared by the name, HAG stands for Hell Raising Anarchist Girls, a Brighton based 'loose collective of anarcha-feminists'.The group originated in February of last year from women attending the Rebel Alliance direct action meetings and the women's nights at the Anarchist Teapot. It combines Feminism and Anarchism to create an alliance better equipped to fight against the forces of capitalism and patriarchy which go hand in hand.

HAG are keen to point out that they are not anti-male, but simply pro-women, a big difference. "Within HAG we can share confidences, humour and experiences. It helps us see things from a different perspective and gives us increased confidence and skills", said a spokeswoman.In their first year, the HAGs have tackled a wide range of issues. Their first action, to coincide with International Women's Day 99 involved a procession round Brighton bringing to the public's attention the large and colourful history of female activists in the town. Since then, they have produced a radio programme (wimminz hour) for pirate Radio 4A, attended the J18 Carnival Against Capitalism in London, took part in International No Diet day with the message 'Riot Not Diet', organised self-defence lessons...and much, much more!

Feeling inspired yet? Here's a quick run-down of what the HAGs have in store for the future...more self defence lessons, anti-GMO actions, climbing training days, making links with other 'anarch-fem' groups, and of course... more fun on this year's International Women's Day.

HAG meet every two weeks, at 6pm on Sundays at The Hag House, 14-16 Newmarket Road (off Lewes Road gyratory). They always need more people to get involved, so get along and get active!

## PAINT IT BLACK

Women in Black is a worldwide organisation that aims to address 'the whole continuum of violence, from male violence against women, to militarism and war.' It was formed in 1998 in Israel out of the women's protests against Israel's occupation of the Palestinian West Bank and Gaza, and now has bases in Yugoslavia, Belgium, the United States, Spain, Italy and many other countries. Women in Black Belgrade have been particularly active of late, highlighting the ongoing troubles caused by the Kosovo conflict, raising awareness and addressing those in power.

Women in Black (London) c/o The Maypole Fund, PO Box 14072 London N16 5WB. www.chorley2.demon.co.uk/wib.html) 0171 482 5670.

## ...and finally...

Sussex Women Magazine needs you now! This is a forthcoming publication that hopes to be up and running in the Summer. It will focus on women's experience in the Sussex area with an emphasis on the positive aspects. "News and information on positive, constructive things women are doing, rather than focusing on the ways in which women are downtrodden."

Contributions are urgently needed, and also people to get involved with the running of the magazine So, if you're a Sussex woman with something to say, get writing. Contact Jacqueline Seamon on 01273 240044 for more details

**disclaimer**

SchNEWS warns all readers that we'll be on strike next week, but will be back the week after with a new agenda. Honest.

*Brighton Prevent the Terrorism Bill squatted community centre, March 2000*

Pic: Alec Smart

# Women make the world go round

"Life in this society being, at best, an utter bore and no aspect of society being at all relevant to women, there remains to civic-minded, responsible, thrill-seeking females only to overthrow the government, eliminate the money system, institute complete automation, and destroy the male sex". So, perhaps shooting men is not quite the solution to global capitalism, but Valerie Solanas still said it with style. Female resistance has taken loads of different shapes across space and time, and the world's never been short of wayward women and impudent girls who say no, and mean no, to a system that consistently denies both women and men any sense of real freedom.

This year's International Women's Day established a feisty agenda for women, with the first ever global women's strike (see SchNEWS 250) demanding that women's lives and work be valued. Tired of being ignored and written out of history women kicked off the new millenium with spectacular assertions of their presence and demands. Sex workers, students, housewives, mums, workers, and loads more went on strike to make the world stop and notice their unpaid or poorly paid work.

Irish women first called the strike, demanding a paid day off work for all women, and the vibe was contagious. "Ni pocas ni locas" (we're neither few nor crazy) was heard all over Argentina, as the Housewives Union coordinated a mass strike calling for pensions without contributions for workers without wages. In Peru 5000 women marched through Lima. In Barcelona a department store that insists its female sales staff stay slim was occupied. British students walked out, claiming that the government should be paying for the work they do. Zapatista women marched in San Cristobal de las Casas demanding the withdrawal of the army from Chiapas, whilst other Mexican women on strike called for the release of women students recently arrested. Women in every town of Macedonia marked the day with a peaceful protest against all kinds of discrimination. Italian Reclaim the Streets occupied the streets from Piazza Venezia to Termini Station, whilst Italian women distributed kits for artificial insemination, protesting against a new law which recognises the embryo as a human being. New Zealand's 'Parents as Partners' organised a "Bad Hair Day" in frustration about the lack of recognition in government policy of unpaid parenting work.

In London the Strike was launched by sex workers. Hiding their identity behind masks, more than half the area's sex workers marched through Soho, in protest at council attempts to evict them from the flats where they work, leaving potential clients with their hands in their trouser pockets. The council's 'clean up' operation to gentrify the area could make over 100 women homeless and working on the streets, where it is 10 times more dangerous than working indoors.

Hey, not only is female resistance older than capitalism, but it has also toppled it before. The 1917 International women's day was marked in Russia on February 23rd, at a time when even the most militant Bolshevik organisations were opposing strikes for fears that the time was unripe for militant action. They were waiting for revolutionary action at some indefinite time in the future. The women textile workers, however, were ready to act there and then. Trotsky testifies to the power of these striking women in his History of the Russian Revolution, where he states that "in spite of all directives the women textile workers in several factories went on strike. It had not occured to anyone that it might become the first day of the revolution". The striking factory women began by mobilising support from the metal workers, and then the whole thing exploded into a mass strike of 90,000 workers! Thus the revolution was kicked off by women workers, a case of grassroots action overcoming resistance even from its own revolutuionary organisations.

Back here in old Blighty, the women of the seventeenth century English revolution remind us that just because hardly anyone's heard of them, it doesn't mean that women revolutionaries haven't been active throughout history. Leveller women attacked lords, lawyers, legislators, and abusive taxes, claiming their rights as women to petition and be heard,

"Come clowns, and come boys,
  Come hober-de-hoys,
  Come females of each degree,
  Stretch your throats, bring in your votes,
  And make good the Anarchy!"
goes one of the ballads of the revolution.

As old as the trees and as varied as women, female resistance is not going away, so, those pesky politicians and bully boy multinationals can quit fucking up the world and do as the girls say. Women's global resistance is stronger than global capital any day, and we're doing it for ourselves!

# WHAT'S REALLY GOING ON IN WORTHING

# The Pork-BoLTeR

ISSUE 25   MARCH 2000   FREE/DONATION

ISSUE 25   MARCH 2000   FREE/DONATION

## Sussex Police reveal protesters' new secret weapon . . .

# YES, IT'S RIOT GRRRAN!

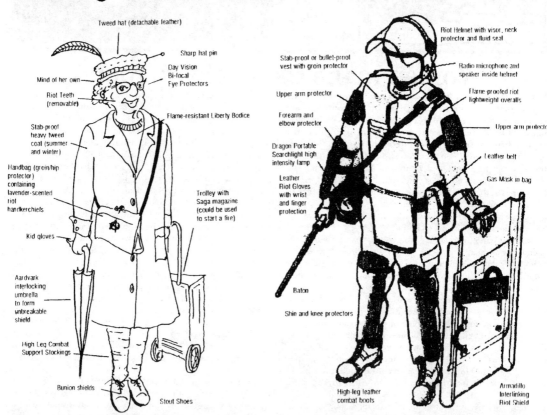

Tweed hat (detachable leather)

Sharp hat pin

Day Vision Bi-focal Eye Protectors

Mind of her own

Riot Teeth (removable)

Flame-resistant Liberty Bodice

Stab-proof heavy tweed coat (summer and winter)

Handbag (groin/hip protector) containing lavender-scented riot handkerchiefs

Trolley with Saga magazine (could be used to start a fire)

Kid gloves

Aardvark interlocking umbrella to form unbreakable shield

High Leg Combat Support Stockings

Bunion shields

Stout Shoes

Riot Helmet with visor, neck protector and fluid seal

Stab-proof or bullet-proof vest with groin protector

Radio microphone and speaker inside helmet

Upper arm protector

Flame-proofed riot lightweight overalls

Forearm and elbow protector

Upper arm protector

Dragon Portable Searchlight high intensity lamp

Leather belt

Leather Riot Gloves with wrist and finger protection

Gas Mask in bag

Baton

Shin and knee protectors

High-leg leather combat boots

Armadillo Interlinking Riot Shield

## Elite Riot Grrran v Elite Riot Cop – how they square up

IT must be jolly stressful to be a top cop with Sussex Police in this day and age, but poor _Assistant Chief Constable Tony Lake_ is clearly now one rubber bullet short of a full baton round.

In a letter to the _Evening Argus_ (February 22), Mr Lake defended the police's treatment of protesters opposed to Shamrock Farm monkey holding centre at Small Dole, near Henfield. He bizarrely condemned **"extremists who seek out older and less agile protesters to use as 'human shields' to escape arrest and provoke confrontation"** ! Even more eccentrically, he claimed that there have **never** been any **"riot police"** at Shamrock, with people under the false impression that **police tooled up in riot gear** amounts to the same thing.

Cynics might ask whether Mr Lake really thinks older people have somehow been tricked into opposing Shamrock and are so stupid they can be 'used'. They might also suggest that he is really just rather frustrated that at Shamrock his non-riot squads cannot merrily weigh into groups of younger protesters, who they can always get away with portraying as violent trouble-makers...

**But we're having none of that!** No, we applaud Mr Lake for **exposing** the growing menace of _"rent-a-granny"_ mobs deployed by evil protesters.

And we can also assist him with his confusion over what is a riot cop and what isn't. A reader has sent us a cutting from a _Daily Telegraph_ supplement (January 25) with the commendably truthful title of _Business Benefits from Technology_ (The Luddites could have told them that much...) This features a charming article about a company called _Civil Defence Supply_ which is doing awfully well thanks to its Internet site selling "police and security specialist products" (**www.civil-defence.org** if you're interested, Mr Lake).

Their splendid illustration reproduced above shows **"an elite riot officer"** equipped with the full fetishistic range of the firm's first class products, including stuff like handy **Leather Riot Gloves** (quite different from non riot gloves, of course) and a lovely **baton** for smashing people's heads in.

If any wishy-washy liberal types think all this is rather over the top, think again – we also show here the fearful might of the **Elite Riot Grrran** being used by protesters, against which the police must obviously be protected.

Only one question mark remains – who was Mr Lake referring to when he wrote of **"cowardly thugs"** involved in the Shamrock conflict? Surely he doesn't mean those non-riot blokes with crash helmets and nasty big sticks?

# SchNEWS INDEX

# 5 THINGS YOU SHOULD TRY TO DO EVERYDAY

**1.** eat some food

**2.** have a meaningful conversation with another person

**3.** read something that adds to your knowledge of the world

**4.** create a new thing

**5.** make a contribution, however small, to the downfall of the existing social order

Isy 2000

# Legal        Warning

## Section    6    (clause    B.2)
### Right To Lunch Out Act 2000

Stick this up on your washing up or kitchen
sink particularly when under eviction:

## Take        Notice

**That**    these are our pots, pans, cutlery and crockery.

**That**    this washing up is not to be done. This is our washing up
and we have the right to not do it.

**That**    you will have to wash out a cup for yourself if you want a
cup of tea.

**That**    if you use violence or threaten violence trying to get us
to do the washing up this could lead to us lunching it out
for a further SIX MONTHS.

**That**    if YOU WANT to come in and do our washing up YOU
ARE QUITE WELCOME.

**That**    no cup in this building has a handle.


## Signed

## The     Occupiers

> **NB This notice is valid no-matter how
> lunched out the rest of the building is.**

# Legal Warning

Section 6 Criminal law Act 1977
As amended by the Crmininal Justice and Public Order Act 1994

# TAKE NOTICE

That: *we live in this house,* it is our home and *we intend to stay here.*

That: *at all times there is at least one person in this house*

That: *any entry into this house without our permission* is a **CRIMINAL OFFENCE** as any of one of us who is in physical possession is opposed to any entry without their permission.

That: *if you attempt to enter by violence* or by threatening violence we **WILL PROSECUTE YOU**, you may receive a sentence of up to **SIX MONTHS IMPRISONMENT** and/or a **FINE** of up to £5,000

That: *if you want us to leave* you will have to take out a summons for possession In the County Court or in the High Court, or produce to us a written statement or Certificate in terms of S. 12a Criminal Law Act 1977 (as inserted by Criminal Justice And Public Order Act 1994.

That: it is an offence under S. 12 a (8) Criminal Law Act 1977, (as amended), to knowingly make a false statement to obtain a written statement for the purposes of S. 12a. A person guilty of such an offence may receive a sentence of up to **SIX MONTHS** imprisonment and/or a fine of up to £5,000.

**The Occupiers**

*n.b. SIGNING THIS LEGAL WARNING IS OPTIONAL. IT IS EQUALLY VALID WHETHER IT IS SIGNED OR NOT.*

COPY THIS FOR YOUR MOMENT OF NEED...

From the heart of D.I.Y Culture comes the ultimate Tree Love Story: True tales from the environmental movement that stalled the British roads building programme, written and published by Kate Evans and her dog.

"*Copse* gives a real idea of what being involved in direct action site counter-culture is really like. It's vibrant, it's alive, it's hungover, it's radical – it's a bit weird. It's life on the edge; it's life under the table. It's intense conflict with the State followed the next week by sun shimmered skinny dipping with your friends... Kate's one of the crew, so people trust her. By basing it on interviews she's got the stories of dozens of people who'd never talk to the media... Read this book and you'll be privy to some really honest conversations with some incisive, interesting and fuckin' funny people.
"The photos are some of the most breathtaking images of our lives that I've seen and the beautifully drawn cartoons encapsulate site life brilliantly – resistance, porridge, passion and mud."

**Also includes *A Beginners Guide to Tree Protesting*: a practical section on how to set up your own environmental protest camp.**

# Copse: the Cartoon Book of Tree Protesting

**£4** **SchNEWS Round**
**issues 51-100**: Reclaim the Streets... Squatters Estate Agents... 3rd Battle of Newbury... The Land Is Ours!... cartoons... and loads more...

**£4** **SchNEWS Annual**
**issues 101-150:** Anarchy + Networks + Ecology + Campaigns + Information + Sabotage + @nti-Copyright + Weird Shit + Comics and more...

**£5** **SchNEWS Survival Handbook issues 151-200:** Genetic crop sites get a good kicking; streets reclaimed all over the world; docks occupied in protest at death at work; protesters rude about corporate plans for world domination...PLUS everything you need to know to survive the 21st century...

Add £1.50 p+p to each order **OR get all three books for a tenner!** plus £4.20 p+p

# Do or Die – Voices From the Ecological Resistance
**Sabotage... Anarcho-feminism... Riots... Anti-Biotechnology... Pirates... June 18th...**

Do or Die No.8 is 350 A5 pages crammed with reports and analysis from the worldwide ecological frontlines.
From tribal resistance against Indonesia to the festive attack on the financial heart of London on June 18th, these are the voices of those involved in the struggles themselves. In these times of concrete alienation here are voices that shine hope from movements aiming to defend nature, create revolution and rewild humanity...

**Send a cheque or postal order made payable to 'Do or Die' for £5 (inc. p&p) to Do or Die, c/o Prior House, 6 Tilbury Place, Brighton BN2 2GY.**

**Yes!** I have been bitten by your cleverly placed anarcho-shopping promotion. Please rush* me at least one copy of **Copse: the Cartoon Book of Tree Protesting.**

Name........................................................................................

Address.....................................................................................

................................................................................................

................................................................................................

Number of copies.............................................@ £9.50 plus £3 p+p each

Cheques payable to 'Orange Dog Productions' please. 1-19 Townhead Cottages, Dunford Bridge, Sheffield, S36 4TG. Copse can also be ordered at bookshops and public libraries. ISBN: 0 9532674 0 7
                                                                        *orders may be despatched in hippy time.

---

**Yes!** I understand the contradiction that consumerism can never make me happy, yet still wish to purchase funky **SchNEWS books!** Please despatch the following volumes to me at once*:

**SchNEWS round** Number of copies @ £4 plus £1.50 p+p each.....................................
ISBN: 0 9529748 0 0
**SchNEWS annual** Number of copies @ £4 plus £1.50 p+p each.....................................
ISBN: 0 9529748 1 9
**SchNEWS Survival Guide** Number of copies @ £5 plus £1.50 p+p each..................
ISBN: 0 9529748 2 7                                            **Total** .....................

**Or!** I have been suckered by your three-for-a-tenner offer. Somehow it just makes sense to spend more when I think how much I save! (?)

**Set of three co-ordinated SchNEWS books** Number of sets @ £14.20 each..................
                                                                        **Total** .....................

Name.........................................................................................

Address.....................................................................................

................................................................................................

Cheques/postal orders payable to 'Justice?' c/o On the Fiddle, PO Box 2600, Brighton, East Sussex, BN2 2DX. SchNEWS books are published by 'Justice?' - or - order them for your local library.
                                                                        *please allow hippy time for delivery.

---

**Please, please, quickly*** send me at least one shining ray of hope to allieviate the concrete cancer of my soul...

                                    Number of copies @ **£5** all in ......................

Name.........................................................................................

Address.....................................................................................

................................................................................................

................................................................................................

................................................................................................

Send a cheque or postal order made payable to 'Do or Die' to Do or Die, c/o Prior House, 6 Tilbury Place, Brighton BN2 2GY.  *yes, quickly! No hippies involved.

---

*Top tip: photocopy this page to save you cutting your book up*

# THE SCHNEWS
# CONTACTS LIST

After the chaos, here's yer list of over 700 groups,
organisations, zines, websites, people and places...

Most of the entries have been checked March to May 2000, with the descriptions usually written by the people themselves. This year web addresses have been included too. There are links on the SchNEWS website, where the full list also appears. International phone numbers often don't have the country's code included, so check in the phone book. SAE means send a stamped, self-addressed envelope.

To make life easier we've included both an alphabetical list, where all the details appear, and a list sorted by categories, where only the organisation's name appears.

If we have the time and technical bods, the site will be (irregularly) updated, so send any updates, contact info for groups not included, etc to Justice? P.O. Box 2600, Brighton BN2 2DX or via email to schnews@brighton.co.uk The database that this list was produced from is available as a Micro$oft Access file or text file on the Web site for mailshots or whatever.

And finally: the list is by no means complete. A few examples will hopefully inspire you to get ideas for what isn't around already and fill in the gaps – the contacts list is a campaigning tool (information for action). Some of the publications listed have many further contacts.

Entries look like: <u>Name</u> (Abbreviation) Address *T* Phone number *F* Fax number wwwebsite email@ddress *Description*

See http://www.schnews.org.uk for updates and a *classified index* for the list.

# Alphabetical Contacts Directory

**1990 Trust, The** South Bank Technopark, 90 London Rd, London, SE1 6LN *T* 020 7582 1990 *F* 020 7735 9011 www.blink.org.uk blink1990@gn.apc.org or jasper@gn.apc.org *A national Black organisation set up to represent the communities at all levels and disseminate and reciprocate information concerning our communities. (Black = African, Asian, & Carribean).*

**1in12 Club** 21-23 Albion St, Bradford, BD1 2LY *T* 01274 734160 http://www.legend.org.uk/1in12 1in12@legend.co.uk *Members social club based on the principles of self-management.*

**56a Infoshop** 56 Crampton St, London, SE17 www.safetycat.org/56a 56a@safetycat.org *We are a space that includes a radical bookshop, a wholefood co-op and an open-access bike workshop...And we rock. Plus a large open-access archive plus squat advice.*

**5th May Group (Turkish and Kurdish Anarchists in Exile)** P.O. Box 2474, London, N8 *T* 0181 374 5027 *F* as phone *We mostly campaign around local issues (eg: JSA, New Deal etc). We also campaign against Compulsory Military Service in Turkey, and propagandise anarchist ideas.*

**A-Infos** www.ainfos.ca/ *A multi-lingual news service by, for, and about anarchists.*

**A27 Action Group** 56 Firle Village, Lewes, BN8 6LG *T* 01273 858365 *F* as phone *We aim to stop with research into the departments facts and figures the building of a new A27 between Lewes and Polegate.*

**Abolition 2000 (A2000 UK)** 601 Holloway Rd, London, N19 4DJ *T* 020 7281 4281 *F* 020 7281 6281 www.abolition2000.org A2000UK@gn.apc.org *To achieve for the new millenium a global treaty to eliminate nuclear weapons.*

**Action Against Injustice (A.A.I)** P.O. Box 858, London, E9 5HU *Co-ordinating prisoner justice campaigns & fighting corruption within the legal system.*

**Action For Social Ecology** Box 34089, 10026, Stockholm, Sweden, ekologisten@usa.net

**Action South West (The Westcountry Activist Network Newsletter)** Box 80, Greenleaf, 82 Colston St, Bristol, BS1 5BB *T* 07931 268966 wca99@hotmail.com *A forum for direct action campaigners in the southwest, aiming to encourage practical solidarity and mutual support.*

**Active Distribution** BM Active, London, WC1N 3XX hon@active.free-online.co.uk *Anarchist distribution, wholesale, mailorder and retail (!). Non-profit DIY project of 10 years! Active isn't super efficient but it's very committed to spreading the message without profiteering from*

**Active-Sydney** Sydney, Australia, www.active.org.au/ webkids@active.org.au *Activist news, views and humour online - a website and email lists for Sydney and soon all over Australia.*

**Activists Legal Project** 16B Cherwell St, Oxford, OX4 1BG *T* 01865 268966

**Adbusters** 1243 West 7th Av, Vancouver, BC, Canada, V6H 1B7 *T* 604 736 9401 *F* 604 737 6021 http://adbusters.org/ adbusters@adbusters.org *We are a global network of artists, activists, writers, students, educators and entrepreneurs who aim to launch the new social activist movement of the information age.*

**Advisory Service for Squatters (A.S.S)** 2 St. Paul's Rd, London, N1 2QN *T* 0171 359 8814 *F* 0171 359 5185 www.squat.freeserve.co.uk advice@squat.freeserve.co.uk *Daily (Sunday to Thursday) legal and practical advice for squatters and homeless people (ring before calling).*

**Agitator, The** c/o Haringey Solidarity Group, P.O.Box 2474,

London, N8 *T* 020 8374 5027 *F* as phone http://home.clara.net/hsg/hhome.html hsg@clara.net *A directory of autonomous, non-hierarchical groups & such like in Britian and Ireland. Free (donations much needed).*

**Agroforestry Research Trust** 46 Hunters Moon, Dartington, Totnes, Devon, TQ9 6Jt

**Ahimsa** 40452 Ditmus Court, Fremont, U.S.A, CA 94538 http://members.xoom.com/ahimsazine ahisazine@xoommail.com *Zine specifically by and for Anarchopacifists. Ahimsa advocates nonviolent non-cooperation, sit-ins, strikes, and all other forms of non-violent resistance.*

**AK Distribution** P.O.Box 12766, Edinburgh, EH8 9YE *T* 0131 555 5165 *F* 0131 555 5215 ak@akedin.demon.co.uk *Distribute and publish a wide range of anarchist, left and counterculture books, pamphlets, magazines, t-shirt and audio. Send for catalogue.*

**Aldermaston Women's Peace Camp** awtt@hotmail.com or sian@aldercamp.freeserve.co.uk *Monthly camps fri-sun at Aldermaston Nuclear weapons establishment near Reading. Workshops, street stalls, arrestable/non arrestable actions, fun, networking.*

**Allotments Coalition Trust, The (ACT)** *T* c/o Sophie 01865 722016

**Alpha** http://www.geocities.com/capitolhill/lobby/4002 *Greek anarchists.*

**Alt-Tech** Glyn Meibion Mawr, Groceslon, Caernarfon, Gwynedd, Wales, LL54 7DP *T* 01286 882199/07802 782187 nik.jenkie@btinternet.com *Provide education and info on renewable energy and power for outdoor events.*

**Amazon Alliance** 1367 Connecticut Ave, N.W Suite 400, Washington DC 20036-1860, USA *T* 202 785 3334 *F* 202 785 3335 www.amazoncoalition.org amazoncoal@igc.org *An initiative born out of the partnership between indigenous peoples of the Amazon and groups and individuals who share their concerns for the future of the Amazon and its peoples.*

**An Phoblacht (Republican News)** 58 Parnell Square, Dublin 1 *T* +353 1 873 3611 *F* +353 1 873 3839

**Anarchist Black Cross (ABC), Brighton** c/o 6 Tilbury Place, Brighton, E.Sussex, BN2 2GY katchoo22@chickmail.com *Prisoner support group, supporting people from our 'movements' who get sent down & other class struggle prisoners. Info/leaflets available.*

**Anarchist Black Cross Innsbruck** LOM, Postlagernd, 6204 Innsbruck, Austria, abcibk@hotmail.com *We support: anarchists, revolutionaries and others, who have been imprisoned because of their resistance against those in power and their system.*

**Anarchist Federation (AF)** c/o 84b Whitechapel High St, London, E1 7QX *T* 01523 786692 http://burn.ucsd.edu/~acf/ acf@burn.ucsd.edu *Unemployed/workers/environmentalist/anti-oppression struggles. Prisoner support. Publishes Organise! Magazine, Resistance newssheet & pamphlets. Previously called ACF.*

**Anarchist Graphics** Box 5, 167 Fawcett Rd, Southsea, Hants, PO4 0DH *Anti-copyright graphics for working class solidarity and social revolution. Loose association of anarchists creating graphics for the anarchist movement.*

**Anarchist Teapot Mobile Kitchen, The** Box B, 21 Little Preston St, Brighton, BN1 2HQ *T* pager: 01523 101729 katchoo22@chickmail.com or savage@easynet.co.uk *Mobile kitchen coooking quality but cheap vegan food for radical events. Non profit. Info/bookstalls also available. We're able to cook meals for up to 400 people.*

**Anarchist Trade Union Network (@TU)** Box EMAB, 88 Abbey St, Derby, DE22 3SQ grrp7763@aol.com *@TU acts as a network,* *information sharing, discussion forum and news exchange for anarchists in trade unions or interested in union or work place issues. Produces regular Bulletin.*

**Anarcho-Syndicalism 101** http://flag.blackened/huelga/ *Anarcho-syndicalism: workers solidarity; direct action; self-management. Articles, resources, contacts, links.*

**Angelltown Community Project Ltd (A.T.C.P Ltd)** Unit 4, Warwick House, Overton Rd, London, SW9 7JP *T* 020 7737 7977 *F* 020 7924 9022 *Charitable organisation - economic, social, environmental regeneration (estate-based).*

**ANIMAL** P.O.Box 467, London, E8 3QX *T* mobile: 07931 301901 *Attacking right wing people/ideas in the environmental movement and encouraging people to build a movement to liberate ourselves & the planet.*

**Animal Contacts Directory** Veggies, 180 Mansfield Rd, Nottingham, NG1 3HW www.veggies.org.uk/acd acd@veggies.org.uk *Networking for Humans, Animals and the Environment. Excellent comprehensive directory of animal rights contacts, listing thousands of campaigns across the world, £4.50/£3.50.*

**Animal Defenders** 261 Goldhawk Rd, London, W12 9PE *T* 0181 846 9777 *F* 0181 846 9712 http://www.cygnet.co.uk/navd navd@cygnet.co.uk *Campaigns for animals and the environment. Current main focus is circus animals.*

**Animal Liberation Front Press Office** BM4400, London, WC1N 3XX *T* 01954 230542/mobile: 0961 303680 *F* as phone *The ALF press office acts as news agency and spokesperson for radical animal liberationists.*

**Animal Rights Calendar** c/o Veggies, 180 Mansfield Rd, Nottingham, NG1 3HW *T* 0115 958 5666 *F* phone first www.veggies.org.uk/calendar arc@veggies.org.uk *Nationally co-ordinated & comprehensive listing of all the main animal rights protests in the UK. Updated monthly. Send sae + extra stamp to the address shown, or check web site.*

**Animal Rights Directory** www.vegggies.org.uk *Lists thousands of campaigns across the world.*

**Anti-Corruption Politics** P.O.Box 187, Chesterfield, Derbyshire, S40 2DU *T* 01246 555713 *F* as phone

**Anti-Fascist Action (AFA)** BM 1734, London, WC1N 3XX *T* 07000 569569/0976 406870 www.anl.org.uk anl@anl.org.uk *Fighting fascism physically and ideologically.*

**Anti-Genetix Network** www.lakota.clara.net

**Anti-Nazi League (ANL)** P.O.Box 2566, London, N4 1WJ *T* 020 7924 0333 *F* 020 7924 0313 anl@anti-nazileague.demon.co.uk *We oppose Nazi ideas and organisations. everyone is welcomed to join us in: promoting Black & White unity, Don't Vote Nazi campaigns, supporting victims of racist attacks.*

**Anti-Slavery International** Thomas Clarkson House, The Stableyard, Broomgrove Yard, London, SW9 9TL *T* 020 7501 8920 *F* 020 7738 4110 www.antislavery.org antislavery@antislavery.org *Anti-Slavery works to eliminate slavery around the world through campaigning, raising awareness, research and lobbying.*

**ARCNEWS** P.O.Box 339, Wolverhampton, WV10 7BZ *T* 01902 711935/0411 430446 *F* as phone (call first) www.arcnews.co.uk/ james@arcnews.co.uk *ARCNEWS is an independent monthly animal rights magazine available for a subscription of £7 per year.*

**Ark Environment Centre, The** 2-6 St Martins Walk, Leicester, LE1 5DG *T* 0116 262 0909 *F* 0116 233 9700 www.environ.org mike@ark99.freeserve.co.uk *Information centre and retail shop for Environ, Leicester's local environmental charity. Vegetarian restaurant upstairs.*

**Arkangel Magazine** BCM 9240, London, WC1N 3XX *Sustainable settlement project information/advice service. Our focus is on ecovillages as a way out of cash-based living. Superb links on web site.*

**Arts Factory** 11 Highfield Industrial Estate, Ferndale, Rhonda, South Wales, CF43 4SX *T* 01443 757954 *F* 01443 732521 www.artsfactory.co.uk elwynjames@artsfactory.co.uk *Working to build a stronger community through enterprise & providing facilities.*

**Asian Coalition for Housing Rights (ACHR)** 73 Soi Sonthiwattana 4, Ladprao Road Soi 100, Bangkok 10310, Thailand *T* (66-2) 538 0919 *F* (66-2) 285 1500 achrsec@email.ksc.net

**Association of Autonomous Astronauts (AAA)** 67 Millbrook Rd, Brixton, London, SW9 7JD *T* 0171 787 2394/mobile: 0793 083 4904 *F* 0171 477 2813 http://www.deepdisc.com/aaa andi@deepdisc.com

*AAA is an independent global collective supporting community space travel and three sided football.*

**Association of Cultural and Artistic Production (KAPA)** Metelkova mesto, Ljubljana, Slovenia *T* 00 386 61 134 4402 *F* 00 386 61 132 2385 www.ljudmila.org/kapa drustvo.kapa@guest.arnes.si *We run concert/performance hall-Gala Hall, we have an audio-recording studio, record label, and we support younger bands, providing them with rehersal space and equipment.*

**Association of Hedgewitches** www.antipope.demon.co.uk/paganlink/uk_info/organis *A contact and social network for witches who work independently (solo or as couples), whether or not they also work in groups.*

**Aston Reinvestment Trust (ART)** c/o Steve Walker or Martin Allcott, Freepost MID 16184, The Rectory, 3 Tower St, Birmingham, B19 3BR *T* 0121 359 2444 http://www.arq.co.uk/art reinvest@gn.apc.org *Local Social Investment Society providing loans to small businesses and voluntary organisations.*

**Asylum Aid** 28 Commercial St, London, E1 6LS *T* 020 7377 5123 *F* 020 7247 7789 www.asylumaid.org.uk info@asylumaid.org.uk *Providing advice and legal representation to asylum-seekers and refugees and campaigning for their fair treatment in the UK.*

**Asylum Rights Campaign** *T* 020 7820 3046 imran.hussain@refugeecouncil.org.uk

**Aufheben** P.O.Box 2536, Rottingdean, Brighton, BN2 6LX http://lists.village.virginia.edu/~spoons/aut_html *Not an organisation, but a magazine dedicated to the theory and practice of revolutionary class struggle.*

**Australian Earth First! Action Update** P.O.Box 12046, Elizabeth St, Brisbane 4002, Australia, www.green.net.au/ozef_update ef_au@hotmail.com *Australian contact point for Earth First!*

**Autonomedia** P.O. Box 568, Williamsburg Station, Brooklyn, New York 11211-0568, USA *T* 718 963 2603 *F* as phone www.autonomedia.org info@autonomedia.org *Autonomedia is a radical media collective.*

**Autonomous Centre of Edinburgh** 17 West Montgomery Place, Edinburgh, EH7 5HA *T* 0131 557 6242/Pager 01426 128984 www.autonomous.org.uk lothian@burn.ucsd.edu *ACE draws together many campaigns for social and ecological justice into a revolutionary struggle to overthrow capitalist social relations ending exploitation.*

**Autonomous Green Action** P.O. Box 4721, Station E, Ottawa, Ontario, Canada, K1S 5H9 soy@igs.net

**Avalon** 73 Fawcett Rd, Southsea, Hants, PO4 0DB *T* 02392 293673 *F* 02392 780444 info@avalonheadshop.co.uk *Portsmouth's only head shop. Stock Undercurrents; distribute SchNEWS as well as information on local, national and international campaigns.*

**Baby Milk Action** 23 St. Andrew's St, Cambridge, CB2 3AX *T* 01223 464420 *F* 01223 464417 www.babymilkaction.org info@babymilkaction.org *Baby Milk Action aims to save infant lives and to end the avoidable suffering caused by inappropriate infant feeding.*

**Backspace** Unit G2, Winchester Wharf, Clink St, London, SE1 9DG http://bak.spc.org/

**Banana Link** 38-40 Exchange St, Norwich, NR2 1AX *T* 01603 765670 *F* 01603 761645 www.laslett.com/bananas blink@gn.apc.org *Banana link campaigns and lobbies for sustainable banana trade and production in collaboration with partners in banana exporting countries.*

**Banner Theatre** Friends Institute, 220 Moseley Rd, Highgate, Birmingham, B12 0DG *T* 0121 440 0460 *F* 0121 440 0459 www.banner theatre.co.uk voices@btinternet.com *Banner Theatre works to promote political change in support of disenfranchised sections of society, through the use of documentary, multi-media cultural productions rooted in radical experiences.*

**Barricade Library Publishing Collective, The** c/o the Barricade Infoshop, 115 Sydney Rd, Brunswick, Melbourne, Australia, infoshop@bedlam.anarki.net *Publish materials on anarchism, direct action, feminism, alternative culture. The Infoshop houses an extensive library and we seek materials for the library and shop.*

**Bay Area Action's Headwaters Forest Project** http://www.headwatersforest.org *www.headwatersforest.org is the main source for news and action alerts from the coalition struggling to protect all 60 000 acres of the endangered ancient redwood ecosystem called Headwaters Forest.*

**Becontree Organic Growers' Association (BOG)** Three Trees, 44 Gale St, Dagenham, Essex, RM9 4NH *T* 0181 592 8941 aandc.poole@cwcom.net *BOG is a 3 acre community garden renowned educational project, developing organic, permaculture methods, regional garden for Plants For A Future.*

**Between the Lines** Box 32, 136 Kingswood High St, London, E8 2WS *T* 07867 652394 *Rebuilding the 17th International for the 19th time. The Loony Left Collective is a secret society closed to those on the outside.*

**Bicycle Recycle Workshop** 107 St Pancras Rd, Kings Cross, London,

**Big Brother Survival Kit** P.O. Box 3157, Brighton, BN2 2SS bbsurvivalkit@yahoo.com

**Big Issue, The** 236-240 Pentonville Rd, London, N1 9JY *T* 0171 526 3200 news@bigissue.com *Current affairs mag sold by homeless people.*

**Bilderberg** www.bilderberg.org/ *The High Priests of Globalisation.*

**Bindman & Partners** 275 Grays Inn Rd, London, WC1X 8QF *T* 020 7833 4433/pager: 01459 136205 *F* 020 7837 9792 *Civil liberties solicitors specializing in defence of eco-protestors, animal rights activists & those arrested for direct action or participation in mass demonstrations etc.*

**Biotech Hobbyist Magazine** www.irational.org/biotech/ *THE place on the Web for biotech thinkers, builders, experimenters, students, and others who love the intellectual challenge and stimulation of hobby biotech!*

**Birmingham Racial Attacks Monitoring Unit (BRAMU)** 339 Dudley Rd, Winson Green, Birmingham, B18 4HB *T* 0121 454 9500 *F* 0121 454 5884 *We are an independent, voluntary organisation, offering free, confidential help, support and advice to anyone suffering racial harassment in Birmingham.*

**Bite Back** Box 47, 82 Colston Rd, Bristol, BS1 5BB info@biteback.u-net.com *Free bi-monthly magazine covering all animal rights issues.*

**Black Environment Network (BEN)** UK Office, 9 Llainwon Uchaf, Llanberis, Wales, LL55 4LL *T* 01286 870715 *F* as phone *Black Environment Network is established to promote equal opportunities, with respect to ethnic communities, in the preservation, protection and development of the environment.*

**Black Flag** BM Hurricane, London, WC1N 3XX http://flag.blackened.net/blakflag blakflageds@hushmail.com *Class struggle anarchist quarterly magazine with strong international coverage, recently revamped. Contact us for subs info. Comprehensive list of UK Anarchist groups.*

**Black Mesa Indigenous Support (BMIS)** P.O. Box 23501, Flagstaff, Arizona 86002, dis-United States of Amerika *T* (USA) 520 773 8086 (voice mail) *F* contact us first www.netmanor.com/unity/unity.html unity@netmanor.com or granmonta@hotmail.com *BMIS is a collective of individuals acting to support the sovereignty of Dine people, who face forced relocation, environmental devastation and cultural extinction.*

**Black Shorts** 125 High Cross Rd, Tottenham Hale, London, N17 6UZ *T* 0181 885 4697 *F* 0961 851054 www.blackshorts.co.uk blackshorts@cerbernet.co.uk *Internet TV and club; concert visuals.*

**Black Women For Wages For Housework** P.O.Box 287, London, NW6 5QU *T* 020 7482 2496 *F* 020 7209 4761 crossroadswomenscentre@compuserve.com *Independent grassroots network fo Black women & other women of colour, which makes visible the unwaged work women do for every community.*

**Blackcurrent Bookshop** 4 Allen Rd, Abington, Northampton, NN1 4NE *Specialises in radical and anti-authoritarian books and journals, with many small press and counter-cultural titles.*

**Blatant Incitement Project (BLINC)** Dept 29, 255 Wilmslow Rd, Manchester, M14 5LW *T* 0161 226 6814 www.eco-action.org/blinc doinit@nematode.freeserve.co.uk *The Blatant Incitement Project exists to empower people to organise themselves without hierarchy, for radical action towards social ecological change, by sharing skills, knowledge and inspiration.*

**Bloody Hell** www.WARisHELL.com/ *Bloody Hell provides a platform for veterans to speak for themselves. Page after page of searing testimony to the brutal, bloody, unmerciful, dehumanising, haunting, destructive grim void of war.*

**Blue** P.O. Box 6696, Dublin 3, blueplanet@ireland.com

**Bougainville Freedom Movement** P.O.Box 134, Erskineville,

Australia, NSW 2043 *T* 61 2 9558.2730 *F* as phone http://www.k2net.co.uk/ef/efhtmls/bvupdate.html v.john@uts.edu.au *Organising protests over the years to expose the death and suffering of the Bougainville people blockaded on their island without food and basic medicine since 1988. Publish a newletter, "Garamut".*

**Brambles** 82 Andover St, Pitsmoor, Sheffield, S3 9EH *T* 0114 279 7164 *Housing co-op, tree planting & saving and that. Direct action & parties & RTS & parties & gardening & garden parties & composting & carnival. Free meeting room, kids stuff, transport to places/parties*

**Brighton & Hove Green Party** 145 Islingword Rd, Brighton, BN2 2SH *T* 01273 600883 *F* as phone www3.mistral.co.uk/greenparty/ greenparty@brighton.co.uk *We hope to win seats at all levels of government to implement ecological and social policies for a sustainable society.*

**Brighton Against Benefit Cuts** Brighton & Hove Unemployed Workers' Centre, 4 Crestway Parade, Hollingdean, Brighton, BN1 7BL babc99@yahoo.co.uk *Resistance to welfare-to-work and other attacks on benefits. Occasional newsletter - 'Where's My Giro?' - free subscription (or via e-mail.*

**Brighton ART (Brighton Arts Resources Technlolgy) incorporating Innerfield, Headspace & Planet Yes** Unit 7d, New England House, New England St, Brighton, BN1 2EF *T* 01273 697579 www.brightonart.co.uk/ info@brightonart.co.uk *Festivals, parties, sound system, projections, geodesic domes, video & audio production, performers, DJs.*

**Brighton Peace & Environment Centre** 43 Gardner St, Brighton, BN1 1UN *T* 01273 692880/620125 *F* 01273 689444 www.oneworld.org/brighpeace/ bripeace@pavilion.co.uk *A fair trade shop, lending library and education unit promoting awareness of peace, justice & environment issues. We provide computer/internet facilities.*

**Brighton Urban Design & Development (BUDD)** c/o Harvest Forestry, 1 New England St, New England Houe, New England St, Brighton, BN1 *T* 01273 681166/389279 *F* 01273 600206 www.solarcity.co.uk/BUDD ktt@solutions-inc.co.uk *We exist to stimulate, encourage and initiate sutainable urban design & development through an inclusive participatory process. Contact us for more details.*

**Bristol Class War** P.O.Box 772, Bristol, BS99 1EG *Bristol group of the national federation. Class struggle anarchists, producing paper & other info/merchandise.*

**British Anti-Vivisection Association (BAVA)** P.O.Box 82, Kingswood, Bristol, BS15 1YF *F* 0117 909 5048 www.eurosolve.com/charity/bava bava@esmail.net *To oppose vivisection entirely and without compromise, on scientific, medical, environmental, economic, moral and ethical grounds.*

**British Trust for Conservation Volunteers** *T* 01491 821600 *F* 01491 839646

**British Union For The Abolition of Vivisection (BUAV)** 16a Crane Grove, London, N7 8NN *T* 020 7700 4888 *F* 020 7700 0252 www.HelpTheDogs.org info@buav.org *Opposes animal experiments. We believe animals are entitled to respect and compassion which animal experiments deny them.*

**Broughton Spurtle** c/o Broughton Books, 2A Broughton Place, Edinburgh, EH *T* 0131 556 0903 *F* 0131 557 6752 www.tpuntis.demon.co.uk *Publish monthly free paper for local area - publicise work of local action groups and generally stir things up a bit.*

**Buckminster Fuller Institute** 11 N. Main Street, Sebastopol, CA 95472, 707 824 2242 *T* 707 824 2242 *F* 707 824 2243 www.bfi.org/index.html info@bfi.org *Devoted to advancing Humanity's Option For Success. We hope to empower site visitors to see the big picture & exercise individual inititiative.*

**Building Worker** c/o 4b Powis Terrace, London, W11 1JP

**Burghfield Women's Peace Camp** c/o 39 Westwood Rd, Southampton, SO17 1DN *T* 01703 554434

**Burma Action Group** Bickerton House, 25-27 Bickerton Rd, London, N19 5JT www.freeburmacoalition.org

**Burma Campaign UK, The** Bickerton House, 25-27 Bickerton Rd, London, N19 5JT *T* 020 7281 7377 *F* 020 7272 3559 www.burmacampaign.org.uk bagp@gn.apc.org *Working for human rights and democracy in Burma. We provide analysis to the media and government, and we lobby and campaign to improve government and commercial policy on Burma.*

CAGE c/o P.O. Box 68, Oxford, OX3 7YS *T* 07931 401962 www.veggies.org.uk/cage prison@narchy.fsnet.co.uk *CAGE network opposes prison building and all forms of detention, bringing direct action to the prisoner support and anti-prison movement.*

**CAHGE (Campaign Against Human Genetic Engineering)** www.users.globalnet.co.uk/~cahge/back1.htm *Addresses the ethical and social problems surrounding human genetic engineering. The impact of Gm foods shows that people can have a say in what science does.*

**Campaign Against Arms Trade (CAAT)** 11 Goodwin St, Finsbury Park, London, N4 3HQ *T* 020 7281 0297 *F* 020 7281 4369 www.gn.apc.org/caat campaigns@caat.demon.co.uk *A broad coalition of groups and individuals committed to an end to the international arms trade and the UK's role; and the conversion of military industry to civil production.*

**Campaign Against Censorship of the Internet** http://omnisite.liberty.org/uk/cacib/artview.ph3? *Self-explanatory.*

**Campaign Against Live Exports** c/o Animal Link, P.O.Box 1176, Kidderminster, DY10 1WQ *T* 01384 828685

**Campaign Against Racism & Fascism (CARF)** BM Box 8784, London, WC1N 3XX *T* 020 7837 1450 *F* 0870 052 5899 www.carf.demon.co.uk/ info@carf.demon.co.uk *Bi-monthly magazine, in-depth analysis of rise of racism/fascism, info on anti-racist campaigns across Europe, refugees, policing, miscarriages of justice and grassroots campaigns.*

**Campaign Against the Child Support Act (CACSA)** P.O.Box 287, London, NW6 5QU *T* 020 7482 2496 *F* 020 7209 4761

**Campaign Against Tube Privatisation (CATP)** 47c Wadeson St, Bethnal Green, London, E2 9DP *T* 020 7387 4771 (HQ)/020 8981 8065 (home) http://keepthetubepublic.listbot.com ohndleach@aol.com *Uniting workers and passengers against the Government's plan to privatise London Underground - for a publicly-owned, publicly-funded, publicly-accountable Tube.*

**Campaign for Free Education** P.O. Box 22615, London, N4 1WT *T* mobile: 0958 556756 *F* 020 7277 8462 www.members.xoom.com/nus_cfe cfe@gn.apc.org *Organising students in mass action, demos, occupations, non payment of fees, to win free education for all and reclaim NUS.*

**Campaign for Nuclear Disamament (C.N.D)** 162 Holloway Rd, London, N7 8DQ *T* 0207 700 2393 *F* 0207 700 2357 www.cnduk.org/cnd cnd@gn.apc.org *C.N.D involves supporters in direct actions, lobbying, press work and local street campaigning to help rid the world of nuclear weapons.*

**Campaign For The Abolition Of Angling (CAA)** BM Fish, London, WC1N 3XX *T* 0870 458 4176 www.anti-angling.com caa@pisces.demon.co.uk *An anti-angling grassroots organisation who campaign to end all fish abuse for entertainment through information, education and direct action.*

**Campaign for the Accountability of American Bases (CAAB)** 8 Park Row, Otley, West Yorkshire, LS21 1HQ *T* 01943 466405/01482 702033 *F* as phone www.gn.apc.org.cndyorks/caab/ caab.lindis_anni@virgin.net *Seeking accountability of American bases/U.S visiting forces through available systems and structures ...and taking non-violent direct action when they fail.*

**Campaign to Close Campsfield** c/o 111 Magdalen St, Oxford *T* 01865 558145/557282/726804 *F* 01865 558145 http://users.ox.ac.uk/~asylum *Demo at immigration centre near Oxford at noon last Saturday every month; other events, meetings; publish Campsfield Monitor. We work to stop immigration detention and close all detention centres.*

**Campaign to Free Vanunu & for a Nuclear Free Middle East** 185 New Kent Rd, London, SE1 4AG *T* 020 7378 9324 *F* as phone www.vanunu.freeserve.co.uk campaign@vanunu.freeserve.co.uk *Working for the release from prison of Mordechai Vanunu, the Israeli nuclear technician who blew the whistle on Israel's nuclear programme and was sentenced for 18 years imprisonment.*

**Campaign To Legalise Cannabis International Association (CLCIA)** 63 Peacock St, Norwich, Norfolk, NR3 1TB *T* 01603 624780 www.paston.co.uk/users/webbooks/index.html webbooks@paston.co.uk *Letters, information, rally; marches, Lobbies, petitions - furthering legalisation. Encouraging formation of local groups and contacts.*

**Canadian Coalition Against the Death Penalty** 80 Lillington Ave,

Toronto, Ontario M1N-3K7, Canada, http://members.tripod.com/ccadp/ ccadp@home.com *We are an inclusive organisation of persons working within the justice system opposed to capital punishment.*

**Cannabis in Avlon (CIA)** P.O.Box 2223, Glastonbury, BA6 9YU *T* 01458 833236/mobile: 0966 396444 http://www.nootopia.com/chic/chicinfo.html cannabisinfo@gn.apc.org *We aim to manifest the total liberation of cannabis to save the planet, heal the body & free the mind.*

**Car Busters Magazine and Resource Centre** Kratka 26, 100 00 Praha 10, Czech Republic *T* +420 2 781 08 49 *F* +420 2 781 67 27 www.antenna.nl/eyfa/cb carbusters@ecn.ez *A quarterly multilingual magazine and resource centre for the international car-free/anti-car movement. To facilitate exchange & co-operation, inspire, reach out, and change the world.*

**Carbon Storage Trust, The** *T* 01865 244151 *Undertaking to ensure carbon dioxide emitted by combustion is absorbed by planting new forests in the UK and elsewhere.*

**Cartoon Art Trust** 7 Brunswick Centre, Bernard St, London, EC1N 8JY *T* 0171 278 7172 *F* 0171 278 4234 skp@escape.u-net.com *Exhibitions of cartoons, comics & animation; children's classics & adult courses; talks, fairs, auctions, sales & awards.*

**Catalyst Collective** (SE) Flat 3, 1 Gladstone Terrace, Brighton BN2 3LB, (SW) Bromley House, Church St, Clastock, Cornwall PL18 9QE *T* 0870 733 4970 http://home.clara.net/greenline/catalyst.htm catalyst@greenline.clara.net *We don't like this corporate capitalist society, so we encourage alternatives: worker co-ops, housing co-ops, common ownership, co-operation, sharing deschooling, low impact lifestyles...*

**Centre for Alternative Technology (C.A.T) & Alternative Technology Association (A.T.A)** Machynlleth, Powys, SY20 9AZ *T* 01654 702400 *F* 01654 702782 www.cat.org.uk info@cat.org.uk *Environmental visitor and information centre.*

**Centre for Environmental Initiatives, The** The Old School House, Mill Lane, Carshalton, SM5 2JY www.a4u.com/cei cei@a4u.com

**Centre for Human Ecology** 12 Roseneath Place, Edinburgh, EH9 1JB *T* 0131 624 1972 *F* 0131 624 1973 www.clan.com/environment/che che@clan.com *Radical Edinburgh Educational Institution offers MSc Human Ecology. Action research includes issues of identity, belonging, place, participation, social and ecological justice.*

**Centre For World Indigenous Studies** PMB 214, 1001 Cooper Point Rd, SW Suite 140, Olympia WA 98502-1107, USA *T* 1 360 754 1990 www.cwis.org usaoffice@cwis.org *Dedicated to wider understanding and appreciation of the ideas and knowledge of indigenous peoples and the social, economic and political realities of indigenous nations.*

**Chapter Seven** The Potato Store, Flaxdrayton Farm, South Petherton, Somerset, TA14 *T* 01460 249204/01935 881975 *F* 01460 249204 www.oneworld.org/tlio chapter7@tlio.demon.co.uk *Campaigns for sustainable planning policies. Low impact planning consultancy. Produce Chapter Seven newsletter, 3 issue per year £5 (£3 concs.).*

**Chiapas Link** Box 79, Green Leaf, Bristol, BS1 5BB

**Children's Participation Project, The** The Children's Society, 92b High St, Midsomer Norton, Bath, BA3 2DE *T* 01761 411771 *F* 01761 411553 cpp@childsoc.org.uk *We work with new traveller families to help them access essential services & safe & secure sites. We have a Tiny Playbus we take on to sites in the South West.*

**Chinese Information and Advice Centre (CIAC)** 1st Floor, 53 New Oxford St, London, WC1A 1BL *T* 020 7692 3476 *F* 020 7692 2476 chineseinformation@yahoo.com *CIAC provides legal advice to disadvantageous Chinese people in nationality, immigration, matrimonial and employment issues, and organisational support to other Chinese organisations.*

**Choice in Education** P.O. Box 20284, London, NW1 3WY *T* 0208 300 7236 *F* 0207 813 5907 www.choiceineducation.co.uk info@choiceineducation.co.uk *The monthly independent publication for home educators, CinE is put together by a collective of home educating volunteers, and is funded purely from subscriptions, sales and advertisements.*

**Chumbawamba** P.O. Box TR666, Armley, Leeds, LS12 3XJ www.chumba.com chumba@chumba.demon.co.uk *A popular beat combo m'lud.*

**Citizen Smith** Old Community Centre, 161 College Rd, Kensal Green, London, NW10 3PH *T* 07931 980534

citizensmithuk@hotmail.com

**Climate Action Network UK (CANUK)** 31 Pitfield St, London, N1 6HB *T* 020 7251 9199 *F* 020 7251 9166 canuk@gn.apc.org *Works to advance public awareness and understanding through education and the provision of information on issues related to climate change.*

**Climate Action NOW!** P.O.Box 324, Redway, U.S.A, CA 95560 http://www.imaja.com/change/environment/can/can/ can@asis.com *Donations go a long way.*

**Club Resistance** Flat 2, 48 Church Rd, Liverpool, L15 9EQ *T* 0151 280 3048 www.resistance.org

**Clun Valley Alder Charcoal** Shropshire Hills Countryside Unit, 2 The School House, Acton Scott Church Stretton, Shropshire, SY6 6QN *T* 01694 781588 *F* 01694 781589 *Renewable sources of charcoal.*

**Coalition to Abolish the Fur Trade (CAFT UK)** P.O.Box 38, Manchester, M60 1NX *T* mobile: 07939 264864 *F* 0870 054 8728 www.arcnews.co.uk caft@caft.demon.co.uk *Grass-roots campaign co-ordinating local and national actions against fur trade. Investigations, demos, education and political work. We publish a magazine 'Anti-Fur News'.*

**Cobalt Magazine** c/o Greenleaf Bookshop, Box 12, 82 Colston St, Bristol, BS1 5BB *F* 08700 522475 http://www.cobaltmagazine.demon.co.uk mid23@cobaltmagazine.demon.co.uk *Free party zine.*

**Collective Against the North American Invasion of Colombia** c/o 36 Vauxhall St, London, SE11

**Common Ground** P.O.Box 25309, London, NW5 1ZA *T* 020 7267 2144 *F* as phone www.commonground.org.uk *Common Ground promotes the importance of our common cultural heritage, everyday nature and buildings, popular history and local places.*

**Commonweal Collection** c/o JB Priestley Library, University of Bradford, Richmond Rd, Bradford, BD7 1DP *T* 01274 233404 www.brad.ac.uk/library/services/commonweal/home.ht commonweal@bradford.ac.uk *A free and independent library specialising in providing literature and other resources around issues of nonviolent social revolution.*

**Communication Workers Union** 150 The Broadway, Wimbledon, London, SW19 1RX

**Communities Against Toxics (CATS)** P.O.Box 29, Ellesmere Port, South Wirral, L66 3TX *T* 0151 201 6780 *F* 0151 339 5473 cats@recycle-it.org.uk *Fighting incinerators - provide info on its chemicals and health dangers. Toxic. Municipal - clinical. Waste. Toxic landfill. SAE for basic info a must!*

**Communities Appeal for Respect for the Environment (CARE)** http://members.tripod.co.uk/care/ *CARE is a North Wales, grass roots, environment organisation based in Cefn Mawr. The main reason for our existence is because of the Monsanto-owned, Flexsys chemical plant.*

**Compassion in World Farming** *T* 01730 264208

**Compendium Bookshop** 234 Camden High St, London, NW1 8QS *T* 020 7485 8944 compbk@dircon.co.uk

**Connolly Association (CA)** 244 Grays Inn Rd, London, WC1X 8JR *T* 020 7833 3022/7916 6172/Mobile: 07775 974980 *F* 020 7916 6172 www.midnet.ie/connolly/ connolly@geo2.poptel.org.uk *An independent non-party, political organisation campaigning for Irish unity and independence.*

**Connolly Association, The** 244 Gray's Inn Rd, London, WC1X 8JR *T* 0171 833 3022/0171 916 6172 *F* 0171 916 6172 connolly@geo2.poptel.org.uk *Campaigning for a united and independent Ireland.*

**Conscience - The Peace Tax Campaign** 601 Holloway Rd, London, N19 4DJ *T* 0171 561 1061 *F* 0171 281 6508 conscience@cablenet.co.uk *Conscience campaigns for the right for people who are ethically opposed to war to have the military part of their taxes spent on peacebuilding.*

**Consumers for Health Choice** 9 Old Queen St, London, SW1H 9JA *T* 0117 925 2624

**Continental Drifts** Hilton Grove, Hatherly Mews, Walthamstow, London, E17 4GP *T* 0181 509 3353 *F* 0181 509 9531 www.continentaldrifts.uk.com christofu@continentaldrifts.uk.com *Works with loads of performance and music from the amazing underground. Festivals are our favourites. Work all over Europe. Not for profit company. Have the best bands there are.*

**Cool Temperate** 5 Colville Villas, Nottingham, NG1 4HN *T* 0115 947 4977 *F* as phone philip.corbett@btinternet.com *Nursery for practical plants (fruit, hedging, nitrogen-fixers, etc) and site-analysis/assessment/design/advice services. All profits are used for researching new methods of sustainable production.*

**Corner House, The** P.O.Box 3137, Station Rd, Sturminster Newton Dorset, DT10 1YJ *T* 01258 473795 *F* 01258 473748 www.icaap.org/Cornerhouse/ cornerhouse@gn.apc.org *Research, advocacy and solidarity work on social & environmental justice issues. Publish regular briefing papers. Free via email.*

**Cornerstone Housing Co-op** 16 Sholebroke Avenue, Leeds, LS7 3HB *T* 0113 262 9365 *F* as phone (call first) www.cornerstone.ukf.net cornerstone@gn.apc.org *Communal housing for people engaged in working for social change. We have a resource centre open to local groups and individuals.*

**Corporate Watch** 16b Cherwell St, Oxford, OX4 1BG *T* 01865 791391 *F* as phone www.corporatewatch.org mail@corporatewatch.org *Corporate Watch is a research and publishing group examining the links between today's social and ecological crisis and the concentration of corporate power.*

**Council for the Protection of Rural England (CPRE)** Warwick House, 25 Buckingham Palace Rd, London, SW1W 0PP *T* 020 7976 6433 *F* 020 7976 6373 www.greenchannel.com/cpre/ cpre@gn.apc.org *CPRE helps people protect & enhance their local countryside keeping it beautiful, productive and enjoyable for everyone.*

**Counter Information Agency (CIA)** Post: Postbus 94115, 1090 GC Amsterdam,, Visiting: The Arkademie, Overtoom 301, Amsterdam, The Netherlands *T* +31 20 665 7743 *F* +31 20 692 8757 www.squat.net/cia cia@arkademie.squat.net *Amsterdam's only squatted inforoom. Books, mags, info archives, films/videos, events, actions, web access, collaborations with activists from Amsterdam and everywhere.*

**counterFEET** P.O. Box 68, Headington, Oxford, OX3 7YS *T* pager: 07654 565992 www.counterfeet.org.uk/ office@counterfeet.org.uk *Broad network of revolutionary artists, culture-jammers and creative campaigners deconstructing media propaganda for postive social change.*

**CREATE (Community Recycling, Environmental Action, Training & Education)** Create Centre, Smeaton Rd, Bristol, BS1 6XN *T* 0117 925 0505 *F* 0117 922 4444 http://www.bristol-city.gov.uk create@bristol-city.gov.uk *CREATE's mission: a showcase of environmental excellence * a centre of influential environmental activity * a base for environmental groups * free entry to recycling exhibition & ecology.*

**Criminal Cases Review Commision (CCRC)** Alpha Tower, Suffolk St, Queensway, Birmingham, B1 1TT *T* 0121 633 1800 *F* 0121 633 1804/1823 www.ccrc.gov.uk info@ccrc.gov.uk *An independent body which investigates suspected miscarriages of justice.*

**Crossroads Women's Centre** 230A Kentish Town Rd, London, NW5 2AB *T* 020 7482 2496 *F* 020 7209 4761 http://ourworld.compuserve.com/homepages/crossroad crossroadswomenscentre@compuserve.com *Lively, welcoming, anti-sexist, anti-racist centre and home to a number of grassroots organisations which highlight the needs and concerns of women who are often overlooked. Volunteers always needed.*

**Crystal Palace Campaign** 95 Belvedere Rd, London, SE19 2HY *T* 020 8656 5524 *F* 020 8670 4395 www.crystal.dircon.co.uk/ crystal@crystal.dircon.co.uk *Crystal Palace Campaign: a voluntary group of local people opposed to a plan to build a huge leisure complex on the historic site of the old Crystal Palace in south London.*

**Cybernetic Culture Research Unit** www.ccru.demon.co.uk

**Cymdeithas Yr laith Gymraeg - The Welsh Language Society** Pen Roc, Rhodfa'r Mor, Aberystwyth, Ceredigion, Wales, SY23 2AZ *T* 01970 624501 *F* 01970 627122 www.cymdeithas.com/ swyddfa@cymdeithas.com *Cymdeithas yr Iaith Gymraeg is a political pressure group campaigning for the future of the Welsh language and Welsh communities.*

**Cymru Goch - Welsh Socialists** P.O. Box 661, Wrecsam, LL1 1EH *T* 01222 830029 www.fanergoch.org *For a free socialist Wales, green, libertarian & decentralised.*

**D.S.4.A** c/o Box 8, 82 Colston St, Bristol, BS1 5BB *Mail order/promoters/fundraising inna class struggle anarchist stylee!*

**DAAA Collective (Direct Action Against Apathy)** c/o Green Action, QUBSU, University Rd, Belfast, BT7 1NF *T* 028 9020 9574

ww.geocities.com/RainForest/Vines/5944 daaa@hotmail.com
*Produce Direct Action Against Apathy magazine (£1.50 + IRC from above address). Contact them for info about other activities in N. reland.*

**Dance Drug Alliance** *T* 020 8889 1361 *Ravers can lodge complaints on a website, expose badly ventilated and overcrowded clubs and stop intrusive searches by bouncers.*

**DARK NIGHT field notes** Dark Night Press, P.O. Box 3629, Chicago, IL 60690-3629, USA *T* 207 839 5794 darknight@igc.apc.org *intended as a way for those deeply involved in the struggle for freedom to share their thoughts and experiences from the field - from the battle lines of that struggle.*

**Dartford Unemployed Group** c/o 34 Saxon Place, Dartford, DA4 JG *T* 01322 865114

**Decadent Action** http://www.underbelly.demon.co.uk/decadent/docs/ i *Find out why it's important to shop to bring down capitalism; also linked to Phone In Sick.*

**Defend Council Housing** c/o Haggerston T.A, 179 Haggerston Rd, London, E8 4JQ *T* 020 7254 2312 *F* as phone *To oppose transfer of council houses to private landlords & to campaign for more and better council housing.*

**DELTA** Box Z, 13 Biddulph St, Leicester, LE2 1BH *T* 0116 210 9652 *F* as phone www.oneworld.org/delta lynx@gn.apc.org *News & background on Ogoni, Shell & Nigeria; globalisation and resistance.*

**Demilitarization For Democracy (DFD)** 2001 S St. NW, Suite 630, Washington, DC, U.S.A, DC 20009 *T* (202) 319 7191 *F* (202) 319 7194 http://www.dfd.net dfd@igc.apc.org *DFD is a leader in the in the movement to promote thegrowth of democratic socieities throughout the world. DFD focusses on the Arms Tarde Code of Conduct, Campaign to Ban Landmines, etc.*

**Des Murphy/Murphys Solicitors** George House, 82 Queens Rd, Brighton, BN1 3XE *T* 01273 733755/mobile: 0973 833693/01459 01982 *F* 01273 733 715 des@witsend00.freeserve.co.uk

**Devonport Claimants' Union (DCU)** c/o 69 Granby St, Devonport, Plymouth *T* 01752 213112 *Campaigning for a just benefits system. Mutual support and advice for claimants. Strike and other direct action support where appropriate.*

**Diggers & Dreamers Publications** BCM Edge, London, WC1N XX *T* 07000 780536 http://ourworld.compuserve.com/homepages/ edgeoftim edgeoftime@compuserve.com *We publish Diggers & Dreamers - a guide to communal living - every two years. UK & overseas communes; articles.*

**Digital Resistance** www.freespeech.org/resistance/ resistance@gmx.net *An archive of some websites that got hacked by activists since 1996, the pages aren't censored in any way and 100% in their original state.*

**Direct Action** P.O.Box 1095, Sheffield, S.Yorks, S2 4YR *T* 0161 232 7889 da@directa.force9.co.uk *Quarterly magazine of the Solidarity Federation - solidarity and direct action in workplaces and communities fighting racism to boycotting Body Shop.*

**Direct Action Media Network (DAMN!)** 444 Melrose St, Morgantown, West Virginia, USA, 26205 *T* (U.S) 304 291 1507 http:/ damn.tao.ca damn@tao.ca *DAMN is a multi-media news service that gathers and distributes news reports about progressive marches, strikes, protests and other in-the-street actions.*

**Direct Action Media Network (DAMN) Video** *Direct action footage on the web.*

**Disabled Action Network** 3 Crawley Rd, Wood Green, London, N22 6AN *T* 0181 889 1361

**Diversitea** 2 Hollow Lane, Shotesham, Norwich, NR15 1YE *T* 01508 550060 *An interactive information tent, raising awareness about: Travellers' issues; Direct action; Planning law; Alternative education; the Terrorism Bill.*

**Do or Die** c/o Prior House, 6 Tilbury Place, Brighton, East Sussex, BN2 2GY www.eco-action.org/dod/ doordtp@yahoo.co.uk *Do or Die is an annual journal dedicated to ecological direct action. Send £5 UK/£6 elsewhere (cheques/P.O.s to 'Dp or Die').*

**Dover Residents Against Racism (DRAR)** c/o Refugee Link, P.O.Box 417, Folkestone, Kent, CT19 4GT *T* 01304 206140 www.canterbury.u-net.com/Dover.html dst@canterbury.u-net.com *DRAR was formed in 1998 to fight racist hostility (from the press, National Front and others) towards asylum-seekers in Dover.*

**Dragon Environmental Network** 23b Pepys Rd, New Cross, London, SE14 5SA www.gn.apc.org/dragon adrian@gn.apc.org

*Exploring and encouraging eco-magic - ritual and spellwork for the Earth. Soon launching The Dragon Journal.*

**Dyfi Eco-Valley Partnership, The** *T* Andy Rowland 01654 705018 *F* 01654 703000 *Promoting the development of small-scale renewable energy and efficiency projects.*

**Earth Centre** Denaby Main, Doncaster, DN12 4EA *T* 01709 512000 www.earthcentre.org.uk

**Earth Circus Network** Create Centre, Smeaton Rd, Bristol, BS1 6XN *T* 0117 907 4074/925 0505 (ask to be put through) *F* 0117 929 7283

**Earth First!** www.k2net.co.uk/ef *Web address's contacts list.*

**Earth First! Action Update (EF! AU)** P.O. Box 1TA, Newcastle-Upon-Tyne, NE99 1TA www.eco-action.org/efau actionupdate@gn.apc.org *The newsletter of Earth First! UK, the network of non-hierarchical environmental direct activists. Edited by a different EF! Group each year.*

**Earth First! Journal** P.O.Box 1415, Eugene, Oregon, U.S.A, OR 97440 *T* 541 344 8004 *F* 541 344 7688 www.enviroweb.org/ef earthfirst@igc.org *The absolutely fabulous Earth First! Journal presents radical voices from the international no compromise environmental movement.*

**Earth Liberation Prisoners** Cornerstone Resource Centre, 16 Sholebroke Avenue, Leeds, LS7 3HB *T* 0113 262 9365 *F* as phone (call first) www.geocities.com/earthlibprisoner earthlibprisoner@hotmail.com *We exist to support those imprisoned for defending animals and the earth and those fighting back against that which oppresses them. We provide a regularly updated webpage of prisoners/addresses.*

**Earthrights Solicitors** Little Orchard, School Lane, Molehill Green, Takeley, Essex, CM22 6PS *T* 07071 225011 *F* as phone www.gn.apc.org/earthrights earthrights@gn.apc.org *Provides legal advice and assistance to environmental campaigners.*

**EarthWise Environmental Consultants Ltd** 12 Bellevue Rd, Southampton, SO15 2AY *T* 0870 7331166 *F* 0870 733 1177 enquiry@earthwise.demon.co.uk *A small workers co-op, providing services and undertaking projects to promote sustainability.*

**East London Association of Autonomous Astronauts (ELAAA)** Box 15, 138 Kingsland High St, London, E8 2NS www.unpopular.demon.co.uk elaaa@unpopular.demon.co.uk *The next thirty seven years will present us with space exploration as both a danger and an opportunity.*

**Eat The State!** P.O Box 85541, Seattle, WA 98145, USA *T* (206) 215 1156 http://EatTheState.org/ ets@scn.org *A shamelessly biased political journal. We want an end to poverty, exploitation, imperialism, militarism, racism, sexism, heterosexism, environmental destruction, television, and large ugly buildings.*

**Ecodefence!** Moskovsky Prospekt, 120-34236006, Kaliningrad/ Koenigsburg, Russia, ecodefence@glas.apc.org

**Ecological Design Association** The British School, Slad Rd, Stroud, Glos, GL5 1QW

**Ecologist, The** Unit 18 Chelsea Wharf, 15 Lots Rd, London, SW10 0QJ *T* 020 7351 3578 *F* 020 7351 3617 www.gn.apc.org/ecologist/ ecologist@gn.apc.org *Monthly international magazine, relaunched April 2000, dedicated to rethinking the current 'development' model and proposing less destructive alternatives.*

**Ecology Building Society** 18 Station Rd, Cross Hills, Keighley, BD20 7EH *T* 01535 635933 *F* 01535 636166 www.ecology.co.uk info@ecology.co.uk *A building society that specialises in mortgages to rescue derelict homes, build energy efficient homes and for housing co-operatives.*

**Ecoseeds/Eco Co-op** 1 Bar View Cottage, Shore Rd, Strangford, BT30 7NN *T* 01396 881227 ecoseeds@dnet.co.uk

**Ecotrip** P.O.Box 22019, London, SW2 2WF *T* 07967 843770 www.ecotrip.co.uk mail@ecotrip.co.uk *DIY cultural and environmental caravan - infoshop, stage, cafe, workshops.*

**Ecovillage Network UK (EVNUK)** Create Centre, Smeaton Rd, Bristol, BS1 6XN *T* 0117 925 0505 (temp) www.ecovillages.org/uk/ network/index.html evnuk@gaia.org *Sustainable settlement project information/advice service. Our focus is on ecovillages as a way out of cash-based living.*

**Ecstacy** http://www.ecstacy.org *Web site of the late Nicholas Saunders, author of the book 'E Is For Ecstacy'.*

**Edinburgh Claimants** c/o Autonomous Centre of Edinburgh, 17 W.

Montgomery Place, Edinburgh, EH7 5HA *T* 0131 557 6242 http://burn.ucsd.edu/~lothian ec@punk.org.uk *We encourage claimants to stick together to overcome benefits hassles, we resist benefit cuts and compulsory workfare schemes e.g New Deal.*

**Education For Sustainable Communities (EFSC)** c/o 3, 35 Carnarlon St, Glasgow, G3 6HP *T* 0141 332 8064 *To educate and inform the public about the nature of democratic schools. For source material contact www.s-hill.demon.co.uk or djjvbbe@prodigy.com/tamariki@clear.net.nz*

**Education Otherwise** P.O. Box 7420, London, N9 9SG *T* 0891 518303

**Education Workers Network** P.O. Box 29, Manchester, M15 5HW

**Ejercito Zapatista de Liberacion Nacional** www.ezln.org/ *The EZLN Page was put together in the Spring of 1994 in order to provide reliable information on the Zapatista uprising and serve as the mouthpiece for the Zapatistas in cyberspace.*

**ELECTRIC GALLERY, THE: The Amazon Project** www.egallery.com/amazon.html rbeckham@egallery.com *The Usko-Ayar is more than an art school. It is an institution devoted to the rescue and preservation of the knowledge and the traditions of the indigenous people of the Peruvian Amazon.*

**Electronic Frontier Foundation, The** 1550 Bryant St, Suite 725, San Francisco, USA, CA 94103 *T* +1 415 436 9333 *F* +1 415 436 9993 www.eff.org ask@eff.org *EFF is a nonprofit organization dedicated to protecting and promoting the civil liberties of the users of online technology. EFF's work includes educating policymakers, law enforcement and citizens.*

**Empty Homes Agency (EHA)** 195-197 Victoria St, London, SW1E 5NE *T* 020 7828 6288 *F* 020 7828 7006 www.emptyhomes.com eha@globalnet.co.uk *Community Action on Empty Houses (CAEH) is a project of the EHA - a grassroots approach to highlighting the waste of resources that occurs when flats, houses & buildings are left empty and unused.*

**Enabler Publications** 3 Russell House, Lym Close, Lyme Regis, Dorset, DT7 3DE *T* 01297 445024 *F* as phone http://members.aol.com/adearling/enabler/ adearling@aol.com *Books about counter culture, new Travellers, protest and creative work with young people. Includes: No Boundaries; Alternative Australia and A Time To Travel.*

**Energy Saving Trust** 21 Dartmouth St, London, SW1H 9BP *T* 020 7222 0101 www.est.org.uk

**English Collective of Prostitutes** Crossroads Women's Centre, P.O.Box 287, London, NW6 5QU *T* 020 7482 2496 *F* 020 7209 4761 *The English Collective of Prostitutes is a network of women, Black and white, of different nationalities and backgrounds working at various levels of the sex industry.*

**Enough anti-consumerism campaign** c/o OWRIC, 6 Mount St, Manchester, M2 5NS *T* 0161 226 6668 *F* 0161 226 6277 www.enviroweb.org/enviroissues/enough/ *Organisers of No Shop Day in Britain.*

**Envirolink** www.envirolink.org *Links to Sustainable Business Network, Animal Rights Resource Site where to buy environmental books. Essential & extensive web directory.*

**Environmental Law Foundation** Suite 309, 16 Baldwins Gardens, London, EC1N 7RJ *T* 0171 404 1030 *F* 0171 404 1032 www.greenchannel.com/elf info@elf-net.org *ELF puts community groups and individuals in touch with specialists in environmental law to resolve environmental problems.*

**Environmental Team, The** http://wkweb5.cablenet.co.uk/eteam
**Environmental Transport Association Services Ltd (ETA)** 10 Church St, Weybridge, KT13 8RS *T* 01932 828882 *F* 01932 829015 www.eta.co.uk eta@eta.co.uk *The ETA is Britain's only ethical alternative to the AA or RAC. All profits gt into campaigning for a sustainable transport system.*

**Environmental Transport Network** 10 Church St, Weybridge, KT13 8RS *T* 01932 828882 *F* 01932 829015 www.eta.co.uk joining@eta.co.uk

**Equi-Phallic Alliance and Poetry Field Club, The** 33 Hartington Rd, Southampton, SO14 0EW www.digital-magic.co.uk/equiphallicalliance/ epa@digital-magic.co.uk *Campaigning for the end of landscape, we 'raise' awareness of the falseness of 'place', deploying ideology within poetic field trips.*

**Ethical Consumer Research Association (ECRA)** Unit 21, 41 Old Birley St, Manchester, M15 5RF *T* 0161 226 2929 *F* 0161 226 6277

www.ethicalconsumer.org/ ethicon@mcrl.poptel.org.uk *ECRA produce a bi-monthly magazine - Ethical Consumer - comparing consumer products according to corporate responsibility issues.*

**Ethical Junction** Fourways House, 3rd Floor, 16 Tariff St, Manchester, M1 2FN *T* 0161 236 3637 *F* 0161 236 3005 www.ethical-junction.org info@ethical-junction.org

**Eurodusnie** http://stad.dsl.nl/~robbel *Dutch anti-authoritarian organisation fighting against economic globalisation. Dutch and international links.*

**Euromarch Liason Committee (ELC) & Unemployed Action Group** The Old Mill, 30 Lime St, Newcastle upon Tyne, NE1 2PQ *T* 0191 222 0299 *F* 0191 233 0578 euromuk@aol.com *Co-ordinates activities of organisations, groups and individuals in the UK affiliated to the European Marches network.*

**Exeter Left** P.O.Box 185, Exeter, EX4 4EW www.exeterleft.freeserve.co.uk davep@exeterleft.freeserve.co.uk *Alliance of socialists, anarchists and greens. Contact point for Red South West (Exeter), Exeter Claimants, Exeter AFA. Our aim is to maximise collaboration and discussion in the movement.*

**Exodus** Long Meadow Community Farm, Sundon Rd, Chalton, Beds LU4 9TU *Luton based party and housing action group. Continue to build a strong collective after years of hassle with police, the press, local council.*

**Expanding Horizons - The Whizzbanger Guide to Zine Distributors** P.O.Box 5591, Portland, U.S.A, OR 97228 *Self-descriptions of 200+ distros from around the world. Three dollars US cash- postage paid worldwide.*

**Exploding Cinema, The** http://bak.spc.org/exponet/ *The EXPLODING CINEMA is a coalition of film/video makers committed to developing new modes of exhibition for underground media. Links to underground film/viewing.*

**Fair Trade Cafe** 2 Ashgrove, Bradford, BD7 1BN *T* 01274 727034 *Not-for-profit cafe that exists to raise awareness about fair trade & other related issues. A largely volunteer run community cafe that aims to provide cheap, healthy, ethical and delicious food.*

**Fairs & Festivals Federation** 27 Kells Neend, Berryhill, Coleford, Glos, GL16 7AD

**Fairtrade Foundation, The** Suite 204, 16 Baldwin's Gardens, London, EC1N 7RJ *T* 020 7405 5942 www.fairtrade.org.uk

**Fans United (Keep Football Alive)** P.O. Box 27227, London, N11 2WY *An open invitation for supporters of rival football teams to stand togther against the exploitation of the traditional game.*

**Farming and Livestock Concern** *T* 01559 384936

**Faslane Peace Camp** 81d Shandon, Helensburgh, Argyll and Bute, Scotland, G84 8NT *T* 01436 820901 *To observe and monitor the Royal navy's activities at HNRB at Faslane; to protest against the Trident nuclear programme.*

**Federation Anarchiste Francophone** 145 Rue Anelot, Paris 75011 *T* 33 0148 053408 *F* 33 0149 299859 http://federation-anarchiste.org/ federation-anarchiste@federation-anarchiste.org *The FA fights with all the exploited against governments, acknowledging the existence of the struggle of the social classes and with final aim an anarchist society.*

**Federation Collective Rampenplan** P.O. Box 780, 6130 At Sittard, The Netherlands *T* +31 (0)46 452 4803 *F* +31 (0)46 451 6460 www.antenna.nl/rampenplan ramp@antenna.nl *This is a collective and a federation of: * A mobile vegetarian/vegan ecological kitchen * A publisher of books on anarchy, environment and (abolition of) work * A video action newsgroup*

**Feminist Library** 5 Westminster Bridge Rd, Southwark, London, SE1 7XW *T* 020 7928 7789 *Promoting feminism and networking between women. Women-only discussion group at the library - alternate Tuesday evenings - 6.30 pm.*

**Festival Eye** BCM 2002, London, WC1N 3XX *T* 01568 760492 *F* phone www.prowse.demon.co.uk/festeye/fe_index.htm festivaleye@stones.com *Listings & reviews of fringe/mainstream/alternative festivals, camps, parties & protests.*

**Fight Poverty Pay Campaign** P.O.Box 14, Accrington, Lancs, BB5 1GG *T* 01254 679605 fightpov@freenetname.co.uk *Fighting against poverty pay.*

**Fight Racism! Fight Imperialism!** BCm Box 5909, London, WC1N 3XX *T* 020 7837 1688 *F* 020 7837 1743 www.rcgfrfi.easynet.co.uk/ rcgfrfi@easynet.co.uk *Newspaper of the Revolutionary Communist Group. Fights imperialism, its barbarism, its destruction of the planet*

Campaigns against poverty pay, the Labour government, supports socialist Cuba.

**Finland Earth First!** Viivinkatu 17 AS 17, 33610 Tampere 61, Finland, ransu@sci.fi

**Flannel** 32A Park Crescent, Brighton, BN1 3HB flannel@wirelock.demon.co.uk *Funkpunk pop with cheese on top. Benefits, balls, barmizvahs - just put petrol in the tank! And featuring guerilla gigs.*

**Food Not Bombs** Box 23, 56a, 56 Crampton St, London, SE17 *T* 020 8766 8813 *F* 020 8703 1111 http://www.webcom.com/~peace/ peactree/stuff/stuff/ fnb@safetycat.org *Free/cheap vegan food for benefits and demos.*

**Football** *There are hundreds of footie fanzines. For a full listing get a copy of When Saturday Comes, available from most newsagents.*

**Football Fans Against the CJA** 352 Southwyk House, Moorlands Estate, Brixton, London, SW9 8TT http://www.urban75.com/footie/ ffacja.html footie@urban75.com *Information and resources dealing with the impact of the Criminal Justice Act on football fans, plus related issues.*

**Forest Stewardship Council (FSC)** Unit D, Station Building, Llanidgoes, Powys, SY18 6EB *T* 01686 413916 *F* 01686 412176 www.fsc-uk.demon.co.uk/ fsc-uk@fsc-uk.demon.co.uk *The FSC is a market mechanism for improving forest management globally. The FSC logo gives the assurance that products originate from well-managed forests.*

**Fourth World Review** 24 Abercorn Place, London, England, NW8 9XP *T* 020 7286 4366 *F* 020 7286 2186 *Human affairs are out of control because of giantism. We promote small nations, small communities and the sovereignty of the human spirit.*

**Free Satpal Campaign (F.S.C)** A.R.C, 101 Villa Rd, Handsworth, Birmingham, B19 1NH *T* 0121 551 4032/pager: 04325 355717 *F* 0121 554 4553 g.s.bhattacharyya@lozells.swinternet.co.uk *We wage a political, anti-racist fight against the government. We have organised many protests and public demonstrations.*

**Free Tibet Campaign** 1 Rosomon Place, London, EC1R 0JY *T* 020 7833 9958 *F* 020 7833 3838 www.freetibet.org/ tibetsupport@gn.apc.org *Free Tibet Campaign engages in non-violent protest, public awareness rasing and political campaigns to end the Chinese occupation of Tibet.*

**Freedom Book Company** 73 Fawcett Rd, Southsea, Hants, PO4 0DB *T* 02392 780600 *F* 02392 780444 www.freedombooks.co.uk/ info@freedombooks.co.uk *Massive range of informative drugs related books and magazines (cultivation, legality, effects etc), Undercurrents videos, radical magazines and periodicals.*

**Freedom Bookshop** 84b Whitechapel High St, London, W1 *T* 0171247 9249 *London's best anarchist bookshop, a wide range of anarchist books & mags.*

**Freedom Network** http://www.freedomnet.demon.co.uk info@freedomnet.demon.co.uk *Internet based information service.*

**Freedom Press** Angel Alley, 84b Whitechapel High St, London, E1 7QX *T* 020 7247 9249 *F* 020 7247 9526 http://freedom.tao.ca/ ~freedom *Anarchist publishers and propagandists since 1886, through our periodicals, books and pamphlets, available from our bookshop or by mail order. Contact us for free sample copy of 'Freedom'.*

**Freedom To Be Yourself, The** 208 Foleshill Rd, Coventry, CV1 4JH www.geocities.com/thehumanmind/ thehumanmind@yahoo.co.uk *Protest naked for the right to be naked in public. The vicious circle must stop: the virtuous circle will begin.*

**Friends of AK Press, The** AK Press, P.O.Box 12766, Edinburgh, EH8 9YE *Pay a monthly minimum amount to support AK's continued existence and in return receive free books.*

**Friends of the Earth (FoE)** 26-28 Underwood St, London, N1 7JQ *T* 020 7490 1555 *F* 020 7490 0881 www.foe.co.uk/ info@foe.co.uk *Friends of the Earth works to improve the conditions for life on earth now and for the future.*

**Friends of the Earth (Scotland)** 72 Newhaven Rd, Edinburgh, EH6 5QG *T* 0131 554 9977 *F* 0131 554 8656 http://www.foe-scotland.org.uk/ foescotland@gn.apc.org *Campaigning for Environmental Justice. No less than a decent environment for all; no less than a fair share of the Earth's resources.*

**Friends of the Garvaghy Rd (London FGR)** BM Box 5519, London, WC1N 3XX *T* 020 8442 8778/mobile: 0956 919871 *F* as phone fgr@brosna.demon.co.uk *We support the Garvaghy Road*

Residents Coalition in the North of Ireland who are under sectarian attack by the Loyalist/Fascist Orange Order.

**Friends, Families & Travellers (FFT)** Community Base, 113 Queens Rd, Brighton, E.Sussex, BN1 3XG *T* 01273 234777/mobile: 07971 550 328 alex@f-f-t.demon.co.uk *Working towards a more equitable society where everyone has the right to travel & stop without constant fear of prosecution because of their lifestyle.*

**Frontline Books** 255 Wilmslow Rd, Manchester, M14 5LW *T* 0161 249 0202 *F* 0161 249 0203 http://www.poptel.org.uk/bookfinder frontline-books@mcr1.poptel.org.uk *Radical bookshop/noticeboards/box nos./etc.*

**Fruitarian/Raw Food Centre of London, The (100% Vegan)** 50 Connell Crescent, Ealing, London *T* 020 8446 2960/441 6252 *Workshops and meetings on the raw vegan lifestyle.*

**Future Fibres** The Ecology Centre, Honeywood Walk, Carshalton, Surrey, SM5 3NX *T* 020 8773 2322 www.bioregional.com

**Future Foods** P.O. Box 1564, Wedmore, Somerset, BS28 4DP icherfas@seeds.cix.co.uk

**Gardens of Gaia, The** c/o Peter Bartlett, Buckhurst Farm, Cranbrook, Kent, TN17 3NS *A 22-acre sculpture park.*

**Gay Veggies & Vegans** GV, BM Box 5700, London, WC1N 3XX *T* 020 8690 4792 *Monthly drop-in in East London;cafe meal; newsletter/ magazine "The Green Queen". Membership is women & men, all ages.*

**Genethics News** P.O.Box 6313, London, N16 0DY *F* 020 7502 7516 genethicsnews@compuserve.com *Newsletter on ethical, social and environmental issues raised by genetic engineering.*

**Genetic Concern** Camden House, 7 Camden St, Dublin 2 *T* 003 531 4760 360

**Genetic Engineering Network (GEN)** P.O.Box 9656, London, N4 4JY *T* 0181 374 9516 *F* as phone (call first) genetics@gn.apc.org *GEN provides information for action against genetic engineering & acts as a first point of contact for those wanting to know of active groups within their area.*

**Genetic Food Alert (GFA)** 4 Bertram House, Ticklemore St, Totnes, Devon, TQ9 5EJ *T* 01803 868523 www.geneticfoodalert.org.uk coodinator@geneticfoodalert.org.uk *We campaign etc. against the introduction of genetic engineering in food. We represent the UK wholefood trade and have a massive membership.*

**Genetically Engineered Free Forests** *T* 020 7561 9146 GEFFcoalition@hotmail.com

**Genetix Snowball** *T* 0161 834 0295

**Get Informed** http://www.getinformed.co.uk *A website set up to question all areas of genetic science and encourage debate.*

**Glasgow Vegan Network** *T* 0141 330 4906/954 6519 *F* 0141 330 6004 http://www.rhizomatics.deom.co.uk/gvn/ m.hersh@elec.gla.ac.uk/rollocroz@aol.com *Promoting veganism and supporting vegans: both campaigning and social activities. We are friendly, informal and very welcoming.*

**Global Partnership** P.O. Box 1001, London, SE24 9NL *T* 020 7924 0974 *F* 020 7738 7512 www.globalpartnership.org/ mail@globalpartnership.freeserve.co.uk

**Gloupgloup** www.gloupgloup.com *A French site of pie flingers with pictures of top politicians and corporate bosses getting a faceful of pie.*

**GM-free Prisoner Support** Dept.29, 255 Wilmslow Rd, Manchester, M14 5LW *T* 0161 226 6814 *Support for prisoners who wish to try and obtain a GM-free diet while in custody. Help with information, prison liaison, media.*

**Gnostic Garden** P.O. Box 242, Newscastle Upon Tyne, NE99 1ED http://gnostocgarden.ndirect.co.uk *Mushroom stuff.*

**Godhaven Ink** Rooted Media, The Cardigan Centre, 145-149 Cardigan Rd, Leeds, LS6 1LJ *T* 0113 278 8617 http:// home.freeuk.net/rooted/godhaven.html merrick@stones.com *Publishers of cheap books and zines about direct action and other countercultural stuff. Promoting a feeling of well-being since 1994.*

**Going for Green** Elizabeth House, The Pier, Wigan, WN3 4EX *T* 01942 612621 *F* 01942 824778 www.gfg.iclnet.co.uk/ gfg@dircon.co.uk *To encourage people to cut waste, save energy and natural resources, travel sensibly, prevent pollution, look after the local environment.*

**Good Bulb Guide, The** c/o Abigail Entwistle, Fauna and Flora International, Great Eastern House, Tenison Rd, Cambridge, CB1 2TT *T* 01223 571000 info@ffint.org

**Grampian Against GM** P.O. Box 248, Aberdeen, AB25 1JE *T* 01224 451140 (answermachine) grampianearthfirst@hotmail.com *A coalition of environmental organisations, political parties and concerned residents. We aim to prevent the introduction of GMOs to the ecology of north-east Scotland.*

**Greater London Pensioners Convention** *T* 020 8764 1047 *Abandoned pens and petitions in favour of roadblocks and occupying buildings.*

**Greater Manchester Socialist Alliance (GMSA)** c/o 58 Langdale Rd, Victoria Park, Manchester, M14 5PN *T* 0161 224 4197 *Aims to create a democratic socialist society, through bringing people together in a united campaign for social justice and ecological sustainability.*

**Green Action** QUBSU, University Rd, Belfast, N.Ireland, BT7 daaa@hotmail.com *Produces topically wide-ranging publication.*

**Green Action Israel** P.O. Box 4611, Tel-Aviv, 61046 Israel *T* 972 (0) 3 516 2349

**Green Adventure** Brockwell Hall, Brockwell Park, London, SE24 9BN *T* 07957 365285 www.greenadventure.demon.co.uk *Brockwell Park GREENHOUSES Community Environmental Centre.*

**Green Anarchist (GA)** BCM 1715, London, WC1N 3XX *T* 0236 223646 http://website.lineone.net/~grandlaf/Sotiga.htm greenanarchist@hotmail.com *Acts as a forum for practical discussion amongst enemies of civilisation. Also carries wide range of anarcho-primitivist/direct action texts.*

**Green Books** Foxhole, Dartington, Totnes, Devon, TQ9 6EB *T* 01803 863260 *F* 01803 863843 www.greenbooks.co.uk greenbooks@gn.apc.org *Publishers and distributors of books on a wide range of environmental issues.*

**Green Events** Swanfleet Centre, 93 Fortess Rd, London, NW5 1AG *T* 020 7267 2552 *F* 020 7813 4889 www.greenevents.com pmccaig@orangenet.co.uk *A monthly newsletter highlighting environmental, human & animal rights issues in and around London.*

**Green Futures** *T* 020 8941 6277 *F* 0870 063 1315 info@gfutures.demon.co.uk *Organisers and consultants for Green Events. Using only renewable energy. Promote a wide range of green ideas, entertainment and campaigns.*

**Green Guide Publishing Ltd** 271 Upper St, Islington, London, N1 2UQ *T* 0171 354 2709 *F* 0171 226 1311 http://greenguide.co.uk info@greenguide.co.uk *We're the best available source of information on organic produce, fair trade goods & environmentally friendly products and services. Produce comprehensive regional guides.*

**Green Leaf Bookshop** 82 Colston St, Bristol, BS1 5BB *T* 0117 921 1369 *Radical bookshop. Mail order. Very fast customer order service - from U.S & U.K.*

**Green Party Drugs Group (GPDG)** 1a Waterlow Rd, London, N19 5NJ *T* 020 8678 9420 *F* as phone www.greenparty.org.uk/drugs greenpartydrugsgroup@gn.apc.org *To campaign and highlight the effects of the war on drug users. To change the law on drugs. To update Green Party drug policy. Making available ecstasy testing kits.*

**Green Pepper** Postbus 94115 (Visiting address: Overtoom 301, Amsterdam), 1090 GC Amsterdam, Netherlands *T* +31 20 665 7743 *F* +31 20 692 8757 www.eyfa.org/greenpepper/ greenpep@eyfa.org *32 page eco alternatives and direct action quarterly magazine produced by a collective active in the eyfa network and beyond.*

**Green Socialist Network** 30 Winterhill Rd, Rotherham, S61 2EN

**GreenNet** 74-77 White Lion Street, London, N1 9PF *T* 020 7713 1941 *F* 020 7837 5551 www.gn.apc.org support@gn.apc.org *GreenNet is part of the APC, the only global computer network specifically designed for environment, peace, human rights and development groups.*

**Grey Owl Centre** 50 Carisbrooke Rd, Hastings, TN38 0JT

**Greyhound Action** P.O. Box 127, Kidderminster, Worcs, DY10 3UZ *T* 01562 745778 greyhoundaction@i.am

**GroenFront! (EarthFirst! Netherlands)** P.O.Box 85069, 3508 AB Utrecht, Netherlands *T* 00 31 30287 0711 www.antenna.nl/nvda/groenfront groenfr@dds.nl *Anticapitalism direct action network, mostly actions against infrastructure (eg: squatting, mass trespassing). NO COMPROMISE!*

**Groovy Movie Picture House, The** www.groovymovie.org mail@groovimovie.org *Sun and wind-powered filmshows, equipment for hire.*

**Groundsell Claimants Action Group** c/o Oxford Unemployed Workers Centre, East Oxford Community Centre, Prince's St, Oxford, OX4 1HU *T* 01865 723750

**Groundswell** 5-15 Cromer St, London, WC1H 8LS *T* 020 7713 2880 *F* 020 7713 2848 www.oneworld.org/groundswell/ groundswell@home-all.org.uk *Groundswell promotes and supports a self-help network with people who are homeless, landless, or living in poverty. We are Cooking Up Change!!*

**Groundwork: Action For The Environment** 85-87 Cornwall St, Birmingham, B3 3BY *T* 0121 236 8565 *F* 0121 236 7356 *Groundwork is an enviornmental regeneration charity. Groundwork believes in using the environment as a tool to engage and motivate local people to improve their quality of life.*

**Guardian Media Guide, The** The Guardian, 119 Farringdon Rd, London, EC1R 3ER *The Media Guide is Britain's leading annual handbook [Hmmm]. It contains the phone numbers of many action groups.*

**Guerilla Press, The (Radical Presses Register)** Tim Telsa, BCM Beetlegeuse, London, WC1N 3XX *Printing literature deliberately intended to further the revolution. Standing for freedom for dissemination of propoganda. Running the Radical Presses Register.*

**Gypsy Council, The (GCECWCR)** 8 Hall Rd, Aveley, Romford, Essex, RM15 4HD *T* 01708 868986 *F* as phone the gypsycouncil@btinternet.com *Advocates, liason, contact point resource centre for Gypsies and people supporting/working with Gypsies.*

**Haggerston Tenants Association (HTA)** Haggerston Community Centre, 179 Haggerston Rd, London, E8 4JA *T* 020 7254 2312 *F* as phone hawk@hotmail.com *Help raise tenancy participation. Fights against privatisation. Defend council housing.*

**Haiti Support Group (HSG)** P.O. Box 29623, London, E9 7XU *T* 020 8525 0456 *F* as phone haitisupport@gn.apc.org *An association of individuals in the UK who support the Haitian people in their struggle for equitable development, justice, and participatory democracy.*

**Haringey Against Privatisation** c/o P.O. Box 8446, London, SE8 4WX *T* 020 7358 1854

**Haringey Solidarity Group (HSG)** P.O.Box 2474, London, N8 0HW *T* 020 8374 5027 *F* 020 8374 5027 http://home.clara.net/hsg/ hhome.html hsg@clara.net *Our aim is to promote solidarity, mutual aid and link working class struggles. We can't rely on politicians or leaders to do things for us - we have to organise and do it ourselves.*

**Haven Distribution** 27 Old Gloucester St, London, WC1N 3XX *Distributes free educational literature to prisoners in the UK. Donations make this possible.*

**Head Mix Collective** 45 Golf Drive, Hollingdean, Brighton, BN1 7HZ *T* 01273 231374/Mobile: 0421 757730 *A band which gigs throughout UK and Europe distributing positive vibes through music and information through merchandise desk.*

**Headspace** *see entry for Brighton ART*

**Health Action Network (H.A.N)/Vaccination Info.** P.O.Box 43, Hull, HU1 1AA *T* 01482 562079 www.vaccinfo.karoo.net yvonne@vaccinfo.karoo.co.uk *Distribute vaccination information, books, tapes. Publish 'Lifeforce' magazine.*

**Hemp Food Industries Association** P.O.Box 204, Barnet, Hertfordshire, EN5 1EP *T* 07000 HEMP 4 U (436748) *F* as phone www.hemp.co.uk/ & www.hempplastic.com hfia@hemp.co.uk *Lots to do with hemp food, ice creams, 9bar's, plastics, paper, fuel, growing, etc.*

**Henry Doubleday Research Association** Ryton Organic Gardens, Coventry, CV8 3LG *T* 02476 303517 *F* 02476 639229 www.hdra.org.uk enquiry@hdra.org.uk *Europe's largest organisation with over 26 000 members. Researching and promoting organic gardening, food, and farming.*

**Herb Society** Deddingtom Hill Farm, Warrington, Banbury, Oxon, OX17 1XB www.herbsociety.co.uk herbs@herbsociety.co.uk *Bringing together amateurs and professionals with interests in herbs. Dissemination of info on herbs.*

**Hiddinkulturz** 174 Deeside Gardens, Mannofield, Aberdeen, Scotland, AB15 7PX *The collection, sharing and dissemination of a wide cross-section of underground information (nationally & internationally). Publish "Hiddinkulturz Zine".*

**Hillsborough Justice Campaign** 134 Oakfield Rd, Anfield, Liverpool, L4 0UG *T* 0151 260 5262 *F* as phone info@hillsboroughjustice.org.uk *We are pro-active organisation, campaigning for the justice denied to all victims of the Hillsborough football disaster.*

**Holistic Education Foundation Co. Ltd., The** 145-163 London Rd, Liverpool, L3 8JA *T* 0151 207 9246 *F* 0151 298 1372 bordencourt@breathemail.net *Established to promote the balanced, organic growth of person-centred learning and holistic health.*
**Home Education Reading Opportunities (H.E.R.O Books)** 58 Portland Rd, Hove, East Sussex, BN3 5DL *T* 01273 775560 *F* 01273 389382 HERObooks@dial.pipex.com *We are trying to make it easier for home educators to obtain the books they want to read via mail order. For a catalogue send a large S.A.E to the address above. Contains list of local newsletters.*
**Home Power magazine** P.O. Box 520, Ashland, OR 97520, USA *T* 541 512 0201 *F* 541 512 0343 www.homepower.com/ hp@homepower.com *The hands-on journal of home-made power.*
**Homeless Information Project** 612 Old Kent Rd, London, SE15 1JB *T* 0171 277 7639 *F* 0171 732 7644 *Squatting and housing advice. Homelessness action pages for the group and individual. Motivation and up-to-date information.*
**Homeless International** Queens House, 16 Queens Rd, Coventry, CV1 3DF *T* 02476 632802 *F* 02476 632911 info@homeless-international.org
**Housmans Bookshop** 5 Caledonian Rd, King's Cross, London, N1 9DX *T* 020 7837 4473 *F* 020 7278 0444 bookshop@housmans.idps.co.uk *Longest surviving radical bookshop in UK. Publisher of Housmans Peace Diary. Sister company to Peace News magazine.*
**Housmans Diary Group** 5 Caledonian Rd, London, N1 9DX *T* 0171 837 4473 *F* 0171 278 0444 *Produces the Peace Diary, including an extensive contacts directory.*
**Housmans Peace Resource Project (HPRP)** 5 Caledonian Rd, Kings Cross, London, N1 *T* 020 7278 4474 *F* 020 7278 0444 worldpeace@gn.apc.org *Produces World Peace Database: 3500 organisations in 170 countries (includes major environmental & human rights groups) - abbreviated annual Directory appears in Housmans Peace Diary.*
**Howard League For Penal Reform, The** 1 Ardleigh Rd, London, N1 4HS *T* 020 7249 7373 *F* 020 7249 7788 www.howardleague.org howard.league@ukonline.co.uk *The Howard League works for humane, effective and efficient reform of the penal system.*
**Human Scale Education** 96 Carlingcott, Bath, BA2 8AW *T* 01972 510709 *F* as phone *Children's needs are best met and their potential most fully realised in human scale settings. Small classes, small schools and large schools restructured into smaller units.*
**Hundredth Monkey, The** 91 South St, St. Andrews, Fife, KY16 9QW *T* 01334 477411 *F* as phone *Radical fair trade workers' co-op. An anticonsumerist shop (?!) - organic wholefoods, fair trade crafts & clothes, ecological alternatives.*
**Hunt Saboteurs Association (H.S.A)** P.O.Box 2786, Brighton, BN2 2AX *T* 01273 622827/Press office only: 0961 113084 *F* as phone - call first. www.envirolink.orglarrs/has/has.html has@gn.apc.org *The H.S.A is dedicated to saving the lives of hunted animals directly, using non-violent direct action.*

**I-Contact Video Network** c/o 76 Mina Rd, St. Werburghs, Bristol, BS2 9TX *T* 0117 914 0188 www.VideoNetwork.org I-contact@gifford.co.uk *We are a non-profit making initiative set up to provide support for those using video for Positive Change. This includes Progressive, Alternative, and Independent Video Makers and Activists.*
**Independent Benefits Advice Service, The** 34 Saxon Place, Horton Kirby, Dartford, Kent, DA4 9JG *T* 01322 865114
**Independent Park Home Advisory Service (IPHAS)** 17 Ashley Wood Park, Tarrant Keynston, Dorset, DT11 9JJ *T* 01732 359655 *F* as phone *Support for U.K.residential mobile home owners with problems. Also seeking changes in legislation to improve protection against rogue landlords.*
**Index on Censorship** 33 Islington High St, London, N1 9LH *T* 020 7278 2313 *F* 020 7278 1878 www.indexoncensorship.org contact@indexoncensorship.org *A bimonthly magazine that covers freedom of expression issues all over the world.*
**Industrial Workers of the World** Secular Hall, 75 Humberside Gate, Leicester, LE1 1WB *T* 0116 266 1835 *The IWW is a revolutionary trade union whose purpose is to gain control over the shop floor and eliminate the bosses.*
**Indymedia** www.indymedia.org/ *Indymedia is a collective of inde-*

*pendent media organizations and hundreds of journalists offering grassroots, non-corporate coverage of the IMF/World Bank protests.*
**IndyMedia UK** www.indymedia.org.uk reports@indymedia.org.uk *An evolving network of media professionals, artists, and DIY media activists committed to using technology to promote social and economic justice. Part of a growing international alliance.*
**Informed Parent, The** P.O.Box 870, Harrow, Middlesex, HA3 7UW *T* 020 8861 1022 *F* as phone *To promote awareness about vaccination in order to preserve the freedom of an informed choice. Produces a quarterly newsletter.*
**Infoshops Network** c/o P.O.Box 4144, Worthing, West Sussex, BN14 7NZ www.eco-action.org/infoshops infoshops@tao.ca or teapot@worthing.eco-action.org *Resource by, and for, infoshops & autonomous centres etc. Keep in touch with infoshops around the world.*
**Inititiative Factory** 29 Hope St, Liverpool *T* 0151 709 2148
**INK - Independent News Collective** 170 Portobello Rd, London, W11 2EB *T* 0171 221 8137 http://www.ink.uk.com ink@pro-net.co.uk *Coodinating alternative magazines.*
**Innerfield** *see entry for Brighton ART.*
**Innocent** Dept.54, 255 Wilmslow Rd, Manchester, M14 5LW http:// innocent.org.uk innocent@uk2.net *Innocent are a mutual support organisation for the families and friends of prisoners who have been convicted of serious crimes.*
**INQUEST** Ground Floor, Alexandra National House, 330 Seven Sisters Rd, London, N4 2PJ *T* 020 8802 7430 *F* 020 8802 7450 www.gn.apc.org/inquest/ inquest@compuserve.com *Monitors and campaigns against deaths in Police, Prison & other State custody; to reform Coroner's Courts, and provides a free legal and advice service to the bereaved on inquests.*
**Institute For Law And Peace (INLAP)** 67 Summerheath Rd, Hailsham, Sussex, Bn27 3DR *T* 01323 844629 *F* as phone or 020 7636 8232 http://I.am/lawpeace lawpeace@I.am *The promotion of international law & the rights of citizens under it, the calling to account of rogue states who disregard the United Nations, and established law.*
**Institute for Social Inventions** 20 Heber Rd, London, NW2 6AA *T* 020 8208 2853 *F* 020 8452 6434 http://globalideasbank.org rhino@dial.pipex.com *Socially innovative ideas & projects plus awards to best. Website allows 3000 best ideas to be rated by reader.*
**Institute of Employment Rights (IER)** 177 Abbeville Rd, London, SW4 9RL *T* 020 7498 6919 *F* 020 7498 9080 www.ier.org.uk ier@gn.apc.org *The Insitute publishes eight booklets a year on all aspects of employment law. The booklets are written by sympathetic lawyers and academics and aimed at the labour movement.*
**Institute of Race Relations** http://www.homebeats.co.uk/ *Resources for researchers, activists, journalists, students and teachers. Useful links to other sites.*
**Interference FM** Box 6, Green Leaf, 82 Colston St, Bristol, BS1 5BB
**International Cannabis Coalition** c/o Green Party, 1a Waterlow Rd, London, N19 5NJ
**International Concerned Family & Friends of Mumia Abu-Jamal** www.mumia.org *Information and networking to save this journalist/activist's life.*
**International Federation of Chemical, Energy, Mine and General Workers' Unions** Ave St Emile de Beco, 109, B-1050 Brussels, Belgium *T* 32 2 626 2020 *F* 32 2 648 4316 www.icern.org icern@geo2.poptel.org.uk
**International Human Rights Association** *T* 00 49 421 557 7093 www.humanrights.de/
**International Institute for Environment and Development (IIED)** 3 Endsleigh St, London, WC1H 0DD *T* 020 7388 2117 *F* 020 7388 2826 humans@iied.org
**International Workers of the World** Secular Hall, 75 Humberstone Gate, Leicester, LE1 1WB *Revolutionary Syndicalist trade union whose aim is to organise and get the bosses off our backs.*
**Irish Network for Nonviolent Action Training and Education (INNATE)** c/o 16 Ravensdene Park, Belfast, BT6 0DA *T* 028 9064 7106 http://members.tripod.com/~innate_news/ innate@net.ntl.com
**Irwin Mitchell Solicitors** St. Peter's House, Hartshead, Sheffield, S1 2EL *T* 0114 276 7777/273 9011 *F* 0114 275 3306 *Produce Claiming Compensation For Police Misconduct- A Guide To Your Rights, a booklet of civil liberties when dealing with the police.*

**ISIP (International Exhibition of Publications)** P.O.Box 325 or Ulica Hrvatske bratske zajednice bb, 10001 Zagreb, Croatia *T* 385 (0)1 616 4055/385 (0)1 6164188 *F* 385 (0)1 616 4188 *Presenting and promoting world literature from all areas of human knowledge.*

**Justice and Freedom For Animals (formerly The Shoreham Protesters)** P.O.Box 2279, Hove, BN3 5BE *T* 01403 782925 *F* 01273 727024 soft.net.uk/brettley willaw@dircon.co.uk *Animal rights group dedicated to fighting animal abuse:- vivisection, blood sports, farming, live exports etc.*

**Justice For Diarmuid O'Neill Campaign** BM Box D. O'Neill, London, WC1N 3XX *T* 020 849 2588/mobile: 07968 361579 *F* as phone www.go.to/justicedoneill justicedoneill@btinternet.com *We are working with the family and friends of Diarmuid O'Neill, a young unarmed Irishman shot dead by police in London in 1996, for truth and justice about the killing.*

**Justice For Mark Barnsley** c/o 145-149 Cardigan Rd, Leeds, LS6 1LJ snide@globalnet.co.uk

**Justice For Ricky Reel Campaign** c/o Southall Monitoring Group, 14 Featherstone Rd, Southall, Middx, UB2 5AA *T* 020 8843 2333 www.monitoring-group.co.uk tmg@monitoring-group.co.uk

**Kate Sharpley Library (KSL)** KSL, BM Hurricane, London, WC1N 3XX http://members.aol.com/wellslake/sharpley.htm kar98@dial.pipex.com *Named after a London anarchist, our extensive collection of libertarian material is devoted to researching and publishing true anarchist history. Website includes an on-line version of our bulletin.*

**Kebele Kulture Projekt** 14 Robertson Rd, Eastville, Bristol, BS5 6JY *T* 0117 939 9469 kebele@marbard.com *Community centre, vegan cafe, and activist resource centre.*

**Kent Socialist Alliance** *T* 01304 216102/mobile: 07803 680053 *Broad network (countrywide) of activists, trade unionists, socialists, anarchists, animal rights, anti-fascists, huntsabs exchanging info & organising activity. Monthly newsletter.*

**Kernow FIN (Free Information Network)** P.O.Box 19, Penzance, Kernow, TR18 2XY *Newsletter & contacts list for the growing network of activists dedicated to creating a socially just & environmentally sustainable Cornwall.*

**Kieran & Co** 31 Clarence Rd, Chesterfield, Derbyshire, S40 1LN *T* 01246 559065/emergency: 01246 568643 *F* 01246 220258 *Specialist criminal defence for animal rights, roads, GM crops, anti-nuclear etc. Protecting your rights nationwide.*

**KK/Collectives** Majdoor Library, Autopin Jhuggi, N.I.T. Faridabad 121 001, India, revelrytion@yahoo.com *Monthly wage-workers' newspaper in Hindi language, 5000 copies, free distribution.*

**KUD Anarhiv** Metelkova Ulika 6, 1000 Ljubljana, Slovenia *T* 386 61 132 33 78 *F* as phone www.ljudmila.org/anarhiv/ anarhiv@mail.ljudmila.org *A resource centre for radical social change.*

**Kurdish Human Rights Project (KHRP)** Suite 319 Linen Hall, 162-168 Regent St, London, W1R 5TB *T* 020 7287 2772 *F* 020 7734 4927 www.khrp.org khrp@khrp.demon.co.uk *committed to the protection of the human rights of all persons within the Kurdish regions, irrespective of race, religion, sex, political persuasion or other belief or opinion.*

**Kurdistan Information Centre (KIC)** 10 Glasshouse Yard, London, EC1A 4JN *T* 020 7250 1315 *F* 020 7250 1317 kiclondon@gn.apc.org *Provides latest news on situation in Kurdistan; expresses human rights violations and repression against Kurds; publishes news bulletin (weekly) magazine "Kurdistan Report".*

**Labour Campaign For Travellers Rights** 84 Bankside St, Leeds, LS8 5AD *T* 01275 838910

**LabourStart** www.labourstart.org/ ericlee@labourstart.org/ *Where trade unionists start their day on the net. Loads on contacts and news etc from around the world.*

**Lancaster Anarchist Group** c/o Single Step Co-op, The Basement, 78A Penny St, Lancaster, LA1 1XN *Anarchist group active in national & community struggles.*

**Land and Liberty** 35 Rayleigh Avenue, Westcliff On Sea, Essex, S20 7DS *T* 01702 303259 *Booklets and pamphlets (mainly self-produced) on veganism, permaculture, land use issues, etc from a libertarian (anarchist) perspective - SAE for list.*

**Land Is Ours, The (T.L.I.O)** 16B Cherwell St, Oxford, OX4 1BG *T* 01865 722 016/0585 132080 www.oneworld.org/tlio/ office@tlio.demon.co.uk *The Land Is Ours campaigns peacefully for access to the land, its resources and the decision making processes affecting them, for everyone - irrespective of race, age, or gender.*

**Land Stewardship Trust** Flat 3, 1 Gladstone Terrace, Brighton, BN2 3LB *T* 01273 672186 lst@greenline.clara.net *LST is an educational charity. We hold land in trust, allowing local people to carry out eco-friendly projects [forming a stewardship group.]*

**Last Chance Saloon** 88 Lower Marsh, Waterloo, London, SE1 7AB *T* 020 7771 7466 sueprince@lastchancesaloon.demon.co.uk *Fringe culture, books, zines, pop art, leftfield gallery and shop. "Twisted pop art".*

**Latin America Solidarity Centre** 5 Merrion Row, Dublin 2 *T* 00 353 1 676 0435 lasc@iol.ie

**Leathes Prior Solicitors** 74 The Close, Norwich, Norfolk, NR1 4DR *T* 01603 610911/mobile: 0468 446800 *F* 01603 610088 tcary@leathesprior.co.uk *Solicitors with considerable experience of representing animal rights pretesters throughout the UK.*

**Leeds Alt-Tech** The Crow, 535 Meanwood Rd, Meanwood, Leeds, LS6 4AW *T* 0113 224 9885

**LeftDirect** www.leftdirect.co.uk/ *More than just a comprehensive directory of all left, radical and progressive organisations in the UK.*

**Legal Aid Head Office** *T* 020 8813 1000

**Legal Defence & Monitoring Group (LDMG)** Bm Haven, London, WC1N 3XX *T* 020 7837 7557 *LDMG provides legal support & back up on demonstrations in London. However we are presently in hibernation and will only come out of it for particular events.*

**Legalise Cannabis Alliance (LCA)** P.O. Box 198, Norwich, NR2 2DE *T* 01603 442215 www.lca.org webbooks@paston.co.uk *Political party campaigning for legalisation and utilisation of canna- bis. Manifesto: Cannabis Legalise and Utilise available £5 inc. p&p.*

**Legends of Peace** Van Blankenburgstr. 25, 2517 XM The Hague, Netherlands *T* 00 31 70 360 2060 *F* as phone www.gn.apc.org/ peacelegends peacelegends@beyondthemask.com *An international project for young people world-wide, creating a culture of peace through the magic of myth and story.*

**Leicester Radical Alliance (LRA)** c/o Dept Z, Littlethorn Books, Humberstone gate, Leicester *T* 0116 251 5967 www.plebs.com/ leicester-radical/ leicesterradical@hotmail.com *Alliance supporting rebels, radicals, and community activists in Leicester and around. Produces free monthly newsletter 'GrassRoots'.*

**Leonard Peltier Defense Committee** P. O. Box 583, Lawrence, Kansas KS 66044, USA *T* 785 842 5774 http://members.xoom.com/ freepeltier/index.html lpdc@idir.net

**Letslink UK** Flat 1, 54 Campbell Rd, Southsea, Hampshire, PO5 1RW *T* 01705 730639 www.letslinkuk.org lets@letslinkuk.org *To empower, educate & inform by advancing & implementing the ethical & sustainable development of local exchange/community-based mutual aid systems inc. LETS.*

**Letterbox Library** Unit 2D, Leroy House, 436 Essex Rd, London, N1 3QP *T* 020 7226 1633

**Levellers** 55 Canning St, Brighton, BN2 2EF *T* 01273 698171 *F* 01273 624884 www.levellers.co.uk/ thelevellers@mistral.co.uk *Band. Produce a magazine, sell merchandise.*

**Lib Ed** 157 Wells Rd, Bristol, BS4 2BU editors@LIBED.demon.co.uk

**Librairie Freecyb** Les Esclargades, Lagnes, F-84800 http:// freecyb.com yann@freecyb.com *Online bookshop. We're offering books & magazines on nomadism, communities, alternatives, energies, spirituality & esoterism.*

**Library of Free Thought (LOFT)** P.O.Box 19, Penzance, Cornwall, TR18 2YP *T* 01736 331236 *Anarchist & alternative books, mags, postcards, noticeboard, meeting space.*

**Light Information and Healing Trust, The (LIGHT)** 28 Devonshire Rd, Bognor Regis, W. Sussex, PO21 2SY *T* 01243 822089 *Working with light, colour, sound - therapy & industry. Quarterly publication.*

**Little Thorn Books** 73 Humberstone Gate, Leicester, LE1 1WB *T* 0116 251 2002 *F* as phone *Radical bookshop.*

**Liverpool Dockers, The** *T* 0151 207 9111 *Have set up a workers' co-op to retrain sacked dock workers. Still having monthly meetings attended by up to 300 people.*

**Lobster** www.lobster-magazine.co.uk/ *The journal of parapolitics,* *intelligence, and State Research.*

**London 21 Sustainability Network** 7 Chamberlain St, London, NW1 8XB *T* 020 7722 3710 *F* 020 7722 3959 http://www. greenchannel.com/slt/index/htm slt@gn.apc.org *Network of people and groups engaged in personal and community-based action for sustainability in London.*

**London Anarchist Black Cross** 27 Old Gloucester St, London, WC1N 3XX londonabc@hotmail.com *We are a revolutionary organisation active in supporting class struggle prisoners. We give direct help by writing, financial support, distributing information and printing articles for prisoners.*

**London Animal Action (LAA)** BM Box 2248, London, WC1N 3XX *T* 020 7278 3068 *F* as phone laa@londonaa.demon.co.uk *Grassroots local animal rights group for London. Against all animal abuse, concentrating on the fur trade with Fur-Free London campaign. Publishes monthly newsletter.*

**London Class War** P.O.Box 467, London, E8 3QX *T* 01582 750601 ambarchik@hotmail.com *Britain's most un-rudely newspaper.*

**London Greenpeace/McLibel Support Campaign** 5 Caledonian Rd, London, N1 9DX *T* 020 7713 1269 *F* as phone www.mcspotlight.org/ mclibel@globalnet.co.uk *We campaign against exploitation and oppression of people, animals and the environment, and for creating a society based on cooperation and sharing.*

**London Hazards Centre** Interchange Studies, Dalby St, London, NW 3NQ *T* 0171 267 3387 *F* 0171 2677 3397 http://www.ihc.org.uk mail@ihc.org.uk *Advice, information and training for trade unions and tenants' organisations on workplace and community health and safety in London.*

**Low Impact** Circus Workshops, Oxford, OX4 1HZ http:// lowimpact.com/ mail@lowimpact.com *Practical ways of treading lightly on the earth: High ideals Low budget.*

**Low Level Radiation Campaign** Ammondale, Spa Rd, Llandrindod, Powys, LD1 5EY *T* 01597 824771 www.llrc.org/ bramhall@llrc.org *Destroying the nuclear industry by revealing the true extent of health damage caused by radioactive pollution.*

**Lydia Dagostino** c/o Kellys - Criminal Defence Specialists, Premier House, 11 Marlborough House, Brighton, BN1 1UB *T* 01273 608311 *F* 01273 674898 l.dagostino@talk21.com *Solicitor.*

**M-Power** www.m-power.org.uk/ stuart_hall@excite.com *This web site is designed to inspire you. If it does not, it has failed. It is designed to be a tool for your own empowerment. If it fails on that aim, it has failed. It is written with love.*

**Mad Pride** www.madpride.net *The entertainment branch of Reclaim Bedlam, putting the humour back into madness.*

**Mahila Milan/National Slum Dwellers Federation (NSDF)** Society for Promotion of Area Resource Centre, P.O. Box 9389, Mumbai 400 026, India *T* (91-21) 285 1500 admin@sparc.ilbom.ernet.in

**Maloka Anarcho Collective** BP 536, 21014 Dijon Cedex, France *T* +33 3 8066 8149 *F* +33 3 8071 4299 www.chez.com/maloka/ maloka@chez.com *We promote anarchism & act for social change, through different activities: infoshop, weekly vegan restaurant, organise lectures, demos & actions, independent gigs, records, newsletter, non-profit.*

**Manchester Environmental Resource Centre initiative (MERCi)** c/o O.W.C, 6 Mount St, Manchester, M2 5NS *T* 0161 819 1139 *F* 0161 834 8137 merci@gn.apc.org

**McLibel Support Campaign** 5 Caledonian Rd, London, N1 9DX *T* 020 7713 1269 *F* as phone www.mcspotlight.org mclibel@globalnet.co.uk

**Medical Marijuana Foundation** The Old Farmhouse, Crylla, Common Moor, Lisheard, Cornwall, PL14 6ER *T* 01579 346592 robin@lifetech.fsnet.co.uk *Camapiging for the legalisation of cannabis, and the creation of a cannabis pill for medical purposes.*

**Microzine** spor23@yahoo.com *Underground arts zine. Printed in French and English. Events include squatting buildings to create "Artspace 23" and experimental sound-scapes.*

**Millimations Animation Workshop** P.O.Box 2679, Brighton, BN1 3QX *T* pager: 04325 370122 www.brighton.co.uk/millimations millie@hiatus.demon.co.uk *Millimations provides workshops, training and productions in animation by, with and for the community. Particularly 'Animate the Earth' education pack.*

**Mind Body and Spirit** Swindon, SN99 9XX

**Minewatch** Methodist Clubland, 54 Camberwell Rd, London, SE5 0EN *T* 020 7277 4852 *F* 020 7277 4853 minewatch@gn.apc.org

**Minority Rights Group International** 379 Brixton Rd, London, SW9 7DE *T* 020 7978 9498 *F* 020 7738 6265 www.minorityrights.org minority.rights@mrgmail.org *Work to secure rights for ethnic, religious and linguistic minorities worldwide, and to promote cooperation and understanding between communities.*

**Miscarriages of Justice UK (MOJUK)** *T* 0121 554 6947 *F* 0870 055 4570 www.ncadc.demon.co.uk/ ncadc@ncadc.demon.co.uk *Hostages in UK prisons are often isolated and have no knowledge of other hostages. MOJUK keeps a list of hostages and their campaigns and encourages people to write to those inside. Newssheet too.*

**Misereor** Mozartstrasse 9, D-52064 Aachen, Germany *T* (49-241) 4420 *F* (49-21) 442188 meerpohl@misereor.de

**Mobile Office, The (MO)** *T* 01226 764279 pp3mo@aol.com *Provide office facilities for any person or group engaged in environmental campaigning.*

**Modern Alternative Disco (M.A.D)** 120 Stanley Way, Ashby Fields, Daventry, Northants, NN11 5SE *T* 01327 300784/mobile: 07977 781213 *We are a Techno free system, playing a mix of music from ska to crappy eighties disco music, with lots of other stuff in between. We run the system on a co-operative basis, between ourselves & others.*

**Monkey Pirates! Multimedia (Mo.PI)** # 8-110 Stirling Ave, Ottawa, Canada, K1Y 1R1 *T* 613 722 8112 www.monkeypirates.com soy@igs.net *Alternative media, anarchist production co-op with digital camera and editing facilities, rentals, resources, links. Documentaries, shorts, features.*

**Monkey-Wrench Graphix** P.O.Box 12802, Edinburgh, EH7 5ZH monkey@punk.org.uk *Non-profit DIY operation printing t-shirts and designing graphics for campaigns and struggles for social justice.*

**Morgenmuffel** Box B, 21 Little Preston St, Brighton, BN1 2HQ *An irregular self published zine with autobiographical cartoons and rants by an anarchist woman in Brighton.*

**Movement Against the Monarchy (MA'M)** P.O. Box 14672, London, E9 5UQ *T* Pager: 01523 160145 www.geocities.com/ capitolhill/lobby/1793/index moveagainstmon@hotmail.com *Organising popular opposition to the Royals using any means necessary as often as possible.*

**Movement For Justice (MFJ)** P.O.Box 16581, London, SW2 2ZW *T* 07957 696636/0976 916956 *Organising against racism & police brutality, building community action against racist attacks and part building a national civil rights movement.*

**Multimap.Com** http://uk8.multimap.com/map/places.cgi *A complete interactive atlas on the web!*

**Mumia Must Live!** BM Haven, London, WC1N 3XX mumia@callnet.uk.com

**'Mushroom Cultivator, The'**, P .Stamets & J.S. Chilton, (Agarikon Press)

**National Anti-Hunt Campaign (NAHC)** P.O.Box 66, Stevenage, SG1 2TR *T* 01442 240246 *F* as phone - call first nahc@nahc.freeserve.co.uk *Uses a wide range of tactics, from lobbying to occupations, investigations and n.v.d.a to oppose hunting with hounds. Free newsletter and campaign pack on request.*

**National Assembly Against Racism (NAAR)** 28 Commercial St, London, E1 6LS *T* 020 7247 9907/07958 706834 *F* as phone http:// ourworld.compuserve.com/homepages/aa_r aa_r@compuserve.com *Bring together an alliance of Black organisations, Jewish and other faith groups, students, trade unions & others to oppose racism & the far right in all forms.*

**National Campaign Against CS Spray** c/o Newham Monitoring Project, Suite 4, 63 Broadway, London, E15 4BQ *T* 020 8555 8151 *F* 020 8555 8163 nmp@gn.apc.org or kevin@copwatcher.freeserve.co.uk *Compiles information & press cuttings on use of CS spray and campaigns for abolition of its use by the police.*

**National Coalition of Anti-Deportation Campaigns (NCADC)** 110 Hamstead Rd, Birmingham, B20 2QS *T* 0121 554 6947 *F* 0870 055 4570 www.ncadc.demon.co.uk/ ncadc@ncadc.demon.co.uk *NCADC will provide free help and advice to all families & individuals wanting to campaign against deportation.*

**National Federation of Badger Groups (NFBG)** 2 Cloisters Business Centre, 8 Battersea Park Rd, London, SW8 4BG *T* 020 7498

3220/mobile: 0976 153389 *F* 020 7627 4212 www.geocities.com/ rainforest/canopy/6626/ ed.goode@ndirect.co.uk *Promote conservation & protection of badgers. Represent 85 local voluntary badger groups. Provide information & advice, membership system.*

**National Federation of City Farms** The Green House, Hereford St, Bedminster, Bristol, BS3 4NA *T* 0117 923 1800

**National Federation of Credit Unions** Unit 1.1 &1.2, Howard House Commercial Centre, Howard St, North Shields, Tyne and Wear, NE30 1AR *T* 0191 257 2219 *F* 0191 259 1884 *Non-profit making financial co-operative.*

**National Gulf War Veterans and Families Association** 4 Maspin Close, Kingswood, Hull, HU7 3EF *T* 01482 833812 ngvfa13.freeserve.co.uk *Support network, proactive at looking into what veterans have been exposed to.*

**National Homeless Alliance (NHA)** 5-15 Cromer St, King's Cross, London, WC1H 8LS *T* 020 7713 2840 *F* 020 7713 2848 www.home_all.org.uk nha@home_all.org.uk *NHA is the membership organisation for those providing services to homeless people. We provide info, advice & training, develop networks, undertake research and lobby for change.*

**National Pure Water Association** 12 Dennington Lane, Crigglestone, Wakefield, WF4 3ET www.npwa.freeserve.co.uk

**National Small Press Centre, The** BM Bozo, London, WC1N 3XX *Serials, magazines, journals, newsletters, bulletins, comics, periodicals, zines, sporadicals.*

**National Society for Clean Air & Environmental Protection (NSCA)** 136 North St, Brighton, BN1 1RG *T* 01273 326313 *F* 01273 735802 http://www3.mistral.co.uk/cleanair intr@nsca.org.uk *NGO lobbying on air pollution & related environmental issues.*

**National Society of Allotment and Leisure Gardeners Ltd, The** O'Dell House, Hunters Rd, Corby, Northants, NN17 5JE *T* 01536 266576 *F* 01536 264509 *The Society is the national representive body for the allotment movement, representing its members at both national and regional levels. Help and advice service on all allotment matters.*

**Native American Resource Centre** 21 Little Preston St, Brighton, BN1 2 HQ *T* 01273 328357 *F* as phone www.pavilion.co.uk/naet naet@pavilion.co.uk *The centre exists to support and disseminate the voices of native North American peoples. We fund various projects on reservations and produce our own journal, "Talking Stick".*

**Native Americas Journal** c/o Akwe:kon Press, 450 Caldwell Hall, Cornell University, Ithaca, NY 14853 *T* (607) 255 4308 *F* (607) 255 0185 nativemaericas@cornell.edu *Issues of concern to Native (ndigenous/aboriginal) peoples throughout the Western Hemisphere.*

**Natural Death Centre, The** 20 Heber Rd, London, NW2 6AA *T* 020 8208 2853 *F* 020 8452 6434 www.naturaldeath.org.uk rhino@dial.pipex.com

**Naturewise** 20 The Triangle, 1 Cromartie Rd, London, N19 3RX *T* 020 7281 3765 *Promotion of: sustainable land use and lifestyles in cities, growing food in cities, education through permaculture courses. The creation of forest gardens in cities. Permaculture consultations given.*

**Network 23 = Manchester Division** *T* 07091 102463 - don't leave messages www.ffwd.to/network23 teknopaul23@yahoo.com *Net magazine: subjects freeparties primarily + anything current and underground.*

**Networking Newsletter Project** 6 Mount St, Manchester, M2 5NS *T* 0161 226 9321 *F* 0161 834 8187 http://ds.dial.pipex.com/toen/ terrace/gdn22/NNP/in networking.newsletter@dial.pipex.com

**New Economics Foundation (NEF)** Cinnamon House, 6-8 Cole St, London, SE1 4YH *T* 020 7407 7447 *F* 020 7407 6473 www.neweconomics.org info@neweconomics.org *NEF works to put people and the environment at the centre of economic thinking.*

**New Futures Association** 6, Snednore, Wellgreen Lane, Kingston, Lewes, E. Sussex, BN7 3NL *T* 01273 479621 *F* as phone nfauk@hotmail.com *Practical support & lobbying on behalf of travellers, homeless, & socially excluded groups. We aim to buy/rent a bit of land/farm to turn into a resource centre.*

**New Internationalist** Tower House, Lathkill St, Market Harborough, LE16 www.newint.org/

**Newham and District Claimants Union** Durning Hall, Earlham Grove, Forest Grove, London, E7 9AB *Meetings 7.30 pm alternate Thursdays. We deal with benefit problems as a collective. Our aim is to involve everyone in everyone else's fights.*

**Newham Monitoring Project (NMP)** 63 Broadway, Stratford,

London, E15 4BQ *T* 020 8555 8151 *F* 020 8555 8163 nmp@gn.apc.org *Grassroots community organisation providing support, advice & campaigning on issues of racial harassment & civil injustice.*

**News From Nowhere Bookshop** 96 Bold Street, Liverpool, L1 4HY *T* 0151 708 7270 *F* 0151 707 0540 *Radical & community bookshop run by a women's collective, now in its 26th year! Sells lots of books & world music CDs.*

**Nighttime Gardener's Guide** www.tao.ca/~ban/1299/ nighttimegardeners.htm nighttimegardeners@angelfire.com *We publish the Nighttime Gardeners Guide: a guide to pulling GE crops in Amerika!*

**Ninfomania c/o Protein** 53 Great Eastern St, London, EC2A 3HP *T* 020 7684 9176 *F* 020 7684 9187 www.ninfomania.com/ info@ninfomania.com *The number one weekly newzfeed for the contemporary digirati.*

**NLP & DHE** www.nlp.com/NLP *Neuro-Linguistic Programming and Design Human Engineering general information server.*

**No Alignment Action Group** c/o Milton Bridge, Penicuik, Midlothian, EH26 0NX www.spokes.org.uk/naag/ naag@ic24.net *Campaigning against the destructive A7101 road realignment outside Edinburgh.*

**No Opencast** 28 Wandle Rd, London, SW17 7DW *T* 020 8672 9698 *Campaigning against opencast mining and trying to circulate information between local groups and successful groups fighting against opencast mines.*

**no.problem.distribution** 82.whitethroat.walk, birchwood, oakwood, warrington.cheshire, wa3 6pq *anarcho. non.profit. d.i.y. newsletter. zine.+benefit. sound.recording. distribution. tape.trading. also. warrington.+ mid. cheshire. animal.rights.+ concern. group.*

**Non Payment Collective** non-payment@onelist.com

**Non-Violent Resistance Network (NVRN)** 162 Holloway Rd, London, N7 8DQ *T* 020 7607 2302 *F* 020 7700 2357 c/o cnd@gn.apc.org *To network non-violent direct action activists in the UK and supply with information about NVDA events.*

**Nonviolent Action (NVA)** 5 Caledonian Rd, Kings Cross, London, N1 9DY *T* 020 7713 6540 *F* 020 7278 0444 nva@gn.apc.org *Monthly publication covering peace, environmental and other campaigning - with news, listings, debate. Plugs the gap since "Peace News" went quarterly.*

**North Devon Animal Defence** c/o Earth Angel, 63-64 Boutport St, Barnstable, North Devon, EX31 1HG *T* 01271 814177

**North/East London Solidarity Federation International** P.O.Box 1681, London, N8 7LE *T* 0181 374 5027 *F* as phone http:// gn.apc.org/solfed *We are anarcho-syndicalists and believe that workers ourselves are the best people to take control of deciding how we work, what is produced, and how things should be run.*

**Northern Animal Rights Coalition** P.O. Box 1JY, Newscastle-Upon-Tyne, NE99 1JY

**Notes From the Borderland** Bm Box 4769, London, WC1N 3XX *T* Pager: 01523 492994 *We publish cutting edge parapolitical research into the secret state, fascists, etc - material that is too sharp for Guardian/Red Pepper. £2.50 each issue, cheques/pos payable to Larry O'Hara.*

**Nottingham Claimants Action (NCA)** Box NCA, 176-188 Mansfield Rd, Nottingham, England, NG1 3HW *T* 0115 958 5666 *F* as phone - call first http://www.geocities.com/capitolhill/lobby/7638/ ncajsa@yahoo.com *Fighting the imposition of JSA, New Deal, and poverty pay. A few activists and a useful website.*

**Nuclear Information and Resource Service (NIRS)** 1424 16 St NW #404, Washington, U.S.A, DC20036 *T* 202 328 0002 *F* 202 462 2183 www.nirs.org/ nirsnet@nirs.org *Information and networking clearinghouse fro grassroots groups and people concerned with nuclear power, radioactive waste, radiation and sustainable energy issues.*

**Oil Companies** www.oilcompanies.org/ shout@oilcompanies.org \find out about Shell. Find out about Chevron. Find out about murder, environmental chaos and the destruction of homes.

**Older Feminists Network (OFN)** c/o Astra, 54 Gordon Rd, London, N3 1EP *T* 020 8346 1900 www.ofn.org.uk rinar@dial.pipex.com *Bi-monthly newsletter/monthly meetings (2nd sat of every month)/shared lunch/workshops/& or speaker/letter writing to MPs, ministers, etc. re issues involving older women.*

**On the Right Track** 84 Bankside St, Leeds, LS8 5AD *Free quarterly magazine for Gypsies, Travellers and supporters. Send five 20p stamps to cover one year's postage.*

**Oneworld** www.oneworld.org *Oneworld reports on current news events, & lists jobs, volunteering and training. Also has a page called Community Web, a search engine indexing UK sites containing community issues and needs info.*

**Ontario Coalition Against Poverty**
www.welfarewatch.toronto.on.ca/ ocap@tao.ca

**Open Spaces Society (OSS)** 25A Bell St, Henley-On-Thames, Oxon, RG9 2BA *T* 01491 573535 www.oss.org.uk osshq@aol.com *We campaign to create and conserve common land, village greens, open spaces, public rights of access, in town and country.*

**OPM Support** c/o 43 Gardner St, Brighton, BN1 1UN www.eco-action.org/opm/ *Solidarity camapign with the indigenous peoples of West Papua. Also produce newsletter.*

**Opposition To Destruction of Open Green Spaces (OTDOGS)** 6 Everthorpe Rd, London, SE15 4DA *T* 020 8693 9412 *F* as phone *Giving advice on how to prevent food stores being built on green land. Produce 'Save Green Spaces From Destruction By Food Giants' by John D. Beasley, £3.40 inc p&p.*

**Orangi Pilot Program (OPP)** Street 4, Sector 5/A, Quasba Colony, Manghopir Rd, Karachi 75800, Pakistan *T* (92-21) 665 2297/665 8021 *F* (92-21) 666 5696 opprti@digicom.net.pk

**Outlook Children's Project** #2, 22 West Heath Drive, London, NW11 7QH *T* 020 8905 5014 outlooktrg@aol.com

**OutRage!** P.O.Box 17816, London, SW14 8WT *T* 020 8240 0222 *F* 020 7403 1790 www.OutRage.org.uk outreach@OutRage.org.uk *OutRage! is a broad-based, non-violent direct action group dedicated to achieving equal civil and human rights for gays people.*

**Oxyacetylene** Box G, 111 Magdalen Rd, Oxford,
www.oxfordcity.demon.co.uk/oxyace

**Paganlink Network** BM Web, London, WC1N 3XX http://www.antipope.org/paganlink/

**PaRTiZans** 41A Thornhill Square, London, N1 1BE *T* 020 7700 6189 *F* as phone partizans@gn.apc.org *To campaign against the worldwide activities of Rio Tinto mining corporation in solidarity with directly affected communities.*

**Payday Men's Network** P.O.Box 287, London, NW6 5QU *T* 020 7209 4751 *F* 020 7209 4761

**Peace Brigades International British Section (PBI)** 1A Waterlow Rd, London, N19 5NJ *T* 020 7281 5370 *F* 020 7272 9243 www.igc.org/pbi pbibritain@gn.apc.org *We send teams of international observers to provide protective accompaniment to local human rights defenders who are at risk as a result of their work for social justice.*

**Peace News** 5 Caledonian Rd, London, N1 9DX *T* 020 7278 3344 *F* 020 7278 0444 peacenews@gn.apc.org *Quarterly publication - in-depth articles, debates, practical tools, & reviews from activists around the world.*

**Pedestrians Association, The** 31-33 Bondway, London, SW8 1SJ *T* 020 7820 1010 *F* 020 7820 8208 www.pedestrians.org.uk/ info@pedestrians.org.uk *Providing advice and information to those seeking to improve their local walking environment through a UK-wide network of 100 volunteers.*

**Pensioners Rights Campaign (PRC)** Rivanner, 77 Holme Rd, Market Weighton, York, YO43 3EW *T* 01430 873637 pensionersrights@frith28.freeserve.co.uk *Fighting for rights & a decent pension for the elderly and generally enhancing their quality of life.*

**People & Planet (P&P)** 51 Union St, Oxford, OX4 1JP *T* 01865 245678 *F* 01865 791927 www.peopleandplanet.org people@peopleandplanet.org *National network of student groups campaigning on international issues of poverty, human rights and the environment (formerly Third World First).*

**Peoples' Global Action** c/o Canadian Union of Postal Workers (CUPW), 377 Bank St, Ottawa, Ontario, Canada, www.agp.org/ pga@agp.org *This new platform will serve as a global instrument for communication and co-ordination for all those fighting against the destruction of humanity and the planet by the global market.*

**Permaculture Association (Britain)** BCM Permaculture Association, London, WC1N 3XX *T* 07041 390170 *F* as phone www.permaculture.org.uk office@permaculture.org.uk *An education and research charity that supports groups and individuals to develop permaculture in their homes, gardens, communities and workplaces.*

**Permaculture Magazine** Hyden House Ltd., - Permanent Publications, The Sustainability Centre, East Meon, Hampshire, GU32 1HR *T* 01730 823311 *F* 01730 823322 www.permaculture.co.uk/ hello@permaculture.co.uk *Permaculture Magazine publishes solutions for sustainable living, supplies a free Earth Repair catalogue of over 350 books on permaculture and related subjects.*

**Pesticides Trust, The** Eurolink Centre, 49 Effra Rd, London, SW2 1BZ *T* 020 7274 8895 *F* 020 7274 9084 www.gn.apc.org/ pesticidestrust/ pan-uk@pan-uk.org *The Pesticides Trust is a scientifically based charity concerned with the health, environmental and policy aspects of pesticide manufacture, trade and use.*

**Philippines Homeless People's Federation/Vincentian Missionaries Social Development Foundation (VMSDFI)** 221 Tandang Sora Avenue, P.O. Box 1179, NIA Road 1107, Quezon City, Philippines *T* (63-2) 455 9480 *F* (63-2) 454 2834 vmsdfi@info.com.ph

**Photon Press** 37 The Meadows, Berwick-Upon-Tweed, Northumberland, TD15 1NY *Publishes "Light's List" of literary independent magazines (1450 titles in 25 countries publishning in English). Independent publisher of self-generated material only.*

**Pilotlight** 15-17 Lincoln's Inn Fields, Holborn, London, WC2A 3ED *T* 020 7396 7414 *F* 020 7396 7484 pilotlight@brunswickgroup.com

**Plain Wordz** P.O. Box 381, Huddersfield, HD1 3XX *Plain Wordz is a distributor of anti-authortarian, pro-working class material - pamphlets, books, zines, t-shirts, music...The proceeds from the material we sell goes to prisoner support campaigns.*

**Planning Aid** *T* 01963 230045

**Platform** 7 Horselydown Lane, Bermondsey, London, SE1 2LN *T* 020 7403 3738 *F* as phone platform@gn.apc.org *Interdisciplinary group of artists and social scientists making projects aimed at creating a democratic and ecological London and Tidal Thames bioregion.*

**Poland Earth First!** P.O. Box 40, 43-304, Bielsko-Biala 4, Poland *T* 48 33 183153 wapienica@pnrwi.most.org.pl

**Poor People's Economic Human Rights Campaign, The** Kensington Welfare Rights Union, P.O. Box 50678, Philadelphia, PA 19132, USA *T* 215 203 1945 *F* 215 203 1950 kwru@libertynet.org *A national effort led by poor and homeless women, men and children of all races to raise the issue of poverty as a human rights violation.*

**Pork-Bolter, The** P.O.Box 4144, Worthing, West Sussex, BN14 7NZ www.worthing.eco-action.org/porkbolter/ porkbolter@worthing.eco-action.org *Radical local newsletter with historically-vindicated pig obsession. Rages against CCTV, Big Business, councils, police etc etc. Free with SAE.*

**Portsmouth Anarchist Network (PAN)** Box A, 167 Fawcett Rd, Southsea, Hants, PO4 0DH *Discusses and organises prisoner support, solidarity with workers in dispute, anti-militarism, annual May Day event, opposes capitalism.*

**Positive News** 5 Bicton Enterprise Centre, Clun, Shropshire, SY7 8NF *T* 01588 640022 *F* 01588 640033 www.positivenews.org.uk office@positivenews.org.uk *Publishes quarterly the newspaper Positive News and magazine Living Lightly.*

**Primal Seeds** www.primalseeds.org/ *A network to actively engage in protecting biodiversity and creating local food security. It is a response to industrial biopiracy, control of the global seed supply and of our food.*

**Prisoners Advice Service (P.A.S)** Unit 305, Hatton Sq, 16/16a Baldwins Gardens, London, EC1N 7RJ *T* 020 7405 8090 *F* 020 7405 8045 *We independently provide information and help to all prisoners in England and Wales regarding your rights as a serving prisoner. We offer advice on complaints, and more.*

**Privacy International** P.O.Box 3157, Brighton, BN2 2SS www.privacy.org/pi/ *International anti-surveillance organisation. Campaigns on Big Brother issues like data tracking, ID cards, CCTV, encryption, police surveillance, corporate biometrics.*

**Project Underground** 1847 Berkeley Way, Berkeley, California, U.S.A, CA 94703 *T* 510 705 8981 *F* 510 705 8983 www.moles.org porject_underground@moles.org *Project Underground supports communities threatened by the oil and mining industries and exposes corporate environmental and human rights abuses.*

**Proof!** 4 Wallace Rd, London, N1 2PG *T* 0171 354 4592 *F* 0171 354 8907 *Quarterly newsletter on Alternative Therapies.*

**Protest Camps** *See regular SchNEWS as they change on a regular*

*basis.*

**Protest.Net** www.protest.net/ rabble-rouser@protest.net *Protest.Net is a community of activists who are working together to create our own media. By publishing a public record of our political activities on the web we are taking a stand against est. media.*

**Public Citizen's Global Trade Watch** 215 Pennsylvania Ave, SE, Washington, USA, DC 20003 *T* 202 546 4996 *F* 202 547 7392 www.tradewatch.org gtwinfo@citizen.org *Global Trade Watch is the Public Citizen division that fights for international trade and investment policies promoting government and corporate accountability, consumer health and safety etc.*

**Public Law Project** *T* 020 7467 9800 admin@plp.bbk.ac.uk

**R.E.C.Y.C Ltd** 54 Upperthorpe Rd, Sheffield, S6 3EB *T* 0114 263 4494/275 5055 *Sheffield is a now a very exciting place to be for recycling. Recyc is a shop and newsletter.*

**Radical Routes** c/o Cornerstone Resource Centre, 16 Sholebroke Av, Leeds, LS7 3HB *T* 0113 262 9365 *F* as phone (call first) www.radicalroutes.org.uk/ cornerstone@gn.apc.org *Network of Housing and Workers co-ops. A number of publications available. Support and low cost loans available to member co-ops.*

**Radio 4A** radio4a@hotmail.com *Radio 4A is a free speech radio station serving the Brighton area on 106.6FM during special occasions.*

**Rainbow Centre** 178-180 Mansfield Rd, Nottingham, NG1 3HW *T* 0115 958 5666 *F* phone first www.veggies.org.uk/rainbow rainbow@veggies.org.uk *Resource centre for campaigning groups & individuals; library, fair-trade shop, recycling, vegan cafe, internet access, office facilities.*

**Rainbow Keepers** P.O. Box 52, Kasimov 391330, Russia *T* +7 09131 4 15 14 www.chat.ru/~rk2000 rk@lavrik.ryazan.ru *Radical environmental movement Rainbow Keepers, every summer protest camp against dangerous objects in Russia, Ukraine, Belorussia, Czech Republic. Alternative projects.*

**Raise Your Banners** P.O.Box 44, Sheffield, S4 7RN *T* 0114 249 5185 www.ryb.org.uk pete@ryb.org.uk *Britain's only festival of political music and campaigning arts, every other year, in Sheffield. Next one: November 2001.*

**Rational Trust, The** Finn Oak House, Street Rd, Glastonbury, Somerset *T* mobile: 07880 562600 *Eco-warriors fighting unnecessary developments.*

**Re-Cycle** 60 High St, West Mersea, Essex, CO5 8JE *T* 01206 382207/mobile: 07970 731530 *F* 01206 385729 www.re-cycle.org/ re-cycle@cerbernet.co.uk *Charity relieving poverty by taking second-hand bicycles overseas, setting up workshops to refurbish them and turn some into work-bikes.*

**Reading International Solidarity Centre (RISC)** 35-39 London St, Reading, Berks, RG1 4PS *T* 0118 958 6692 *F* 0118 959 4357 www.risc.org.uk risc@risc.org.uk *A Development Education Centre with community meeting rooms, fair trade shop and organic cafe.*

**Reading Roadbusters** c/o RIS Centre, 35-37 London St, Reading, RG1 4PS *T* 0118 954 6430 www.roadbusters.clara.net/ roadbusters@clara.net *Environmental and Social Justice Activist Group. Supports non-violent direct action locally and globally. Meets 6pm every 1st Sunday at RISC.*

**Real Nappy Association** P.O.Box 3704, London, SE26 4RX *T* 0181 299 4519 www.realnappy.com *The Real Nappy Association is the central source of information & advice on all nappy-related issues for individuals, local authorities, health professionals and the media.*

**Reclaim the Streets** P.O.Box 9656, London, N4 4JY *T* 0171 281 4621 www.gn.apc.org/rts/ rts@gn.apc.org *M-ways into allotments; no electric cars; streets for people; free public transport; part of global resistance movement against capitalism; all these and more via non-hierarchical direct action.*

**Reclaim the Streets -The Film** *T* mobile: 07941 025493 www.come.to/rtsfilm reclaim_streets_film@yahoo.com *Video clips, background info and ordering details for this essential documentary, taking a frantic look at RTS actions in the UK and abroad.*

**Red Pepper** 1b Waterlow Rd, London, N19 5NJ *T* 020 7281 7024 *F* 020 7263 9345 www.redpepper.org.uk redpepper@redpepper.org.uk

**Red South West** 1 Blake Place, Bridgwater, Somerset, TA6 5AV *T* 01278 450562 www.redsw.fsnet.co.uk glen@redsw.fsnet.co.uk *Journal aimed at developing discussion and co-operation between socialists and anarchists in the South West.*

**Redwood Coast Watersheds Alliance** P.O.Box 90, Elk, U.S.A, CA95432 *T* 707 877 3405 or 415 731 9062 www.elksoft.com/gwa pirohuck@men.org or chalice@weo.com *Saving redwoods from destruction by the Gap clothing store chain.*

**Reforesting Scotland** 62-66 Newhaven Rd, Edinburgh, EH6 5QB *T* 0131 554 4321/mobile: 07666 775263 *F* 0131 554 0088 www.gn.apc.org/ReforestingScotland/ reforscot@gn.apc.org *Promotes the ecological & social restoration of Scotland. Produces 'Reforesting Scotland Journal'. Currently campaigning for community ownership and management of woodlands.*

**Release** 388 Old St, London, EC1V 9LT *T* 0171 729 5255/24hr helpline: 0171 603 8654 *F* 0171 729 2599 http://www.release.org.uk *24 hour drugs and legal helpline. Also free phone drugs in schools helpline: 0808 8000 800. Also produces publications, such as the bustcard, and runs training programmes.*

**Renewable Energy in the Urban Environment (RENUE)** Unit 9, Merton Abbey Mills, Watermill Way, London, SW19 2RD *T* 020 8542 8500 *F* 020 8542 7789 cleanpower@renue.freeserve.co.uk *Tackling Climate Change at a community level by installing renewable energy systems and energy efficient measures, conducting education and arts projects in Wandsworth and Merton.*

**Resurgence** Ford House, Hartland, Bideford, Devon, EX39 6EE *T* 01237 441293 *F* 01237 441203 www.resurgence.org ed@resurge.demon.co.uk *Publish magazine (6 times a year) covering ecology, spirituality, sustainable living, human scale education, organic living. Free sample copy available.*

**Revolution Centre** Darvell, Robertsbridge, E.Sussex, TN32 5DR *T* 01580 883300 *F* 01580 883319 www.blumagazine.net revcenter@hotmail.com *Our aim is to raise spiritual & social consciousness, and to give an audience to other activists, creative workers, human beings. We work for revolution in souls & society.*

**Right To Protest Forum** J-B Louveaux, Flat 7, 10A Airlie Gardens, London, W8 7AL *T* 0171 727 0590/mobile: 0403 210069 *F* as phone jb1@netlane.com *Explores & develops ways to better protest the rights of protesters and improve the law relating to peaceful public protest. Setting up a permanent funded legal observer organisation.*

**Rising Sun Arts Centre** 30 Silver St, Reading, RG1 2ST *T* 0118 986 6788 *Arts centre run by volunteers aiming to provide local access to arts activities. Programme of live music and workshops.*

**Rising Tide** c/o Cornerstone Resource Centre, 16 Sholebroke Av, Leeds, LS7 3HB *T* 0113 262 9365 *F* as phone (call first) http://www.sol.co.uk/d/diffusion/cornerstone/crc/r cornerstone@gn.apc.org *Rising Tide is a campaign aimed at preventing the global environmental and social disasters that would be associated with a change in the global climate.*

**River Ocean Research & Education (RORE)** 113-117 Queens Rd, Brighton, BN1 3XG *T* 01273 234032 *F* 01273 234033 www.rore.org.uk info@rore.org.uk *Working for sustainable use of all areas of the water environment.*

**RoadPeace** P.O.Box 2579, London, NW10 3PW *T* 020 8838 5102/ national helpline: 020 8964 1021 *F* 020 8838 5103 www.roadpeace.org.uk roadpeace@roadpeace.org.uk *RoadPeace provides information and support to bereaved & injured road traffic victims through its helpline & contact with people who have suffered the same.*

**Robert Hamill Justice Appeal Fund** c/o 8 William St, Lurgan, Co. Armagh, BT66 1JA

**Royal Town Planning Institute (RTPI)** 26 Portland Place, London, W1N 4BE *T* 020 7636 9107 *F* 020 7323 1582 www.rtpi.org.uk online@rtpi.org.uk *To provide free and independent town planning advice to groups and individuals that cannot afford professional fees.*

**RTMark** www.rtmark.com/ *RTMark supports the sabotage of corporate products, with no risk to the public investor.*

**RTP (Ragged-Trousered Philanthropic) Press** c/o 103 Northcourt Av, Reading, Berks, RG2 7HG *(Very small!) publisher. Publisher of "The Activist's Unofficial Guide To Industrial Action" by Joe Hills (£2.50 plus 40p p+p) - all profits to workers in dispute.*

**Rural Advancement Foundation International (RAFI)** HQ: 110 Osborne St, Suite 202, Winnipeg MB R3L 1Y5, Canada *T* (204) 453 5259 *F* (204) 925 8034 www.rafi.org rafi@rafi.org *RAFI is dedicated to the conservation and sustainable improvement of agricultural diversity, and to the socially responsible development of technologies useful to rural societies.*

**Rural Media Company, The** Sullivan House, 72-80 Widemarsh St,

Hereford, HR4 9HG *T* 01432 344039 *F* 01432 270539 info@ruralmedia.co.uk *We're a charity who use media to create and collect evidence of rural needs through video, design work and photography.*

**Rwanda UK Goodwill Organisation, The** www.netrigger.co.uk/rugo mikeahughes@compuserve.com

**Safe Alliance, The** 94 White Lion St, London, N1 9PF *T* 020 7837 8980 *F* 020 7837 1141 www.gn.apc.org/safe safe@gn.apc.org *Bringing agricultural, food, environmental and development organisations together for a more sustainable food production system.*

**Scarborough Against Genetic Engineering (SAGE)** c/o 7 Palace Hill, Scarborough, North Yorkshire, YO11 1NL *T* 01723 375533/ 370046 *F* none sage@envoy.dircon.co.uk *SAGE campaigns against the use of genetic engineering in food and farming.*

**SchNEWS** c/o on the fiddle, P.O.Box 2600, Brighton, E. Sussex, BN2 2DX *T* 01273 685913 *F* 01273 685913 http://www.schnews.org.uk/ schnews@brighton.co.uk *The UK's weekly direct action newsletter. Heavily into 'informal networking'.*

**Schumacher Society Bristol Desk** The Create Centre, Smeaton Rd, Bristol, BS1 6XN *T* 0117 903 1081 *F* as phone www.oneworld.org/ schumachersoc schumacher@apc.gn.org *Running lectures, publishing briefings, offering book service all on human scale living & working.*

**Scientists for Global Responsibility (SGR)** P.O. Box 473, Folkestone, CT20 1GS www.sgr.org.uk sgr@gn.apc.org *Research, education and related activities aiming to ensure the responsible use of science and technology.*

**Scottish Human Rights Centre (SHRC)** 146 Holland St, Glasgow, G2 4NG *T* 0141 332 5960 *F* 0141 332 5309 www.shrc.dial.pipex.com shrc@dial.pipex.com *Promotion of human rights through public education & advice, research, scrutiny of legislation & monitoring application of international human rights realities within Scotland.*

**Scottish Opencast Action Group** c/o 42 Woolfords, by West Calder, West Lothian, EH55 8LH *T* 01501 785202 soag.info@virgin.net *A network of people campaigning against inappropriate opencast coal mining in scotland (it's definitely heading north!!).*

**Sea Shepherd Conservation Society U.K (S.S.C.S)** 35 Vicarage Grove, London, SE5 7LY *T* 01303 872570 http:// www.seashepherd.org/ seashepherd@seashepherd.org *Direct action to enforce international laws for marine conservation.*

**Sea Turtle Restoration Project (STRP)** Turtle Island Restoration Network, P.O.Box 400/40 Montezuma Av, Forest Knolls, U.S.A, CA 94933 *T* 415 488 0370 *F* 415 488 0372 www.seaturtles.org seaturtles@igc.org *STRP works to protect sea turtle populations in ways that meet the needs of the turtles & the local communities who share the beaches & waters with these endangered species.*

**Selavip Foundation** S.J. House, 7-1 Kioi-cho, Chiyoda-ku, Tokyo 102-8571, JAPAN *T* (81-3) 3238 5056/3465 8630 e-anzore@hoffman.cc.sophia.ac.jp

**SELFED** P.O. Box 1095, Sheffield, S2 4YR da@directa.force9.co.uk *Empowerment through self education. Reclaiming education from the state and academia. For confidence in ideas, organising, and direct action. Contact for details/samples of recent projects.*

**Sellafield Women's Peace Camp** c/o Cornerstone Resource Centre, 16 Sholebroke Av, Leeds, LS7 3HB *T* 0113 262 1534 cornerstone@gn.apc.org *A camp every 2 months at Sellafield. Call for more info.*

**Sexual Freedom Coalition** P.O.Box 4ZB, London, W1A 4ZB *T* 0171 460 1979 *F* 0171 493 4479 http://www.sfc.org.uk sfc.org.uk *The SFC campaigns against laws restricting consensual adult activity and against the mass media's tawdry, and invasive puerile approach to sex.*

**Shack Dwellers Federation of Namibia/Namibia Housing Action Group (NAHG)** P.O. Box 21010, Windhoek, Namibia *T* (09-264-61) 239398 *F* (09-264-61) 239397 nhag@iafrica.com.na

**Shared Interest Society Limited** 25 Collingwood St, Newcastle upon Tyne, NE1 1JE *T* 0191 233 9110 *F* as phone http:// www.shared-interest.com post@shared-interest.com *Co-operative lending society investing in Third World trade and finance.*

**Shop, The** c/o AEEU Strike Fund, 249 Thorold Rd, Ilford, Essex, IP1 4HE *Set up by workers on the Jubilee Extension, The Shop is a workplace-run union organisation, now 500 strong and "carrying out the activities that unions were originally built for".*

**Shoreham Protesters, The** c/o 7 Stoneham Rd, Hove, Sussex, BN3 5HJ *T* 01273 885750/mobile:07974 201999 *F* as phone www.shoreham-protester.org.uk spaaa@cwcom.net *Animal rights protest group - hunt protest & sabs. Campaign & demonstrate against all animal abuse. We meet every Tues evening 7.30-10 pm at Hove Lagoon Cafe, Kingsway, Hove.*

**Simon Jones Memorial Campaign** P.O.Box 2600, Brighton, BN2 2 DX *T* 01273 685913 *F* as phone www.simonjones.org.uk/ action@simonjones.org.uk *Campaigns for justice for Simon Jones, killed on his first day as a casual worker on a Shoreham dock, and to expose the dangers of casualisation.*

**Single Mothers' Self-Defence (SMSD)** Crossroads Women's Centre, P.O.Box 287, London, NW6 5QU *T* 020 7482 2496 *F* 020 7209 4761 *Single-Mothers Self-Defense is a network of single mothers who got together to defend our benefits, families and communities from government cuts in welfare.*

**Single Mothers' Self-Defense (SMSD)** Box 14, 1 Newton St, Manchester, M1 1HW *T* 0161 344 0758 *As London group.*

**Single Step Co-Op** 78A Penny St, Lancaster, LA1 1XN *T* 01524 63021 *Wholefood Co-Op selling wholefoods etc. Also stock wide range of political literature/magazines.*

**Slough Environmental Education Development Service (SEEDS)** 1st Floor, 29 Church St, Slough, Berkshire, SL1 1PL *T* 01753 693819 *F* as phone *Environmental education and community based environmental projects in Slough & district.*

**Social Anarchism** Atlantic Center For Research and Education, 2743 Maryland Avenue, Baltimore MD 21218, USA, www.nothingness.org/sociala/ *As both political philosphy and personal lifestyle, social anarchism promotes community self reliance, direct participation in political decision-making, respect for nature. Produce magazine.*

**Socialist Party (Headquarters)** 3/13 Hepscott Rd, London, E9 5HU *T* 0181 533 3311 socialistparty.org.uk/index.htm membership@socialistparty.org.uk *An end to the rule of profit, for a socialist society to meet the needs of all. Struggle, solidarity and socialism.*

**Socialist Party - Manchester Branch** c/o Hugh Caffrey, Grosvenor Place, Grosvenor St, Manchester, M1 7HR *T* 0161 933 4707 manc_sfe@hotmail.com *Campaigning for decent pay, for free education, against all the attacks of Government and bosses. For struggle, solidarity, and socialism.*

**Society For the Promotion of Nutritional Therapy** P.O. Box 47, Heathfield, E.Sussex, TN21 8ZX

**Soil Association** Bristol House, 40-56 Victoria St, Bristol, BS1 6BY *T* 0117 929 0661 *F* 0117 925 2504 info@soilassociation.org *Campaigning for organic food and farming and sustainable forestry.*

**Solar Energy Society, The (UK Section of The International Solar Energy Society)** c/o School of Engineering, Oxford Brookes University, Gipsy Lane Campus, Headington, Oxford, OX3 0BP *T* 01865 484367 *F* 01865 484263 uk-ises@brookes.ac.uk

**Solidarity and the Urban Poor Federation (SUPF)/Urban Poor Development Fund** P.O. Box 2242, Phnon Penh, Cambodia *T* (855-23) 720890 *F* as phone updf@forum.org.kh

**South African Homeless People's Federation/People's Dialogue** P.O. Box 34639, Groote Shuur, 73937 Cape Town, South Africa *T* (27-21) 4474 740 *F* (27-21) 4474 741 joelb@dialogue.org.za

**South Wales Activist Network (SWAN)** every Tuesday, 7.30 pm, Ecocentrig, Wood St, nr Cardiff Central station *A support network and direct action group to campaign on most issues based around neo-liberalism (so that's about everything that's bad then).*

**South Yorkshire Genetic Engineering Network** 1-19 Lower Townhead, Dunford Bridge, Sheffield, S36 4TG *T* 01226 762359/ journalist line: 01226 764279 pp3mo@aol.com *Referendum campaign advice line. Anything from the legal aspects involved, through to networking locally, regionally and nationally. We can advise on media, campaign funding etc.*

**Southall Black Sisters** 59 Norwood Rd, Southall, Middlesex, UB2 4DW

**Southall Monitoring Group** 14 Featherstone Rd, Southall, Middx, UB2 5AA *T* 020 8843 2333 www.monitoring-group.co.uk tmg@monitoring-group.co.uk *Anti-racism.*

**Southwark Homeless Information Project (SHIP)** 612 Old Kent Rd, London, SE15 1JB *T* 020 7277 7629 *F* 020 7732 7644 *Advising on rights and tactics in homelessness and helping secure tenancies.*

**Speakout (Homeless Persons Charter For Scotland)** c/o 100 Piccadilly St, Glasgow, G3 8DR *T* 0141 204 1072 *F* 0141 221 7473 www.speakout-scotland.co.uk speakout@uk2.net *A group of homeless and ex-homeless people campaigning in Scotland for a better deal for all homeless people.*

**Spiral Objective** P.O.Box 126, Oaklands Park, South Australia 5046 *T* +618 8276 5076 www.popgun.com.au/spiralobjective spiralob@adelaide.on.net *DIY Music/Record Label/Fanzine Mailorder with emphasis on activist information distribution. We carry books & music from all over the world.*

**Sprawl Busters** 21 Grinnell St, Greenfield, MA 01301 *T* 413 772 6289 www.sprawl-busters.com/ info@sprawl-busters.com *How you can stop superstore sprawl in your hometown.*

**Spunk Library, The** www.spunk.org/ spunk@spunk.org *The Spunk Library collects and distributes literature in electronic format, with an emphasis on anarchism and related issues. Links, archives, and more. Excellent resource.*

**Squall Magazine** P.O.Box 8959, London, N19 5HW www.squall.co.uk/ squall@squall.co.uk *A regularly updated, investigative and accurate UK online magazine covering social justice, environment and culture. Produce A5 monthly hardcopy magazine 'Squall Download': £10 for 12 issues.*

**[Squat!net]** www.squat.net/ squat@squat.net/ *[Squat!net] is an international internet magazine with main focus on squatted houses, car sites and other free spaces.*

**Statewatch** P.O.Box 1516, London, N16 0EW *T* 020 8802 1882 *F* 020 8880 1727 www.statewatch.org/ office@statewatch.org *Statewatch is an independent european network of researchers & activists working on a broad range of civil liberties issues.*

**Stonehenge Campaign** c/o 99 Torriano Av, London, NW5 2RX *T* 07970 378572 www.geocities.com?Soho/9000/scn9909.htm stonehenge@stones.com *Campaign to reinstate the Stonehenge Peoples Free Festival and open access; to protect the Stonehenge environment. Produce magazine containing list of all Free Information Networks (FINs).*

**Stonewall** 16 Clerkenwell Close, London, EC1R 0AA *T* 020 7336 8860 info@stonewall.org.uk

**Stop Huntingdon Animal Cruelty (SHAC)** P.O. Box 381, Cheltenham, Glos, GL50 1UF *T* 0121 632 6460 *F* as phone - call first www.welcome.to/shac info@shac.u-net.com *Campaign to close down Huntingdon Life Sciences, Europe's biggest animal testing laboratory. Send details for a free info pack. Get active!*

**Stop Quintiles' Animal Tests (SQAT)** P.O. Box 27, Kidderminster, Worcs, DY10 3UZ *T* 01562 745778 100302.1616@compuserve.com

**Strike Support Group** Regular Monday meetings 7.30 pm Cock Tavern, Pheonix St., London, NW1 *T* 0171 249 0041 *Practical support for people on strike: picketing, leafleting, organising. Meetings are strictly no paper-selling, no faction talk just action. Publish monthly newsletter Workers of the World UNITE*

**Student Action India** http://www.gn.apc.org/sai

**Student Environment Network (SEN)** c/o Grassroots Office, Manchester University Students Union, Oxford Rd, Manchester, M13 9PR *T* 0161 275 2942 *F* 0161 275 2936 s.e.n@mailexcite.com *SEN aims to an inclusive support/campaigning network for green group societies, environment officers and other green students.*

**Subversion** Dept.10, 1 Newton St, Piccadilly, Manchester, M1 1HW http://www.geocities.com/athens/acropolis/8195 knightrose@geocities.com *Revolutionary communist politics.*

**Subvertise!** c/o Box E, 111 Magdalen Rd, Oxford, OX4 1RQ www.subvertise.org *An archive of 100s of subverts, political art, cartoons and articles.*

**Sunrise Screenprint Workshop** The Old Schoolhouse, Kirkton of Menmuir, by Brechin, Angus, Scotland, DD9 7RN http://www.gn.apc.org/sunrise *We're vegans who print t-shirts inc. lots of animal rights/anarchist/stonehenge designs and print for groups and campaigns using environmentally safe inks.*

**Sunseed Technologia del Desierto/Sunseed Desert Technology** P.O.Box 2000, Cambridge, CB4 3UJ *T* 01273 387731 *F* 0034 950 525 770 www.sunseed.clara.net *Community of volunteers in southern Spain, researching regeneration of lands, solar energy, appropriate technology. Also, sustainable organic living; education about issue of desertification.*

**Surfers Against Sewage** www.sas.org.uk/ *Formed in 1990, one of the fastest growing pressure groups in the country, SAS call for full non-chemical treatment of sewage discharged into our seas.*

**Survival International** 11-15 Emerald St, London, WC1N 3QL *T* 020 7242 1441 *F* 020 7242 1771 www.survival-international.org info@survival-international.org *Survival International is a worldwide organisation supporting tribal peoples. It stands for their right to decide their own future and helps them protect their lives, lands and human rights.*

**Sussex Non-Payment Campaign** susxnonpay@hotmail.com

**Sustain 2020** Tir Gaia, East St, Rhayader, Mid Wales, LD6 5DY *T* 01597 810929 *F* as phone www.sustain2020.co.uk sustain2020@zen.co.uk *Promoting new radical political process of sustainability through Citizen's Income, which removes the need to sell bits of the Earth to each other to earn a living.*

**Sustrans** *T* 0117 929 0888 www.sustrans.org.uk *Sustrans is a civil engineering charity which designs and builds routes for cyclists, walkers, and people with disabilities.*

**Swansea Earth Action (SEA)** Swansea University SU, Singleton Park, Swansea, SA2 8PP http://members.tripod.co.uk.nolorjustus nolor_justus@hotmail.com or SwanEA@hotmail.com *Direct action for radical change stopping environmental destruction; creating the alternatives; broadening our network and existing links; many local campaigns - contact for more info.*

**Tactical Media Crew** c/o Radio Onda Rossa, Via dei Volsci, 56, Roma, Italy, 00185 *T* ++ 39 06 491750 *F* ++ 39 06 4463616 http://www.tmcrew.org/ tactical@tmcrew.org *Tactical Media Crew was born to introduct in the Internet many social realities, starting from what is usually called the radical-Autonomous Movement.*

**Taiga Resue Network (TRN)** Box 116, Jokkmokk, Sweden, S-962 23 *T* +46 971 17039 *F* +46 971 12057 www.snf.se/trn taiga@ajtte.com *Taiga Resue Netwok was established to give the voice to those wanting to see sensitive development in the Boreal region rather than a quick grab for profit.*

**Talamh Housing Co-Op** Birkhill House, nr. Coalburn, Lanarkshire, MZ12 0NJ *T* 01555 820555/820400 *F* 01555 820400 talamh@gn.apc.org *Permaculture/organic garden activist safe haven, involved in local anti-open cast trident ploughshares, rts/free party stuff & anything & everything anti-state.*

**TAPOL, The Indonesia Human Rights Campaign** 111 Northwood Rd, Thornton Rd, Surrey, CR7 8HW *T* 020 8771 2904 *F* 020 8653 0322 www.gn.apc.org/tapol tapol@gn.apc.org *TAPOL campaigns against all categories of human rights violations in Indonesia, West Papua, Aceh and East Timor, providing up to date information and detailed analysis in English. Website links.*

**Thai Community Networks/Urban Community Development Office (UCDO)** 2044/31-33 New Phetchburi Road, Khet Huai Khwang, Bangkok 10320, Thailand *T* (66-2) 716 6000 *F* (66-2) 716 6001 ucdo@mozart.inet.co.th

**Thameside Strike Committee** 29 Booth St, Ashton-under-Lyne, OL6 7LB *T* 0161 308 2452 *Care workers on strike over pay and conditions.*

**The Borders Forest Trust** FREEPOST SCO 2459, Jedburgh, Scotland, TD8 0BR

**Thespionage** 47 Queens Rd, Brighton, BN1 3XB *T* 01273 388079/ mobile: 0411 809438 *F* as phone *Brighton's own agit/prop theatre company puts plays on about social issues, squatting in 'Tatting Down', JSA & undercover cops in 'Grief Encounter', drugs in 'Tick a Teenth'.*

**Think Globally Act Locally** P.O.Box 1TA, Newcastle, NE99 1TA www.newcastle54.freeserve.co.uk/think_index ne991ta@yahoo.com *We are a monthly newsletter that reports and informs campaigns and direct action in North East England.*

**Third Battle of Newbury (3BN)** P.O.Box 5642, Newbury, Berkshire, RG14 5WG *T* 07000 785201 www.gn.apc.org/newbury thirdbattle@hotmail.com *Still meeting on the first Thursday of each month, 3BN continues to campaign on pollution and major infill planning issues.*

**Thr@ll** P.O.Box 22-076, Christchurch, New Zealand/Aotearoa, cybersmog@geocities.com *Anarchist news and views from Aotearoa. The South Island's leading magazine.*

**Tibet Foundation** 100 Bloomsbury Way, London, WC1A 2SH *T* 0171 404 2889 *F* 0171 404 2366 http://www.gn.apc.org/tibetgetza getza@gn.apc.org *A forum for Tibetan culture in the UK.*

**Tineril Prieteni ai Naturii (TPN) - Romanian Young Nature Friends** OP nr 12, CP 986, 1900 Timisoara, Romania *T* +40 (56) 183418 *F* as phone www.banat.ro/tpn/index.htm tpn@banat.ro *Traffic pollution campaigning, practical ecological education, raising public awareness of ecological issues. We are hosting Towards Car Free Cities II (TCFCII)*

**Tinkers Bubble** Little Norton, Stoke-Sub-Hamdon, Somerset, TA14 *T* 01935 881975 *Community small holding. We live in low-impact dwellings and try to earn our livings through sustainable forestry, organic growing, processing, & woodcraft. We invite willing workers - call first.*

**Tools For Solidarity (TFS)** Unit 1B1, Edenberry Industrial Estate, 326 Crumlin Rd, Belfast, BT14 7EE *T* 01232 747473 colle-system@ic24.net *Organisation whilch collects and repairs broken or unwanted handtools for tradespeople in Africa who have the skills but are without the tools to practise their trades.*

**Totnes Genetics Group** *T* 01803 840098 info@togg.freeserve.co.uk

**Tourism Concern** Stapleton House, 277-281 Holloway Rd, London, N7 8HN *T* 020 7753 3330 *F* 020 7753 3331 www.tourismconcern.org.uk tourconcern@gn.apc.org *Tourism Concern is an educational charity promoting awareness of the impact of tourism on people and their environment.*

**Transform** 1 Roselake House, Hudds Vale Rd, St.George, Bristol, BS5 7HY *T* 0117 939 8052/mobile: 07970 174747 *F* 0117 939 8867 www.transform-drugs.org.uk steve@transformuk.freeserve.co.uk *Campaign for effective drug policy - to repeal prohibition & replace with regulated drugs market.*

**Transport 2000** Impact Centre, 12-18 Hoxton St, London, N1 6NG *T* 0171 613 0743 *F* 0171 613 5280 *Campaigns & lobbies for a sustainable transport policy.*

**Traveller Law Research Unit (TLRU)** Cardiff Law School, P.O.Box 427, Cardiff, CF10 3XJ *T* 01222 874580 *F* 01222 874097 http://www.cf.ac.uk/uwcc/claws/tlru/ tlru-l@cf.ac.uk *Research and publication of Traveller-related legal issues; provide referral to UK-wide network of 'Traveller-friendly' legal practitioners and other service providers. Runs a variety of seminars.*

**Travellers' Advice Team (TAT)** The Community Law Partnership, 3rd Floor, Ruskin Chambers, 191 Corporation St, Birmingham, B4 6RP *T* 0121 685 8595/emergency phone: 0468 316755 *F* 0121 236 5121 partnership@communitylaw.freeserve.co.uk *Providing advice (& representation when necessary) to travellers throughout England & Wales on evictions, planning matters, & problems on official sites. Training for groups is possible.*

**Travellers' School Charity** P.O.Box 36, Grantham, NG31 6EW *T* 01558 650621/pager: 01426 218424 *Distributing culture-friendly resources & educational advice to home-educating traveller parents.*

**Tree Council** 51 Catherine Place, London, SW1E 6DY *T* 0171 828 9928 *F* 0171 828 9060 *Promotes the improvement of the environment through the planting and conservation of trees. Free magazine: Tree News.*

**Trees For Life** The Park, Findhorn Bay, Forres, Moray, IV36 3TZ *T* 01309 691292 *F* 01309 691155 www.treesforlife.org.uk trees@findhorn.org *Scottish charity restoring the Caledonian Forest to 600sq. miles of Highland wilderness and advocating the eventual reintroduction of missing wildlife. People can get their hands dirty planting trees!*

**Trident Ploughshares 2000 (TP 2000)** 41-48 Bethel St, Norwich, Norfolk, NR2 1NR *T* 01324 880744 *F* 01436 677529 www.gn.apc.org/tp2000/ tp2000@gn.apc.org *Open, accountable & non-violent disarmament of the British nuclear Trident system.*

**Troops Out Movement (TOM)** P.O.Box 1032, Birmingham, B12 8BZ *T* 0121 643 7542/0961 361518 *F* 0121 643 7681 tomorg@ndirect.co.uk *The TOM has two demands: British withdrawal from Ireland, and self-determination for the Irish people as a whole.*

**Turners' Field Permaculture** Compton Dundon, Somerset, TA11 6PT *T* 01458 442192 *Permaculture introductory weekends, working holidays, camps, student volunteers; structures for sustainable living.*

**Tyneside Action For People & Planet (TAPP)** P.O. Box 1TA, Newcastle upon Tyne, NE99 1TA www.newcastle54.freeserve.co.uk/subvert_menu.htm *Name says it all really!*

**Uncaged** 14 Ridgeway Rd, Sheffield, S12 2SS *T* 0114 253 0020/mobile: 07990 584158/9 *F* 0114 265 4070 www.uncaged.co.uk/uncaged.anti-viv@dial.pipex.com *Dynamic campaign to end all animal experiments on moral and scientific grounds.*

**Undercurrents** 16B Cherwell St, Oxford, OX4 1BG *T* 01865 203662 *F* 01865 243562 www.undercurrents.org underc@gn.apc.org *Producing and distributing grassroot environmental/social justice news (on video). Offers training, lectures (video activism/media). Maintains a radical archive.*

**Unemployed Action Group (UAG)** The Old Mill, 30 Lime St, Newcastle upon Tyne, NE1 2PQ *T* 0191 222 0299 *F* 0191 233 0578 www.seriousforehead.free-online.co.uk neuag@aol.com *Independent unemployed group, self-help for mutual aid, agitate/direct action at home and with the French and overseas unemployed movements.*

**United Systems - The International Party Network** *T* 020 8959 7525 *F* 020 7688 0413 www.united-systems.freetekno.org *Information on events & gatherings in the UK & abroad. Repetitive bleeps & source unknown information teknowlogy flow state hotline: 020 8959 7525.*

**UpStart Services** Court Ash, Yeovil, Somerset, BA20 1HG *T* 0870 733 2538 *F* 01935 431222 www.gn.apc.org/ss/upstart upstart@co-op.org *UpStart provides accountancy and training services for new & existing co-ops & community enterprises. We have a wide range of free briefings on co-op issues.*

**URBAN 75** 352 Southwyk House, Moorlands Estate, Brixton, London, SW9 8TT www.urban75.com/ info@urban75.com *One the UK's busiest independent websites with the latest underground eco-protest news, rave reports, drug information, legal rights, direct action, reclaim the streets, photos, football etc.*

**Urban Ecology Australia (UEA)** Centre for Urban Ecology, 84 Halifax St, Adelaide, Tandanya Bioregion, South Australia, 5000 *T* +61 8 8232 4866 *F* as phone www.urbanecology.org.au urbanec@metropolis.net.au *A United Nations accredited non profit community group committed to the evolution of ecologically sustaining human settlements - ecocities - through education and example.*

**Urban Regeneration and Greenfield Environment Network (URGENT!)** Box HN, 16B Cherwell St, Oxford, OX4 1BG *T* 01865 794800 www.urgent.org.uk/ info@urgent.org.uk *Information/skill sharing network for campaigners wanting sane, sustainable housing policies not unaffordable new houses on greenfield sites. Donations: "Urgent".*

**VAN UK National Vaccination Centre** 178 Mansfield Rd, Nottingham, NG1 3HW *T* 0115 948 0829 *F* 0115 950 3858 www.van.org.uk enquiries@van.org.uk *VAN UK provides unbiased information on all childhood and adult vaccines to enable you to make an informed decision.*

**Vegan Organic Network (VON)** Anandavan, 58 High Lane, Chorlton, Manchester, M21 9DZ *T* 0161 860 4869 *F* as phone - call first veganorganic@supanet.com *Promotion of vegan organic/stockfree horticulture & agriculture// advice//courses//placements voluntary &. Paid. Join us & help make the vegan revolution! Grow it//sow it & if GM then mow it!*

**Vegan Prisoners Support Group (VPSG)** P.O.Box 194, Enfield, EN1 3HD *T* 020 8292 8325 *F* as phone hvpc@vpsg.freeserve.co.uk *Helps vegan prisoners of conscience with diet, toiletries, footwear, nutritional information whilst being detained in prison, or held in police stations.*

**Vegan Society, The** Donald Watson House, 7 Battle Rd, St. Leonards On Sea, E. Sussex, TN37 7AA *T* 01424 427393 *F* 01424 717064 http://www.vegansociety.com info@vegansociety.com *Educational charity promoting ways of living whicg avoid the use of animal products - for the benefit of people, animals and the environment.*

**Vegan Village** *T* 0113 293 9385 www.veganvillage.co.uk postie@veganvillage.co.uk *A website listing vegan organisations in the UK, with a noticeboard, newstand and links to hundreds of vegan websites.*

**Veganarchy** http://veganarchy.freeserve.co.uk *Against the exploitation of people, animals and the environment.*

**Vegetarian Society, The** Parkdale, Dunham Rd, Altringham, Cheshire, WA14 4QG *T* 0161 928 0793 *F* 0161 926 9182 www.vegsoc.org info@vegsoc.org *The Society works to promote a vegetarian diet in order to reduce animal suffering, benefit human health and safeguard the environment.*

**Vegfam** "The Sanctuary", nr. Lydford, Okehampton, Devon, EX20 4AL *T* 01822 820203 *F* as phone call first www.veganvillage.co.uk/vegfam vegfam@veganvillage.co.uk *Feeds the hungry WITHOUT*

*exploiting animals. The world cannot feed humans AND their food animals WITHOUT RUINING THE ENVIRONMENT. Vegan based projects for over 30 years.*

**Veggies Catering Camapign** 180 Mansfield Rd, Nottingham, NG1 3HW *T* 0115 958 5666 *F* phone first www.veggies.org.uk info@veggies.org.uk *Providing catering for demos, green events and any other occasion, using no animal ingredients whatsoever, and giving support to the animal rights (and other) campaign movements.*

**Video Activist Journalist Survival Kit** www.gifford.co.uk/l-contact *Support/information network for those using video for positive change.*

**Viva!** 12 Queen Square, Brighton, E.Sussex, BN13 3FD *T* 01273 777688 *F* 01273 776755 www.viva.org.uk/ info@viva.org.uk *A national campaigning vegan/vegetarian animal charity dedicated to saving animals. Regularly launch hard-hitting campaigns. Loads of info on going vegetarian or vegan, plus free campaign materials.*

**Voice of Irish Concern for the Environment** 14 Upper Pembroke St, Dublin 2, Ireland *T* +353 1 661 8123 *F* +353 1 661 8114 www.voice.buz.org avoice@iol.ie *VOICE is a grassroots organisation campaigning for clean and fluoride-free water, sustainable resource use, bio-diverse Irish forestry, an end to global biopatents and a ban on GE crops.*

**Voices in the Wilderness UK** 16b Cherwell St, Oxford, OX4 1BG *T* 01865 243232 www.nonviolence.org/vitw voices@viwuk.freeserve.co.uk *Voices breaks the economic sanctions on Iraq by taking medical supplies to Iraqi children without applying for export licences.*

**Wages Due Lesbians** P.O.Box 287, London, NW6 5QU *T* 0171 482 2496 *F* 0171 209 4761 *Multi-racial network campaigning for social, economic, civil & legal rights for lesbian women & against all forms of discrimination.*

**Wages For Housework Campaign** P.O.Box 287, London, NW6 5QU

**Water Meadows Defence Campaign, Bury St Edmonds** c/o Windrush, Ashfield Rd, Elmswell, Bury St Edmunds, Suffolk, IP30 9HJ *T* 01359 240365 *F* as phone (sometimes) www.bradgate.u-net.com/ johnmatth@hotmail.com *Defence of the water meadows around Bury St Edmunds from road building and other development threats. The outlook is grim.*

**Water Pressure Group, The** P.O. Box 10046, Dominion Rd, Auckland, New Zealand *T* 0064 09 828 4517/mobile: 025 2666 552 *F* as phone www.water-pressure-group.org.nz/ jimg@pl.net *To bring down the council-owned company running water services here. Our turn-on squads reconnect, in some cases we have re-excavated, replaced the pipework, and buried the lot in concrete.*

**Web Directory** www.webdirectory.com *"Earth's biggest environmental search engine" - say no more!*

**West Australian Forest Alliance** 2 Delhi St, West Perth 6005, Australia *T* 61 8 9420 7265 *F* 618 9420 7273 www.wafa.org.au/ *The campaign to save Western Australia's ancient south west forests continues to gather momentum.*

**West London Anarchists & Radicals (WAR)** c/o BM Makhno, London, WC1N 3XX war1921@altavista.com *Local class struggle anarchist/communist group. We are always interested in making contact with people who live/work in West London. Bi-monthly newsletter.*

**What Doctors Don't Tell You (WDDTY)** 4 Wallace Rd, London, N1 2PG *T* 020 7354 4592 *F* 020 7354 8907 www.wddty.co.uk wddty@zoo.co.uk *Provides a critical view of modern and orthodox medicine.*

**White Dot** P.O.Box 2116, Hove, East Sussex, BN3 3LR www.whitedot.org/ info@whitedot.org *Campaign against television, fake friends, fake living and the gradual domestication of the human species. Run International TV Turnoff Week in Britain, 22-28 April.*

**William Morris Society** Kelmscott House, 26 Upper Mall, Hammersmith, London, W6 9TA *T* 020 8741 3735 www.ccny.cuny.edu/wmorris/morris.html wmsoc@compuserve.com *Exists to spread knowledge and encourage appreciation of the life, work and ideas of William Morris. Regular events. Newsletter (4 p.a); Journal (2 p.a); occasional other publications.*

**Willing Workers On Organic farms (WWOOF)** P.O.Box 2675, Lewes, E.Sussex, BN7 1RB *T* 01273 476286 *F* as phone www.phdcc.com/wwoof fran@wwoof-uk.freeserve.co.uk *Involvement and access to organic growing, like minded people worldwide.*

*Hard work in exchange for b&b. Opportunities with vast variety of host organic farms & holdings.*

**Wind Fund, The** Brunel House, 11 The Promenade, Clifton, Bristol, BS8 3NN *T* 0117 973 9339 *F* 0117 973 9303 mail@windfund.co.uk *Investment fund for renewable energy sources.*

**WinVisible: Women with Visible and Invisible Disabilities** Crossroads Women's Centre, 230A Kentish Town Rd, London, NW5 2AB *T* 020 7482 2496 *F* 020 7209 4761 crossroadswomenscentre@compuserve.com *Multi-racial self-help network of women with visible and invisible disabilities from different backgrounds and situations. Support, information, campaigning. Publications and speakers available.*

**Wolfe Tone Society (WTS)** BM Box 6191, London, WC1N 3XX *T* 020 8442 8778/mobile: 07956 919871 *F* as phone wts@brosna.demon.co.uk *This is the organisation which supports the Irish Republican movement (Sinn Fein) in England.*

**Wolfs Head Press** P.O.Box 77, Sunderland, SR1 1EB *Autotelic activities among the flotsam and jetsam of the universe. And other stuff. Oysters are ambisexual, starting life as male, and changing back and forth several times.*

**Woman and Earth Global Eco-Network (WE)** 467 Central Park West, Suite 7F, New York, New York, USA, 10025 *T* +1 212 866 8130 *F* as phone www.dorsai.org/~womearth Tatyana V. Mamanova <womearth@dorsai.org *Publish almanac in English & Russian; produce eco/women videos; annual world conference, film festival, expo; web site; international & girls chapters; lectures.*

**Woman and Earth UK** c/o Elinor Burdett *T* 0113 216 7819 *F* as phone *UK chapter of Woman and Earth Global Eco-Network.*

**Women Against Rape (WAR)** Crossroads Women's Centre, 230A Kentish Town Rd, London, Nw5 2AB *T* 0171 482 2496 *F* 0171 209 4761 crossroadswomenscentre@compuserve.com *Support, legal advice, information, campaigning.*

**Women In Black, London** c/o The Maypole Fund, P.O.Box 14072, London, N16 5WB *T* 0171 482 5670 *F* as phone www.chorley2.demon.co.uk/wib.html jane@gn.apc.org *Women In Black is a loose network of women worldwide committed to peace with justice and actively opposed to war and violence.*

**Women in Prison** 22 Highbury Grove, London, N5 2EA *T* 020 7226 5879 *Support group for women in prison.*

**Women's Bank** 151/13, E-Zone, Seevali Pura, Borella, Colombo 8, Sri Lanka *T* (94-1) 681355 womensbank@lankanet.jca.apc.org

**Women's Development Bank Federation** No.30 Kandy Road, Galtotmulla, Yakkala, Sri Lanka *T* (94-33) 27962/27396 janawomented@lanka.ccom.lk

**Womens Environmental Network (W.E.N)** 87 Worship St, London, EC2A 2BE *T* 0171 247 3327 *F* 0171 247 4740 www.gn.apc.org/wen wenuk@gn.apc.org *WEN is a membership organisation which researches and campaigns on environmental issues, informing & empowering women to implement change. Men can join too!*

**WoMenwith Womyn's Peace Camp** Kettlesing Head Layby, nr. Harrogate, N.Yorks, HG3 2RA

**Woodland Trust, The** Autumn Park, Grantham, Linc, NG31 6LL

**Word Power Bookshop** 43 West Nicholson St, Edinburgh, EH8 9DB *T* 0131 662 9112 *F* as phone *Radical bookshop - Scotland's only! Organise Edinburgh Radical Book fair in May each year - publishers' stalls, speakers, etc.*

**Workers Solidarity Movement** P.O.Box 1528, Dublin 8 *Anarchist organisation fighting for a 32-county Workers' Republic. Produces pamphlets.*

**Workers' Aid for Kosova/Workers' Aid For Bosnia** Flat 301, 41 Old Birley St, Hulme, Manchester, M15 5RF *T* 0161 226 0404/226 0908/0708 521715 *F* 0161 226 0404/226 0422 www.redbricks.org.uk/ workersaid workersaid@redbricks.org.uk *Convoys of aid and solidarity to pro-democracy groups and Unions. Set up your own local group and get on the road!*

**Workshop For All Beings** P.O. Box 40, 43-304 Bielsko-Biala 4, Poland *T* ++48 33 81 83 153 *F* as phone www.sll.fi.TRN/ network.allbeings/index.html wapienica@pnrwi.most.org.pl *What we do: * Public campaigns to promote different forms of nature protection * Traditional rituals and ceremonies * Publications * Collaborations with communities, parks, and any others.*

**World Animal Net** 24 Barleyfields, Didcot, Oxon, OX11 0BJ *T* 01235 210775 www.worldanimal.net/ worldanimalnet@yahoo.com *The world's largest network of animal protection societies with over 1500 affiliates in more than 80 countries campaigning to improve the*

status and welfare of animals.

**World Development Movement (WDM)** 25 Beehive Place, London, SW9 7QR *T* 020 7737 6215 *F* 020 7274 8232 www.wdm.org.uk wdm@wdm.org.uk *WDM is a membership organisation, campaigning to expose and change the political causes of global poverty.*

**World Information Service on Energy International** P.O.Box 59636, 1040 LC Amsterdam, The Netherlands *T* 31 20 612 6368 *F* 31 20 689 2179 http://antenna.nl/~wise wiseamster@antenna.ul *Campaigning and networking against nuclear energy, 20 years old networking experience. 11 relays around the world. Publish the WISE News Communique (20 issues a year).*

**World Socialist Web Site** www.wsws.org/ *Contacts and info from around the world.*

**Worthing Anarchist Teapot** c/o P.O.Box 4144, Worthing, W. Sussex, BN14 7NZ www.worthing.eco-action.org/teapot/ teapot@worthing.eco-action.org *Provides free tea and coffee, plus anarchist and radical info, from squats and town centre stalls. Monthly events first Tuesday of every month, 7.30 pm, 42 Marine Parade, Worthing (above Paiges bar).*

**Worthing Eco-Action** P.O. Box 4144, Worthing, www.eco-action.org/ *Worthing eco-action.org is a local domain providing free web-hosting service to community groups involved in environmental campaigning and direct action.*

**Wowarea** www.wowarea.com/ *Wowarea is a free 'reference point for all people on the internet. About our services: the first one is a sort of search engine. The second one is a very comprehensive internet guide.*

**y ddeilen werdd** www.ddeilenwerdd.free-online.co.uk/ *Radical green and Welsh internet newsletter.*

**YearZero (YZ)** P.O. Box 26276, London, W3 7GQ http://freespeech.com/yearzero yearzero@flashmail.com *The quality print mag for the disaffected.*

**Yorkleaf (York's Local Environmental Action forum)** S.U., Goodricke, York University, Heslington, York, YO10 5DD www.users-york.ac.uk/~socs203/ socs203@york.ac.uk *Dedicated to awareness raising regarding a wide array of environmental issues. Contact us for further details about Neo-Luddism!*

**Youth & Student Campaign for Nuclear Disarmament (Y&SCND)** 162 Holloway Rd, London, N7 8DQ *T* 0171 607 3616/ pager: 07666 833117 *F* 0171 700 2357 youth_cnd@hotmail.com *Campaigning to trash Trident through actions, demonstrations, awareness raising & letter writing. New volunteers are welcome. We love getting anti-nuke articles for the mag.*

**Youth Against Racism in Europe (YRE)** P.O.Box 858, London, E7 5HU *T* 0181 533 4533 *F* 0181 985 2932 *Campaigning against racism, fascism & prejudice in all their forms, across Europe. Also provide anti-racist educational material & speakers.*

**Zeme Predevsim! (Earth First! Prague)** P.O.Box 237, 16041 Praha 6, Czech Republic, www.ecn.cz/zemepredevsim zemepredevsim.ecn.cz *Radical ecology, anti globalisation campaign, RTS activity, anti nazi activity, information, propaganda, network of Czech activists.*

**Zimbabwe Homeless People's Federation/Dialogue On Shelter** P.O. Box CH 934, Chisipite, Harare, Zimbabwe *T* (263-4) 704027 *F* (263-4) 704123 bethc@omnizim.co.zw

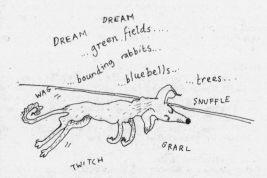

# Contacts Directory By Categories

For full descriptions and addresses etc see the individual entries in the alphabetical list. Many organisations etc appear in more than one category, use yer imagination as to why that's the case! The order of the categories is as follows:

Anarchy/Class Struggle;
Animal Rights/Hunt Saboteurs;
Music/Parties/Festvals/Theatre/Culture;
Drugs;
Direct Action;
Education;
Environment/Pollution/Quarrying/Opencast;
Alternative Energy;
Parenting;
Food/Vegan and Veggie;
Genetics;
Health;
Homeless/Housing/Co-ops;
Indigenous Peoples/Travellers/Solidarity Campaigns;
Networking Support/Information Networking;
Infoshops/Radical Bookshops/Cafes;
Media/Distribution/Film and Video;
Justice and the Law/Solicitors/Prison and Prisoners;
Land Rights/Gardening/Organics/Trees;
Peace/Anti-Nuclear/Arms and Military;
Social Change;
Anti-Capitalism;
Anti-Racism;
Benefits and JSA;
Economics;
Industrial Action and Workers' Rights;
Transport/Alternatives;
Women

## Anarchy/Class Struggle

5th May Group; A-Infos; Active Distribution; Agitator, The; Ahimsa; AK Distribution; Alpha; Anarchist Federation (AF); Anarchist Graphics; Anarchist Teapot Mobile Kitchen, The; Anarchist Trade Union Network; Anarcho-Syndicalism 101; Aufheben; Big Issue, The; Black Flag; Brighton Against Benefit Cuts; Bristol Class War; D.S.4.A; Do or Die; Earth First!; Earth First! Journal; Earth First! Action Update; Eat The State!; Federation Anarchiste Francophone; Freedom Bookshop; Freedom Press; Friends, Families and Travellers; Green Anarchist; Haringey Solidarity Group (HSG); Kate Sharpley Library; Lancaster Anarchist Group; Land and Liberty; London Class War; Maloko Anarcho Collective; Monkey Pirates! Multimedia; Morgenmuffel; Movement Against the Monarchy (MA'M); no.problem.distribution; North/East London Solidarity Federation International; Plain Wordz; Portsmouth Anarchist Network; Reclaim the Streets; Red South West; SchNEWS; Social Anarchism; Squall; Land Is Ours, The; Shop, The; Spunk Library, The; Thespionage; Thr@ll Unemployed Action Group; Veganarchy; West London Anarchists & Radicals; Workers Solidarity Movement; Worthing Anarchist Teapot

## Animal Rights/Hunt Saboteurs

Animal Contacts Directory; Animal Defenders; Animal Liberation Front Press Office; Animal Rights Calendar; Animal Contacts Directory; ARCNEWS; Bite Back; British Anti-Vivisection Association; British Union for the Abolition of Vivisection; Campaign Against Live Exports; Campaign for the Abolition of Angling; Coalition to Abolish the Fur Trade (CAFT UK); Envirolink; Farming and Livestock Concern; Green Events; Hunt Saboteurs Association (H.S.A.); Justice and Freedom for Animals; London Animal Action (LAA); London Greenpeace/McLibel Support Campaign; National Anti-Hunt Campaign; National Federation of Badger Groups; North Devon Animal Defence; SchNEWS; Shoreham Protesters, The; Squall; Stop Huntingdon Animal Cruelty (SHAC); Vegetarian Society, The; Uncaged; Viva!; World Animal Net

## Music/Parties/Festivals/Theatre/Culture

Association of Cultural and Artistic Production (KAPA); Brighton ART; Chumbawamba; Club Resistance; Cobalt Magazine; Common Ground; Continental Drifts; Diversitea; Earth Circus Network; Ecotrip; Exodus; Flannel; Football Fans Against the CJA; Green Futures; Groovy Movie Picture House, The; Head Mix Collective; Headspace; Innerfield; Kartoon Kate/Orange Dog Productions; Levellers; Maloka Anarcho Collective; Millimations Animation Workshop; Mobile Alternative Disco; Network 23 = Manchester Division; no.problem.distribution; Paganlink Network; Platform; Polyp; Raise Your Banners; Rising Sun Arts Centre; SchNEWS; Socialist Party; Spiral Objective; Squall; Stonehenge Campaign; Subvertising; Sunrise Screenprint Workshop; ELECTRIC GALLERY, THE: Amazon Project; Rural Media Company, The; Thespionage; Tiocfaidh Ar La; United Systems; URBAN 75

## Drugs
Campaign to Legalise Cannabis International; Cannabis in Avlon; Ecstacy; Freedom Book Company; Green Party Drugs Group; Legalise Cannabis Alliance; Release; Transform

## Direct Action
Action South West; Active-Sydney; Animal; Action For Social Ecology; 5th May Group; Agitator, The; Anti-Fascist Action; Anti-Nazi League; Australian Earth First! Action Update; Autonomous Centre of Edinburgh; Autonomous Green Action; Bay Area Action's Headwaters Forest Project; Black Environment Network; Brambles; Bristle; Broughton Spurtle; Campaign Against Arms Trade (CAAT); Campaign Against Live Exports; Campaign Against Tube Privatisation; Campaign for Free Education; Campaign for the Accountability of American Bases; Coalition to Abolish the Fur Trade; Crystal Palace Campaign; DAAA Collective (Direct Action Against Apathy); Digital Resistance; Direct Action; Direct Action Media Network (DAMN); Do or Die; Earth First!; Earth First! Action Update; Earth First! Journal; Ecodefense!; Free Tibet Campaign; Freedom To Be Yourself, The; Godhaven Ink; Genetic Engineering Network (GEN); Grampian Against GM; Green Action; Green Anarchist; Green Pepper; Groen Front! (Earth First! Netherlands); Haringey Solidarity Group (HSG); Hunt Saboteurs Association; Irish Network for Nonviolent Action Training and education (INNATE); Kebele Kulture Projekt; Kent Socialist Alliance; Leicester Radical Alliance; London Animal Action (LAA); London Greenpeace/ McLibel Support Campaign; Maloka Anarcho Colective; Mobile Office, The; National Anti-Hunt Campaign; Nighttime Gardener's Guide; No Alignment Action Group; No Opencast; Non-Violent Resistance Network; Protest.Net; Rainbow Centre; Rainbow Keepers; Rational Trust, The; Reading Roadbusters; Redwood Coast Watersheds Alliance; SchNEWS/Justice?; Scottish Opencast Action Group; Sea Shepherd Conservation Society UK; Shoreham Protesters, The; Simon Jones Memorial Campaign; South Wales Activist Network; South Yorkshire Genetic Engineering Network; Sprawl Busters; Squall; Stop Huntongdon Animal Cruelty (SHAC); Strike Support Group; Student Action India; Surfers Against Sewage; Swansea Earth Action; Taiga Rescue Network; Talamh Housing Co-op; Think Globally Act Locally; Third Battle of Newbury; Tineril Prieteni ai Naturii; Tools For Solidarity; Totnes Genetics Group; Trees For Life; Trident Ploughshares 2000; Tyneside Action For People & Planet; Unemployed Action Group; URBAN 75; Water Pressure Group, The; Western Australia Forest Alliance; Women Against Rape; Women in Black; Womens Environmental Network (WEN); World Development Movement; Worthing Anarchist Teapot; Worthing Eco-Action; Zeme Predevsim!

## Education
Adbusters; Campaign for Free Education; Centre for Human Ecology; Centre for World Indigenous Studies; Choice in Education; Education for Sustainable Communities; Education Otherwise; Education Workers' Network; Holistic Education Foundation Co. Ltd, The; Home Education Reading Opportunities (H.E.R.O. Books); Human Scale Education; NLP & DHE; SchNEWS; Scientists for Global Responsibilty; SELFED; Squall; Sunseed Desert Technology; Tineril Prieteni ai Naturii; Traveller' School Charity; Urban Ecology Australia; White Dot

## Environment/Pollution/Quarrying/Opencast
A27 Action Group; Action For Social Ecology; Agroforestry Research Forestry; Amazon Alliance; Animal Contacts Directory; Animal Defenders; Autonomous Green Action; Bay Area Action Headwaters Forest Project; Black Environment Network; Blatant Incitement Project (BLINC); Blue; Borders Forest Trust, The; Brighton & Hove Green Party; Brighton Peace & Environment Centre; British Trust for Conservation Volunteers; Carbon Storage Trust, The; Climate Action Network UK; Climate Action NOW!; Clun Valley Alder Charcoal; Communities Against Toxics (CATS); Communities Appeal for Respect for the Environment (CARE); Cool Temperate; Corner House, The; Corporate Watch; Council for the Protection of Rural England (CPRE); CREATE (Community Recycling, Environmental Action, Training & Education); Crystal Palace Campaign; Do or Die; Dragon Environmental Network; Earth First! Action Update; Earth First! Journal; Earth Liberation Prisoners; Earthwise Environmental Consultants Ltd; Ecologist, The; Ecodefense!; Ecoseeds/Eco Co-op; Ecotrip; Envirolink; Environmental Law Foundation; Equi-Phallic Alliance and Field Poetry Club, The; Forest Steward-ship Council; Friends of the Earth (FOE); Friends of the Earth (Scotland); Gardens of Gaia, The; Global Partnership; Gnostic Garden; Going For Green; Green Adventure; Green Books; Green Events; Green Futures; Green Guide Publishing Ltd; Greenpeace; Green Pepper; GreenNet; Groundwork: Action for the Environment; Hemp Food Industries Association; Hundredth Monkey, The; International Institute for Environment and Development; Land Stewardship Trust; Light Information and Healing Trust, The; London 21 Sustainability Network; Low Impact; Low Level Radiation Campaign; Manchester Environmental Resource Centre initiative (MERCi); Mobile Office, The; Multimap.Com; National Society for Clean Air & Environmental Protection; New Economics Foundation; No Alignment Action Group; No Opencast; Oil Companies; Open Spaces Society; PaRTiZans; Pedestrians Association, The; People & Planet; Pesticides Trust, The; Platform; Positive News; Project Underground; R.E.C.Y.C. Ltd, Rainbow Keepers; Rational Trust, The; Re-Cycle; Reading Roadbusters; Reclaim the Streets; Reforesting Scotland; Resurgence; Rising Tide; River Ocean Research & Education (RORE); Royal Town Planning Institute; Rural Advancement Foundation International (RAFI); SchNEWS; Scottish Opencast Action Group; Sea Shepherd Conservation Society; Sea Turtle Restoration Project; Slough Environmental Education Development Service; Squall; Student Environment Network; Sunseed Desert Technology; Surfers Against Sewage; Swansea Earth Action; Taiga Rescue Network; Dyfi Eco-Valley Partnership, The; Environmental Team, The; Natty Trust, The; Safe Alliance, The; Woodland Trust, The; Third Battle of Newbury; Tourism Concern; Tree Council; Trees For Life; Urban Ecology Australia; Vegfam; Voice of Environmental Concern for the Environment; Water Meadows Defence Campaign; Web Directory; West Australian Forest Alliance; Womens Environment Network (WEN); Workshop For All Beings; Worthing Eco-Action; y ddeilen werdd; Yorkleaf; Zeme Predevsim!

## Alternative Energy
Alt-Tech; Alt-Tech Leeds; Centre for Alternative Technology (C.A.T.) & Alternative Technology Association (A.T.A.); Groovy Movie Picture House; Home Power magazine; Institute for Social Inventions; Renewable Energy in the Urban Environment; Resurgence; Solar Energy Society, The; Wind Fund, The

## Parenting (see also: Education)
Baby Milk Action; Campaign Against the Child Support Act; Children's Participation Project, The; Informed Parent, The; Outlook Children's Project; Real Nappy Association; SchNEWS; Single Mothers' Self-Defence; Squall; VAN UK National Vaccination Centre

## Food/Vegan and Veggie
Anarchist Teapot Mobile Kitchen, The; Baby Milk Action; Banana Link; Consumers For Health Choice; Federation Collective Rampenplan; Food Not Bombs; Fruitarian/Raw Food Centre of London, The (100% Vegan); Gay Veggies & Vegans; Gloupgloup; Hemp Food Industries Association; Henry Doubleday Research Association; Land and Liberty; Maloka Anarcho Collective; Naturewise; Primal Seeds; Rural Advancement Foundation International (RAFI); SchNEWS; Single Step Co-op; Squall; Safe Alliance, The; Vegetarian Society, The; Vegan Organic Network; Vegan Prisoners Support Group; Vegan Society, The; Vegan Village; Veganarchy; Vegfam; Veggies Catering Campaign; Viva!

## Genetics
Anti-Genetix Network; Biotech Hobbyist Magazine; Corporate Watch; Earth First! Action Update; Genethics News; Genetic Engineering Network (GEN); Genetic Food Alert; Genetix Snowball; Get Informed; Glasgow Vegan Network; GM-Free Prisoner Support; Greenpeace; Nighttime Gardener's Guide; Rural Advancement Foundation International; Scarborough Against Genetic Engineering; SchNEWS; South Yorkshire Genetic Engineering Network; Squall; Totnes Genetics Group; Vegan Organic Network

## Health
Baby Milk Action; Communities Against Toxics (CATS); Consumers for Health Choice; Ecologist, The; Gnostic Garden; Health Action Networ/Vaccination Info; Holistic Education Foundation Co. Ltd; Informed parent, The; Medical Marijuana Foundation; National Campaign Against CS Spray; 'Mushroom Cultivator, The'; Proof!; SchNEWS; Squall; VAN UK National Vaccination Centre; Voices in the Wilderness UK; What Doctors Don't Tell You

## Homeless/Housing/Co-ops
Advisory Service for Squatters (A.S.S); Arkangel Magazine; Asian Coalition for Housing Rights; Brambles; Buckminster Fuller Institute; Catalyst Collective; Chapter Seven; Cornerstone Housing Co-op; Defend

Council Housing; Diggers & Dreamers Publications; Ecovillage Network UK; Empty Homes Agency; Exodus; Grounswell; Haggerston Tenants Association; Homeless Information Project; Homeless International; Independent Parks Advisory Service; Mahila Milan/National Slum Dwellers Federation; Misereor; National Homeless Alliance; Orangi Pilot Project; Philippines Homeless People's Federation; Pilotlight; Poor People's Economic Human Rights Campaign, The; Radical Routes; SchNEWS; Selavip Foundation; Shack Dwellers Federation of Namibia; Solidarity and the Urban Poor Federation; Southwark Homeless Information Project; Speakout (Homeless Persons Charter for Scotland); Squall; [Squat!Net]; Talamh Housing Co-op; Thai Community Networks; Big Issue, The; Natty Trust, The; Tinkers Bubble; UpStart Services; Urban Ecology Australia; Urban Regeneration and Greenfield Environment Network (URGENT!); Zimbabwe Homeless People's Federation

**Indigenous Peoples/Travellers/Solidarity Campaigns**
5th May Group; Amazon Alliance; Black Mesa Indigenous Support; Bougainville Freedom Movement; Brighton Against Benefit Cuts; Burma Action Group; Burma Campaign UK, The; Centre For World Indigenous Studies; Chiapas Link; Collective Against the North American Invasion of Colombia; Connolly Association; Cymdeithas Yr Iaith Gymraeg – The Welsh Language Society; Cymru Goch – Welsh Socialists; DARK NIGHT Field Notes; DELTA; Do or Die; Earth First! Action Update; Ejercito Zapatista Liberacion Nacional; Free Tibet Campaign; Friends of the Garvaghy Rd (London); Gypsy Council, The; Haiti Support Group; Kurdish Human Rights Project; Kurdistan Information Centre; Minority Rights Group International; Native American Resource Centre; Native Americas Journal; New Futures Association; On the Right Track; SchNEWS; Squall; Statewatch; Survival International; TAPOL, The Indonesia Human Rights Campaign; ELECTRIC GALLERY: Amazon Project; Rwanda UK Goodwill Organisation, The; Tibet foundation; Tools For Solidarity; Tourism Concern; Traveller Law Research Unit; Travellers' Advice Team; Travellers' School Charity; Troops Out Movement; Voices in the Wilderness UK; Wolfe Tone Society; Workers Solidarity Movement; Workers' Aid For Kosova/Workers' Aid for Bosnia

**Networking Support/Information Networking**
A-Infos; Action South West; Active-Sydney; Ahimsa; An Phoblacht (Republican News); Anarchist Teapot Mobile Kitchen, The; Anarchist Trade Union Network; Animal Liberation Front Press Office; Animal Rights Calendar; ARCNEWS; Arkangel Magazine; Association of Hedgewitches; Australian Earth First! Update; Big Brother Survival Kit; Building Worker; Blatant Incitement Project (BLINC); Blue; Bristol Class War; Bristle; Broughton Spurtle; Corner House, The; Corporate Watch; DAAA Collective; Direct Action Media Network (DAMN); Do or Die; Earth First! Action Update; Earth First! Journal; Eat The State!; Exeter Left; Fight Racism! Fight Imperialism!; Freedom Network; Friends, Families and Travellers; Frontline Books; Green Action; Green Anarchist; Green Events; Green Pepper; 'Guardian Media Guide, The'; Hiddinkulturz; IndyMedia; IndyMedia UK; Infoshops Network; INK – Independent News Collective; ISIP (International Exhibition of Publications); Kent Socialist Alliance; Kernow FIN; KK/Collectives; Kurdistan Information Centre; LeftDirect; Leicester Radical Alliance; Letslink UK; London Class War; Manchester Environmental Resource initiative (MERCi); Microzine; Networking Newsletter Project; Nonviolent Action; Oneworld; Peace News; Peoples' Global Action (PGA); Porkbolter, The; Positive News; Protest.Net; Rainbow Centre; Red South West; SchNEWS; South Wales Activist Network; Squall; Stonehenge Campaign; Strike Support Group; Student Environment Network; Swansea Earth Action; 1990 Trust, The; Agitator, The; Spunk Library, The; Think Globally Act Locally; Thr@ll; Undercurrents; United Systems; URBAN 75; Vegan Village; Veganarchy; Web Directory; What Doctors Don't Tell You; Woman and Earth Global Eco-Network; Workshop For All Beings; World Animal Net; World Information Service on Energy International; World Socialist Web Site; Worthing Anarchist Teapot, Worthing Eco-Action; y ddeilen werdd; Year Zero; Zeme Predevsim!

**Infoshops/Radical Bookshops/Cafes**
1 in 12 Club; 56a Infoshop; Anarchist Teapot Mobile Kitchen, The; Ark Environment Centre, The; Autonomous Centre of Edinburgh, Avalon; Barricade Library Publishing Collective, The; Blackcurrent Bookshop; Brighton Peace & Environment Centre; Citizen Smith; Compendium Bookshop; Counter Information Agency (CIA); Diversitea; Fair Trade Cafe; Freedom Bookshop; Frontline Books; Green Leaf Bookshop; Housmans Bookshop; Hundredth Monkey, The; Infoshops Network; Kebele Kulture Projekt; KUD Anarhiv; Librairie Freecyb; Library of Free Thought (LOFT); Little Thorn Books; Maloka Anarcho Collective; Manchester Environmental Resource Centre initiative

(MERCi); News From Nowhere Bookshop; Rainbow Centre; Reading International Solidarity Centre (RISC); Revolution Centre; Rising Sun Arts Centre; Single Step Co-op; Veggies Catering Campaign; Word Power Bookshop; Worthing Anarchist Teapot.
If any infoshops/radical bookshops/cafes want to be sent x9 SchNEWS every week, drop us a line.

**Media/Distribution/Film and Video**
Active Distribution; Adbusters; AK Distribution; Anarchist Graphics; Autonomedia; Avalon; Backspace; Barricade Library Publishing Collective, The; Black Shorts; Campaign Against Cemsorship of the Internet; Cartoon Art Trust; counterFEET; Cybernetic Culture Research Unit; D.S.4.A; Digital Resistance; Direct Action Media Network (DAMN); Direct Action Media Network (DAMN) Video; Frontier Foundation, The; Enabler Publications; Expanding Horizons; Exploding Cinema, The; Federation Collective Rampenplan; Freedom Book Company; Freedom Press; Friends of AK Press, The; Godhaven Ink; Green Books; Green Guide Publishing Ltd; Green Leaf Bookshop; GreenNet; 'Guardian Media Guide, The'; Guerilla Press, The (Radical Presses Register); Haven Distribution; Hiddinkulturz; Home Education Reading Opportunities; i-Contact Video Network; IndyMedia; IndyMedia UK: INK – Independent Media Collective; Kartoon Kate/Orange Dog Productions; Librairie Freecyb; Monkey Pirates! Multimedia; Monkey-Wrench Graphix; Morgenmuffel; Multimap.Com; National Small Press Centre, The; Ninfomania; no.problem.distribution; Photon Press; Plain Wordz; Radio 4A; Reclaim the Streets – The Film; RTMark; RTP (Ragged Trouser Philanthropic) Press; SchNEWS; Spiral Objective; Squall; Subvertising; Sunrise Screenprint Workshop; Tactical Media Crew; Spunk Library, The; Undercurrents; Video Activist Journalist Survival Kit; Web Directory; White Dot; Wolfs Head Press; Woman and Earth Global Eco-Network; Word Power Bookshop; Worthing Eco-Action; Wowarea; y ddeilen werdd; Zed Books

**Justice and the Law/Solicitors/Prison and Prisoners**
Action Against Injustice; Activists' Legal Project; Anarchist Black Cross (ABC), Brighton; Anarchist Black Cross Innsbruck; Bindmans and Partners; CAGE; Campaign to Close Campsfield; Campaign to Free Vanunu and for a Nuclear Free Middle East; Canadian Coalition Against the Death Penalty; Chinese Information and Advice Centre; Criminal Cases Review Commission; Des Murphy/Murphys Solicitors; Earth Liberation Prisoners; Earthrights Solicitors; Environmental Law Foundation; Football Fans Against the CJA; Free Satpal Ram Campaign; Freedom To Be Yourself, The; GM-Free Prisoner Support; Green Party Drugs Group; 'Guardian Media Guide, The'; Haven Distribution; Hillsborough Justice Campaign; Howard League For Penal Reform, The; Index On Censorship; Innocent; INQUEST; Institute for Law and Peace; Institute of Employment Rights; International Concerned Family & Friends of Mumia Abu-Jamal; Irwin Mitchells Solicitors; Justice For Diarmuid O'Neill Campaign; Kieran & Co; Leathes Prior Solicitors; Legal Aid Head Office; Legal Defence & Monitoring Group (LDMG); London Anarchist Black Cross; Lydia Dagostino; Miscarriages of Justice UK; Movment For Justice; National Campaign Against CS Spray; Newham Monitoring Group; Portsmouth Anarchist Network; Prisoners Advice Service; Right to Protest Forum; SchNEWS/Justice?; Scottish Human Rights Centre; Squall; Statewatch; Big Issue, The; Transform; Traveller Law Research Unit; Travellers' Advice Team; URBAN 75; Vegan Prisoners Support Group; Wages Due Lesbians; Women in Prison

**Land Rights/Gardening/Organics/Trees**
A27 Action Group; Agroforestry Research Trust; Allotments Coalition Trust, The; Becontree Organic Growers' Association (BOG); Borders Forest Trust, The; Brambles; Brighton Urban Design & Development (BUDD); Carbon Storage Trust, The; Catalyst Collective; Chapter Seven; Clun Valley Alder Charcoal; Compassion in World Farming; Connolly Association; Cool Temperate; Council for the Protection of Rural England (CPRE); Crystal Palace Campaign; Diggers & Dreamers Publications; Ecovillage Network UK; Exodus; Forest Stewardship Council; Global Partnership; Gnostic Garden; Good Bulb Guide, The; Green Adventure; Green Guide Publishing Ltd; Groundswell; Gypsy Council, The; Henry Doubleday Research Association; Land and Liberty; Land Stewardship Trust; Low Impact; National Society of Allotment Gardeners Ltd, The; Naturewise; New Futures Association; Open Spaces Society; Opposition to Destruction of Open Green Spaces; 'Mushroom Cultivator, The'; Permaculture Association, Britain; Permaculture Magazine; Primal Seeds; Reclaim the Streets; Reforesting Scotland; Resurgence; SchNEWS; Soil Association; Squall; Stonehenge Campaign; Sunseed Desert Technology; Sustain 2020; Talamh Housing Co-op; Land Is Ours, The; Rural Media Company, The; Woodland Trust, The; Tinkers Bubble; Tree Council; Trees For Life; Turners' Field Permaculture; Water Pressure Group, The; Willing Workers On

Organic Farms (WWOOF)

## Peace/Anti-Nuclear/Arms and Military
Abolition 2000; Aldermaston Women's Peace Camp; Amnesty International; Burghfield Women's Peace Camp; Campaign Against Arms Trade (CAAT); Campaign for Nuclear Disarmament (CND); Campaign for the Accountability of American Bases; Campaign to Free Vanunu & for a Nuclear Free Middle East; Chernobyl Children's Project; Conscience – The Peace Tax Campaign; Demilitarization for Democracy; Faslane Peace Camp; Food Not Bombs; Housmans Diary Group; Housmans Peace Resource Project; Human Rights Watch; Legends of Peace; Nonviolent Action; Nuclear Information and Resource Service; Peace Brigades International British Section; Peace News; SchNEWS; Sellafield Women's Peace Camp; Squall; Statewatch; Trident Ploughshares 2000; WomenWith Womyn's Peace Camp; World Information Service on Energy International

## Social Change
5th May Group; Angelltown Community Project Ltd; Animal; Anti-Corruption Politics; Arts Factory; Aston Reinvestment Trust; Autonomous Centre of Edinburgh; Between the Lines; Bicycle Recycle Workshop; Blatant Incitement Project (BLINC); Brighton & Hove Green Party; Campaign to Close Campsfield; Campaign to Legalise Cannabis International; Canadian Coalition Against the Death Penalty; Commonweal Collection; counterFEET; Crossroads Womens Centre; Direct Action; Disabled Action Network; English Collective of Prostitutes; Eurodusnie; Exodus; Federation Anarchiste Francophone; Fourth World Review; Friends, Families and Travellers; Gloupgloup; Greater Manchester Socialist Alliance; Groundswell; Haringey Solidarity Group (HSG); Kebele Kulture Projekt; KK/Collectives; Letslink UK; Lobster; London 21 Sustainability Network; London Class War; M-Power; Microzine; Movement for Justice; NLP & DHE; Notes From the Borderland; Oneworld; OutRage!; Payday Men's Network; Pensioners Rights Campaign; Privacy International; Re-Cycle; Redwood Coast Watersheds Alliance; SchNEWS; Schumacher Society Bristol Desk; Scientists For Global Responsibility; Sexual Freedom Coalition; Single Mothers' Self-Defence; Squall; Subversion; Sustain 2020; Big Issue, The; Connolly Association; Land Is Sours, The; Thespionage; UpStart Services; Wages Due Lesbians; Wages For Housework Campaign; WinVisible: Women With Visible and Invisible Disabilities; Women's Development Bank Federation; World Development Movement

## Anti-Capitalism
Adbusters; Anarchist Federation (AF); Anti-Slavery International; Bilderberg; Black Environment Network; Bloody Hell; Corporate Watch; Decadent Action; Enough anti-consumerism campaign; Ethical Consumer Research Association; Groen Front! (Earth First! Netherlands); London Greenpeace/McLibel Support Campaign; Opposition to the Destruction of Open Green Spaces; PaRTiZans; People & Planet; Peoples' Global Action; Porkbolter, The; Primal Seeds; Project Underground; Public Citizens' Global Trade Watch; Reclaim the Streets; RTMark; SchNEWS; Sprawl Busters; Squall; Statewatch; Trident Ploughshares 2000; Troops Out Movement; White Dot; Women in Black

## Anti-Racism
Anti-Fascist Action (AFA); Anti-Nazi League; Anti-Slavery International; Asylum Aid; Asylum Rights Campaign; Birmingham Racial Attacks Monitoring Unit; Campaign Against Racism & Fascism (CARF); Campaign to Close Campsfield; DARK NIGHT Field Notes; Dover Residents Against Racism; Exeter Left; Fight Racism! Fight Imperialism!; Free Satpal Ram Campaign; Gypsy Council, The; Human Rights Watch; Institute of Race Relations; Kent Socialist Alliance; Minority Rights Group International; National Assembly Against Racism; National Coalition of Anti-Deportation Campaigns; Newham Monitoring Group; Southall Black Sisters; Southall Monitoring Project; 1990 Trust, The; Youth Against Racism in Europe

## Benefits and JSA
Brighton Against Benefit Cuts; Dartford Unemployed Group; Devonport Claimants' Union; Edinburgh Claimants; Unemployed Action Group; Groundswell Claimants Action Group; Newham and District Claimants Union; Nottingham Claimants Action; Unemployed Action Group;

## Economics
Ecology Building Society; National Federation of Credit Unions; New Economics Foundation; Poor People's Economic Human Rights Campaign, The; Shared Interest Society Ltd; Women's Bank

## Industrial Action and Workers' Rights
Anarchist Trade Union Network; Anarcho-Syndicalism 101; Building Worker; Campaign Against Tube Privatisation; Euromarch Liason Committee; Fight Poverty Pay Campaign; Hillingdon Hospital Workers; Industrial Workers of the World; Institute of Employment Rights; International Workers of the World; LabourStart; Liverpool Dockers, The; london Hazards Centre; Simon Jones Memorial Campaign; Strike Support Group; Thameside Strike Committee; Shop, The

## Transport/Alternatives
A27 Action Group; Association of Autonomous Astronauts (AAA); Car Busters Magazine and Resource Centre; Disabled Action Network; East London Association of Autonomous Astronauts (ELAAA); Environmental Transport Association Services Ltd; Going For Green; Pedestrians Association, The; Reclaim the Streets; RoadPeace; SchNEWS; Squall; Sustrans; Tineril Prieteni ai Naturii; Transport 2000; Zeme Predevsim!

## Women
Aldermaston Women's Peace Camp; Baby Milk Action; Burghfield Women's Peace Camp; Crossroads Women's Centre; English Collective of Prostitutes; Feminist Library; News From Nowhere Bookshop; Older Feminists Network; SchNEWS; Sellafield Women's Peace Camp; Single Mothers' Self-Defence; Southall Black Sisters; Squall; Wages Due Lesbians; Wages for Housework Campaign; Winvisible: Women with Visible and Invisible Disabilities; Woman and Earth Global Eco-Network; Women Against Rape; Women in Black; Women in Prison; Women's Bank; Women's Development Bank Federation; Women's Environmental Network (WEN); WomenWith Womyn's Peace Camp

---

### ...and finally...
### a SQUOTE

*So what I propose,*
*with all the weight of last words,*
*is that we embrace each other in commitment:*
*We'll go to the open spaces,*
*we'll risk ourselves for the other,*
*we'll hope along with those who are putting out*
*their arms,*
*so that a new wave of history will raise us up.*
*Perhaps it's already raising us up, silently,*
*underground,*
*like shoots stirring beneath the winter earth.*

**Ernesto Sabato,** *Before the End*

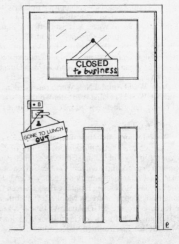